RUSSIAN CAMPAIGN

Miles

0   100   200   300   400   500

Main Railways ┼─┼─┼─┼─   Oil Pipelines ─ ─ ─ ─ ─

BRITISH INTELLIGENCE
IN THE SECOND
WORLD WAR

ITS INFLUENCE ON STRATEGY
AND OPERATIONS

VOLUME THREE
PART I

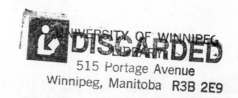

The authors of this, as of other official histories
of the Second World War, have been given free access
to official documents. They alone are responsible
for the statements made and the views expressed

BRITISH INTELLIGENCE IN THE SECOND WORLD WAR

Its Influence on Strategy and Operations

VOLUME THREE

PART I

by

F. H. HINSLEY
Master of St John's College and Emeritus
Professor of the History of International Relations
in the University of Cambridge

with
E. E. THOMAS
C. F. G. RANSOM
The late R. C. KNIGHT

LONDON
HER MAJESTY'S STATIONERY OFFICE

HER MAJESTY'S STATIONERY OFFICE

Government Bookshops

49 High Holborn, London WC1V 6HB
13a Castle Street, Edinburgh EH2 3AR
Brazennose Street, Manchester M60 8AS
Southey House, Wine Street, Bristol BS1 2BQ
258 Broad Street, Birmingham B1 2HE
80 Chichester Street, Belfast BT1 4JY

*Government Publications are also available
through booksellers*

Printed in the United Kingdom for
Her Majesty's Stationery Office
Dd 716922 C90 10/83

ISBN 0 11 630935 0*

CONTENTS

*A bibliography covering the whole of this history will be included in
Volume III Part 2.*

PREFACE

WE THINK it will be helpful if we repeat here the conditions under which we have worked as we stated them in the prefaces to Volume I and Volume II.

In carrying out our brief, which was to produce an account of the influence of British intelligence on strategy and operations during the Second World War, we have encountered two problems of presentation. The first was how to furnish the strategic and operational context without retelling the history of the war in all its detail; we trust we have arrived at a satisfactory solution to it. The second arose because different meanings are given to the term intelligence. The value and the justification of intelligence depend on the use that is made of its findings; and this has been our central concern. But its findings depend on the prior acquisition, interpretation and evaluation of information; and judgment about its influence on those who used it requires an understanding of these complex activities. We have tried to provide this understanding without being too much diverted by the problems and techniques associated with the provision of intelligence. Some readers will feel that we have strayed too far down the arid paths of organisation and methods. Others, to whom such subjects are fascinating in themselves, will wish that we had said more about them.

It is from no wish to disarm such criticisms that we venture to point to the novel and exceptional character of our work. No considered account of the relationship between intelligence and strategic and operational decisions has hitherto been possible, for no such account could be drawn up except by authors having unrestricted access to intelligence records as well as to other archives. In relation to the British records for the Second World War and the inter-war years, we have been granted this freedom as a special measure. No restriction has been placed on us while carrying out our research. On the contrary, in obtaining access to archives and in consulting members of the war-time intelligence community we have received full co-operation and prompt assistance from the Historical Section of the Cabinet Office and the appropriate government departments. Some members of the war-time community may feel that we might have made our consultation more extensive; we have confined it to points on which we needed to supplement or clarify the evidence of the surviving archives. As for the archives, we set out to see all; and if any have escaped our scrutiny we are satisfied that over-sight on our part is the sole explanation.

In preparing the results of our research for publication we have been governed by a ruling that calls for a brief explanation. On 12 January 1978, in a written reply to a parliamentary question, the Secretary of State for Foreign Affairs advised war-time intelligence staff on the limited extent to which they were absolved from their undertakings of reticence in the light of recent changes of policy with regard to the release of war-time records. He drew a distinction between the records of the Service intelligence directorates, which will be placed with other departmental archives in the Public Record Office, and 'other information, including details of the methods by which this material was obtained'. He explained that this other information 'remains subject to the undertakings and to the Official Secrets Act and may not be disclosed'. And he concluded with a reference to this History: 'if it is published, the principles governing the extent of permitted disclosure embodied in the guidance above will apply in relation to the Official History'. This statement has not prevented us from incorporating in the published History the results of our work on records which are not to be opened. The records in question are the domestic records of some of the intelligence-collecting bodies. We have been required to restrict our use of them only to the extent that secrecy about intelligence techniques and with respect to individuals remains essential.

The need to apply this restriction to the published History has at no point impeded our analysis of the state of intelligence and of its impact, and it has in no way affected our conclusions. It has, however, dictated the system that we have adopted when giving references to our sources. Government departments, inter-governmental bodies and operational commands – the recipients, assessors and users of intelligence – have presented no difficuly; to their intelligence files, as to their other records, we have always supplied precise references. This applies not only to documents already opened in the Public Record Office, and those to be opened after a stated period of extended closure, but also to individual files and papers which, though they may not be available for public research for a considerable time to come, nevertheless fall into categories of war-time records whose eventual opening in the Record Office may be expected. But it would have served no useful purpose to give precise references to the domestic files of the intelligence-collecting bodies, which are unlikely ever to be opened in the Public Record Office. We have been permitted – indeed encouraged – to make use of these files in our text and we have done so on a generous scale, but in their case our text must be accepted as being the only evidence of their contents that can be made public. This course may demand from our readers more trust than historians have the right to expect, but we believe they will agree that it is preferable to the alternative, which was to have incorporated no evidence for which we could not quote sources.

The above limitations have arisen from the need for security. We turn now to others which have been imposed on us by the scale on which we have worked. The first of these is that not merely when security has required it but throughout the book – in the many cases where security is no longer at stake and where readers may regret our reticence – we have cast our account in impersonal terms and refrained from naming individuals. We have done so because for our purposes it has generally sufficed to refer to the organisations to which individuals belonged; the exceptions are a few activities which were so specialised or were carried out by such small staffs, and thus became so closely associated with individuals, that it has been convenient sometimes to use names. In addition, however, we must admit to a feeling for the appropriateness of Flaubert's recipe for the perfect realistic novel: *pas de monstres, et pas de héros*. The performance of the war-time intelligence community, its shortcomings no less than its successes, rested not only on the activities of a large number of organisations but also, within each organisation, on the work of many individuals. To have identified all would have been impossible in a book of this canvas; to have given prominence to only a few would have been unjust to the many more who were equally deserving of mention.

As for the organisations, it has been impossible to deal at equal length with all. In some cases we have had to be content with a bare sketch because they kept or retained few records. With others we have dealt briefly because most of their work falls outside our subject. This applies to those responsible for counter-intelligence, security and the use of intelligence for deception purposes; like the intelligence activities of the enemy, we have investigated them in these volumes only to the extent that they contributed to what the British authorities knew about the enemy's conduct of the war. Lack of space has restricted what we have been able to say about intelligence in the field – about the work that was carried out, often in hazardous conditions, by Service intelligence officers with fighting units and by the people who were responsible in the field for signal intelligence, for reporting to the SIS and SOE, for examining enemy equipment and for undertaking photogaphic intepretation, POW examination and many similar tasks. As for the contribution of the many men and women who carried out essential routine work at establishments in the United Kingdom and overseas – who undertook the continuous manning of intercept stations or of cryptanalytic machinery, the maintenance of PR aircraft and their cameras, the preparation of target information for the RAF or of topographical information for all three Services, the monitoring of foreign newspapers, broadcasts and intercepted mail, and the endless indexing, typing, teleprinting, cyphering and transmitting of the intelligence output – only occasional references to it have been possible in an account which sets out to reconstruct the influence of intelligence on the major decisions, the chief operations and the general course of the war.

Even at this last level there are unavoidable omissions. The most important of these is that we have not attempted to cover the war in the Far East; when this was so much the concern of the United States, it is not possible to provide an adequate account on the basis of the British archives alone. A second derives from the fact that while the archives are generally adequate for reconstructing the influence of intelligence in Whitehall, there is practically no record of how and to what extent intelligence influenced the individual decisions of the operational commands. It has usually been possible to reconstruct what intelligence they had at their disposal at any time. What they made of it under operational conditions, and in circumstances in which it was inevitably incomplete, is on all but a few occasions a matter for surmise. And this is one matter which, after stating the facts to the best of our ability, we have left to the judgment of our readers and to the attention of those who will themselves wish to follow up our research by work in the voluminous records which are being made available to the public.

That room remains for further research is something that goes without saying. Even on issues and episodes for which we have set out to supply the fullest possible accounts, the public records will yield interpretations that differ from those we have offered. At the opposite extreme there are particular undertakings and individual operations to which we have not even referred. In our attempt to write a co-ordinated yet compact history we have necessarily proceeded not only with a broad brush but also with a selective hand, and we shall be content if we have provided an adequate framework and a reliable perspective for other historians as well as for the general reader.

□

We must again make special references to the contribution of Miss Eve Streatfeild. In addition to sharing in the research, she has for several years carried out with great skill and patience the bulk of the administrative work that the project has involved. We wish to express our indebtedness for help during the preparation of this volume to Mr C A G Simkins, CB, CBE for his research on the archives relating to the Italian campaign, and to Mr H J C Dryden, CBE for the valuable assistance we have received from his war-time knowledge of the British effort against enemy cyphers.

ABBREVIATIONS

AAPIU	Army Air Photographic Interpretation Unit
ACAS(I)	Assistant Chief of Air Staff (Intelligence)
ACIU	Allied Central Interpretation Unit
ADGB	Air Defence of Great Britain
ADI (K)	Assistant Director of Intelligence (Prisoners of War)
ADI (Ph)	Assistant Director of Intelligence (Photographic)
ADI (Sc)	Assistant Director of Intelligence (Science)

(at the Air Ministry)

AFHQ	Allied Force Headquarters
AFV	Armoured Fighting Vehicle
AI	Air Intelligence (Branch of the Air Ministry)
ASI	Air Scientific Intelligence
ASV	Anti-Surface Vessel Radar
BNLO	British Naval Liaison Officer
'C'	also CSS: Head of the Secret Service
CAS	Chief of the Air Staff
CBME	Combined Bureau Middle East
CCS	Combined Chiefs of Staff (Anglo-US)
CIC	Combined Intelligence Committee (Anglo-US)
CIGS	Chief of the Imperial General Staff
CIU	Central Interpretation Unit
CNO	Chief of Naval Operations (US)
CNS	Chief of Naval Staff (First Sea Lord)
COHQ	Combined Operations Headquarters
COS	Chiefs of Staff (British)
COSSAC	Chief of Staff to the Supreme Commander (Designate)
CPD	Controller of Projectile Development (Ministry of Supply)
CSDIC	Combined Services Detailed Interrogation Centre
CSS	Chief of the Secret Service, also 'C'
DD (C)	Deputy Director (Civil) (at GC and CS)
DD (S)	Deputy Director (Services) (at GC and CS)
DDI	Deputy Director of Intelligence (Air Staff)
DDMI	Deputy Director of Military Intelligence
DDMI (I)	Deputy Director of Military Intelligence (Intelligence)
DDMI (O)	Deputy Director of Military Intelligence (Operations)
DDMI (P)	Deputy Director of Military Intelligence (Planning)
DDMI (PW)	Deputy Director of Military Intelligence (Prisoners of War)
DDMI (Y)	Deputy Director of Military Intelligence (Y Service)

DDNI	Deputy Director of Naval Intelligence
DF	Direction Finding
DMI	Director of Military Intelligence
DNI	Director of Naval Intelligence
ETOUSA	European Theatre of Operations United States Army
GAF	German Air Force
GC and CS	Government Code and Cypher School
GCI	Ground Controlled Interception
HDU	Home Defence Unit
IAF	Italian Air Force
IFF	Identification Friend or Foe
IS (O)	Intelligence Section (Operations)
ISTD	Inter-Services Topographical Department
JIC	Joint Intelligence Sub-Committee (of the COS)
JIS	Joint Intelligence Staff
JPRC	Joint Photographic Reconnaissance Committee (Anglo-US)
JPS	Joint Planning Staff (of the COS)
MAAF	Mediterranean Allied Air Forces
MAIU	Mediterranean Army Interpretation Unit
MEW	Ministry of Economic Warfare
MI	Military Intelligence (Branch of the War Office)
MIRS	Military Intelligence Research Section
NID	Naval Intelligence Division
OIC	Operational Intelligence Centre (Admiralty)
OKH	Oberkommando des Heeres (High Command of the German Army)
OKL	Oberkommando der Luftwaffe (High Command of the GAF)
OKM	Oberkommando der Kriegsmarine (High Command of the German Navy)
OKW	Oberkommando der Wehrmacht (High Command of the German Armed Forces)
OSS	Office of Strategic Services (US)
PIU	Photographic Interpretation Unit
PR	Photographic Reconnaissance
PRU	Photographic Reconnaissance Unit
PWE	Political Warfare Executive
Pzkw	Panzerkampfwagen
RAE	Royal Aircraft Establishment

RFP	Radio Finger Printing
R/T	Radio Telephony

SAAC	Scientific Adviser to the Army Council
SACMED	Supreme Allied Commander Mediterranean
SCU	Special Communications Unit
SD	Sicherheitsdienst
SHAEF	Supreme Headquarters Allied Expeditionary Force
Sigint	Signal Intelligence – the general term for the processes of interception and decryption and the intelligence they produced
SIME	Security Intelligence Middle East
SIS	Special or Secret Intelligence Service
SLU	Special Liaison Unit
SOE	Special Operations Executive

TA	Traffic Analysis – the study of wireless communication networks and procedure signals, call-signs, low-grade codes and plain language, together with DF (see above
TINA	(Not an abbreviation) – the study of morse characteristics of individual wireless operators
VCAS	Vice-Chief of the Air Staff
VCIGS	Vice-Chief of the Imperial General Staff
VCNS	Vice-Chief of the Naval Staff

W/T	Wireless Telegraphy
Y	The interception, analysis and decryption of wireless traffic in low and medium-grade codes and cyphers. The term 'low-grade' refers to the degree of security provided by a code or cypher and does not imply that the traffic in it was either unimportant or easy to break and interpret

LIST OF MAPS

PART VIII

Strategic Intelligence Assessments from June 1943 to June 1944

CHAPTER 29

Strategic Assessments

AT THE Casablanca conference in January 1943 the British Chiefs of Staff had obtained US agreement to a strategy which limited the war against Japan in favour of Mediterranean operations. They had argued that such operations would bring about the collapse of Italy, and that that was the best means of putting pressure on Germany and relieving Russia. But the US Joint Chiefs of Staff had not been wholly won over from their wish for a cross-Channel invasion in 1943 in preference to exploitation in the Mediterranean. The only Mediterranean operation explicitly approved by the conference was the invasion of Sicily (Operation *Husky*), and for some months after Casablanca – months in which enormous Allied losses in the battle of the Atlantic and German resistance in Tunisia were making it impossible to find the shipping to carry out the conference's further decision that in the Far East the Allies should at least reconquer Burma in the autumn of 1943– uncertainty reigned as to what the Allies should do after capturing Sicily.

In its first contribution to the debate the Joint Intelligence Committee (JIC) wondered whether, in view of Germany's growing difficulties, even the attack on Sicily might be abandoned in favour of a cross-Channel invasion in 1943. Arguing that the German military machine had been 'damaged to such an extent that it is questionable whether it can ever be repaired', and even that the collapse of organised German resistance in Russia could not be ruled out, it did not doubt that Germany would transfer troops from the west to enable her to hold a line in Russia as far to the east as possible. But it did not believe that she could move troops from Russia to meet a large-scale Anglo-American attack; in that eventuality she would withdraw divisions from various parts of occupied Europe until such time as she was left in one area or another with insufficient troops to maintain control.[1] The Chiefs of Staff felt that this assessment was unduly influenced by Germany's recent defeat at Stalingrad, and that it under-rated her ability to switch her forces westward; but it persuaded them that the Joint Planners should re-examine the strategy laid down at Casablanca.[2]

---

1. CAB 66/34, WP(43) 76 of 22 February (JIC(43) 64 of 15 February).
2. CAB 79/80, COS(43) 24th (o) Meeting, 19 February.

On the Joint Planners the JIC's view had a considerable impact. Hesitating between recommending that *Husky* should still proceed or recommending that it should be abandoned in order to permit an Anglo-American cross-Channel invasion later in 1943, when the situation on the eastern front might have created favourable conditions for it, they asked the JIC early in March for an assessment of the scale of resistance likely to be encountered by a landing in France in 1943.[3] The JIC remained optimistic. It thought that by mid-summer Germany might be failing to stabilise the eastern front sufficiently to protect the Romanian oil and avoid trouble with her satellites; in this situation she would not hesitate to draw more and more divisions from the west.[4] On the assumption that she had done this to the point of reducing her western garrisons to the minimum, and on the assumption that Italy remained in the war as her unstable partner, the Allies having carried out no Mediterranean operations since the clearance of Tunisia, it thought that, as compared with the existing 32, she would have 22 divisions in France, of which only one Panzer division, one SS division and one infantry division would be capable of rapid movement over large distances, and that her air opposition to a determined Allied assault would also be limited. An initial force of 450 aircraft might be raised to 850 by reinforcements, but their numbers and serviceability would quickly deteriorate under Allied attack.[5]

The Chiefs of Staff were not impressed by the JIC's argument and on 19 March they asked the Joint Planners to consider what Mediterranean operations should follow *Husky*.[6] The Joint Planners' reply began by noting that if *Husky* had produced Italy's collapse by the late summer, and if this had sufficiently weakened Germany's power, a cross-Channel operation might produce the quickest dividends; but it conceded that Italy might not collapse, or her collapse might not sufficiently weaken Germany, and that since these uncertainties would not be resolved before *Husky* had taken place and Russia had launched her summer campaign, *Husky* should be followed by a further Allied offensive in the Mediterranean.[7] But would the Chiefs of Staff give approval for such an operation if it made the offensive in Burma impossible?* The response of the Chiefs of Staff

---

* By the time of the Cairo conference in November 1943 the reconquest of Burma had been replaced by a smaller operation against the Andaman Islands in 1944 (see below, pp 16, 17).

3.   CAB 84/6, JP(43) 13th and 14th Meetings, 2 and 3 March.
4.   JIC(43) 99 of 9 March.
5.   JIC(43) 100 (o) of 9 March; JIC(43) 14th Meeting, 16 March.
6.   CAB 121/128, SIC file A/Policy/ME/3, Hollis note to JPS, 19 March 1943.
7.   ibid, JP(43) 140 of 7 April.

was to repeat their demand for an assessment of what could best be done in the Mediterranean after *Husky* to drive Italy out of the war and draw German forces from the Russian front, they themselves suggesting in their impatience that the seizure of airfields in Sardinia might be an alternative to a descent on the Italian mainland.[8]

On 13 April the Chiefs of Staff approved as a basis for the work of the Joint Planners a JIC paper which assessed the rate of German build-up in southern Italy on the assumption that the Axis had been driven out of Tunisia and Sicily, but that Italy remained in the war.[9] This appreciation expressed the view that Germany, lacking offensive reserves, was not in a position to fight on new fronts without risking disaster elsewhere, and argued that she would abandon Italy rather than take that risk in Russia or if she judged that Italy was about to collapse. But it conceded that to keep Italy in the war she might find nine divisions from France and either Norway or Russia, of which no less than three would have to replace divisions that Italy would have withdrawn from the Balkans and southern France.[10] It was followed on 23 April by a JIC appreciation for the Joint Planners on Germany's reaction to an Italian collapse; this again concluded that she would be unable to do more than take up defensive positions in the north – with two or three divisions along the Maritime Alps and two divisions to the east on the river Adige. 'We have weighed up the possibility that the Germans, if they had any forces in Italy at the time of her collapse, might reinforce them and try temporarily to hold a line as far south as Ravenna-Pisa. We conclude however that the serious security problem involved in the occupation of Italy and the additional commitments which the Germans would have to meet in the Balkans and southern France would entail such risks as to make this course unacceptable'.[11] In yet a third paper the JIC advised the Planners on the feasibility of defeating Italy by air attack alone between August and October 1943; it thought it reasonable to expect that the results of an intensive bombing offensive over this period would force Italy to sue for peace.[12]

The Joint Planners reported to the Chiefs of Staff on 17 April. They recommended that the main Allied effort should be a bomber offensive against Italy, for which it would be necessary to divert resources from the bombing of Germany but not to seize Sardinian and Corsican airfields. To ensure and accelerate Italy's collapse,

---

8. ibid, COS(43) 69th (o) Meeting, 8 April.
9. ibid, COS(43) 74th (o) Meeting, 13 April.
10. ibid, JIC(43) 160 of 11 April.
11. CAB 84/6, JP(43) 32nd Meeting, 19 April; JIC(43) 186 (o) of 23 April.
12. CAB 121/128, JP(43) 145 of 17 April, Appendix H (JIC(43) 167 (o) of 16 April).

they also recommended that the Allies should land in the Toe of
Italy as soon as possible after *Husky*, to establish a position from
which they could attack the Heel and advance to the north if the
landings had not produced Italy's collapse.[13] The Planners' report
failed to satisfy the Chiefs of Staff. They questioned the omission of
action against Sardinia and asked for a closer assessment of the risks
that would follow if Italy did not collapse after the landing, or if
Italy did collapse but Germany did not withdraw to the Brenner.
Nor were the Chiefs of Staff reassured on learning in reply to this
enquiry that success in operating against the Heel and advancing
to Bari and Naples would depend on Soviet success in the summer
campaign in Russia and the certainty that Axis opposition would
not exceed four divisions (including one German) building up to
eight (4 or 5 German) by D + 60.[14]

The Joint Planners completed on 3 May another paper in which,
in close consultation with the JIC, they considered what the Allies
should do if Italy collapsed before or as a result of *Husky*. It accepted
the JIC's view that in this eventuality Germany would probably
withdraw to the Maritime Alps and the Adige, though allowing that
she might try to deny the Allies the northern Italian airfields by
temporarily holding the Pisa-Rimini line. It recommended that the
Allies should not try to drive her from that line or try to advance to
Austria or Istria if she abandoned northern Italy altogether. To
prevent German infiltration, and to take over the airfields in the
Milan-Turin area should Germany withdraw from them, they
should occupy Corsica and Sardinia and move a force to central
Italy, but otherwise 'any forces we have to spare would be better
employed in exploiting the very favourable situation likely to develop in the Balkans'. In the first instance the Allies should use the
forces landed in Italy and the bases seized there to assist the
establishment of a bridgehead in the Durazzo area in support of the
guerrillas; should develop mass air attacks on Balkan targets, particularly the oil at Ploesti; and should if possible occupy the Dodecanese at the same time, this being an essential preliminary to the
entry of Turkey into the war.[15]

The JIC and the Joint Planners had been interested since the
end of 1942 in the opportunities that might arise for Allied action
in the Balkans. On 27 November 1942, when they first reached the
conclusion that Germany would give the defence of that area priority
over the occupation of Italy when Italy collapsed, they had been
inclined to recommend that the Allies should carry the war to the

---

13.   ibid, JP(43) 145 of 17 April.
14.   ibid, COS(43) 81st (o) Meeting, 22 April, 93rd (o) Meeting, 4 May.
15.   ibid, JP(43) 99 of 3 May.

Balkans rather than land in Italy.[16] On 3 December, relying on Sigint about the Balkans, which had been increasing in volume since the previous spring,* the JIC had stressed that the German garrisons there were 'even now barely sufficient to retain control';[17] and on 5 December the Joint Planners had listed the capture of Crete and the Dodecanese, to be followed by the seizure of air bases in Greece and air attacks to open the way for landings in support of the Yugoslav guerrillas, as operations which the Allies might undertake after landing in southern Italy.[18] In February and March 1943, notwithstanding the decision of the Casablanca conference to confine further operations in the Mediterranean to Sicily and possibly mainland Italy, the Planners and the JIC had underlined the extent to which the German economy was dependent on Balkan raw materials in papers which listed the areas that would be most suitable for operations in conjunction with the guerrillas should the Allies decide to act in the Balkans when Italy collapsed.[19] In the appreciation of 3 May they revived these projects, but only as projects which might follow an unopposed landing in Italy and which would even then remain secondary and subordinate to the Allied advance on the Italian mainland.

The Chiefs of Staff were not attracted by these limited proposals for exploiting the situation in the eastern Mediterranean and the Balkans. They dismissed the idea of preparing for the occupation of the Dodecanese, vetoing at the same time a proposal from the C-in-C Middle East for an attack on Rhodes, and they showed little interest in the project for establishing a bridgehead in the Adriatic. Nor was this solely because they recognised that such operations would not be acceptable to the US authorities. They thought it premature to encourage Turkey when the Allies were unable to give her substantial support. They suspected, moreover, that to take that course might incite Germany to strengthen the Ploesti defences and perhaps to attack in Thrace. But above all they continued to be sceptical of the JIC's argument that, if only because she would have to give priority to retaining control of the Balkans, Germany would withdraw to northern Italy if Italy collapsed before or soon after the Allies had established themselves on the mainland; they concluded that if Germany did divert large forces to Italy, a move

---

* See below, p 138 and Appendix 6.

16. CAB 84/5, JP(42) 192nd Meeting, 27 November; JIC(42) 466 (o) of 28 November.
17. CAB 121/412, SIC file D/Germany/1, Vol 1, JIC(42) 462 of 3 December.
18. CAB 121/127, SIC file A/Policy/ME/2, JP(42) 990 of 5 December.
19. CAB 84/51, JP(42) 1027 (o) 2nd Revise of 24 February 1943; JIC(43) 115 of 22 March.

which would take pressure off the Russians, the Allies should seize Corsica and Sardinia but that further decisions about the development of Allied operations must be deferred.[20]

It was in this frame of mind that they went to the Anglo-US conference which took place in Washington from 12 to 25 May. In Washington they found that distrust of the damage 'the suction pump' of Mediterranean operations might do to the project for a cross-Channel invasion had in no way abated. In preparation for the conference the US Chiefs of Staff had drawn up a brief which, after emphasising the close relationship between the war in Europe and the war in the Far East, insisted that no other operation must be allowed to jeopardise preparations for the invasion of north-west Europe and the progressively increasing air offensive that was to precede it. It ruled out all operations in the eastern Mediterranean and accepted that operations in the western Mediterranean immediately following the occupation of Sicily might have some merit only provided they did not impinge on the plan for north-west Europe by preventing a reduction in Allied forces in the Mediterranean.[21] To meet the US view the conference agreed to earmark a defined force of 29 divisions for a cross-Channel invasion on 1 May 1944 (Operation *Overlord*). To meet the British view it was agreed that limited operations in the Mediterranean to eliminate Italy would be carried out after Operation *Husky* by all the Allied forces in the theatre other than seven divisions which were to be ready for withdrawal from 7 November to meet the target date for the cross-Channel operations.[22] It was further agreed that the Allied Combined Chiefs of Staff must approve any specific Mediterranean operation and that they would meet again in July or at the beginning of August to review the situation in the light of the progress of Operation *Husky* and of developments on the eastern front.[23]

These agreements governed the planning for Mediterranean operations to follow the capture of Sicily that were under continuous discussion between Whitehall, Washington and Allied Force HQ (AFHQ) until on 26 July, the day after Mussolini's dismissal, the Combined Chiefs of Staff ordered General Eisenhower to carry the war to the Italian mainland at the earliest possible date.* The British authorities regretted the American tendency to neglect the need to make adequate provision for action in the event of Italy's

---

* For a detailed account of the discussions at the Washington conference see M Howard, *Grand Strategy*, Vol IV (1972), Chapter XXII.

20.   CAB 121/153, SIC file A/Strategy/9, COS(43) 256(o) of 17 May (JP(T) 5 and 6 of 8 May, 9 and 11 of 10 May).
21.   M Howard, *Grand Strategy*, Vol IV (1972), pp 420–421.
22.   ibid, p 433.   23.   ibid, p 433.

collapse – a sentiment which was answered by Washington's belief that British thinking under-estimated Germany's capacity for rising to emergencies, as well as by its determination to avoid delays to *Overlord* – but they accepted that the agreement to withdraw divisions and assault shipping from the Mediterranean after the capture of Sicily could not be reconsidered until the next Allied conference, if at all. Before the next conference met at Quebec in the middle of August they had already concluded that, unless the opportunity arose to take it cheaply, an assault on Rhodes must be deferred; that other operations in the Dodecanese and the Aegean must be limited to such small raids and unopposed landings as could be undertaken by existing British forces in the area; that in the Balkans the Allies would not be able to achieve a decisive success in time to assist *Overlord*; and that at least until the spring of 1944 operations on the Italian mainland would leave insufficient troops and shipping for assaults on Sardinia and Corsica or for the establishment of a bridgehead at Durazzo from which to support and supply the Yugoslav guerrillas.[24] They had accepted, indeed, that it only remained to settle the scope of Allied operations on the Italian mainland and their relationship to *Overlord* and developments on the Russian front. The British Chiefs of Staff went to the Quebec conference hoping that it would give priority to discussing the Mediterranean, but they had decided to stress only the need for 'vigorous action in Italy in order to draw still more German forces in that direction to relieve pressure on the Russian front, and to pave the way for *Overlord*'.*

On this account, and also because the British Chiefs of Staff had on 20 July imposed a standstill order stopping the dispersal of Mediterranean resources until the situation was clarified, the US Chiefs of Staff suspected that the British government would try to retreat from its existing agreements, and were determined to oppose any change. In the event the Quebec conference, coinciding as it did with Italian approaches to the Allies for armistice negotiations,†

---

* See below, p 103. But the Prime Minister showed a continuing interest in the Balkans. Shortly before leaving for Quebec he arranged for General Alexander to be sent an account from Ultra and other sources of the 'marvellous resistance recently put up by the so-called partisan followers of Tito in Bosnia and the powerful cold-blooded manoeuvres of Mihailovic in Serbia' and in doing so suggested that Alexander should consider as 'quite a good secondary gambit', should he feel that German strength around Naples or Rome was beyond his powers, the capture of the Toe, Ball and Heel of Italy; from there he might reach out with seaborne supplies, agents, commandos and air power into Albania and Yugoslavia.[25]

† See below, p 104 et seq.

24. CAB 121/128, JP(43) 216 of 3 July, JP(43) 221 of 12 July, COS(43) 158th (o) Meeting, 15 July; CAB 121/154, SIC file A/Strategy/10, COS(43)513(o) of 11 September, Part A.

25. PREM 3/228/5, PM telegram to Alexander, T/1033/3 of 22 July 1943; Howard, op cit, Vol IV, p 505.

unavoidably devoted much time to discussing the scope and the objectives of Allied operations in Italy; and the American views on that subject did not greatly differ from the British. The British Chiefs of Staff urged that an advance initially to the Pisa-Rimini line and ultimately to positions covering the Milan and Turin airfields would be the best means of forcing Germany to withdraw divisions from north-west Europe; they also argued that it would force her to divert up to a third of her day and night-fighters from that theatre since 65 per cent of her fighters were produced in areas most easily bombed from northern Italy, on which flank her air defences were weak. The US Chiefs of Staff agreed that the mainland advance should establish air bases as far north as Rome, and felt that the Allies should seize Sardinia and Corsica. But they also insisted that since Italy was a secondary theatre, and one in which logistical difficulties and the terrain precluded decisive operations against the heart of Germany, the limits already laid down for the resources to be retained in the Mediterranean should be strictly adhered to.[26]* The British Chiefs of Staff fought hard against what they regarded as American inflexibility on the allocation of forces, stressing not only the importance for *Overlord* of acquiring bomber bases in northern Italy but also the fact that the success of *Overlord* would depend on the relative strength of the opposing forces at the point of the landings, rather than on the absolute strength of the forces which the Allies assembled for the follow-up stages of the invasion. And with assistance not only from the evidence that Italy was anxious for an armistice, but also from the conclusions reached in the outline plan for *Overlord*, which the Chief of Staff to the Supreme Allied Commander (COSSAC) had submitted to the conference,† they had some success – though not to the extent of persuading the Americans to reconsider the decision to withdraw seven divisions from AFHQ.

Given that the invasion force would have to be maintained in the assault area until ports had been put in order, COSSAC's plan stipulated three conditions for *Overlord's* success. The enemy's over-all strength in fighter aircraft must be severely reduced by D-day; on D-day the number of first-class enemy divisions in France and the Low Countries, over and above the three static divisions employed on coast defence in the assault area, must not exceed twelve; and the enemy must not be allowed to increase that number

---

* For details see Howard, op. cit., Vol IV, Chapter XXIX.
† For details of the *Overlord* planning see Volume III Part 2.

26. CAB 121/154, COS(43)513(o) of 11 September, Part B, (COS(Q) of 6 August), COS(43)513(o), Part A, (CCS 106th and 108th Meetings, 14 and 15 August); Howard, op cit, Vol IV, pp 567–570.

by more than fifteen from other fronts in the two months following the landings.[27] The conclusions of the Quebec conference largely reaffirmed the strategy agreed in May 1943, but in principle they recognised that interdependence between *Overlord* and operations in the Mediterranean might justify flexibility in the allocation of forces. The bombing offensive was to continue to have highest priority, the destruction of Germany's military, industrial and economic resources, the dislocation of her lines of communication and the reduction of her air strength being prerequisites for *Overlord*. *Overlord*, allotted twenty-nine divisions, target date 1 May, was to be the primary Allied effort in 1944. Operations elsewhere were to be carried out with the main object of ensuring the success of *Overlord* and, except insofar as this was varied by the Combined Chiefs of Staff, operations in the Mediterranean would be carried out with the reduced forces allocated at the Washington conference. In Italy the first objective would be to establish air bases in the Rome area, the second the seizure of Sardinia and Corsica, the third the maintenance of pressure on German forces in the north to create the conditions required for *Overlord* and for eventual landings in the south of France (Operation *Anvil*) to create a diversion in connection with *Overlord*. Strategic bombing would be carried out from Italy against targets in the Balkans, as well as against Germany, but operations in the Balkans would otherwise be confined to supplying the guerrillas.[28]

□

When the Quebec agreements were concluded it was already apparent that, as the JIC had foretold, Germany would not abandon the Balkans when Italy collapsed. By the beginning of July 1943, when the Enigma reported the arrival in Greece of an armoured division (1st Panzer) from France, and a Japanese diplomatic telegram from Sofia referred to persistent rumours that Rommel had been appointed C-in-C Balkans, with his HQ at Sofia,[29] it had been estimated on the basis of the high-grade Sigint that since the spring the numbers of German divisions in the area had risen from seven or eight to fifteen.* From the same source it was known that the modest front-line strength of the GAF in Greece and Crete had

---

* The actual increase was from eight divisions in March to eighteen by 10 July. For details see below, pp 144–145.

27.   CAB 121/154, COS(43)513(0), Part B (COS(Q)8 of 7 August).
28.   ibid, COS(43)513(0), Part A, (CCS 313/3 of 17 August); Howard, op cit, Vol IV, Appendix VIII (CCS 319/5 of 24 August).
29.   Dir/C Archive, 3808 of 9 July 1943.

been doubled between May and June, and that a new GAF Command for south-east Europe had been established.* Like the despatch of German army reinforcements to Rhodes, beginning in April and accelerating in May as the Enigma disclosed,† these considerable changes in the enemy's order of battle had been sufficiently explained by decrypts which had confirmed that until the Allied landings in Sicily in the second week of July the Germans were unable to exclude the possibility that the Allies would attempt landings in the eastern Mediterranean as well as, or instead of, in Sicily.‡ Nor were they entirely discounting that threat when they withdrew from Sicily in August; Sigint showed that, while recognising that southern Italy would be the next Allied objective, they still feared that landings in Italy would be accompanied or followed by landings in the Balkans if they themselves relaxed their grip there. More positively, Sigint had by then disclosed that they were determined to retain their grip should the Italians defect. On 26 July – the day after Mussolini was dismissed as head of the Italian government – an Enigma decrypt had shown that the German naval authorities in the Aegean had been ordered to be ready to seize the Italian W/T stations.[30] High-grade Army decrypts – bearing out the Japanese diplomatic rumours – had reported on 28 July that Army Group E was to move from Salonika to Belgrade and that a new Army Group B was to be created under Rommel at Salonika;[31] on 31 July that German units were moving into Italian-occupied Croatia;[32] and on 4 August that, under the code-name *Achse*, the German forces in the Balkans had been given preliminary instructions for the disarming of Italian troops in the event of an armistice.[33]

Towards the end of August, amid widespread rumours that an armistice was imminent, Sigint provided more detailed information about Germany's preparations. Army Group E was to remain at Salonika because Rommel's Army Group B was now ordered to cover northern Italy, and a new Army Group F under von Weichs as C-in-C South East was being formed in Belgrade. HQ Second Panzer Army was being brought in from Russia to control Yugoslavia with a new XXI Mountain Corps (commanding Serbia from Mitrovica), a new III SS Panzer Corps (commanding northern Croatia from Zagreb) and XV Mountain Corps (resuscitated to

---

* For details see below, pp 80, 82.   † For details see below, pp 119–120.
‡ For details see below, p 77 et seq.

30.   DEFE 3/573, CX/MSS/C 157, 158; DEFE 3/610, ZTPGM 27872; Dir/C Archive, 4014 of 27 July 1943.
31.   DEFE 3/831, ML 9625 of 2 August 1943.
32.   CX/MSS/2999/T23.
33.   CX/MSS/3180/T12.

command the remainder of Croatia from Banja Luka). XXII Mountain Corps had been transferred from Russia to northern Greece.[34]* At the same time, the GAF was creating new commands for Greece and Albania.[36] From 26 August the decrypts disclosed that German troops in Yugoslavia were entering Italian-held territory, assuming control in Ljubljana, moving to the Albanian and Montenegrin borders and taking over some of the Dalmatian airfields.[37] By early September it was clear from the German and Italian dispositions given in these decrypts and in field reports from the guerrillas that Germany had put herself into a position in Yugoslavia from which she could oppose any threat from the sea and disarm many of the Italian divisions, and had done so with meagre reinforcements, having brought in as yet only some Corps troops, elements of one SS Panzer Grenadier Division, two independent regiments and one garrison division.

Within hours of the announcement of the Italian armistice on 8 September she was disarming the Italians in Yugoslavia and taking over the remaining mainland areas held by them; and despite fierce resistance in some areas, she had all but completed the work by the end of the month. By the middle of October she had driven the Yugoslav Partisans out of Istria, which they had occupied after Italy's collapse,[38]† and recovered most of the areas they had seized in Dalmatia. In the Aegean her response to the armistice was no less prompt; she secured the capitulation of the Italian garrison on Rhodes on 11 September and by October had captured Cos from a British garrison landed there when Italy collapsed.‡ The British authorities found these set-backs all the more galling because they knew the German garrisons in the eastern Mediterranean and the Balkans to be so thinly spread; at the end of September the JIC feared that Germany would consolidate her hold on south-eastern Europe and her unwilling allies in Hungary, Romania and Bulgaria

---

* In the autumn of 1943 III SS Panzer Corps moved to Russia and V SS Mountain Corps moved into Yugoslavia from Germany. The destination of III SS Panzer Corps could only be inferred from decrypts until its presence in Russia could be confirmed in January 1944. But the replacements of its divisions in the area it quitted in Yugoslavia were recorded currently in the Sigint.[35]

† See below, p 157.   ‡ See below, p 121 et seq.

34. DEFE 3/573, CX/MSS/C 172; DEFE 3/875, JP 2427 of 20 August 1943; Dir/C Archive, 4248 and 4255 of 27 and 28 August; WO 208/3573, MI 14 Appreciation for the CIGS of 30 August 1943; CX/MSS/3123/T4 and 6, 3132/T52, 3204/T5.
35. DEFE 3/130, VL 4447 of 21 January 1944.
36. DEFE 3/753, CX/MSS/C 172; WO 208/3573 of 23 and 30 August 1943; CX/MSS/3078/T38, 3123/T56, 3132/T52, 3134/T15, 3138/T25, 3204/T5.
37. CX/MSS/2985, 3034, 3049/T24, 3093, 3123/T56, 3130, 3167, 3173/T10.
38. J Ehrman, *Grand Strategy*, Vol V (1956), pp 79–80.

'even with her present inadequate forces'.[39] But they were even more disconcerted to learn from Sigint at the beginning of October that Germany, contrary to her earlier intention to withdraw her forces in Italy to the Pisa-Rimini line when Italy capitulated, had decided to hold a line as far south as possible.

The first firm intelligence about what Germany would do in Italy when Italy collapsed had been received towards the end of August. Sigint had then disclosed that Rommel would cover the north with Army Group B and had listed the forces to be placed at his disposal, three Army Corps comprising eight divisions, while emissaries from Italy had reported that the Germans intended to defend Sardinia and Corsica and to resist on the mainland on a line from Pisa to Rimini.* These initial indications were not belied by the Sigint which recorded Germany's response to the announcement of the Italian armistice and the Allied landings at Salerno from 8 September. The decrypts dealing with the execution of Operation *Achse* showed that having failed to secure one of its important objectives, the seizure of the Italian Fleet, the Germans were moving into the Italian zones in the south of France and along the Dalmatian coast and had ordered Rommel to hold northern Italy and Corsica, and by 13 September they had disclosed that the Germans were evacuating Corsica as well as Sardinia. By the same date the decrypts covering the battle at Salerno had strongly suggested that Germany did not intend to commit any of the divisions from the north against the Allied bridgehead, and subsequent decrypts had disclosed that following their failure to contain the bridgehead the German divisions in south and central Italy were preparing a staged withdrawal.†

The JIC accordingly reiterated on 29 September its long-standing view that the enemy intended to evacuate the south and the centre, including Rome and its important airfields, and would eventually withdraw to a line in the north. On 2 October, however, the Enigma disclosed that Hitler had decided that as little ground as possible should be given up in Italy. This change of mind was no doubt influenced by the fact that since the middle of September, as Sigint had also disclosed, the Germans had come to fear that the activities of the Partisans in Dalmatia and Albania indicated that an Allied landing was imminent [40] – and so much so that on 3 October, as the Japanese Ambassador reported in a telegram decrypted on 8 October, Hitler thought a Balkan invasion more likely than an

---

* See below, pp 104–105.   † See below, pp 115–116.

39. CAB 121/529, SIC file F/Balkans/2, JIC (43) 385(0) of 25 September.
40. eg DEFE 3/883, JP 6219 of 4 October 1943.

advance on the Italian mainland.[41] But it was also prompted, as we now know, by the slow pace of the Allied advance and by evidence that Allied assault shipping was leaving the Mediterranean for the United Kingdom.*

It was in these circumstances that in the middle of October, when operations in the Dodecanese and the Aegean had been frustrated for lack of troops and assault shipping and arms were failing to reach the Yugoslav guerrillas for lack of planning and resources, but when divisions awaiting transfer to the United Kingdom remained idle in north Africa and Sicily and assault shipping was engaged in ferrying an air force to bases in Italy which did not yet exist, and might not now be taken without a long and arduous struggle, the British Chiefs of Staff began to doubt the wisdom of the agreements they had accepted at Quebec. They did not question the high priority given to *Overlord*; on the contrary, it was because they feared that the Allies might otherwise fail to secure the conditions laid down for *Overlord's* success that they argued for a more flexible, though still limited, Mediterranean strategy based on a more vigorous campaign in Italy and the diversion of resources for the capture of the Dodecanese. They recognised that this strategy would require the retention of landing craft in the Mediterranean, and thus some delay to *Overlord*, but felt that the delay would have the compensating advantage that more time would be available for the production of assault shipping and the development of the United States build-up in the United Kingdom.[42]

On 19 October, in response to their representations, the Prime Minister requested that 'a staff study of the situation in the Mediterranean . . . be conducted in a secret manner and on the assumption that commitments into which we have already entered with the Americans particularly as regards *Overlord* can be modified to meet the exigencies of a changing situation'.[43] In making the study, which was issued on 8 November under the title 'Relation of Mediterranean to *Overlord*', the Joint Planners accepted the JIC's view that the Germans would not be able to bring enough divisions to Italy to enable them to strike a decisive blow there; this was ruled out by Germany's difficulties in Russia and in Italy itself, by her needs in the Balkans, without which she could not continue the war economically and strategically, and by her inability to stage a major counter-offensive in Italy without running grave risks elsewhere.†

---

* See below, p 173.   † See below p 176.

41. Dir/C Archive, 4595 of 8 October 1943. See also R Lewin, *The American Magic* (1982), p 237.
42. Ehrman, op cit, Vol V, pp 113–115.
43. ibid, p 106; CAB 121/128, COS(43)639(o) of 19 October.

But the Planners also accepted that the Allied offensive in Italy could not be taken beyond Rome without unacceptable delay to *Overlord*, and thus concentrated attention on the remaining possibilities. Assuming that Turkey could be brought into the war by the end of 1943* and that Russia maintained the initiative on the eastern front, there was a good chance that by sending limited forces to Turkey the Allies could secure the surrender of some of the Balkan satellites, Bulgaria being the most vulnerable. Given Turkish co-operation, Rhodes could be neutralised from air bases in south-west Anatolia, thus permitting the Allies to pass convoys to Russia and Turkey through the Aegean and enabling them to cut off the German-occupied islands for later occupation. So much could be done without affecting *Overlord*. To increase support for the guerrillas and further the enemy's collapse in the Balkans the best course would be to establish a bridgehead in Albania. But this could not be done without drawing on forces from the United Kingdom; it would require the postponement of *Overlord* for one month, to 1 June 1944, and would also mean that Operation *Anvil* in the south of France would have to be abandoned unless it became clear that enemy resistance in that area would be slight.[44]

The Chiefs of Staff accepted these proposals as the basis of the argument they would develop at the next meeting with the Americans, that which took place in Cairo from 22 to 26 November and which was resumed there on 3 December, after the western Allies had met the Russians in conference at Tehran. During the first half of the proceedings at Cairo the Prime Minister made a vigorous statement of the case for revising the existing Mediterranean strategy. In an examination of the seaborne operations that would be possible during the coming winter the British Chiefs of Staff argued for a landing on the west coast of Italy in December 1943 or January 1944 and an attack on Rhodes in February 1944 in addition to the agreed operations across the Bay of Bengal against the Andaman islands in March 1944 (Operation *Buccaneer*). The United States authorities, who were anxious to concentrate discussion on strategic planning for the Pacific and south-east Asia, stipulated that operations in the Dodecanese must not interfere with plans for the operation against the Andamans, but otherwise accepted the British proposals 'as the basis for discussion with the Soviet staff'. At Tehran, however, the Russian authorities pronounced firmly against any postponement of *Overlord* and – to the

---

* A meeting of the Russian, American and British Foreign Ministers, held in Moscow on 29 and 30 October to brief the Russian government on the decisions reached at the Quebec conference, had agreed that efforts to bring Turkey into the war should be renewed.

44. CAB 121/128, JP(43) 390 of 8 November.

surprise of the western delegations, which had so far ceased to give serious attention to *Anvil* that they did not take AFHQ's plan for the operation to the Tehran meeting – argued almost as powerfully against any dispersal of Allied forces in the Mediterranean; they preferred that all available Allied forces should take part in a landing in the south of France in conjunction with the *Overlord* invasion.[45]

After much discussion, the British and US Chiefs of Staff concluded that they must undertake to launch *Overlord* during May 1944 and to support it with a landing in the south of France on the largest scale permitted by the number of landing craft available. Together with an undertaking by Stalin to launch an offensive to coincide with *Overlord*, in order to prevent the transfer of German forces from the eastern to the western front, this commitment was written into the military conclusions of the Tehran conference. The other conclusions provided for the support of the Yugoslav Partisans with supply and commando operations, for continued efforts to persuade Turkey to enter the war and for measures to secure close co-operation between the three military staffs in the planning of their European operations.[46]

For the British and US military staffs, returning to Cairo with considerable anxiety at the narrow margin of safety allowed for in the existing plans for *Overlord* and *Anvil*, the problems that remained were those of reconciling their plans for the Mediterranean and their plans for the Pacific and south-east Asia with their Tehran commitments. The first problem was solved by an agreement to limit the advance in Italy to the Pisa-Rimini line and to make operations in the Aegean dependent on the entry of Turkey into the war.[47] The second was solved by deferring the invasion of the Andaman islands. These agreements were incorporated in the final report of the Combined Chiefs of Staff of 6 December which, after reaffirming that the continued repression of the U-boats and the strategic air offensive were among the first charges on resources for the war against Germany, went on to say that in the light of the Tehran decisions 'we have reached agreement as follows regarding operations in the European Theatre:-

(a) "Overlord" and "Anvil" are the supreme operations for 1944. They must be carried out during May 1944. Nothing must be undertaken in any other part of the world which hazards the success of these two operations.

---

45. Ehrman, op cit, Vol V, pp 165–167.
46. CAB 80/77, COS(43)791(0) Part III of 8 March 1944 (CCS 426/1 of 6 December 1943); Ehrman, op cit, Vol V, pp 172–183.
47. Ehrman, op cit, Vol V, pp 181–182, 184, 186.

(b) "Overlord" as at present planned is on a narrow margin. Everything practicable should be done to increase its strength.

(c) The examination of "Anvil" on the basis of not less than a two-division assault should be pressed forward as fast as possible. If the examination reveals that it requires strengthening, consideration will have to be given to the provision of additional resources.

(d) Operations in the Aegean, including in particular the capture of Rhodes, are desirable, provided that they can be fitted in without detriment to "Overlord" and "Anvil".

(e) Every effort must be made, by accelerated building and conversion, to provide the essential additional landing craft for the European Theatre'.[48]

□

The British and American authorities held their debates and took their decisions of the last four months of 1943 in the knowledge that on the eastern front Germany had lost the initiative after the failure of her Kursk offensive in July. The Russian counter-attack against Army Group South in the Kursk salient early in August took the Germans by surprise. They abandoned Kharkov on 23 August and by the end of September the Russians had forced them to pull back beyond the Dnieper and to evacuate the Taman peninsula across the Kerch straits. In October they held the Russians to the south of Kiev; but further south they lost Zaporozhe, Dniepropetrovsk and Melitopol while further north – having lost Smolensk in September – they were unable to stem the Russian offensive towards Vitebsk which cut the rail communications between Army Group Centre and Army Group North. In November they held Vitebsk with difficulty but lost Kiev and Zhitomir. By the end of that month they had retaken Zhitomir but had failed to retake Kiev. At the end of the year the Russian thrust from Kiev threatened to separate Army Group South, which had by then lost the northern half of the Dnieper, from Army Group Centre. What London and Washington learned from the communiqués about the course of the fighting was supplemented by a steady supply of intelligence.

Sigint continued to provide the most reliable information on the course of the fighting. The main Sigint sources were the Enigma and the Fish, which now increasingly rivalled the Enigma in importance, but Japanese diplomatic decrypts also added a little. Of the Enigma keys, the GAF general key (Red) and the naval keys in

---

48.   CAB 80/77, COS(43)791(o) Part III of 8 March 1944 (CCS 426/1 of 6 December 1943), para 10; Ehrman, op cit, Vol V, p 189.

use in the Black Sea (Porpoise and, from October 1943, Grampus) were again the most valuable. Of the Fish links,* GC and CS was by May 1943 reading those with Army Group South (Squid), with Army Group A and Seventeenth Army (Octopus), and with the GAF mission in Romania (Tarpon) and the German authorities in Memel (Trout); and the link with Army Group Centre (Perch) was broken in August. These links produced a steady rise in the volume of Sigint, and because they yielded a high proportion of decrypts of long-term significance they more than made up for the fact that GC and CS had no success at this stage against the army Enigma keys on the eastern front and broke few of the GAF Enigma keys. Of the GAF Enigma keys in that theatre, only that of Fliegerkorps I in the Ukraine (Ermine), first broken in February 1943, was read with any regularity between the autumn of 1943 and the summer of 1944.†

In addition to Sigint, Whitehall was now receiving what it regarded as good reports from SIS. Some of these came from Switzerland; others, including those from a SIS agent in touch with the German military intelligence agency (the Abwehr), were valuable because they covered developments on the northern sector of the front, from which there was little intelligence from the Sigint sources. As before, however, the Soviet authorities supplied little information. They continued to be reserved about their own plans and intentions. About the German forces they confined themselves mainly to providing occasional retrospective analyses of battles, some of which included technical intelligence about enemy tanks.[49]‡

The reticence of the Soviet authorities about themselves made it difficult for Whitehall to predict the onset of the battles, but Whitehall's intelligence about the German forces enabled it to follow the day-to-day fighting on the eastern front in considerable

---

* See Appendix 2.
† For details of GC and CS's progress against the Enigma cyphers see Appendix 3.
‡ At the Tehran conference in November 1943 arrangements were made for the regular briefing of the Russian General Staff on Allied operational plans.[50] But nothing was said about the exchange of intelligence, and while the Russians continued to make frequent requests for information on such subjects as German manpower and equipment, and were also given specially prepared versions of the JIC's regular assessments of the results of the bombing of Germany, they still supplied little or nothing in return. In the spring of 1944,

49. CAB 121/464, SIC file D/Russia/4, MIL 9703 of 15 August and 9818 of 2 September 1943 (advance copies of COS(43)265 of 27 September in CAB 121/465, SIC file D/Russia/5, Vol 1); CAB 121/466, SIC file D/Russia/5, Vol 2, BMM report no 5 of 4 January 1944 (issued by MI 17 on 27 January); CAB 121/464, Account of visit to Leningrad front, 17 February 1944; JIC(44)81(o) of 8 March.
50. CAB 80/77, COS (43) 791 (o) Part III of 8 March 1944 (CCS 426/1 of 6 December 1943).

detail without great delay. It also received from time to time enemy
assessments of the broader strategic outlook. In a telegram to the
embassy in Berlin, decrypted at the beginning of May 1943, the
Japanese Foreign Minister had emphasised that Soviet Russia's
industrial potential and ability to wage war were steadily increasing.[33] It was learned on 9 August, from a SIS report from Switzerland, that 'the highest German authorities' recognised that they
had under-estimated Russian strength and feared that they might
not be able to prevent a break-through.[54] On 13 August Whitehall
obtained the decrypt of the comments of the Japanese Ambassador
on an interview he had had with Ribbentrop at the end of July; the
Ambassador thought Germany would probably put up a more
effective defence than she had managed during the past two winters,
but he discounted any prospect of 'a brilliant German victory'. By
16 August Sigint had established that Army Group South lacked
reserves and was having to be reinforced from other parts of the
front, and another SIS report had claimed that the Germans had
decided to construct a fortified line from Riga to the Black Sea.[55]*
This line was again referred to, this time as the *Ostwall*, in another
Japanese diplomatic decrypt from Berlin towards the end of September, when the Military Intelligence Branch (MI) surmised that
it might run along the rivers Bug and Dniester.[57] Meanwhile, GAF
and Porpoise Enigma decrypts had revealed that the German
evacuation of Taman had been in progress since the first week of
September,[58] while by 19 September GAF Enigma decrypts and an

---

when a new head of the British Military Mission in Moscow was appointed, yet another
attempt to achieve some reciprocity encountered reluctance.[51] The head of Mission was able
to report on 29 April that a Tiger tank was being shipped from Murmansk and that a
Ferdinand gun was promised as soon as one was available; but he had no other evidence of
any desire to co-operate.[52] An authority in the Ministry of Economic Warfare has confirmed
that though MEW made contact with the Russian Mission in London and devoted a good
deal of time to answering Moscow's questions the Russians supplied nothing in return. From
the spring of 1944, however, the Russian General Staff did supply some order of battle
intelligence on the German Army, as we shall see in Volume III Part 2.

* Hitler gave permission for all four Army Groups to begin work on this line, the Panther
line or *Ostwall*, on 12 August.[56]

51. JIC (44) 8th, 9th and 10th (o) Meetings, 22 and 29 February, 7 March;
       CAB 121/466, SIC file D/Russia/5, Vol 2, JIC (44) 81 (o) of 8 March,
       COS (44) 80th (o) Meeting, 9 March.
52. CAB 121/466, MIL 1183 of 29 April, COS (44) 555 (o) of 22 June.
53. Dir/C Archive, 3171 of 2 May 1943.
54. WO 208/3573 of 9 August 1943.
55. ibid of 16 August 1943.
56. A Seaton, *The Russo-German War 1941–1945* (1971), p 378.
57. WO 208/3573 of 27 September 1943.
58. ibid, 27 September 1943; eg DEFE 3/583, ZTPGMs 34139, 35749, 36732,
       37198, 37233, 37419, 38247.

Abwehr decrypt had foreshadowed the German decision to withdraw to the Dnieper.[59]

If intelligence showed that the German Army was stretched to the utmost, with many divisions below establishment, it left no doubt that the German Air Force was in a still more parlous state. During September the Air Ministry calculated that the first-line strength of the GAF on the entire eastern front was 1,550 to 1,600, compared with 2,000 in July, and that in most units serviceability was no higher than 50 per cent; and it pointed out that the concentration of most of this force south of Kharkov had left the Kiev-Smolensk front with 'totally inadequate' air support.[60] The Air Intelligence Branch (AI) attributed the GAF's weakness in Russia mainly to the over-riding claims of the defence of the Reich and of the fighting in other western theatres.[61] Another factor, as AI noted in October, was that whereas Germany was drawing on obsolete and obsolescent aircraft, the Russians were building modern planes and benefiting from US and British production.[62] These conclusions were to be amply borne out; fighters withdrawn from the eastern front in the autumn of 1943 to bolster the defence of the Reich were never to be replaced, and the continuing demands of the ground fighting in Russia made it impossible for the GAF to carry out its plans for withdrawing dive-bomber and fighter formations for re-equipment with modern types.[63] The GAF was also handicapped by the effects of a change of policy to which – no doubt because the enemy again encountered delay and difficulty in carrying it out – the Air Ministry did not attach sufficient importance at the time. By the summer of 1943 the High Command of the GAF (OKL), realising that the policy of close support for the Army, which had hitherto engaged four-fifths of its bombing on the eastern front, could not be decisive, had decided to devote more effort to strategic bombing. In the face of opposition from Hitler and the High Command of the Armed Forces (OKW) it was unable to start on the necessary reorganisation until after the Kursk offensive, and by the spring of 1944, when it was ready to carry out a larger bombing effort against Soviet industrial production, the German retreats on the eastern front had put the Soviet targets out of range. Meanwhile, however, the withdrawal of bombers for training for the new programme had increasingly reduced the German bombing effort in support of army operations since November 1943, and during the Russian advances of March and April 1944 the disengagement for

59. WO 208/3573 of 12 and 19 September 1943.
60. CAB 80/41, COS(43)267 of 30 September (213th résumé), para 46.
61. ibid, COS(43)248 of 2 September (209th résumé), para 31.
62. CAB 121/464, JIC(43)409(0) of 2 October.
63. AIR 41/10, *The Rise and Fall of the German Air Force*, p 243.

training of Fliegerkorps IV was to reduce to 165 the number of first-line bombers immediately available for the entire eastern front.[64]

On 2 October 1943, in the light of the available intelligence and of Soviet reports that the Germans were withdrawing only when forced to do so,[65] the JIC concluded that the enemy had resisted the Russian offensive with all available forces, but had done so to no avail, and it judged that he might be driven back as far as the line Bug-Dniester-Pripet marshes if the Russians kept up their hammer blows during the next few weeks, while the weather held, and might be unable to hold even that line throughout the winter.[66] During October several diplomatic reports from Sweden, Switzerland and Turkey claimed that the Germans had already decided to withdraw to the *Ostwall*, described as a line that was being developed in depth from Riga to Odessa,[67] and they received some confirmation from a Japanese diplomatic decrypt. This gave details of such a defence line and reported that the retreat was not going according to plan because of Russian pressure; it added that according to Ribbentrop Hitler had spoken of having to withdraw on the eastern front 'in addition to sparing 24 divisions for the Mediterranean theatre'.[68] At about the same time, however, Sigint from the eastern front disclosed that of four additional divisions brought in to meet the Soviet attacks in the Kirovograd area after the fall of Zaporozhe, three had come from other fronts – 24th Panzer Division from Italy, and 376th and 389th Infantry Divisions from France and the Low Countries.[69]

On 15 November, after the Soviet capture of Kiev, the JIC forecast that the Soviet forces, with large reserves of manpower and with superiority in the air and in winter warfare, would maintain the offensive throughout the winter, and that until the thaw of 1944 Germany would have no choice but to withdraw as slowly as possible to Riga in the north, to Korosten in the centre and to the Dniester in the area of Army Group South.[70] It made this appreciation in the course of a debate with the US JIC, which suspected that Germany was falling back to shorter lines in order to release five to ten divisions from Russia and which was pointing out that

---

64. ibid, pp 223–234, 239–240, 242, 243–244.
65. WO 208/3573 of 19 September 1943; CAB 121/464, MIL 9943 of 15 September 1943.
66. CAB 121/464, MIL 9943 of 15 September, JIC(43)409(o) of 2 October; WO 208/3573 of 19 September 1943.
67. WO 208/3573 of 11 and 18 October 1943.
68. ibid, 11 October 1943; Dir/C Archive, 4595 of 8 October 1943.
69. WO 208/3573 of 25 October 1943; Dir/C Archive, 4567 of 8 October; CX/MSS/3329/T14.
70. JIC(43)457 of 15 November.

relatively small withdrawals from Russia would constitute a considerable accretion of German strength on other fronts.[71] The JIC did not agree. Drawing on Sigint which by mid-November had provided still more evidence to confirm Russian 'indications' that divisions were being transferred to the eastern front by disclosing the presence there of 1st Panzer Division from the Balkans, of SS Division Adolf Hitler and 76th Infantry Division from Italy and of 25th Panzer Division from France, it estimated that these arrivals had raised the total of German divisions from 200 to 205* and the number of offensive divisions from 167 to 174, of which the number of Panzer divisions had risen from 17 to 20; and it pointed out that neither the new arrivals nor the reinforcement of the Dnieper front by between 28 and 30 divisions from other sectors of the eastern front had enabled Germany to stem the Russian advance. As for the coming months, the German divisions, many of which were on average 40 per cent below strength, would be further weakened in a fighting withdrawal; in the absence of German reserves, all would require re-organisation and re-equipment; and the GAF was unable to make up for the Army's numerical inferiority to the Russians. The JIC's conclusion was that until the spring of 1944 Germany would move divisions from Russia – and then only two or three – only if she was confronted by disastrous developments in south-eastern Europe, and that in the spring, when she would have to decide whether she was more threatened in the east or west, she would probably decide to withdraw only depleted divisions from the eastern front.[73]

It did not yet know that on 3 November Hitler had already issued a directive laying down that priority was to be given to the western front. But it was soon to learn from a diplomatic decrypt that in an interview on 24 January 1944 he had told the Japanese Ambassador that he was having to conduct the war in Russia on the principle of not jeopardising the defence of the west; the need for increased preparations against the western invasion was now adding itself to the consequences of Italy's collapse, which had called for the reinforcement of Italy and the Balkans by 35 German divisions at the expense of the eastern front.[74]

□

---

* The actual total of German divisions in Russia in November 1943, including Finland, was 195, as compared with 177 (presumably excluding Finland) in October.[72]

71. JIC(43)441 of 28 October.   72. Seaton, op cit, p 394.
73. WO 208/3573 of 9 August, 11 October, 15 November 1943; CAB 121/464, MIL 331 of 7 November 1943; JIC(43)457 of 15 November, paras 2 and 12 et seq.
74. Dir/C Archive, 5595 of 5 February 1944.

The agreements reached at the Cairo conference had involved the Allies in establishing a unified command in the Mediterranean under a Supreme Allied Commander (SACMED) and making new provisions to meet the shortage of landing craft; those due to leave the Mediterranean for *Overlord* were to be retained until mid-January 1944, while those earlier allocated to the operation against the Andaman islands were re-allocated to *Overlord* and *Anvil*.[75] At the end of December 1943 as a result of their slow progress in the campaign in Italy – and of the conclusion that the campaign could not, in the Prime Minister's words, be allowed 'to stagnate and fester' without crippling the *Anvil* preparations and increasing the difficulties of *Overlord* – the Allies agreed that an amphibious operation on the Italian west coast should be launched at Anzio (Operation *Shingle*) on 22 January 1944. Partly because of lack of progress in negotiations aimed at getting Turkey to enter the war, but mainly to ensure that the required assault shipping was available for Operation *Shingle*, operations in the Aegean and against Rhodes were deferred until after Operation *Anvil* had taken place. The smaller seaborne operation in Arakan which had been substituted for the operation against the Andamans was abandoned.[76]

The Allies were frustrated in their hope that the Anzio landing would enable them to gain Rome by the end of January; and intelligence on the enemy's reaction to the landing, which showed that it included the transfer of divisions from other theatres, confirmed that he remained determined to devote considerable resources to resisting the Allied advance.* Nor was this the only setback for Allied planning. In December AFHQ had requested that the initial *Anvil* assault force be raised from two to three divisions; in January, following General Eisenhower's arrival at SHAEF as Surpreme Allied Commander, SHAEF recommended that the *Overlord* assault force should be increased from three to five divisions and its front widened, that its rate of supply and reinforcement should be accelerated and that the operation must therefore be postponed. In the ensuing Allied debate about strategy, which revolved around 'the defence of *Anvil* against the combination of *Shingle* and its sequel with the claims of *Overlord*',[77] the US Chiefs of Staff sought to retain *Anvil*, General Eisenhower became prepared to reduce *Anvil* to a mere threat if the needs of *Overlord* so required, and the British Chiefs of Staff, convinced that *Anvil* would be of less

---

* See below, p 186 et seq.

75. CAB 80/77, COS (43)791(o) Part III of 8 March 1944 (CCS 426/1 of 6 December 1943), paras 12, 13, 24.
76. Ehrman, op cit, Vol V, pp 209–223.
77. ibid, p 225.

assistance to *Overlord* than a vigorous continuation of the Italian campaign, pressed for its cancellation.[78]

Thus far, intelligence had contributed nothing to the discussions. On 12 January, assisting the Joint Planners to examine SHAEF's recommendation that *Overlord* should be strengthened and *Anvil* reduced to a threat, the JIC had suggested that the land opposition to *Overlord* was 'unlikely to be less, and in the early stages may exceed', what the COSSAC plan had allowed for, but that it would not be any greater if *Anvil* was reduced to a threat. But it had had no evidence for the view that the reduction of *Anvil* would not lead to any substantial changes in the enemy's dispositions; it had supported it only with the belief that Germany had been unable to assess the strength of Allied shipping resources in the Mediterranean and was likely to remain so.[79] On 24 February the JIC had revised this belief – there were signs, it then said, that the enemy was beginning to doubt whether the Allies had enough assault shipping in the Mediterranean for another amphibious operation on the scale of the Anzio landings in the near future – and had emphasised that the most effective way of preventing the transfer of German troops into the *Overlord* area was to keep him guessing about Allied intentions and resources in the Mediterranean area as a whole. Not entirely consistently, it had also said the enemy 'appeared to be most nervous' about a threat to the south of France, and had suggested that this nervousness might be allayed if the Allies concentrated shipping in the Adriatic for an assault on Istria which, if carried out at the earliest possible moment after the beginning of *Overlord*, would be preferable to *Anvil* as a means of assisting *Overlord*.[80]

The debate had been driven into a temporary compromise by Germany's successes against the Anzio beachhead and at Cassino. On 22 February SACMED, General Wilson, unwilling to withdraw forces from Italy before the main Allied force in Italy had made a junction with the Anzio bridgehead, recommended the cancellation of *Anvil*. On 26 February the Combined Chiefs of Staff gave him a new directive. The campaign in Italy was to have over-riding priority over other Mediterranean operations and be the first call on his resources, but so far as possible without prejudice to that campaign he was to prepare to carry out alternative amphibious operations with the object of contributing to *Overlord* by containing the maximum enemy forces. Among these alternatives, he was to

---

78. ibid, pp 229–242.
79. JIC(43)524(o) of 30 December, JIC(44)10(o) of 8 January; CAB 121/405, SIC file D/France/10, Vol I, JP(44) 4 of 12 January.
80. JIC(44)64)(o) and 72(o) of 24 February.

give priority to *Anvil*, as a two-division assault launched simultaneously with *Overlord*, until the situation was reviewed in a month's time. *Overlord* itself was to be postponed until early in June.[81]

In the second week of March the high-grade Sigint disclosed that despite the failure of his efforts to destroy the Anzio beachhead, Field Marshal Kesselring still intended to withdraw from the present defence line, the *Gustav* line, only if he proved unable to hold the line and contain the beachhead with his existing forces, and that in that event he would fall back to a line, the *Caesar* line, from which he could still cover Rome.* It was in the light of this intelligence, as well as of the course of the fighting, that on 22 March, in response to a request from the Combined Chiefs for his latest appreciation, SACMED again recommended that *Anvil* should be cancelled. He argued that, as the Germans were preparing the *Caesar* line from which to cover Rome when the Allies had succeeded in forming a junction between the Anzio bridgehead and their main front, no forces should be withdrawn from Italy until he had taken Rome, and that if he took Cassino in the present fighting and was able to relieve the bridgehead by the middle of May, he would still be unable to launch *Anvil* before late July, too late to help *Overlord*. Moreover, while the Allies after the fall of Rome would be able to choose between *Anvil* and a full-scale offensive in Italy, he already felt that the latter course of action would make the greater contribution to *Overlord*.[82] On 24 March the US Chiefs of Staff agreed that *Anvil* should be postponed until July but refused to abandon it. Another fierce and lengthy debate ensued. As General Eisenhower told the British Chiefs of Staff, the US Chiefs remained reluctant to abandon *Anvil* mainly because they feared that the Germans would carry out a swift and voluntary withdrawal from Italy shortly before *Overlord* was launched. When the British Chiefs of Staff, strongly in favour of SACMED's recommendation, countered this argument by claiming that all the available intelligence showed that the Germans had every intention of holding on to Rome and that, given that the enemy had already brought in eight divisions to the Rome front from elsewhere, the Italian campaign was admirably fulfilling the purpose of containing his forces, the Americans fell back on another argument. Once the Germans had been driven north of Rome they would be able to carry out delaying actions in Italy with six to eight divisions, releasing nine divisions to oppose *Overlord*, and would have their nine divisions in southern France unengaged.

---

* See below, pp 197–198.

81. Ehrman, op cit, Vol V, pp 229–242.
82. ibid, pp 243–247.

The British conceded that this contingency had to be allowed for and that, if it arose, an *Anvil*-type operation would be necessary as a diversion to help *Overlord*, but urged that the options should be kept open till the latest possible date. The Americans, convinced that *Anvil* would otherwise not be launched at all, insisted that a specific date should be set for it. Nor was the deadlock broken by an approach to General Marshall from the Prime Minister, who relied on Sigint to point out that the Allies were tying down no less than 34 divisions, 25 in Italy (of which 18 were south of Rome) and nine in the south of France. It was not until 19 April, when General Alexander had persuaded the Combined Chiefs of Staff that the Allies should not resume the offensive in Italy until the middle of May, so that they would not be able to carry out *Anvil* in July, that a new directive was sent to SACMED.[83]

The new directive laid it down that with the objective of destroying or containing the maximum German formations, SACMED was to launch an all-out offensive in Italy. He was also to develop the greatest possible threat to contain German forces in the south of France by *Overlord* D – 5 and to maintain it for as long as possible after D-day. And in order to ensure that his available amphibious lift could be used either to support operations in Italy or to exploit opportunities arising in the south of France or elsewhere, he was to push forward with all preparations which did not prejudice the main offensive.[84] In proposing this compromise the British Chiefs of Staff implicitly recognised that while they had excellent intelligence about the dispositions and the order of battle of the German Army and about its present strategy in Italy, conclusive intelligence about Germany's intentions in the future, in contingencies which had not yet arisen, was necessarily lacking. After SACMED had received the new directive they explicitly recognised that this was the case when the Prime Minister told them that the Americans were still anxious lest the Germans in Italy 'suddenly withdraw at full speed leaving rearguards and nip through the tunnels into the *Overlord* battle', and asked for their comments; they replied that they had always allowed that this might happen and that, if it did, *Anvil* might be the best Allied response.[85] And it is indeed the case that uncertainty on this score greatly hampered the JIC when it was drawing up the appreciations it issued after the end of February.

At the beginning of March the JIC had been confident that, in order to prevent the Allies from reaching the south-eastern frontier

---

83. ibid, p 245 et seq: CAB 121/406, SIC file D/France/10, Vol 2, PM telegram to General Marshall OZ 1895 of 12 April 1944.
84. Ehrman, op cit, Vol V, pp 259, 561.
85. CAB 121/406, COS(44)361(o) of 22 April, COS(44) 133rd (o) Meeting, 25 April, Annex.

of France and making contact with the Yugoslav Partisans through Istria, Germany would delay her retreat to the Pisa-Rimini line for as long as possible; but it had recognised that she might be able to withdraw up to eight divisions from other fronts, including Italy, if the Allies had not broken the Pisa-Rimini line, in the event that she needed reinforcements to prevent the Allies from exploiting the *Overlord* bridgehead.[86] At the end of March the JIC had concluded that the Germans would continue to fight in southern Italy with the utmost vigour provided that developments on the Russian front or as a result of *Overlord* did not compel them to reinforce either or both of those theatres; in this case, however, they would be forced to try to withdraw from Italy.[87] On 13 April, in a paper which examined the implications for *Overlord* of the situation on the Russian front, the JIC had thought that if Germany was compelled to send reinforcements to the east she would draw them from other theatres than France and the Low Countries even at the expense of withdrawing to the Pisa-Rimini line, in which case she could take up to six divisions from Italy.[88] In all these appreciations the British authorities took the view that their intimate knowledge of Germany's stance in Italy made it reasonable to discount a voluntary German withdrawal. She would withdraw divisions from Italy only if the necessity of defeating *Overlord* or of responding to a sudden deterioration on the eastern front compelled her to change her strategy.

☐

They maintained the same view with regard to her policy in the Balkans, and did so with the help of intelligence that was no less detailed and comprehensive.

At the time of the Italian capitulation the JIC had estimated that the Germans had some sixteen divisions in the Balkans, six and a half (including four offensive divisions: 100th, 114th and 119th Jäger, and 7th SS Mountain (Prinz Eugen)) being in Yugoslavia, none in Albania and seven (including the sole Panzer Division, 1st Panzer) in Greece and the Greek islands. It had believed that when Italy collapsed Germany would have to increase the total from sixteen to at least twenty-four if she were to hold the area, and that even if six of the additional divisions were kept in Yugoslavia and two sent to Albania, to make up for the loss of some fourteen Italian divisions, her forces would be thin on the ground; they would have

---

86. CAB 121/413, SIC file D/Germany/1, Vol 2, JIC(44)66(0) of 1 March.
87. CAB 121/406, JP(44)88 of 26 March, para 6.
88. JIC(44)138(0) of 13 April.

to be disposed so as to retain control in the north-west, to hold the lines of communication to the Dalmatian coast and the bauxite region round Mostar and to cover the vital rail link between Salonika and Belgrade, thus abandoning most of Bosnia, Hercegovina and Montenegro to the guerrillas. But there was no doubt that she would do her utmost to meet these minimum requirements.[89] The accuracy of these forecasts was fully borne out by the ample Sigint coverage of the German Army's order of battle and of the fighting in Yugoslavia during the winter of 1943–1944.

Between September 1943 and February 1944 Germany reinforced the Balkans by a net seven divisions. Of the twelve brought in, nine were newly raised, one came from the rear in Italy, one from Norway and one (8th SS Cavalry Division together with elements of 5th SS Panzer Division) from Russia after a brief refit in Germany. Seven of the twelve were predominantly German, the rest had German cadres; some, it was clear, were well below establishment strength. Five were moved out of the Balkans – one to France, one to Italy and three to Russia. The timing of the transfers was such that the total strength in the area, as estimated by MI, was between twenty-one divisions in November 1943 and twenty-four in the first week of January 1944; after dropping to twenty-two divisions by the end of February it rose at the beginning of March to twenty-five.[90]

In December 1943 AFHQ estimated that in an effort to contain the Partisans no less than nineteen of the available divisions were in Yugoslavia and Albania.[91] This estimate included divisions in transit through Yugoslavia and German-Croat formations that were being used to release field formations for the more important fronts, but the decrypts left no doubt that Greece was being denuded of troops by the needs of other fronts and the pressures in Yugoslavia. The movement of 1st Panzer Division to Russia, where it was located by the Enigma at the end of October 1943, left only one division in the Peloponnese (117th Jäger).[92] When that had been reinforced by an incompletely trained Fortress Division from Germany, the Germans were forced from the end of November to transfer 1st Mountain Division from Greece and a Bulgarian division from Macedonia, as well as 371st Infantry Division from northern Italy, because they could no longer delay the attempt to

---

89. JIC(43) 336 (o) of 14 August.
90. WO 208/3573, passim to 6 March 1944; WO 204/968, AFHQ Intelligence Summaries Nos 74 of 24 January, 80 of 7 March 1944; and, eg, DEFE 3/887, JP 8253 of 27 October; DEFE 3/9 VL 1126 of 4 December 1943.
91. WO 208/968, No 69 of 22 December 1943.
92. WO 208/3573 of 15 November 1943; CX/MSS/3491/T50.

clear the Partisans from south of Zagreb and the Sarajevo area until they had completed the occupation of the Adriatic islands.[93]

The detailed Sigint coverage of the fighting in Yugoslavia fully confirmed that Germany was making do with the bare minimum of troops. Her first attempt to clear the Partisans from the Zagreb-Ljubljana area was delayed by the pressing need to secure the Dalmatian coast and provide for the capture of the islands as far south as Split, and was brought to an inconclusive close in November by the need to recall divisions to northern Italy. In December her operations in the Zagreb and Sarajevo areas, resumed with the divisions newly arrived from Italy and Greece, delayed her programme for the capture of the islands between Split and Dubrovnik; and in January 1944, while that programme itself was largely completed despite the all but total lack of air and naval support, the drives inland again ended indecisively and 371st Infantry Division was being transferred to the Russian front.[94]*

In January the Germans also ordered the transfer to Italy of 114th Jäger Division from the coast and the hinterland between Sinj and Split.[95] The decrypts had shown that the possibility of a major landing there by Allied forces from Italy had continued to give them cause for grave anxiety till the end of October 1943, but that they had begun to discount the risk of Balkan invasion, either from Italy or in the eastern Mediterranean, during November and had then dismissed it entirely.[96] At the end of December the decrypt of an appreciation by Fremde Heere West took the appointment of General Eisenhower to be Supreme Allied Commander in northwest Europe as evidence of 'the manifest decision of the enemy command to concentrate its main effort in the England area'.[97] In an appreciation decrypted on 22 February GAF South East judged that Allied dispositions in the Mediterranean precluded the possibility of any Allied action in the Adriatic other than commando raids.[98]

---

    * For further details see below, p 157 et seq.

    93. CX/MSS/T31/95; WO 208/3573 of 13 December 1943; WO 204/968, No
          66 of 27 November 1943; CAB 121/529, Balkan sitreps Nos 6, 12 and 25 of
          22 and 28 November, 12 December 1943.
    94. eg DEFE 3/129, VL 3999 of 15 January; DEFE 3/135, VL 5406 of 2
          February 1944; WO 204/968, No 73 of 18 January 1944.
    95. As examples of many decrypts about the move of 114th Jäger, DEFE 3/
          18, VLs 3361 of 6 January, 3406 of 7 January; DEFE 3/129, VLs 3797 of
          12 January, 3916 of 14 January; DEFE 3/130, VL 4146 of 17 January;
          DEFE 3/131, VLs 4253 and 4280 of 19 January, 4321 and 4346 of 20
          January, 4435 of 21 January; DEFE 3/132, VL 4513 of 22 January 1944.
    96. eg DEFE 3/16 VL 2755 of 27 December 1943; CX/MSS/T36/44.
    97. DEFE 3/17, VL 3053 of 1 January 1944.
    98. DEFE 3/141, VL 6878 of 22 February 1944.

In March, far from being able to resume operations against the Partisans in Serbia, Germany had to give ground to them as a result of her withdrawal from Yugoslavia and Greece of the forces initially used to occupy Hungary. The first indication that new movement was afoot was given by a decrypt in mid-February. It suggested that 1st Mountain Division was leaving Split for a destination outside Yugoslavia; Transport HQ Vienna was involved in the transfer.[99] On 22 and 23 February, however, decrypted signals from Second Panzer Army, dated 9 February and ordering 1st Mountain Division from Split to Skoplje and SS Division Prinz Eugen from Mostar to the Sarajevo area, stated that the SS Division was being shifted so as to be available for rapid rail movement in the event of an Allied landing. These decrypts persuaded MI that the two divisions were to form a mobile reserve against a perceived Allied threat, probably to Greece.[100] Together with signals decrypted on 11 and 12 March, ordering the move of two infantry divisions to the Zara-Sibenik area and the formation of a mobile reserve on the Dalmatian coast against the danger of an Allied landing,[101] they seemed to be explained by Allied deception measures aimed at suggesting that landings in Greece and Dalmatia were to be expected.[102] Partly on this account, and partly because other decrypts ordering troop movements refrained from mentioning destinations and were thought to be in preparation for new offensives against the Partisans,[103] it did not emerge until after the invasion of Hungary that they had been part of an elaborate deception plan devised to conceal Germany's intentions from her own troops.*

Although GAF Enigma decrypts relating to the stocking of airfields in the area of Luftgau XVII (which included Wiener Neustadt and Vienna-Aspern) had suggested to AI by 25 February that Germany was perhaps apprehensive about the 'recalcitrant satellites', Sigint gave no warning of the invasion of Hungary, which

---

* For a similar deception measure, carried out with the aim of impressing the Italians with the strength of Germany's forces in Italy, see below, p 108 n†. Others were to find their way into the high-grade decrypts in connection with the Ardennes offensive in the winter of 1944 and the attack in south Hungary in March 1945. On none of these occasions was the deception carried out in the fear that Germany's cyphers were insecure.

99. DEFE 3/139, VL 6452 of 17 February 1944.
100. DEFE 3/141, VL 6852 of 22 February, 6896 of 23 February 1944; WO 208/3573 of 28 February 1944.
101. DEFE 3/146, VLs 8199 and 8244 of 11 March; DEFE 3/147, VL 8272 of 12 March 1944; WO 208/3573 of 13 March 1944.
102. For decrypts reporting alarms about Allied landings see DEFE 3/145, VLs 7816 of 6 March, 7899 of 7 March; DEFE 3/148, VL 8587 of 16 March; DEFE 3/150, VLs 9129 and 9144 of 22 March 1944.
103. DEFE 3/144, VL 7885 of 7 March; DEFE 3/146, VL 8039 of 9 March; DEFE 3/148, VLs 8632 of 13 March, 8725 of 18 March 1944.

began on 19 March, until late on 18 March.* Other GAF signals, one containing Fliegerführer XIV's orders for the operation and another revealing that on 15 March 1st Mountain Division's line of march had been towards the Hungarian frontier, were then decrypted.[105] A subsequent review of the Sigint evidence established that the invasion had been carried out under the over-all command of C-in-C South East with ground forces which, apart from slight assistance by XXII Mountain Corps from Greece, were entirely drawn from Yugoslavia; they included LXIX Mountain Reserve Corps, 1st Mountain Division and elements of 42nd Jäger and 8th SS Cavalry Divisions.[106]

Despite this sizeable diversion and despite the transfer of two further divisions from Yugoslavia and Albania to the eastern front – the Enigma disclosed on 9 April that 100th Jäger Division and 367th Infantry Division were moving to Russia[107] – Germany resumed the offensive against the Partisans in the middle of April, and in May she made a determined effort to eliminate their stronghold in the central mountains.† To make these operations possible she brought up additional police battalions for garrison duties and railway protection;[108] recalled most of the formations used against Hungary;[109] and by various devices, including a new locally-raised division, 21st SS Mountain (Skanderbeg) in Albania,[110] again increased the number of divisions in the Balkans. At the beginning of April MI estimated Germany's total strength in south-eastern

---

* There was no warning from the non-Sigint sources. Reports from the liaison officers at Tito's HQ and elsewhere in Yugoslavia were usually received less promptly than the decrypts, and the information they gave about the enemy, especially about his movements and intentions, were almost without exception either imprecise or (as Sigint showed) inaccurate. On this occasion they reported in advance of the invasion that 1st Mountain Division was moving westward, probably to Germany, and on the day of the invasion that one Panzer division and two SS divisions were ready to move into Hungary from Austria.[104]

† See below, p 163 et seq.

104. WO 202/153, GX/M No 490 of 26 February, GX/M No 680 of 12 March 1944.
105. DEFE 3/149, VL 8760 of 18 March 1944.
106. WO 209/3573 of 27 March 1944; DEFE 3/150, VLs 9039 of 20 March, 9144 of 22 March; DEFE 3/151 VLs 9385 of 25 March, 9417 of 26 March; DEFE 3/152, VLs 9547 of 27 March, 9625 of 28 March 1944.
107. WO 208/3573 of 10 April 1944; CX/MSS/T147/67.
108. DEFE 3/152, VL 9621 of 28 March 1944; WO 208/3573 of 3 April 1944; WO 204/969, AFHQ Intelligence Summaries, No 90 of 17 May 1944.
109. WO 204/969, No 90 of 17 May 1944.
110. WO 208/3573 of 3 and 10 April 1944; DEFE 3/35 (1), KV 139 of 3 April 1944; WO 204/969, No 88 of 2 May 1944; WO 202/165, BLO Sitrep No 275 of 24 May 1944; WO 202/249, B1/3/597/1317 of 26 May 1944.

Europe, including Hungary, as 27, the highest yet.[111]* Except that they left some uncertainty about the whereabouts of the divisions involved in exchanges between Hungary and Yugoslavia, the high-grade decrypts provided evidence for all these measures, as they did for the last-minute temporary reinforcement of the GAF for the drive against Tito's HQ.

They also disclosed that, as was only to be expected, the Germans were coming to feel beleaguered by the increasing pressure on all their fronts. Another appreciation by Fremde Heere West, dated 21 March, had pointed out that the diversion of German forces from Yugoslavia to Hungary provided the Allies with an incentive for a descent on the north-east coast of the Adriatic.[113] At the end of April a signal from Jodl was decrypted ordering the formation of a strategic reserve of divisions which were not to to be used without the consent of OKW†; the divisions in south-east Europe included in the order were 1st Mountain and 42nd Jäger, which had returned from Hungary to Yugoslavia, and three SS divisions then in Hungary (8th Cavalry, 16th and 18th Panzer Grenadier).[114] Commenting on the first of these decrypts on 10 April, MI thought it now unlikely that Germany would be able to reinforce western Europe with forces from the Balkans.[115] And from the end of May this view received further support, as did the JIC's conclusion that Germany would continue to resist on the Italian front, from decrypts which disclosed her first use of the strategic reserve. They reported on 29 May that 16th SS PG Division was moving to Italy[116] and on 1 June that 42nd Jäger was also moving there.[117] On the eve of the landings in Normandy, therefore, the Balkan theatre, according to MI's estimates, was once more holding down 25 divisions: on the western front, according to MI, there were 58 divisions and on the eastern front 187[118]

☐

---

* The actual figure was indeed 27 divisions, of which fifteen were fully German. Of these fifteen, six were unfit for operations; of the total force, thirteen were available for active operations.[112]

† See Volume III Part 2.

111. WO 208/3573 of 3 April 1944.
112. Molony, *The Mediterranean and Middle East*, Vol VI Part 1 (forthcoming) Chapter VII.
113. WO 208/3573 of 10 April 1944.
114. ibid, 1 May 1944; DEFE 3/44 (1), KV 2388 of 29 April 1944.
115. WO 208/3573 of 10 April 1944.
116. WO 208/3573 of 5 June 1944; DEFE 3/162, KV 5685 of 29 May 1944.
117. WO 208/3573 of 5 June 1944; DEFE 3/163, KV 5964 of 1 June; DEFE 3/164, KV 6156 of 2 June 1944.
118. WO 208/3573 of 5 June 1944.

By that time a lull had set in on the eastern front where the Russian offensive, begun in January 1944, had forced the Germans to retreat on all sectors.

The offensive had struck against the Leningrad area and in the Ukraine. In the north it had threatened to envelop the whole of Army Group North by mid-February, when Hitler was forced to allow withdrawal out of Russia to the *Ostwall*. Further south, administering heavy defeats on the German armies, it had reached Galicia and the Romanian and Czechoslovak borders by the beginning of April, and by the middle of April another Russian thrust across the Perekop isthmus and from Kerch had compelled the German forces in the Crimea to evacuate from Sevastopol. During this fighting Whitehall had continued to obtain good intelligence from the Sigint sources,* to which GC and CS added after the opening of the offensive the Enigma keys of Seventeenth Army in the Crimea (Owl), which was read regularly after February 1944, and of First Panzer Army (Pelican), which was read for only a few days in March, and a new Fish link with Army Group A (Stickleback), which had replaced Octopus for Army Group A in October 1943 and was read from February 1944.

In December 1943, before the offensive began, the decrypts, especially of signals from the naval liaison officer with Army Group A, had disclosed that following the failure of the German effort to retake Kiev, the Soviet armies had regained in a few days' fighting much of the ground they had lost to the German counter-offensive.[119] From the GAF Enigma Whitehall also knew that although the Germans had thrown into the counter-offensive two-thirds of their total air strength on the eastern front, the GAF had been ineffective; largely because so many fighters had been withdrawn to Germany, but also because, as the Enigma showed, there was a growing shortage of long-range reconnaisance aircraft, it had been frittered away in unescorted bomber and dive-bomber daytime raids in close support operations made at the request of local military commanders and following no general plan.[120] On 20 January 1944, summing up the voluminous intelligence received since the opening of the Soviet advance, the JIC appreciated that out of a total of 2,100 Axis first-line aircraft on the eastern front, of which at least 1,100 were obsolete or obsolescent, some 1,775 were German, and two-thirds of these 1,775 had been concentrated in the southern

---

* See above, pp 18–19.

119. CAB 80/42, COS (43) 321 of 30 December (226th résumé), para 24.
120. CAB 80/42, COS (43) 318 of 23 December (225th résumé), para 45;
        AIR 41/10, p 242; CX/MSS/T60/10, T61/52, 66 and 103.

sector for the past six months. It also estimated that the German Army on the Russian front totalled about 4 million men in some 209 divisions, many much reduced in strength and equipment if not as yet in morale, of which 95 (including twenty-two Panzer divisions) were in the south and 67 (four Panzer) in the centre; in July 1943 88 (nine Panzer) had been disposed in the centre and 65 (ten Panzer) in the south. It knew that these forces had no reserves and estimated that they faced a Soviet Army of some 7–8½ million men, high in morale and steadily improving in fighting value, and a Soviet Air Force of at least 5,000 mainly modern operational aircraft.[121]

This JIC paper opened with the familiar warning that in relation to the Soviet forces it was 'subject to a wide margin of error because we have so little intelligence about Russian strength and intentions, and at this critical time no information official or unofficial from Moscow other than communiqués'. But the JIC had some evidence from Sigint that Russia had built up concentrations against all the German Army Groups and that her offensive was taking place in 'a series of co-ordinated thrusts in widely separated sectors with the object of fully exploiting the German inferiority in numbers, their supply difficulties and lack of reserves'. It knew from the same source that Germany intended to hold the Crimea as a fortress, was clinging on to the eastern tip of the Dnieper bend and the Nikopol bridgehead despite the fact that her forces there were in grave danger, and would be unable to reinforce the much reduced Army Group North against what it expected to be a major Soviet offensive on the Leningrad front. And it concluded that she would have no choice but to avoid encirclement by carrying out a fighting withdrawal with such counter-attacks as she could manage without dangerously weakening her forces elsewhere, especially in France.

During the course of the Soviet offensive Sigint provided, as usual, relatively little detailed intelligence about the fighting on the front held by Army Group North. The GAF Enigma made it clear that the GAF in that sector, comprising some 250 first-line aircraft after being reinforced from the centre and the south, was 'totally inadequate', particularly in fighters, and that its performance was 'singularly weak'.[122] It also revealed that although Army Group North was receiving ground reinforcements from the south, its losses were not being made good from the end of January.[123] But most of

---

121. CAB 121/464, JIC (44) 21 of 20 January, Appendices I and II.
122. CAB 80/43, COS (44) 20 of 27 January (230th résumé), para 44, COS (44) 24 of 10 February (232nd résumé), para 48, COS (44) 37 of 24 February (234th résumé), para 45.
123. CX/MSS/T73/70, T84/68, T101/51.

the decrypts from this sector dealt less with the fighting than with the question of which line the enemy would withdraw to. From early in January they indicated that the Germans were intending to hold the line Narva-Lake Peipus; this conclusion was supported by SIS reports, and in mid-February the decrypt of a telegram from the Japanese Ambassador in Berlin disclosed that on 8 February authorities there had been nervous as to whether that line could be held.[124] By 15 February the SIS had learned that the Finns had been told that Germany was preparing to withdraw to, and hold, the line of the 1939 Soviet frontier.[125] The Soviet advance was then within five hundred miles of Gdynia, the German Navy's most important base for refitting main units and working-up U-boats, and in particular for the construction of the new type U-boats, and there were indications that she was planning to transfer U-boat training to Swinemünde. These received some support from the fact that photographic reconnaissance (PR) operations there began to encounter a heavy smoke screen.

Sigint threw still less light on the first phase of the Soviet advance south of Pripet, between Army Group Centre and the left flank of Army Group South. Beginning on 27 January the offensive reached the river Styr, well inside Poland's 1939 borders, by the end of the month; this was not reflected in the decrypts until 24 February.[126]

About developments on the front held by Army Group South the more voluminous flow of Sigint began with a long appreciation dated 8 January by the Army Group's intelligence HQ. It disclosed that the Soviet forces were shifting their attack from the southern to the northern sector, from which they were expected to develop encircling movements to the north and the south;[127] presumably on the strength of this decrypt MI concluded on 13 January that the Germans risked another Stalingrad if they did not quickly decide to withdraw from the Kiev-Dnieper bend.[128] Another decrypt from Army Group South's intelligence staff revealed on 28 January that the Russians had completed the encirclement of elements of the German Eighth Army in the Cherkassy pocket.[129] Decrypts of Luftflotte 4's reconnaissance reports for 28 January, received on the following day, told the same story.[130] The German efforts to supply and relieve the surrounded divisions – estimated by the Soviet General Staff to be ten in number, and reported as seven in a

---

124. WO 208/3573 of 17 and 31 January, 14 February 1944.
125. Dir/C Archive, 5726 of 15 February 1944.
126. CX/MSS/T105/78.
127. CX/MSS/T59/19.
128. CAB 80/43, COS (44) 8 of 13 January (228th résumé), para 31.
129. CX/MSS/81, para D40.
130. Dir/C Archive, 5505 of 29 January 1944; CX/MSS/T77/109.

Japanese diplomatic decrypt – were well covered by Sigint. On 13 February it disclosed that they had been ordered to try to break out, and it later reported that 12,000 men had been brought out. On 29 February two diplomatic decrypts, one from the Japanese Ambassador in Berlin and the other from the German Foreign Ministry, showed that the Germans were claiming that most of their forces had got away. But the Soviet claim to have destroyed ten divisions (55,000 men killed and 18,000 taken prisoner) was accepted by Whitehall on the strength of negative evidence from the military Sigint; most of the ten divisions named in the Soviet claim disappeared from the decrypts for several months.[131]

In the extreme south, where a Soviet offensive beginning on 27 January took Nikopol on 7 February and Krivoi Rog on 22 February, the Fish decrypts supplied many German intelligence assessments of Soviet intentions. On 20 February they showed that the Germans were expecting the Russians to advance on Krivoi Rog and attack from Kirovograd in a pincer movement that would be the start of far-reaching operations towards the Bug between Voznesensk and Nikolayev.[132] Decrypts reporting on the delays which held up this further offensive until 6 March revealed that the Germans were expecting it at any moment.[133] On 6 March itself GAF Enigma signals emphasised that in this sector the Russians were exercising unprecedentedly close control over their armies, particularly by concentrating and holding back their armour, and that on this evidence the Germans were again deducing that the Soviet objective was to smash Sixth Army* and break through to the Bug northwards of Nikolayev.[134]

Once the Russian advance had begun Sigint about Sixth Army's front became prolific, not least because a series of reports from the naval liaison officer with Army Group A on Sixth Army's plight were decrypted. On 9 March he warned that Sixth Army was in danger of being encircled; on 13 March he reported that it was almost entirely surrounded, and that the Soviet forces might well seize the Bug crossings to the north of Nikolayev before it could fight its way out.[135] On 20 March he reported that the Soviet advance was across the Bug and threatening Nikolayev 'in order to

---

* Reconstituted, since the loss of the original Sixth Army at Stalingrad.

131. CX/MSS/T82/7, T88/35, T89/22 and 124, T93/48, 110 para D16; WO 208/3573 of 7, 14, 21 and 28 February 1944; CAB 80/43, COS (44) 24 of 10 February (232nd résumé), para 26.
132. CX/MSS/T93/26, T112/46; WO 208/3573 of 14 February 1944.
133. CX/MSS/T113/82, T117/120, T118/72, T119/14, 123 para D6.
134. CX/MSS/T121/6.
135. CX/MSS/T122/25, T123/101; WO 208/3573 of 13 March 1944.

be able to carry out [the] strategical intention of a thrust towards Odessa'; and warned that Army Group A would be in grave danger if the Russians, who were already across the Dniester at Yampol, were to develop from there a deep thrust in the area between the Dniester and the Pruth that was held only by weak Romanian covering forces.[136] Three days later, announcing that this thrust had begun, he foresaw the development of operations which might encircle Sixth and Eighth Armies, 'thus finally eliminating resistance on the southern wing of the eastern front'.[137] By that date MI 14 had concluded from a mass of detailed decrypts about the course of the fighting that Sixth Army had already sustained very serious losses, although it could not fully confirm the Soviet claim to have routed ten divisions (including one Panzer), to have heavily defeated eleven (including two Panzer divisions) and to have inflicted severe damage on four others.[138]

On 27 March Fish and GAF Enigma decrypts disclosed that Soviet forces had crossed the Pruth in several places and that for Sixth Army's withdrawal the High Command of the Army (OKH) had set a 'final line' at the bridgehead Odessa-Tiraspol.[139] On 30 March the decrypt of a signal of 29 March had shown that Army Group South and Army Group A were being re-organised and had been ordered to retreat to a planned defence line in Romania.[140] From further decrypts the German intentions emerged in great detail in the next few days. The Army Groups had been redesignated as Army Group North Ukraine, comprising First and Fourth Panzer Armies, and Army Group South Ukraine, comprising Sixth and Eighth German Armies and Third and Fourth Romanian Armies. The HQ of Army Group South Ukraine was moving from Tiraspol to Galatz. Its tasks, as summarised by GC and CS, were to be as follows:

'The Fourth Romanian Army, which had been brought in on the west flank of the Eighth Army to fill the gap created by the Soviet drive through the First Panzer Army, was to hold as long as possible the sector between Cernauti and Lipcani from positions behind the Pruth, and to prevent an advance across the Pruth between Lipcani and Jassy until superior enemy pressure forced it to withdraw by sectors to a position adjoining the Eighth Army and running through Jassy westwards through Targul and Neamtu, and resting on the Carpathians. Special importance was attached to holding bridge-

---

136. CX/MSS/T130/66, 136 para D13; WO 208/3573 of 27 March 1944.
137. CX/MSS/T136/102.
138. WO 208/3573 of 20 and 27 March 1944; CAB 80/43, COS (44) 52 of 23 March (238th résumé), para 24.
139. CX/MSS/T128/16 and 82, T147/16.
140. DEFE 3/765, VL 9771 of 30 March 1944.

heads across the Pruth in the area of Sculeni and Ungheni. Army Group A had asked for forces from Hungary to hold the entrances to the Carpathians between Neamtu and Radauti; but until the request had been granted, troops of the Fourth Romanian Army were to hold the passes, and only when the bringing up of the requisite forces had been assured could those troops join the remainder of the army on the line to be finally defended.

The south flank of the Eighth Army was to swing round to follow the withdrawal of the Sixth Army. At the same time, it was to act as a blocking force to prevent a Russian thrust between Balta and Rybnitsa into the deep flank of the Sixth Army. The Army's final line was to run westwards from the Dniester through Orhei to Sculeni on the Pruth . . . the Sixth Army, with the Third Romanian Army, was to hold the bridgehead Odessa-Tiraspol until Odessa could be completely evacuated'.[141]

Thereafter the Sigint which covered the progress of the Soviet advances against Army Group South Ukraine disclosed Sixth Army's intention to begin the evacuation of Odessa on 10 April and traced the withdrawal of Sixth and Eighth Armies to the line of the Dniester, and westward through Jassy to the Carpathians, which the Germans were to hold from the middle of April until the following August.[142]

The Russian offensive on the northern sector of Army Group South's front, launched against Fourth Panzer Army in the Zhitomir area on 4 March, to coincide with the southern thrust, had meanwhile surrounded First Panzer Army in the Skala pocket south-east of Tarnopol. As early as 14 March the decrypts had shown that Luftflotte 4 was using bombers to supply First Panzer Army; by 26 March they had established that the Army was completely encircled; and its dire straits had been illustrated by a report on 24 March to the effect that 6th Panzer Division had been reduced to one tank and a few anti-tank guns.[143] On 4 April, however, a decrypt from the German naval liaison staff in Romania had disclosed that First Panzer Army was counter-attacking in an attempt to break out westward towards Lvov and join up with Fourth Panzer Army. Two days later another decrypt from this staff added that II SS Panzer Corps with 9th and 10th SS Panzer Divisions, was advancing southwards some 40 miles south-west of Lwow,[144] and that a Jäger

---

141. CX/MSS/T138/96; WO 208/3573 of 3 April 1944.

142. eg CX/MSS/T146/73, T147/61 and 69, T149/4, T152/6, 152, para D13 (1); DEFE 3/701, ZTPGR 10363; WO 208/3573 of 10 April 1944.

143. DEFE 3/151, VL 9455 of 26 March 1944; CX/MSS/135 para D13, T135/24, 28 and 51, 136 para D25, T137/Para D30(2), 157 para D35.

144. DEFE 3/35 (1), KV 189 of 4 April; DEFE 3/36 (2), KV 325 of 6 April 1944.

division from the Balkans was also taking part in the relief operation. That an infantry division from Croatia was also involved was revealed by the decrypt of an Army situation report of 6 April.[145] Sigint had located II SS Panzer Corps at Alençon at the end of 1943; had established at the end of February 1944 that 10th SS Panzer Division was in north-west France; and had disclosed that 9th SS Panzer Division was moving from the French Mediterranean coast on 27 March to an unknown destination.[146] The speed of 9th SS Panzer Division's move was remarkable, as Whitehall realised at the time; its spearheads were driving towards First Panzer Army, supplied by air, a mere ten days after the beginning of its journey from France.[147] The advance of II SS Panzer Corps, which linked up with First Panzer Army on 8 April, was fully covered by the decrypts, as were the efforts of Fourth Panzer Army to assist the encircled forces to break out and of Luftflotte 4 to supply First Panzer Army and the relieving forces.[148] First Panzer Army, comprising six Panzer divisions, one Panzer Grenadier division, one artillery division and ten infantry divisions, got away some 200,000 to 300,000 men, but had to abandon most of its equipment and heavy weapons.[149]

From the middle of April there was a lull in the fighting on all sectors of the eastern front except the Crimea. In that sector, where Hitler had vetoed evacuation, the Russians launched an offensive on 8 April across the Perekop isthmus and the Lazy Sea bridgehead in the north and from Kerch in the east. GC and CS's analysis of earlier decrypts had shown that the Germans had expected the attack to come at the beginning of March, to coincide with the other Soviet offensives, and it was not long before the decrypts indicated preparations for withdrawal in the face of a rapid Russian advance. On 10 April GC and CS decrypted Seventeenth Army commander's orders for a withdrawal, presumably to Sevastopol, and a Grampus decrypt showed that he was ignoring the cancellation of his order by Berlin.[150] The numbers of troops arriving in Sevastopol and awaiting evacuation were disclosed by the decrypts at regular intervals until 18 April, when they reported that Seventeenth Army's twelve divisions (five of which were German) were badly battered and were left with only 30 per cent of their artillery and 25

---

145. CX/MSS/T147/67.
146. DEFE 3/140, VL 6626 of 19 February 1944; CX/MSS/T121/38, T143/97.
147. CX/MSS/T147/88.
148. CX/MSS/T143/52, T147/88, T148/94, T149/4; WO 208/3573 of 10 April 1944.
149. Seaton, op cit, pp 425–426.
150. CX/MSS/ T151/43 and 52; DEFE 3/701, ZTPGRs 10600, 10601.

per cent of their anti-tank guns.[151] A decrypt of 18 April disclosed that Hitler, learning that Seventeenth Army intended to hold Sevastopol only until embarkation was completed, had forbidden the evacuation of any fit troops; another of 27 April showed that he had rejected an appeal by Seventeenth Army commander against this order, though it did not reveal that he had dismissed the commander.[152] Early in May it became evident from the decrypts of returns from the Sevastopol port authorities that he had agreed to the withdrawal of Romanian troops, but the decrypt giving his reluctant consent to complete evacuation did not come until 9 May.[153]

The evacuation was covered in great detail by Sigint. It was carried out by the Navy and the GAF, the decrypts showing that 121,000 men were taken off by sea and 21,500 by air.[154] The GAF did what it could to protect the evacuation, transferring one Gruppe of heavy fighters from Germany, two Gruppen of long-range bombers from the central sector of the eastern front and some 80 other aircraft – torpedo-bombers and fighters – from the western Mediterranean, the Balkans and Austria.[155]

Germany's difficulties on the Dniester and in the Crimea were accentuated by Allied interference with shipping on the Danube, which carried her bulk-supplies for those sectors of the fronts and was needed for the withdrawal of her forces as well as for carrying imports of oil and other essential industrial raw materials.* On three nights in the middle of April and in four further raids in May, Liberators and Wellingtons of No 205 Group RAF laid 531 mines in 152 sorties, and in May and June US bombers attacked ports and installations on the river.[157] On 11 April a naval Enigma decrypt reporting the first response to the minelaying stated that the German Danube Flotilla feared that the Allies were aiming at a systematic disturbance of the traffic.[158] In the next few days Enigma decrypts

---

* It was learned after the war that OKW informed Hitler in the middle of May that the mining had not only held up 10,000 tons of ammunition for the Dniester front but had also contributed to the halving of imports of Romanian oil.[156]

151. DEFE 3/40(2), KV 1275 of 17 April; Dir/C Archive, 6286 of 18 April; WO 208/3573 of 17 and 24 April 1944.
152. CX/MSS/T165/107, T168/91; DEFE 3/702, ZTPGRs 11654, 11909; Dir/C Archive, 6471 of 29 April 1944.
153. DEFE 3/46 (1), KV 2937 of 5 May; DEFE 3/153, KV 3317 of 9 May 1944; DEFE 3/703, ZTPGRs 12549, 12550, 12554.
154. CX/MSS/T 187/21; DEFE 3/704, ZTPGR 13021.
155. CX/MSS/T179/20, T181/59; DEFE 3/702, ZTPGR 11804; AIR 41/10, p 245.
156. Cabinet Office Historical Section, EDS/Appreciation/17, Chapter 3, pp 19–20.
157. Molony, op cit, Vol VI, Part I, Chapter VII.
158. DEFE 3/38 (2), KV 757 of 11 April 1944.

disclosed that on account of the shortage of mine-spotting aircraft and the lack of sweeping gear, the river had been closed and traffic paralysed for days at a time when it was urgently needed for the evacuation of the Crimea.[159] The Germans eventually organised counter-measures against what another Enigma decrypt described as the 'extremely menacing' mining offensive,[160] but an Abwehr decrypt received on 24 April complained that the Allies were paralysing the traffic in the cheapest possible way, as the river was still being closed wherever a raid took place or was suspected.[161] On 26 April, on reading some of these decrypts, the Prime Minister sent minutes to the CAS: 'You seem to have struck a soft spot here'; 'You are on a good thing'.[162] At the end of April the Enigma reported that the Germans had reopened the Danube for the whole of its length from Regensburg,[163] but the NID suspected they had been forced to do so prematurely by Hitler's order that Sevastopol must be held. In May, as the Enigma showed, they continued their efforts to bring in minesweeping equipment and personnel, to improve the Flak defences and to replace tugs, lighters and cargo-towing vessels sunk in the Allied attack,[164] but were still forced to close sections of the Danube at frequent intervals.[165] By the end of that month the number of minesweepers, tows, tugs and barges reported by Enigma signals to have been sunk since 28 April totalled 34, with a further 32 damaged.[166]*

---

* After the war it emerged from German documents that over 170 vessels were destroyed or damaged between April and June.[167]

159.   ibid, KV 861 of 13 April; DEFE 3/38 (1), KV 919 of 13 April; DEFE 3/39 (1), KVs 1148 and 1180 of 16 April 1944.

160.   DEFE 3/40 (2), KV 1273 of 17 April 1944. See also DEFE 3/40 (1), KV 1381 of 19 April; DEFE 3/41 (1), KV 1747 of 23 April; DEFE 3/42 (2), KV 1788 of 23 April; DEFE 3/44 (1), KV 2473 of 30 April 1944.

161.   Dir/C Archive 24 April 1944.   162.   ibid and 6345 of 26 April 1944.

163.   DEFE 3/44 (2), KV 2353 of 29 April; DEFE 3/144 (1), KVs 2468 of 30 April, 2493 of 1 May 1944.

164.   eg DEFE 3/43 (1), KV 2245 of 28 April; DEFE 3/44 (2), KV 2350 of 29 April; DEFE 3/44 (1), KVs 2473 of 30 April, 2493 of 2 May; DEFE 3/46 (2), KV 2867 of 5 May; DEFE 3/153, KV 3490 of 11 May; DEFE 3/154, KVs 3503 of 11 May, 3704 of 13 May; DEFE 3/158, KV 4744 of 21 May; DEFE 3/160, KV 5195 of 25 May; DEFE 3/162, KV 5587 of 28 May; DEFE 3/163, KV 5996 of 1 June 1944.

165.   eg DEFE 3/47 (1), KV 3227 of 8 May; DEFE 3/157, KV 4399 of 19 May; DEFE 3/158, KV 4521 of 19 May; DEFE 3/162, KV 5587 of 28 May; DEFE 3/162, KV 5564 of 28 May; DEFE 3/163, KV 5791 of 30 May; DEFE 3/164, KVs 6155 of 2 June, 6248 of 3 June 1944.

166.   DEFE 3/159, KV 4942 of 23 May; DEFE 3/160, KV 5198 of 25 May; DEFE 3/162, KV 5587 of 28 May 1944.

167.   BR 1736 (56) (1), *British Mining Operations 1939–1945*, Vol I (1973), pp 658–659, 663–664.

The JIC had meanwhile issued appreciations on the implications for *Overlord* of developments on the eastern front. On 2 May 1944 it had considered how Germany would react if, before *Overlord* was launched, the Russians advanced into Hungary or broke through the Galatz gap: in the first eventuality she would be compelled to withdraw forces, particularly armour, from the west, but might also be faced with collapse on her home front; in the second case she could withdraw to some defence line from which she could delay the Russian advance without having to withdraw divisions from other fronts. And while allowing that Russia might make her main effort on some sector other than Galatz in order to get more rapid and more decisive results, it had concluded that she was unlikely to be able to advance into the Hungarian plain.[168] On 13 May, in the last such appreciation it issued before *Overlord*, the JIC emphasised that Russia was determined to defeat Germany in 1944, and it recognised her ability to launch offensives in more than one sector; but it concluded that her offensives would probably be delayed to coincide with *Overlord* and that the lull in the fighting, by enabling Germany to strengthen her grip on Romania, Hungary and Finland, had relieved her of the need to transfer any further divisions from west to east before *Overlord* was launched.[169]

☐

On 1 May 1944, in its latest periodical review of the effects being obtained by Allied strategic bombing, the JIC, leaving aside such developments as might take place on the Russian front, expressed the view that no German withdrawal in north-west Europe was to be expected before the date set for *Overlord*, nor any disintegration within Germany itself.[170]* This appreciation did no more than update a conclusion the JIC had reached in December 1943. But it stood in sharp contrast to assessments issued by the JIC in the previous summer.

A JIC paper of 1 August 1943 argued that the strain on Germany was becoming so great that 'a major development such as the collapse of Italy might have very great results';[171] and on 9 September, the day after the Italian surrender, in a paper entitled 'Probabilities of a German Collapse', it took up a suggestion aired by the

---

* For a full account of the attempts to assess the effects of the strategic bombing offensive on German morale see below, p 298 et seq.

168.   JIC (44) 171 (o) of 2 May.
169.   JIC (44) 198 (o) of 13 May.
170.   JIC (44) 177 (o) of 1 May.
171.   JIC (43) 282 of 1 August, para 243.

Foreign Office since the summer of 1942* that, as she had in 1918, Germany might collapse 'with startling rapidity':

'In the late summer of 1918 the Allies were studying, as we study today, the impact on Germany of great reverses of fortune. The records of that period show that the Allied estimate of Germany's power and will to continue the struggle was then very wide of the mark . . . because they attached too much importance to intelligence of a purely military character, and too little to political and economic intelligence, which is necessarily more indefinite. The experience of 1918 emphasises the danger of letting the enemy's apparent military strength blind us to fundamental weaknesses in his position as a whole. . . . If it were not that the political situation in Germany today is very different from that of 1918, we should unhesitatingly predict that Germany would sue for an armistice before the end of the year'.

And even after allowing for the political discipline of the Nazi regime, the JIC still believed that:

'We must be prepared for a situation where further military reverses, the Allied air offensive and the defection of Germany's Allies produce even this year a crisis. . . . A study of the picture as a whole leads us inevitably to the conclusion that Germany is if anything in a worse position today than she was at the same period in 1918'.[172]

This argument clearly owed a great deal to the euphoria induced by Italy's collapse; since December 1942 the JIC had referred from time to time to 'the possibility of a German collapse', but, except that in February and March 1943, following Germany's defeat at Stalingrad, it had briefly discussed the possibility that her difficulties on the eastern front might prevent her from providing adequate military opposition to a cross-Channel invasion carried out later that year, it had hitherto discounted the possibility as unlikely to arise in the near future.† In January 1943, however, at the Casablanca conference the Allied authorities had considered for the first time the need to provide at the planning level, as a matter of common prudence, for the contingency of a German collapse before the date set for *Overlord*.[173] Discussion of this eventuality (Operation *Rankin*) had been resumed in August 1943 at the Quebec conference, where COSSAC had tabled a paper urging immediate preparations for three contingencies: the weakening of Germany's armed forces to a point which permitted an Allied assault before the *Overlord* date;

---

* See Volume II, pp 98, 114, 159.   † See above, pp 3–4.

172. JIC (43) 367 of 9 September.
173. CAB 121/152, SIC file A/Strategy/8, COS (43) 33 (o) of 28 January (CCS 169), para 2(b)).

Germany's withdrawal from the occupied territories; and Germany's acceptance of unconditional surrender, which the Allies had announced as their war aim at Casblanca.[174]

On 16 September, on their return from Quebec and no doubt in response to the recent JIC paper, the British Chiefs of Staff instructed the JIC to advise them if circumstances arose which indicated that they should consider the need either to mount Operation *Rankin* or to bring forward the date of the full-scale *Overlord* assault.[175] The JIC had issued no such alert, however, by December 1943, when the Combined Chiefs of Staff decided at the Cairo conference that the Allied Combined Intelligence Committee (CIC) should make a monthly report on Operation *Rankin*.[176] It explained why on 20 December in the first of the briefs it drew up to assist its JIC (Washington) in compiling the CIC appreciations with the American JIC; in spite of the loss of her Italian ally, her failure in Russia and her difficulties in the Balkans, and in spite of the intensification of the Allied bombing offensive, Germany's strategic situation had not deteriorated 'anything like as rapidly as had appeared probable in early autumn'. More positively, although her industrial output was declining, the central control of her economic machine remained unbroken, her work-force remained fairly well disciplined and her population was adequately fed.[177]

While not entirely ruling out organised revolt or a military coup – for such crises might arise without warning in the Nazi political system – the December brief advised that Operation *Rankin* could not be carried out during the next six weeks without meeting opposition; and the American JIC believed with more confidence, or more pessimism, that *Rankin* could be regarded as impracticable for a month longer, until mid-March 1944.[178] Nor were these assessments modified in the next few months. The reports issued by the CIC at the end of January and the end of February updated the earlier predictions and reproduced the original divergence between the British and American JICs, the former forecasting that circumstances favourable for *Rankin* would not develop in the next six weeks, the latter that they would not develop for ten weeks to come.[179] Towards the end of March the JIC could still find no

174. CAB 121/387 SIC file D/France/6/10 Vol I, COS (43) 465 (o) of 13 August.
175. CAB 79/64, COS (43) 217th (o) Meeting, 16 September.
176. CAB 80/77, COS (43) 791 (o) Part II of 25 February 1944 (CCS 134th Meeting, 4 December 1943); Part III of 8 March 1944 (CCS 426/1 of 6 December 1943, para 20).
177. CAB 121/419, SIC file D/Germany/4, JIC (43) 511 (o) of 20 December.
178. CAB 88/59, CIC 41/2 of 1 January (JIC (44) 13 (o) of 9 January).
179. ibid, CIC 41/4 pf 28 January (JIC (44) 56 (o) of 10 February), 41/6 of 29 February (JIC (44) 90 (o) of 8 March); JIC (44) 12 (o) of 11 January, 18, (o) of 17 January, 62 (o) of 17 February.

evidence that the German economy or the Nazi administration would break down in the next two months.[180] After the end of March no more *Rankin* briefs were issued, the two JICs having agreed that estimates of the German build-up in France against *Overlord* as far ahead as D + 60 should in future be substituted for assessments of the prospects for *Rankin*.[181]

On 10 April the first of the new-style CIC reports concluded that a collapse of German resistance, or a German surrender, was 'most improbable' prior to *Overlord*, and the evacuation by Germany of any part of western Europe 'improbable'.[182] To this the JIC added in a separate review on 13 April that, while the ability of the German economy to sustain prolonged operations on all fronts was declining, the decline was not likely to affect her opposition to *Overlord* in the early stages.[183] And on 1 May, as we have already recorded, it reaffirmed its belief that there would be no enemy withdrawal in north-west Europe, and no disintegration in Germany, before the Allied invasion.[184]

We have noted already that this conclusion stood in sharp contrast to the optimism expressed by the JIC in the summer of 1943. But it had been retreating from that optimism since the beginning of 1944, and it has to be added that from the autumn of 1943, in one direction or another, the intelligence sources, while they were re-assuring in that they continued to give no indication that the enemy was making progress with nuclear weapons or preparing for the first use of gas,* had left little doubt that the Germans were striving to recover the initiative with major technological innovations which would alter the course of the war – indeed, the entire complexion of warfare – if only they could win the time required to make them operationally effective. And ever since the same date this intelligence had given rise to anxieties which made it more and more imperative that the Allies should neither delay the launching of the cross-Channel invasion nor fall short of quick success in carrying it out.

As early as July 1943, in the light of intelligence received since the spring, the Air Ministry had issued the first of a series of alerts:

---

* For further details, see Volume III Part 2. Meanwhile, on 31 January 1944, information was received from a SIS agent who was an Abwehr official to the effect that OKW was alarmed at the possibility that in response to a V-weapon offensive the Allies would turn to chemical and biological warfare; he reported that the German population was not prepared for these types of warfare.

180. JIC (44) 109 (o) of 23 March.
181. JIC (44) 9th (o) Meeting, 29 February, 13th (o), 21 March; CAB 88/59, CIC 46/D of 24 March (JIC (44) 149 (o) of 12 April).
182. CAB 88/59, CIC 46/1 of 10 April (JIC (44) 157 (o) of 17 April).
183. JIC (44) 138 (o) of 13 April.
184. JIC (44) 177 (o) of 1 May.

it was clear that the Germans were at last giving high priority to the development of jet propelled aircraft and were also experimenting with rocket powered aircraft which might 'outclass and render practically obsolete all aircraft designs with gas-turbine engines or combined power units.'[185] This warning had prompted the British authorities to accelerate the production of the first British jet fighter and inaugurate the serious study of the problems associated with supersonic flight.* It had been followed by a set-back which occasioned more immediate anxiety when, in August and September 1943, Germany achieved complete surprise with the deployment against Royal Navy ships and the Italian Fleet of the first-ever radio guided rocket missile (the Hs 293) and a radio controlled bomb (the FX 1400).† And before the end of 1943 the Allies had sustained still greater shocks.

In November the Admiralty had received the first evidence that the Germans were phasing out the construction of the existing types of U-boat and experimenting with new types incorporating, amongst other advanced features, unconventional methods of propulsion that gave higher underwater speeds.‡ In December a longer-standing anxiety – the result of the receipt since the previous spring of signs that the enemy was developing a long-range rocket propelled missile and of the suspicion, which had dawned only in October, that she was also developing a long-range jet propelled pilotless aircraft – had suddenly escalated into an alarm of panic proportions following the receipt of evidence suggesting that the threat from the pilotless aircraft might be imminent. The alarm had been raised by the detection during November of over 80 suspicious sites in the Pas de Calais and the Cherbourg area; it was all the greater because it had proved impossible to associate the sites firmly with the pilotless aircraft for nearly a month.§

Of all these disturbing developments, the last appeared to be the most dangerous throughout the first half of 1944. It had the most serious bearing on Operation *Overlord*, both directly for its possible threat to the preparation of the invasion and indirectly because a timely and successful invasion might well be the only effective means of averting or reducing large-scale enemy bombardment of London and southern England. Whitehall's first response to it, and particularly to the further discovery that some of the sites were aligned on targets other than London, had been to ask COSSAC to consider the need for *Overlord* bases outside the range of the flying

---

* See below, p 336. † See below, p 337 et seq.
‡ See below, p 238 et seq. § See below, p 403.

185. AIR 20/2690, D of I (Ops) Report No 3004 of 19 July 1943.

bomb, as alternatives to Portsmouth, Southampton and Plymouth.[186]* It is clear from the official history of the USAAF that initially the American authorities took a serious view of the threat, envisaging in connection with the V-weapons 'extreme possibilities' such as the use of biological and chemical warfare and 'unusually violent' explosives of a revolutionary character, which might enable the Germans to stop the Allied bombing offensive by the devastating bombardment of England, and believing that if the Germans withheld the V-weapon attack till D-day they might disrupt the entire operation.[187]† They were perhaps influenced by a decrypt of a telegram from the Japanese Ambassador in Berlin to Tokyo to the effect that the Germans had plans to destroy not only London but the whole of Britain with the V-weapons. In January 1944 COSSAC calculated that the *Overlord* plan could still be carried out if the capacity of London, Southampton and Portsmouth to handle shipping were to be reduced by up to 50 per cent, but that if damage rose above that figure it would become increasingly impracticable to undertake the operation on anything like the planned scale. The Air Ministry and SHAEF then worked out in detail, as best they could in the light of the available intelligence, the effects the flying bomb offensive might have on the *Overlord* ports and the nearby camps. In February, on the basis of what was known about the accuracy of the weapon and the number of sites, and of what seemed to be reasonable rates of enemy attack, their interim conclusion was that in its scale and timing the offensive was unlikely to preclude the launching of *Overlord* from the Thames and the south coast to the east of Southampton. This conclusion was confirmed on 28 March and adopted for planning purposes.[188]

The conclusion made several assumptions. The most important of them were that although the flying bomb had reached such a state of development that it could become operational at any time, it would remain subject to a good deal of inaccuracy, and that sustained Allied bombing would keep the number of serviceable

---

* See below, p 417.

† As stated above, (p 46) there is no evidence that the British had grounds at this time for fearing that the Germans would resort to biological or chemical warfare or to nuclear weapons.

186. CAB 121/211, SIC file B/Defence/2, Vol 1, COS (43) 306th (o) and 311th (o) Meetings, 16 and 21 December; CAB 121/212, B/Defence/2, Vol 2, COS (43) 312th (o) Meeting, 23 December.
187. W F Craven and J L Cate, *The Army Air Forces in World War II*, Vol III (1951), p 97.
188. CAB 121/212, COS (44) 21 (o) of 9 January, 107 (o) of 2 February, DO (44) 4th Meeting, 3 February, COS (44) 139 (o) of 7 February, COS (44) 290 (o) of 28 March.

launching sites available to the enemy down to twenty (including two in the Cherbourg area).[189] Between the end of March and the beginning of June these assumptions were undermined. Sigint disclosed that in their trial firings of the weapon the Germans were steadily improving its accuracy and reliability. At the end of April Whitehall was shocked by the sudden and belated discovery that the Germans were abandoning the existing launching sites, those which had absorbed so much of the Allied bombing resources since the previous December, and constructing simpler ones which presented much more difficult targets for Allied air attack. The intelligence authorities were meanwhile having to take account of an increasing amount of intelligence about the long-range rocket and were, on the other hand, failing in all their efforts to acquire information about the German programme for launching the offensive with either weapon, as also about the essential characteristics of the two missiles. In all the circumstances it is not surprising that the possible effects of the flying bomb and the rocket on the preparations for *Overlord* remained a source of grave and mounting anxiety.*

In the Admiralty the receipt of further, but still inconclusive, intelligence on Germany's new U-boats was generating alarm on the same score. By February it was known that in addition to carrying out experiments with new types, the Germans were equipping the existing U-boats with the *Schnorchel* equipment which made them less vulnerable to radar detection and helped them to cruise submerged for long periods; moreover, it was believed that, among the new U-boats, they were giving priority to the development of a small anti-invasion vessel incorporating a revolutionary closed-cycle propulsion system, which gave it a high underwater speed, and might already have built a considerable number. In March, it was finally established that few if any U-boat hulls of the old type had been laid down since the previous autumn. In April photographic reconnaissance of the U-boat yards administered a double shock; it detected not only that U-boats of new types were already building, but also that they were being assembled rapidly from pre-fabricated pressure-hull sections. One such U-boat, indeed, was seen to have been launched already, after being on the slip for no more than six weeks; and it had taken a minimum of five months to build the old-type U-boat. Nor was it until May 1944 that the Admiralty could feel sure that there was no immediate threat to *Overlord*, Sigint having reliably established that the Germans were hoping to return

---

* See below, Chapters 41 and 42.

189.   ibid, COS (44) 290 (0) of 28 March.

to the Atlantic offensive with two new types of U-boats (Type XXI and Type XXIII) in the autumn of 1944. Later in May, on the other hand, the same source disclosed that although the new boats were transitional in that they retained the existing methods of propulsion, they had a novel hull, greatly increased power and new and formidable aids to navigation and attack,* as well as the *Schnorchel*; and the Admiralty did not doubt that they represented a 'revolution' in U-boat design and construction.†

In May, again, the Air Ministry was disturbed by new intelligence about Germany's latest aircraft. It had been aware since the beginning of the year that she was producing not only three new conventional or jet-assisted twin-engined fighters or fighter-bombers – the FW 154, the He 219 and the Do 335 – but also the twin-engined jet propelled Me 262 fighter, the rocket propelled Me 163 fighter and the AR 234 jet propelled reconnaissance bomber – all of novel type and superior to any Allied aircraft.‡ In May it received firm intelligence from Sigint that the Me 262 and the Me 163 were about to become operational.§

In the event, though by only a narrow margin, the Germans failed in their efforts to mount an offensive with their long-range missiles before the Allies had completed their preparations for the cross-Channel invasion. By the time the Allied forces landed in Normandy, moreover, the Allied air forces had suppressed the serious threat presented by the entry of new types of aircraft into Germany's defences. In the process of establishing decisive daytime command of the air over Germany in the spring, and subsequently intensifying the strategic bombing offensive against Germany's communications, synthetic oil production and airframe and aero-engine factories, they had not only delayed the V-weapon offensive, but had also inflicted great damage on, or forced the dispersal of, the German aircraft industry and severely curtailed the enemy's ability to train aircrew for such of the new aircraft as continued to be produced despite the Allied depredations. In the second quarter of 1944 the Germans were forced by the bombing to abandon or suspend production of the FW 154, the He 219 and the Do 335.** They persevered with the production of the Me 262 and the Me 163, but the bombing delayed until August 1944 the entry of these aircraft into service and they were thereafter unable to produce

---

* These aids included an improved acoustic homing torpedo, a device for the automatic patterned firing of torpedoes designed to hit many ships with one salvo, and improved methods of detection and evasion. But intelligence did not provide these details at the time.[190]
† See below, p 239 et seq.   ‡ See below, p 344 et seq.   § See below, p 351.
** See below pp 344–346.

190.   ADM 234/68, BR 305 (3), p 5.

them in quantity or to train sufficient pilots good enough to fly them.* The Allied air offensive had meanwhile also dislocated the dispersed pre-fabrication system adopted for the production of the new U-boats, of which only five Type XXIII and one Type XXI were to become operational before the end of the war.

What consequences would have followed if Germany had taken these developments in hand earlier, or if she had succeeded in prolonging the war by delaying *Overlord* or checking the Allies on the Normandy beaches?† It would serve no purpose to attempt to answer such questions. Suffice it to say that during the first half of 1944, in the light of the intelligence at their disposal, the Allies had to accept that, bound up as it was with the prospects for *Overlord*, the outcome of their strategy remained in the balance. Nor have we yet completed the catalogue of their anxieties. Over and above the other uncertainties that complicated the preparations for *Overlord*, they faced the serious possibility that the intelligence at their disposal might at any time be reduced by the loss of a considerable part of the product of GC and CS.

In January 1944 the Chiefs of Staff referred to GC and CS as 'our most important source of intelligence during the war'.[191] But from the autumn of 1943 it had become apparent that the German armed forces had embarked on a thorough overhaul of their wireless procedures and cypher precautions with a view to improving the security of the Enigma which, despite the rise of Fish, remained the mainstay of their communications and the principal source of Sigint for GC and CS. They introduced from that date a series of innovations which were prompted by the belief that stricter security was demanded by the passage of time, and particularly by the danger that Enigma machines and keys were increasingly subject to capture, rather than from any suspicion that the cypher was radically insecure. The changes were nevertheless more fundamental than any that had been brought into force since the U-boats had adopted

---

* See below, pp 351–352.

† Only after the Normandy landings had succeeded and the Allies were established in strength on the continent did the intelligence sources disclose that the Germans had embarked on other technological innovations in their effort to restore their fortunes by inaugurating a new phase of warfare. Before the end of the war it would be discovered that in addition to more advanced fighters and fighter-bombers, these included a larger longer range Hs 293 for attacking cities (the BV 246); a winged version of the V 2 rocket and a two-stage rocket capable of reaching the United States; jet propelled bombers with the same capability (the Ju 287 and the Ju 338); anti-aircraft surface-to-air guided missiles (the *Wasserfall*, *Natter*, *Schmetterling* and *Rheintochter*) and an air-to-air guided missile (the X 4); and an ocean-going U-boat (Type XXVI W) that was still more revolutionary in design than Types XXI and XXIII.

191. Dir/C Archive, Memo from the Chiefs of Staff to the Prime Minister, 20 January 1944.

the four-wheel key (Shark) in 1942,* and they created at GC and CS from November 1943 a succession of emergencies. With the mastery it had previously established over the Enigma machine, GC and CS was able in the event to call on such reserves of ingenuity and such resources in machinery and manpower that, until *Overlord* was launched, it surmounted the crises without any marked decline or delay in its output. But from the end of 1943 until they landed in Normandy the Allies could at no time exclude the possibility that they would lose access to a large part of the Enigma traffic on which they depended for their intimate knowledge of Germany's strengths, dispositions, movements and other responses to developments in every theatre of the war.

---

* See Volume II, p 228 and its Appendix 19.

CHAPTER 30

Intelligence on the German Economy

IF THE the optimism of August – September 1943 about the prospects of an early German collapse had evaporated by the end of the year, and if it did not re-surface before *Overlord* was launched, this was largely because it could not withstand the evidence derived from operational experience and strategic intelligence about Germany's continuing military resilience in the face of so many reverses. But increasing respect for her military capacity was reinforced by the recognition that her economic system was responding far more effectively than had been expected to the demands made upon it. During the first half of 1943 it was generally believed that German industrial production was declining steadily after reaching a peak early in the year.[1] In February 1943, for example, the JIC had reported that 'economic shortages are making themselves increasingly felt in Germany, and economic difficulties are having a growing effect on the armed forces [which] must, we believe, make it impossible for her High Command to carry out any offensive strategy on land, in Russia or anywhere else'.[2] In March, again, the JIC had believed that 'the decline in industrial output, mainly due to the comb-out of manpower from industry, and the effects of air bombing, will make it impossible for Germany adequately to equip in 1943 her own armed forces and still less those of her satellites'.[3] By the end of 1943 these expectations had been revised: it was still accepted that Germany could not take the offensive on any significant scale but it was no longer being suggested that her power to resist might before long be undermined by economic crisis.[4]

Like the corresponding revision of Whitehall's assessments of the state of Germany's morale,* the re-appraisal of the performance of her economy owed little to improvements in intelligence. The volume of information available to the authorities greatly increased

---

* For this process see below, p 298 et seq.

1. eg JIC (43) 40 of 11 February, JIC (43) 99 of 9 March, JIC (43) 142 (o) of 2 April, JIC (43) 239 (o) of 5 June; FO 837/17, Editorial article in MEW Weekly Intelligence Report No. 72/A of 3 July 1943.
2. JIC (43)) 64 of 15 February.
3. JIC (43) 99 of 9 March.
4. JIC (43) 510 (o) of 14 December.

from the middle of 1943, but its sources continued to be those, all for one reason or another inadequate, on which they had relied since the early years of the war. Of the 3,144 'Classified Intelligence Reports' summarised in the Weekly Intelligence Report issued by the Enemy Branch of the Ministry of Economic Warfare (MEW)* between 1 January 1943 and 30 June 1944, almost one-third originated from overt sources (Press reports, broadcasts, published speeches, statutes and decrees) and the bulk consisted of agents' reports, the remainder being summaries of PR evidence and technical analyses.† A high proportion of the agents' reports were from countries outside Germany and Austria,‡ and most of the comparatively small number that were substantial in content dealt with France and Poland; this source thus threw an oblique rather than a direct light on the German economy. No documentary and first-hand evidence of the situation in Germany was obtained before the Allied armies began to advance into north-western Europe. Nor was it until the summer of 1944, after German police decrypts became available on the state of heavy industry, the coal industry and the petrol shortage, that Sigint contributed regularly and directly to the fund of intelligence on such subjects§. The Enigma decrypts increasingly referred from the middle of 1943 in operational contexts to shortages of trained manpower, of fuel and of aircraft and tanks, and to the effects of Allied air attacks on specific factories as well as on cities; but they were by no means comprehensive and did not provide an adequate guide to the performance and the problems of the economy. If it remained as difficult as ever to assemble reliable data on the scale required for accurate description, let alone for reasoned forecasting, it was increasingly recognised that the limitations of economic intelligence called for greater caution in assessments.

From the time of Germany's victories in the summer of 1940 until after the Casablanca conference Allied strategic thinking had believed that Germany's superiority in military strength would eventually be off-set by economic deficiencies induced by blockade, strategic bombing and losses in military operations. It had also

---

* In April 1944 control of Enemy Branch passed to the Foreign Office.[5]

† This review of the sources for economic intelligence is based on the summaries of the reports that were printed in the Weekly Intelligence Report issued by the Ministry; the reports themselves, as received by MEW, have mostly been destroyed.

‡ There was in this period a total of 86 reports on aircraft production, of which 24 related to Germany and Austria, 25 to France, 7 to Poland and 30 to other occupied countries, and a total of 121 reports on land armaments production, of which 47 related to Germany and Austria, 29 to France, 5 to Poland and 40 to other countries.

§ For further details see Volume III, Part 2.

5. JIC (44) 16th (o) Meeting, 25 April.

assumed that the balance between her military power and her economic decline could be calculated with sufficient accuracy to guide strategic decisions about the scale and timing of Allied operations. As late as May 1943, indeed, the Combined Chiefs of Staff made this assumption when defining the mission of the US and British bomber forces. They were 'to accomplish the progressive destruction and dislocation of the German military, industrial and economic systems to a point where her capacity for armed resistance is fatally weakened. This is construed as meaning so weakened as to permit of final combined operations on the Continent'.[6] By then, however, the economic intelligence authorities had recognised that it was not possible to answer with this degree of precision questions of such generality about Germany's current or prospective economic performance, and the scale and timing of the offensives which took the Allied armies back to the Continent after the middle of 1943 were in fact determined without reference to forecasts of Germany's economic situation.

At this stage of the war, on the other hand, while the military power of the Allies was growing so fast and the planning of their strategic initiatives no longer called for calculating how long Germany's economy would remain viable, there was a growing demand for estimates of economic elements in the strength with which the enemy would be able to oppose the operations which the Allies had decided to carry out. Under the pressure of this demand the nature of economic assessments underwent a change. Speculative studies of the long-term dynamics of the German economy gave way to analyses that were operational rather than strategic in their thrust, and notable for their comparatively greater realism. By the end of 1943 they had brought the German economy into focus as an economy that was under strain but not, for all the weight of the Allied air attack, in so critical a condition as to threaten the ability of the armed forces to continue fighting.

□

Foremost among the indications of greater realism was the fact that MEW now gave some weight to the administrative reforms which had put armaments production under Speer's control in the spring of 1942.* In December 1943 it showed considerable understanding of the changes which these reforms, to which it had scarcely referred during 1942, were bringing to the structure of the German

---

* See Volume II, pp 151–153.

6. C Webster and N Frankland, *The Strategic Air Offensive against Germany*, Vol IV, (1961) Appendix 23.

economy;[7] and by the spring of 1944 it had recognised that it was 'no mean achievement' on Speer's part to have completed a massive reorganisation in time for the decisive stage of the European war.[8]

MEW had some evidence, indeed, that the reorganisation was failing in one direction during the first half of 1944. The Kriegsauf-lageprogramm of 1942, designed to increase the supply of essential consumer goods as Allied area bombing grew in power and destructiveness,* was being frustrated by wastage due to military disasters and air raid damage: Speer's effort to meet the minimum requirement of consumer goods for maintaining the health and working capacity of the population had been unsuccessful; nor could drastic cuts in civilian standards of life, imposed by the effects of bombing, be made good. As against the increasing shortages of manufactured consumer goods, however, MEW recognised that, assisted by a mild winter in 1943–1944 and guided by a highly developed system of production and market control under the long-established Reich 'Estate' for food production (Reichsnähr-stand), agricultural production was being well maintained. By March 1944 the food ration for German civilians was estimated to give 2,500 calories a day, comparing favourably with that of 1918.[9] In the months immediately before *Overlord* MEW saw stability in German food supply, civilian diet still at the level of September 1943 and calorie intake 90 per cent of the pre-war level. The Germans had been far more successful in maintaining the level of nutrition than in 1918 because a much higher level of self-sufficiency had been achieved, agricultural production having been preserved and efficiently mobilised throughout the war.[10]

With regard to the major raw materials in German Europe, MEW continued to under-estimate the enemy's position down to July 1944, when it issued the last of its annual tabulated estimates of supplies, consumption and stocks.[11]† It recognised, however, that its knowledge of the pre-war levels of stocks was incomplete and that it lacked reliable information on subsequent levels of supply and consumption. Moreover, despite its exaggeration of the rate of decline in the level of stocks, its view in the months before *Overlord*

---

* See Volume II, pp 152–153, 154, 155.

† See Appendix 4, Table (a) (MEW estimates) and Table (b) (Official German statistics).

7. FO 837/19, MEW Weekly Intelligence Report No 108 of 29 February 1944 (Survey of six months ending 31 December 1943).
8. FO 837/20, MEW WIR No. 134 of 31 August 1944 (Survey of six months ending 30 June 1944).
9. FO 837/19, MEW WIR No 110 of 16 March 1944.
10. FO 837/20, MEW WIR No 134 of 31 August 1944.
11. ibid.

was that shortages of raw materials were not seriously affecting the German output of armaments. In May 1944 it reached a similar conclusion with regard to rubber, which had not been included in its regular statistical series: apart from her stocks of reclaimed rubber and of natural rubber acquired by blockade-running, Germany's capacity to produce synthetic rubber was sufficient for her requirement.[12]*

Despite their exhaustive study of evidence bearing on the supply and consumption of oil,† the intelligence authorities were unable to estimate the effects of the oil situation on the economy as a whole. But with the approach of D-day for *Overlord* they argued that Germany's military operations would be hampered by shortage of oil if the Allied air forces attacked the oil industry.‡ In November 1943 they estimated that the shortening of Germany's lines in Russia and the Mediterranean would enable her to increase her resources by about one million tons by February 1944 – and this despite a slowing down in the construction of new synthetic plants and the fact that Romania and Hungary were resisting her demands for a reduction in their fuel consumption – if the Allies did not launch an all-out attack on Germany's oil industry; and they broadened this hint by pointing out that the refineries had become more vulnerable to bombing since the collapse of Italy, which had put her air bases at the disposal of the Allies.[13] In April they noted that Germany would soon be losing the Romanian, Hungarian, Polish and Estonian oil-fields to the Soviet armies, but added that stocks in western Europe were sufficient to meet her operational requirements against an invasion for at least two months.[14] And at the end of May, their earlier hints having had no influence on Allied bombing directives, they expressed the belief that a sustained air attack on Germany's oil production would 'within a period of from 3 to 6 months produce a shortage of oil so serious that it would render it impossible for her to carry out full-scale operations on three major fronts. . . . Both on the short and the long view, oil has therefore become a vital factor in German resistance'.[15]

A systematic offensive against the oil targets was given first priority on 8 June 1944.§ At the end of July the JIC reported that

---

* See Appendix 4, Table (c) (MEW estimates) and Table (d) (German statistics).
† A full account of the sources used and the problems involved in the study of the oil situation will be given in Volume III Part 2.
‡ See Volume III Part 2.   § See Volume III Part 2.

12. MEW's German Handbook, Economic Survey Section P, pp 2–3.
13. JIC (43) 477 of 22 November, 480 of 26 November.
14. JIC (44 153 of 14 April.
15   JIC (44) 218 (o) of 27 May.

Germany was reduced to strategic stocks, with no free reserves, and calculated that shortage of oil would bring about her military collapse by December.[16] Although she was still fighting hard in December, this estimate did not greatly differ from that made by Speer. He reduced the supply of oil to the economy by 35 per cent in June and by a further 23 per cent in July, but still informed Hitler at the end of August that 'the flow necessary for the supply of the troops and the country will be paralysed in the late autumn of this year unless hard weather gives Germany a large amount of luck'.[17] In the event the extremely hard weather of October and November 1944 was a factor enabling Germany to struggle through into 1945.*

On the eve of *Overlord* the intelligence authorities accepted that manpower both in the armed forces and in the civilian labour force was being maintained at a higher level than had been expected. In February 1943 an *ad hoc* committee of the JIC had estimated that, by substituting some 1.75 million foreigners and POW for men called up in 1942, the Germans had maintained the civilian labour force at about 36 million, equal to figures for January 1942; but it had foreseen either a serious decline in the strength of the armed forces or an inevitable loss of production in essential industries if the labour force was further 'combed-out.[18] In February 1944, however, MEW's calculations indicated that by September 1943 there had been a heavy switch-over of manpower from the distribution services, like trade and banking, to the metals, engineering and chemicals industries without any effect on the armed forces.[19]† In the same month the JIC concluded that the labour force had remained at approximately the same size as at the beginning of 1943, and this despite a comb-out from industry that was even more extensive in 1943 than in previous years; transfers to the armed forces had helped to increase the strength of the German Army, as had the incorporation of foreign personnel, but these transfers had been off-set by some mobilisation of women and the importation of a further one million foreign workers.[20]

MEW could find little evidence that the dilution of the labour force by foreign workers and POW,‡ which together stood at an

---

* See Volume III Part 2.   † See Appendix 4, Table (e).

‡ MEW must have known that not all POW were put into industry, as British POW, for example, were not so used. Under 'foreign workers' it presumably included, but never specified, forced labour and the inmates of concentration camps.

16   JIC (44) 320 (o) of 24 July.
17.   CAB 77/29, AO (46) 1 of 9 March, pp 130, 134.
18.   JIC (43) 40 of 11 February; JIC (43) 56 of 9 February.
19.   FO 837/19, MEW WIR No 107 of 22 February 1944.
20.   JIC (44) 42 of 18 February.

estimated total of 6.5 million, by the recruitment of women and by the loss of skilled men to the armed forces had reduced the quantity or quality of Germany's industrial output. In the reviews it made of the engineering and armaments industries in the first half of 1944 it detected no decline that could be attributed to shortage of manpower. The Allied bombing was creating difficulties for the machine tool industry, as for German industry as a whole,* but there was no threat to the supply of essential machine tools to the priority industries.[21]† In the general engineering industries a loss of capacity due to shortages of men and materials in the second half of 1943 had been overcome by requisitioning idle plant and transferring resources from less essential to priority work.[24] The output of the aircraft industry was believed to be well maintained, the industrial reorganisation of 1942 and 1943 having simplified production and reduced the number of man-hours spent on each aircraft.[25] The production and quality of land armaments had similarly been maintained, in MEW's view, because rationalisation and standardisation had off-set the dilution of labour.[26]

---

* For detailed estimates of the effect of the bombing offensive see below p 298 et seq.

† The US Strategic Bombing Survey[22] severely criticised MEW after the war for being unaware of the large excess of machine tool capacity available to the Germans. It claimed that MEW's estimates were made on the incorrect assumption that machine tools were utilised as intensively in Germany as in Great Britain, and this despite the fact that 'it was comparatively easy to obtain intelligence on the utilisation of machinery'. It gave the following figures to illustrate the resulting under-estimation –

Year	Actual Inventory	MEW Estimate
1938	1,327,000	658,000
1939	1,498,000	706,200
1940	1,664,000	746,400
1941	1,840,000	766,000
1942	2,007,000	838,000
1943	2,150,000	981,400

MEW published revised estimates in January 1945[23] when it gave the following figures –

	MEW Estimates
1938	1,473,000
1939	1,764,000
1940	1,994,000
1941	2,143,000
1942	2,280,000

21. FO 837/20, MEW WIR No. 134 of 31 August 1944.
22. US Strategic Bombing Survey, Synoptic Volume (1945), Table 18, p 44.
23. MEW's German Handbook, Economic Survey Section, issued January 1945.
24. FO 837/20, MEW WIR No 134 of 31 August 1944.
25. FO 837/19, MEW WIR No 108 of 29 February 1944.
26. FO 837/17, MEW WIR No 72/A of 3 July 1943.

As for the over-all performance of the economy, MEW had concluded by the spring of 1944 that although its ability to sustain prolonged operations on all fronts was declining, the decline was unlikely to affect Germany's resistance to *Overlord* in the early stages.*

When MEW issued in August 1944 its report on the German economy in the second quarter of the year, it recognised that 'Every branch of war production, however severely hit, still climbs back steadily unless methodically and severely "policed".' 'To sum up – an economy decreasing in efficiency but still under control is competing as best it can with demands far exceeding its capacity. It is still responsive to changes in priority of demand and still capable of profitting by any respite which is given to it . . .'[27] In the same month, and again in September, the JIC concluded that Germany's collapse would be brought about by military defeat in the field, rather than by economic difficulties.[28]

□

In the months before these appreciations were issued MEW nevertheless continued to under-estimate the enemy. Despite the greater caution and realism of its appreciations after the autumn of 1943, it was still reaping the consequences of its misconception of Germany's economic programme in the first three years of war, which prevented it from fully grasping the thrust and significance of the reorganisation effected in 1942. Having believed for so long that the German economy had been close to full mobilisation before the reorganisation took place, it did not realise the scope for move-ment towards total war that existed when the reorganisation was brought into force. On the other hand, the greater caution it displayed after the autumn of 1943 led it to infer from some of its evidence, notably the fact that many women in Germany were still employed in domestic service,† that the reorganisation had not achieved the complete mobilisation of the enemy's resources. For these reasons it was not until June 1944 that it finally realised, in a

---

* See above, p 46.
† In December 1943 MEW concluded that no more than 30–40 per cent of the women recruited under Sauckel's decree of January 1943 on the mobilisation of labour for Reich defence were yet engaged in full-time war work, and in June 1944 it still felt that the absence of large-scale measures for the mobilisation of labour, including that of women, was 'most striking'.[29]

27. FO 837/20, MEW WIR No 134 of 31 August 1944.
28. JIC (44) 349 of 10 August; JIC (44) 407 of 16 September.
29. FO 837/19, MEW WIR No 108 of 29 February 1944; FO 837/20, WIR No 134 of 31 August 1944.

critical advance in understanding which invalidated most of the assumptions it had previously made about Germany's economic mobilisation, that the reforms of 1942 had involved 'not only the switch-over from semi-total to total war, but also from short-term to long-term conceptions' in an effort to adapt the war machine to the requirements of a defensive strategy.[30]

The best test of the degree of under-estimation that followed from the absence of this insight, as also of the dearth of corrective intelligence, is provided by the estimates of Germany's capacity for armaments production. Except in relation to U-boat construction, for which the Enigma and PR supplied reliable information,* the lack of intelligence was fully realised, and the estimates advanced were highly tentative. But the fact that from the beginning of 1944 they consistently and increasingly fell short of actual production figures of aircraft was not fully recognised until in May 1944 the JIC decided to make no further use of production estimates.[31]

It was difficult to obtain information about the production of tanks because the entire German engineering industry participated in it; and the problem of arriving at reasonable estimates on the basis of scanty intelligence on factory output was further complicated from the middle of 1943 by the knowledge that Germany was devoting a good deal of her capacity to the manufacture of new types – the Panther, the Tiger I and the Tiger II.† Towards the end of 1943 MEW embarked in collaboration with the US authorities on an analysis of the manufacturing serial numbers marked on German tanks and found that they provided a reasonable basis for calculations. But the analysis established that tank production had been over-estimated during 1942 and 1943,[36] and MEW accordingly

---

* See below, p 240.

† MEW's review of the first six months of 1943 dated the commencement of Tiger I production as early 1942 and its operational debut as January 1943. (According to Speer the first six of this tank were tried out on the Russian front, and destroyed, in the early summer of 1942).[32] MEW also recognised that a new medium tank, the Panther, intended to replace Pzkw III and Pzkw IV, was in production.[33] Information available in February 1944 to Enemy Branch showed that the Germans were concentrating upon the construction of the new tanks.[34] By April 1944 Enemy Branch had come to the conclusion that the Panther had failed as the principal fighting tank and the Tiger was playing a subsidiary role. In view of these failures the Germans had decided to retain Pzkw IV as a temporary measure.[35]

30. FO 837/20, MEW WIR No 134 of 31 August 1944; MEW's German Handbook, Part II, Administration, issued in April 1944, the contents 'valid for conditions up to October 1943'.
31. Webster and Frankland, op cit, Vol IV, Appendix 49, p 500.
32. A Speer, *Inside the Third Reich* (Sphere Books 1971), pp 335–336.
33. FO 837/17, MEW WIR No 72/A of 3 July 1943.
34. FO 837/19, MEW WIR No 108 of 29 February 1944.
35. JIC(44) 144 (o) of 15 April; FO 837/20, MEW WIR No 134 of 31 August 1944.
36. FO 837/19, MEW WIR No 108 of 29 February 1944.

reduced its estimate of monthly production. In August 1943 it had set the figure at 700. For the first three months of 1944 it set it at between 300 and 350.[37] This figure was further below actual output (over 2,000 tanks in the first quarter of 1944) than the 1943 estimates had been above it. Nor was it until 1945, with the acquisition of voluminous first-hand information, that revised estimates of tank production since 1940 were produced that were close to actuality.*

With regard to the German aircraft industry, Whitehall had recognised from the beginning of 1943 that it was expanding and giving priority to fighters;[38] in April the JIC had noted that the increase in the fighter establishment from 1,360 operational units in August 1940 to 2,050 in April 1943, and the re-equipment of practically the whole of the single-engined fighter force with Me 109s and FW 190s, were remarkable achievements which, if not checked, might seriously blunt the Allied air offensive.[39] Thereafter the authorities concerned – AI 2(a), MEW and the JIC – knew that aircraft production was continuing to receive high priority, and that by means of a rigorous policy of conservation and as a result of a rationalisation of the production processes, initiated in 1942 to reduce the number of man-hours spent on each aircraft, output was being maintained at a higher level than before the spring of 1943.[40]† But they seriously under-estimated the scale of production, setting it consistently at a total monthly production of about 1,500 aircraft, including about 900 fighters, when with only a brief intermission in November and December 1943, due to the redeployment of some of the industry to avoid Allied bombing, actual production rose steadily from 2,100 aircraft a month, including 936 fighters, in April 1943 to 4,219 aircraft, including 2,954 fighters, in July 1944.‡

These miscalculations arose generally from lapses in organisation within the Air Intelligence Branch. Thus, there was no central recording section, which should have been regarded as essential in view of the number of sections interested in such things as call-signs and works numbers, each of which was keeping records for its own

---

* See Appendix 4, Table (f).

† Interrogation in September 1943 of an aeronautical engineer in close touch with the German Air Ministry disclosed that at the beginning of the war, 7,000–8,000 man-hours had been required to produce one Me 109, but that this figure had been reduced to 6,500 in 1942 and that it was 3,900 at Wiener Neustadt in June 1943.[41]

‡ See Appendix 4, Tables (g) (h) and (i) and Volume II, pp 521–522.

37. JIC (44) 241 of 13 June.
38. AIR 19/543, Memo from AI 2(a) to D of I (O) of 24 November 1943
39. JIC (43) 185 of 23 April.
40. FO 837/17, MEW WIR No 72/A of 3 July 1943; FO 837/19, MEW WIR No 108 of 29 February 1944; JIC (44) 42 of 18 February.
41. AIR 19/543, ADI (K) Report No 473/1943.

purposes; there should have been separation of estimates of production rates from those of locations of factories for target purposes; and it might have been useful to have a joint working party from AI 2(a) and AI 3(b) – the order of battle section – to estimate production rates and wastage.[42] In these circumstances the immediate reason for the inaccuracy lay with the method of estimating production adopted by AI 2(a) in 1942. This relied on the numbers carried by German aircraft, and it had produced reasonably accurate results, especially from the autumn of 1942. From the spring of 1943, when the Germans introduced random gaps in the number sequences, there was little check from other sources on the method's increasing unreliability.[43] Although the Japanese diplomatic decrypts from time to time provided valuable reports on Germany's policy and plans for aircraft production,* neither they nor the Enigma threw a steady light on the progress Germany was actually making with her expansion programme. Photographic reconnaissance and SIS agents provided good intelligence about the location of aircraft factories but little or no information about their output.[44] The discrepancy between estimated and actual output was concealed, moreover, by another consideration. The wastage rate in the GAF from the autumn of 1943 arising from poor training and Allied attacks on factories and aircraft on the ground, as well as from combat losses, almost equalled the number of new and repaired aircraft allocated to units;[45]† but this was not suspected till the end of the war. The outcome was that Allied estimates of the output of new aircraft did not conflict with Allied estimates of the first-line strength and order of battle of the GAF which, based as they were on Sigint, and relying very little on estimates of production, were at all times highly accurate.[46]

---

* See below, pp 294–295 and Appendix 16.

†Quarter ending	Total Allocation[a]	Total Wastage[b]	First-line Strength	Reserve Training Unit	Change in Strength
31.3.43	?	3,950	6,527	1,527	+ 1,504
30.6.43	?	5,641	7,193	1,595	+ 734
30.9.43	?	7,178	6,186	1,542	– 1,000
31.12.43	6,452	5,344	6,688	1,665	+ 625
31.3.44	7,441	7,094	6,777	1,600	+ 24
30.6.44	10,983	9,914	6,746	1,569	– 62

a. ie *new* aircraft, plus repaired aircraft, allocated.
b. ie aircraft destroyed, missing or damaged.

42. Air Historical Branch, *Air Ministry Intelligence*, p 239.
43. JIC (44) 177 (0) of 1 May; JIC (44) 228 (0) of 3 June; *Air Ministry Intelligence*, pp 236, 238.
44. *Air Ministry Intelligence*, pp 228, 240.
45. Webster and Frankland, op cit, Vol IV, Appendix 49, p 500.
46. *Air Ministry Intelligence*, pp 170, 177.

On the contrary, as it became obvious from Sigint and operational reports during the air battles of the spring of 1944 that the GAF's wastage rate was rising,* it was the estimates of front-line strength which made the Air Ministry and the JIC uneasy about the estimates of aircraft production, particularly in relation to fighters. Early in April 1944 the JIC thought that the front-line strength of the GAF 'may be expected to show a considerable decline . . . up to and including the *Overlord* target date'[47]. In May, however, it warned that because of lack of information all aircraft production estimates for recent months must be regarded as tentative,[48] and by June it had modified its optimistic forecast of a decline in front-line strength in the light of order of battle intelligence.[49]

In view of the fact that, except in relation to U-boats, estimates of arms production and wastage,† however tentative, were so wide of the mark, it is not surprising that in their efforts to foresee the effects of shortages of armaments on Germany's actual strengths, and thus on her strategy, the intelligence authorities were able to add little of value to the conclusion they had reached by the spring of 1943, to the effect that she was no longer capable of taking the offensive on any large scale. In June 1943, within that framework, they reported that training in the GAF was already so severely restricted by shortage of aircraft and fuel that she would be unable to resume sustained strategic bombing, but that there was as yet no evidence that land operations were being seriously affected by shortages.[50] In November the JIC noted that there was a shortage of tanks for equipping new divisions,[51] and by February 1944 it knew that the Army had suffered from shortages of tanks and motor transport in operations on the Russian front, where Panzer formations were frequently below strength.[52] A general review of German shortages by the JIC in April 1944, concluding that the Army was inadequately equipped with tanks, motor transport and heavy weapons, though not short of ammunition or signals equipment, and that the GAF was 'wholly inadequate' to meet Germany's mounting defensive requirements, foresaw that the disparity between production and requirements would have serious effects on one of the three fronts when Germany became engaged on land in the west as well as in the east and the south; it also expected that the GAF, acutely short of spare parts and accessories, would decline

---

* See below, p 317 et seq.
† MEW frequently pointed out that it was extremely difficult to calculate the rate at which the Germans were losing tanks in action.

47. JIC (44) 127 (o) of 3 April.   48. JIC (44) 177 (o) of 1 May.
49. JIC (44) 228 (o) of 3 June.   50. JIC (43) 239 (o) of 5 June.
51. JIC (43) 458 of 12 November.   52. JIC (44) 42 of 18 February.

in front-line strength by the target date for *Overlord* to no more than 4,000 aircraft, of which 1,800 would be on the western front.[53]

In May the JIC noted the worsening supply situation in the GAF, which was barely maintaining its first-line strength, and repeated that production for the Army, though still considerable despite a continuing decline in overall industrial production, was not meeting requirements; periodical shortages of ammunition were appearing alongside shortages of heavy equipment and motor transport.[54] By June it believed that the Army's over-all shortage of tanks might amount to some 5,000 but, as we have already seen, it had raised its estimate of GAF front-line strength*; the figures given were a total of 5,250 aircraft of which 2,350 were in the west.[55]

---

* See above p 64.

53. JIC (44) 144 (o) of 15 April.   54. JIC (44) 190 of 9 May.
55. JIC (44) 228 (o) of 3 June, 241 of 13 June.

PART IX

The Mediterranean from June 1943 to June 1944

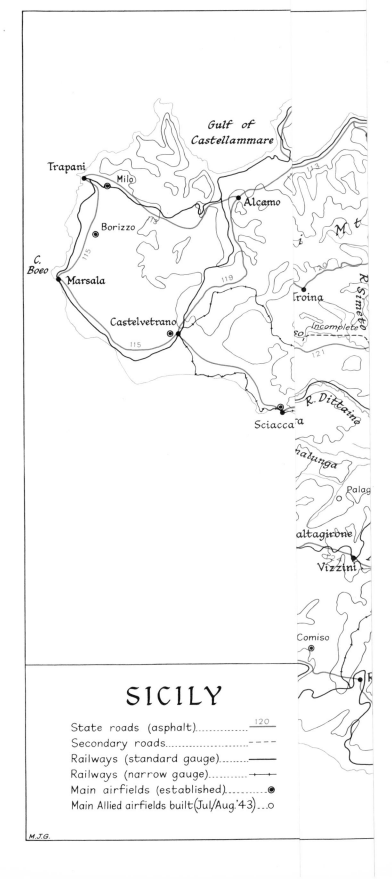

Gulf of
Castellammare

Trapani

Milo

Alcamo

Borizzo

C.
Boeo

Marsala

Castelvetrano

Troina

Incomplete

R. Dittaino

Sciacca

Palag

altagirone

Vizzini

Comiso

SICILY

State roads (asphalt)............ ———
Secondary roads.................... - - - -
Railways (standard gauge)........ ————
Railways (narrow gauge)......... +-+-+
Main airfields (established).......... ◉
Main Allied airfields built(Jul/Aug.'43)...o

M.J.G.

CHAPTER 31

The Capture of Sicily and the Italian Surrender

THE ANGLO-AMERICAN decision to undertake the invasion of Sicily (Operation *Husky*) as soon as possible after the completion of the Tunisian campaign was taken at the Casablanca conference in January 1943.* Intelligence contributed nothing to the Allied decision apart from general estimates of Germany's over-all strengths. In reaching the decision the Combined Chiefs of Staff took into account an estimate by the JIC that should Germany fall back to a shortened line in Russia, should Italy have fallen out of the war and Germany be on the defensive in the Mediterranean area – these being the worst case assumptions for the Allies – Germany would be able to oppose a cross-Channel invasion in 1943 with 41 divisions and 1,500 aircraft, and to assemble against a landing in the Cotentin peninsula – the only feasible locality – 15 divisions in the first two weeks.[1] They agreed that these calculations ruled out any attempt to open 'the second front' in north-west Europe 1943 before Germany's reserves had been greatly reduced.

Intelligence also contributed little to the discussion of the choice of Sicily as the first target. Partly on the ground that Germany might riposte by invading Spain and partly on the ground that the operation would deflect effort from other theatres, the Pacific as well as western Europe, there was some residual American reluctance to mount an attack across the Mediterranean, but it was overcome by strategic and political arguments.[2] These arguments included the possibility that the attack would topple Mussolini's regime and force Italy out of the war. But although the British

---

* For details of the discussions leading to this decision see M Howard, *Grand Strategy*, Vol IV (1972), Chapters XIII and XIV, and M Matloff and E Snell, *Strategic Planning for Coalition Warfare 1943–1944* (Washington DC 1959).

1. CAB 121/145, SIC file A/Strategy/2, JIC (42) 490 of 11 December (JP (42) 1005 of 12 December, Annex 6), COS (42) 452 (o) of 31 December (tabled at Casablanca as CCS/135/1); CAB 121/152, SIC file A/Strategy/8, CCS 167 of 22 January 1943, CCS 68th Meeting, 23 January 1943 (both in COS (43) 33 (o) of 28 January).
2. CAB 121/152, COS (S) 1st, 3rd and 4th Meetings, 13, 15 and 16 January 1943, CCS 55th, 57th and 60th Meetings, 14, 15 and 16 January 1943 (all filed in COS (43) 33 (o) of 28 January).

authorities pressed the point, they were aware that they could not support it with firm evidence. In November 1942, following the Allied victory at Alamein, the JIC was instructed to weigh up the prospects of an Italian collapse and during December it had argued that while the collapse of the Italian government and a request for a separate peace were unlikely before Sardinia, and possibly Sicily also, were in Allied hands, there was some evidence that high-ranking Italians were already contemplating an attempt to over-throw Mussolini. The intelligence authorities in Cairo had been more sceptical; on the strength of their interrogations of POW, they had questioned whether any Italians were seriously contemplating a *coup*, and they had doubted whether any Italian government would be sufficiently independent of Germany to be able to ask for a separate peace. To the first of these objections the JIC had retorted that it had better evidence than POW interrogation.* But it had been somewhat nonplussed by the second; and when the Casablanca conference opened, it was still deferring for lack of evidence consideration of the extent to which Italy would be free to pursue an independent policy even supposing Mussolini was over-thrown.[6] At the conference itself the JIC delegate maintained that the capture of Sardinia would be no less effective in forcing Italy out of the war than the capture of Sicily, given that it could be

---

* The JIC was referring to the fact that several tentative approaches had been made to SOE's agents by individual Italians in recent weeks. The War Cabinet was first informed of these approaches on 3 December 1942, when it decided that no response should be made to them.[3] While the Casablanca conference was in session the Cabinet returned to the subject on 18 January 1943, when, without minuting the fact, it discussed a report to the effect that an Italian industrialist who had been in touch with the SOE in Berne since the previous spring had intimated that Generals Badoglio and Caviglia wanted to send an emissary to Cyrenaica to discuss with the British authorities a plan to overthrow Mussolini and form an anti-Fascist army, and that the SOE had asked the Chiefs of Staff for approval to proceed. The Cabinet ordered that no reply should be given; it was unlikely that any force recruited by Badoglio would have real military value and any advantage to be derived from talks was outweighed by the disadvantage of having to give undertakings to him, which might cause grave discouragement throughout the Balkans.[4] The Cabinet's view was shared at the Casablanca conference, where the Prime Minister, the President and the Combined Chiefs of Staff agreed that 'we should be very careful of accepting any invitation to support an anti-Fascist insurrection. To do so might only immobilise a considerable force to no useful purpose.'[5]

3.   CAB 65/32, WM (42) 164 CA of 3 December. For details of the approaches see CAB 101/144, Cabinet Office Historical Section paper on the Italian Armistice, p 10 et seq.
4.   CAB 66/33, WP (43) 27 of 4 January; CAB 65/33, WM (43) 9 of 18 January.
5.   CAB 121/152, CCS 58th Meeting, 16 January 1943 (in COS (43) 33 (o) of 28 January).
6.   JIC (42) 442 (o) of 11 November, 447 (o) of 14 November, 462 of 3 December, 474 of 8 December, 497 (o) of 15 December; 498 (o) of 16 December; JIC (42) 62nd Meeting, 22 December, JIC (43) 2nd Meeting (o) of 5 January.

carried out two months earlier, but the conference chose Sicily because it was intrinsically of greater strategic importance rather than because there was any great expectation that *Husky* would produce the collapse of Italy.[7]

Intelligence figured more prominently in the outline plan for *Husky* which the Combined Chiefs of Staff issued to General Eisenhower. Drawn up by the British Joint Planners during the autumn of 1942 as part of Whitehall's preparations for the Casablanca conference,[8] the plan listed the main prerequisites for the success of the operation after considering the JIC's estimates of the nature and the scale of the enemy's resistance. Calculating that the effective strength of the Italian Fleet would be six battleships, eight cruisers (two of them heavy), sixteen destroyers and one aircraft carrier, the JIC drew the obvious conclusion that the scale of the naval covering forces required for the invasion would depend on how far the Allies had previously succeeded in driving the opposition into the Adriatic.[9] It estimated that by late April 1943, out of a total of 1,200 German and 1,450 Italian aircraft in the Mediterranean theatre, 840 German and 1,100 Italian aircraft would be based in the Sicily-Sardinia-Pantellaria area; and it judged that, since existing airfields in that area already allowed for rapid reinforcement and might be increased, the Allied landings would encounter a formidable scale of attack by some 795 aircraft, of which 545 would be German,[10] unless steps were taken in advance to cut back the enemy air forces and destroy their bases. As for the enemy's ground forces, the JIC estimated that the existing Italian garrison in Sicily – correctly assumed to consist of three infantry divisions, one regiment of medium tanks, three battalions of light tanks and 54 low category static defence battalions – might be reinforced after the end of the Tunisian fighting by between three and five field divisions, of which two or three might be German.[11] This last estimate dictated the recommended scale of the Allied expedition – eight divisions – and a further calculation guided the proposals made for the landings. The outline plan expressed anxiety not only about 'the chances of success against a garrison which includes German formations',[12]

---

7. CAB 121/152, COS (S) 12th Meeting, 21 January 1943; Howard, *Grand Strategy*, Vol IV, pp 265–266; M Matloff and E Snell, *Strategic Planning for Coalition Warfare 1943–1944* (Washington DC 1959), p 25.
8. CAB 121/578, SIC file F/Italy/5A, vol 1, JP (43) 7 of 10 January.
9. ibid, JP (43) 7, Annex 1, p 2 para 9, p 4 para 25.
10. ibid, JP (43) 7, Annex 1, p 3 para 14 and Appendices A and D.
11. ibid, JP (43) 7, Annex 1, p 3 para 16 and Appendices A and E, JP (43) 18 of 9 January; C J C Molony, *The Mediterranean and Middle East*, Vol V (1973), pp 13–14.
12. CAB 122/578, JP (43) 7, p 1 para 4.

but also about the rate at which the enemy might bring in the expected reinforcements, which could be as high as one German division or one and a half Italian divisions per week by the ferry service to Messina alone.[13] For these reasons, although this called for a great increase in the scale of the attack, the Joint Planners advocated two landings – one by British forces in the Catania area, the other by US forces on the west coast with the object of taking Palermo – 'as the only way to conquer the whole island if the enemy is in strength'.[14] They urged that a single landing in the Catania area should be contemplated only if intelligence established that the strength of the enemy's ground forces and his ability to reinforce them were less than they had allowed for.[15]

The outline plan was handed to General Eisenhower at the Casablanca conference, on his appointment to be Supreme Commander of the expedition. His instructions were to report not later than 1 March 1943 whether the operation could be carried out in the July moon period; if not, he was to confirm by 1 March that it would take place in August. At the insistence of the President and the Prime Minister he was also asked to consider during the next three weeks whether 'by contrivance or ingenuity' it could be brought forward to June.[16] The Combined Chiefs of Staff named General Alexander as General Eisenhower's deputy and made him responsible for the detailed planning, preparation and execution of Husky. They also appointed Admiral Cunningham as naval C-in-C and, as air C-in-C, the commander of the new Mediterranean Air Command, Air Chief Marshal Tedder. Alexander established a new operational and administrative staff (later to become 15th Army Group) at which Cunningham had a special planning section and near to which the Mediterranean Air Command and the HQs of its tactical and strategic forces were in due course also grouped. The force commanders – General Montgomery of the Eastern Task Force (comprising the British Eighth Army) and General Patton of the Western Task Force (comprising US Seventh Army) – each had his own operational and administrative staff with a naval component and associated air forces.[17] The arrangements proved to have some major disadvantages. Eisenhower's three generals were all deeply involved in the conduct of the fighting in Tunisia until the Axis surrender on 13 May. None of them was able to give undistracted attention to the detailed planning for Husky, nor was it easy for them to meet for planning discussions. Subordinate commanders were

---

13.   ibid, Annex 1, p 3 para 16, Appendix E, para 5.
14.   ibid, Annex 1, p 4 para 24.
15.   ibid, Annex 1, p 4 para 26.
16.   Molony, op cit, Vol V, pp 3–4.
17.   ibid, pp 4, 7, 8; AIR 41/52, *The Sicilian Campaign*, pp 15, 17–18.

similarly preoccupied and dispersed. Thus, for example, the commander of Eighth Army's XXX Corps, who from mid-May was acting as Montgomery's deputy in Cairo where the Eastern Task Force's planning for *Husky* was carried out, was able to collect his formation commanders together for only one conference – and that before detailed planning had begun – before meeting them again in Sicily.[18] Similar problems impeded co-ordination between the intelligence staffs. No intelligence section was attached to Alexander's staff until late February; until then it had to rely on a liaison section at AFHQ to meet its needs for operational intelligence. The Eastern Task Force obtained the intelligence it required from GHQ ME in Cairo.[19]

The staffs attached to Eisenhower at AFHQ and to his army commanders accepted the estimates made by the Joint Planners in London of the probable scale of the enemy's ground opposition: up to eight active divisions, of which two would be German, and five coastal divisions. But in their anxiety about the risks involved in making what was to be the first amphibious assault against substantial German forces, and about the need to effect the early capture of the airfields and important ports, they tended to depart from the recommendation of the Joint Planners that the Allied effort should not be concentrated in the Catania area unless it became clear that the enemy's ground forces were to be less than had been estimated. In March the Combined Chiefs of Staff averted a proposal that one US division should be transferred from the Western Task Force to the Eastern Task Force, at the expense of delaying the assault on Palermo, by agreeing to provide an additional division for the Eastern Task Force; even so, it was then accepted that because of difficulties in allotting ships and landing craft, the western landings must be postponed from D + 2 to D + 5. On 24 April, a fortnight after these adjustments had been agreed to, General Montgomery demanded a still greater strengthening of the Eastern Task Force at the expense of abandoning the assault on Palermo altogether. Despite the misgivings of other commanders, he had got his way by the time the final plan was approved by the Combined Chiefs of Staff at the Trident conference in Washington on 13 May.*

---

* For detailed discussion of the planning see Howard, op cit, Vol IV, pp 363–368: C J C Molony, *The Mediterranean and Middle East*, Vol V (1973), pp 18–24; A Garland and H Smyth, *Sicily and the Surrender of Italy* (Washington DC 1965), pp 59–60. For the final Allied plan see below, p

18. WO 279/164, R D Q Henriques, *Planning* (War Office 1954), p 143.
19. E E Mockler-Ferryman, *Military Intelligence Organisation*, p 170; CAB 121/579, SIC file F/Italy/5A, Vol II, General Eisenhower's despatch, *The Sicilian Campaign*, pp 4, 56.

The lack of advance information about the enemy's intentions and expectations was among the considerations underlying the pressure for these adjustments. So long as the fighting in Tunisia continued it remained difficult to distinguish between troops which were to be based in Sicily and troops which were in transit to Tunisia. Despite this fact there was no lack of evidence that the Germans were preparing to defend the island. On 18 April the Enigma disclosed that a Battle Group of unknown composition was being established in Sicily and that OKW had ordered that the Hermann Göring Panzer Division was to be retained in Italy for the reinforcement of the island.[20] An Enigma decrypt of 12 May gave the dispositions that the Hermann Göring Division would adopt when it moved to Sicily.[21] By that date it was known that the German troops already in Sicily, which had increased from about 5,000 to 10,000 since the middle of April, were being formed into an *ad hoc* division under Colonel Baade, with his HQ at Enna in the centre of the island, and that Baade's intention was to distribute them among the main ports, Palermo, Catania and Trapani.[22] But it was impossible to predict how many reinforcements would be sent to Sicily before the launching of the Allied assault, the date for which had on 10 April been fixed as 10 July. As the Eighth Army's Chief of Staff was later to write in connection with General Montgomery's request for modifications to the *Husky* plan, 'the ultimate size of the German garrison and the strength of the GAF in Sicily by the date of the invasion were, of course, unknown and not very easy to assess. We had therefore to prepare for a considerable [enemy] reinforcement'.[23]

This uncertainty was progressively reduced from the middle of May, and it was finally established that the ground opposition was to remain below the estimate made by the Joint Planners. In relation to the German measures, the Allies owed this improvement to high-grade Sigint. At first the amount of Enigma traffic fell off drastically following the end of the Tunisian fighting and there was some fear that, with the enemy's withdrawal to Europe and its landlines, it would not recover. In the event, the GAF in Italy and Sicily again resorted to wireless when its defensive preparations increased and the German Army formations opened up wireless links on their arrival in Sicily. As was always the case in the absence of active fighting, the GAF Enigma keys were read with less

---

20. DEFE 3/811, VM 9717 of 18 April 1943; DEFE 3/812, ML 24 of 18 April 1943; Dir/C Archive, 3011 of 18 April, 3054 of 22 April 1943.
21. DEFE 3/815, ML 1840 of 12 May 1943; Dir/C Archive, 3267 of 13 May 1943.
22. WO 208/3573, MI 14 Appreciations of 19 April and 27 May 1943; DEFE 3/814, ML 1057 of 4 May 1943.
23. F de Guingand, *Operation Victory* (1947), pp 274, 277.

difficulty than those of the German Army. However, a new operational army key (named Albatross at GC and CS), which was first identified as in use in Sicily in May, was broken from 2 June about 50 per cent of the time and the GAF decrypts continued to yield intelligence about army formations.* At the end of May, moreover, GC and CS had broken the non-morse teleprinter link connecting the German High Command in Italy with OKH (Bream); as was to be the case throughout the Italian campaign the traffic on this link furnished from the outset a more comprehensive guide to the enemy's dispositions and intentions than did any of the Enigma keys. By contrast, Sigint on the Italian Army had now declined in significance, most of the high-grade being no longer readable, and the principal source for the Italian preparations was the examination of mail addressed to Italian POW.[24]†

In the third week of May, from these sources, the Allies learned that the German troops already in Sicily had acquired divisional status as the Sicily Division, with its HQ at Caltanissetta in the centre of the island, and that it was to be reorganised as a two-regiment Panzer Grenadier (PG) Division, its third regiment being kept for reinforcement of particularly threatened points on the coast. Between 20 June and the beginning of July the decrypts showed the Hermann Göring Division arriving with 18,000 men, 96 guns and 53 tanks, but minus its third infantry regiment. Before it arrived, the knowledge that the Chief Quartermaster to Field Marshal Kesselring, the C-in-C South, was arranging for supplies for two divisions to be equally divided between bases in the Trapani-Palermo area and bases north and north-west of Catania had made it clear that the German defence of the island was to rest on having one division in the east and one in the west: and by the end of June it was established that the Hermann Göring Division was to be in the east, with its HQ probably in the Paterno area south of Mount Etna. At the same time, it emerged from further references to the

---

* See below, pp 81–82 for the GAF keys.

† The SIS was of no assistance during the planning of *Husky*. At the end of April SIS Algiers concluded that 'Sicily must now be so closely guarded – also the islands – that it would be wasteful to expend . . . trained agents on such a hot target'; nor was it until June that the SIS stations in the Mediterranean began their preparations for entering Italy in the wake of the Allied forces (see below, p 178). The War Report of the American Office of Strategic Services shows that the same applied to the OSS. General Alexander's despatch on *Husky* stated:

'So good was the police and counter-espionage system in Sicily that we were unable to obtain any information direct from the island.'[25]

24. CAB 106/594, General Alexander's despatch, *The Conquest of Sicily*, p 15 fn; D Hunt, *A Don at War* (1966), p 186.
25. CAB 106/594, p 16; US War Department, *War Report of the OSS*, Vol II (1976), p 63.

use of the third regiment of the Sicily Division that the enemy judged Catania to be the most threatened area. On 8 July (D – 2) last-minute intelligence showed that at the beginning of the month the Sicily Division had been transferring its Tiger company, with about 15 Tiger tanks, to the Hermann Göring Division, and that the Sicily Division was being re-named 15th Panzer Division.[26]*

In the Allied appreciations issued on the eve of *Husky* the two German divisions were shown as being divided into four battle groups, disposed so as to act as stiffeners to the Italian divisions. It was calculated that the number of Italian coastal divisions had remained at five, though it was thought that they had been strengthened by the transfer of artillery and machine gun units from northern Italy; they varied in quality, but the one facing the Eighth Army's assault area was known to be poorly equipped. It was known that the Italian field divisions had been increased from three to four, making a total of six enemy field divisions in all. From many reports about their armament, training and morale it was judged that only one of the Italian field divisions, the Livorno Division, was at all formidable. From their dispositions, as from the German evidence, it was clear that while the enemy expected the south-east and the east to be the most likely areas for the Allied landings, he was not discounting a landing in the west: it was known that the Italians were organised into two Corps under the Sixth Army, XII Corps holding the western half of the island and XVI Corps holding the east.[28] Sixth Army had tactical command of the German forces; Hitler's personal liaison officer with Sixth Army was General von Senger und Etterlin.

Although to the end they remained subject to some uncertainty,† these order of battle estimates were substantially correct. Captured documents subsequently disclosed that the enemy's plans had been the subject of disagreements between the Axis partners. The Italians, initially opposed to having any German divisions in Sicily, had then wanted to hold back the two German divisions with other

---

* It was in fact a Panzer Grenadier Division with only one tank battalion,[27] and was soon to be called 15th Panzer Grenadier.

† A fifth Italian field division had been mistakenly identified in the Catania area for a time, but the error was corrected before the final appreciations were made.[29]

26. DEFE 3/817, ML 2755 of 25 May; DEFE 3/819, ML 3982 of 6 June; DEFE 3/822, ML 5499 of 26 June; DEFE 3/825, ML 6635 of 8 July 1943; Dir/C Archive, 3397 of 28 May, 3505 of 11 June, 3683 of 28 June, 3704 of 30 June 1943.
27. Molony, op cit, Vol V, p 45; CAB 106/594, p 16.
28. CAB 44/23, AL 1200/12, para 5A; CAB 44/24, AL 1200/13, paras 1–7 sketch maps 2 and 3 and Table A; Molony, op cit, Vol V, p 39 et seq.
29. CAB 106/594, p 16; Hunt, op cit, p 186.

mobile reserves in the belief that the Allies would attack on a broad front, whereas the Germans had wanted the reserves disposed close to the most likely landing places. On the other hand, the Italians and the German Command in Sicily had both wanted to have 15th PG Division in the east, where it had become accustomed to the terrain, but had been over-ruled by Kesselring who had insisted that the Hermann Göring Division, more strongly armoured, should be in the east, where the terrain was more suitable for tanks. With all agreeing that the south and south-east were the areas most threatened, the final arrangement had been a compromise by which the Hermann Göring Division, with one Battle Group of 15th PG Division attached to it, was disposed in the south-east in Sixth Army reserve, the second Battle Group of 15th PG Division was in the west and the third in the centre near Caltanissetta, while the Italian divisions were disposed inland.[30]

□

If the Allies knew that they could not hope to surprise the enemy by the location and relative weight of their landings, they knew, too, that they could not conceal the timing of their assault. Sigint showed that the German and Italian air forces between them maintained an 'entirely thorough' reconnaissance coverage of the whole Mediterranean; it had to be assumed that 'any large sea-going force is unlikely to escape detection and a warning would be received in ample time'.[31] Only by persuading the Axis that Sicily was not the objective of the expedition, or not its sole objective, could these handicaps be off-set.

The attempt to do this was all the more necessary, and all the more difficult, in that Sigint showed that from the end of February the enemy was pre-supposing that Sicily was the obvious Allied target. At the end of February 1943, when he was allowing that a landing on a fairly large scale was possible as early as March, the GAF Enigma disclosed that he thought the most threatened areas were Sicily, Crete, Sardinia and Corsica, in that order.[32] From an analysis of the Sigint received during March it was deduced that, while he was uncertain whether the attack would come before or after the fall of Tunisia, he continued to think Sicily its most likely objective: reports of Allied preparations against Crete, Rhodes and the Greek mainland had not been borne out by PR; Allied preparations in the north African ports made the western Mediterranean more probable than the Atlantic coast of France; in the western

---

30. Molony, op cit, Vol V, pp 42–43; A Garland and H Smyth, *Sicily and the Surrender of Italy* (Washington DC 1965), pp 73–75, 83–87.
31. ADM 223/209, 'The GAF and *Husky*'.
32. DEFE 3/802, VM 5072 of 27 February 1943.

Mediterranean he was discounting Spain and judging that Sardinia and mainland Italy were less likely than Sicily. A month later it was clear that the Germans had all but excluded all areas other than the western Mediterranean in the light of their observation of Allied military, naval and air concentrations in Gibraltar, Malta and the north African ports. Though allowing for a limited attack on Crete, they believed there was no threat to the Balkans; in the western Mediterranean they continued to think Sicily the most probable Allied objective.

It was in these circumstances that, to reinforce deception measures already in progress in the Middle East, the Allies developed their strategic deception plan (Operation *Mincemeat*). Early in May a corpse in British uniform was washed ashore on the Spanish coast bearing a letter to General Alexander which indicated that the Allies were planning an assault landing in Greece (named *Husky*) and that the idea of using Sicily as the cover target for this operation had been rejected in favour of using it as cover for another operation (Brimstone)* for which the target was unspecified.[33] Although it was not the only factor influencing Germany's dispositions – her anxiety about the possibility of an Italian collapse was no less important – Sigint established that the plan had a considerable, if declining, effect, not least because it chimed with Hitler's fears for the Balkans. On 14 May GC and CS decrypted a signal from OKW to Kesselring and other German commanders in the Mediterranean; it conveyed the 'absolutely reliable' information that large-scale Allied landings were being mounted both in the eastern and the western Mediterranean, the objective of the former (cover name *Husky*) being the Peloponnese.[34] Until the beginning of June there were other decrypts indicating that the enemy expected early Allied action against southern Greece as well as in the western Mediterranean;[35] and as late as a week before *Husky* the decrypts of the German C-in-C South East's day reports showed him believing that concentrations of guerrillas in western Greece gave some support to rumours that the Allies intended to land there.[36] But after the Allied capture of Pantellaria on 11 June† the Sigint evidence,

---

* *Brimstone* was in fact the name of the plan to invade Sardinia which had been rejected by the Combined Chiefs of Staff at Casablanca.
  † See below, pp 84–85.

33. Howard, op cit, Vol IV, p 370.
34. CX/MSS/2571/T4; JIC (43) 219 (o) of 19 May; ADM 223/209, 'Operation *Husky*'.
35. CX/MSS/2608/T35; ZTPI 32152, 32156, 32713; Air Sunset 66 of 21 May 1943.
36. DEFE 3/824, ML 6306 of 5 July 1943.

becoming more voluminous as the enemy increased his defence preparations in the danger areas, left little doubt that although not ruling out a simultaneous descent on the Peloponnese or Crete, he was convinced that the biggest danger lay in the western Mediterranean.[37] On 27 June GC and CS decrypted an order of the day from Kesselring to all German forces in the Mediterranean; it said that the hour of decision was at hand and they must be prepared to protect the homeland 'on Italian soil'.[38]

In the western Mediterranean, as the Sigint showed, the Axis authorities remained to the end unable to exclude a threat to Sardinia or southern Italy,[39] but they concentrated increasingly on Sicily and in the week before D-day decrypts about minelaying and other defensive measures by the GAF left little doubt that they regarded Sicily as the most probable Allied objective.[40] The Italians finally reached this conclusion on 4 July: on that day, when the Germans were still inclined to believe that there would be simultaneous landings in Sicily, Sardinia and Greece, and that the danger was not imminent, the Italian High Command in Sicily appreciated from reconnaissance of Allied convoys and naval concentrations that Sicily, particularly eastern Sicily, was the target and that the attack would come on 10 July.[41] The decrypts did not give this appreciation in so many words, but they left little doubt that the Allies would not achieve surprise.

A C 38m decrypt* expected an Allied assault to take place on 10 July.[42] On 25 June the decrypt of a signal from the Japanese Military Attaché in Stockholm to Tokyo disclosed that he had heard that the Allies had decided to land in Sicily; though the date was not yet arranged, their First Army was already concentrating in the Bizerta/Tunis area.[43] Enigma decrypts of 5 July showed that the GAF had deduced from PR of the north African ports that some 250,000 tons of merchant shipping was about to leave with 120 landing craft and a large escort force and presumed that some of it was destined for the eastern Mediterranean.[44] By 8 July it was known that the Italian

---

* The C 38m was a medium-grade cypher used by the Italian navy, see Volume II, p 22 n.

37. ADM 223/209, 'Operation *Husky*'; JIC (43) 251 (o) of 16 June, 262 (o) of 23 June; Air Sunset 69 of 15 June 1943
38. Dir/C Archive, 3677 of 27 June 1943; CX/MSS/2800/T19.
39. JIC (43) 270 (o) of 30 June, 277 (o) of 7 July; ADM 223/209, 'Operation *Husky*'.
40. JIC (43) 279 (o) of 7 July; ADM 223/209, 'Operation *Husky*'; Air Sunset 70 of 20 June.
41. Garland and Smyth, op cit, p 110.
42. DEFE 3/822, ML 5163 of 24 June 1944; Dir/C Archive, 3652 of 25 June.
43. Dir/C Archive, 3742 of 4 July 1943; SMA 2038 of 25 June.
44. DEFE 3/824, ML 6352 of 6 July 1943.

Admiralty had estimated on the basis of the known dispositions of landing craft that the Allies had embarked some seven divisions in north African ports, about one division in Malta and 1½ divisions in the eastern Mediterranean, and that Kesselring, on the evidence of Allied air raids and other indications that the offensive was imminent, had ordered increased vigilance.[45] Another decrypt ordered a first state of readiness at 1630 on 9 July following the sighting of 150 to 200 vessels north of Malta and Gozo:[46] this alert applied only to Sardinia and the Allies did not decrypt the signals in which, following GAF sightings of convoys travelling at high speed near Pantellaria, the Italian Command in Sicily concluded that an invasion of the Gela-Catania area was imminent and ordered a preliminary alert at about 1900.[47]

□

Between March and D-day for Operation *Husky* the number of German divisions in the Balkans as a whole rose from eight to eighteen, and those in Greece from one to eight.* While it is difficult to say how far the Allied deception measures were instrumental in provoking this build-up, they had little if any effect on the dispositions of the German Air Force. The Air Ministry estimated that the strength of the GAF in Greece and Crete increased from 125 to 265 aircraft between the fall of Tunisia and the *Husky* D-day,[48] but the bulk of its available resources and of the reinforcements it brought in from other theatres were concentrated in the central Mediterranean.

Early in March the JIC reviewed the estimate of GAF strengths and dispositions in the Mediterranean that it had supplied for the original *Husky* plan: a total of 1,200 aircraft by the end of April, of which 840 would be in the Sicily-Sardinia-Pantellaria area.† It concluded that the total was now 930 and did not expect it to change by more than 10 per cent.[49] In May, after the end of the Tunisian campaign, the Air Intelligence Branch estimated that the total was 820, of which 695 were in the central area,[50] and the newly established JIC Algiers estimated that the figure for Sicily, Sardinia and Italy was then 585 and would rise by D-day to 870.[51] A week before

---

* See above, p 11.   † See above, p 71.

45. ZTPI 34197; DEFE 3/825, ML 6515 of 7 July 1943.
46. ADM 223/209, 'Operation *Husky*'.
47. Garland and Smyth, op cit, pp 110–111.
48. Air Sunsets 61, 71 and 73 of 17 May, 28 June and 5 July 1943.
49. JIC (43) 92 (o) of 3 March.
50. Air Sunset 61 of 17 May 1943.
51. JIC (43) 231 (o) of 27 May.

D-day AI's estimate was that 990 German aircraft were in the central area out of a total of 1,260 for the whole of the Mediterranean, and it noted that the increase during recent weeks, mainly in single-engined fighters and fighter-bombers, had been achieved by diversions from other fronts, mainly western Europe, and by the formation of new units with aircraft direct from the factories.[52]* The actual strength of the GAF in the central Mediterranean on the eve of *Husky* was 960 aircraft.[54] The March JIC estimate of the total strength of the Italian Air Force was 1,275 aircraft.[55] In May the JIC Algiers estimated that the number of Italian aircraft based in Sicily, Sardinia and Italy was 825, and forecast that it would rise to 1,060 by D-day.[56] A week before *Husky* AI's estimate of the total strength of the IAF was 1,695 aircraft of which 880 were in the central Mediterranean.[57] The actual total was 1,500 aircraft of which about 700 were in the central Mediterranean and another 100 or so in Albania and Yugoslavia.[58]

There was little Sigint evidence to support these estimates in the case of the Italian Air Force. The interception of R/T now provided some information about the methods used for controlling the fighters in Sicily, Sardinia and southern Italy: this gave some indication of the fighter strength in Sardinia and western Sicily, but not elsewhere, and conveyed the general impression that the IAF's defence preparations were poor. But the IAF's high-grade cyphers were no longer readable, and its medium and low-grade W/T traffic was insufficient to give a reliable guide to its order of battle. In the case of the GAF, on the other hand, high-grade Sigint was again abundant after the temporary lull following the end of the Tunisian fighting. The GAF general Enigma key (Red) was decrypted currently. The key used by the GAF ground organisation in Italy (Primrose) was read regularly and often currently, as was that used by Fliegerkorps II for army-air liaison traffic (Locust). About half of the traffic in two other keys, that used by Luftflotte 2's bomber units (Squirrel) and that used by the transport organisation, Fliegerkorps XIV (Mayfly), was read, some of it currently. It was the

---

* The Enigma disclosed that the GAF's Inspector of Fighter Aircraft was to make a tour of the Mediterranean area presumably in order to speed up the supply of fighters and improve their efficiency.[53]

52.   Air Sunset 75 of 5 July 1943.
53.   CX/MSS/2862/T17. See also Molony, op cit, Vol V, p 47 (n).
54.   Molony, op cit, Vol V, p 46.
55.   JIC (43) 92 (o) of 3 March.
56.   JIC (43) 231 (o) of 27 May.
57.   Air Sunset 72 of 2 July 1943.
58.   AIR 41/52, Appendix 4.

fact that GC and CS decrypted most of the strength and service-ability returns transmitted in these keys that explains the accuracy of the estimates of GAF strengths.*

The main changes in the GAF's command structure in the Mediterranean after the fall of Tunisia, as disclosed by the Enigma, centred on Luftflotte 2. Its area of responsibility was restricted to Italy and the central Mediterranean, a new command being established for south-east Europe and given control of Fliegerkorps X. At the same time, Luftflotte 2's HQ staff was strengthened; it came to comprise Fliegerführer Sicily and Fliegerkorps II, and a new bomber organisation was established within Fliegerkorps II comprising all the bombers in Sicily, Italy and southern France, under the command of Colonel Peltz.[60] Peltz, transferred from his post as Angriffsführer England,† arrived in Piacenza on 17 June.[61]

GAF bomber strength in the Mediterranean was not increased after the end of May.[62] By the beginning of June, moreover, the Enigma indicated that the bomber units previously based in Sicily were being withdrawn to the mainland, and during the first week of the month it showed that some of them were moving from central Italy to northern Italy and southern France.[63] The withdrawal reduced the GAF's counter-attacks on Allied invasion ports and convoys, which had little effect on the preparations for Husky. This, too, was reflected in the GAF Enigma, which frequently reported confusion and changes of plan in the enemy's bombing operations.‡ Such was the degree of air superiority achieved by the Allies by D-day that whereas it had been assumed that 300 ships might be lost to air attack off the beaches, in fact only twelve were destroyed.[64]

The withdrawal of the bombers was made in response to the Allied air offensive in which, in its first phase up to 3 July, the

---

* The decrypts were also the reason why the CAS could reassure the Prime Minister in the third week of June that none of the GAF moves had been unexpected or had merited any action not already taken. The CAS considered that Allied air forces in the Mediterranean were quite strong enough to deal with the situation and that the German moves were a sign of irresolution in the High Command and a further result of being thrown on the defensive.[59]

† See Volume II, pp 510–511.

‡ On this account, however, advance intelligence of GAF raids, though sometimes obtained from the Enigma, was of little value to the Allies, times and targets for raids being changed at short notice.

59. Dir/C Archive, 3598 (CAS Minute of 21 June 1943).
60. CX/MSS/2570/T4 and 13, 2747/T19 and 34, 2766/T28 and 31, 2800/T33; Air Sunsets 70 and 71 of 20 and 28 June 1943; Molony, op cit, Vol V, p 47 fn.
61. Air Sunset 70 of 20 June 1943.
62. AIR 41/10, The Rise and Fall of the German Air Force, p 258.
63. AIR 41/10, p 259; Air Sunset 67 of 7 June 1943; and, as examples, CX/MSS/2630/T16, 2636/T10, 2640/T16, 2698/T23, 2735/T28, 2736/T20, 2747/T19.
64. D Richards, The Royal Air Force 1939–1945 (1953), Vol II, p 310.

bombing of the principal airfields and ports in Sicily, Sardinia and central and southern Italy was supplemented by raids against northern Italy carried out from the United Kingdom by Bomber Command and against eastern Mediterranean targets by bombers from the Middle East. But the number of GAF fighters and fighter-bombers in Sicily and Sardinia continued to be increased until 3 July, when the Allied air offensive, entering on its final phase and concentrating against land, sea and air communications with and within Sicily, achieved some reduction of their strengths. On the evidence of the Enigma Sicily had 185 fighters and 79 fighter-bombers by 3 July and Sardinia had 81 fighters and 68 fighter-bombers.[65] On the same evidence the number of fighters in Sicily was down to about 135 on the eve of Operation *Husky* and the fighter-bombers had been withdrawn.[66] There were 130 fighters and fighter-bombers in Sardinia, but the serviceability of the 55 or so fighter-bombers was down to 35 per cent compared with 55 per cent on 3 July. It was clear, moreover, that fuel shortages had frustrated the intention to build up a main concentration of fighters in Sardinia, where total fuel stocks were by 6 July sufficient for only two days of restricted operations.[67] These estimates may be compared with what is known about actual German strengths at the time: some 300 fighters in Sicily and the Toe of Italy, with 70 in Sardinia, and some 130 fighter-bombers.[68]

The pre-*Husky* air offensive was guided by PR as well as by Sigint, high and low-grade, about the GAF, the operational intelligence section of the Mediterranean Air Command at La Marsa putting the product of both sources together on an hour to hour basis.* In addition to special reconnaissance of industrial areas and lines of

---

* PR operations for *Husky* were the responsibility of the Northwest African PR Wing, which also had a detachment at Malta, though it was not until June that there was a courier service between Malta and north Africa.[69] The operations were hampered by a shortage of aircraft even after the end of the fighting in Tunisia, when, as a result of a personal appeal by Eisenhower, four Mark IX PR Mosquitoes were temporarily made available.[70] Interpretation was the responsibility of the Northwest African Central Interpretation Unit, whose work was based on material supplied by the CIU at Medmenham, and the Army Air Photographic Interpretation Unit (AAPIU) in Cairo. For the *Husky* planning Eighth Army's divisional interpreters returned to Cairo, its Interpretation Section moving to Malta a few weeks before the landings. US Seventh Army relied largely on British interpreters but it, too, had its own interpretation section in Sicily after the landings.[71]

65. Air Sunset 73 of 5 July 1943.
66. Air Sunset 74 of 9 July 1943.
67. Air Sunset 74 of 9 July 1943.
68. AIR 41/52, p 49 and appendices 3 and 4.
69. Molony, op cit, Vol V, p 50; AIR 41/7, *Photographic Reconnaissance*, Vol II, p 121.
70. AIR 41/7, pp 121–123; Mockler-Ferryman, op cit, p 189.
71. AIR 41/7, pp 122, 123; Mockler-Ferryman, op cit, p 190.

communication, airfields in Corsica, Sardinia, Sicily and Italy were photographed at least once a day, those in the western Balkans somewhat less frequently.[72] It was clear that only two of the airfields in Sicily remained entirely serviceable by D-day – Sciacca in the south-west and Milo in the extreme west – and that some, including Palermo, had been practically abandoned.[73] But it was also clear that the enemy resorted to the construction of emergency landing strips; including these, the nineteen airfields believed to exist in Sicily at the start of the planning for _Husky_ had increased to over thirty by the end of June.[74] Thus the important Gerbini system near Catania, comprising a major airfield and satellite landing grounds, had nine satellite landing grounds by the end of June and had three more added to it in the week preceding the invasion;[75] and though it was the target of many attacks, it was never put out of action entirely.[76] As for the rail traffic on Sicily, this had been virtually brought to a standstill by D-day through the destruction of rolling-stock and repair facilities.[77] In addition to the attacks on airfields and on communications generally, there were two other particular targets in the Allied bombing offensive. It was known from Sigint that the Germans were having trouble with the Messina ferry service as a result of the Allied attacks. On 7 June, for example, the railway ferry was temporarily out of action with the sinking of the last serviceable ferry and arrangements had to be made to use very small craft for the transport of troops and light equipment.[78] On 9 July the HQ of Fliegerkorps II at the Hotel San Domenico at Taormina was raided by Spitfires; it had been located by Sigint as well as by the Polish Intelligence Service, and Sigint showed that the damage done by the raid had dislocated the GAF effort on the day of the landings.[79]

Photographic reconnaissance was the chief source of intelligence during the preparations for the capture of Pantellaria, which were part of the pre-_Husky_ air offensive. From various sources – POW, Sigint and PR – enough was known about its garrison and defences

---

72. Molony, op cit, Vol V, p 50; Richards, op cit, Vol II, pp 301–306.
73. AIR 41/7, p 123; AIR 40/2323, Humphreys, _The Use of Ultra in the Mediterranean and Northwest African Theatres of War_, pp 15–16.
74. CAB 121/579, Eisenhower's despatch, p 19; Garland and Smyth, op cit, p 53 fn 1.
75. CAB 121/579, Eisenhower's despatch, p 19.
76. AIR 41/52, p 43.
77. S Zuckerman in _The Sunday Times_, 22 January 1978; see also Cabinet Office Historical Section, EDS Appreciation 14 Part I, Chapter 1, pp 45–46.
78. WO 208/3573 of 7 and 14 June 1943; JIC (43) 234 (0) of 2 June; CX/MSS/2624/T25; ZTPI 32901; CAB 106/594, p 15.
79. CX/MSS/2870/T45, 2872/T18, 2873/T34; AIR 41/52, p 43.

to suggest that an opposed landing would involve a heavy expenditure of Allied men and equipment.[80] In the middle of May, when it was decided that the base must be taken to remove the threat to *Husky* posed by its radar stations and its capacity to accommodate about 100 fighter aircraft, it was accordingly decided that it must be reduced primarily by bombing. Until 6 June it was subjected to increasingly intense air attack, as well as to naval bombardment, and a special effort was made to achieve greater than normal density of bombing against targets such as gun positions and pill-boxes which were either small and difficult to locate or so heavily concreted as to be able to withstand even direct hits from 1,000 lb bombs. The work called for constant PR cover of the bomb damage, and careful study of the photographs of every hit and crater with a view to estimating not only the extent of the destruction, but also how many hits were made with each bomb-load and which types of bomb were the most effective. It was undertaken by a team of experts from the Air Ministry and the Ministry of Home Security, working alongside the PRU detachment at Malta.[81] In the event, the saturation bombing proved to be less effective in destroying guns and other fixed defences than in undermining the morale of the garrison, which surrendered within the day when the Allied assault convoys arrived on 11 June.[82] The nearby island of Lampedusa surrendered on 12 June.

The quality of the intelligence provided about the invasion beaches in Sicily, for which PR was again the chief source, is difficult to assess. Despite the fact that in the original *Husky* plan the Joint Planners had pointed out the lack of information about Sicily's beaches, particularly about their slopes and exits, and had stressed the dependence of detailed planning on accurate beach intelligence,[83] complaints about the failure of PR in this direction continued to be made in many quarters throughout the planning period.[84] Towards the end of April the JIC noted that the planning was having to rely on charts and navigational maps, often pre-war, with

---

80. CAB 121/578, JP (42) 944 of 11 November, JP (43) 7 of 10 January; CAB 121/575, SIC file F/Italy/3, Algiers telegram to ETOUSA No 1409 of 27 February; JIC (43) 38 (o) of 30 January; Garland and Smyth, op cit, p 69.

81. CAB 121/575, Summary of Eisenhower's despatch on Pantellaria; AIR 41/7, p 122; Garland and Smyth, op cit, p 70; Air Historical Branch, *Air Ministry Intelligence*, p 35.

82. CAB 121/575, AFHQ telegram to War Office No 1595 of 17 June. See also K Strong, *Intelligence at the Top* (1968), p 98.

83. CAB 121/578, JP (43) 7, Annex 1, p 2 para 5.

84. ibid, COS (43) 30th (o) Meeting, 26 February and Washington telegram R 6393 of 5 March; CAB 121/579, COS (43) 73rd (o) Meeting, SSF, 10 April; JIC (43) 25th (o) Meeting, 11 May.

only 'scanty additional information'.[85] At the end of June, after a visit to Algiers, the Director of Military Intelligence (DMI) reported to the JIC that inadequate beach intelligence had been, and still remained, the chief obstacle facing the planners.[86] After the landings, however, tributes to the excellence of the beach photography, particularly the very low altitude photography carried out by the RAF, were equally widespread.[87] The discrepancy is in all probability largely explained by the fact that although the PR cover became very good, it did not do so in time to reduce uncertainty and anxiety during detailed planning, much of which had to be completed down to company level by D − 30 and all of which had to be carried out in the knowledge that, following the abandonment of the plan to land in western Sicily, the entire Anglo-American expedition would have to be maintained across the beaches for a considerable time. This is borne out not only by the nature of the complaints,[88] but also by General Eisenhower's request to the Combined Chiefs of Staff in July for PR for post-*Husky* operations; in this he stressed that the results of PR had hitherto been received so late that all but a fraction of their potential value had been wasted.[89] But this was not the sole problem. The naval C-in-C commented in his despatch on *Husky* that 'the estimation of beach conditions and gradients by air photography and study of wave velocities* have now reached a fine pitch of efficiency; but where sand bars exist there is no present substitute for swimming reconnaissance . . .'.[91] This was a reference to the Combined Operations Pilotage Parties, who were taken into the beaches by submarines from the end of February to supplement the work of PR. Despite the heavy casualties incurred during March and April,† this most hazardous method of collecting beach intelli-

---

* Part of the PR preparations for *Husky* was the development of a new method of calculating the slope of beaches by a mathematical formula measuring the interval between crests of waves in different wind conditions, the interval showing up in photographs in parallel white lines.[90]

† Of the 14 officers and 17 ratings made available, 11 officers and 4 ratings had been lost by mid-March; during April the number of officers lost rose to 14.[92]

85.   CAB 121/579, JIC (43) 182 (0) of 21 April.
86.   JIC (43) 33rd (0) Meeting, 29 June.
87.   Molony, op cit, Vol V, p 50; de Guingand, op cit, p 277; AIR 41/7, p 123.
88.   WO 279/164, pp 64, 109–110, 193 et seq; Garland and Smyth, op cit, p 99.
89.   CAB 88/2, CCS 100th Meeting, 2 July 1943; CAB 88/12, CCS 259.
90.   CAB 121/578, COS (43) 48th (0) Meeting, 18 March; CAB 121/579, JIC (43) 182 (0) of 21 April; WO 279/164, p 109; Hunt, op cit, pp 185–186.
91.   Quoted in CAB 106/3, *History of the Combined Operations Organisation 1940–1945*, p 50.
92.   CAB 121/578, COS (43) 144 (0) of 21 March; CAB 121/579, COS (43) 73rd (0) Meeting, SSF, 10 April.

gence was again used with good results during the dark period at the end of May and the beginning of June.[93]

In view of the fact that the Italian high-grade naval cyphers were unreadable, PR was also the main source of intelligence about the strength and distribution of the Italian Fleet. Each port harbouring warships was photographed daily and even the meanest port was photographed at least once a week. The results showed that the strength and distribution of the Italian Fleet on the west coast of Italy remained much as had been expected in the original *Husky* plan, so that the Allies had to provide large naval covering forces for their expedition at the expense of the Home Fleet. Until May, six battleships, two heavy cruisers and six light cruisers were identified, distributed about equally between Taranto and La Spezia with freedom to concentrate through the Straits of Messina.[94] In May the number of battleships increased by one and the number of light cruisers by two.[95] But between 11 and 18 June PR showed that a new battleship (later identified as the *Roma*) had been damaged by bombing in La Spezia and withdrawn to Genoa, where she remained until PR reported her return to La Spezia on 11 August. The Italian Fleet at the time of the invasion of Sicily in fact consisted of seven battleships, two heavy cruisers and nine light cruisers, but because of fuel shortage and the lack of adequate air protection, Comando Supremo had already decided in May to commit it against the Allied invasion only if an exceptionally good opportunity presented itself.[96] On 10 July PR reported that two battleships in La Spezia were outside their baffle and that three of the cruisers had steam up; on 12 July it reported signs that the battleships at Taranto were ready to sail. But no ships moved until, as was disclosed by the Enigma and the C 38m, two cruisers were despatched to bombard Palermo on the night of 6–7 August, and again on the following night. They turned back on the first attempt after a brush with destroyers and on the second after being sighted by aircraft.[97]

□

93. CAB 121/578, C-in-C Med telegram 1847A/7 March, COS (43) 44th (o) Meeting, 14 March, C-in-C Med telegram 2234A/18 March, COS (43) 51st (o) Meeting, 22 March; CAB 121/579, Admiralty to C-in-C Med 1619A/24 March, JIC (43) 182 (o) of 21 April.
94. CAB 121/579, Eisenhower's despatch, p 15; CAB 106/594, p 17.
95. JIC (43) 231 (o) of 27 May; ADM 223/209, 'Operation *Husky*'.
96. Howard, op cit, Vol IV, p 467; Garland and Smyth, op cit, p 82.
97. DEFE 3/871, JPs 191 and 264 of 7 August, 319 of 8 August; DEFE 3/872, JP 523 of 10 August 1943; DEFE 3/612, ZTPGM 29542; ZTPI 36026, 36056; CX/MSS/3034/T26.

In the final Allied invasion plans the object of the seaborne and airborne assaults was the capture of the airfields in the south-east and of the ports of Syracuse on the east and Licata on the south coasts with a view to establishing a firm base from which to take Augusta and Catania and the Gerbini group of airfields. The Eighth Army, comprising XIII Corps (5th and 50th Divisions) and XXX Corps (51st Highland Division, 1st Canadian Division and 231st Infantry Brigade), was responsible for capturing Augusta, Catania and the Gerbini airfields from landings at Syracuse and Pozallo. US Seventh Army, comprising II Corps (1st and 45th Divisions) and 3rd Division operating directly under General Patton, was responsible for capturing Licata and the airfields in its neighbourhood and for protecting the left flank of the Eighth Army in the Ragusa area.[98] Once the armies were established across the south-east corner on the line Catania-Licata General Alexander intended to bring about the reduction of Sicily by cutting the island in half, seizing the road network in the centre and leaving only the northern coast road open to the enemy.[99] It was estimated that Catania would be taken between D + 7 and D + 14.[100] No date was set for the capture of the whole island; on 13 May however, the Combined Chiefs of Staff had expected that if *Husky* began as planned on 10 July it should be completed in about a month.[101]

Despite the lack of tactical surprise* and the hazards of combined operations, all the Allied assault forces secured their beachheads. Against opposition described as 'slight or negligible', XIII Corps on the right secured positions round Cassibile and Avola and took Syracuse on the evening of D-day, by which time XXX Corps was firmly established in the Pachino peninsula. Forty-five miles to the west US II Corps suffered more severely from poor weather and encountered tougher opposition, but by the end of D-day was holding beachheads around Scoglitti, Gela and Licata.[102]†

At the time of the landings the enemy's ground forces were disposed as follows. A Battle Group under Colonel Schmalz with elements of the Hermann Göring Division and a regiment from 15th PG Division covered Catania. The Napoli Division was in the south-east corner with the rest of the Hermann Göring Division

---

* See above, pp 79–80.
† For the small scale of U-boat operations against *Husky* see below, p 232 n†.

98.   Molony, op cit, Vol V, pp 26–29.
99.   CAB 106/594, pp 11–12.
100. AIR 41/52, p 23.
101. CAB 121/153, SIC file A/Strategy/9, CCS 83rd Meeting, May 1943 (in COS (43) 286 (o) of 7 June).
102. Molony, op cit, Vol V, pp 59–64.

and the Livorno Division on its right in the area Caltagirone-Caltanissetta. The two other Italian field divisions and the main body of 15th PG Division were in the west of the island.[103] Early on 10 July the Commander of the Italian Sixth Army decided to recall the main body of 15th PG Division to Caltanissetta to protect his right flank; he also ordered a counter-attack on II Corps's beachhead at Gela and the reinforcement of the Syracuse sector to prevent the Eighth Army from breaking out into the Catania plain.[104]

Eighth Army's intelligence summary for 10 July noted that 15th PG Division was moving back from the west by 1900 on that day.[105] This information was almost certainly provided by air reconnaissance: no further news of the division was obtained during the next two days, and it was not until 14 July that GC and CS was able to inform the Allied commands that it had been moving to the Caltanissetta area on the evening of 10 July to protect the Axis right flank.[106] But the decrypts of orders issued at 2300 on 10 July for operations by GAF ground attack aircraft against the Gela beachhead at first light on 11 July were signalled by GC and CS at 0231 on 11 July;[107] the news that a German Battle Group was moving south from Catania through Lentini followed immediately (this was Battle Group Schmalz);[108] and an hour later GC and CS reported that at 1715 on 10 July Kesselring had instructed the Hermann Göring Division to attack at once, Hitler having ordered all forces to be brought into operation immediately to prevent the Allies from establishing themselves.[109]

The counter-attack on Gela on 11 July failed after hard fighting and on 13 July, while US Seventh Army advanced northwards to Vizzini, north-west towards Caltanissetta and west towards Porto Empedocle and Agrigento, Eighth Army took Augusta and launched its main thrust towards Catania across the Simeto river. Meanwhile, on 11 July Hitler had ordered that HQ XIV Panzer Corps under General Hube should move from southern Italy to give unified direction to the German units in Sicily, and that those units should be reinforced by 1st Parachute Division, flown in from Avignon, and 29th Panzer Grenadier Division from Calabria. But on 13 July, following the Italian collapse at Augusta, he defined the German task as being 'to delay the enemy advance as much as possible and bring it to a halt in front of Mount Etna along a line

---

103. ibid, pp 41–43.
104. Garland and Smyth, op cit, p 147.
105. WO 169/8519 of 10 July 1943.
106. DEFE 3/826, ML 7394 of 14 July 1943.
107. DEFE 3/825, MLs 6964 and 6966 of 11 July 1943.
108. ibid, ML 6967 of 11 July 1943.
109. ibid, ML 6976 of 11 July 1943.

running approximately from San Stefano via Aderno to Catania', and while confirming the transfer of 1st Parachute Division, ordered that 29th PG Division should be held at Reggio di Calabria until the prospects of maintenance across the straits of Messina had become clearer. On 15 July Kesselring and Roatta, Chief of the Italian Army High Command, agreed to establish a defensive front round Mount Etna. On 16 July Hube took over from the Italian Sixth Army the tactical command of all sectors containing German troops; on 2 August command of the whole front was formally transferred to him.[110]

From 13 July Sigint became plentiful. In addition to the cyphers already mentioned, notably the Red and Locust keys of the GAF, the Albatross army Enigma key and the Bream traffic,* the German naval Enigma key (Porpoise) provided a good deal of intelligence about the ground fighting as well as adding to the shipping intelligence derived from the C 38m.† Moreover, although it was little used as yet, a high-level Army key (named Puffin) was now introduced for communications between OKH and German forces in Italy and Sicily, and GC and CS broke it for the first time on 23 July. There was thus no lack of Sigint, about either the enemy's intentions or the state of affairs on the battle-front, for transmission to the Allied commands. In addition to transmitting to the principal commands in Tunisia and north Africa, GC and CS transmitted directly to Seventh and Eighth Armies when their commanders moved into Sicily.

On 14 July it became clear that the enemy was abandoning western Sicily; the decrypts of that day included orders to the supply staff at Palermo to expedite the evacuation of the supply base in west Sicily by every possible means. These were followed by orders on 15 July to ration depots at Palermo and Trapani to issue as much of their stocks as possible to the armed forces and prepare to destroy the remainder; a GAF order early on 15 July for the immediate evacuation of all ground elements in the Palermo area; a report that

---

* See above, pp 75, 81.

† The C 38m was now decrypted in the Mediterranean theatre for the first time. As part of the preparations for *Husky* a small party of cryptanalysts from GC and CS was attached to C-in-C Mediterranean's HQ at Algiers to exploit on the spot Italian low-grade tactical codes and cyphers which had hitherto been exploited only at GC and CS and at Alexandria. When the party arrived at the end of May, however, it found that, partly because of changes made by the Italians and partly for lack of interception facilities at Algiers, it could not work these codes and cyphers, but the presence of the party was turned to account: improvised arrangements were made before D-day by which it moved to Malta with the C-in-C Mediterranean and decrypted the C 38m there.

110.   Molony, op cit, Vol V, pp 44, 85, 90, 91; Garland and Smyth, op cit, pp 203, 211–217.

Trapani harbour had been blown up at noon on 15 July and Milo evacuated; an order in the evening of 15 July that all landing craft not on urgent supply traffic were to be sent from the Messina Straits to Palermo 'for important return cargoes'; directions for the removal of stores in short supply; and orders on the morning of 16 July that a named general was to be responsible for carrying out the orderly evacuation of western Sicily.[111]

At the same time, it was established that the enemy intended to reinforce eastern Sicily. Instructions to the Rations Office at Reggio to expect 26th Division* and HQ XIV Panzer Corps, together comprising about 14,000 men, within the next few days were decrypted on 13 July.[112] Soon after midday on 14 July the Allied Command learned that the German liaison staff with Sixth Army had been informed that for the present only a detachment of 29th PG Division (one battalion of 15th PG Regiment, one heavy infantry gun platoon, one light battery and three Panzer reconnaissance troops) would go to Sicily that day, and that by Hitler's orders this detachment was to be used to protect the flank and rear of Battle Group Schmalz.[113] The announcement that HQ XIV Panzer Corps would be moving on 15 July was decrypted on 16 July.[114] The fact that on 17 July its staff was to be routed via Taormina to battle HQ six kilometres east of Randazzo was passed to the Allied commands at 1349 on 18 July,[115] by which time they had already been informed that General Hube had been appointed C-in-C German Armed Forces in Sicily on 14 July and that General von Senger und Etterlin was in command of German Army formations.[116] Between 13 and 17 July Sigint showed the Axis forces to be under heavy pressure on the whole front. It was known on the evening of 13 July that at 1530 Battle Group Schmalz had asked for artillery and anti-tank support at Francofonte[117] (ten miles east of Augusta) and, from a message intercepted in the morning of 12 July but not decrypted in time for counter-action, that the Battle Group had been reinforced on the afternoon of 12 July by a Parachute regiment which had been dropped 15 km south-west of Catania.[118] A report that the Hermann Göring Division had lost 200 men on 12 July and that Schmalz had had moderate losses was available shortly before midnight on 13 July.[119] An order by Kesselring late on 13 July to the Hermann

---

* It soon became clear that this was a mistake for 29th PG Division.

111. DEFE 3/827, MLs 7534 of 15 July, 7649, 7654, 7681 and 7710 of 16 July 1943.
112. DEFE 3/826, ML 7288 of 13 July.   113. ibid, ML 7390 of 14 July.
114. DEFE 3/827, ML 7729 of 16 July.   115. ibid, ML 7887 of 18 July.
116. ibid, ML 7812 of 17 July; DEFE 3/573, CX/MSS/C 142, 149, 150 and 151.
117. DEFE 3/826, ML 7286 of 13 July.
118. ibid, MLs 7285 and 7303 of 13 July.   119. ibid, ML 7324 of 13 July.

Göring Division to put its mobile reserve immediately at the disposal of Battle Group Schmalz was signalled by GC and CS to the Mediterranean authorities at 0332 on 14 July,[120] and at 1334 on 14 July the decrypt of a message sent by Kesselring to von Senger that morning read: 'What are the possibilities of rapid reinforcement of east wing? If it should not be possible to hold east flank in Catania area for much longer am of opinion it must be withdrawn immediately to area east of Etna'.[121] Later messages on 14 July continued to convey an impression of crisis. Kesselring ordered a battalion of another PG regiment from Reggio to reinforce Schmalz;[122] more units of 1st Parachute Division were dropped (the message was again out of date as an intention by the time it was decrypted);[123] and according to a situation report signalled by GC and CS at 2237 Schmalz was engaged in heavy defensive fighting, the Hermann Göring Division was being violently attacked by tanks and strong infantry forces, the situation of the Axis forces in the Catania basin was seriously endangered and at 1500 the Italians had hauled down the flag over Catania (but had promised to hoist it again).[124]

In the small hours of 15 July GC and CS informed the Mediterranean authorities that the Hermann Göring Division had been ordered at noon on 14 July to restore the situation at Catania with its main body;[125] and that Schmalz had asked for fighter protection over Lentini to cover his withdrawal on 14 July,[126] but had been told that this was impossible because the GAF was fully committed.[127] A report on the GAF's operational intentions in support of the Army on 13 July had already shown that Fliegerkorps II had 'only weak forces available'.[128] At noon on 15 July GC and CS signalled orders issued at 0700 to Fliegerführer Sardinia. He was instructed to send aircraft to carry out continuous reconnaissance to establish the front line; if German parachutists were surrounded east of Lentini they were to be told to fight their way through to Catania; it was thought that British tanks were probably already on the Catania plain.[129]

The decrypts circulated on 16 July showed Fliegerkorps II telling Sixth Army that more support was impossible as its whole effort was needed for the Schmalz section[130] where at 1600 on 15 July Schmalz had reported severe fighting with heavy losses and an urgent need for reinforcements.[131] They disclosed that Kesselring

---

120. ibid, ML 7347 of 14 July.
122. ibid, ML 7398 of 14 July.
124. ibid, ML 7447 of 14 July.
126. ibid, ML 7487 of 15 July.
128. ibid, ML 7323 of 13 July.
129. DEFE 3/827, ML 7527 of 15 July.
131. ibid, ML 7713 of 16 July.

121. ibid, ML 7393 of 14 July.
123. ibid, ML 7448 of 14 July.
125. ibid, ML 7478 of 15 July.
127. ibid, ML 7495 of 15 July.

130. ibid, ML 7751 of 17 July.

had made General Conrad, commanding the Hermann Göring Division, entirely responsible for the Axis left flank and had asked von Senger personally to superintend the clearing up of the situation there by counter-attack.[132] They also showed that early on 15 July 15th PG Division and the Hermann Göring Division had been ordered to hold their positions unless annihilation was imminent, in which case withdrawal or continued contact was to be at the discretion of the divisional commander,[133] and that the Hermann Göring Division's intention on 15 July was to withdraw to the line of the river Gornalunga in the event of strong Allied pressure.[134] A signal to the Mediterranean authorities at 1657 on 16 July told them that by 2200 on 15 July the Hermann Göring Division was in the new defence line from Gerbini along the railway line from Catania to Catenanuova with outposts on the Gornalunga. Its withdrawal had exposed the left flank of 15th PG Division.[135] An order from Kesselring at 1000 on 16 July was signalled to the Mediterranean at 2211; it forbade the Hermann Göring Division to withdraw to the intended main defence line and said that although the left wing might have to withdraw in the event of heavy pressure, the remainder of the front was to be held by offensive operations.[136]

At 0514 on 17 July GC and CS signalled an appreciation of the position in the Schmalz sector at 1700 the previous day. This indicated some easing of the pressure. Allied attacks on battle outposts had been beaten off and ten tanks had been knocked out; elements of the Parachute Regiment which had been cut off had fought their way through.[137] Luftflotte 2's situation reports at 1600 on 16 July, signalled to the Mediterranean authorities at 1436 on 17 July, noted that the main Allied effort that day had been against the German right wing where a breakthrough had been prevented. Strong Allied pressure on the Catania plain had caused withdrawal northward.[138]

The immediate crisis was in fact over. A frail but connected German front had come into being.[139] The Allied thrust for Catania across the Simeto river had failed and, although Montgomery was still optimistic,[140] the attempt to reach the town through Paterno and Misterbianco was to fare no better during the next three days.[141] Eighth Army's Intelligence Summary of 19 July remarked that, except in the west, where the enemy had given up the unequal struggle and the city of Palermo and two Italian divisions awaited

---

132. ibid, ML 7610 of 16 July.
134. ibid, ML 7685 of 16 July.
136. ibid, ML 7720 of 16 July.
138. ibid, ML 7817 of 17 July.
139. Molony, op cit, Vol V, p 110.
141. ibid, pp 114–117.

133. ibid, ML 7647 of 16 July.
135. ibid, ML 7694 of 16 July.
137. ibid, ML 7755 of 17 July.

140. ibid, pp 114, 120.

capture, 'the complexion of the battle has now changed. Instead of the speedy capture of beaches and ports we are engaged in a slower slogging match to gain bridges and crossings with valuable airfields as the prize'. The arrival of XIV Panzer Corps HQ suggested that 'the enemy is far from selling out of his remaining bridgehead in Sicily with the great natural advantages of the Etna position and the defensive line he holds in front of it'.[142]

The check to Eighth Army produced a change in Allied plans. On 13 July General Alexander had accepted General Montgomery's proposal that Eighth Army should advance on two axes, one to capture Catania (XIII Corps) and the other to secure the network of roads in the Enna area, and that Seventh Army should side-step to the west to protect Eighth Army's flank. Whether and to what extent he was influenced by the intelligence which showed the enemy to be under great pressure it is impossible to establish, but on 16 July he issued a directive by which Eighth Army was to capture Catania and then, advancing on three main lines, drive the enemy back to the Messina peninsula, while Seventh Army protected its rear. General Patton, who then had Caltanissetta, Porto Empedocle and Agrigento almost in his grasp and was hoping for permission to strike for Palermo, protested. His representations secured a modification of the directive on 18 July, when he was told that Seventh Army should push to split the island in two and then mop up western Sicily.[143] Seventh Army took Palermo on 22 July. On 23 July it was ordered to thrust eastward with maximum strength to assist Eighth Army's advance against the enemy's defensive positions. The eviction of the enemy from these positions involved heavy fighting until Catania fell on 5 August, when the enemy began a step by step withdrawal to a shortened bridgehead position on a line from six miles south of Cape Orlando across Mount Etna to a point twelve miles north of Catania.[144]

During this phase of the campaign the high-grade Sigint disclosed the arrival in Sicily between 19 and 25 July of two reinforced regiments of 29th PG Division and the assumption by this division of responsibility for the northern sector of the front.[145] On 27 and 28 July, however, decrypts of 26 July disclosed that no more motor transport or troops were to be ferried to Sicily at present other than personnel of 1st Parachute Division.[146] The high-grade Sigint also

---

142. WO 169/8519 of 19 July 1943.
143. Molony, op cit, Vol V, pp 88, 107–119; Garland and Smyth, op cit, pp 235–236, 254.
144. Molony, op cit, Vol V, p 92.
145. DEFE 3/828, MLs 8199 of 20 July, 8497 of 23 July; DEFE 3/829, ML 8973 of 27 July; DEFE 3/830, ML 9115 of 28 July 1943.
146. DEFE 3/829, ML 8980 of 26 July; DEFE 3/830, ML 9099 of 28 July.

disclosed the withdrawal from Sicily of the GAF's close support forces, which began on 16 July and was completed by 22 July.[147] But it provided little intelligence that was of tactical value to the Allied forces; and the same was true of Army Y.* Except that it provided details about the activities of the Hermann Göring Division during the last week of July,[148] and was at all times a useful check on other sources of field intelligence, Army Y during the Sicilian campaign was unable to fulfil the high expectations aroused by its performance during the desert campaigns and in the later stages of the Tunisian fighting; by such measures as more frequent changes of field codes and keys, new map reference systems and more complex call-sign systems the Germans and the Italians had greatly improved the security of their field communications.[149]

□

On 26 July OKW ordered Kesselring to prepare for the eventual evacuation of the German forces, and plans were drawn up for this operation by 1 August. In the event the main evacuation was delayed by the need to counter the Allied advances. But the German Army had meanwhile retreated to successive defensive positions, holding each for a short time and disengaging a proportion of troops at each stage for embarkation, and over 12,000 men, 4,500 vehicles and 5,000 tons of equipment were withdrawn to the mainland by this means between 1 August and the night of 11 August, when the main evacuation began. The Italians, organising their evacuation separately, followed a similar policy, preliminary withdrawals beginning on 3 August, the main evacuation taking place from 9 August. By 17 August, when the Allies entered Messina, some 60,000 German troops had been transported safely and the Italians had brought away some 75,000 men.[150]

Apart from a somewhat ambiguous Enigma decrypt of 18 July which discussed arrangements for the defence of 'the Fortress of the

---

* Learning from experience during the *Torch* landings (see Volume II, Appendix 18) provision was made in the *Husky* plan for a small Army Y party to accompany Advance British Corps HQ; in the event Eighth Army's Y section landed ahead of the 'advance' party. The *Husky* plan also provided for ship-borne Y, but it achieved so little that for future operations such plans were abandoned in favour of serving ships from shore stations. But for the use of ship-borne Y during the *Dragoon* landings in southern France in August 1944 see Volume III Part 2.

147. Air Sunsets 78 of 19 July, 79 of 23 July 1943.
148. WO 169/8519 of 23, 25 and 30 July, 6 and 7 August 1943; CAB 121/589, SIC file F/Italy 5H, Alexander telegram to CIGS MA 334 of 30 July 1943.
149. *History of Sigint in the Field*, p 90.
150. Molony, op cit, Vol V, pp 161, 179–182; Garland and Smyth, op cit, pp 374, 375.

Straits of Messina' – on which, also ambiguously, the Prime Minister commented: 'A significant phrase'[151] – the first indication from intelligence that an evacuation might be in the offing was received on 1 August, when the decrypts disclosed that ferrying in the Straits of Messina 'for practice and experimental purposes' had been ordered for the previous night and that ferrying points had been assigned to each of the German formations – 15th PG Division, 29th PG Division and the Hermann Göring Division with elements of 1st Parachute Division.[152] This was followed by a request from the German Sea Transport Officer Messina for more barrage balloons for vessels, and for equipment to improve the night lighting at berthing places, which was decrypted and distributed by GC and CS early on 5 August.[153] There was no further Sigint on the subject until 6 August. Nor were the intelligence authorities in the Mediterranean impressed by these early and admittedly inconclusive signs. On 4 August the JIC Algiers concluded from decrypts referring to the transfer of a fortress battalion to Sicily as late as 30 July that no evacuation was intended.[154] Eighth Army's intelligence summary for 5 August wondered, however, whether it was significant that of three Siebel ferries seen by PR that morning one was returning loaded to the mainland and two were arriving in Sicily empty.[155]

On the morning of 6 August GC and CS informed the Mediterranean commands that on 4 August the Hermann Göring Division had asked that assault boats and inflatable rafts with crews from the bridging company of its Panzer Engineer Battalion should be sent to Catona, 4½ miles from Messina across the Straits.[156] That evening Eighth Army's intelligence summary noted that 'evacuation measures include calling for names of personnel of the Hermann Göring Engineer Battalion trained in the use of assault boats'.[157] But AFHQ remained sceptical about the imminence of evacuation. Its intelligence summary for the week ending 7 August, issued on 10 August,[158] found 'no adequate indications that the enemy intends an immediate evacuation of the Messina bridgehead'. A certain amount of surplus material had probably been evacuated and it was likely that advance plans for an eventual evacuation had been put

---

151. Dir/C Archive, 3948 of 21 July 1943; CX/MSS/2932/T28 of 18 July 1943.
152. DEFE 3/831, ML 9601 of 1 August 1943.
153. ibid, ML 9978 of 5 August.
154. ibid, ML 9632 of 2 August; WO 204/1006, JIC (A) 16/43.
155. WO 169/8519 of 5 August 1943.
156. DEFE 3/871, JPs 74 and 101 of 6 August.
157. WO 169/8519 of 6 August 1943.
158. WO 204/967, AFHQ Weekly Intelligence Summary, No 50 of 10 August 1943.

in hand. For both prestige and strategic reasons, however, it was to the enemy's advantage to maintain resistance in Sicily, 'and despite the strain of sustained heavy defensive fighting with little air support it is anticipated that the enemy will continue to defend the north eastern tip of the island'. The summary claimed that lighters and Siebel ferries had maintained their normal scale of activity and concluded that although Siebel ferries had been seen arriving empty on the Sicilian side in order to load return cargoes, including personnel, for the mainland, the reduction in the intake to Sicily was probably due partly to the dislocation of railways in southern Italy, while the return cargoes to the mainland were probably mainly surplus motor transport, anti-aircraft and coast defence material, wounded 'and other normal L of C traffic'.

By the time this appreciation was issued on 10 August its conclusions had been invalidated by further intelligence. On the evening of 8 August, by which time decrypts of Enigma signals from Kesselring and from the German naval authorities in Sicily had established that the gradual withdrawal of the Axis front to shortened bridgehead positions had been proceeding according to plan since 6 August,[159] GC and CS had decrypted a signal in which XIV Panzer Corps stated on 6 August that priority delivery of fuel was essential for the coming heavy demands on the entire ferry system[160] and a signal giving the Italian naval authorities in Messina instructions about the removal of stores.[161] On the same evening Eighth Army's intelligence summary had noted that interpretation of PR photographs of the previous day had confirmed that ferries to the mainland were full while those moving to Sicily were empty; and it had added the comment that 'the enemy has started his evacuation early and in the best conditions any evacuation has had in this war'.[162]

At midnight on 10 August, nearly twenty-four hours before the main German evacuation began, the commands received the information from German naval Enigma decrypts that fourteen landing craft were on passage to the Straits of Messina for 'a special operation' and that eight others were being brought down to Naples from the north as a reserve.[163] And on the evening of 11 August, on the basis of PR evidence, Eighth Army's intelligence summary described the evacuation as being in full swing, employing about 75 ferry craft under cover of fierce Flak.[164] Thereafter, PR and Sigint both recorded the progress of the operation. In the early hours of 12

---

159. DEFE 3/871, JPs 228 of 7 August, 292 and 298 of 8 August 1943.
160. DEFE 3/871, JP 357 of 8 August.   161.   ibid, JP 347 of 8 August.
162. WO 169/8519 of 6 August 1943.
163. DEFE 3/872, JP 572 of 10 August.
164. WO 169/8519 of 11 August.

August GC and CS informed the commands in an emergency signal that the GAF had ordered the concentration of fighters over the operations area of XIV Panzer Corps and the Straits of Messina.[165]* On 13 August PR found that about 75 ferry craft were being used.[167] During 14 August Army Y detected the move of the HQ of the Hermann Göring Division to the mainland,[168] and during the night of 14–15 August high-grade decrypts reported that the evacuation had proceeded well up to the evening of 13 August, the ferry service having proved more efficient than expected, and that General Hube would be staying behind with a small operations staff until all forces that could be saved had left the island.[169]

In their criticism of the Allied failure to prevent the escape of the Axis forces, two of the official histories of the war have referred to the intelligence dimension. 'While it appears that the Allied commanders knew of the impending operation . . . it also appears that these same commanders had no overall plan for thwarting such an evacuation'.[170] 'Our intelligence services were late in drawing the correct conclusions, but even when the enemy's intention was plain the action taken suffered from lack of inter-Service co-ordination'.[171] It will be clear that the intelligence authorities at AFHQ were indeed slow to appreciate the significance of the available intelligence, which was sufficient to enable those at Eighth Army HQ to draw the correct conclusions as early as the evening of 6 August. Moreover, the intelligence summary, somewhat defensive in tone, which AFHQ issued on 17 August suggests that its authors may have remained unconvinced until as late as 13 August that a general evacuation was in progress; it stated that traffic across the Straits up to the second week of August had indicated that all material not essential for the delaying action in the bridgehead was being removed, but that the figures for the transport of personnel had risen steadily between 7 and 13 August, by which date the scale of the ferry traffic had indicated that the momentum of the evacuation was being considerably accelerated.[172] And if this were the case, and

---

* In the last few days of the fighting the GAF Enigma showed that despite being hampered by having to operate at extreme range the GAF increased its fighter sorties by an average of 60 in twenty-four hours to an average of 150.[166]

165. DEFE 3/872, JP 689 of 12 August.
166. AIR 41/10, p 260.
167. WO 169/8519 of 13 August.
168. ibid; *History of Sigint in the Field*, p 93.
169. DEFE 3/872, JPs 986 of 14 August, 1020 and 1027 of 15 August; Dir/C Archive, 4167 of 15 August 1943.
170. Garland and Smyth, op cit, pp 378, 379, 410–412.
171. S W Roskill, *The War at Sea*, Vol III Part 1 (1960), p 149.
172. WO 204/967, No 51 of 17 August 1943.

if 15th Army Group was relying on AFHQ's assessments, this would explain why on 11 August, when Eighth Army's intelligence staff was confident that the evacuation was in full swing, General Alexander informed the CIGS that 'the general impression, and only an impression, is that the Germans may withdraw across the Straits shortly',[173] why it was not until the afternoon of 13 August that the Tactical Air Force was told that 'evacuation is held to have begun',[174] and why General Alexander's signal to Air Chief Marshal Tedder, stating that 'it now appears that evacuation has really started', did not follow until 14 August.[175]

These communications between them suggest that, strictly speaking, it may not be correct to claim that 'the Allied commanders knew of the impending operation'.* As is only to be expected, however, they did envisage that the enemy would attempt to evacuate his forces. AFHQ in the intelligence summary issued on 10 August allowed that he had probably put in hand advance plans for an eventual evacuation. As early as 3 August, presumably in response to the intelligence sent out on 1 August,† General Alexander notified Admiral Cunningham and Air Chief Marshal Tedder that there were signs that the enemy was preparing to withdraw to the mainland and promised timely advice about when they should strike. 'We must', he added, 'be in a position to take advantage . . . by using full weight of navy and air power. You have no doubt co-ordinated plans to meet this contingency'.[177] In the event, as we have seen, although timely intelligence was available, the advice was not provided. But how far the Allied failure to interrupt the withdrawal was due to this fact, and how far it was due, rather, to the weakness of the Allied command structure, the efficiency of Axis planning and the circumstances which favoured the enemy – the difficulty of the terrain in north-eastern Sicily and the ease with which the short crossing from Messina could be defended against air and naval attack – must remain an open question.

□

---

* In Enigma signals decrypted at the end of August, Hitler and Kesselring made a similar claim. In Kesselring's words: 'The enemy recognised early this decision to evacuate. It would have been an easy thing for him to impede the withdrawal by the employment of his fleet, his numerous landing craft etc., but he did not dare'.[176]

† See above, p 96.

173.   CAB 120/98, PM registered file 402/33/B Vol I, Concrete telegram no 125 of 12 August 1943.
174.   Roskill, op cit, Vol III Part 1, p 148.
175.   ibid, p 149.
176.   Dir/C Archive, 4240 of 26 August 1943; CX/MSS/3085/T6, 3115/T2.
177.   Roskill, op cit, Vol III Part 1, p 148.

In January 1943, when they settled on the invasion of Sicily, the Allies had not reached agreement on the strategy they would adopt in the Mediterranean after the capture of Sicily. Operation *Husky* itself had been given limited objectives – to round off the north African campaigns by re-opening the Mediterranean shipping routes; to increase the pressure on Italy – and further decisions had been left open in deference to the wish of the United States authorities to devote a minimum of resources to the exploitation of the Mediterranean theatre. In May at the Washington conference the Allies had agreed in principle that the occupation of Sicily should be followed by further operations against Italian territory; but on US insistence they had placed limits on their scope – seven divisions from the theatre must be ready for withdrawal to the United Kingdom by early November; and any Mediterranean operation must be approved by the Combined Chiefs of Staff, who would meet again in July or at the beginning of August to review the matter in the light of the progress of operation *Husky* and developments on the Russian front.* Nor had the British authorities succeeded in their subsequent efforts to get US agreement to an earlier decision 'to invade Italy should Sicily be taken'. In further meetings between 29 May and 3 June in Algiers, where General Marshall had accompanied the Prime Minister and the CIGS after the Washington conference, it had been decided that General Eisenhower should set up two HQs, one to prepare for operations against Sardinia and Corsica, the other to plan for a landing on the Italian mainland, and should make a recommendation to the Combined Chiefs as between the two alternatives as soon as possible after the invasion of Sicily had begun.[178]

General Eisenhower had submitted detailed plans for a descent on the mainland or an invasion of Sardinia, with the object of forcing Italy to sue for peace and on the assumption that she would have enough freedom from German control to be able to do so, on 30 June. The plans had called for the retention in the Mediterranean of some of the assault shipping that was scheduled for withdrawal after *Husky*, and had thus not appealed to the US Chiefs of Staff. Following the early success of the *Husky* landings, however, not only Whitehall but also General Marshall having concluded that the Allies ought to take calculated risks to exploit their advantage with such of their Mediterranean resources as had not been earmarked for withdrawal, the Combined Chiefs of Staff had advised General Eisenhower on 16 July to consider a landing in the Naples area

---

* See above, p 8.

178.   Howard, op cit, Vol IV, Chapters XXII and XXVI.

instead of in Calabria or against Sardinia. He had expressed doubt about the risks of landing so far north as Naples, but when approving his recommendation of 18 July that the war should nevertheless be carried to the mainland as soon as Sicily was captured, they had given him firm instructions to extend his operations in Italy as far to the north as his shore-based fighter cover would permit. And on 26 July they had ordered him to mount the assault on the mainland at the earliest possible date. Like the order to prepare for the evacuation of Sicily, which Kesselring received on the same day, their decision was precipitated by the dismissal of Mussolini from office on 25 July.[179]

The fall of Mussolini vindicated one of the forecasts of the Whitehall JIC. On 11 April the JIC had argued that an Allied landing on the mainland following the invasion of Sicily might well result in an Italian collapse, such was the unpopularity of the Germans in Italy.[180] By the middle of April it had actively canvassed the possibility that Italy might collapse under air attack alone, concluding that when the weight of bombing was increased after the capture of Sicily 'the Italian government would ... probably sue for peace'.[181] On 22 May, responding to a warning from the Cs-in-C Middle East that the Italians might fight with much more determination in defence of Sicily than they had done in north Africa, it had insisted that the fighting value of the Italian forces in Sicily would be much the same as it had been in Africa – initial resistance would be stiff, but it would be short-lived – and had again asserted that the loss of Sicily might well lead to an Italian collapse.[182] And on 6 July, in the last appreciation it issued before the Sicily landings, it had concluded that the loss of Sicily, combined with heavy and sustained air attack on northern and central Italy and a landing in southern Italy, might well produce a breakdown in civil administration or an Italian request for an armistice.[183] But the JIC had been no less emphatic in expressing its belief that, in the event of an Italian collapse, the Germans would not remain in occupation of Italy. It had so argued in March,[184] and on 23 April, casting aside the hesitation it had felt on the point at the beginning of the year,* it had been confident that, while Germany would make every effort to deny the Allies possession of the air bases in northern

---

* See above, p 5.

179.   ibid, pp 502–508; Matloff and Snell, op cit, pp 157–161.
180.   JIC (43) 160 (o) of 11 April.
181.   JIC (43) 163 (o) 165 (o), 167 (o) of 13, 14 and 16 April.
182.   JIC (43) 210 (o), 218 (o) of 13 and 22 May.
183.   JIC (43) 276 (o) of 6 July.
184.   JIC (43) 94 (o), 135 (o) of 5 and 27 March.

Italy, she would not be able to prevent the creation of an Italian government that would be both anxious to negotiate a separate peace and free to do so.[185] The JIC may, in reaching this conclusion, have taken into account the disclosure by Sigint from mid-April that Italian air and ground forces were being withdrawn from the Russian front.[186]

When General Eisenhower was instructed on 26 July to proceed with the attack on the mainland the Allies had no firm evidence about the readiness of the new Italian government to negotiate with them; there had earlier been informal contacts between the SOE and individual Italians, but these had been broken off in the spring.* As to how Germany would respond if the Italians entered into negotiations with them, they had some grounds for believing she would take over the Italian positions in the eastern Mediterranean

---

* On 18 March the Cabinet had reconsidered an offer to send an Italian general to Cyrenaica for discussions, and had agreed that the project could go forward provided the Italian emissary presented himself constitutionally and that no Allied commitments to him were made without ministerial authority. Either because these stipulations had proved unacceptable to the Italians, or because the Italian offer had not been genuine, this reply put an end to the Italian approaches to the SOE in Berne.[187] There were no further contacts between the Italians and the Allies until the first Italian peace emissary presented himself formally at the British embassy in Lisbon on 4 August – although it had been learnt from diplomatic decrypts as early as February 1943 that the Italian Cabinet had been discussing the possibility of taking advantage of Mussolini's illness to send an emissary to Lisbon to negotiate with the Allies.[188] It was suggested in a variety of quarters that the Allies should take the initiative in approaching the Italians, or should at least modify their propaganda towards Italy. In April AFHQ proposed that high-ranking Italian POW should be used to approach the commanders of Italy's island garrisons, in an attempt to undermine their will to resist, and that the Allies should reconsider the tone of their propaganda to Italy, which had hitherto discouraged hopes for a separate peace and insisted on unconditional surrender.[189] Nothing appears to have come of the first of these proposals. The second was taken up in the same month by the Cs-in-C Middle East, who recommended that Allied propaganda should begin to emphasise the contrast between the consequences of German occupation that would follow an Axis victory and the fair treatment that would be obtained under the Atlantic Charter.[190] On 2 May the SOE strongly supported this suggestion, urging on the Chiefs of Staff the view that the time had come for the Allies to assure Italy that her future position would be safeguarded.[191] On 19 May the Vice-Chiefs of Staff agreed that the change to a softer propaganda line should be made soon. But the Foreign Office opposed the change and this led to a sharp difference of opinion between the British government and General Eisenhower as to the timing of the switch.[192]

185. JIC (43) 186 (o) of 23 April.
186. For example, CX/MSS/2451/T35.
187. CAB 65/37, WM (43) 42 CA of 18 March; L Woodward, *British Foreign Policy in the Second World War*, Vol II (1971), p 468.
188. Dir/C Archive, 2295 of 16 February.
189. CAB 121/579, Algiers telegram to War Office, 3 April 1943, COS (43) 226 (o) of 30 April.
190. JIC (43) 210 (o) of 3 May.
191. CAB 80/69, COS (43) 233 (o) of 2 May.
192. CAB 101/144, p 35 et seq; CAB 65/38, WM (43) 72 and 73 CA of 20 and 21 May; CAB 69/5, DO (43) 10 of 19 May; CAB 105/140, NAF 221 of 17 May 1943; CAB 105/145, FAN 127 of 24 May 1943.

and the Balkans,* but there was no intelligence on what she would do in Italy itself. In the spring occasional decrypts had made it clear that Hitler was concerned about 'the wavering attitude of Italy', but there had been no other reference to the subject apart from a Japanese diplomatic decrypt which showed at the end of May that the Japanese embassy at Berne believed, like the JIC, that Germany would hold a line in the north if Italy collapsed.[193] Thus on 19 July, discussing an estimate of the scale of opposition the Allies would meet if they landed near Naples – an estimate in which the JIC had noted that there had been so many Axis orders and counter-orders since the launching of *Husky* that it was 'most difficult to foresee with any certainty the development of enemy plans during the next few weeks' – the British Chiefs of Staff had 'felt considerably handicapped by the inability of the Intelligence Services to obtain reasonably accurate and up-to-date information of the enemy dispositions', and had feared that an advance on the Italian mainland 'would be the prelude to extensive land operations which would inevitably affect the date of *Overlord* and of operations in the Indian theatre'.[194]

Thereafter, the JIC became more confident. On 27 July it forecast that a landing in Italy would precipitate peace overtures and surrender by the Italian government, and expected the Italians to facilitate a German withdrawal.[195] On 3 August it argued that while Germany might make a temporary stand on the Pisa-Rimini line or on the Po when Italy collapsed, it was more likely that, since she would be unable to send more than four divisions to Italy to join the three already in the south and such forces as she could extricate from Sicily, she would hold the line of the Maritime Alps in the west and positions covering Venezia and the Tyrol in the east.[196] But the Chiefs of Staff were not wholly convinced by these forecasts, least of all by the second, as may be judged by the conclusion they reached on 5 August on their way to the Quebec conference. They decided that with the object of relieving pressure on Russia and improving the prospects for *Overlord* they would urge the conference to take vigorous action to eliminate Italy from the war and compel Germany to send reinforcements to Italy and the Balkans.[197]

---

* See above, pp 11–12.

193. Dir/C Archive, 3449 of 29 May 1943.
194. CAB 121/590, SIC file F/Italy/6 Vol I, JP (43) 253 of 19 July (Appendix I of which is JIC (43) 296 (o) of 18 July), COS (43) 165th (o) Meeting, 19 July.
195. JIC (43) 313 (o) of 27 July.
196. CAB 121/413, SIC file A/Germany/1, Vol II, JIC (43) 324 of 3 August.
197. CAB 121/154, SIC file A/Strategy/10, COS (Q) 1st and 6th Meetings, 5 and 9 August 1943, COS (Q) 3 (Revise) of 6 August (all in COS (43) 513 (o) Part B of 11 September).

Even as they were reaching this conclusion the Italian government was making the first of its formal approaches to the Allies,* and before long the evidence obtained from the Italian emissaries was not only indicating that their government might lack the freedom to take Italy out of the war, but was also casting doubt on the assumption that Germany would withdraw from southern Italy without a fight.† On 4 August Italy's first emissary, the Marchese d'Aieta from the Italian Foreign Office, approached the British embassy in Lisbon. He reported that the King and the Army leaders were preparing to break with the Germans and, as evidence of good faith, provided information about German plans to send reinforcements to Italy. His information was received sceptically in Whitehall, where its accuracy had not yet been borne out by Sigint.[198] A week later a second emissary, Signor Berio, also from the Italian Foreign Office, presented himself to the British authorities in Tangier. He reported that Badoglio was ready to treat with the Allies but could not yet do so as the Italian government was entirely under Germany's control. He was told that the Allies would not in any case negotiate; they required unconditional surrender.[199] A third emissary, General Castellano, Chief of Staff to the Italian Chief of General Staff, made contact with the British Ambassador in Madrid on 15 August. He had full authority from Badoglio to say that, if Italy could reach agreement on armistice terms with the Allies, she would fight with them against Germany when they landed on the mainland, and would meanwhile offer to co-operate with Mihailovic against Germany in Yugoslavia‡ and provide the Allies with the fullest possible information about the German forces in Italy. He added that there were already thirteen German divisions in Italy and that more were likely to arrive.[200]

---

* For the details of these approaches see L Woodward, *British Foreign Policy in the Second World War*, Vol II (1971), p 481 et seq.

† The same impression was soon being conveyed by Axis diplomatic decrypts. At the end of July these had shown that Italy's partners had been taken by surprise by Mussolini's dismissal, as had Italy's own ambassadors. In the first week of August they showed that the German Foreign Ministry and the Japanese embassies in Berlin and Rome were either inclined to think that Italy did not intend to make peace or were convinced that the new Italian government realised that it could not get out of the war even if it wanted to do so. At the end of August the Japanese reported that the Germans believed the Italians were strongly inclined to continue the war, and they themselves could find no confirmation of the persistent rumours that Italy was engaged in armistice negotiations. The decrypts of signals from the Japanese embassies in Berlin and Rome in September showed that the announcement of the armistice had come as a surprise to the Japanese.

‡ See below, pp 146–148.

198. Garland and Smyth, op cit, p 297; FO 371/37264, Lisbon telegram 1455; CAB 101/144, p 80.
199. CAB 101/144, p 81; PREM 3/249, Tangier telegram 405 of 6 August 1943.
200. CAB 101/144, p 85; Howard, op cit, Vol IV, pp 520–521; Garland and Smyth, op cit, pp 443–444; CAB 120/99, PM file 402/33(B) Vol II, Concrete telegram 231 of 16 August 1943.

Details of Castellano's offer and of his information about the German order of battle in Italy were forwarded from Whitehall to the Quebec conference on 16 August. With regard to the statement that thirteen divisions were already in Italy, the JIC advised its representative at the conference that these presumably consisted of the four in Sicily, one in Sardinia, three in southern Italy, one in central Italy and four in the north.[201] Sigint had by then identified, over and above the forces in Sicily, only three divisions (16th Panzer, 26th Panzer and 3rd Panzer Grenadier) in southern and central Italy and one (90th Panzer Grenadier) in Sardinia.[202] With regard to the offer, the Foreign Secretary advised the Prime Minister that the Allies should not depart from their present policy of making no bargains with or promises to the Italians in return for surrender: they could not concert operations with the Italians without revealing their operational plans; it was reasonable to assume that the Italians would co-operate even if unconditional surrender was still insisted on.[203] But the conference decided to override the advice of the Foreign Office. Later on 16 August it instructed General Eisenhower to send two officers to Lisbon to negotiate with Castellano; they were to seek his agreement to unconditional surrender on the basis of the 'Short Terms' and to state that the extent to which the terms could be modified would depend on the amount of assistance Italy provided to the Allies.[204]

The 'Short Terms', drawn up at AFHQ following the fall of Mussolini, at a time when detailed armistice terms drafted in the Foreign Office were still the subject of discussion between London and Washington, had been submitted to the Combined Chiefs of Staff together with a proposal from General Eisenhower that they should be broadcast in order to give Italy an opportunity for honourable surrender; and they had avoided using the phrase 'unconditional surrender' in the hope of securing Italian assistance for the Allied landings on the mainland. AFHQ's proposal had provoked acrimonious opposition from those who preferred to wait until Italy made approaches to the Allies and then to present her with a comprehensive statement of the consequences of unconditional surrender.[205] The Allied leaders in Quebec decided that General Castellano should nevertheless be presented with the 'Short Terms' – the knowledge that the Germans had succeeded in withdrawing their divisions from Sicily was already creating misgivings

201. CAB 120/99, Concrete telegram 255 of 16 August 1943.
202. WO 208/3573 of 23 and 30 August 1943.
203. CAB 101/144, p 86; CAB 120/99, Concrete telegram 231 of 16 August 1943.
204. CAB 101/144, p 89; CAB 121/154, COS (Q) 14th Meeting, 17 August, Annex I (in COS (43) 513 (o) Part B, of 11 September).
205. CAB 101/114, p 63; Howard, op cit, Vol IV, p 517.

about the prospects for the Allied landings. Nor did these misgivings decline in the next few days. By 20 August Sigint had confirmed Castellano's warning about Germany's intention to reinforce her divisions in Italy. It had established that sixteen divisions, including the four withdrawn from Sicily, were in mainland Italy or were due to arrive there, and that a newly-formed Army Group B was to control those in the north. The latter were to comprise 76th, 94th and 305th Infantry Divisions under LXXXVII Corps; 44th Infantry Division and Brigade Doehla under LI Mountain Corps; and SS Division Adolf Hitler, 24th Panzer Division and 65th and 71st Infantry Divisions under an unspecified SS Panzer Corps.[206] On 20 August Whitehall received from the AFHQ officers who had met Castellano on 19 and 20 August a list of the German divisions that he knew to have been in or intended for Italy on 12 August. Except that it included two SS divisions and made a mistake in the numbering of 65th Infantry Division, it tallied with the Sigint evidence.[207]

Castellano had provided further information; it was forwarded to the Quebec conference on 23 August with the comment that it was trustworthy. The two most important items were that there were several thousand SS troops in Rome, which was also threatened by 3rd PG Division and 2nd Parachute Division, and that the Germans intended to defend Sardinia and Corsica and to make the Genoa-Ravenna position their main line of resistance, defending the line of the Po if the Genoa-Ravenna line was penetrated.[208]* At the same time, arguing that Badoglio would require a fortnight's notice of the date of the Allied landings, Castellano had expressed reservations about the proposal made to him by AFHQ whereby General Eisenhower would grant an armistice five or six hours before the main landing and General Badoglio would respond by proclaiming Italy's cessation of hostilities, and he had left it uncertain whether Italy would accept the 'Short Terms' without further parley. After making arrangements to return to Sicily for further discussions about the end of August, he had then left to consult his government.[209]

It was in these circumstances that on 24 August the Quebec conference finally accepted AFHQ's plans for landings by the

---

* This line was sometimes given as Pisa-Rimini, sometimes as Pisa-Ravenna, and occasionally as Genoa-Rimini or Spezia-Rimini.

206.   CAB 120/100, PM file 402/33(B) Vol III, Concrete telegram 403 of 20 August 1943.
207.   CAB 80/73, COS (43) 482 (o) of 21 August.
208.   CAB 120/100, Concrete telegram 518 of 23 August.
209.   CAB 101/144, p 98; Howard, op cit, Vol IV, pp 524–525.

Eighth Army across the Straits of Messina (Operation *Baytown*) and by US Fifth Army in the Gulf of Salerno (Operation *Avalanche*) and laid down the objectives of the campaign in Italy:

'First phase – the elimination of Italy as a belligerent and the establishment of air bases in the Rome area and if possible further north. Second phase – seizure of Sardinia and Corsica. Third phase – maintenance of unremitting pressure on German forces in north Italy and the creation of the conditions required for *Overlord* and of a situation favourable for the eventual entry of our forces into southern France'.[210]

It did so after hearing that AFHQ, while it still believed that 'the German intention seems to be to deny us the Po valley by holding a line Pisa-Rimini' and that 'it looks as if they intend to withdraw their divisions in southern Italy to the north', was no longer confident about these forecasts and was, moreover, anxious that even if Germany did not bring down the new divisions from the north, she might endanger *Avalanche* by concentrating against it the divisions she already had in the south. The Deputy Chief of Staff, AFHQ, reported to the Combined Chiefs of Staff during the conference that *Baytown* was unlikely to meet very strong opposition, but that 'there is of necessity some anxiety about *Avalanche*. The assault may be opposed within a few hours by comparable German forces. If and when the Germans realise that our assault is not in very great strength they may move divisions to the sound of the guns and attack us with up to six divisions some time during September'.[211]

AFHQ spelled out this threat in more detail on 31 August. In reply to an urgent request of 27 August from the British Vice-Chiefs of Staff for an appreciation of the consequences for *Avalanche* of 'the changing situation and the latest intelligence reports of German dispositions in Italy', it estimated that the initial opposition – one armoured division and possibly two or three parachute battalions – would be increased by D + 5 to two and a half armoured divisions (one and a half of them weak), one and a half Panzer Grenadier divisions (equal to one full-strength Panzer division) and one parachute division; between D + 5 and D + 10 this force might be further increased by one armoured division and one weak PG division.[212] MI 14 thought this estimate optimistic in assuming that the Germans would not release any divisions from the north: they might bring down one armoured division and one PG division, in which case they could have three armoured divisions and four and

---

210. CAB 121/154, CSS 319/5 of 24 August 1943 (in COS (43) 513 (0) (Part A) of 11 September).
211. ibid, CCS 116th Meeting of 24 August 1943.
212. CAB 121/590, COS (43) 198th Meeting, 27 August, NAF 345 of 31 August 1943.

a half others in action by D + 10, and by D + 17 the margin in their favour might be at least 1¹/₃ divisions.[213]

Both of these appreciations were based on full and accurate intelligence about the German Army's order of battle in southern Italy. By 28 August the high-grade Sigint had disclosed that a new Tenth Army (AOK 10) had taken control of XIV and LXXVI Panzer Corps,[214] that LXXVI Panzer Corps had 29th PG Division, 1st Parachute Division and 26th Panzer Division in Calabria and Apulia, that XIV Panzer Corps had 15th Panzer Division at Gaeta, the Hermann Göring Division at Caserta and 16th Panzer Division at Salerno, and that 2nd Parachute Division and 3rd PG Division were in the Rome area.[215] As for northern Italy, where it was known from high-grade military Sigint as well as from the decrypt of a Japanese diplomatic telegram that Rommel had been appointed C-in-C Army Group B,* Enigma decrypts had by 30 August referred to the arrival in the Parma-Piacenza area of advanced elements of XXXIX Panzer Corps with 18th Panzer Division and 14th PG Division, thus raising the number of divisions in or destined for mainland Italy (excluding Sardinia) to eighteen.[216]† But as to how Germany would use her forces in the rapidly changing situation, no further intelligence was received before the Allies landed at Salerno. On 29 August OKW approved the proposal from Kesselring, who remained C-in-C South, that LXXVI Panzer Corps should withdraw gradually northwards to a line from Scalea on the west coast to Taranto and Brindisi, and on 6 September it ordered Rommel to remain north of the Apennines. But these orders were not decrypted. Nor was it known at the time of the landing at Salerno that under the German plan for the contingency of Italy's desertion (Operation

---

* See above, p 12.

† This Panzer Corps and its divisions were eliminated by MI 14 from the German order of battle in Italy in October[217] when it was established that Army Group B had been using a new Enigma key (named Shrike at GC and CS) to pass signals simulating their presence in Italy when they were in fact on the Russian front. It later transpired that the purpose of the deception was to impress the Italians that German strength in Italy was to be greater than was actually intended.[218] This was the first of several occasions on which the Germans used the Enigma to pass information to be used for deception purposes. (See above, p 31). On none of these occasions were they assuming that the Enigma was insecure. Nevertheless, this first occasion caused considerable alarm at GC and CS.

213. CAB 121/591, SIC file F/Italy/6, Vol II, COS (W) 779 of 2 September 1943, WO estimate of comparative rates of build-up (excluding Calabria) of 12 September 1943, prepared for COS (43) 214th Meeting, 13 September.
214. CX/MSS/3096/T1 and 20.
215. WO 204/967, No 53 of 30 August 1943.
216. WO 208/3573 of 30 August 1943.
217. WO 208/3573 of 4 October 1943.
218. Cabinet Office Historical Section, Enemy Documents Section, AL 1455b.

Achse) German troops were to be removed from Sardinia and Tenth Army to be pulled back to the Rome area.[219] Not until the day of the landing, moreover, when it was too late to make terms for Italian assistance, did the Allies complete a settlement with the Italian government.

Castellano had returned to Sicily on 31 August to request information about the strength and whereabouts of the Allied landings and to report that his government could not agree that the armistice should be announced before it was sure that the landings had been successful. His request had been refused and his government's condition rejected; to help the Italians to defend Rome the Allies had, however, undertaken to mount a hazardous additional airborne operation, for which the President and the Prime Minister had given their approval on 1 September. On 3 September, when Castellano had succeeded in obtaining only 'implicit acceptance' of the Allied terms from Badoglio, and the Allies had accordingly cancelled their offer of an armistice, Badoglio had finally authorised Castellano to sign the 'Short Terms', but the Italians had requested the cancellation of the airborne operation, on the grounds that it would only provoke more drastic German action, and they had also pleaded that the announcement of the armistice would only precipitate the German occupation of Italy and the creation of a quisling government. General Eisenhower had agreed to cancel the airborne operation but had insisted that, as AFHQ had originally proposed, he and General Badoglio should broadcast a few hours before landing. They did so on 8 September.[220]*

□

The Germans offered little opposition to the Eighth Army's landing in Calabria on 3 September. The GAF effort fell off rapidly after the first day; the high-grade Sigint showed the enemy making a planned withdrawal; and it gave no sign that the divisions in the Gaeta-Salerno area were being moved south.[221]† Since the middle

---

* After Castellano's return to Italy the Italian government communicated with AFHQ, and also with Castellano when in Sicily, on a W/T link provided by SOE. Castellano had taken back with him from Lisbon a W/T set and a signal plan provided by SOE, and SOE had also informed him that an experienced British W/T operator was a POW in Milan. Badoglio had had the POW brought to Rome to operate the link.

† For U-boat operations against *Avalanche* – on an even smaller scale than those against *Husky* – see below, p 232 n†.

219. Molony, op cit, Vol V, p 239; Garland and Smyth, op cit, pp 473–497.
220. CAB 101/144, pp 130–141; Howard, op cit, Vol IV, p 528 et seq.
221. As examples CX/MSS/3154/T25, 3164/T3, 3166/T47 and 53, 3173/T13, 3178/T12, 3180/T10, 3181/T30; DEFE 3/617, ZTPGM 34215; ZTPI 37572.

of August, on the other hand, the same source had established that the Axis expected another landing further to the north, and it was clear that the Allies could not expect Operation *Avalanche* to achieve surprise.

In an Abwehr decrypt of 14 August the head of the Italian Intelligence Service was reported to be forecasting an Allied landing between Naples and Salerno, as well as landings in Sardinia and Corsica, and on 15 August an Abwehr message from Istanbul was decrypted which forecast landings in the Gulf of Salerno and Calabria.[222] A GAF Enigma decrypt of 20 August quoted the Abwehr as expecting a landing in the Salerno area to follow the capture of Sicily, and on 28 August the danger of a landing in the Gaeta-Naples-Salerno area was referred to in another GAF Enigma decrypt.[223] On 26 August an Italian Admiralty appreciation was decrypted which argued that Allied preparations pointed to plans for landing beyond the range of fighter aircraft, in southern Italy, Sardinia or Corsica.[224] On 1 September the Allies received an appreciation of 28 August by the German naval authorities. This pointed out that the Allies had assembled forces in excess of what would be required for attack on Sardinia or Corsica and that, while southern France could not be excluded, southern Italy was probably the objective; it also expected the attack in the near future.[225] Thereafter, as the decrypts showed, the intensification of Allied air attacks and GAF sighting reports of Allied convoys left the enemy in little doubt about the location and the imminence of the threat. On 6 September the Abwehr in Naples reported to Berlin that heavy air raids on the area of the Volturno estuary on 4 and 5 September were judged to be in preparation for a large-scale landing near Naples. During 7 and 8 September the GAF Enigma disclosed frequent sighting reports of convoys and requests for reconnaissance,[226] and on 8 September GC and CS was able to report at 0739 that German naval forces south of Rome had been placed at half an hour's notice and those north of Rome at two hours' notice;[227] at 1358 that the German Navy expected a landing in the Naples-Palinuro area;[228] and at 2159 that Fliegerkorps II's intention for 9 September was to employ all forces against a landing in the Naples-Salerno area.[229]

---

222.   Dir/C Archive, 4167 of 15 August 1943.
223.   Dir/C Archive, 4207 of 20 August 1943.
224.   DEFE 3/875, JP 2293 of 26 August.
225.   DEFE 3/876, JP 2959 of 1 September.
226.   DEFE 3/878, JPs 3552 and 3596 of 7 September, 3601, 3607, 3616, 3642, 3688 and 3715 of 8 September.
227.   ibid, JP 3627 of 8 September.
228.   ibid, JP 3655 of 8 September.
229.   ibid, JP 3708 of 8 September 1943.

The GAF's attack with fighter, ground attack aircraft and bombers against the *Avalanche* forces,* which had begun during the night of 8–9 September, was covered in detail in the Enigma decrypts.† The intelligence was of little tactical benefit; though it included advance notice of intentions and orders as to target priorities, its chief operational value lay in the fact that it gave an accurate account of the formations involved and of the scale of the effort. It showed that the daily number of fighter and ground attack sorties began to decline after 12 September, when the close support effort was concentrated in aid of the German ground offensive against the beachhead, and that it slumped heavily after 16 September, when the enemy's greatly overmatched close support forces began to be withdrawn to the Rome area. A feature of the intelligence about the bomber effort was the disclosure that it included anti-shipping operations by III/KG 100, a formation equipped with the new FX 1400 radio controlled bomb, which was mentioned in connection with an attack on Allied naval forces off south Calabria on 2 September,[231] and also by II/KG 100, the group which had already used the new Hs 293 radio guided rocket missile with success against British naval forces in Biscay and whose return from Atlantic bases to Istres in southern France was reported on 7 September.[232]‡ Orders that bombers were to begin withdrawal from Foggia, the main bomber base, were decrypted early on 19 September.

On the response of the German Army to the landing no intelligence was obtained for more than two days. Army Y produced no information during the fighting at Salerno.[233]§ Ultra intelligence from GC and CS was passed to HQ US Fifth Army in the invasion command ship by naval channels from 15th Army Group at Bizerta during the first three days of the battle.** During 9 and 10 September

---

* The *Avalanche* forces, under the command of US Fifth Army, were organised into a Northern Attack Force comprising the British X Corps of Eighth Army, and a Southern Attack Force comprising US VI Corps. Landing south-east of Salerno, X Corps's objective was the capture of Naples; US VI Corps's was to secure its share of the bridgehead, to protect the right flank of X Corps and gradually free the British Corps for the blow against Naples.[230]

† For details see Appendix 5.   ‡ For its earlier operations from Istres see below, p 339.

§ Neither British nor US Y units could land for some days after the assault. An RAF R/T unit landed but was prevented from operating for 48 hours, because of casualties to personnel and vehicles, and even then could only operate on a limited scale because it could not reach a position on high ground.

** On 12 September a SLU officer and two signallers were landed on the beachhead with General Clark,[234] but few signals were sent to them between 12 and 19 September by this route, presumably because of the risk of compromise so long as the situation remained uncertain.

---

230. Molony, op cit, Vol V, p 259.   231. CX/MSS/3151/T9, 13.
232. DEFE 3/878, JP 3575 of 7 September 1943.
233. *History of Sigint in the Field*, p 107.
234. *The History of the Special Liaison Units*, pp 34–35.

the Enigma decrypts disclosed only that the German forces in Calabria were withdrawing according to plan and that those in the Rome area were fully occupied in securing the capitulation of Italian divisions.[235] It was thus because so much anxiety had been aroused by the pre-battle intelligence about the German order of battle that on 10 September, the day after the landings, General Alexander pressed General Clark, in command of Fifth Army, for a decision as to how he wanted to use US 82nd Airborne Division, which had been relieved by the cancellation of the airborne operation in the Rome area and made available to General Clark as an immediate reinforcement on 8 September, and suggested sending part of it to Salerno in landing craft.[236] As General Eisenhower reported on the evening of 10 September, the Allied Command remained anxious about the speed of Fifth Army's build-up because it feared that the enemy might reinforce his left flank with the troops from the south and did not exclude the possibility that he would bring some units down from the north by the east coast route.[237] On the morning of 11 September, when General Eisenhower asked to be allowed to retain eighteen landing craft which were under orders for India,[238] these fears had still not been confirmed.

Information that the enemy intended to use all his immediately available forces against the beachhead followed during the evening of 11 September. At 2053 on that day GC and CS reported that the Enigma had disclosed that lack of fuel was seriously delaying the movement of units of LXXVI Panzer Corps to the Salerno front.[239]* At 2120 it transmitted to the Mediterranean commands the orders issued by Kesselring to the Tenth Army that afternoon; Tenth Army was to leave strong elements of one division in northern Calabria and a reinforced regiment in the Foggia area, but was to concentrate all its other forces in the Naples-Salerno area and throw the Allies into the sea.[241] During the night of 11–12 September

---

* A message decrypted on 7 September from Kesselring's Chief Quartermaster had described the disorganisation of the Italian railway system as a result of air attack and had asked for special priority for fuel trains; if this was not granted – and in spite of coastal shipping having been brought in to help – the fuel situation would soon become so strained that it would be impossible to ensure that necessary movements could be carried out.[240] This is a tribute to the efficiency of the Allied air offensive which had been continuous since before the launching of *Husky* – see above, pp 82–84.

235. DEFE 3/878, JPs 3809 and 3832 of 9 September 1943.
236. M Blumenson, *Salerno to Cassino* (Washington DC 1969), p 122.
237. CAB 121/591, W 9647/3045 of 11 September 1943.
238. ibid, NAF 398 of 11 September 1943.
239. DEFE 3/879, JP 4081 of 11 September 1943.
240. DEFE 3/878, JP 3555 of 7 September 1943.
241. DEFE 3/879, JP 4082 of 11 September 1943.

several earlier signals were decrypted, some dating back to 9 September, which carried similar orders and reported movements associated with them.[242]

During 12 September the bridgehead battle developed unfavourably to the Allies and on 13 September the situation became critical. Eighth Army, ordered on 12 September to press ahead from the south regardless of the administrative consequences,[243] was in no position to assist. Nor did matters improve until the night of 13–14 September, when US 82nd Airborne Division made a parachute drop in the beachhead. With this reinforcement, which was repeated on the following night and supplemented on 15 September by troops brought in by cruisers from Tripoli and by powerful naval and air support of the beachhead, the scale began to turn in favour of the Allies.[244] General Clark had ordered this first use of the Airborne Division on the morning of 13 September, well before the Allies received the next advance intelligence about the enemy's intention – a decrypt on the evening of 13 September disclosing that the Hermann Göring, 16th Panzer and 29th PG Divisions were to advance during the night of 13–14 September for the main counter-thrust to the Gulf of Salerno.[245] The British official history has described Salerno as a soldiers' battle.[246] Certainly there is no evidence that intelligence influenced the battle significantly. It is possible that it might have done so and that the crisis which developed during 13 September might have been averted if, in the light of the information received on the evening of 11 September, a decision had been taken forthwith to reinforce the beachhead with US 82nd Airborne Division on 12 September.

On 15 September Kesselring, learning that Tenth Army commander did not want to launch a fresh attack, told OKW that Allied naval and air power had forced LXXVI Panzer Corps on to the defensive and that whether a decisive success could be obtained now depended on the efforts of the Hermann Göring Division and 26th Panzer Division and the arrival of reinforcements from 1st Parachute Division in Apulia. The following day an appreciation he had requested from Tenth Army admitted that Allied naval and air supremacy had prevailed, and advised that to continue the battle would only lead to heavier losses, and Kesselring agreed.[247] The Allied commanders learned nothing of these exchanges until 17

---

242.   ibid, JPs 4087, 4094 and 4106 of 11 September, 4137 and 4147 of 12 September 1943.
243.   Molony, op cit, Vol V, p 305.
244.   ibid, p 305; Blumenson, op cit, pp 122–123.
245.   DEFE 3/879, JP4331 of 13 September 1943.
246.   Molony, op cit, Vol V, p 326.
247.   ibid, p 324.

September, when the decrypts disclosed that on 14 September Kesselring had urged Tenth Army to bring up its last reserves from Apulia if necessary, and that on 15 September a Battle Group of 1st Parachute Division was being put under the command of LXXVI Panzer Corps in the Salerno area.[248] But other decrypts obtained on 17 September included reports of the fighting during 16 September which showed the enemy meeting strong resistance and incurring heavy losses,[249] and at noon on 18 September GC and CS reported the news that on the previous day, at 1100, LXXVI Panzer Corps had announced its intention to begin the withdrawal at dusk.[250] The German situation reports for 17 September were decrypted in the afternoon of 18 September; they showed the enemy on the defensive on the whole front.[251]

□

On the broader question of Germany's intentions in the Italian theatre as a whole, there was no lack of high-grade Sigint during the battle at Salerno. It is true that during the first two days of the fighting it remained uncertain whether she would commit the divisions newly arrived in the north against the Allied landings; on the evening of 10 September General Eisenhower did not exclude the possibility that she might bring some of them down to Salerno.[252] On 11 September, however, AFHQ's intelligence summary considered that such a move was likely only in the event of a marked German success;[253] and on 14 September, in response to an enquiry from the Combined Chiefs of Staff, the JIC endorsed this view and reiterated the belief that it was 'the German intention eventually to withdraw to the north, possibly holding as far south as Pisa-Rimini'. 'German tactics will be to delay and render as expensive as possible Allied operations in south and central Italy without, however, risking the cutting off of their forces . . . Only a rapid and major success in eliminating the Allied bridgeheads might encourage the Germans to delay their withdrawal'.[254]

These appreciations were based not only on the absence of any Sigint evidence that any German formation was preparing to move south, but also on the receipt since 9 September of many decrypts

---

248. DEFE 3/880, JPs 4614 and 4655 of 17 September 1943.
249. ibid, JPs 4626, 4642 and 4688 of 17 September 1943.
250. ibid, JP 4743 of 18 September 1943.
251. ibid, JP 4752 of 18 September 1943.
252. CAB 121/591, W 9647/3045 of 10 September 1943.
253. WO 204/967, No 55 of 11 September 1943
254. JIC (43) 381 (o) of 14 September.

which reported Germany's reactions to the Italian armistice (Operation *Achse*).* The earliest of these decrypts had dealt with Germany's attempts to seize the Italian Fleet† and her decision to evacuate her forces in Sardinia to Corsica.[258] There had followed on 10 September the decrypt of a message from the German Foreign Office to all naval attachés, who were informed that Germany intended to hold north Italy and Corsica with Rommel in command; that her troops in southern Italy would if necessary make a fighting retreat to the north; and that German troops were moving into the Italian occupied zones of France and securing the Dalmatian coast. On 11 September the GAF Enigma had disclosed that the GAF Command and all GAF operational units in Sardinia had been ordered to Corsica the previous evening.[259] On 13 September, following earlier decrypts reporting Italian and 'de Gaullist' resistance in Bastia and German operations against the town, the naval Enigma had announced that the Germans had ordered the evacuation of Corsica.[260] Other decrypts had included the daily reports of Army Group B. They had revealed on 12 and 13 September that it was moving its HQ from Munich to Garda, and that its southern boundary was to be Elba-Piombino-Perugia-Civita Nova, and had shown it to be fully occupied in establishing its control; according to its report of 14 September it had by that date disarmed 340,000 Italians.[261] By that time decrypts of Sicherheitsdienst (SD) messages

---

* For the aspects of Operation *Achse* which concerned the Balkans see above, pp 13–14.

† Signals from the German Naval Command Italy on the evening of 8 September, decrypted on 9 September, informed subordinate units that the German Army had been ordered to take over Italian warships and merchant ships, instructed German naval units to force all Italian ships encountered at sea to proceed to ports north of Civita Vecchia and ordered the naval authorities at Taranto to use mining and E-boats to prevent the escape of Italian Fleet units.[255] At noon on 9 September further naval decrypts disclosed that Operation *Achse* had failed at Genoa and Spezia, the Italian warships there having sailed, and that III/KG 100 had eight aircraft ready to attack the Italian Fleet with radio guided bombs; and an Italian report that the battleship *Roma* had been sunk and the battleship *Italia* damaged on the afternoon of 9 September was decrypted in the early hours of 10 September.[256] Italian signals decrypted during 9 September had included a general announcement from the Admiralty warning that communications might shortly be interrupted, as German troops were marching on Rome, and ordering the Navy in the King's name faithfully to fulfil the terms of the armistice and sail to Malta.[257]

255. DEFE 3/878, JPs 3738 and 3759 of 9 September.
256. ibid, JPs 3780 and 3789 of 9 September, 3814 of 10 September 1943.
257. ibid, JP 3769 of 9 September 1943.
258. DEFE 3/876, JP 2742 of 1 September; DEFE 3/878, JP 3799 of 9 September 1943.
259. CX/MSS/3186/T23.
260. DEFE 3/878, JPs 3760 of 9 September, 3908 of 10 September; DEFE 3/879, JP 4297 of 13 September 1943.
261. DEFE 3/879, JPs 4192 of 12 September, 4273 of 13 September; DEFE 3/880, JP 4533 of 15 September 1943.

had revealed that Himmler was confident that he knew of Mussolini's whereabouts and had given the SD complete freedom of action to effect his release; and on 12 September they had added that Mussolini had been taken from Pranica di Mare by air to Vienna.

During the next ten days the high-grade Sigint seemed to substantiate the JIC's judgment, as did developments on the fighting front. As well as confirming that Tenth Army had abandoned the attempt to smash the Salerno bridgehead and that the GAF was being withdrawn from southern Italy, it reported the completion of the evacuation of Sardinia on 17 September[262] and covered in great detail the evacuation of Corsica, which began on 15 September with the embarkation at Bastia of 90th Division, recently arrived from Sardinia,[263] until its completion early in October. To these indications was added on 21 September the decrypts of a report by the Japanese Ambassador in Berlin of a talk with the German Vice-Minister of Foreign Affairs. The report stated that 'from the first Germany had had no intention of fighting a decisive battle in the centre or the south of Italy . . . even the fighting in the Salerno area had been carried out with the purpose of inflicting as great a loss as possible on the enemy with the forces already there, and once these operations were over Germany would resolutely order the retirement of her army. Rome would remain in Germany's hands for the present but she had no idea of holding it for a long time, because militarily that would be an extremely difficult thing to do and because it would be disadvantageous to Germany to have to manage the food supplies of Rome during the coming winter. An additional reason was that Hitler could not bear to see the capital of culture and the fine arts devastated by war'.[264] Thereafter, although they did not disclose that Kesselring had received from Hitler during the Salerno fighting a directive ordering him to withdraw the Tenth Army to the Rome area whatever the outcome of the battle, the many decrypts reporting on the fighting in southern Italy showed that Tenth Army, eschewing stubborn resistance, was making a staged withdrawal before growing Allied pressure. On 23 September they disclosed that LXXVI Panzer Corps intended to withdraw to four successive lines of resistance on 23, 25, 27 and 30 September, the final line running roughly from south of Avellino to Manfredonia,[265] and in the early hours of 28 September they reported that XIV Panzer Corps had begun to retire to a line running between Vesuvius and a point south-west of Avellino.[266]

---

262.   DEFE 3/880, JP 4737 of 18 September.
263.   ibid, JP 4706 of 18 September.
264.   Dir/C Archive, 4412 of 21 September 1943.
265.   DEFE 3/881, JP 5242 of 23 September.
266.   DEFE 3/882, JP 5719 of 28 September.

It was in these circumstances that on 29 September the JIC reiterated, in bolder terms than it had used on 14 September, the view that the Germans were preparing to evacuate southern and central Italy and, abandoning Rome and the important airfields north and south of it, would withdraw to a defence line in the north, possibly Pisa-Rimini. It believed that the GAF units moving from Rome, Naples and Foggia would be based in Turin, Milan, Verona and Venice, from which they could provide only limited support to land forces south of such a line, and it deduced from the evacuation of Sardinia and Corsica, which exposed the German right flank, that the process of withdrawal would not be protracted.[267] Nor was this appreciation out of line with the conclusions of the Allied commanders. On 21 September General Alexander had already issued to his army commanders his forecast of the course of operations. They would develop in four phases: consolidation on the line Salerno-Bari; capture (by 7 October) of Naples and the Foggia airfields; capture (by 7 November) of Rome and the road and rail centre at Terni; and capture (by 30 November) of Leghorn and the communications centres of Florence and Arezzo.[268]

Eighth Army duly reached Foggia on 27 September and on 2 October the Allies entered Naples, but the remainder of General Alexander's programme was not to be achieved. When he laid it down, 'in the well-founded belief that the bulk of AOK 10 covered by delaying forces was withdrawing to the area of Rome', he had had 'no reason to suspect that within a fortnight German policy would change'.[269]

---

267. JIC (43) 395 (o) of 29 September.
268. Molony, op cit, Vol V, pp 332–333.
269. ibid, p 332.

CHAPTER 32

The Eastern Mediterranean

IN May 1943, before going to the Washington conference, the British Chiefs of Staff had declined to give approval to proposals by which, in order to exploit 'the very favourable situation likely to develop in the Balkans', the C-in-C Middle East should be ready to carry out his plans for capturing Rhodes and occupying the Dodecanese once the Allies had taken Sicily. At the conference they agreed with the US authorities that the Allies would undertake no large-scale operations in the eastern Mediterranean.* On 28 June, by which time it had emerged in discussions between AFHQ and Cairo that the Middle East Command could not meet its commitments in support of the invasion of Sicily unless it cancelled its programme for supplying military aid to Turkey, the Chiefs of Staff directed the C-in-C Middle East to continue planning for the capture of Rhodes (Operation *Accolade*) only with the limited object- ive of seizing a foothold, to be exploited at a later date, when Italy surrendered.[1] Hitherto, outline planning for *Accolade* had envisaged three eventualities: a walk-in if Italy collapsed and Germany with- drew; a rapid occupation if Italy collapsed and Germany stood firm; and a large-scale invasion against Italian and German opposition.[2]

When the decision of the Washington conference and the directive of the Chiefs of Staff ruled out action in the last of these eventualities, intelligence had already established that Germany intended to hold on to Rhodes and thus eliminate the first. At the beginning of March 1943, according to Cairo's estimate, there had been only 300 GAF personnel on Rhodes[3], but before the end of April a high-grade decrypt had disclosed that a convoy carrying 1,250 men of a German Assault Brigade had been due in Rhodes at the end of March[4] and from the middle of May it became clear that the German reinforce- ment was continuing. On 14 May high-grade decrypts revealed that the Italians had given approval to German reinforcements at a recent conference in Rome, and that the Germans were discussing the need to bring in an air transport Gruppe with fighter escorts to

---

* See above, pp 7–8.

1. Howard, *Grand Strategy*, Vol VI (1972), pp 383, 411, 416, 428, 487.
2. Molony, *The Mediterranean and Middle East*, Vol V (1973), pp 533–534.
3. CAB 121/130, SIC file A/Policy/ME/4, COS (43) 79 (o) of 2 March, App- endix B para. 20.
4. DEFE 3/811, VM 9857 of 20 April 1943.

help with the transfer of army units to Rhodes and Lemnos.[5]* Early in June, when GHQ ME estimated that the Germans had 3,000–4,000 men and 20 guns on Rhodes,[10] decrypts showed that artillery and anti-tank troops were beginning to arrive.[11] By the middle of June GHQ ME estimated that the Germans had brought in 30 tanks,[12] and a month later it believed that the troops arriving in March had been the first elements of a motorised division, probably an *ad hoc* formation, which was still not up to strength.[13]

At the news of Mussolini's dismissal the Prime Minister re-opened discussion of the advantages that would follow from a quick operation to seize Rhodes. But he was forced to bow to the intelligence evidence that Germany was reinforcing the Aegean and to the fact that, since the operation would require the diversion of air and naval forces from the central Mediterranean, General Eisenhower was recommending that Operation *Accolade* should be cancelled altogether. In August at the Quebec conference the British delegation, which was in any case intent on securing higher priority for vigorous Allied action in Italy, accepted that Allied action in south-eastern Europe should be restricted to strategic bombing and supply operations in support of the guerrillas.† Accordingly, the Middle East Command confined itself to arranging that on the announcement of Italy's surrender it would send a SAS detachment to Castelrosso, other detachments to other islands, Cos in particular,

---

* Although the German reinforcement of Rhodes, like the reinforcement of the German divisions in Greece and the Balkans, had begun earlier, it seems probable that this acceleration of it was due to the success of Operation *Mincemeat*, carried out by the deception authorities in the first week of May, in persuading the enemy that the Allied preparations for Operation *Husky* were preparations for a landing in the eastern Mediterranean (see above, p 78). Another decrypt of 14 May indicated that the Germans were impressed by the *Mincemeat* evidence,[6] and it was followed in June by Sigint which showed that a full-strength armoured division (1st Panzer) was arriving in the Peloponnese from France.[7] Allied deception measures aimed at suggesting that the Allies intended to go over to the offensive in the eastern Mediterranean had, of course, begun well before May 1943, but it is difficult to judge how effective they had been before then. The German decrypts often reported alarms and anti-invasion preparations in the Dodecanese, Rhodes, Crete and southern Greece after the beginning of 1943, [8] but one decrypt at the end of February had revealed that OKW was aware that the Allies were practising deception on a large scale.[9]

† See above, p 11.

5. DEFE 3/815 ML 1942 of 13 May; Dir/C Archive, 3290 of 15 May 1943.
6. CX/MSS/2571/T4.
7. WO 208/3573, MI 14 Appreciation of 14 June 1943; CX/MSS/2607/T17.
8. WO 208/3573 of 19 April, 17 and 24 May 1943 as examples.
9. CX/MSS/2180/T28.
10. WO 201/2167, MI GHQ ME Periodical Intelligence Note No 42 of 8 June 1943, Appendix B.
11. DEFE 3/819, ML 3603 of 5 June 1943; Dir/C Archive, 3463 of 7 June 1943.
12. DEFE 3/821, ML 4857 of 21 June 1943; Dir/C Archive, 3623 of 22 June 1943.
13. WO 201/2167, No 47 of 18 July 1943.

and a small mission to Rhodes to try to persuade the Italian forces to round up the German garrison – the last to be followed by a brigade and tanks if it succeeded.[14]

On 8 September, the day of the Italian armistice, the Italian garrison on Castelrosso surrendered to the British detachment. Between then and 16 September British forces occupied Cos, Calymnos, Leros, Samos and other smaller islands without meeting Italian resistance.[15] On Rhodes, however, the British mission, landed on the night of 9–10 September, failed to forestall the Germans: they seized the Italian commander and on 11 September, making effective use of dive-bombing Ju 87s, secured the capitulation of the garrison;[16]* and by 16 September, as Sigint showed, they were organised as an 'Assault Division' for the defence of the island.[18] Nor were the British authorities able to recover from this set-back. Because the retention of the positions acquired in the other islands, not to speak of their expansion, depended on the possession of Rhodes with its harbours and airfields, the Middle East Command drew up a plan for taking Rhodes from the Germans – an operation which it had previously set aside as being beyond its resources. But even as it was obtaining permission from the Chiefs of Staff to carry out the plan before the end of October its hopes were again frustrated. The German capture of Cos on 3–4 October finally destroyed the British chances of exercising air and naval control to the extent required for an attack on Rhodes.

Despite the loss of Rhodes these chances had perhaps remained reasonable until 18 September. We now know that even after 12 September, when Hitler ruled that the chain of islands between the Peloponnese and Rhodes must be held, OKW doubted whether the British could be ejected from the positions they had taken, and it could not spare any additional army reinforcements.[19]† But the

---

* A C 38m decrypt of 10 September disclosed that the Italian commander considered resistance useless in view of the German superiority in equipment. This news was signalled to the Prime Minister in Washington and is an early example of the military Sigint which was by then going daily from 'C' to the Foreign Office (see below, p 139).

† The DMI noted in November 1943 after the German capture of Leros that a parachute unit sent from Italy for that operation represented 'the only additional troops which the Germans have brought into the Balkan-Aegean theatres for the express purpose of meeting the Allied threat to the islands'.[20]

14. Molony, op cit, Vol V, p 537.
15. ibid, p 539; ADM 234/364, BR 1736 (40), Aegean Operations, p 8.
16. Molony, op cit, Vol V, p 538.
17. Dir/C Archive, CX 527 of 12 September 1943; DEFE 3/879, JP 4144 of 10 September 1943.
18. CX/MSS/3217/T41.
19. Molony, op cit, Vol V, pp 532, 542–544; S W Roskill, *The War at Sea*, Vol III Part 1 (1960) pp 192–193.
20. AL 3000/E, Account of Land Operations on Leros, p 12.

British prospects had faded rapidly from 18 September. The GAF had by then begun to bring in reinforcements; among them, as the Enigma had disclosed by 27 September, were twenty single-engined fighters to Greece from Vienna and two long-range bomber formations, each of thirty aircraft – II/KG 51 from southern Russia to Salonika and II/KG 6 from northern France to Larissa.[21] This intelligence was reflected in GHQ ME's and AI's estimates of German air strength in Greece and the Aegean at the end of September and early October: a total of 350 aircraft, including 75 fighters, 85 long-range bombers and 65 dive-bombers.[22] Early in September, by way of comparison, the Air Ministry had estimated that the GAF had 250 aircraft in Greece and Crete, including 60 fighters, about the same number of dive-bombers, and 20 long-range bombers,[23] while at the end of August the actual GAF strength in the area had been 215 aircraft, excluding transport aircraft, of which 29 were fighters and 75 dive-bombers.[24]

Germany's success in capturing Cos owed much to the ability of her Air Force to rise to emergencies, as the Air Ministry recognised at the time.[25] The GAF's bombing of Cos, which started on 18 September, prevented the British, who in any case lacked adequate shipping, from establishing a protected advanced base on the island for Allied aircraft.[26] Its local air superiority throughout the area hampered the build-up of British troops and other supplies – so that only 2,700 men, 27 guns and 7 vehicles had been transported in all, mainly to Cos, Leros and Samos, by the end of September – and greatly increased the difficulties imposed on the Allied naval forces by their lack of advanced refuelling bases.[27] And so much was this the case that it may be doubted whether the Allies would have been able to intercept the German seaborne expedition against Cos even if they had received more intelligence, or had made better use of the intelligence they received.

In his subsequent report to the Prime Minister the C-in-C Middle East wrote that there was 'no intelligence at our disposal which would have led us to foresee that the enemy would be able to collect and launch at such short notice an expedition of the magnitude which made the assault on Cos.'[28] This statement is consistent with

---

21.   AIR 41/10, *The Rise and Fall of the GAF*, pp 262–264; Air Sunsets 103, 104 and 106 of 21, 27 September, 3 October 1943; CX/MSS/3250/T43.

22.   CAB 121/572, SIC file F/Italy/2 Vol 1, CC/314 of 28 September 1943.

23.   Air Sunset 92 of 2 September 1943.

24.   AIR 41/53, *Operations in the Dodecanese Islands*, Appendix I.

25.   Air Sunset 107 of 7 October 1943.

26.   AIR 41/53, p 19.

27.   Molony, op cit, Vol V, p 542.

28.   CAB 105/12, Hist (B) 12, No 55, CIC/132 of 7 October 1943.

the appreciations issued by GHQ ME and the War Diary kept by Force 292, the planning authority responsible in Cyprus for the operations in the Aegean, during the second half of September. They show that the intelligence authorities were aware that the enemy would attempt to occupy all the islands; that they thought he was unlikely to attempt seaborne landings until he had neutralised the air threat from Cos; but that, having no evidence that he was preparing for seaborne landings, they believed that in his effort to reduce Cos, which would probably be his first objective, he would rely on dive-bombing attacks and airborne landings.[29] The subsequent report of the fortress commander on Cos claimed that he studied the appreciations 'with care', and came to the conclusion that a seaborne landing was unlikely and that he should expect a small-scale airborne attack aimed at capturing the airfield.[30] In fact, a considerable movement of enemy shipping had been detected at the end of September, but the authorities in the theatre assumed from the outset that it was destined for Rhodes.

On 30 September PR detected the arrival in Crete of an enemy convoy from the Piraeus; and on 2 October, having detected the arrival of more ships in Crete on the previous day, it reported that all the shipping had left Crete that morning by 1025.[31] By then, moreover, Sigint had hinted that a seaborne landing was being contemplated: in a signal decrypted in the middle of September the German Navy had advised that dive-bombers should be used against garrison troops during landing operations, rather than for attacks on harbours and defence installations which would destroy valuable war material.[32] But the PR that was carried out daily over Crete from towards the end of September was on the 'watch for active shipping which might attempt a fast night passage to Rhodes'.[33] On 2 October, on receipt of the first PR warning of the convoy's arrival in Crete, one British and two Greek destroyers were sailed against it from Alexandria in the belief that it was bound for Rhodes; they found nothing during the night of 1–2 October, and having to lie up during daylight on 2 October to avoid air attack, they were unable to follow up air sightings of the convoy before being forced to return for refuelling at midnight.[34] The convoy

29. AL 3000/E, Account of Land Operations in Cos Island, p 18, Appendix C; ADM 234/364, p 42, Appendix E.
30. WO 106/3145, Narrative of the Cos operation, p 7 paras 28, 29, p 11 para 44.
31. AIR 41/54, *The RAF in Maritime War*, Vol VII Part 1, p 364; AIR 41/53, p 23.
32. DEFE 3/879, JP 4469 of 15 September; Naval Headlines, No 803 of 15 September; Dir/C Archive, 4375 of 15 September.
33. AIR 41/53, p 20; AIR 41/54, pp 361–363; AIR 41/7, *Photographic Reconnaissance*, Vol II, p 125.
34. AL 3000/E, Cos report, p 7; ADM 234/364, p 12; AIR 41/53, p 23.

was sighted on 2 October first off Paros and then off Naxos, steering east. At 2005 the Senior Naval Officer Aegean informed Force 292 that contact had been lost at 1530 but that, as the timing indicated that the convoy was not making for Leros, its destination was possibly Rhodes.[35] The authorities on Cos appear to have received no news of the sightings before 0300 on 3 October, when they were informed that a convoy had been sighted off Melos at 1120 on 2 October and was expected to reach Rhodes during the night: and on this evidence the fortress commander was satisfied that it was taking reinforcements to Rhodes until, from about 0545 on 3 October, his patrols began to report shipping off the coast.[36].

The presupposition that Rhodes would be the destination of the enemy force was referred to in the C-in-C's report to the Prime Minister; 'We did of course foresee the possibility of seaborne attack but intelligence from all sources including Most Secret Sources* pointed strongly to the probability that this would be preceded by the reinforcement of Rhodes'.[37] The inclusion of 'Most Secret Sources' in this reference may have owed something to the fact that on 23 September the destroyer *Eclipse* had sunk a merchant ship off the south-west point of Rhodes, where it had been landing reinforcements, after the Enigma had disclosed that the ship was to make its return journey under escort from a torpedo-boat.[38] But Sigint gave no other pointer to the objective of the expedition until late on 2 October. German naval signals of 1 October were then decrypted which mentioned preparations for sailings from Suda Bay and referred to a landing craft for the use of 'Battalion Staff'. The reference to a landing craft should perhaps have suggested that the objective was not Rhodes; but the evidence was slight, and it came when time was running out. GC and CS, signalling a summary of the decrypts to Cairo at 0054 on 3 October, felt able only to add the comment that some unspecified operation was to be carried out during 3 October.[39] The next relevant Sigint was the decrypt of a report from the 'Suda Group' to the effect that it had been sighted by Allied reconnaissance at 0820 on 2 October; this intelligence was signalled to Cairo at 0647 on 3 October.[40] By that time the small German assault force, brought in four transports and a few naval

---

  * ie the Enigma.

35.   AIR 41/53, p 23.
36.   ibid, pp 23–24, AL 3000/E, Cos report, p 8.
37.   CAB 105/12, No 55, CIC/132 of 7 October 1943.
38.   ADM 234/364, p 11; DEFE 3/619, ZTPGMs 36601, 36625; DEFE 3/620, ZTPGM 37717.
39.   DEFE 3/883, JP 6094 of 0054/3 October 1943.
40.   ibid, JP 6134 of 0647/3 October 1943.

ferries and landing craft, was getting ashore on Cos, where at 0630 a small number of paratroopers dropped on the airfield.

Enjoying almost total control of the air and continuous close support from Ju 87 dive-bombers, the Germans quickly over-whelmed the Italian and British defenders; organised resistance ceased early on 4 October. GS and CS decrypted the German account of the operation, which nevertheless described the opposition as 'tough', the following day.[41]

□

The official historian of the war at sea, after criticising the decision to embark on the Aegean operations in the knowledge that Rhodes could not be captured, was still more critical of the decision to continue with them 'when it had become clear that we could not exercise adequate maritime control over the disputed waters – and that unpleasant fact was abundantly plain after the fall of Cos on 3 October, if not earlier'.[42] The situation might still have been re-trieved had it been possible for AFHQ to give air support in the Aegean. Alarmed by the build-up of the GAF, the Prime Minister had pressed for this since the end of September, but without success; the day after Cos fell General Eisenhower advised the Combined Chiefs of Staff that he could divert resources only at the expense of the campaign in Italy, where it had become clear that Germany intended to offer determined resistance.[43] The Prime Minister there-upon appealed to the President for some relaxation of the US insistence that nothing must deflect the Allies from carrying out *Overlord* on the agreed date and securing in Italy a line north of Rome. He failed again; and on 9 October a military conference in Tunis, also attended by all three Middle East Cs-in-C, unanimously agreed that the situation in Italy did not permit any diversion to the Aegean.[44] The Prime Minister did not take this decision grace-fully. On 12 October, on reading the most recent decrypts about German preparations for the attack on Leros, he expressed some anger to the CAS that the Mediterranean Air Command had withdrawn air support from the eastern Mediterranean following the decision not to try to capture Rhodes. He was still keeping up the pressure two days later when, on reading further decrypts about the German difficulties in carrying out the attack on Leros, he

---

41. ibid, JPs 6292 and 6355 of 5 and 6 October; Dir/C Archive, 4555 of 5 October, 4567 of 6 October 1943.
42. Roskill, op cit, Vol III Part 1, pp 204–205.
43. Molony, op cit, Vol V, p 545
44. Ehrman, *Grand Strategy*, Vol V (1956), pp 94–99.

signalled to the C-in-C ME that 'a little more strength on our part might turn the scales'.[45]

The Cs-in-C Middle East, with the support of the Prime Minister and the British Chiefs of Staff, nevertheless decided that every effort must be made to hold Leros and Samos. In reaching their decision they were influenced, it may be assumed, by the fact that their forces had recently scored the first success against an enemy convoy in the Aegean. On the morning of 7 October a minelayer and at least part of a convoy from the Piraeus had been sunk off Stampalia in attacks by HM submarine *Unruly* and an Allied force of two cruisers and two destroyers.[46] The surface forces involved in the attack were protected by USAAF Lightning long-range fighters, made available by AFHQ for a few days, and RAF coastal Beaufighters already under ME command.[47] The Lightning squadrons were withdrawn to the central Mediterranean on 11 October. But it was not long before naval reinforcements – amounting eventually to four British cruisers and six British destroyers, together with two British and four Italian submarines to assist in running supplies to Leros – were diverted from Malta. For it soon emerged that the attack on the convoy had forced the Germans to postpone their attack on Leros, and that they were having great difficulty in remounting the operation and were hesitating about its practicability.

The Enigma had not given advance notice of the convoy's departure from the Piraeus, but it had disclosed after the attack that it had been bound for Cos. Early on 8 October it was confirmed that at least part of the convoy had been destroyed. Later on 8 October an Enigma decrypt strongly indicated that, though bound for Cos in the first instance, the convoy had formed part of German preparations for the attack on Leros; the decrypt ordered that despite the loss of the convoy the Battle Group on Cos was to carry out Operation *Leopard*, which was 'of decisive importance for the whole situation', on 9 October at the latest.[48] Early on 9 October another decrypt established that *Leopard* had been postponed for 24 hours on the morning of 8 October.[49] On the morning of 10 October the decrypt of a signal from Army Group E disclosed that *Leopard* was

45. Dir/C Archive, minutes between the Prime Minister and the CAS 12 to 15 October, and C 4690 of 16 October 1943; PREM 3/3/9, PM telegram to Wilson T/1616/3 of 14 October 1943.

46. Molony, op cit, Vol V, p 547; CAB 105/12, No 50 of 7 October 1943; ADM 234/364, p 13.

47. Roskill, op cit, Vol III Part 1 pp 196–197; Molony, op cit, Vol V, pp 546–547; ADM 234/364, pp 13–14; AIR 41/53, Chapter 3.

48. DEFE 3/883, JP 6499 of 7 October; DEFE 3/884, JPs 6503, 6504, 6505, 6544 of 7 October, 6574 and 6603 of 8 October 1943.

49. DEFE 3/884, JP 6637 of 0414/9 October 1943.

to be carried out as a surprise operation on that day or during the night of 10–11 October. [50] Later decrypts of 10 October showed that it had again been postponed until the early hours of 12 October, and that the German naval and air commands were nervous about its prospects.[51] In signals of 11 October, decrypted on 12 October, the German naval authorities considered that *Leopard* would not be possible unless air reconnaissance could establish in good time that there were no Allied warships in the Aegean or in Turkish waters; they also ordered minelaying on the night of 11–12 October and recommended continued minelaying should *Leopard* be further postponed.[52] On the morning of 12 October the Enigma disclosed that the operation had again been postponed;[53] and from then until 12 November the decrypts showed that, either because of unfavourable weather or because of fear of the risks arising from the lack of information about Allied naval movements, postponements were being made almost daily. At the same time, Sigint made it clear that Hitler, though he increased the risks and prolonged the postponements by vetoing attacks on Allied warships as they lay up in Turkish territorial waters,[54] nevertheless remained determined that *Leopard* should be carried out, as a surprise move, at the first opportunity.[55] On learning of Hitler's determination the Prime Minister commented to the First Sea Lord: 'This should give us a good chance. Pray do all you can to help our defences'.[56]

There had been other indications in the Sigint of Hitler's determination to hold on to his position in the Aegean. With the Italian capitulation the German Navy in the Mediterranean faced the problem that, because of the enforced division of its control into three separate compartments, the merchant shipping at its disposal was inequitably divided, with tonnage immobilised in one area that was urgently needed in another. The Aegean was acutely short of shipping, and for this reason in mid-September Hitler ordered the transfer there of as much as possible from the then less hard-pressed resources in the Adriatic. To execute this order was a dangerous operation in view of the Allied occupation of southern Italy and the lack of escorts available to the German naval authorities in the

---

50. ibid, JP 6745 of 1049/10 October 1943.
51. ibid. JPs 6763 of 10 October. 6824 and 6848 of 11 October.
52. ibid, JP 6926 of 12 October; Naval Headlines, No 830 of 12 October 1943.
53. DEFE 3/884, JP 6928 of 12 October 1943.
54. ibid, JP 6941 of 12 October; DEFE 3/885, JP 7122 of 14 October; DEFE 3/866, JP 7558 of 19 October; DEFE 3/890, JPs 9522 and 9764 of 12 November 1943; Naval Headlines, Nos 831, 833 and 839 of 13, 15 and 21 October 1943.
55. DEFE 3/886, JP 7558 of 19 October; WO 208/3573 of 25 October 1943.
56. Dir/C Archive, 4747 of 21 October 1943.

Adriatic, but the risk was accepted in a decision to try to pass fast ships through the Straits of Otranto, sailing independently.[57] Of the ten that sailed, eight failed to reach the Piraeus; two of them were taken in prize by the Royal Navy, one was destroyed by the Yugoslav Partisans, two by Allied surface ships, one by submarine and one by Allied aircraft; the eighth disappeared on passage. Decrypts about the movements of all ten ships were plentiful. They were not always received in time to be of operational use but, in conjunction with air sightings which may themselves have been based on decrypts, they certainly contributed to one of the sinkings by surface attack (the *Olimpia*) on 15 October and to one of the captures (the *Argentina*) on the same day.[58]

In the Aegean, other successes against enemy shipping had a direct effect on the problem of fixing a date for Operation *Leopard*. The Enigma having reported that two merchant ships had left the Piraeus in convoy on 14 October, a submarine sank one of the ships on 16 October and the other was badly damaged by destroyers in a bombardment of Port Calymnos.[59] On 29 October a submarine sank the troop-carrier SS *Ingeborg* after decrypts had disclosed that she was moving via Naxos to Calymnos.[60] Her loss and that of the SS *Sinfra* (4,470 tons) on the night of 18–19 October, following an aircraft sighting,[61] were considerable additions to those reported by the German Admiral Aegean in a signal decrypted on 18 October: three merchant ships sunk or damaged up to that date in addition to one minelayer, two torpedo-boats and eight landing craft.[62] But while these losses severely reduced the enemy's limited resources – the Admiral's signal added that his effective force had been reduced to four landing craft, one torpedo-boat, three harbour defence vessels and one armed fishing vessel – they were inconsiderable in comparison with those incurred by the Allies. After the withdrawal of the USAAF Lightnings on 11 October the Allied warships had been forced to abandon daytime operations; the Beaufighters could

---

57. DEFE 3/618, ZTPGMs 35634, 35637.
58. Naval Headlines, No 833 of 15 October 1943; DEFE 3/885, JPs 7193 of 15 October, 7278 and 7304 of 16 October 1943; AIR 41/54, p 395.
59. DEFE 3/885, JPs 7108 and 7154 of 14 October, 7176 and 7182 of 15 October, 7275 of 16 October, 7320 of 17 October 1943; Naval Headlines, Nos 832 and 833 of 14 and 15 October, 835 and 836 of 17 and 18 October 1943; ADM 234/364, p. 15.
60. DEFE 3/886, JPs 7733 and 7758 of 22 October; DEFE 3/887, JPs 8292 and 8303 of 28 October; Naval Headlines, Nos 840 of 22 October, 848 of 30 October 1943; ADM 234/364, p 20.
61. DEFE 3/886 JP 7555 of 19 October 1943; WO 106/3149, C-in-C ME Cositrep of 19 October 1943.
62. DEFE 3/885, JP 7428 of 18 October; Naval Headlines, No 836 of 18 October 1943.

not provide adequate cover. Lying up by day in Turkish waters, they confined themselves to operations in areas which the destroyers could reach during the night, cruisers providing anti-aircraft fire and fighter direction as the destroyers entered and retired from the Aegean.[63] Even so, six destroyers had been sunk and four destroyers and four cruisers had been damaged by the end of the Aegean operations, in addition to the loss of two submarines and ten minesweepers and coastal vessels.[64]*

Some of the naval casualties were brought about by enemy minelaying; this accounted for damage to a Greek destroyer and the sinking of the British destroyers *Hurworth* and *Eclipse* in the last week of October.[65] The remainder were inflicted by the GAF, which continued to receive sufficient reinforcements to off-set its own heavy losses.† On 21 October, when the Enigma had recently disclosed the transfer of ten dive-bombers from Yugoslavia, of a few aircraft from Reserve Training Units in Yugoslavia and the Baltic and of 30 long-range bombers from Austria, and had reported that a further thirty bombers were to follow, AI estimated the GAF's strength in the eastern Mediterranean as 190 aircraft, including 70 bombers, 55 fighters and 30 dive-bombers.[67]‡ Its actual strength on that date was 246 (excluding transport aircraft), of which 33 were bombers, 55 were fighters and 56 were dive-bombers.[69] This had risen to 265, including 94 bombers, 69 fighters and 28 dive-bombers, by 12 November.[70] AI, which had recently learned from Sigint that twenty fighters were moving from Albania to Athens, that the bombers included ten from France equipped with Hs 293,§ and that bombers had begun to operate from Rhodes and Cos, then estimated its strength as 305, including 105 bombers, 80 fighters and 55 dive-bombers.[71]**

---

* The Allies also lost 113 aircraft in the campaign, including 50 per cent of the Beaufighters they committed.

† Its total losses in the Aegean campaign were 92 aircraft destroyed by Allied action and 64 which did not return from operations.[66]

‡ But by 23 October a single-engined fighter Gruppe had been moved from the Dodecanese to Montenegro because of losses to dive-bombers in Yugoslavia through Allied interception.[68]

§ For details of the Hs 293 radio guided rocket missile see below, p 337 et seq. Hs 293 was probably used in night attacks for the first time during the Aegean operations.

** Compare the September figures and estimates on p 122 above.

63. Molony, op cit, Vol V, p 547; ADM 234/364, p 14.
64. Molony, op cit, Vol V, pp 531, 557.
65. Roskill, op cit, Vol III Part 1, p 199.
66. Molony, op cit, Vol V, p 557.
67. Air Sunsets 110 of 17 October, 111 of 21 October 1943.
68. Air Sunset 112 of 24 October 1943.
69. AIR 41/53, Appendix 1.   70. ibid.
71. Air Sunsets 116 of 1 November, 120 of 15 November; DEFE 3/890, JPs 9531 and 9542 of 12 November 1943.

As the GAF took its toll, and the difficulty of building up and supplying the Allied garrisons on Leros and Samos increased, the prospects of fending off the enemy's descent on Leros declined. On 23 October the Cs-in-C Middle East informed Whitehall that although the Allied position was precarious and could not be made secure without considerable air reinforcements, so that 'further heavy losses, especially naval losses, may be incurred', they intended to 'do all in our power to retain Leros with the limited forces at our disposal. . . .'; they believed that Germany's difficulties were at least as great as their own and that 'if [she] breaks, [the] moral and political effect on the whole of south-east Europe should be considerable'.[72] In Whitehall doubts were by then setting in. On 19 October the Defence Committee, drawing attention to the Sigint evidence on Germany's preparations against Leros, had appealed in vain to the Mediterranean Air Command for any help against them that might be possible without prejudice to the operations in Italy.[73] On 25 October the CIGS questioned the wisdom of the Middle East's decision,[74] and on 27 October the Joint Planning Staff, after considering the Joint Intelligence Staff's assessment of the probable scale of the German attack, concluded that 'in the light of the situation in Italy' the large-scale diversion of air forces needed to secure Leros was not justifiable.[75] But when the Chiefs of Staff considered this advice it emerged that the Chief of the Air Staff and the Vice-Chief of the Naval Staff preferred to accept the risks of trying to hold on, and the Chiefs of Staff accordingly recommended that an effort should be made to persuade the Turkish government to allow Allied aircraft to operate from bases in Anatolia.[76]

The Turks had helped the Allies by ferrying supplies to Samos in September and had since then continued to turn a blind eye to the use of their territorial waters by Allied warships, but they rejected this request at a meeting with the Foreign Secretary in Cairo on 7 November.[77]* Nor would a favourable reception of it have been in time to prevent the situation in the Aegean from swinging rapidly in Germany's favour. By 28 October Sigint had disclosed that Luftflotte 2 was supplying troops, equipment and Ju 52s for a paratroop operation in the area. The decrypts of signals sent on 29

---

* The Soviet government agreed to join the British in making the approach to Turkey but the US government decided not to be associated with it.

72.   CAB 105/12, No 94, CC/327 of 23 October 1943.
73.   ibid, No 90, CAS to Tedder, Punch 63 of 19 October 1943.
74.   CAB 121/573, SIC file F/Italy/2 Vol 2, COS (43) 259th (o) Meeting, 25 October.
75.   ibid, JP(43) 382 of 27 October.
76.   ibid, COS (43) 262nd (o) Meeting, 28 October.
77.   Ehrman, op cit, Vol V, pp 100–102.

October had carried orders for a landing on Samos to take place on 31 October. On 31 October it emerged from Sigint that, while the Samos operation had been postponed, the authorities involved in the Leros operation had received a weather forecast for the early hours of that day. By 1 November Cairo had learned from agents' reports that landing craft and naval personnel had been arriving in the Piraeus since 28 October, and on 3 and 4 November naval Enigma decrypts, agents, PR and air sightings all indicated that what were taken to be these craft were exercising in the Gulf of Athens. By 5 November, when the force was reported moving eastwards, naval Enigma decrypts had associated it with D-day for the Leros assault and had referred to the build-up of airborne troops. On the following day agents reported that troop reinforcements had arrived in Greece, one report specifying that they were airborne troops for attacks on 'two islands'.[78] Between 7 and 11 November, when they disclosed that D-day was to be 12 November, the Enigma decrypts traced in great detail and with little delay the passage of the expedition to Cos and Calymnos, showing that it was dispersing and lying up by night and moving under heavy fighter protection by day. On 7 November they reported that 13 of its initial 38 ships had already dropped out, some from technical defects and others as a result of Allied action.[79]* But Allied efforts to intercept the convoy in the later stages of its passage came to nothing. The Beaufighters, no match for the GAF, suffered heavy losses but did no damage. The destroyers were handicapped in night operations by GAF shadowing in moonlight conditions. By day they were under instructions to lie up unless they received orders to the contrary from the naval C-in-C; and their last opportunity to forestall the landings slipped by when aircraft sighted two groups of ships steering north-west to the east of Calymnos. The destroyers were too distant to be able to engage before daylight,

---

* With no hint of his source, the Prime Minister gave the gist of these decrypts, up to 8 November, to the War Cabinet. Two days later 'C' sent him a précis clarifying 'the situation of the convoys'. The intelligence the decrypts contained also went to the Foreign Office from 'C'.[80]

78. DEFE, 3/887 JPs 8002 of 24 October, 8185 of 26 October, 8397 of 29 October, 8451 and 8472 of 30 October; DEFE 3/888, JPs 8579 and 8586 of 31 October, 8806, 8811, 8829, 8834 and 8852 of 3 November, 8930, 8935 and 8952 of 4 November, 8959, 8975 at 5 November; DEFE 3/889, JPs 9004 and 9025 of 5 November 1943; Naval Headlines, Nos 848 and 849 of 30 and 31 October 1943; WO 106/3149, passim; WO 208/3573 of 1 November 1943; ADM 234/364 pp 21, 49, 50.

79. DEFE 3/889, JPs 9109, 9112, 9114, 9121, 9123, 9153 of 7 November, 9193, 9195, 9197 of 8 November, 9259, 9264, 9278 of 9 November, 9341 and 9350 of 10 November, 9391 and 9421 of 11 November 1943.

80. Dir/C Archive, 4943 of 8 November, 4973 of 10 November 1943.

and they had withdrawn before the C-in-C's Operations Room realised that it was the invasion force that had been sighted.[81]

The German landings on Leros began at 0600 on 12 November. Within half an hour GC and CS had sent to Cairo the contents of decrypts giving details of the enemy's last-minute plans: the first wave of the assault was to be made from 0300 by two separate Battle Groups, one for the west coast and the other for the east coast.[82] Between then and the evening of 16 November, when the British commander of the garrison surrendered, the C-in-C Middle East derived no benefit from such Sigint as cast light on the development of the battle. During 12 November the decrypts disclosed that the western Battle Group had returned to Calymnos after failing to get ashore, and was under orders to return that night to reinforce the eastern group's beachhead.[83] Sigint later reported that it had done so by 0500 on 13 November,[84] but a destroyer sweep on the night of 12–13 November found no enemy forces. A Sigint reference to paratroops on the morning of 12 November indicated that their operation had been delayed, but the decrypts made no further mention of the airborne troops before they made their drop on the west coast near Gurna Bay in the afternoon.[85] Nor was it until the afternoon of 13 November that they disclosed that a second airborne operation had been ordered for the morning of that day.[86] By early on 15 November the decrypts disclosed that troops for a follow-up landing were expected to arrive at Cos later that day, and that that date was the earliest on which E-boats from the Adriatic and urgently needed torpedo-boats could reach the operational area, but they provided no further information until the following day.[87] They then disclosed that this 'vital' landing, bringing in heavy guns, had taken place at Pandeli Bay on the east coast during the night of 15–16 November.[88] In the event, assault craft en route for Leros had been sighted by air reconnaissance about 2100 on 15 November, but the Allied destroyer force did not sail to act on the report till dawn on 16 November; it was lying up in Turkish waters after being continually shadowed by aircraft during the previous

---

81.   Roskill, op cit, Vol III Part 1 p 201; Molony, op cit, Vol V, p 554; ADM 234/364 pp 21–24, 50–53; AIR 41/53, pp 42–44.
82.   DEFE 3/890, JP 9503 of 0626/12 November 1943.
83.   ibid, JPs 9514 and 9577 of 12 November, 9591 of 13 November; Naval Headlines, No 862 of 13 November 1943.
84.   DEFE 3/890, JP 9614 of 13 November 1943.
85.   ibid, JP 9567 of 12 November 1943; Molony, op cit, Vol V, p 555.
86.   DEFE 3/890, JP 9645 of 13 November 1943.
87.   ibid, JPs 9713 of 14 November, 9743, 9750, 9757, 9776 of 15 November, 9808 of 16 November; Naval Headlines, No 864 of 15 November 1943.
88.   DEFE 3/890, JPs 9821, 9827 and 9833 of 16 November 1943; AL 3000/E, Leros report, p 10.

night, and Allied operations were by then being affected by severe delays in W/T communications.[89] Sigint reported that Allied resistance to the Pandeli Bay landing had been 'peculiarly' weak.[90] Hitherto the decrypts had reported the Allied resistance in the land fighting to be 'unbroken' and 'tough', and had described the German situation as 'critical' for lack of heavy guns.[91]

The German plain text announcement of the capitulation of the Leros garrison was intercepted just after midnight on 16–17 November, two hours before the Enigma report of the capitulation was decrypted.[92] On the following day all Allied troops except a small garrison on Castelrosso were ordered to withdraw from the Aegean. The Samos garrison was evacuated during the night of 19–20 November and the Germans occupied Samos on 22 November.[93]

□

After the fall of Leros the Germans were desperately short of shipping in the Aegean. By the end of November 1943, as the Enigma disclosed, they had lost 23 per cent (10,000 tons) of the shipping available at the beginning of the month and were having to divert some of the remainder to assist their troops in the Crimea.[94] In January 1944, moreover, the Enigma also disclosed that the Allied landing at Anzio had forced them to transfer all their bomber strength from Greece; which left the GAF with only about 100 aircraft for the protection of the Aegean.[95] But during that month they were able to strengthen their island garrisons and establish something approaching a regular supply system by bringing ships back from the Black Sea.[96]

In February 1944 the Allies stepped up their operations, and their successes, hitherto limited to the sinking of a few small ships by submarines and naval coastal forces, increased. The Germans

---

89. ADM 234/364, p 27; AIR 41/53, p 48.
90. DEFE 3/890, JP 9833 of 16 November 1943.
91. ibid, JPs 9701 of 14 November, 9799 of 15 November, 9827 of 16 November 1943.
92. WO 106/3149 of 17 November 1943; DEFE 3/890, JP 9875 of 0211/17 November 1943.
93. Molony, op cit, Vol V, p 559; Roskill, op cit, Vol III Part 1, p 203; CAB 80/42, COS (43) 303 (121st résumé) of 25 November, para 29.
94. Naval Headlines, Nos 875 of 26 November, 881, 883 and 886 of 2, 4 and 7 December 1943; DEFE 3/8 (1), VL 908 of 1 December 1943.
95. Roskill, op cit, Vol III Part 1, p 317; AIR 41/10, pp 266, 269; Air Sunset 139 of 25 January 1944.
96. Roskill, op cit, Vol III Part 1, pp 317–318; DEFE 3/635, ZTPGM 52612.

lost two large supply ships to air attack – one of them, the *Leda*, after the Enigma had disclosed that she was due to sail from Leros to Crete with the Battle Group used in the attack on Leros – and a third was sunk by HM submarine *Sportsman*.[97] And at the end of the month they failed in their attempt to transfer a large ship from the Adriatic to the Aegean: the *Diedrichsen* was sunk by French light cruisers soon after leaving Pola, the Enigma having given notice of the intention to transfer her and of her time of departure.[98] At the same time the Allies undertook commando raids on the islands with the Special Boat Squadron and the Long Range Desert Group.

The Germans continued to be nervous about the commando raids in April and May, when the Enigma showed them to be increasing their supervision of the island populations, planning descents on the smaller islands to forestall the establishment of Allied bases and complaining of the casualties inflicted by the raids.[99] But Allied successes against the German supply shipping fell off after the end of February; no ship of any importance was sunk between then and the end of April, when HMS *Sportsman* sank the *Luxembourg* on passage from Piraeus to Crete.[100] By then, moreover, as the JIC had noted in March, Germany had increased air transport in the area by sending an additional GAF transport Gruppe to Greece.[101] Nor was it long before the Enigma provided further evidence that, however limited her resources, she would do her utmost to hold on to her Aegean bases.* In May, in a movement which had been planned for weeks but which took place only after she had abandoned hope of capturing the island of Vis, she succeeded in transferring three R-boats from the Adriatic to the Aegean, a fourth

---

* Although their reasoning was obvious enough, it was not known until after the war that the German authorities believed that six or seven British divisions were standing by in Egypt for a descent on Rhodes and Crete, or, as Hitler believed in May, for an invasion of the mainland via Crete and the Peloponnese.[102]

97. Molony, op cit, Vol V, pp 827–828; Roskill, op cit, Vol III Part 1, p 318; Naval Headlines, Nos 940 of 30 January, 942 of 1 February 1944; DEFE 3/134 VL 5109 of 30 January 1944.
98. Naval Headlines, Nos 957, 958, 959 of 16, 17 and 18 February, 971 and 972 of 1 and 2 March 1944; AIR 41/54, p 416; Air Sunsets 148 and 150 of 25 February and 1 March 1944; WO 208/3573 of 21 February 1944; DEFE 3/140, VLs 6536 and 6564 of 18 February 1944; DEFE 3/143 VLs 7311 of 28 February, 7414 of 29 February 1944.
99. Naval Headlines, Nos 1011 of 10 April, 1023 of 22 April, 1034 of 3 May 1944; DEFE 3/37 (2), KV 607 of 9 April; DEFE 3/41 (1), KV 1638 of 21 April; DEFE 3/45 (1), KV 2683 of 3 May 1944.
100. Molony, op cit, Vol VI Part 1 (forthcoming), Chapter VII; Roskill, op cit, Vol III Part 1, p 318.
101. JIC (44) 91 (0) of 13 March.
102. Molony, op cit, Vol VI, Part 1, Chapter VII.

being sunk by Allied aircraft off Corfu.[103] In the same month she managed to re-furbish her Aegean garrisons by withdrawing ships from the Black Sea as soon as she completed the evacuation of the Crimea.[104] As the Enigma showed, the transfer of ships from the Black Sea continued into June despite the fact that the Turkish government was by then refusing some clearances.[105]

At the beginning of June the German supply position received a serious set-back. From a convoy of three merchantmen, which was sighted soon after it left the Piraeus, Allied aircraft sank two of the merchantmen and three of the escorts as they neared Crete; the surviving supply ship was sunk by submarine on its return passage on 8 June. The Enigma had not reported the sailing of the convoy; but it had disclosed the preparations for its departure and it reported the results of the air attack.[106] This disaster convinced the Germans that they could no longer risk sailing large ships in convoy in the Aegean, and it inaugurated the worsening of their supply situation under increasing Allied attacks which forced them to begin their withdrawal from the area in the autumn.

---

103. Naval Headlines, Nos 1029 of 28 April, 1033–1035 of 2–4 May, 1043 of 12 May, 1047 of 16 May, 1049–1052 of 18–21 May 1944; DEFE 3/43 (1), KV 2230 of 28 April; DEFE 3/45 (2), KV 2514 of 1 May; DEFE 3/45 (1), KVs, 2697 and 2720 of 3 May; DEFE 3/154, KV 3550 of 12 May; DEFE 3/155, KV 3968 of 12 May; DEFE 3/156, KVs 4237 and 4239 of 18 May; DEFE 3/157, KV 4286 of 18 May; DEFE 3/158, KVs 4524 and 4535 of 19 May, 4589 and 4600 of 20 May 1944.

104. Molony, op cit, Vol VI Part 1, Chapter VII; Roskill, op cit, Vol III Part 1, pp 329–330.

105. Naval Headlines, Nos 1056–1059 of 25–28 May, 1061 and 1062 of 30 and 31 May, 1063 of 1 June, 1065 and 1066 of 3 and 4 June 1944; DEFE 3/165, KV 6313 OF 4 June; DEFE 3/704, ZTPGR 13769.

106. Molony, op cit, Vol VI, Part 1 Chapter VII; Roskill, op cit, Vol III Part 1, p 329; Naval Headlines, Nos 1051 of 20 May, 1065–1067 of 3–5 June 1944; DEFE 3/157, KV 4459 of 19 May; DEFE 3/164, KVs 6180 and 6199 of 3 June; DEFE 3/165, KV 6302 of 4 June 1944.

THE CENTRAL & EASTER
MEDITERRANEAN

0   100   200   300   400   5
LAND MILES

AUSTRIA   HUNGARY
CARINTHIA   ROMA
Ljubljana SLOVENIA   BARANJA
Trieste   Zagreb   BACKA
           CROATIA   BANAT
Venice
Pola   Senj Bihac   Banja Luka BELGRADE
Ravenna   Drvar Jajce   BOSNIA
Rimini   Zara   DALMATIA   SERBIA
Ancona   SANDJAK
           Split
           Mostar   BU
           MONTENEGRO
Pescara   Vis   Dubrovnik   Podgorica   Skoplje
Termoli   SEA   ALBANIA
ROME
Anzio   Durazzo Tirana   Salon
Pontine Is.   Naples   Bari   Fleri Berat   S
Ischia   Salerno   Brindisi Valona
           Taranto   Saseno   Larissa
                   Corfu   Volos
                   GREECE
                   Levkas
Ustica   Cephalonia   Corin
Messina   IONIAN   Peloponne
SICILY   SEA
Augusta

MALTA

Lampedusa

MEDITERRA

Tripoli
Misurata
Benghazi Berka

CY

TRIPOLITANIA

CHAPTER 33

Developments in Yugoslavia

THE LOSS of Leros destroyed all prospect of early Allied operations in the eastern Mediterranean. But the capitulation of Italy's forces in the Balkans and the advance of the Allied armies in Italy had meanwhile opened up an important, if peripheral, theatre of Allied operations in Yugoslavia.

British involvement with the Yugoslav resistance movements began in September 1941,* when Captain Hudson, the first of many officers to be sent on missions, was put ashore by the SOE with instructions to contact all groups opposing the enemy and report on them by W/T.[1] Except that occasional Italian and German decrypts had mentioned 'Communist' activity in Montenegro, Bosnia and Slovenia,† and that the then Colonel Mihailovic had broadcast an appeal for help,[2] little was then known about the nature and strength of the resistance groups or the relations between them. Nor was the position much clearer when, in the middle of October, the British government accepted Mihailovic as the leading insurgent and instructed Hudson, whose first encounters had been with the Communist-led Partisans, to make contact with him.[3] This decision was made after Mihailovic had established a W/T link with the Yugoslav government in London and had sent messages announcing that he was launching a national revolt as head of 'The Royal Yugoslav Army in the field'; but except that King Peter had shown these to the Prime Minister, the situation remained obscure.[4]

---

* A vast literature has grown up on this subject in recent years, and it should be noted that the following pages make no attempt to survey it in detail. As stated in the preface, the aim of the volume is to provide only so much of the operational and strategic context as readers must have if they are to be in a position to judge the influence exerted by the intelligence that was avilable at the time, as distinct from information that has come to light since.

† One of these decrypts was a German police message. The source of the others cannot be traced, but the German Air Force general Enigma key was the most informative cypher at this stage. See Appendix 6.

1. CAB 101/126, Cabinet Office Historical Section paper on Yugoslavia, pp 1, 4.
2. L Woodward, *British Foreign Policy in the Second World War*, Vol III (1971), p 282.
3. CAB 101/126, p 5.
4. WO 208/2014, Enclosure 1a, 'Summary of events in Yugoslavia', p 1; Woodward, op cit, Vol III, p 282; CAB 121/676, SIC file F/Yugoslavia/3, COS (41) 626 of 13 October.

Whitehall accepted Mihailovic's claim in the belief that all the guerrilla groups could be brought together in a single resistance movement. The Foreign Office responded sympathetically to the Soviet suggestion that the best way of creating a diversion in Yugoslavia was to grant support to all groups irrespective of their political colour.[5]* A series of meetings between Mihailovic and Tito and their staffs took place in November 1941. But Hudson's report on this conference was not encouraging. Having previously reported that fighting had broken out between the two groups in Serbia, he now gave the first of many warnings that Tito's Partisans suspected that Mihailovic's Cetniks were collaborating with Nedic's government in Serbia and with other pro-Axis elements against them.[7]

Hudson's message, which reached London via Cairo on 13 November, was quickly followed by the first Axis winter offensive against the guerrillas. This dispersed both groups and severed British contacts with Yugoslavia.[8]† The resulting dearth of information from Yugoslavia was relieved only by GC and CS's high-grade Sigint, which from the spring of 1942 included decrypts from German Army and GAF area keys as well as from the GAF general key.‡ The decrypts by no means provided a comprehensive picture; but by showing that the Cetniks and the Partisans were fighting each other, and that the Cetniks were collaborating with the Italians and the Axis-controlled Croat state, they established that the fragile truce between Tito and Mihailovic had not survived the Axis offensive. At the end of December 1941 two decrypts showed that the Germans were keeping an anxious eye on Mihailovic's forces; and in April 1942 there were references to a German plan to capture him with a special unit trained in Serbia. In a decrypt dated 18 April, on the other hand, the German General, Zagreb reported that the Cetniks were negotiating with Croat elements, and on 30 May he added that 'the split between the Serbo-Nationalist elements

---

* In the summer of 1941 there had been British/Soviet/Yugoslav discussions in Istanbul about the possibility of sending a joint mission into Yugoslavia to try to heal the breach between the resistance movements. The scheme came to nothing, apparently because of objections by the Yugoslav government.[6]

† Hudson remained out of touch with Mihailovic until the spring of 1942 and was not able to re-establish W/T contact with Cairo till May. Mihailovic re-established contact with the Yugoslav government in London in January, when the King appointed him Minister for War.

‡ See Appendix 6.

5. Woodward, op cit, Vol III, p 282.
6. M Wheeler, *Britain and the War for Yugoslavia 1940–1943* (1980), p 95–96; J Amery, *Approach March* (1973), pp 259–260.
7. CAB 101/126, pp 5a–7; for Hudson's telegrams see WO 202/128; Deakin, *The Embattled Mountain* (1971), pp 135–142.
8. Woodward, op cit, Vol III, pp 284, 285; CAB 101/126, pp 9–10.

of the rebels and the Partisans is widening throughout Croatia' and that 'the former are more and more inclined to co-operate with the Croat government. . . .'. In the same signal he reported that the Italians continued to use Cetniks in operations against the Partisans. There had been several references in the decrypts since the beginning of May to collaboration between Cetniks and Italians.[9]

From the beginning of June 1942, on the basis of information supplied by the Partisans, the Soviet government drew the attention of the Foreign Office to its belief that Mihailovic's forces were collaborating with Nedic and the Italians. No doubt because Hudson had already made it, the Foreign Office was prepared to accept the charge insofar as it related to Nedic, and even to draw comfort from it: if true, it might indicate that Nedic was half-hearted in his support of the Axis. It dismissed the allegations of Cetnik collaboration with the Italians, distrusting their Partisan origins and being unable to suppress the suspicion that the Soviet government was sacrificing the immediate advantage of securing a united front among the guerrillas to its longer-term interest in establishing a Communist regime in Yugoslavia.[10] In doing so, it was unaware that Enigma decrypts had confirmed the allegations; until the autumn of 1943 it did not receive Enigma intelligence, though its Permanent Under-Secretary and its representative on the JIC were aware of its existence.*

In MI, which had seen the decrypts, neither they nor the Russian charges made any impact. In February 1942 MI had believed that the meetings between Mihailovic and Tito had produced 'a greater degree of co-ordination in the guerrilla movement as a whole'.[11] In June, when the Enigma had belied this view, it urged SOE Cairo to renew its attempts to settle the differences between Cetniks and Partisans,[12] and advised the Prime Minister and the CIGS that the existing policy of backing Mihailovic's efforts to curb 'the wilder elements' among the Partisans should be retained on military grounds. It argued, as Mihailovic had often claimed, that the wilder elements were an embarrassment to the Allies: by threatening political anarchy, they would drive more moderate opponents of the Axis into collaboration with the enemy and thus destroy the chances of establishing Allied control over the rebel movement and building up a serious threat to Germany's flank.[13] And in August, after

---

* See Volume II p 5. By the autumn of 1943, however, the Foreign Office was receiving a regular summary of the Service Enigma decrypts from 'C'.

9. CX/MSS495/T3, 564/T2, 575/T23, 903/T14, 911/T13, 1031/T14 and 16, 1033/T5, 1036/T8; WO 208/2014, Enclosure 19a.
10. CAB 101/126, pp 10–12; Woodward, op cit, Vol III, pp 285–289.
11. WO 208/2104, Enclosure 4b.   12. ibid, Minute 24 of 25 June 1942.
13. ibid, Enclosure 22a of 3 June 1942.

reviewing the intelligence evidence in the light of the Soviet allegations and of similar accusations then being broadcast by Free
Yugoslavia Radio, which was based in Russia, MI remained of the
same mind: Mihailovic was 'indubitably' the man to back.[14]

Following a meeting of all the interested authorities in Whitehall
at which the suggestion that contact should be made with Tito was
raised but not followed up, the Foreign Office had meanwhile, on
8 August, decided to launch further appeals to Mihailovic and the
Soviet government for help in establishing a settlement between the
Cetniks and the Partisans.[15] By then, however, Hudson's reports
had led SOE in Cairo to question existing policy. In the autumn of
1942 he claimed that several of Mihailovic's subordinates – Djurisic,
Bircanin, Jevdjevic, Djukanovic – were collaborating with the Italians against the Partisans; quoted Mihailovic as saying that he
hoped to negotiate a settlement with the Italians and eventually to
seize Italian arms; and while making it clear that he had not 'the
slightest evidence that Mihailovic himself had ever contacted Italians or Germans', hinted briefly that he might already have reached
a secret understanding with both.[16] On the strength of these reports,
and of others still more critical of Mihailovic from a Yugoslav officer
who had recently joined Hudson after failing to make contact with
the Partisans,[17] SOE Cairo warned London on 8 December that it
had to be concluded that all Mihailovic's bands in Montenegro,
Hercegovina and Dalmatia were 'legalised' by the Italians on the
understanding that they attacked the Partisans and left the Italians
undisturbed.[18]

The authorities in London did not dissent from this conclusion,
but were not deflected by it. The SOE, which was then replacing
Hudson with a more senior liaison officer, Colonel Bailey, noted
that Hudson had become so antipathetic to Mihailovic that he
would be driven before long to recommend that all support should
be directed to the Partisans.[19] MI, which had continued to assert
that inter-guerrilla conflicts were declining, argued with reference
to Cetnik collaboration with the Italians that it was understandable
that Mihailovic did not want to risk reprisals which would jeopardise his plans for 'perfecting his organisation against the day'.[20] On
19 December, as part of its preparations for the Casablanca conference, the JIC produced its first appreciation of the situation in

14.   ibid, Minutes 28 and 30 of 18 and 23 August 1942.
15.   Woodward, op cit, Vol III, pp 285–289.
16.   WO 202/356, in particular GESH 171 of 15 November, 195 of 23 November
      1942; Deakin, op cit, pp 152–153.   17.   CAB 101/126, pp 9, 12.
18.   WO 202/356, Cairo telegram to London B1 3192 of 8 December 1942.
19.   CAB 101/126, p 12.
20.   WO 208/2014, Minutes 31 to 15 September, 33 of 18 October, 35 of 21
      November, 37 of 17 December 1942.

Yugoslavia; with the advice of MI, this concluded that support for the resistance movement should be concentrated on Serbia and Montenegro, where 'General Mihailovic already has an organisation'.[21]

It need not be doubted that these endorsements of existing policy stemmed mainly from political and military considerations – the political preference for Mihailovic as against Tito and the belief that Mihailovic's policy of keeping his forces in being suited Allied military requirements so long as Allied strategic plans for the Mediterranean remained unsettled. But MI may also have been influenced by the high-grade Sigint. During the last three months of 1942, while disclosing that Communist-led guerrilla activity was increasing,[22] the decrypts, which included Abwehr Enigma decrypts from October,* sometimes cast doubt on the argument that Mihailovic's forces were doing no fighting at all. In September, for example, when sections of the European Press were claiming that the Partisans had captured Foca, a town south-east of Sarajevo, the Enigma had attributed the achievement to the Cetniks.[23] More important, the decrypts had shown that the Germans increasingly disliked what they learned of Cetnik-Italian collaboration, suspecting a secret understanding between the two, and that far from collaborating with the Cetniks themselves, they remained determined to eliminate Mihailovic's organisation.[24]

At the end of January 1943 SOE Cairo opened a new stage in the debate by giving a paper to the Prime Minister during his visit to the Middle East. The paper was based on the latest reports from the mission with Mihailovic and on Cairo's decrypts of German medium-grade and low-grade hand cyphers, chiefly of those used by the Abwehr and the Police.[25]† It accepted that there was no

---

* See Appendix 6, p 502.

† The SIS objected to the dissemination of decrypts of Abwehr traffic to or in Cairo until after the arrival of an officer to set up the necessary organisation. This meant that although CBME had increasing success on the Abwehr material from May 1941 the results were sent only to GC and CS until about the middle of 1942 when local dissemination of decrypts to the SIS was authorised. At the same time material from the decrypts of Abwehr traffic made at GC and CS was incorporated in GC and CS's SCU/SLU signals (see Volume I Appendix 13) to the Middle East and Mediterranean HQs. Copies of the local decrypts would not normally have been available to SOE in Cairo, but between January and May 1943 they were seen by two officers under restrictions imposed by SOE's Chief of Staff in Cairo and used solely in connection with planning the first operations to contact the Partisans. The Chief of Staff is said to have remained on the circulation list for the decrypts fortuitously after leaving a previous appointment in MI 14. For further details about the nature of the decrypts see Appendix 6.

21. JIC (42) 507 (0) of 19 December.
22. CX/MSS/1350/T2, 1352/T11, 1374/T1; ZTPI 24039, 24040.
23. WO 208/2104, Minute 31 of 15 September 1942; CX/MSS/1350/T12.
24. CX/MSS/1559 para 37, 1546 para 18.
25. P Auty and R Clogg (eds), *British Policy towards Wartime Resistance in Yugoslavia and Greece* (1975), pp 210–214; Deakin, op cit, pp 185–186, 197.

evidence from these sources that Mihailovic was collaborating with the Germans. As for his collaboration with the Italians, it repeated that his subordinates had concluded local arrangements which amounted to a mutual non-aggression pact and an agreement to co-operate against the Partisans, but recognised the force of his own motives. He was determined to conserve Serb manpower not only for advantage in the future political struggle with other Yugoslav groups, but also because he wanted to be able to assemble an effective military force at the right moment; in particular, he clearly hoped to acquire the equipment of the six Italian divisions in Montenegro when that moment came. At the same time, SOE Cairo's report pointed out that of the 40 Axis divisions in Yugoslavia (of which 6 were German and 19 Italian), Mihailovic's forces were holding down only 9 (3 German and 6 Bulgarian), and stressed that the resistance movement in Croatia and Slovenia that was holding down the rest of the Axis divisions could not be of real military value to the Allies unless it was supplied independently of the programme of aid to Mihailovic's forces.[26]

MI's order of battle calculations did not wholly agree with SOE's; in its estimation, there were about 17 Axis divisions in the Partisan areas and 14 in Mihailovic's at the beginning of 1943.[27] But it is noticeable that although SOE Cairo had not yet suggested that aid to Mihailovic should be stopped – only that aid to Tito should begin – discussion in Whitehall was increasingly concerned from February 1943 with the question whether or not to break with Mihailovic completely, and the explanation is to be found in the fact that developments in the Mediterranean, combined with the evidence that the Partisans were a more effective military force, were lending persuasiveness to the military argument for aiding the Partisans. This is indicated by the change which took place in MI's response to the Sigint evidence. Receiving from the Enigma decrypts confirmation that the Cetniks operating under Italian auspices were fighting the Partisans, it commented in distinctly defensive terms, saying that there was no case for breaking with Mihailovic since, if the Germans replaced the Italians in Montenegro and Dalmatia, Mihailovic would fight them rather than persist in the 'degrading' policy of collaboration against the Partisans, but adding that 'while it is not perhaps true that these Cetniks are actually fighting for the Germans, there is no doubt that the latter recognise and ultimately regulate their activities'. Sigint also disclosed that the Axis was mounting an offensive against the Partisans in the Mostar area,*

---

* See below, p 146.

26.   CAB 121/676, COS (43) 44 of 11 February (B1/2/134/78 of 30 January).
27.   WO 106/5689A, MI 3(b) Appreciation of 19 February 1943.

and the possibility that this would reduce Partisan activity against the Axis provided MI with another argument for maintaining support for the Cetniks: otherwise, in the event that the Partisans were dispersed, the Allies would be left without local support of any kind.[28] But this reasoning was, to say the least, half-hearted, as the operations staff at the War Office (MO 5) recognised on 21 February, when it summed up as follows: 'The argument in favour of supporting Mihailovic thus depends mainly on sabotage and similar action, which he is in a better position to carry out. That in favour of the Partisans on actual guerrilla action against the enemy'.[29] Nor were the Foreign Office and SOE London much more positive in support of Mihailovic. The Foreign Office agreed with MI that it would be a mistake to drop Mihailovic, since he controlled Serbia, but was nevertheless inclined to think that contact should be made with the Partisans.[30] SOE London argued that he should continue to receive supplies at least until there was good and sufficient cause for extending support to other elements in Yugoslavia.[31]

On 4 March the Chiefs of Staff concluded that 'on balance, taking the long view', the better military alternative was to continue to back Mihailovic; 'he would provide some organisation and control whereas under the Partisans chaos would probably ensue when the Axis forces were defeated.'[32] By then, however, under the influence of further unfavourable reports from SOE missions in the Cetnik areas, SOE Cairo was coming to the conclusion that Mihailovic ought to be abandoned,[33] and in London the arguments in his defence were becoming still weaker. By 17 March MI was so bewildered in its efforts to follow the course of the continuing Axis operations against the guerrillas, on which it was receiving a lot of high-grade Sigint*, that it could not decide whether the better course was to break with Mihailovic or to stay with him; the only thing that was clear was that 'the hands of all are against the Partisans.'[34] The Foreign Office remained sceptical towards the criticism of Mihailovic by the missions attached to him, but it also felt that Bailey, who was claiming that the Partisans were losing influence, was in no position to judge that.[35] It was supported by 'C', who could not reconcile the claim with reports of pro-Partisan

---

* See below, p 144 et seq.

28. ibid, Appreciations of 15 and 19 February 1943.
29. ibid, MO 5 note of 21 February 1943.
30. Woodward, op cit, Vol III, p 290.   31. CAB 101/126, pp 16–17, 23.
32. CAB 121/676, COS (43) 34th (o) Meeting, 4 March.
33. CAB 101/126, pp 19–23.
34. WO 208/2019, Minute 15 of 17 March 1943.
35. Woodward, op cit, Vol III, pp 289–290; CAB 101/126, pp 14–16, 25.

and anti-Mihailovic feeling that he was receiving from all areas.[36]* The Prime Minister put in a good word, if an ambivalent one, for Mihailovic: perhaps on the strength of Mihailovic's interest in eventually acquiring their arms, he thought Mihailovic was double-crossing the Italians.[37]

The outcome of this uncertainty was that by the end of March 1943 the government had decided to send officers from Cairo to contact the Partisans in Croatia and Slovenia and to defer the question whether to give support to Tito until they had reported.[38]

□

This decision followed upon a considerable increase in Axis, and more particularly in German, involvement against the Partisans, and was accompanied by firm evidence of preparations for a still more determined offensive against both of the resistance movements. The evidence came mainly from the German high-grade Sigint.† The sole reliable guide to enemy resources and intentions, this had steadily increased in volume since the autumn of 1942 and was now becoming prolific as the German armed forces intensified their activities in an area where, in the absence of landlines, they relied entirely on W/T for their signals.

Until the autumn of 1942 Sigint, though limited in amount and by no means giving a comprehensive account of the situation in south-eastern Europe, was nevertheless useful as a reliable check on information supplied by other sources. It helped to establish that three Italian Armies, in Slovenia – Dalmatia, in Albania – Montenegro and in Greece, comprised a total of 28 divisions (24 of them infantry divisions) in October 1941, and that these divisions had risen to between 30 and 32 in number by September 1942. For the German forces in Serbia, Croatia and Greece, organised under C-in-C South East at Twelfth Army HQ in Athens until the creation of Army Group E at Salonika in the autumn of 1942, the Enigma

---

* The reports were not being supplied by the SIS (see below, note †) and their source is not mentioned; they were presumably the Abwehr and German police decrypts.

† The SIS played little part in developments in Yugoslavia. Not much of the SIS and SOE stay-behind networks survived the coup of March 1941, and the SIS's attempts to build up a new one were frustrated by the competing demands of the SOE for the limited transport available. The SIS established a Yugoslav section in Italy after the Allied landings there, but was even then unable to recruit agents who were independent of the resistance organisations. Although the SOE liaison missions in Yugoslavia regularly submitted reports on Axis order of battle and military operations these were not usually received as promptly as the Sigint, nor were they always accurate or sufficiently definite to be useful for Allied operations.

36. CAB 101/126, pp 17–18.
37. Woodward, op cit, Vol III, p 291.   38. ibid, p 290.

provided frequent, though not continuous, divisional identifications and locations; these included an almost complete divisional order of battle for Yugoslavia in November 1941, when there were four infantry divisions in Serbia, one on the Serbo-Croat frontier and one in Belgrade. By the autumn of 1942 it was clear from the combination of Sigint with reports from other sources that of a total of seven divisions under C-in-C South East, only one of which was of first-class quality, one SS Division and four infantry divisions were in Yugoslavia.[39] The detailed dispositions of these German divisions illustrated Germany's policy of treating the Croatian government as an ally, as did Sigint's disclosure of the role of the German General, Zagreb in developing the Croatian Army, and the decrypts established the strength of that army and threw some light of the activities of the Ustasa, the Croatian government's political troops.[40]

Throughout the period to the autumn of 1942 Sigint provided regular information about the railway sabotage carried out by the guerrillas in both the German and the Italian zones of Yugoslavia, as also in Greece, conveying clearly the Axis feeling that such action presented an insoluble problem.[41] It also gave a reasonably full account of the German effort to crush the guerrillas in Serbia in the last two months of 1941; and from May 1942, after showing that the situation in Croatia had deteriorated since the beginning of the year, it covered in still greater detail the operations carried out by German, Italian and Croatian forces in the Foca area. The decrypts revealed that this area was still not pacified in July, when the Germans feared a threat to the Sarajevo – Mostar railway and were critical of Italian inaction because the bauxite mines at Mostar, though lying in the Italian area of control, were of crucial importance for the German economy;[42] they showed, indeed, that this problem continued to worry the Germans until they occupied the area in March 1943[43].

From the autumn of 1942 the army Enigma decrypts disclosed a steady increase in the number of German divisions in the Balkans: the total reached fifteen by June and sixteen by August 1943, about one additional division a month having reached Yugoslavia and the number in Greece having risen to five.* Although the enemy was obviously unwilling or unable to send first-class troops to the area, it was evident that he was also improving the quality of the occupying forces; garrison-type divisions had been upgraded to infantry

---

* For the actual totals see above, p 11.
39. eg CX/MSS/126 para 20, 406 para 9, 410 para 4, 1384 para 26.
40. eg CX/MSS/919 paras 25–26, 1176 para 52, 1333 paras 48, 49.
41. eg CX/MSS/1356/T25.
42. CX/MSS/1250/T13, 1350/T2, 1588 para 29.
43. CX/MSS/1421, para 46, 1477 para 33, 1986 para 36.

divisions by March 1943.[44] It was also evident that the reinforcements were being made not only in response to the fear of Allied action* but also because of the need to take action against the increase in guerrilla activities in Yugoslavia. The Sigint provided detailed coverage of three main Axis operations carried out against the guerrillas in the first half of 1943. Of these operations, the first two, *Weiss I* and *II*, involved four German and three Italian divisions and were directed mainly against the Partisans. The decrypts showed that *Weiss I* in January 1943 was not a marked success and that *Weiss II*, carried out against a new threat to the bauxite mines in the Mostar area in February and the first half of March, was also inconclusive.[45] In the third operation (*Schwarz*), which involved five German and three Italian divisions and was launched on 15 May, the Germans set out to annihilate Mihailovic's forces before resuming the offensive against the Partisans; the decrypts revealed that they failed to catch Mihailovic himself (though taking many Cetnik prisoners) or to prevent Tito's forces from withdrawing to the north and regrouping in Bosnia.[46]

In the course of these operations the Enigma left no doubt that the fighting value of the Cetniks was greatly inferior to that of Tito's Partisans. This was particularly marked during operation *Schwarz*; in the middle of June the German C-in-C South East reported that since 15 May his forces had captured 3,050 Cetniks and killed 15 as compared with 5,697 Partisans killed and 1,150 taken prisoner.[47]† But the Enigma decrypts contained no evidence of Cetnik collaboration with the Germans. On the contrary, they showed that though the Germans had long been aware of the existence of complex rivalries between Mihailovic and non-Mihailovic factions among the Cetniks,[49] they were becoming increasingly alarmed about the collaboration of Mihailovic's forces with the Italians – and so much so that when planning Operation *Schwarz* they were determined to override Italian objections to the rounding-up and disarming of Mihailovic's bands. They initially insisted in the face of Italian opposition that all Cetniks should be rounded up and on Hitler's orders took measures to withhold the plan from the Italians for as long as possible. In reply to Italian demands for exemption

---

* For details of Axis assessments of Allied intentions see above, pp 77–78.

† The decrypt of the C-in-C's final report on *Schwarz* gives Cetnik casualties as 17 killed and 3,764 captured; of the Partisans' losses of 12–13,000, counted dead totalled 7,489, estimated dead 3,000 and dead from hunger and disease 1–2,000.[48]

44. WO 208/3573, MI 14 Appreciation of 14 June 1943.
45. JIC (43) 285 (o) of 3 August.   46. ibid.
47. DEFE 3/822, ML 5054 of 23 June 1943.
48. Dir/C Archive, 3634 of 24 June 1943; CX/MSS/2782/T21.
49. eg CX/MSS/495 para 27, 1384 para 24.

at least for Cetniks outside the fighting area, they then warned the Italians that they had Sigint evidence that the Cetniks were playing off Germany against Italy and instructed their own forces that 'no Cetnik formations whose leaders were proved to be in touch with Mihailovic are to be spared'.[50] The Prime Minister was given a summary of this intelligence on 17 March after he had expressed interest in a Japanese diplomatic decrypt of 11 March which had similarly referred to Gemany's dislike of the Italian attitude to Mihailovic's forces and to her wish to disarm them without delay.[51]

The grounds for the anxiety of the Germans were not in doubt. They were fully aware that they were meeting with greater resistance from the Partisans* but they also realised that they might soon be having to disarm the Italians themselves and that the links between the Italians and the Cetniks would then increase their problems. It was known from the Enigma that the Germans were decrypting Cetnik signals† which disclosed Mihailovic's interest in eventually turning Italian arms against the Germans and his anxiety lest the Italians should turn against the Cetniks, as well as the fact that in the spring, as a result of a general fear among the Cetniks that they would be at the mercy of the Germans if the Partisans were defeated, he had limited his attacks on the Partisans in the hope that Tito would keep the Germans fully occupied.[53] During operation *Weiss II* an Enigma signal had referred to 'the menacing consequences' of the Italian wish to use Cetnik forces against the Partisans in the bauxite area near Mostar, and in yet another decrypt the German C-in-C South East had informed the GOC Second Italian Army that he had been ordered by the German Supreme Command to treat the Cetniks as enemies.[54] Although MI realised that the German disquiet about Italian-Cetnik relations and the German decision to act against the Cetniks in operation *Schwarz* were closely connected, it could not yet know that *Schwarz* was to be the last offensive before the Italian capitulation. But Sigint was soon to

---

* An Abwehr decrypt suggested that as late as June 1943 uncertainty as to Tito's identity remained. But the puppet Croatian authorities had identified him correctly by April 1943 and parts of his police file also appeared in the Axis Press at that time.[52]

† For Enigma evidence that the Germans were also decrypting the Partisan signals, see below, p 164 n*.

50. CX/MSS/1564 para 18, 2256/T10, 2574 para 6, 2597/T8, 2627 para 11, 2750 para 7; WO 208/2019, Minute 13 of 14 March 1943.
51. Dir/C Archive, 2604 of 17 March 1943.
52. Deakin, op cit, p 206 fn.
53. CX/MSS/2152 para 18, 2256/T10, 2262/T2; WO 202/2019, Minute 13 of 14 March 1943.
54. CX/MSS/2228/T9; WO 208/2019, Minutes 10 and 11 of 5 and 10 March 1943.

disclose that, having prepared for the contingency of an Italian collapse, Germany had with a minimum of troop transfers into Yugoslavia put herself in a position to deal with it by stationing forces within striking distance of the vital coastal area and of almost all the Italian divisions they would have to disarm.*

☐

It had been obvious when Whitehall decided to send officers to contact the Partisans that one result might be to deepen Mihailovic's hostility to them and produce a civil war. The JIC, referring to this as 'the principal Allied difficulty', had warned that, should Mihailovic succeed in seizing Italian arms, he might try to exterminate Tito's forces. But it had also believed that his followers were 'entirely anti-German', though collaborating with Italy, and that Croats who were with the Partisans might be expected to join him if he acquired Italian arms, and had therefore concluded that there was a reasonable chance that, having also made contact with Tito, the Allies might finally persuade the two men to sink their differences and operate together against the Germans when Italy collapsed.[55]

This expectation was severely shaken after the conclusion of Operation *Weiss II*. The fighting, moving into Hercegovina, then took place mainly between the rival resistance organisations, and by the end of April the Enigma decrypts and Bailey's reports had left MI in no doubt that Mihailovic's forces had suffered a major reverse.[56] With the launching of Operation *Schwarz* the prospects of reconciling the Cetniks and the Partisans declined further, and so much so that on 26 May, arguing that the poor performance of Mihailovic's forces in resisting the latest Axis offensive against the guerrillas had confirmed that he was a spent force even in Serbia, the Middle East Defence Committee ordered him to break with the Axis and withdraw into Serbia, leaving the non-Serbian lands in the hands of the Partisans.[57]

The Foreign Office and SOE London protested against this action, denying that Mihailovic was a spent force. They argued that he had 20,000 men in Serbia and 150,000 mobilisable but admittedly unarmed in other areas, and pointed out that while the Partisans must have some 65,000 men, their main body was threatened with

---

* For the German preparations against an Italian collapse (Operation *Achse*) see below p 156 and above, pp 11–12.

55. JIC (43) 115 of 22 March.
56. WO 208/2019, Enclosure 9a (map of fighting based on 'Most Secret Sources'), Minutes 5 of 25 March, 8 and 9 of 23 and 24 April 1943.
57. Woodward, op cit, Vol III, pp 292–293.

encirclement by the Germans.[58] The Chiefs of Staff, briefed by MI, defended the Middle East Defence Committee's action, agreeing with the Committee that resistance to the Axis must be the 'paramount consideration'.[59] MI was impressed by the initial reports from the first officers sent to the Partisans, which indicated that Mihailovic's authority was now restricted to Serbia. As the Chiefs of Staff told the Foreign Office, MI had also concluded from 'Most Secret Sources' that it was the well-organised Partisans who had held down the enemy in the recent fighting and that the Cetniks were 'hopelessly compromised in relations with the Axis'.[60]

At the end of June 1943 this dispute ended in a compromise incorporating another step in Tito's favour. The Middle East Defence Committee withdrew its ultimatum to Mihailovic, but the Foreign Office conceded that the Partisans might be given arms on condition that they did not use them against Mihailovic's forces.[61] This concession was followed in July by the appointment of a mission headed by Brigadier Fitzroy Maclean to Tito's headquarters; at the same time Brigadier Armstrong was appointed to join Bailey at Mihailovic's HQ, to take charge of military relations, Bailey remaining until January 1944 as political adviser.[62] Maclean arrived in Yugoslavia on the night of 17–18 September and before submitting his comprehensive report, which reached the Foreign Office on 12 November,* kept Whitehall and Cairo informed of his immediate reactions to the situation in the areas in which the Partisans were operating. At the same time the liaison officers with Mihailovic and with his local commanders pressed for more active measures against Germany, and the new policy of supporting both sides and hoping to persuade them to stop fighting each other escaped revision. But in this interval evidence accumulated to the effect that the Cetniks were collaborating with the Germans and that they were losing power relative to the Partisans.

Captain Deakin, the officer appointed in the spring of 1943 to contact Tito's HQ, had arrived at the height of Operation *Schwarz*, on 28 May. By the summer he had acquired much evidence of Cetnik collaboration with the Germans, as well as with the Italians,

---

* See below, p 153.

58.   CAB 121/676, COS (43) 175 of 15 June, COS (43) 336 (o) of 23 June, Annex
       1 (letter to PM 18 June 1943).
59.   ibid, COS (43) 128th (o) Meeting, 17 June, Annex IV.
60.   ibid, loc cit; WO 208/2026, MI 3(b) Minute 14 of 28 May, DMI minute to
       CIGS, 4 June 1943.
61.   Woodward, op cit, Vol III, pp 293–294; Howard, *Grand Strategy*, Vol IV
       (1972), pp 481–483.
62.   Woodward, op cit, Vol III, p 299.

from Cetnik prisoners and captured documents in Partisan hands. At the end of August he summed it up in a report to the effect that collaboration with Germany had been 'close, constant and increasing' over the past two years.[63] Thereafter, the missions to the Partisans reported that the collaboration was continuing in various areas.[64] After the launching of Operation *Schwarz* in the middle of May, moreover, Cairo's decrypts of the Abwehr and Police traffic had indicated that some Cetnik leaders were working with the Germans or offering to do so.[65] By the end of September the SOE in Cairo had concluded on the basis of this local intelligence that the Cetniks were definitely collaborating with the Germans in Hercegovina and the parts of Dalmatia and Montenegro immediately bordering it, that elsewhere in Montenegro their attitude remained uncertain and that in the Sandjak they were still anti-German.[66] As to Mihailovic's own complicity, however, the local sources were not conclusive. The captured documents had included one which purported to be instructions from him to his commanders to stop fighting the Partisans and liaising with the Germans, and to prepare to assist possible Allied landings, from 27 September.[67] But it was recognised that his links with his commanders were not close,[68] and while the decrypts had included a report to the effect that one of the collaborating Cetnik bands had declared that it was unconnected with him,[69] it was known from reports from the field that some Cetniks were fighting the Germans.[70]

There was further ground for uncertainty on this point. The Enigma traffic decrypted at GC and CS, far from providing evidence of Cetnik-German collaboration,* continued to leave no doubt that

---

* Only two Enigma decrypts referred to collaboration before November 1943. The first was a signal in March 1943 from the German Intelligence Branch (Fremde Heere Ost) reporting that an agent had claimed that contacts existed between Mihailovic and German troops in Hercegovina and asking C-in-C South East whether the matter should be followed up. GC and CS had not decrypted a reply from the C-in-C.[71] The second, distributed by GC and CS on 29 August, was a signal probably from the German liaison officer with Italian VI

63. -WO 202/297A, B1/304/821.
64. eg WO 202/135, B1/51/302 and 355 of 17 and 30 September 1943.
65. WO 202/132A Part III, Undated (? Dec 1943) review of Most Secret Sources; WO 202/162, reviews of 19 and 23 September 1943.
66. WO 202/162, reviews of 19, 23, 24 and 28 September 1943; WO 202/132A Part III, review of MSS ? Dec 1943.
67. WO 202/141, Addendum to report on Cetnik collaboration, 4 September 1943; WO 202/135, B1/51/166 of 12 August, B1/51/262 of 9 September 1943.
68. WO 202/297A, Message 108 of 23 August 1943; F Maclean, *Disputed Barricade* (1957), p 263.
69. WO 202/132A Part III.
70. WO 202/2026, Minute 21 of 9 September 1943; WO 202/135, B1/51/227 of 29 August 1943.
71. CX/MSS/2250/T10.

at least at the highest level the Germans remained set on Mihailovic's destruction. In July Hitler had suggested that the C-in-C South East should put a higher price on the heads of Mihailovic and Tito.[75]† In August, amid growing rumours of the imminent withdrawal of the Italian divisions, it was learned that the Abwehr had warned Berlin from Dubrovnik that the Cetniks were thirsting for revenge on German troops, and the C-in-C South East had complained that he did not have enough forces to engage the Cetnik bands.[76] In September the Enigma showed that the Germans had arrested the staffs at Mihailovic's HQs in Croatia, Slovenia, Baranja, Backa and the Banat at the outset of the campaign to disarm the Italian forces (Operation *Achse*).[77] On 1 October an Abwehr decrypt drew attention to the danger that if the Cetniks took over the arms of the Italian Venezia Division Germany's hold over the whole of the southern Sandjak would become untenable. Towards the end of September the decrypt of a telegram to the German diplomatic missions threw further light on Germany's attitude; in what Ribbentrop described as a satisfactory meeting with Nedic on 18 September Ribbentrop had spoken of the 'traitorous machinations' of Mihailovic, which would hand over the Serbs to the Bolsheviks, and Nedic had expressed his determination to fight Mihailovic as well as Tito.[78]

On the strength of this intelligence MI was still unconvinced at the end of September, as was the Foreign Office, that Mihailovic was himself involved in the collaboration with Germany; both accepted, moreover, that he considered his policy of collaboration with Italy and opposition to the Partisans to be justified and both felt that Tito, while deserving support on military grounds, was politically dangerous.[79] For these reasons the general view in Whitehall was that there was no alternative to the policy of supporting

---

Corps. It claimed that Jevdjedic, who was in charge of Cetnik formations with Italian VI Corps, was ready to work with the Germans against the Partisans even if they would not conclude a formal agreement with him; it added that 'Mihailovic and Nedic are of the same opinion'.[72] But Jevdjedic was not then in communication with Mihailovic, with whom he had had differences. In September the Sigint provided by CBME showed that Jevdjedic was in contact with the German military authorities in Zagreb and with the Abwehr, and was to be introduced to the Sicherheitsdienst.[73] In November Mihailovic, who remained in contact with the Allies, claimed that he had not been in touch with Jevdjedic for months.[74]

† In July posters offering 100,000 gold marks for either man dead or alive were put up throughout Serbia.

72. DEFE 3/573, CX/MSS/C 181.
73. WO 202/162 of 23 September and WO 202/132A Part III.
74. WO 106/5690, Stevenson telegram to FO, No 116 of 27 November 1943.
75. CX/MSS/2905/T8.   76. CX/MSS/3045 para 17.
77. DEFE 3/573, CX/MSS/C 181.
78. Dir/C Archive, 4464 of 26 September 1943.
79. WO 208/2026, Minute 22 of 28 September 1943; Woodward, op cit, Vol III, pp 297–298.

both sides and trying to persuade them to stop fighting each other. The Chiefs of Staff in the second week of October agreed with the Prime Minister that SOE should meet a recent appeal from Mihailovic for more rifles, feeling that, though less active than Tito, Mihailovic had been 'showing good form' and still deserved support.[80] But the contrast between the limited sabotage activities carried out by his forces and the more extensive operations of the Partisans had been increasing. Already in the middle of August, on learning that the SOE in Cairo was minded to recommend that relations with Mihailovic should be broken off and all support switched to the Partisans, MI had advised the CIGS that it could but approve of this course in view of Mihailovic's 'consistently unsatisfactory attitude'.[81] During September MI had been impressed by the energy shown by the Partisans in exploiting the Italian collapse.[82]* And from the middle of October opinion in MI and in SOE London [83] hardened against Mihailovic on military grounds.

By 20 October MI had learned from the Enigma that a German thrust to clear the southern Sandjak had forced the Cetniks to retreat.[84] Between then and 4 November it saw decrypts in which the intelligence staff of the C-in-C South East appreciated that since the start of the expected fighting between the Cetniks and the Partisans, 'under the personal guidance of Mihailovic and Stab Tito', Tito had made a decisive advance and Mihailovic had suffered a severe pyschological defeat.[85] Commenting on this fighting on 1 November MI noted without disapproval that the Partisans were carrying out operations against the Cetniks apparently with the object of liquidating them in Montenegro and the Sandjak before extending their own control into Serbia; it also noted that Tito, unlike Mihailovic, was succeeding in persuading Serbs and Croats to fight side by side.[86] On 3 November the DMI, who regularly submitted the Sigint evidence together with illustrative maps to the CIGS, remarked in a covering note to the latest instalment that if the Partisans were to keep up their pressure on the Germans the

---

* See below, p 157.

80. CAB 121/531, SIC File F/Balkans/4, GHQ ME Cositrep No 20 of 10 October, PM to COS 11 October, COS (43) 246th (o) Meeting and Minute of 12 October.
81. WO 208/2026, Minutes 19 and 20 of 14 and 16 August 1943.
82. ibid, Minute 22 of 28 September 1943.
83. CAB 121/531, COS (43) 626 (o) of 14 October, Annex and Appendix A.
84. DEFE 3/886, JP 7590 of 20 October 1943.
85. DEFE 3/888, JP 8899 of 4 November 1943.
86. WO 208/2026, Minute 24 of 1 November 1943.

need to supply them would become increasingly important.[87] Nor was it long before the same message began to reach Whitehall from other quarters.

In the middle of November the liaison officers with Mihailovic reported that they had failed in their attempts to persuade him to take more active measures against the German lines of communication; and they recommended that the British authorities should either try to remove him from the leadership of the Cetnik movement or abandon the movement altogether.[88] On 20 November, Mr Ralph Stevenson, the British Ambassador accredited to the Yugoslav government, which was based in Cairo from mid-September 1943, drew the Foreign Office's attention to the news that in the last six weeks the Germans had moved 1st Panzer Division from Greece to Russia over railways passing through Mihailovic-held territory.[89]* A few days earlier Maclean's report on his mission to Tito had reached Whitehall. He recommended that support for Mihailovic should be discontinued and aid to Tito increased, and did so on operational and political grounds. The Partisans were a well-organised force of 200,000 men; except in Old Serbia and Montenegro, they had liberated large areas from the enemy and established effective political control; they exercised power on overwhelmingly Communist lines; but their strength was such that nothing less than large-scale Allied military intervention could prevent them from taking over the country when the Germans withdrew. Mihailovic, in contrast, had no chance of uniting the country; his strongly reactionary pan-Serb policy was discredited, and the Partisans had so much evidence that his forces were collaborating with the Germans, as previously with the Italians, that they regarded him as a traitor.[91]

Maclean's report did not quote this evidence or waste time on the question of Mihailovic's complicity. His conclusion was that Mihailovic 'may possibly deny that he himself has acted in direct collaboration with the enemy, but he cannot deny the active and open collaboration of many of his principal commanders, of which there is irrefutable evidence'. And for this conclusion, at least, there was now no lack of evidence in London. At the end of October

---

* Enigma decrypts, which had located 1st Panzer Division in Macedonia on 17 October, had reported its arrival on the Russian front by 24 October.[90]

87. WO 208/2015, Minute 26 of 3 November 1943.
88. CAB 101/126, p 44.
89. CAB 121/531, Stevenson telegram to FO No 103 of 20 November 1943.
90. DEFE 3/885, JP 7432 of 18 October 1943.
91. CAB 121/531, JIC (43) 474 (o) of 17 November; Woodward, op cit, Vol III, pp 296–297.

Stevenson had informed the Foreign Office that, while Mihailovic himself remained 'on the extreme edge of his forces', Cairo was still receiving reports of collaboration with the Axis from all areas except Serbia.[92] The liaison officers with the Partisans had for some weeks been reporting that Cetnik units were assisting the Bulgarian forces in Serbia, mobilising under Djuic in support of the Germans in Croatia, receiving arms from the Germans in Bosnia and operating under Djuric in south Serbia alongside Nedic's forces.[93] Since the middle of November, moreover, there had been indications that Mihailovic was himself involved. On 20 November the Foreign Office had been warned by Stevenson that it was being rumoured that Mihailovic had instructed Djuric to collaborate with Nedic, but that Djuric and the majority of his men were refusing to obey unless ordered to do so by the King.[94] More important – for in the middle of November Mihailovic had already denied the 'base lie' that he had reached an agreement with Nedic,[95] and Stevenson was still checking the latest rumour with the liaison officers at Mihailovic's headquarters – the C-in-C Middle East had advised the CIGS on 14 November of a development which, in his view, called for a change of policy by the Foreign Office. The material decrypted by CBME had disclosed that at the end of October Mihailovic had ordered all Cetnik units to co-operate with Germany against the Partisans, and there were indications in the decrypts and from captured documents supplied by the Partisans that the Germans were making overtures to Mihailovic's representatives in the belief that the order had had the approval of the Yugoslav government.[96] Finally, GC and CS's Abwehr decrypts, while they still threw no light on Mihailovic's attitude,* had indicated that the German attitude towards collaboration with the Cetniks was changing. In a decrypt of 7 November the Abwehr in Belgrade had protested

---

* Except that one decrypt of 19 November perhaps illustrated his declining faith in British support. This showed that Army Group F had intercepted a signal from Mihailovic on 12 November ordering fires to burn on the hills throughout the night of 25 November in the shape of the word 'America'. Army Group F's message instructed the German forces not to interfere with this 'good means of diverting Bolshevik hopes'.[97]

92.   CAB 121/531, Stevenson to FO No 34 of 28 October 1943.
93.   WO 202/135, B1/51/355 of 30 September, B1/51/543 of 16 November 1943; WO 204/967, No 64 of 13 November 1943; WO 204/968, Nos 65 of 20 November, 67 of 4 December 1943; CAB 80/42, COS (43) 301 (220th résumé of 18 November) para 33.
94.   CAB 121/531, Stevenson telegrams to FO, Nos 102 and 103 of 20 November 1943.
95.   WO 106/5690, Stevenson to FO, No 136 of 1 December; WO 106/5692, No 142 of 4 December 1943.
96.   CAB 121/531, GAD/CO 625 of 14 November 1943.
97.   CX/MSS/T9/43.

against an order to collect 'well-disposed' Cetniks and employ them against the Partisans; this would be prejudicial to current military operations. On 12 November, on the other hand, the Abwehr had reported that, as a result of the infiltration of the Partisans and of 'the well-known fact' that the Balkans were to become a Soviet sphere of influence, the Cetniks in Montenegro were 'strongly interested on Germany's behalf'. And by 22 November another Abwehr decrypt had disclosed that the German C-in-C South East had signed a secret treaty with Lukacevic, commander of a Cetnik HQ in Montenegro, covering a cease-fire in the Uzice area, west of Sarajevo, as a preliminary to joint action against the Partisans. This decrypt was sent to Cairo – where the Allied conference was in progress – with a comment from 'C' that there was no evidence that Mihailovic himself was involved but that it was very possible he was conniving in the arrangement.[98]*

In the course of the discussions about Maclean's report, the JIC and the Foreign Office took somewhat different views of this evidence about collaboration. The JIC, accepting Maclean's assessment of the military strength and effectiveness of the Partisans, agreed that aid to them should be increased – and added that unless it was increased as a matter of urgency 'the German hold on Yugoslavia may become so effective as to enable the Germans even to reduce their garrisons'. It also agreed that supplies to Mihailovic should be discontinued in view of the fact that he was 'encouraging or, at best, failing to prevent' collaboration between his forces and the enemy; and in support of this argument it referred to the rumour about Djuric and the decrypts about Lukacevic as part of the 'increasing evidence that he is collaborating with the Germans or that his control over his commanders is so weak that he cannot control them'.[100] The Foreign Office accepted that the political and military strength of Tito's forces was growing and conceded that Mihailovic was handicapped by his anti-Partisan stance; it thus abandoned the hope that the two men could be reconciled. But it insisted that there was no proof that Mihailovic had ordered collaboration with Germany or was even conniving in the activities of his subordinates – indeed, it regarded the decrypt about Lukacevic as the first reliable evidence that collaboration was even taking place.[101]

---

* It was learned after the war that the C-in-C South East had concluded by 1 November that Tito's forces had to be treated as a full military threat and not merely as insurgents, and that it was more important to defeat them than to prepare against the less likely threat of an Allied landing; and that OKW had agreed with this assessment on 10 November.[99]

98. Dir/C Archive, of 24 November 1943.
99. Molony, *The Mediterranean and Middle East*, Vol V (1973), p 568.
100. CAB 121/531 JIC (43) 488 (o) of 25 November.
101. Woodward, op cit, Vol III, p 298 fn.

On this account, and also because it believed that Maclean had under-estimated the personal following Mihailovic still enjoyed in Serbia, it was unwilling to break with the Cetnik movement altogether, but because it recognised that Mihailovic and Tito would never work together it now favoured an attempt to persuade the Yugoslav government to replace Mihailovic with a more moderate Cetnik leader.[102]

The Foreign Office's response to the Maclean report did not avert an immediate decision effectively to abandon Mihailovic: he received virtually no supplies after the end of November 1943, and at a plenary meeting of the Tehran conference on 29 November the three Allied heads of government decreed that Tito must be supplied to the greatest possible extent in an effort to help him to withstand the German drive to re-establish control in Yugoslavia.[103]*

□

At the news of the Italian armistice the Germans had acted quickly to put into effect the measures they had prepared in advance for securing the surrender of the Italian forces (Operation *Achse*).† On 12 September the decrypt of a report from C-in-C South East had claimed that all the main Italian units had been disarmed.[105] Sigint, in the form of German military, Abwehr and SS Enigma and occasional decrypts of the Italian C 38m and Military Attaché cyphers, had indicated that the claim was somewhat premature. According to these decrypts – which seem, however, to have exaggerated the resistance put up by the Italians – the Italian commanders in Albania and Montenegro had surrendered on 11 September; but in Montenegro two divisions had put up fierce resistance around Kotor Bay until 20 September and, further inland, two others had not been completely subdued by the middle of

---

* The amount of supplies sent into Yugoslavia up to the Italian armistice was negligible (71 tons to the Partisans; 118 to Mihailovic). The amount increased to 125 tons a month during the winter of 1943–1944, but remained well below the target of 350 tons a month on account of bad weather, the shortage of aircraft and the fact that airborne supply still had to be by parachute because of the lack of landing facilities. In the spring of 1944 the number of aircraft available to SOE was increased from 32 to 113, and 3,100 tons were dropped to Tito in the second quarter of the year. Seaborne supplies, very limited before the beginning of 1944, had temporarily outstripped those sent by air in the first quarter, but were reduced as the air supplies improved.[104]

† See above pp 11–12, 148.

102.   Woodward, op cit, Vol III, pp 298–299, summarising COS (43) 733 (0) of 26 November (copy in CAB 121/531).

103.   Ehrman, *Grand Strategy*, Vol V, (1956) pp 179–181.

104.   ibid, p 273; Molony, op cit, Vol V, p 569, Vol VI Part I (forthcoming) Chapter VII.

105.   DEFE 3/879, JP 4231 of 12 September; Dir/C Archive, 4370 of 12 September 1943.

October,[106] while in Dalmatia and north-west Croatia some units of the Second Italian Army, the only higher command to order resistance *à outrance*, had fought stubbornly around Dubrovnik, Split and Zara till towards the end of September.[107] But inland in the north-west almost all the Eleventh Italian Army had obeyed its orders to offer no resistance.[108] By the beginning of October it was clear that most of the fifteen Italian divisions in Yugoslavia had been disarmed or dispersed.[109] On the other hand, the Partisans had also responded quickly to the Italian capitulation. By the beginning of October they had seized Istria, an area behind Split and most of the Dalmatian islands; were profiting from the diversion of German troops by threatening the main railway to Belgrade in the area around Zagreb; and had themselves disarmed some Italian divisions and enlisted support or acquired arms from others.[110]

From the beginning of October bulletins from the Partisans, reports from the British liaison officers and the German high-grade Sigint – above all the Sigint, which had become even more copious – had left no doubt that the Germans were making a determined effort to recover the lost ground. They had cleared the Istrian peninsula, the coastal plain east of Udine and the area around Fiume by the middle of October. On 20 October II SS Panzer Corps from Rommel's Army Group B in northern Italy, up-graded for the occasion as First SS Panzer Army, had embarked on a campaign to recover the Zagreb-Ljubljana area with five full divisions, elements of five other divisions and some smaller formations – the largest force ever employed by Germany in anti-guerrilla operations.[111] This had ended indecisively on 21 November, when First SS Panzer Army withdrew into northern Italy.[112] But by the

---

106. DEFE 3/879, JP 4224; of 11 September; Dir C/Archive, 4370 of 12 September 1943; CX/MSS/3202/T1, 3218/T1, 3247/T39, 3348/T2, 3389/T14, T28/100.

107. WO 208/2264, WO (Restricted) Intelligence Summary No 6 of 23 September 1943; eg CX/MSS/3235/T30, 3247/T39, 3294/T10; ZTPI 37773.

108. WO 208/2264, No 6 of 23 September 1943; eg CX/MSS/3196/T40, 3208/T41; MSE (Italian MA series) 1485, 1486.

109. WO 208/2026, Minute 22 of 28 September 1943; eg CX/MSS/3396/T1.

110. Ehrman, op cit, Vol V, pp 87–80; WO 208/3573 of 19 and 27 September 1943; WO 208/2026, Minute 22 of 28 September 1943.

111. WO 208/2026 and 2015, Minutes of 1 and 3 November 1943; DEFE 3/886, JPs 7539 of 19 October, 7719 of 21 October, 7807 of 22 October 1943; DEFE 3/887, JPs 8022 and 8089 of 25 October, 8154 of 26 October, 8460 of 30 October 1943; DEFE 3/889, JPs 9196 of 8 November, 9607 and 9631 of 13 November 1943, as examples.

112. WO 202/2015, Minute of 18 December 1943; and for examples of the decrypts, DEFE 3/889, JP 9347 of 10 November; DEFE 3/890, JPs 9559 of 12 November, 9663 of 13 November, 9820 of 16 November, 9913 of 17 November 1943; DEFE 3/5 (2), VL 43 of 19 November; DEFE 3/6 (2), VL 297 of 23 November, DEFE 3/9 (2), VL 1026 of 2 December 1943.

beginning of December it was known from the decrypts that 371st Infantry Division, recently arrived from Italy, was among the formations which Second Panzer Army – in command in Yugoslavia under Army Group F – was about to use in another offensive in the Zagreb area, and that in the Sarajevo area, where it had carried out preliminary clearing operations since early in November, V SS Mountain Corps had just launched a major attack with 1st Mountain Division (brought in from Greece) and 7th SS Mountain Division (the Prinz Eugen) transferred from the Dalmatian coast. On the coast, moreover, recent decrypts had disclosed that the Germans, who had relieved the ports and temporarily re-captured islands as far south as Split during November and early December,[113] were now preparing to attack the large islands between Split and Dubrovnik, where they had hitherto been held up by fierce guerrilla resistance and the lack of GAF support against Allied air attacks,[114]* and where the Allies were soon to join up with the Partisans by establishing detachments on the islands of Lagosta and Vis and an airfield on Vis. A decrypt of 1 December had given details of the assembly of landing craft for an assault on the island of Solta; Allied aircraft had destroyed the whole of this force on the following day.[115] On 3 December GC and CS decrypted Second Panzer Army's orders of 2 December for the recapture of the other islands; they gave no dates, but laid it down that they were to be re-taken in the sequence Brac, Hvar, Korcula, Mljet, Lagosta and Vis.[116]

These being the circumstances in which the Allies decided to step up supplies to Tito as a matter of urgency at the beginning of December 1943, it was the subsequent development of Yugoslavia into a theatre where Allied support to the Partisans could tie down substantial German forces† which led to the decision formally to

---

* For the weakness of the GAF see below, pp 169–170.

† For the assessment of the number of German divisions tied down in Yugoslavia out of the total available for deployment see above, p 28 et seq.

113.   Naval Headlines, No 855 of 6 November 1943; Air Sunset 118 of 8 November 1943; DEFE 3/887, JP 8439 of 30 October; DEFE 3/888, JPs 8503 of 30 October, 8590 of 31 October, 8924 of 4 November; DEFE 3/889 JPs 9026 of 5 November, 9323 of 10 November, 9447 and 9478 of 11 November 1943; DEFE 3/7 (2), VLs 541 and 596 of 26 November; DEFE 3/8 (2), VL 974 of 29 November; DEFE 3/8 (1), VLs 832 of 30 November, 945 and 968 of 1 December 1943.

114.   WO 208/2015, Minute of 6 December 1943; Air Sunset 118 of 8 November 1943; DEFE 3/887, JPs 8007 of 24 October, 8084 of 25 October; DEFE 3/888, JPs 8648 and 8651 of 1 November, 8882 of 3 November; DEFE 3/889, JPs 9148 of 7 November, 9419 of 11 November 1943.

115.   Naval Headlines, No 884 of 5 December 1943; DEFE 3/8 (1), VL 952 of 1 December 1943.

116.   DEFE 3/9 (2), VL 1077 of 3 December 1943.

break with Mihailovic. During December 1943 and January 1944 the Germans, persisting and failing in their effort to establish a grip on the countryside, were handicapped by increasing Allied supplies to the Partisans as well as by their own shortages of troops and aircraft; and persisting and not quite succeeding in their effort to take and hold all the islands which were vital for their defence of the mainland and the maintenance of their supply-line, they encountered increasing air and naval opposition from the Allies.* At the same time the Allies not only learned that Mihailovic was trying to step up Cetnik attacks on the Partisans but also received further evidence that, to save his precarious position in Serbia, he was throwing in his lot with Nedic and the Germans.

A copy of an order from Mihailovic for general mobilisation against the Partisans, dated 13 November, had reached Cairo on 29 November and London by 2 December.[117] By 4 December the liaison officers with Tito's forces had reported that some of Mihailovic's influential subordinates were reluctant to obey, preferring to make agreements with Tito, that Mihailovic was threatening death to Cetniks unwilling to fight the Partisans, and that desertions by his followers were forcing him to turn to Nedic for support.[118] By the same date GC and CS had decrypted an Abwehr signal of 1 December which reported that Mihailovic was negotiating with the SS in Zagreb about the formation of volunteer bands in northern Greece, and this decrypt – the first Enigma message, as NID 12 noted, to refer to his personal involvement in collaboration with the Germans – was followed by one dated 2 December which confirmed the information supplied by the liaison officers. It disclosed that the Abwehr, exploiting the knowledge that Mihailovic had been alienated from Great Britain by her decision to support Tito, was furthering unofficial negotiations between him and Nedic. During the rest of December the extent to which his mobilisation order was being disobeyed remained unclear,[119] but the liaison officers sent in further evidence that Cetniks were fighting with Nedic's forces and the German Army against the Partisans in Croatia, Serbia and Dalmatia,[120] and their reports were again confirmed by Sigint. GC

---

* see below, p 167 et seq.

117. WO 106/5690, Stevenson, to FO, No 130 of 29 November; CAB 80/42, COS (43) 306 (222nd résumé of 2 December), para 31.
118. CAB 121/531, Stevenson to FO, No 135 of 30 November; WO 204/968, AFHQ Intelligence Summary No 67 of 4 December 1943, p 11; WO 202/2015, Minute 29 of 6 December 1943.
119. WO 202/2015, Minute of 18 December 1943.
120. CAB 121/529, Balkan sitreps 26 and 30 of 13 and 16 December 1943, 46 of 1 January 1944.

and CS decrypted several Enigma messages to this effect, including a signal of 14 December in which Abwehr HQ in Belgrade, noting that many small Cetnik bands were reaching agreements with the Germans, reminded its subordinates that such agreements required the approval of Germany's roving ambassador in the Balkans.[121] In CBME's decrypts there were references to 'Cetnik leaders collaborating with the Germans with the approval of Mihailovic but denying to the Germans that they were connected with him'.[122]

On his return to Cairo with the Foreign Secretary and his military advisers after the Tehran conference, the Prime Minister was convinced by 'all reports received', and by talks with Maclean and Deakin, that Mihailovic was 'in active collaboration with the Germans'.[123] From the immediate military point of view this conclusion was of no great significance: the decision to support Tito had already been taken. But it created considerable difficulties when the Prime Minister, embarking on the political task of complementing that decision by persuading the Yugoslav government to dismiss Mihailovic and reach a working agreement with the Partisans, saw King Peter and told him that the case against Mihailovic was 'irrefutable'.[124] The first difficulty was that the best evidence for Mihailovic's personal involvement in collaboration with the Germans came from Sigint sources. As a means of circumventing this difficulty, the military authorities in Cairo proposed that the effort to persuade King Peter to dismiss Mihailovic should be furthered by setting a test; the Allies would abandon Mihailovic if he failed to comply with an order to attack railway lines in Serbia by 29 December. The Foreign Secretary subscribed to this proposal before leaving Cairo, but encountered the second difficulty when he returned to London. In the Foreign Office the test – which Mihailovic duly failed – was not accepted as a realistic, or indeed a respectable, substitute for conclusive documentary evidence that Mihailovic had approved of collaboration with Italy and Germany.[125] On 28 December the Foreign Secretary informed Cairo, where Stevenson was pressing for an immediate break with Mihailovic, that 'as yet the Foreign Office has received no such conclusive evidence'.[126] On 1 January 1944 he wrote in the same vein to the Prime Minister: 'if

---

121. DEFE 3/7, VL 590 of 26 November; DEFE 3/9, VLs 1113 and 1130 of 3 and 4 December; DEFE 3/11, VL 1526 of 9 December; DEFE 3/12, VL 1797 of 13 December; DEFE 3/15, VL 2698 of 26 December 1943; WO 204/968, No 67 of 4 December 1943.
122. WO 202/132A Part III.
123. Churchill, *The Second World War*, Vol V (1952), pp 415–416.
124. Woodward, op cit, Vol III, p 300.
125. ibid, pp 300, 301; CAB 101/126, pp 47, 49–50.
126. Woodward, op cit, Vol III, p 307.

we have a public and spectacular breach with Mihailovic our case against him for treachery must be unanswerable. I am still without evidence of this'.[127]

Meanwhile Deakin had prepared for SOE Cairo a statement of the evidence against Mihailovic. Received in the Foreign Office on 12 January 1944, it could not make use of the Enigma sent out to the Middle East and added little to the intelligence which had already reached London from the Middle East; its main sources were the reports of the liaison officers with the Partisans, documents captured by the Partisans with dates running from February 1942 to April 1943, and POW interrogation.[128] It did not convince the objectors in the Foreign Office. The Foreign Office agreed that it proved that Cetnik commanders in most areas except Serbia had long had contacts with German, Italian and Croatian forces, and even that they had regarded themselves as acting with Mihailovic's approval, but it would not accept that they could not have done so without Mihailovic's knowledge, and it insisted that there was no evidence that they had done so under Mihailovic's orders.[129]* SOE London was equally sceptical: it felt that, though pointed up by carefully selected documentary support, the situation set out in the statement did not seriously differ from that which had all along been conveyed by the reports of the missions attached to Mihailovic. Nor were the sceptics converted when later in January Maclean reported not only that newly captured documents – Gestapo files dated December 1943 from the Banja Luka area of central Bosnia – had provided further evidence of Cetnik collaboration with German and Croatian troops, but also that a captured Cetnik W/T operator equipped with a British set, and claiming to be from Mihailovic's HQ, had confessed to passing German signals traffic. The Foreign Office minute of 24 January on this report reads as follows: 'More proof of collaboration and always indirect.[130] The Foreign Office, in its reluctance to accept that Mihailovic was associated with the collaborationist activities of his commanders, had already re-drafted Deakin's statement before sending it to the Prime Minister on 22 January.†

---

* Although summaries of Enigma decrypts were reaching the Foreign Office by the autumn of 1943 (see above, p 139) it must be presumed that those who were handling the problem at desk level at the Foreign Office had not seen the evidence implicating Mihailovic.

† As received in Whitehall, the statement was itself only a summary of the original report, parts of which are in the Public Record Office.[131]

127. CAB 101/126, p 71.
128. Woodward, op cit, Vol III, p 311; FO 371/44245, R1115/143/92. For examples of POW interrogation see WO 202/137 and 141.
129. Woodward, op cit, Vol III, pp 311, 315 fn 1.
130. FO 371/44245, R1199/143/92.   131. WO 202/137.

Even before the statement had reached the Foreign Office from Cairo, however, the Foreign Secretary had conceded in a paper circulated to the War Cabinet on 10 January that Mihailovic was accepting assistance from Nedic, and 'even' from the Germans;[132] and on the following day the Chiefs of Staff had again displayed their earlier indifference to the process of trying to hang a breach with Mihailovic on charges of treachery. After considering the Foreign Secretary's paper, they had agreed to recommend the withdrawal of the missions with Mihailovic in the belief that the best way of containing the German forces in Yugoslavia, 'a matter of great importance to our whole European strategy', was to give support only to Tito; 'even if the evidence of Mihailovic's treachery is incomplete, there is no doubt that he is doing nothing to help in the defeat of Germany'.[133]

A final decision to implement this recommendation was deferred by the opposition of SACMED, who argued that Mihailovic was at least holding down two Bulgarian divisions. On 9 February, however, the C-in-C Middle East proposed the immediate withdrawal of the missions, his main reason being that Tito was otherwise unwilling to accept the full Allied missions which were essential if Allied support for him was to be effective. SACMED agreed, and on 17 February, under pressure from the Prime Minister, the Foreign Office accepted the proposal.[134]

□

The missions attached to Mihailovic's force could not make their way out at once; the last of them did not leave until the end of May. Meanwhile, the political and diplomatic effort to achieve an agreement between King Peter and Tito still delayed the dismissal of Mihailovic until 16 May 1944, when the King dismissed his entire government. But these delays were of no significance in view of the development of the military situation in Yugoslavia.

Between the beginning of December 1943 and the middle of February 1944 the main German operations were Second Panzer Army's offensive south of Zagreb and V SS Mountain Corps's offensive in the Sarajevo area.* The decrypts showed that the former, beginning on 6 December, drove the Partisans north-eastward towards Zagreb but was called off on 22 December without

---

* see above, p 158.

132.   CAB 121/531, WP (44) 19 of 10 January.
133.   ibid, COS (44) 8th (o) Meeting, 11 January.
134.   Woodward, op cit, Vol III, pp 311 fn 1; 313–314.

having eliminated their threat to the area;[135] and that during January 114th Jäger Division was engaged in further inconclusive fighting there in the course of its transfer from Yugoslavia to Italy.[136] In the Sarajevo area the decrypts showed that 1st Mountain Division and 7th SS Mountain Division, having narrowly failed to encircle some 9,000 Partisans by 11 December, drove them back to the banks of the river Bosna before turning to capture the Partisan capital, Jajce, on 9 January.[137] In the course of this fighting GHQ Middle East and AFHQ found it difficult to assess the extent of the German success or the scale of the Partisan losses; but they believed that the Partisans would recover some of the lost ground, and by the middle of February the Partisans had indeed re-captured Jajce.[138]

Since January the Enigma had recorded a steady increase in sabotage operations by the Partisans against the railway system and similar targets, which were also subjected to heavier Allied air raids,[139] and from mid-March the Partisans, resuming the offensive in Serbia, made progress against garrisons of satellite troops at a time when the Russian advance from the east and the German occupation of Hungary were forcing redeployment on the Germans.* By the middle of April, however, they were in retreat before a German advance which aimed to eliminate Tito's stronghold in the central mountains. It culminated on 25 May in a concerted attack on Drvar in southern Bosnia by units of the Brandenburg Division and battle groups from V and XV SS Mountain Corps, spearheaded by an airborne drop by SS paratroops.[140] In an effort

---

* For the occupation of Hungary, see above, pp 31–32.

135. DEFE 3/15 (2), VLs 2531 of 23 December, 2556 and 2574 of 24 December 1943; DEFE 3/18 (1), VL 3435 of 7 January 1944.
136. CAB 80/43, COS (44) 3 (227th résumé of 6 January).
137. As examples of decrypts DEFE 3/8 (1), VL 903 of 1 December; DEFE 3/10 (2), VLs 1266 and 1381 of 5 and 7 December; DEFE 3/12 (2), VL 1785 of 13 December; DEFE 3/13 (1), VL 2215 of 19 December; DEFE 3/14 (2), VL 2320 of 21 December, part 4 ff; DEFE 3/14 (1), VL 2500 of 25 December; DEFE 3/15 (2), VL 2556 of 24 December; DEFE 3/16 (1), VL 2951 of 31 December 1943; DEFE 3/17 (2), VL 3056 of 1 January; DEFE 3/18 (1), VLs 3435 of 7 January, 3466 and 3500 of 8 January; DEFE 3/19, VL 3554 of 9 January; DEFE 3/19 (1), VL 3636 of 10 January; DEFE 3/129, VL 3926 of 14 January; DEFE 3/130, VL 4201 of 18 January; DEFE 3/131, VL 4362 of 20 January; DEFE 3/134, VL 5158 of 30 January 1944.
138. eg CAB 121/529, Nos 8 of 24 November, 29 of 15 December 1943; WO 204/968, Nos 29 and 70 of 22 and 28 December 1943, 71 and 74 of 4 and 24 January 1944.
139. eg WO 204/2015, Minute of 11 March 1944; WO 208/3573 of 10 April; CX/MSS/T111/2, T142/11.
140. Ehrman, op cit, Vol V, pp 276–277; Molony, op cit, Vol VI Part 1, Chapter VII.

to hold up the German advance the Allies stepped up supply drops* to the Partisans and air attacks on the enemy's lines of communication. Whereas GAF South East had reported in a decrypt in January that Allied raids were inflicting little damage,[145] many decrypts during April and May reported that attacks on railway stations and bridges were causing heavy disruption.[146] On 19 May, however, the Enigma, which had previously carried an appreciation from XV SS Mountain Corps to the effect that the Partisans would hold Drvar with all available forces, disclosed that the Germans had been discussing on 12 May a large-scale operation in XV SS

---

* Since the autumn of 1943 the Mediterranean commands had on several occasions been warned that the enemy either knew the exact locations of supply dropping points and landing grounds or had received information about them which was enabling him to try to locate the sites by PR. These warnings were derived from Enigma decrypts which themselves contained decrypts of Tito's W/T traffic; other Enigma decrypts showed that the Germans learned something from the same source about the recognition signals given to aircraft approaching the dropping points and landing grounds.[141] The warnings were of some use, as is indicated by the decrypt of a report from GAF South East early in January 1944, which noted that the Allies were changing the destination of the supply flights almost nightly, and by a report from Fliegerführer Croatia, decrypted in March, which noted that the recognition signals were constantly being changed.[142] But nothing could be done to deny this source to the Germans, and the fact that it was known to exist was concealed from Tito and the liaison officers on security grounds. Needless to say, the Germans claimed a good deal of information from the same 'sure source' about the operational plans and intentions of the Partisans, and this was disclosed in Enigma decrypts from the autumn of 1943.[143] The British Mission with Tito was aware of the risk that his cyphers might not be secure; and on at least one occasion it warned that German POW had claimed that the Germans were getting good results from the Partisan cyphers. But apart from offering to supply cyphers to the Partisans there was no way of solving this problem and negotiations with them on the subject came to nothing.[144]

141. eg DEFE 3/887, JP 8110 of 26 October; DEFE 3/889, JP 9464 of 11 November 1943; DEFE 3/12 (1), VL 1899 of 15 December; DEFE 3/13 (2), VL 2092 of 17 December; DEFE 3/15 (1), VL 2732 of 27 December; DEFE 3/17 (1), VL 3157 of 3 January 1944; DEFE 3/132. VL 4511 of 22 January; DEFE 3/146, VL 8150 of 10 March; DEFE 3/148, VL 8558 of 15 March; DEFE 3/37 (2), KV 626 of 10 April; DEFE 3/39 (1), KV 1248 of 17 April; DEFE 3/40 (1), KV 1389 of 19 April; DEFE 3/41 (1), KV 1655 of 22 April; DEFE 3/156, KV 4142 of 16 May 1944.
142. DEFE 3/18 (2), VL 3311 of 6 January 1944; DEFE 3/151, VL 9367 of 25 March.
143. DEFE 3/883, JPs 6009 of 2 October, 6279 of 5 October 1943; DEFE 3/13 (2), VL 2167 of 19 December; DEFE 3/13 (1), VL 2241 of 20 December; DEFE 3/14 (2) VL 2323 of 21 December; DEFE 3/19 (1), VL 3729 of 11 January 1944; DEFE 3/138, VL 6015 of 11 February; DEFE 3/151, V.L 9442 of 26 March 1944.
144. WO 202/332 Bari telegram 476 of 12 April 1944; WO 202/339, telegrams between Cairo and British Mission 19 July and 19 September 1943.
145. DEFE 3/18 (2), VLs 3311 and 3336 of 6 January 1944.
146. DEFE 3/35 (2), KV 117 of 3 April 1944; DEFE 3/35 (1), KV 216 of 4 April; DEFE 3/39 (2), KV 1087 of 15 April; DEFE 3/40 (1), KV 1378 of 19 April; DEFE 3/41 (2), KV 1517 of 20 April; DEFE 3/43 (2), KV 2016 of 25 April; DEFE 3/153, KV 3432 of 10 May 1944.

Mountain Corps's area; and on 22 and 23 May it indicated that for an important operation to be carried out in the next few days 300 men were to be accommodated at the airfields at Bihac and Banja Luka and Fliegerführer Croatia was to receive temporary aircraft reinforcements.[147] On 24 May a decrypt disclosed that an operation was scheduled to take place on 25 May.[148] On 25 May GC and CS decrypted a further signal of 24 May in which GAF Zagreb had notified an SS Parachute Battalion that all was ready for loading.[149]

When AFHQ in Italy received the decrypt obtained on 24 May the Germans were about to deliver their attack on Drvar, and they carried out the attack early on 25 May, some hours before GC and CS decrypted the signal to the Parachute Battalion. AFHQ could have sent an alert to the British Mission at Tito's HQ on the basis of the decrypts it had received between 19 and 23 May, but it clearly did not do so. Although the officer in command of the Mission decided to move it to a new location about a mile from the centre of Drvar during 22 May, his subsequent report records that he did so because 'very careful' German photographic reconnaissance of the area on that day persuaded him that a bombing attack was imminent.[150] Moreover, the file of signals from Bari to the Mission[151] contains no warning signal and the officer in charge of the Mission's communications at the time is certain that no such signal was received. There is some indication, on the other hand, that by the morning of 25 May AFHQ had prepared a general warning for transmission to the Mission but that it was overtaken by events. The Mission first reported the German attack at 0910 on 25 May, but was obliged to move again before it could receive at least one emergency signal awaiting transmission to it. On the copy of the Mission's report in the Public Record Office there is a pencilled note by the Bari duty officer which includes the words ' . . . (3) General warning late? . . .' [152] What was the reason for AFHQ's inaction – or, perhaps, its delay? Was it due to unwillingness to help the Partisans? Apart from the fact that this explanation is incompatible with the efforts made to support the Partisans before and after the German attack on Drvar, it fails to take account of the policy laid down for preserving the security of Ultra. The authorities in Whitehall had decided in December 1943 that the Mission should

---

147. DEFE 3/47 (1), KV 3103 of 6 May; DEFE 3/157, KV 4483 of 19 May; DEFE 3/159, KVs 4788, 4842 and 4845 of 22 May, 4912 and 4948 of 23 May 1944.
148. DEFE 3/160, KV 5059 of 24 May 1944.
149. ibid, KV 5157 of 25 May 1944.
150. WO 208/2002, Appendix A to Colonel Street's account.
151. WO 202/232.
152. WO 202/333, folio 225 of 25 May 1944.

receive no intelligence based on high-grade Sigint, the main considerations being the knowledge that the Partisan cyphers were insecure, the fact that the Mission's own cypher was not of the highest grade and, not less important, the risk that, if taken without proper precautions, action based on Ultra might arouse German suspicions about the vulnerability of the Enigma.*

After the attack on Drvar the Allied air forces helped to contain the German drive against the Partisans by launching a sustained offensive against the airfields from which the GAF was supporting it. On Sigint evidence AI estimated that the offensive, destroying 45 aircraft on the ground and damaging 96 others, virtually eliminated the GAF as a combat force in Yugoslavia.[154] Although Tito's HQ had to be evacuated to Bari by Allied aircraft early in June – it was subsequently established on Vis – the Partisans were able to resume active operations in July.[155]

Meanwhile, despite the fact that the Sigint covering Germany's operations on the Adriatic coast was obtained mainly from the GAF general Enigma key, from the key of GAF South East (Gadfly) and from the naval Enigma key (Porpoise), all of which were decrypted with little delay, the Allies had been unable to prevent her occupation of most of the important islands. On 13 December 1943 OKM had issued a revised programme for the capture of the islands lying between Split and Dubrovnik.† Decrypted and disseminated by GC and CS on the following day, this specified that Korcula should be attacked on 16 December, Mljet on 24 December, Hvar on 3 January, Brac on 9 January, and that assaults should follow on Solta and, if sufficient naval forces remained available, on Lagosta and Vis.[156] Further decrypts disclosed that the assault on Korcula was delayed by the shortage of troops and shipping,[157] the inability

---

* 'C' and the DMI used these arguments to dissuade the Prime Minister when, on 9 March 1944, he wanted to ignore the security decision and send the Mission some information obtained from Enigma decrypts.[153]

† See above, p 158, for the original plans.

153. Dir/C Archive, 5947 and 5955 of 9 March 1944.
154. CAB 80/44, COS (44) 102 and 104 (248th and 249th résumés), 1 and 8 June; WO 208/3573 of 11 June 1944.
155. Ehrman, op cit, Vol V, p 277; Molony, op cit, Vol VI Part 1, Chapter VII; CAB 101/126, pp 135–136.
156. Naval Headlines, No 893 of 14 December 1943; DEFE 3/12 (1), VL 1845 of 14 December 1943.
157. For troop shortages, see eg DEFE 3/12 (2), VL 1751 of 12 December 1943. For examples of shipping shortages, see Naval Headlines, Nos 891–893 of 12, 13 and 14 December, 900 of 21 December 1943; DEFE 3/12 (2), VL 1813 of 13 December; DEFE 3/12 (1), VL 1900 of 15 December; DEFE 3/14 (1), VL 2395 of 22 December; DEFE 3/15 (2), VL 2505 of 23 December 1943.

of the GAF to provide fighter support,[158] and the damage done by British attacks; for example, the RAF created considerable disruption with a heavy raid on Zara, the rear supply base, on 16 December,[159] and on 22 December torpedo-boats sank the ex-Italian Flak cruiser *Niobe* after she had been crippled in an air attack.[160] But the assault went forward without Allied intervention, and by 28 December, meeting only token guerrilla opposition, the Germans had completed the capture of the island. By the end of January, making the short sheltered sea crossings at night and exploiting bad weather to avoid Allied interference, they had occupied Mljet, Solta, Brac and Hvar with little or no air and naval support but without meeting serious resistance, the Partisans having left behind only small rear-guards to fight delaying actions.[161]

This marked the limit of German expansion down the Yugoslav coast. It was obvious that the Germans would try to take Vis, and in the middle of February 1944 the Enigma disclosed that, having earlier ruled out an airborne assault for lack of aircraft, they were preparing a sizeable combined operation against Vis and Lagosta.[162] Before the end of February, however, after giving full details of the forces engaged, the Enigma reported that GAF objections, the weather and nervousness about the size of the Allied garrison had led to the postponement of the attack on Vis;[163] and it later added that a detachment which had sailed against Lagosta on 1 March

---

158. eg Naval Headlines, Nos 897–899 of 18–20 December; Air Sunset 131 of 20 December; DEFE 3/13 (2), VLs 2103 and 2116 of 18 December; DEFE 3/13 (1), VLs 2169 and 2200 of 19 December 1943.
159. Naval Headlines, No 897 of 18 December; AIR 41/54. *The RAF in Maritime War*, Vol VII Part 1, pp 399–400; DEFE 3/13 (2), VL 2108 of 18 December; DEFE 3/13 (1), VLs 2186 and 2194 of 19 December; DEFE 3/14 (1), VL 2390 of 22 December 1943.
160. For examples of the Sigint leading up to the sinking of the *Niobe* see Naval Headlines, Nos 898 and 900 of 19 and 21 December; DEFE 3/13 (2), VL 2018 of 18 December; DEFE 3/13 (1), VL 2167 of 19 December; DEFE 3/14 (2), VLs 2254 and 2295 of 20 December, 2337 of 21 December; DEFE 3/14 (1), VL 2374 of 21 December 1943.
161. JIC (44) 36 (o) of 31 January; WO 204/968, No 72 of 25 January 1944, p 10; and as examples of the Sigint Naval Headlines, Nos 914 of 4 January, 918–924 of 9–14 January, 927 and 928 of 17 and 18 January, 930 of 20 January; DEFE 3/17 (1), VL 3210 of 4 January; DEFE 3/18 (1), VLs 3418 and 3499 of 7 and 8 January; DEFE 3/19 (1), VLs 3704 and 3731 of 11 and 12 January 1944.
162. Naval Headlines, Nos 928 and 929 of 18 and 19 January 1944; DEFE 3/19 (1), VL 3640 of 10 January; DEFE 3/130, VLs 4171 and 4209 of 18 January; DEFE 3/138, VL 6134 of 12 February 1944.
163. Naval Headlines, Nos 957 of 16 February, 959 of 18 February, 967 of 26 February 1944; DEFE 3/139, VL 6318 of 15 February; DEFE 3/140, VLs 6507, 6564 and 6576 of 18 February; DEFE 3/142, VL 7094 of 25 February; DEFE 3/143, VL 7311 of 28 February 1944.

had been shelled by Allied destroyers.[164] Proposals for attacks on the two islands continued to figure in the decrypts long after the Enigma disclosed that the Führer had decided on 25 April that they should be abandoned, but the local German commanders had recognised before the end of March that, far from permitting any further expansion, Allied naval and air superiority already threatened their ability to defend their coastal supply routes and retain the islands they had recently taken.[165]*

Germany's determination to seize the islands had arisen from the crucial importance of seaborne traffic to her entire supply system in Yugoslavia, as the JIC had recognised in January 1944,[167] but her success in taking them only increased the strain on the limited air and naval forces she could provide for the defence of shipping. It greatly enlarged the opportunities for Allied attacks on the coastal supply route at a time when, with No 242 Group RAF of the Coastal Air Force establishing itself in Taranto in January and increasing in strength as it moved its bases up the Italian peninsula, the Allies were expanding their anti-shipping operations.[168] At the end of January the JIC estimated that of the 143,000 tons of merchant shipping available to Germany in the Adriatic, some 60,000 tons had already been immobilised or damaged,[169] and that the German naval forces in the area consisted of 2 destroyers, 10 torpedo-boats, 2 corvettes, 4–10 E-boats, 8 R-boats, 3 U-boats and 7 Italian motor torpedo-boats (MAS).[170] These estimates rested on a stream of naval Enigma decrypts giving reports on the damage done by air attacks to ships and port installations at Dubrovnik, Zara, Split and Sibenik in November and December 1943[171] and at Fiume, Pola,

---

* After reading recent decrypts the Prime Minister had telegraphed to SACMED on 19 March 1944 that the enemy's intention to make an important effort to recover Vis was clear; he expressed the hope that Vis would not become 'another Kos', 'having started up here we ought surely to carry it through'.[166]

164. CX/MSS/T110/32.
165. Naval Headlines, Nos 1001 of 31 March, 1028 of 27 April, 1045 of 14 May, 1053 of 22 May, 1062 of 31 May 1944; eg DEFE 3/765, VL 9862 of 30 March; DEFE 3/43 (2), KV 2122 of 26 April; DEFE 3/154, KV 3663 of 13 May; DEFE 3/158, KV 4714 of 21 May; DEFE 3/162, KV 5650 of 29 May 1944.
166. DEFE 3/149, VL 8803 of 18 March 1944; Dir/C Archive, PM telegram to Wilson T/609/4 of 19 March 1944.
167. JIC (44) 36 (0) of 31 January.
168. AIR 41/54, pp 331 (Figure 11), 382, 383, 386, 414.
169. JIC (44) 36 (0) of 31 January.   170. ibid, Annex A.
171. eg Naval Headlines, Nos 869 of 20 November, 878 of 29 November, 879 of 30 November, 881 of 2 December; DEFE 3/5 (2), VL 63 of 19 November; DEFE 3/6 (2), VL 339 of 23 November; DEFE 3/6 (1), VL 377 of 24 November; DEFE 3/7 (1), VL 746 of 28 November; DEFE 3/8 (2), VLs 764, 784 and 802 of 29 November, 867 of 30 November; DEFE 3/8 (1), VL 969 of 1 December; DEFE 3/9 (1), VL 1229 of 4 December; DEFE 3/12 (1), VL 1963 of 16 December; DEFE 3/13 (2), VL 2108 of 18 December 1943.

Sibenik and Trogir in January 1944.[172] Thereafter, the Allied air offensive was intensified. With over 300 aircraft available from the end of January, and a growing participation by the Italian Air Force from the spring, it was able not only to make more frequent attacks on the main ports and naval bases but also to attack the remoter harbours and ships on passage.[173] The results of the offensive were again reflected in Sigint, the Enigma decrypts providing immediate accounts not only of the increasingly heavy raids on the main ports, but also of the many small encounters in which individual ships were sunk or damaged.[174]

The Allied air attacks met with negligible air opposition until February 1944. Throughout the previous autumn, as the GAF Enigma had disclosed, Fliegerführer Croatia and Fliegerführer Albania, their resources cut to the bone by withdrawals to other theatres, which reduced the strength of the GAF in the Mediterranean theatre as a whole from 1,280 aircraft in July 1943 to 575 in January 1944,[175] and denied all but temporary reinforcements by the fact that the GAF's first concern in the eastern Mediterranean after the Italian armistice was to strengthen its position in the Ionian islands and the Dodecanese, had been quite unable to meet the many demands made upon them for the defence of the Adriatic ports, the protection of the sea routes and support of the Army's operations against the islands and the Partisans inland.[176] From January 1944 their ability to meet these demands was further reduced. Sigint disclosed that aircraft were being withdrawn from

---

172.   AIR 41/54, pp 409A–412, 414; Naval Headlines, Nos 920 of 10 January, 927 of 17 January, 928 of 18 January, 933 of 23 January 1944; eg DEFE 3/17 (2), VL 3102 of 2 January; DEFE 3/18 (2), VL 3327 of 6 January; DEFE 3/18 (1), VL 3410 of 7 January; DEFE 3/19 (2), VL 3609 of 10 January; DEFE 3/19 (1), VLs 3668, 3673 and 3696 of 11 January; DEFE 3/129, VLs 3820 of 13 January, 3877 and 3903 of 14 January, 3965 of 15 January; DEFE 3/130, VLs 4138 of 17 January, 4203 of 18 January, 4245 of 19 January; DEFE 3/132, VL 4538 of 23 January; DEFE 3/133, VL 4855 of 26 January; DEFE 3/134, VL 5211 of 31 January; DEFE 3/135, VL 4327 of 1 February 1944.

173.   AIR 41/54, pp 414–415, 417–418, 430.

174.   ibid, pp 418–419, 429. And as examples of the Sigint Naval Headlines, Nos 951 of 10 February, 967 of 26 February, 971 of 1 March 1944; DEFE 3/137, VLs 5773 of 8 February, 5893 and 5902 of 9 February, 5998 of 10 February; DEFE 3/141, VL 6972 of 24 February; DEFE 3/142, VL 7079 of 25 February; DEFE 3/151, VLs 9305 of 24 March, 9429 and 9458 of 26 March 1944.

175.   AIR 41/10, *The Rise and Fall of the GAF*, pp 265–266.

176.   Naval Headlines, No 898 of 19 December 1943; Air Sunsets 110 of 18 October, 118 of 8 November, 131 of 20 December 1943; eg DEFE 3/884, JPs 6584 of 8 October, 8651 of 1 November 1943; DEFE 3/13 (2), VL 2022 of 16 December; DEFE 3/13 (1), VL 2169 of 19 December; DEFE 3/14 (2), VL 2327 of 21 December 1943.

the Dalmatian coast for the air defence of Bulgaria in January,[177] when AI estimated that of some 125 aircraft available in the whole of Yugoslavia and Albania only 55 were first-line aircraft.[178] Another 40 single-engined fighter aircraft were transferred from Yugoslavia to Bulgaria and Romania in February.[179] From the same month the GAF was driven to concentrating fighters in northern Italy from several areas, including Yugoslavia, against the Allied strategic bombing raids on the Reich that were being made from Italian bases. As a result, the Allied attacks on the north Adriatic ports, which were sometimes chosen as alternative targets by bombers unable to get through to Germany, at last met fighter opposition; but by being forced to adopt this measure, the GAF had to reduce still further the number of aircraft available for escorting shipping in the Adriatic.[180] GAF South East was before long faced with another problem: towards the end of March the Enigma disclosed that it had been ordered to give up trained men for the defence of the Reich and to carry out a ruthless comb-out of such spare parts as could contribute to the maximum mobilisation of fighters for the home front.[181] In April another decrypt showed that GAFSE's Albanian command was already so short of men that it had been exempted from the order to release operational crews.[182] In May it emerged from the Enigma that the GAF had been forced to transfer fighters from Greece for operations against the Allied air-lift of supplies to the Partisans.[183]

From mid-March, in conjunction with their plans for commando raids and landings on the islands, the Allies concentrated their Adriatic air offensive against the enemy's naval vessels. The Monfalcone ship-yards at Trieste were bombed in the middle of the month, when the Enigma reported that the raid had suspended all work on E-boat construction.[184] A month later the Enigma added that the construction of landing craft had been delayed by more attacks on the yards.[185] In air raids on the islands, as the Enigma confirmed, four Siebel ferries were sunk in the third week of March.[186] In the last week of the month the decrypts showed that in

177. Air Sunset 138 of 20 January 1944.
178. JIC (44) 36 (0) of 31 January.
179. Air Sunsets 148–150 of 25 and 29 February, 1 March 1944.
180. AIR 41/54, pp 409a–412.
181. DEFE 3/152, VLs 9536 and 9724 of 27 and 29 March 1944.
182. DEFE 3/14 (1), KV 1741 of 23 April 1944.
183. Air Sunset 170 of 9 May 1944.
184. DEFE 3/150, VL 9159 of 22 March; DEFE 3/152, VL 9528 of 27 March 1944.
185. DEFE 3/40 (1), KV 1497 of 20 April 1944.
186. DEFE 3/149, VL 8832 of 19 March; DEFE 3/151, VL 9269 of 24 March, 9337 of 25 March 1944.

naval sweeps and air attacks in support of the first Allied commando raids the German navy lost 1 R-boat (plus 2 damaged), 3 Siebel ferries, 3 landing craft, 4 motor launches and 7 motor coasters [187] – not in itself an impressive haul, but sufficient to produce a critical situation for the German navy, which had seen its effective strength in the islands reduced to seven small craft, and which had already complained that shipping along the Dalmatian coast would be at a complete standstill unless the sea and air defences were at once improved.[188]

In the absence of air support Admiral Adriatic attempted to bring E-boats into the Dalmatian harbours. It was known from Sigint that bomb-proof berths for E-boats and R-boats were being prepared there since the previous January, but that no E-boats had been available before March, when two arrived at Kotor.[189] Two more arrived early in April,[190] but the Allies bombed Kotor in the third week of April and by the end of the month E-boat operations were confined to the hours of darkness for lack of fighter protection.[191] Oil stocks at Kotor were running low by then, and an attempt to replenish them by sending four tanker barges from Pola, of which the Enigma provided full details in advance, was seriously disrupted when two of the barges were sunk by air attack on 19 May.[192] Despite these many difficulties, three E-boats operated against the Allied commando raid on Solta on 10–11 May, sinking one of the ships.[193] This, their first real success in the Adriatic, was not repeated before they were withdrawn on 4 June; but at the end of May they were being relieved by five E-boats of a new flotilla.[194]

Allied commando raids on the islands were by then giving the Germans cause for increasing alarm. Raids against Solta and Hvar

---

187. Naval Headlines, Nos 998 of 28 March, 1006 of 5 April 1944; AIR 41/54, p 417; DEFE 3/151, VLs 9435 of 26 March, 9500 of 27 March; DEFE 3/152, VLs 9525 of 27 March, 9551 of 27 March; DEFE 3/35 (1), KV 186 of 4 April 1944.
188. Naval Headlines, No 983 of 13 March; DEFE 3/147, VL 8338 of 13 March 1944.
189. Naval Headlines, No 995 of 25 March 1944; DEFE 3/130, VL 4128 of 17 January; DEFE 3/148, VL 8556 of 15 March 1944.
190. DEFE 3/36 (1), KV 432 of 7 April 1944.
191. Naval Headlines, No 1030 of 29 April 1944; AIR 41/54, p 429; DEFE 3/43 (1), KV 2237 of 28 April 1944.
192. Naval Headlines, Nos 1031 of 30 April, 1034 and 1036 of 3 and 5 May 1944; eg DEFE 3/44 (1), KVs 2382 of 29 April, 2410 of 30 April; DEFE 3/45 (1), KV 2707 of 3 May; DEFE 3/46 (2), KVs 2813 of 4 May, 2872 of 5 May; DEFE 3/155, KV 3980 of 15 May; DEFE 3/157, KVs 4258 of 18 May, 4456 and 4482 of 19 May; DEFE 3/158, KV 4564 of 20 May 1944.
193. Naval Headlines, No 1043 of 12 May; DEFE 3/153, KVs 3433 of 10 May, 3446 of 11 May 1944.
194. DEFE 3/160, KVs 5107, 5133 and 5177 of 25 May; DEFE 3/161, KVs 5293 and 5301 of 26 May; DEFE 3/165, KV 6464 of 5 June 1944.

in March, against Mljet and Korcula in April, and Solta again in May had been followed by a larger-scale landing on Mljet on the night of 22–23 May. It failed to make contact with the German garrison as a result of 'faulty information on German dispositions'.[195] These operations derived little immediate benefit from the Enigma, which was rarely decrypted in time to be of tactical value. But they caused many signals to be made complaining of the lack of air support and the shortage of ferries and transports, and some which confirmed that, despite these deficiencies, the Germans were anxious to maintain the garrisons for as long as possible as a means of delaying Allied landings on the coast.[196] On 25 April AFHQ estimated that the raids had had the effect of compelling the enemy to use practically the whole of 118th Jäger Division on the islands to the detriment of their operations on the mainland.[197] Between 2 and 4 June an Allied landing on Brac, staged to help Tito during his retreat, succeeded in diverting further German troops to the coast, the Enigma revealing that the enemy regarded the raid as more serious than its forerunners and was fearful that Split would be threatened if it succeeded.[198]

195.   CAB 121/528, SIC file F/Balkans/1, Wilson telegram to PM 29 May 1944.
196.   Naval Headlines, Nos 1025–1028 of 24–27 April 1944, eg. DEFE 3/151, VL 9407 of 25 March; DEFE 3/42 (2), KV 1790 of 23 April; DEFE 3/42 (1), KVs 1980 and 1910 of 24 April.
197.   WO 204/969, No 87 of 25 April 1944.
198.   Naval Headlines, Nos 1067 and 1068 of 5 and 6 June 1944; DEFE 3/165, KVs 6444, 6447 and 6475 of 5 June; DEFE 3/166, KV 6502 of 5 June 1944.

ARBARA LINE ....
OV SANGRO LINE ─ ∙ ─
ERNHARDT LINE ────
KTOR LINE ─ ─ ─
USTAV LINE ────
TLER LINE ∙∙∙∙∙∙∙∙∙

S. Gothard
Pass

A

Simplon
Tunnel

Mt. Cenis
Pass

METRES
1500 and over
1000
500
Sea level

CHAPTER 34

From Naples to Rome

FOR TWO weeks after the battle of Salerno Germany had had no plans for holding Italy south of Rome. Hitler had instructed Kesselring to withdraw to the Rome area, delaying the Allies by rear guards and a scorched earth policy, whether or not his counter-attack at Salerno succeeded; these instructions had remained unchanged till the end of September 1943. At the end of September, however, Hitler ordered Kesselring to use delaying tactics only so far as a line from Gaeta to Ortona. He was to hold this line and, if the Allies did not attempt to break it, he was to plan to take the offensive into Apulia. Army Group B was to protect his lines of communication and coastal flanks, to organise defence in the Apennines and to crush the Partisans in Istria and Slovenia. These new instructions, which were embodied in a formal directive on 4 October, were prompted by the slow pace of the Allied advance and reports that assault shipping was leaving the Mediterranean for the United Kingdom; from this evidence Hitler deduced that in Italy the Allies aimed only at the political prize of Rome and a base from which to attack southern France or, more probably, the Balkans.[1]

Sigint quickly disclosed the change in German policy. Enigma signals of 1 October, decrypted on 2 October, revealed that in a recent interview with Kesselring Hitler had said that it was 'of the utmost importance' that as little ground as possible should be given up, particularly on the left flank of Tenth Army, and had ordered active defence along the whole front.[2] On 8 October two further decrypts of signals from the GAF's liaison officers* with LXXVI Panzer Corps provided firm evidence that the Germans intended to hold a line south of Rome for the winter: they gave details of the line to which the Panzer Corps was to retire during the night of 7–8 October, of a further line of resistance along the river Trigno (line *Barbara*) and of 'the final winter position' (line *Bernhardt*, which lay a little north of the river Sangro), as well as of sector boundaries between LXXVI Panzer Corps on the German left and XIV

---

* Fliegerverbindungsoffiziere (Flivos).

1. Molony, *The Mediterranean and Middle East*, Vol V (1973), pp 318–319, 377–379.

2. DEFE 3/883, JP 6048 of 2 October 1943; Dir/C Archive, 4535 of 2 October 1943.

Panzer Corps on the German right.[3] References to the *Bernhardt* line in XIV Panzer Corps's sector, though less conclusive, showed that it ran through the Cassino area.[4] Other decrypts of 7 October disclosed that 65th and 305th Infantry Divisions were being transferred from Army Group B to C-in-C South[5] and that Hitler and Ribbentrop had told the Japanese Ambassador in Berlin that the German forces were looking for an opportunity to take the offensive and drive the Allies out of Italy.

This intelligence caused the Allied commands to abandon their earlier expectation of occupying Rome early in November and reaching Leghorn, Florence and Arezzo by the end of that month.[6] For some weeks, indeed, it induced them to give serious attention to the possibility of a major German counter-offensive in Italy. The Prime Minister and the Chiefs of Staff had already considered this possibility in September,[7] and at the beginning of October AFHQ had been anxious lest Germany might free divisions for use in Italy by withdrawing to an *Ostwall* in Russia.[8]* On 20 October, after weighing the recent intelligence, JIC Algiers thought that a German offensive could not be precluded and that, as air support for it would be minimal, it would be more likely to come that winter than in the spring.[9] Expressing a similar anxiety to General Eisenhower on 24 October, General Alexander judged that Germany had at least 24 divisions in Italy; that she could maintain some 60 divisions there if she could make them available; and that she was shortening her lines elsewhere in order to create a reserve.[10] On 26 October AFHQ feared that Germany might take the offensive.[11]

These anxieties were not shared in Whitehall. Among the high-grade decrypts received on 19 October (and forwarded to the Mediterranean commands on the same day) one had contained instructions from Keitel to the effect that first priority in transport arrangements in Italy was to be given to the movement of troops

---

* For intelligence on the building of an *Ostwall*, see above, pp 20, 22.

3.   DEFE 3/884, JP 6578 of 8 October 1943; Dir/C Archive, 4587 of 8 October 1943.
4.   For examples, CX/MSS/3234/T1, 3242/T51, 3776/T16.
5.   DEFE 3/884, JP 6545 of 7 October 1943.
6.   WO 204/967, AFHQ Weekly Intelligence Summaries Nos 59 and 60 of 12 and 19 October 1943; WO 204/1006, JIC (AF) 19/43 of 20 October 1943.
7.   CAB 121/128, SIC file A/Policy/Middle East/3, JP (43) 321 of 10 September, Concrete telegram 853 of 11 September 1943.
8.   JIC (43) 412 (o) of 4 October.
9.   WO 204/1006, JIC (AF) 19/43 of 20 October 1943.
10. CAB 121/128, NAF 486 of 24 October 1943.
11. WO 204/968, AFHQ Weekly Intelligence Summary No 61 of 26 October 1943.

from Italy to other fronts, and in another the C-in-C GAF had sent orders to Luftflotte 4 for the movement of transport aircraft from Italy to Russia.[12] On 21 October the Prime Minister sent the following comments on these decrypts to the CIGS: 'These transfers *away from* Italy are significant'; 'The pressures in S Russia must be heavy. Also the Italian front is definitely given second place'.[13] On 29 October, asked to comment on General Alexander's appreci- ation, the JIC made the same point. Assessing German strength in Italy as 22 to 25 divisions, of which five or six were facing the Partisans in Istria and Slovenia, it was confident that the number could not be increased to anything like 60, and doubted whether it could be increased at all. The argument that Germany was trying to create a reserve by shortening her lines in Russia was contrary to all the evidence. There was no question of divisions being transferred from Russia; the contrary was more probable. No forces were likely to be moved from the Balkans. It was highly improbable that any would be moved from France and the Low Countries. At most 16 or 17 of the divisions in Italy could be made available for a counter-offensive, and many of these were below strength. On these grounds, and because air support would be quite inadequate, the JIC was 'convinced . . . that the enemy would not feel he was in a position to launch . . . a large-scale attack'.[14]

The JIC's appreciation was entirely accurate: on 22 October, as we now know, Kesselring had reported that he would need six divisions and large air reinforcements for an offensive into Apulia, and as a result of his report Hitler shelved the project.[15] Nor was it long before high-grade Sigint* provided significant support for the appreciation by disclosing that Germany was transferring a number of crack divisions from Italy to the Russian front. By 7 October the Enigma had mentioned that 24th Panzer Division was under orders

---

* The German Army Enigma keys used in Italy were not very productive at this period owing to the static nature of the fighting and the enemy's use of line communications. Thus the key and staff key of Tenth Army (named Albatross I and II by GC and CS) and the keys used for communications between OKH and German forces in Italy (Puffin I and II) were broken only very occasionally, and there was very little traffic from Army to Army Group and to OKH. But Army Group B's key (Shrike) was broken four or five days a week from early in October 1943 until the traffic died out in the spring of 1944, and the shortage of high level army Enigma decrypts was off-set by the fact that GC and CS was still reading regularly with about a week's delay the non-morse teleprinter link between C-in-C South and OKH (Bream). In addition the GAF general key (Red), which was also still read regularly and currently, provided some high level intelligence about the Army, and other GAF keys produced a great deal of tactical information about the ground fighting.

12. DEFE 3/886, JPs 7644 and 7647 of 19 October 1943.
13. Dir/C Archive, 4744 of 21 October 1943.
14. JIC (43) 442 (o) (Draft) of 29 October; CAB 121/128, JP (43) 377 of 28 October.
15. Molony, op cit. Vol V p 378.

to move to Russia; it had established that the division was on the eastern front by 25 October.[16] Other decrypts had referred on 26 October to the 'transfer away' of 76th Infantry Division and SS Panzer Division Adolf Hitler;[17] both were identified in Russia by mid-November.[18] On 18 November GC and CS decrypted instructions to Kesselring which showed that 16th Panzer Division was being transferred, though it was to move without its armoured observation battery following a plea from Kesselring that he could not spare it.[19] The move to Russia of 2nd Parachute Division, which had been in the Rome area since August, was also revealed by the Enigma decrypts during November.[20]

The JIC, no doubt fortified by its knowledge of the earlier of these transfers, refused to change its view when the CIGS criticised its appreciation of 29 October for being complacent and over-optimistic.[21] In further reports in the first week of November it allowed that, if given the benefit of every doubt, the enemy might be able to assemble 15 or 16 of his divisions in Italy for an offensive and seven more for reliefs, and calculated that, if he was prepared to accept the risks of stripping every other theatre, he could assemble as many as 31 divisions. But in each of these reports it emphasised that the calculations were hypothetical and repeated its conclusion that the Germans were in no position to deal the Allies a decisive blow. The JIC could not envisage 'any circumstances under which the enemy will be able to increase his air power in Italy to a scale in any way sufficient to support a major offensive . . ., especially in view of the overwhelming Allied air superiority'.[22]

On 8 November, in their report on the 'Relation of Mediterranean to *Overlord*', the Joint Planners accepted the JIC's assessment. They advised the Chiefs of Staff that 'the present German intention in Italy is to hold us as far south as possible for as long as possible, and when forced to retire to hold us firmly on the Pisa-Rimini line. Owing to their air inferiority, which they cannot rectify, and to deterioration on other fronts, the Germans will be unable to stage a major counter-offensive without running the gravest risks else-where . . .'[23] The Prime Minister and the Chief of Staff incorporated

---

16. CX/MSS/3329/T14; WO 208/3573, MI 14 Appreciation of 25 October 1943
17. DEFE 3/887, JP 8188 of 26 October 1943.
18. WO 208/3573 of 15 November 1943.
19. DEFE 3/890, JP 9971 of 18 November.
20. ibid., JPs 9561 of 12 November, 9606 of 13 November 1943; WO 208/3573 of 29 November 1943.
21. CAB 121/128, COS (43) 263rd (o) Meeting, 29 October.
22. CAB 121/413, SIC file D/Germany/1, Vol II, JIC (43) 444 (o) of 1 November, JIC (43) 456 (o) of 8 November.
23. CAB 121/128, JP (43) 390 of 8 November.

the conclusions of the JIC and the Joint Planners in the aide memoire which they drew up for use at the forthcoming Anglo-US conference in Cairo. This made no reference to the possibility of a German counter-offensive and proposed only that the Allied offensive in Italy 'should be nourished and maintained until we have secured the Pisa-Rimini line . . .'.[24]

□

In Italy by the middle of November a temporary stalemate had been reached along the whole front, with both sides exhausted by operations in which the Allies had forced the delaying positions in front of the German winter line and made their first efforts to penetrate the winter line itself, and Generals Eisenhower and Alexander had issued new directives. Dated 8 November, these laid it down that after securing Rome the Allied forces would pause and reorganise for a further big advance and establish heavy bomber units in Italy for operations against central Europe. For the approach to Rome they instructed Eighth Army to get across the lateral road Pescara-Collarmele so as to threaten through Avezzano the lines of communication of the enemy facing US Fifth Army, which was to capture Frosinone. When Frosinone had been captured a seaborne landing directed against the Alban hills would be made south of Rome.[25] By the end of 1943, however, the Allied forces were far from gaining these new objectives. Eighth Army had crossed the Sangro, broken through the Adriatic end of the *Bernhardt* line and taken Ortona, but was held up at Orsogna. Fifth Army had forced the line on a front of about 20 miles between Mignano and Acquafondata, but XIV Panzer Corps was doggedly holding new ground.[26] The resolution with which the enemy had contested every vital feature had made it plain that, even if a serious counter-offensive was beyond his means, he remained determined to hold the Allies south of Rome for as long as possible.

Intelligence threw much light on the enemy's determination to carry out this objective by providing a wealth of detail about his order of battle, the state of his divisions, his supply situation and the development of his defence positions. On the last of these subjects PR provided good evidence,* but with this exception the

---

* As the Allied advance progressed, both the RAF and the USAAF formed PR Wing HQs to control their squadrons moving forward in Italy.[27] The Northwest African PR Wing, in overall command of the PR operations, remained under American command when the

24. ibid; CAB 80/76, COS (43) 708 (o) of 14 November, Annex I.
25. Molony, op cit, Vol V, pp 332–333, 360, 383–384, 429, 438, 447, 450–453.
26. ibid, pp. 488–491, 494, 513–520.
27. Air 41/7, *Photographic Reconnaissance*, Vol II, pp 66–67, 124.

intelligence was almost entirely obtained from high-grade Sigint and Army Y. The SIS, which had re-organised its Mediterranean resources in the summer and established a forward unit in Sicily, had transferred that unit to Bari by October 1943 with instructions to develop an independent network and an organisation to operate in collaboration with SIM (the Italian Secret Service). It did not produce much information before the beginning of 1944, when most of SIS Algiers moved to Naples,* but it obtained useful intelligence from Rome before the city's capture and later rendered a valuable additional service in that the considerable supply of military intelligence that SIS received after the capture of Rome provided cover for the dissemination of Ultra to a far wider circle of users than would otherwise have been possible.† SOE was also a source of intelligence from the autumn of 1943 when the first of its liaison missions to the infant resistance movement in Italy arrived.[30]

High-grade Sigint disclosed all movements of divisions from Army Group B to the battle area – the transfer of 65th, 305th and 94th Infantry Divisions in October,[31] of 44th Infantry Division in November,[32] and of 90th Panzer Grenadier (PG) Division, 5th Mountain Division and 334th Infantry Division (the latter to replace

---

Allied air forces in the Mediterranean were amalgamated in January 1944 and to convey to the Wing the PR requirements of the Mediterranean Allied Air Forces (MAAF) an inter-Allied Mediterranean Photographic Intelligence Centre was established at the same time. A Mediterranean Army Interpretation Unit (MAIU) was also set up, whose western component, under the control of the new Mediterranean PR Wing, met the requirements of the main theatre of operations, including those of Eighth Army.[28] It has been claimed that the fullest stage of development in Corps and Divisional interpretation was attained during the Italian campaign, with senior officers appreciating the potentialities of air photographs and interpretation sections becoming an integral, though individual, part of an HQ.[29] See Appendix 1 for further details.

* The Bari unit, which had about five agents and W/T operators in enemy-held territory by the end of 1943, and 35 W/T operators in northern Italy by the end of the war, concentrated on organising the production of military intelligence from SIM and the resistance movements in German-occupied areas in Italy; particularly reliable contacts for the production of military intelligence were built up with the Communist resistance in the north from the autumn of 1943. In January 1944 the SIS section collaborating with SIM transferred from Bari to Naples. SIS Naples also concentrated on political intelligence, in particular on coverage of the activities of the Italian authorities in the liberated area. Only general indications of what SIS achieved in Italy survive, but these make it clear that intelligence on German order of battle and troop movements was well received by 15th Army Group and that valuable reports on the effects of Allied air attacks on enemy communications were supplied in answer to special requests for such intelligence from AFHQ (Air).

† See Volume III Part 2.

28. ibid, p 67; Mockler-Ferryman, *Military Intelligence Organisation*, pp 191–192.
29. Mockler-Ferryman, op cit, p. 192.
30. J Beevor, *SOE: Recollections and Reflections 1940–1945* (1981), pp 140–141
31. DEFE 3/884, JP 6545 of 7 October; DEFE 3/887, JP 8040 of 25 October 1943.
32. DEFE 3/5, VL 107 of 20 November 1943; DEFE 3/8, VL 763 of 29 November 1943; WO 208/3573 of 22 November 1943.

the much-battered 65th Infantry Division) in December.[33] The dispositions and movements of the enemy divisions in the front line were known both from the Enigma and Army Y. At the beginning of October Army Y disclosed the transfer of 16th Panzer Division from XIV Panzer Corps to LXXVI Panzer Corps to meet Eighth Army's offensive at Termoli.[34] On the last day of the month the Enigma reported the intended withdrawal of the Hermann Göring Division and 29th PG Division into reserve and, in the middle of the month, the rather precipitate return of 29th PG Division to the front to restore a critical situation.[35] An Enigma decrypt of 29 November disclosed the move of the 26th Panzer Division to support the German left wing (as did Army Y) and listed all the divisions in the line, from right to left.[36] Further important adjustments in the battle area were revealed by high-grade Sigint during the second half of December; they included the withdrawal of 90th PG Division into reserve and the creation of Corps Group Hauck, comprising 305th Infantry Division and some Alpine battalions, to hold a section of the front between the two Panzer Corps under the direct control of Tenth Army.[37] On 20 November, as well as revealing the new appointment of Kesselring as C-in-C South-West and GOC Army Group C, which took over all formations of Army Group B, the decrypts carried a general appreciation from Kesselring to OKW. In it he announced that he would try to relieve the front-line divisions periodically, to conserve their strength, and that, to permit the withdrawal of 26th Panzer Division and 29th PG Division for rest and refitting and employment in a mobile role, he intended to bring up 44th Infantry Division from Istria to the front. He thought there was an urgent need for mountain troops at the front and asked OKW to consider the exchange of Panzer Grenadier or infantry divisions for Mountain divisions.[38] Throughout the autumn Sigint was supplemented by PR, which supplied excellent evidence about the lay-out of the enemy's defences, particularly in the eastern sector of the *Bernhardt* line.[39]

33. DEFE 3/8, VLs 957 of 1 December, 976 of 2 December 1943; DEFE 3/9, VL 1146 of 4 December 1943; DEFE 3/11, VLs 1685 of 11 December, 1689 of 12 December 1943; DEFE 3/12, VLs 2006 of 16 December, 2424 of 22 December 1943; WO 208/3573 of 13, 20 and 27 December 1943.

34. *History of Sigint in the Field*, p. 107.

35. DEFE 3/888, JP 8554 of 31 October, DEFE 3/889, JPs 9070, 9075 and 9078 of 6 November; DEFE 3/890, JP 9575 of 12 November 1943.

36. DEFE 3/8, VL 821 of 29 November 1943; *History of Sigint in the Field*, p 108.

37. DEFE 3/13, VL 2006 of 16 December; DEFE 3/14, VL 2424 of 22 December 1943; DEFE 3/15, VLs 2569 of 24 December, 2734 of 27 December 1943; DEFE 3/16, VLs 2758 of 27 December, 2934 and 2939 of 30 December 1943; WO 208/3573 of 20 and 27 December 1943.

38. DEFE 3/5, VL 107 of 20 November 1943.

39. AIR 41/7, pp 121–124; AIR 41/34, *The Italian Campaign*, Vol I, p 212: WO 204/968, No 63 of 9 November 1943; Molony, op cit, Vol V, p 483.

During December the high-grade Sigint provided further evidence that the Allied pressure had not been sufficient to oblige the enemy to relent in his determination to hold a line south of Rome. In a signal of 4 December, decrypted on 14 December, Kesselring ordered the construction of a new reserve position on the left flank following Eighth Army's crossing of the river Sangro;[40] and an order of 26 December for the transfer of a labour battalion to develop defence lines on the river Foro, just north of Ortona, was decrypted on 31 December, three days after Eighth Army had captured Ortona.[41] The decrypts of three lengthy reports from Kesselring in December gave details of the state of development of prepared positions along the whole front.[42] At the same time it was clear that the enemy was managing to sustain his strength in tanks and guns.

This information came from two different series of German decrypts. C-in-C South's evening situation reports sometimes included a statement on tanks from early October 1943 and ten of these were decrypted in the next month. A more important series was that issued by the C-in-C's Chief Tank Officer, the first of which was decrypted on 8 November; thereafter, though rarely decrypted completely, they were decrypted sufficiently and sufficiently frequently to permit a reasonably accurate reconstruction of the situation, except between 30 November 1943 and 25 January 1944 and again between 5 September and 11 November 1944. From 30 November 1943, when this latter series of returns adopted a new and comprehensive pro-forma incorporating a statement of the number of captured Italian armoured fighting vehicles (AFVs) and assault guns issued to German formations, they became the chief source of information on the subject. It was known that Tenth Army had 149 tanks serviceable on 13 October (60 Pzkw III and 89 Pzkw IV), of which 82 were with 26th Panzer Division, 35 with the Hermann Göring Division, 21 with 15th PG Division and 11 with 16th Panzer Division; it had 112 assault guns and 85 heavy anti-tank guns.[43] On 30 November the returns showed that it had 182 tanks, 22 Armoured Command Vehicles (ACVs) of which four were Italian, 173 assault guns and 320 heavy anti-tank guns; and Kesselring also had under his command a newly arrived Panzer Operational Company with 40 tanks, Tiger Unit Meyer with seven serviceable Tiger tanks, and Fourteenth Army, which had no tanks but mustered 54 assault guns (42 Italian) and 193 heavy anti-tank guns.[44]

---

40. DEFE 3/12, VL 1909 of 15 December 1943.
41. DEFE 3/16, VL 2946 of 31 December 1943.
42. DEFE 3/13, VLs 2051 and 2055 of 17 December 1943; DEFE 3/17, VL 3006 of 1 January 1944; DEFE 3/18, VL 3322 of 6 January 1944.
43. DEFE 3/885, JP 7260 of 16 October 1943.
44. DEFE 3/11, VL 1664 of 11 December 1943.

Intelligence on the enemy's supply situation told a similar tale. During October and November the regular decryption of day returns from the Chief Quartermasters of C-in-C South and Tenth Army showed that rations were well maintained, that stocks of ammunition, though low to begin with, steadily improved, and that, though small, fuel stocks were kept above the danger level.[45] This was despite the Allied strategic bombing of railway communications in central Italy; the effectiveness of this, to which there were frequent references in the high-grade decrypts,[46] including one in which Kesselring deduced from the careful planning of the attacks that the Allies were being advised by the Italian transport authorities,[47] was mitigated by the enemy's increasing use of coastal shipping. It was possible to calculate from the decrypts, particularly those of the naval Enigma, that during November, despite the bombing of ports and other Allied action, about 17 per cent of all deliveries to Tenth Army and 20 per cent of all fuel deliveries had been made by sea. During December there was a decline in the amount of intelligence about supplies, particularly those of Tenth Army, but it was clear that although the enemy had been unable to build up stocks, so that those of ammunition and fuel came under strain, he was managing to meet his current needs and was under no necessity to withdraw his defence line further north for supply reasons.[48]

The overall position was summed up in the second half of December in two appreciations by JIC (AFHQ). In the middle of the month the committee appreciated that in addition to eleven divisions in the battle zone and the equivalent of four in Istria/Slovenia, the Germans had a reserve in Italy of six divisions, two of which were defensive and one, or possibly two, were still forming; this slender reserve formed a barely adequate base for the defensive battle in the south, for which the divisions at the front were only just sufficient.[49] But on 28 December it nevertheless concluded that the enemy had never yet been thrown so far off balance by Allied pressure as to be obliged to change his plans; he still intended to deny Rome to the Allies and to build up on each flank reserves for counter-attack.[50]

□

---

45. eg DEFE 3/887, JP 8352 of 28 October 1943.
46. Molony, op cit, Vol V, p 467; AIR 41/34, Chapter VI; DEFE 3/886, JP 7830 of 22 October; DEFE 3/888, JP 8754 of 2 November; DEFE 3/889, JPs 9115 of 7 November, 9169 of 8 November, 9302 of 9 November, 9398 of 11 November 1943; DEFE 3/8, VL 803 of 29 November; DEFE 3/11, VL 1541 of 9 December; DEFE 3/12, VL 1984 of 16 December; DEFE 3/13, VL 2139 of 18 December; DEFE 3/15, VLs 2728 and 2736 of 27 December 1943.
47. DEFE 3/887, JP 8198 of 26 October 1943.
48. DEFE 3/14, VL 2448 of 22 December 1943.
49. WO 204/968, No 68 of 15 December 1943.
50. ibid, No 70 of 28 December 1943.

Tactical intelligence was in plentiful supply during the hard-fought battles of the last three months of 1943, particularly after the beginning of November when a GAF Enigma key which had been first used for army-air co-operation in Sicily (known to GC and CS as Puma) became the key of the GAF liaison officers with Tenth Army. The almost daily decryption of the reviews by these officers of events on their divisional fronts made it possible to view the battlefield through German eyes. The naval Enigma key (Porpoise), which continued to be broken regularly, also made a considerable contribution to Allied knowledge of the German supply situation. With the development of the fighting in Italy, moreover, Army Y redressed the disappointments in its performance during *Husky* and at the time of the Salerno landings* and again provided a picture of enemy activity as comprehensive as that which it had given in the Western Desert and during the later stages of the Tunisian campaign. German field security was steadily improving, so that the amount of intelligence derived from Traffic Analysis and from the interception, DF-ing and exploitation of traffic on low and medium W/T frequencies greatly declined. Fortunately, however, the rediscovery in October of the enemy's VHF networks proved a turning point and restored the declining prestige of Army Y. VHF was intercepted mainly at battalion level, though internal regimental links were occasionally heard. Most of the traffic was in plain language or in plain language mixed with simple alphabetical codes; it provided something like 60 per cent of the intelligence obtained from Army Y throughout the Italian campaign.

Examples of the intelligence obtained from Army Y and the Enigma suggest that the Allies often knew almost as much about the enemy's formations as he did himself.[51] Enigma decrypts of 12 November disclosed that 3rd PG Division, badly mauled in the fighting round Venafro, was to be relieved by 29th PG Division, Kesselring having concluded that the Allied advance in that area had created a grave situation.[52] An Enigma decrypt of 7 December described the situation of 15th PG Division on 6 December as critical and disclosed that the Allied penetration into the main defence line in the Monte Camino sector was creating serious anxiety.[53] During November Army Y provided a great deal of information about the heavy fighting on the fronts held by 1st Parachute Division and 16th Panzer Division, and disclosed the

---

* See above, pp 95, 111.

51. *History of Sigint in the Field*, p 91
52. DEFE 3/890, JPs 9575 and 9579 of 12 November 1943.
53. DEFE 3/10, VL 1352 of 7 December 1943.

transfer of 26th Panzer Division to the German left wing. From the end of November, when 90th PG Division was committed on Eighth Army's front and Eighth Army embarked on the Sangro offensive, Army Y again produced valuable intelligence.[54] That good use was made of both sources, which often gave full particulars of divisional fronts, is indicated by the report of a remark by Kesselring to General Lemelsen, acting Commander of Tenth Army – 'the enemy always comes on the boundaries' – and of Lemelsen's reply – 'the Devil knows how he always finds out where they are'.[55]

The high-grade Sigint also provided regular intelligence, often in advance, about the GAF's effort in battle reconnaissance and close support of the Army.[56] Throughout the autumn, however, this effort was spasmodic, rising to peaks on the Volturno front in mid-October, during the struggle for the Mignano gap in the first half of November and at the beginning of December, and during Eighth Army's offensive across the Sangro in December, but at other times falling to almost negligible proportions.[57]

Intelligence on the GAF bomber raids against Allied bases and shipping was rarely prompt enough to be of operational value. Between 21 October and the end of November the GAF, whose bomber effort had hitherto been crippled by the transfer of the bombers from Foggia to north Italian bases, bombed Naples six times by night and once by day. In the case of the night raids, the GAF Enigma disclosed that bomber operations had been ordered without being able to specify the target.[58] During November there were also three attacks on convoys by aircraft from southern France; two of them inflicted serious damage with torpedoes and the Hs 293, and only in the case of the third, on 26 November, did the defences receive good warning.[59] In advance of the GAF's most

---

54. WO 109/8520 Eighth Army Intelligence Summaries, Nos 611 of 27 November, 612 of 28 November, 617 of 3 December and 619 of 6 December 1943; *History of Sigint in the Field*, pp 90, 91, 106–109.
55. Molony, op cit, Vol V, p 494.
56. DEFE 3/886, JPs 7596 of 20 October, 7722 of 21 October, 7935 of 23 October, 7955 and 7969 of 24 October; DEFE 3/887, JPs 8034 of 25 October, 8210 of 27 October; DEFE3/888, JPs 8787 and 8800 of 2 November, 8910 and 8926 of 4 November; DEFE 3/889, JPs 9064 of 6 November, 9095 of 7 November, 9366 of 10 November, 9442 of 11 November; DEFE 3/6, VL 441 of 24 November; DEFE 3/7, VLs 510 of 25 November, 549 of 26 November, 616 of 27 November 1943.
57. AIR 41/34, Chapter VI.
58. ibid; DEFE 3/886, JPs 7763, 7934 and 7979 of 22, 23 and 24 October; DEFE 3/889, JPs 9019, 9073 and 9477 of 5, 6 and 11 November 1943; DEFE 3/7, VL 579 of 26 November 1943.
59. DEFE 3/5, VLs 217, 241 and 245 of 22 November; DEFE 3/6, VLs 272 of 22 November, 293, 340 and 358 of 23 November, 368 and 370 of 24 November; DEFE 3/7, VL 591 of 26 November 1943.

damaging blow, the raid on Bari by aircraft from northern Italy on the night of 2–3 December which destroyed seventeen ships and caused about 1,000 casualties,[60] the Enigma decrypts provided reports on the enemy's reconnaissance of the harbour and the airfields. A second raid on Bari, which did no serious damage, followed on 13 December; the decrypts gave good warning that this was being planned, but the signal which disclosed the time of the attack and the fact that it was to be made by aircraft from Greek bases was not decrypted till 14 December.[61]

In the second week of December the GAF Enigma revealed that most of the bombers in northern Italy were being withdrawn to airfields in Germany.[62]*

□

At the conferences at Cairo and Tehran in November/December 1943 the Allies decided to launch Operation *Overlord* in May 1944 in conjunction with a secondary operation against the south of France (which became known as Operation *Anvil*) and meanwhile to continue the advance in Italy to the Pisa-Rimini line. At the end of December, convalescing at Marrakesh, the Prime Minister discussed the furtherance of the advance with the Mediterranean commanders. He pressed for a landing at Anzio (Operation *Shingle*) to cut the German line of communications south-east of Rome and threaten the rear of XIV Panzer Corps, arguing that the task in Italy must be finished by the time the Allies undertook *Overlord* and *Anvil*. The commanders conceded that only by such a landing could they obtain a quick decision; that a two-divisional assault, supported by airborne troops and followed up by an armoured formation based on the elements of a third division, should be sufficient to achieve success; and that the operation could be carried out about 20 January. The Prime Minister secured the agreement of the President to the operation, and to the necessary deferment of the transfer of tank landing ships (LSTs) from the Mediterranean, on 28 December. On 8 January 1944, after holding a further conference 'to clear up all outstanding difficulties', he informed the Defence Committee and the Chiefs of Staff in London that the landing would take place on 22 January.[63]

---

* See below, p 324.

60. AIR 41/34, p 221.
61. DEFE 3/11, VLs 1583 of 10 December, 1692 of 12 December; DEFE 3/12, VLs 1826 and 1841 of 14 December 1943.
62. DEFE 3/11, VL 1739 of 12 December; DEFE 3/12, VLs 1760, 1788 and 1795 of 13 December 1943.
63. CAB 121/592, SIC file F/Italy/6/1, Vol I, Frozen telegrams 873, 892, 893, 897 all of 25 December, Grand telegram 864 of 28 December 1943, Frozen telegram 1171 of 8 January 1944.

At this further conference AFHQ advised that by D + 3 the Germans would be able to oppose the landing with at most two divisions, some tanks and one or two parachute battalions.[64] This appreciation was based on excellent intelligence about the enemy's order of battle in Italy and was to prove accurate.* It is doubtful whether the elements of five divisions which the Germans managed to assemble against the Anzio landing by 26 January amounted to as much as two divisions.[65] But it does not appear that any systematic attempt was made at Marrakesh to look beyond the enemy's immediate capacity to resist and to assess what his strategic reaction was likely to be. If the Allied commanders had this consideration in mind on 3 January, when they noted that *Shingle* was 'obviously a hazardous operation although the prize to be gained was so high that the risk might well be worth taking',[66] they did not develop it into an argument against the Prime Minister's enthusiasm.[67] Nor was it until 16 January that US VI Corps, the force made responsible for the landing, completed its detailed estimate which, crediting the Germans with some twenty-eight battalions on the Anzio front by D + 6, went some way to foreseeing the formidable enemy build-up which eventually materialised.[68]

In preparation for VI Corps's landing, US Fifth Army was ordered to thrust as strongly as possible towards Cassino and Frosinone, its objectives being to attract German reserves that might otherwise be used at Anzio and to break XIV Panzer Corps's front with a view to linking up with VI Corps, and the British Eighth Army was ordered to press against LXXVI Panzer Corps to prevent it from transferring troops to the western flank.[69] Eighth Army's two attempts to take the offensive in January were quickly abandoned, and throughout the fighting at Anzio and Cassino in February and March its front remained static following the withdrawal of its major formations to reinforce Fifth Army.[70] Fifth Army's advance crossed the Garigliano in the Minturno sector and broke into the main German defence line on the night of 17–18 January, but its attempts to make a second bridgehead across the Garigliano and to cross the Rapido between 19 and 22 January were all repulsed.[71]

The Allies had very full knowledge of the order of battle and the intentions of the German Tenth Army during the January fighting,

---

* See Appendix 7.

64. ibid, COS (44) 35 (0) of 15 January.
65. Molony, op cit, Vol V, pp 587, 588, 661–665; AIR 41/34, p 218.
66. CAB 121/592, NAF 577 of 3 January 1944.
67. Molony, op cit, Vol V, p. 772.　　　68. ibid, pp 645, 773.
69. ibid, p 593.　　　70. ibid, pp 596–597.
71. ibid, pp 600–601, 603, 604, 605, 609, 613, 616, 617, 619.

intelligence from the main source, high-grade Sigint, having been further increased when, early in the previous month, GC and CS broke the Enigma key (Bullfinch) in which Tenth Army made its day reports to OKH.* In the course of 20 and 21 January, as General Alexander and General Wilson (the Supreme Allied Commander in the Mediterranean) reported to the Chiefs of Staff, they learned from Sigint that in response to Fifth Army's offensive the Germans were counter-attacking strongly and, as had been hoped, appeared to be committing a large part of their reserves.[72] Further details reached them in a priority signal from GC and CS in the early hours of 22 January; this disclosed that I Parachute Corps was to take over operational command of the German front on the right of 15th PG Divison and use 90th PG Division to regain the old main defence line.[73] Later on 22 January a further decrypt told them that I Parachute Corps was under Tenth Army and in command of 94th Infantry Division and 29th and 90th PG Divisions.[74] By this time US VI Corps had landed at Anzio, accompanied by an Army Y party attached to 3rd US Infantry Division and a SCU/SLU unit which landed on the beachhead from the command ship on 25 January.[75]

Except by the GAF which, as the Enigma confirmed, concentrated all its close support forces against it,[76] the Anzio landing was at first unopposed.† Nor was it seriously affected by the enemy's frequent bombing raids on the landing fleet and the beachhead.‡ But on 31 January the attempt to take the offensive from the beachhead, begun the previous day, was brought to a standstill, and VI Corps was on 2 February preparing to defend its existing positions against a determined counter-attack. The landing had achieved tactical but not strategic surprise; and the Germans at once put into effect an existing plan for the reinforcement of Italy in the event of an Allied attack on the west coast (*Marder I*). OKW ordered the transfer to Italy from the Replacement Army in Germany of the HQ of LXXXV Corps, three infantry regiments and

---

* See Appendix 8 for a summary of what was known about Tenth Army's order of battle and its reaction to Fifth Army's offensive, and of the less complete information that was available about the forces under Fourteenth Army in central and northern Italy.

† U-boat operations against operation *Shingle* were on the very small scale that had marked their activities during the landings in Sicily and at Salerno, see p 232 n†, below, p 235.

‡ See Appendix 9.

72. CAB 121/592, MA telegrams 1019 of 20 January, 1021 of 21 January 1944, MEDCOS 5 of 21 January 1944.
73. DEFE 3/131, VL 4464 of 22 January 1944.
74. DEFE 3/132, VL 4506 of 22 January 1944.
75. *History of the SLUs*, p 36; *History of Sigint in the Field*, p 121.
76. DEFE 3/153, VLs 4502 of 22 January, 4542 of 23 January 1944.

some artillery and the transfer from C-in-C West of 715th Infantry Division and a battalion of Panzer Regiment 4. Long-range bombers were despatched to Italy from western Europe and Greece, and the anti-shipping bomber force in the south of France was reinforced and provided with advanced landing grounds at Bergamo and Piacenza. In Italy Kesselring recalled the operational HQ of I Parachute Corps to Grottaferrata on 22 January and on 23 January ordered the HQ of Fourteenth Army to assume tactical command of the Rome area; and by 26 January he had assembled elements of five divisions – 3rd PG, Hermann Göring, 4th Parachute, 65th Infantry and 71st Infantry – around the beachhead. By the end of the month these forces had been strengthened by battle groups of 16th SS PG Division and 114th Jäger Division, 715th Infantry Division was coming up and 26th Panzer Division was at Avezzano under orders to join I Parachute Corps.[77]

The return of long-range bombers from the western front to northern Italy and the reinforcement of the bomber force in southern France were reflected in the Enigma decrypts without delay and detected by RAF Y as they occurred. On 22 January AFHQ's analysis of GAF dispositions gave the long-range bomber strength as nil in northern Italy, 60 in the south of France and 50 in Greece and the Aegean. By 29 January these figures had been changed to 65 in northern Italy, 105 in southern France and nil in Greece and the Aegean. By 5 February the number known to be in northern Italy had risen to 100 – fifteen with II/KG 76, forty-five with I and III/KG Lehr 1, forty with I, II and III/KG 30 – and there was no appreciable change after that date.[78]

The first intelligence of the enemy's decisions affecting his ground forces went out from GC and CS on the morning of 25 January: a report to the effect that 94th Infantry Division and 29th and 90th PG Divisions had reverted to XIV Panzer Corps, that I Parachute Corps was in command against the Allied landing, and that on Tenth Army's front 71st Infantry Division had begun to relieve 44th Infantry Division.[79] Early the following day the Enigma disclosed that the GAF liaison officer attached to 29th PG Division was to join I Parachute Corps at Grottaferrata, and indicated that the relief of 44th Division had been cancelled – possibly in order to permit the switch of some or all of 71st Division to the Anzio front.[80] Later on 24 January further decrypts showed that 3rd PG Division

---

77. Molony, op cit, Vol V, pp 587, 588, 661–665; AIR 41/34, p 218; Air Sunset 140 of 28 January 1944.
78. WO 204/968, Nos 74 to 77 of 24 January to 15 February 1944.
79. DEFE 3/132, VL 4559 of 23 January 1944.
80. DEFE 3/132, VLs 4618 and 4619 of 24 January 1944.

had been at Albano, north of Anzio, the previous morning;[81] that the spearhead of Gruppe Gesele (which was believed to include the SS Panzer Grenadier Regiment from Leghorn) and advanced elements of 65th Infantry Division had passed through Aquapendente on the main road from Siena to Rome;[82] and that troops were being withdrawn to the beachhead from Corps Group Hauck and LXXVI Panzer Corps as well as from XIV Panzer Corps, which had been ordered to go on the defensive against Fifth Army.[83] On 25 January it was established that 26th Panzer Division had left LXXVI Panzer Corps and been placed at the disposal of the Army Group C with temporary headquarters at Avezzano.[84] In the early hours of 28 January GC and CS reported that elements of 26th Panzer Division had left Avezzano to join I Parachute Corps,[85] and by that time it was known that 715th Division was to pass through Aquapendente between 28 and 31 January together with Battle Group Knöchlein of 16th SS PG Division, which, it was learned on 29 January, was being sent to Viterbo.[86] On the evening of 29 January the decrypt of a signal from I Parachute Corps gave the locations at which, over and above 'the divisions already employed', 65th, 715th and 71st Infantry Divisions and 26th Panzer Division were assembling.[87] By 2 February further information about the order of battle at the beachhead had been obtained from a decrypt naming the commanders and chief staff officers of 65th, 71st and 715th Infantry Divisions, the Hermann Göring Division, 3rd PG Division, 26th Panzer Division and 4th Parachute Division,[88] and in a signal to Göring Kesselring had reported that 4th Parachute Division would be concentrated when he was ready to attack.[89] Army Y effectively filled in the broad picture presented to the Allied commanders by the high-grade Sigint. The VHF links of formations were heard as they arrived and the formations were usually identified well before contact identification had been made.[90]

Kesselring and von Mackensen, commanding Fourteenth Army, had initially hoped to make a major assault on the beachhead on 1

81.　DEFE 3/132, VL 4634 of 24 January 1944.
82.　DEFE 3/132, VL 4637 of 24 January 1944.
83.　DEFE 3/132, VLs 4646 and 4654 of 24 January 1944.
84.　DEFE 3/132, VL 4715 of 25 January 1944; DEFE 3/133, VL 4775 of 25 January 1944.
85.　DEFE 3/133, VL 4956 of 28 January 1944.
86.　DEFE 3/133, VL 4949 of 27 January 1944; DEFE 3/134, VL 5038 of 29 January 1944.
87.　DEFE 3/134, VL 5065 of 29 January 1944.
88.　DEFE 3/135, VL 5345 of 1 February 1944.
89.　DEFE 3/135, VL 5349 of 2 February 1944.
90.　*History of Sigint in the Field*, pp 116–118, 121.

February. Following US VI Corps's advance on 30 January, however, they placed I Parachute Corps on the defensive, with orders to prevent any extension of the beachhead, and began to doubt their ability to dislodge the Allies without further reinforcements. Kesselring had decided to strengthen von Mackensen's forces by bringing over the experienced HQ of LXXVI Panzer Corps from Tenth Army and replacing it with the HQ of LI Mountain Corps, brought down from central Italy; these moves took effect on 4 February. On 6 February von Mackensen reported personally to Hitler; he could open the counter-offensive about 15 February, but requested an additional experienced division. Hitler refused a division, but offered the élite Infantry Lehr Regiment from Germany, some Tiger tanks and some new weapons.[91]

One reason for the hesitation of the German commanders was the fact that the supply situation was making it difficult to create reserves for the counter-attack; the Allies learned something about this on 1 February, when the decrypt of a signal from Kesselring of 26 January revealed that although train movements from Germany had improved, supply trains were still not reaching Rome and supply by motor transport was insufficient for daily needs.[92] Not less serious for them was the situation on XIV Panzer Corps's front. In December, in the course of advocating Operation *Shingle*, the Prime Minister had argued that, if carried out in sufficient strength, the landing should be decisive: since it would cut the communications of the forces facing Fifth Army, 'the enemy must therefore annihilate the *Shingle* force by withdrawals from the Fifth Army front or immediately retreat'.[93] AFHQ on 24 January was by no means so sanguine. It noted that the enemy's situation was awkward but not yet grave, and added: 'It is certain he will strain himself to the utmost. To abandon the Cassino line at once would be contrary to his policy, his interests and his nature'.[94] The severe fighting on the Fifth Army front that followed the Anzio landing and the German decision to go on to the defensive against Fifth Army caused the Germans increasing anxiety. In the last ten days of January the French Expeditionary Corps advanced around Monte Abate and Monte Belvedere on this front and X Corps resumed its offensive on the lower Garigliano; and in the first week of February US II Corps embarked on the first battle of Cassino.[95] On 29 and 30 January decrypts of Tenth Army's reports disclosed that an Allied penetration after hard fighting on 29th PG Division's

---

91. Molony, op cit, Vol V, pp 676–678, 725–726, 730–735.
92. DEFE 3/135, VL 5336 of 1 February 1944.
93. Molony, op cit, Vol V, pp 772, 773.
94. WO 204/968, No 74 of 24 January 1944.
95. Molony, op cit, Vol V, pp 625–636, 696–703.

sector had been blocked with the last local reserves and that, after violent fighting on 44th Division's left flank, the Germans feared that the Allies would outflank the Cassino position.[96] Between 1 and 5 February the Enigma decrypts portrayed the desperate efforts that were being made to contain US II Corps's advance north and west of Cassino town, which included bringing 90th PG Division into the Cassino sector from reserve.[97] On 4 February they revealed that German Headquarters were fighting in the foremost front line.[98] During 6 February the decrypts of further reports made on 4 and 5 February disclosed that the Germans intended to relieve the exhausted units of 44th Infantry and 90th PG Divisions by transferring 1st Parachute Division from LI Mountain Corps, on their left flank, and conveyed an unmistakeable air of crisis.[99] On the Garigliano front Army Y's intercepts of the prolific communications of 94th Infantry Division were valuable, as were those of 90th PG Division's signals in the Cassino area.[100]

The Enigma decrypts received on 6 February were the last to be obtained from the Bullfinch Enigma key. As well as providing immediate news of the impact of the Anzio landing on Tenth Army, this source had furnished the Allies with an almost current account of Tenth Army's view of the fighting since December 1943. Its disappearance early in February, before the end of the first battle of Cassino, was followed by a marked decline in the amount of Sigint relating to Tenth Army's front. But Sigint coverage of the enemy's over-all situation, and of his preparations for counterattacking at Anzio, was unaffected. On 2 February the decrypts included, for the first time since 30 November, a return of the AFV holdings of the formations under Kesselring's command on 25 January; it was incomplete, but indicated that there had been no increase in the number of serviceable tanks.[101] By 3 February they had revealed that LI Mountain Corps had relieved LXXVI Panzer Corps at Catignano the previous day.[102] On 3 February GC and CS also provided one of the most valuable decrypts of the whole war. It was the decrypt of a signal dated 28 January which contained Kesselring's intentions for the counter-attack on the beachhead.[103]*

---

* According to the SLU history it was this decrypt which finally convinced General Clark, hitherto sceptical, of the value of Sigint.[104]

96. DEFE 3/134, VLs 5100 of 29 January and 5111 of 30 January 1944.
97. DEFE 3/135, VLs 5431 and 5437 of 3 February 1944.
98. DEFE 3/135, VLs 5362 of 3 February, 5431, 5437, 5467 and 5477 of 3 February; DEFE 3/136, VLs 5568 and 5588 of 5 February 1944.
99. DEFE 3/136, VLs 5630, 5655, 5661 and 5667 of 6 February 1944.
100. *History of Sigint in the Field*, pp 116–118, 121.
101. DEFE 3/135, VL 5398 of 2 February 1944.
102. DEFE 3/135, VLs 5357 of 2 February, 5434 of 3 February 1944.
103. DEFE 3/135, VL 5449 of 3 February 1944.
104. *History of the SLUs*, p 36.

Kesselring reported that the timing depended on the arrival of reinforcements (namely 715th Infantry Division, two reinforced PG regiments, some artillery units, the first battalion of Panzer Regiment 4 and elements of 114th Jäger Division) and the supply of two ammunition issues. Since the necessary movements, mainly by motor transport, could not be completed before 31 January, the attack could not take place before 1 February. It would be prepared by I Parachute Corps, with HQ at Grottaferrata, under Fourteenth Army with HQ at Capranica, and I Parachute Corps would command the following formations: 65th Infantry Division (less one regiment, but with elements of 4th Parachute Division and a GAF Jäger battalion); Gruppe Gräser consisting of 3rd PG Division (less one and a half regiments, but with a reinforced PG Regiment under command); 26th Panzer Division with the first battalion of Panzer Regiment 4 and Tiger Company Meyer; the Hermann Göring Division (less its Panzer regiment, but with SS PG Regiment 35, Parachute Regiment 1 and 4th Panzer Reconnaissance Battalion). After reconnaissance patrols and counter-battery shelling (for which ammunition was limited) the main attack would be made by Gruppe Gräser and 71st Division with 26th Panzer Division echeloned behind, on a five kilometre front with the right wing just west of the Via Anziate in order to break through the Allied main defence zone in the direction of Nettuno. In the nights before the offensive, bombers would attack shipping; for the final twenty-four hours heavy bombers would concentrate on warships, and a special artillery group was being formed in an attempt to neutralise bombardment by medium and heavy naval guns. The task of the close support air forces would be protection of the assault formations and attacks on Allied batteries: considerable fighter reinforcements were needed. If the Allies attacked first the counter-offensive would have to be developed out of defensive fighting.

On 5 February further details about Kesselring's preparations were decrypted, including the fact that from 4 February I Parachute Corps was commanding the German right wing and LXXVI Panzer Corps the left,[105] and in the next few days, while local German counter-attacks on the beachhead were forcing the 1st British Infantry Division to withdraw from the Campoleone salient,[106] Sigint gave more information about the German build-up. It showed that all trains bringing in the first battalion of Panzer Regiment 4 had arrived by 2 February, and 14 of the 16 trains bringing the Lehr Artillery Abteilung; that 715th Division had

---

105. DEFE 3/136, VLs 5594 and 5607 of 5 February 1944.
106. Molony, op cit, Vol V, pp 725–726, 729–735.

taken part in the operations against the Campoleone salient; and that 26th Panzer Division had taken Gruppe Berger (of 114th Jäger Division) under command.[107] Decrypts on 10 and 11 February disclosed that 71st Infantry Division was moving to XIV Panzer Corps in exchange for 29th PG Division from the Garigliano front.[108] On 13 February GC and CS reported that 3rd PG Division had been expected to occupy its advanced battle headquarters that morning.[109] Early on 14 February it added that Gruppe Gräser was being dissolved that day, leaving 3rd PG, 715th Infantry and 114th Jäger Divisions to hold its front as independent commands, and that the Infantry Lehr Regiment was in the front line of 3rd PG Division's sector.[110]

From the afternoon of 15 February the decrypts left little doubt that the enemy had made his final preparations and that the counter-offensive was imminent. At 1345 that day GC and CS signalled that Luftflotte 2's intentions for the coming night and for 16 February were a concentrated bombing attack on beachhead targets, early morning reconnaissance of the area between Naples and Nettuno, and close support of the Army in the beachhead.[111] At 0345 on 16 February it reported that LXXVI Panzer Corps had requested that fighters should be available from first light against aircraft spotting for artillery, and that during the rest of the day it would require battle reconnaissance and, on demand, ground attack aircraft and the intervention of the main fighter force.[112] At 0454 it added that during the evening of 15 February LXXVI Panzer Corps had informed Luftflotte 2 that 'day and time remain as provisionally projected in special order' and that 26th Panzer Division had been ordered to move to its assembly area.[113]

The main thrust of the counter-attack by 3rd PG, 715th Infantry and 114th Jäger Divisions had made sufficient progress by the evening of 17 February for von Mackensen to commit 26th Panzer and 29th PG Divisions to its support. By the evening of 18 February the German spearheads had almost reached the San Lorenzo-Padiglione road. But except for a short time on the following morning, this was the furthest they were to get; on 19 February they were caught off balance by the Allied counter-attack. Kesselring decided

---

107. DEFE 3/136, VLs 5607 of 5 February and 5631 of 6 February; DEFE 3/137, VL 5871 of 9 February 1944.
108. DEFE 3/137, VL 5929 of 10 February; DEFE 3/138, VL 6016 of 11 February 1944.
109. DEFE 3/138, VL 6168 of 13 February 1944.
110. DEFE 3/138, VL 6195 of 14 February 1944.
111. DEFE 3/139, VL 6342 of 15 February 1944.
112. DEFE 3/139, VL 6349 of 16 February 1944.
113. DEFE 3/139, VL 6352 of 16 February 1944; CX/MSS/T95/79.

to regroup before resuming the offensive on another axis, reporting that – as had indeed been the case, thanks to Sigint – the Allies had correctly identified the direction of the main thrust and concentrated their forces against it.[114] The new attack, timed for 18 February but delayed for twenty-four hours by heavy rain, made no significant progress. It was abandoned on the evening of 1 March when Kesselring and von Mackensen, recognising that they could not eliminate the bridgehead without substantial reinforcements, which were not available, fell back on containing it by a policy of active defence.[115] Meanwhile, stalemate had also been reached on the Cassino sector with the failure on the night of 17–18 February of the Allied effort to establish a bridgehead over the Rapido in attacks that were in part designed to prevent Tenth Army from releasing reinforcements to the counter-offensive at Anzio.[116]*

Decrypts on the Cassino battle were confined to two reports by GAF liaison officers on the violent fighting for the railway station and Monastery Hill.[118] From the Anzio front intelligence was more plentiful.[119] There was a delay of about twenty-four hours between the transmission of the enemy signals and the transmission of the decrypts from GC and CS to the front. Thus the fact that 29th PG Division was being committed, reported in a GAF message late on 17 February, was signalled by GC and CS at 0404 on 19 February;[120] and the fact that the division had crossed the San Lorenzo-Padiglione road, reported by LXXVI Panzer Corps at 0700 on 19 February, was forwarded by GC and CS at 0904 on 20 February.[121] By the early hours of 21 February, however, the decrypts had established that the enemy's thrust had failed and that he was

---

* It was during these operations that the abbey at Cassino was heavily bombed by the Allies. Some battlefield observers believed that the Germans were using the abbey for military purposes, but Allied official histories accept that this was not in fact the case before the Allied bombing had wrecked it. No information to contradict the histories' conclusion was provided by any reliable intelligence source either before or after the bombardment.[117] See D Hunt, *A Don at War* (1966), pp 246–247, for the information that although an Army Y intercept suggested that a German Abteilung (Abt.) was in the abbey an intelligence officer realised that the reference to 'Abt' was a reference to the abbot (Abt) and not to the German military.

114. Molony, op cit, Vol V, pp 745–749, 752.
115. ibid, pp 755–756.
116. ibid, pp 697, 704, 705, 715–722.
117. ibid, pp 695, 707–709, 713; M Blumenson, *Salerno to Cassino* (Washington DC 1969), Chapter XXIII; AIR 41/34, pp 283, 289–290.
118. DEFE 3/140, VLs 6650 and 6655 of 19 February 1944.
119. DEFE 3/139, VLs 6469, 6477, 6480 of 17 February 1944; DEFE 3/140, VLs 6520, 6521, 6527, 6542 and 6551 of 18 February, 6585, 6607 and 6615 of 19 February, 6685 of 20 February 1944.
120. DEFE 3/140, VL 6585 of 19 February 1944.
121. DEFE 3/140, VL 6685 of 20 February 1944.

expecting further violent counter-attacks.[122] Nor was the Sigint confined to the land fighting. It revealed that fighters and fighter-bombers had been transferred from northern Italy on 16 February and that more than 200 sorties over the beachhead had been flown on the night of 16 and 17 February, as compared with an earlier average of about 60.[123] During the next fortnight, when bombers from northern Italy and southern France attacked the beachhead on most nights, it showed that fighter reinforcements had reached Italy from France and Germany.[124] It also provided information, often in advance, about the enemy's attempts to carry out seaborne attacks against shipping off the beachhead.

The first warning that Italian assault craft (explosive motor-boats) from Fiumicino and Italian MAS boats (motor torpedo-boats) from San Stefano were to be used against the beachhead was received on the morning of 18 February.[125] Later decrypts revealed that after some postponement two units had operated unsuccessfully on the night of 20–21 February and were to try again on the following night.[126] SIS agents operating from Rome reported on 20 and 21 February that MAS attacks were to be carried out in the next few days and at 1928 on 21 February warning that MAS boats were to attack on the night of 21–22 February was issued by GC and CS.[127] From then until 28 February the decrypts contained frequent warnings of intended attacks by MAS boats but also gave frequent notification that attacks had been postponed or broken off because of the weather.[128] Motor torpedo-boats were intercepted off the beachhead on the night of 20–21 February, when one blew up and another was driven ashore; another attack was intercepted on the night of 23–24 February, one boat being reported sunk.[129] It is not known whether these warnings directly helped the defences on these occasions, but the fact that the Allies had early warning that Germany was planning to use human torpedoes at Anzio no doubt contributed a good deal to their success in frustrating the first attack with these weapons on the night of 20–21 April.

---

122. DEFE 3/140, VLs 6662, 6677, 6679, 6684, 6713, 6720 of 20 November, 6726 and 6731 of 21 February 1944.
123. WO 204/968, No 78 of 22 February 1944.
124. ibid, No 80 of 7 March 1944.
125. DEFE 3/140, VL 6522 of 18 February 1944.
126. DEFE 3/140, VLs 6568 of 18 February, 6616, 6635 and 6656 of 19 February, 6718 and 6723 of 20 February 1944; DEFE 3/141, VL 6789 of 21 February 1944.
127. DEFE 3/141, VL 6784 of 21 February 1944.
128. DEFE 3/141, VLs 6958, 6962, 6971 and 6974 of 24 February; DEFE 3/142, VLs 7017 of 24 February, 7081 of 25 February, 7106 and 7159 of 26 February, 7190 of 27 February; DEFE 3/143, VLs 7268 of 27 February, 7327 of 28 February 1944.
129. WO 204/968, No 79 of 29 February 1944.

The fact that the 10th MAS Flotilla had gone over to the Germans after the Italian surrender, and that the Germans were taking an interest in Italian midget submarines, had been disclosed by Abwehr and Mediterranean naval Enigma decrypts in the autumn of 1943. By the end of that year the Home Waters Enigma had shown that the Germans had salvaged British X-craft in Altenfjord and were examining the towing fitments,[130] and the Naval Attaché Stockholm had obtained reports of the existence of a small U-boat which could be hoisted on board larger ships. Nothing further was learned until the middle of March 1944, but the Admiralty then notified the Mediterranean commands that Enigma decrypts had revealed that the German naval authorities in Kiel were planning an attack on the Anzio beachhead with Italian underwater anti-shipping equipment and would soon be sending 40 special weapons to the area; the decrypts gave the dimensions of the weapons but no other details.[131] At the end of March the Enigma added that the first consignment of the weapons would leave Eckernförde, which was known to be the site of the German Navy's torpedo experimental establishment, in a few days' time. In April it reported that the German Navy had taken over from the Abwehr the control of these specialised units by appointing an admiral to be in charge of a new Small Battle Units Command (KDK).[132]*

The SIS gave the first warning of the attack on Anzio on the night of 20–21 April (Operation *Marder*) which was carried out by motor torpedo-boats, assault craft and long-range bombers as well as by German human torpedoes. On 19 April SIS agents operating from Rome reported the arrival of two human torpedoes at Fumicino for immediate use, and it was to this information that the local naval authorities attributed a large share of the success in frustrating the attack. But Porpoise and GAF Enigma decrypts also gave good notice of the attack. At 1334 on 20 April GC and CS alerted the commands to the fact that four units had been ordered to sail; at 2354 it confirmed that an unspecified number of units had sailed; and at 0008 on 21 April it added the news that bombers from Udine,

---

* A new Enigma key identified at that time (named Bonito by GC and CS) was discovered to be a four-wheel key for use by the KDK when GC and CS broke it for the first time early in May 1944. Except for a brief period in September and October 1944, Bonito was read with ease down to the end of the war, and we shall see that it was to be of considerable operational value in Home Waters for the light it threw on the activities of the enemy's charioteers, swimming saboteurs and midget submarines during and after the Allied invasion of Normandy. In the Mediterranean, however, the enemy had virtually brought these activities to an end by the time it was broken; and it was not broken by the time he made the attack on Anzio on 20–21 April.

130. ADM 223/186, Ultra signal 1420/19 November 1943.
131. ADM 223/191, Ultra signals 1227/14 March, 1310/15 March.
132. DEFE 3/651, ZTPGM 68485.

Verona and Brescia were to make a concentrated attack on the beachhead at 0300.[133] A later decrypt disclosed that by 0530 on 21 April only one unit had returned to base.[134]

Sigint had meanwhile given good notice of the enemy's re-grouping for the renewal of the counter-attack on the beachhead and of the start of the attack on 29 February which was made by the Hermann Göring and 26th Panzer Divisions, by 362nd Infantry Division, brought up from coast defence duties north of the Tiber, and by part of 715th Infantry Division, transferred from the German right to the German left flank, while I Parachute Corps made diversionary attacks on the right and 29th PG Division went into reserve.[135] On 22 February the decrypts disclosed that the Hermann Göring Division had been relieved by 362nd Infantry Division on 21 February.[136] By 25 February they had reported that 3rd PG Division had been placed under command of I Parachute Corps and was taking over the sector held by 26th Panzer Division, and that the Hermann Göring Division was taking over a new sector.[137] On 28 February it became clear that 26th Panzer Division was in the line between 362nd Division and the Hermann Göring Division.[138] During 25 and 26 February Sigint established that 715th Division was moving to the left flank and disclosed that it was to preserve W/T silence until D-day.[139] Nor was this the only indication that the regrouping was being made in preparation for another offensive. Decrypts of 25 February showed that the enemy was issuing air photographs of specified areas extending well into Allied-held territory,[140] and decrypts of 27 February gave the location of 362nd Division's advanced battle headquarters and of the battle headquarters of 29th PG Division.[141] By the evening of 27 February GC and CS had issued the contents of two other decrypts of that day, reporting that ground attack aircraft would take part in 'to-morrow's operation' and announcing that 362nd Division had postponed Operation *Seitensprung* for twenty-four hours.[142] It was thus with some confidence that, as AFHQ reported, the Allies appreciated on the evening of 28 February that the attack would

---

133. DEFE 3/41, KVs 1511 and 1556 of 20 April, 1557 of 21 April 1944.
134. DEFE 3/41, KV 1593 of 21 April 1944.
135. Molony, op cit, Vol V, pp 750, 751.
136. DEFE 3/140, VL 6710 of 20 February; DEFE 3/141, VL 6808 of 22 February 1944.
137. DEFE 3/141, VL 6891 of 23 February 1944; DEFE 3/142, VLs 7040, 7053 and 7098 of 25 February, 1944.
138. DEFE 3/143, VL 7301 of 28 February 1944.
139. DEFE 3/142, VLs 7040 of 25 February, 7117 of 26 February 1944.
140. DEFE 3/142, VLs 7039, 7076 of 25 February 1944.
141. ibid, VLs 7188, 7206 of 27 February 1944.
142. DEFE 3/143, VLs 7266, 7270 of 27 February 1944.

come on the following day, beginning in 362nd Division's sector and being exploited by 26th Panzer and the Hermann Göring Divisions, and perhaps by 29th PG Division, while I Parachute Corps on the right wing and 715th Division on the left made holding attacks.

The offensive began as expected on 29 February. During 1 March decrypts of signals made on 29 February left no doubt of the enemy's discomfiture: the left wing of 26th Panzer Division had gained 500 metres but its right wing had suffered heavy losses; advance elements of 362nd Division had reached the Crocetta crossroads, but its attack on the Colle dei Pozzi had failed and one of its battalions had been smashed on the Carano-Crocetta road; 715th Division had not yet linked up with the Hermann Göring Division's attack; 114th Jäger Division had suffered severe casualties; the Hermann Göring Division had made only slow progress against Allied minefields and artillery fire.[143] By 0800 on 2 March GC and CS was able to issue the news that 362nd Division had reported the previous evening that it was withdrawing to its starting line and that part of 114th Jäger Division was also retiring.[144] On 5 March it decrypted the signal of 28 February in which Kesselring had notified OKW of his plan of operations; this confirmed that the attack had completely miscarried.[145]

On 9 March a still more valuable decrypt gave part of an appreciation made by Kesselring on 1 March, when he had realised that the offensive had failed. He reported that all the divisions, but especially 65th, 715th and 114th Infantry Divisions, needed rest and that 362nd Infantry Division and 4th Parachute Division ought to be taken out of the line for training. He was constructing a defensive position and, if the Allied strength remained constant, his own forces should be just sufficient to prevent an Allied breakthrough; but he could not hope to eliminate the beachhead unless two new battle-trained divisions were made available. If replacements continued on the existing basis, and he had to give up no forces except the Hermann Göring Division* and the Lehr Regiment†, he hoped that, in addition to containing the beachhead and keeping the Allied supply ports under artillery fire, he could stabilise the Cassino front by attacks with limited objectives. If he had to give up more formations, however, and if the long-term defence of the beachhead and of the *Gustav* line‡ proved impossible with the

---

* See Appendix 8, p 508. † See above, p 189
‡ The *Gustav* line ran from Cassino to the mouth of the Garigliano.

143. DEFE 3/143, VLs 7447, 7452, 7454 and 7468 of 1 March 1944; DEFE 3/144, VL 7550 of 2 March 1944.
144. DEFE 3/144, VLs 5738 and 7539 of 2 March 1944.
145. DEFE 3/144, VL 7740 of 5 March 1944.

remaining forces, he would have to withdraw to 'the C position'. The construction of this position would take two months; he would adopt it only in the most extreme emergency; but it would have the merits of permitting a unified conduct of operations and of still covering Rome.[146]

□

After their failure to break through on the Cassino sector on 17–18 February the Allies had planned a further attempt. While successive postponements due to weather were delaying the offensive, Sigint disclosed that 90th PG Division was being relieved by 1st Parachute Division from the Adriatic coastal sector, and Sigint and Army Y VHF intercepts established that 1st Parachute Division was arriving from 25 February.[147] On 6 March a decrypt reported that it was complete in the Cassino area.[148] The Allied attack began two days later with immense air and artillery bombardment of Cassino town. By 23 March it was clear that the enemy could not be dislodged, and the battle was gradually broken off.

Except that it confirmed that the Germans, like the Allies, were sustaining heavy casualties during this fighting, intelligence had no influence on the third battle of Cassino. The yield of high-grade decrypts about the ground fighting was meagre, and Army Y's exploitation of 1st Parachute Division's VHF traffic produced only tactical reports of no great value.[149] The decrypts regularly reported the division's selection of targets for the GAF's close support operations and often revealed the GAF's intentions in advance,[150] but the enemy's air effort was itself of little importance in the battle.

While the Germans were thus succeeding in stabilising the front, with the Anzio beachhead still separated from the main Allied forces, the Allied authorities were engaged in prolonged debate about the scope of the campaign in Italy, and when the debate began to move towards a compromise by which an advance as far as Rome was given priority over the withdrawal of troops for Operation *Anvil* in the south of France* several weeks followed while the Allied armies in Italy were regrouped for the next advance.

---

* See above, p 25 et seq.

146.   DEFE 3/146, VL 8072, of 9 March 1944.
147.   DEFE 3/141, VLs 6797 of 21 February, 6891 of 23 February 1944; DEFE 3/142, VL 7191 of 27 February 1944; *History of Sigint in the Field*, p 118.
148.   DEFE 3/148, VL 8608 of 16 March 1944.
149.   *History of Sigint in the Field*, p 117.
150.   DEFE 3/148, VLs 8571 of 16 March, 8652 and 8655 of 17 March, 8731 of 18 March 1944; DEFE 3/149, VLs 8826 and 8828 of 19 March, 8922 of 20 March 1944.

During this interval Allied planning derived great benefit from Sigint. From the decrypts of Kesselring's appreciation of 1 March* it could be deduced that he would not abandon the attempt to contain and, if possible, reduce the Anzio beachhead or withdraw at Cassino unless 'extreme emergency' forced him to do so, though it could not be ruled out that Hitler might insist that he destroy the beachhead and provide the necessary reinforcements; and it could also be deduced that, when he was forced to retreat, he would still try to hold a line which covered Rome.[151] By the middle of April the lack of decrypt evidence had indicated that reinforcements sufficient for an attempt to destroy the beachhead had not reached him and there was positive evidence that he was concerned about the possibility of being outflanked by another Allied amphibious operation; but there was no indication that he contemplated withdrawal. The damage done to his communications by the Allied air offensive had increased enormously since the beginning of April, but his supplies remained adequate.[152] On 21 April, however, the decrypt of a report of 15 April on the state of the German rearward defence lines and coastal fortifications gave a general account of the *Caesar* position – it ran from the west coast through a point 2½ kilometres south-west of Valmontone and a point 14 kilometres north-west of Avezzano and from there to the east coast – and mentioned a Campagna switch-line running from a point 10 kilometres south-west of Rome to Albano.[153] On 9 May, on the strength of this intelligence, AFHQ concluded that while it would be dangerous for the Germans to delay their retreat to a single front on the *Caesar* line until the Allies had made an irreparable breach in their existing fronts, it would be contrary to their practice to withdraw before the Allies attacked.[154]

On those fronts Sigint had by then disclosed that important changes had been made in the German order of battle. The Hermann Göring Division and 114th Jäger Division had moved from Anzio for rest and refitting and 26th Panzer Division and 29th PG Divisions and the Battle Group of 16th SS PG Division had left the front line, leaving three divisions under I Parachute Corps (4th Parachute, 65th Infantry and 3rd Panzergrenadier) and two divisions under LXXVI Panzer Corps (362nd and 715th Infantry

---

* See above, pp 197–198.

151. WO 204/968, No 81 of 14 March 1944.
152. DEFE 3/39, KVs 1096 of 15 March, 1135 and 1152 of 16 March 1944; DEFE 3/40, KVs 1352 of 18 March, 1469 of 20 March 1944; DEFE 3/42, KV 1912 of 24 April 1944; DEFE 3/43, KVs 2045 and 2047 of 25 April, 2049 and 2119 of 26 April, 2150 and 2153 of 27 April; DEFE 3/44, KV 2405 of 30 April; DEFE 3/145; KVs 2528 of 1 May, 2684 of 3 May 1944.
153. DEFE 3/41, KV 1578 of 21 April 1944.
154. WO 204/969, No 89 of 9 May 1944.

Divisions) to mask the beachhead.[155] At the end of March the main front under Tenth Army had been held by, from left to right, LI Mountain Corps with 305th and 334th Infantry Divisions and a blocking unit, made up mainly of units from 305th Division, and XIV Panzer Corps with 5th Mountain, 44th Infantry, 1st Parachute, 15th PG, 71st and 94th Infantry Divisions;[156] but the enemy had made substantial changes from mid-April. 114th Jäger Division had relieved the blocking group, which had itself relieved a Battle Group of 15th PG Division behind the right wing of XIV Panzer Corps. 71st Infantry Division had taken over the southern part of 15th PG Division's sector. LI Mountain Corps HQ had moved south to the Sora area and taken over 5th Mountain Division from XIV Panzer Corps. A new Corps Group under Hauck (GOC 305th Division) had been set up as an independent command responsible for the Adriatic flank. The bulk of 15th PG Division had been withdrawn from the line south of Cassino to the Fondi area and its sector was held by the Bode Group and the remains of 15th PG Division, under 44th Division HQ which had handed over its own sector to 1st Parachute and 5th Mountain Divisions.[157] On 12 May the decrypt of a signal from Kesselring to OKW had summed up the changes: XIV Panzer Corps, with 15th PG Division and 94th and 71st Infantry Divisions, was responsible for the sector from Terracina to the Liri river and LI Mountain Corps, with 44th Infantry, 1st Parachute, 5th Mountain and 114th Jäger Divisions, was responsible from the river to the boundary of Corps Group Hauck, which was directly under Tenth Army.[158]

The enemy's mobile reserves had meanwhile been disposed so as to guard against the danger of being outflanked by another Allied amphibious operation.* The Hermann Göring Division was at Leghorn and could not be employed without OKW's permission. 26th Panzer Division was to take over the coastal sector south of Tarquinia in the event of an Allied landing between Orbetello and

---

* The threat of which had been projected since 10 April 1944 by the deception staff at AFHQ in order to draw off the enemy's reserves.

155.   WO 208/3573 of 27 March 1944; DEFE 3/146, VL 8045 of 98 March 1944; DEFE 3/151, VL 9336 of 25 March 1944.
156.   WO 204/968, No 83 of 28 March 1944.
157.   DEFE 3/39, KVs 1089 of 15 April, 1119 of 16 April 1944; DEFE 3/42, KV 1854 of 24 April 1944; DEFE 3/44, KVs 2255 and 2290 of 28 April, 2427 of 30 April, 2491 of 1 May 1944; DEFE 3/45, KV 2690 of 3 May 1944; DEFE 3/46, KV 2788 of 4 May 1944; DEFE 3/47, KVs 3075 and 3129 of 7 May, 3145 and 3169 of 8 May, 3245 of 9 May 1944; DEFE 3/153, KVs 3294 of 9 May, 3474 of 11 May 1944; Molony op cit. Vol VI, Part I (forthcoming), Chapter I.
158.   DEFE 3/154, KV 3557 of 12 May 1944.

Ostia. 29th PG Division was north-west of Rome. And while most of 15th PG Division was at Fondi, behind Tenth Army's right flank, 90th PG Division, in Tenth Army reserve, was in the Ostia area.[159]

To the comprehensive intelligence about the German order of battle Sigint had added some information about the fighting capacity, the strengths and state of training of the enemy's formations[160] and, for the first time since November 1943, complete AFV returns. In November 1943 Kesselring's command had had 283 tanks, of which 229 had been serviceable. A return of 3 March 1944 had disclosed that the number had increased to 375, but that only 186 were serviceable.[161] A return of 28 April gave the total as 403 and the number serviceable as 310, of which 197 were with Fourteenth Army, 37 with Tenth Army and the remainder with the Hermann Göring Division and Army Panzer Abteilung 8 in the von Zangen Army Group in the north of Italy.[162] This was the last return received before the Allied offensive (Operation *Diadem*) began on 12 May.

The Allied regrouping in preparation for *Diadem* had moved V Corps, comprising two divisions and an armoured brigade, to the Adriatic front as a defensive sector in place of Eighth Army; Eighth Army, comprising X and XIII Corps, the Canadian Corps and the Polish Corps, had taken over the central sector as far as Cassino; and Fifth Army held the line from Cassino to the sea with US II Corps and the French Expeditionary Corps and also commanded US VI Corps at Anzio. The objects of the operation, as laid down on 5 May, were to destroy the right wing of the German Tenth Army, to drive the Tenth and Fourteenth German Armies north of Rome and thence to pursue the enemy to the Pisa-Rimini line, inflicting maximum losses in the process. The plan required Eighth Army to break through at Cassino and advance to the area east of Rome, and thence through Terni and Perugia to Ancona and Florence, while Fifth Army took Ausonia and advanced parallel to Eighth Army, and also launched an attack from Anzio towards Valmontone, and V Corps held its front and put pressure on the enemy if he attempted to withdraw.[163]

---

159. DEFE 3/39, KV 1119 of 16 April 1944; DEFE 3/40, KV 1284 of 18 April 1944; DEFE 3/42, KV 1953 of 23 April 1944; DEFE 3/44, KV 2388 of 29 April, 1944; WO 204/968, No 84 of 4 April; WO 204/969, No 87 of 25 April 1944.

160. DEFE 3/39, KV 1232 of 17 April 1944; DEFE 3/43, KV 2177 of 27 April 1944; DEFE 3/44, KVs 2305 and 2306 of 28 April 1944; DEFE 3/45, KV 2520 of 1 May 1944.

161. DEFE 3/146, VL 8212 of 11 March 1944.

162. DEFE 3/45 (2), KV 2540 of 11 May 1944.

163. Molony, op cit, Vol VI Part I, Chapters I and II.

From the beginning of the battle on 12 May to 4 June, when the Allies entered Rome, Sigint in large quantities was available with little delay. No less than one-third of the high-grade decrypts of enemy traffic at and above divisional level were forwarded by GC and CS to the front in emergency signals. Army Y was still more valuable as a source of tactical intelligence, performing as well as it had ever done in north Africa, and it provided a detailed running commentary on the fighting while the Germans continued to resist south of Rome.[164] The interrogation of POW, who were taken in fair numbers from the outset, made an important contribution to tactical and order of battle intelligence, though it is difficult to assess the precise value because intelligence was frequently ascribed to prisoners in order to disguise its origin in Sigint. Photographic reconnaissance had provided thorough coverage of the terrain before the battle and it kept a close watch on the enemy's development of the *Hitler** and *Caesar* lines as the advance proceeded.[165]

In the first phase of the advance, which ended with the breaking of the *Gustav* line on 25 May, US Fifth Army quickly broke through on XIV Panzer Corps's front, the French Expeditionary Corps capturing Ausonia on 14 May and Esperia on 18 May and US II Corps taking Formia on 18 May after inflicting severe losses on the German 71st and 94th Infantry Divisions. On the central sector held by LI Mountain Corps the enemy put up fierce resistance to attacks by XIII Corps and the Polish Corps but withdrew during the night of 17–18 May, when Eighth Army began its advance up the Liri valley towards the *Hitler* line. Kesselring, who had brought in his immediate reserves – 15th PG Division from Fondi and 90th PG Division from Frosinone – on 13 May, and who had agreed on 16 May that Tenth Army should withdraw to the *Hitler* line (now renamed the *Senger* line to avoid compromising the Führer's prestige), decided on 17 May to move 26th Panzer Division from the Alban Hills, where it had been in reserve facing the Anzio beachhead, to his right flank, and on 18 May he ordered 305th and 334th Infantry Divisions into the battle from the Adriatic sector, replacing them with 278th Infantry Division from Istria.

From the VHF links of all the enemy formations engaged in this fighting, and particularly of 71st and 94th Divisions on Fifth Army's front who are said to have passed the highest volume of traffic ever

---

* This line had been under development for some time as a switch-line in case the *Gustav* line was breached. It ran from Terracina on the west coast through Fondi, Pico, Pontecorvo, Aquino, Piedimonte to Monte Cairo.

164.　*History of Sigint in the Field*, pp 127–131.
165.　Molony, op cit, Vol VI Part I, Chapter II; WO 170/202, Eighth Army Intelligence Summaries Nos 720, 729, 734 of 13, 23 and 29 May 1944.

intercepted, Army Y once again obtained a great deal of detailed information from the outset.[166] Much of it was of purely local interest; but it also covered the movement of the immediate German reserves (15th and 90th PG Divisions), the southward move to the Liri valley of units from 5th Mountain and 114th Jäger Divisions, the assembly of a Battle Group to protect the southern flank of 1st Parachute Division, the evacuation by that division of Monastery Hill – advance notice of which assisted the Poles to capture some 200 parachutists – and the commitment of 26th Panzer Division.[167] Nor was there any lack of high-grade decrypts on these and other enemy moves. They disclosed on 14 May that 15th PG Division was in the Formia area, and on 18 May that 3rd PG Division on the Anzio front had been ordered to send its reconnaissance unit to 15th PG Division at Fondi.[168] On 14 May they located part of 90th PG at Cassino; on 15 and 17 May they added that, having failed to stabilise the situation there, it was under orders to protect LI Mountain Corps's flank against the Allied breakthrough south of the Liri.[169] On 18 and 19 May they reported that 26th Panzer Division was moving to support XIV Panzer Corps.[170] Between 18 and 20 May they reported that 305th Division was under orders to transfer to XIV Corps's front and was being replaced by 278th Division from Istria, Kesselring having concluded that he could not leave the Adriatic sector unprotected in view of the possibility that the large amount of Allied shipping in Bari meant that the Allies intended an outflanking landing on the east coast.[171]

On 19 May the high-grade Sigint disclosed Kesselring's intentions: he would use the forces withdrawn from Cassino to reinforce the *Gustav* and the *Senger* lines, pull back the right wing of Tenth Army to the *Senger* line, but try to hold on to Gaeta and to annihilate the Allies as they advanced up the Liri and Cassino valleys.[172] By 25 May, however, the Allies had completed the second stage of their advance by breaking through the *Senger* line. On Fifth Army's front US II Corps captured Gaeta on 19 May and Terracina on 23 May,

---

166. *History of Sigint in the Field*, p 128.
167. ibid, pp 127–128; WO 170/202, No 720–725 of 13 to 18 May 1944; WO 170/339, XIII Corps Intelligence Summaries Nos 395–397 of 15, 16 and 17 May 1944; WO 204/969, No 91 of 24 May 1944; WO 170/63, HQ Allied Armies in Italy Intelligence Summary No 45 of 17 May 1944.
168. DEFE 3/155, KV 3788 of 14 May 1944; DEFE 3/157, KV 4263 of 18 May 1944.
169. DEFE 3/155, KVs 3798 of 14 May, 3948 of 15 May 1944; DEFE 3/156, KV 4147 of 17 May 1944; WO 170/202, No 721 of 14 May 1944.
170. DEFE 3/157, KVs 4263 of 18 May, 4393 of 19 May 1944.
171. DEFE 3/157, KVs 4313, 4360, 4363 and 4383 of 18 May, 4400 of 19 May 1944; WO 170/202, No 727 of 20 May 1944.
172. DEFE 3/158, KVs 4525 and 4532 of 19 May 1944.

and the French Corps advanced to Ceprano after fighting a severe battle with elements of 26th Panzer, 90th PG and 30th Infantry Divisions at Pico between 19 and 22 May. On 23 May US VI Corps broke out from the Anzio bridgehead, advancing to Cisterna and joining up with US II Corps's advance from Terracina on 25 May. On Eighth Army's front the Canadian Corps broke through the line at Pontecorvo on 23 May and established a bridgehead over the river Malfa on the following day. On 20 May, Fifth Army's advance having posed a threat to the junction between the German Tenth and Fourteenth Armies, Kesselring had moved 29th PG Division from the coast at Civitavecchia to Fourteenth Army's front at Terracina. On 23 May he had ordered the Hermann Göring Division to move south from Leghorn; two days later it was approaching Valmontone with a regiment of 92nd Infantry Division, which had been forming north of the Tiber, and elements drawn from 4th Parachute and 65th Infantry Divisions on the Anzio front. By then the enemy was bringing in reinforcements from outside Italy – 16th Panzer Grenadier Division and the SS Panzer Grenadier Lehr Division from Hungary; 20th GAF Field Division from Denmark; 42nd Jäger Division from Croatia to Genoa, where it was to relieve 356th Infantry Division for transfer to the south.

Army Y and the high-grade Sigint provided advance information about the German redispositions. By the early hours of 24 May Enigma decrypts had disclosed that 29th PG Division was in the Terracina sector, between 715th Division on its right and 94th Division on its left.[173] By 24 May, when 305th Division had been located in the Pastena area from the decrypts, the Enigma had also disclosed that 334th Division was also leaving the Adriatic sector; on 25 May it added that there would be considerable delay before 334th Division reached the right wing of Tenth Army because bombing had blocked the road at Avezzano.[174] As early as 20 May an Enigma decrypt indicated that the Hermann Göring Division might be preparing to move;[175] but the first evidence that it had come south was provided by Army Y, which placed its advance elements at Viterbo early on 24 May. By 27 May Army Y had suggested that it was near Valmontone,[176] and a high-grade decrypt

173. DEFE 3/159, KVs 4781 and 4813 of 22 May, 4866 and 4875 of 23 May, 4999 of 24 May 1944.
174. DEFE 3/159, KVs 4786 and 4800 of 22 May, 4939 of 23 May, 4990 of 24 May; DEFE 3/160, KVs 5148 and 5163 of 25 May 1944.
175. CAB 121/594, SIC file F/Italy/6/1, Vol III, General Alexander to CIGS, MA/1286 of 22 May 1944; DEFE 3/158, KV 4574 of 20 May 1944
176. CAB 121/594, Special Unnumbered Signal to PM from General Alexander, 24 May 1944; *History of Sigint in the Field*; pp 128, 129; WO 170/63, No 46 of 24 May 1944; WO 170/339, No 404 of 26 May 1944.

had added that the division had incurred considerable losses from incessant fighter-bomber attacks while on the move.[177] On 25 May the Enigma reported that three out of the eleven trains of the SS Panzer Grenadier Lehr Regiment had arrived in Kesselring's command by 23 May, and on 2 June it added that Kesselring had asked Himmler to agree that the regiment should go temporarily to the Tarquinia-Civitavecchia area to replace 92nd Infantry Division, which had been sent to the front.[178] On 29 May it disclosed that the north Italy command had 'taken over' 40 trains of 16th SS PG Division, and on 3 June the decrypt of a signal from Kesselring reported that the division's state of training was very low.[179] From decrypts obtained on 6 and 7 June it emerged that 16th SS PG and the SS PG Lehr Regiment were to be employed as reserves behind the Ligurian coast, and that by 5 June Kesselring had decided that the Lehr Regiment was to be incorporated in 16th SS PG Division, part of which was to be used to cover the coast between Leghorn and Carrara and the remainder to act as a mobile reserve, and that 19th GAF Field Division was also being brought in by rail for coast defence south of Leghorn.[180] Between 31 May and 5 June Sigint established that 356th Infantry Division in the Genoa area was being relieved by 42nd Jäger Division from the Balkans and that 20th GAF Field Division was being sent to the Civitavecchia-Orbetello area as part of Army Group reserve.[181]

By then the Allies had entered Rome. US VI Corps, making its main thrust to the north-west after taking Cisterna, had been held up on its right by the Hermann Göring Division before Valmontone, but had pierced the *Caesar* line with its left wing and taken Valletri on 1 June. US II Corps had captured Valmontone on 2 June. Eighth Army had captured Frosinone on 30 May, Ferentino on 1 June and Anagni on 3 June. On 3 June, having failed to block Fifth Army's breakthrough and stabilise the front on the *Caesar* line, Kesselring had withdrawn the Hermann Göring Division to the Aniene river east of Rome and ordered Fourteenth Army to retire north of the Tiber. Fifth Army entered Rome on 4 June while Eighth Army followed up the retreat of Tenth Army towards Arsoli and Avezzano.

The reduction and retreat of the enemy's formations is amply recorded in the high-grade Sigint signalled to the commands by GC

---

177. DEFE 3/161, KV 5401 of 27 May 1944.
178. DEFE 3/160, KV 5200 of 25 May 1944; DEFE 3/164, KV 6109 of 2 June 1944.
179. DEFE 3/162, KV 5685 of 29 May 1944; DEFE 3/163, KV 5944 of 31 May 1944; DEFE 3/164, KV 6238 of 3 June 1944.
180. DEFE 3/166, KVs 6556 of 6 June, 6700 and 6728 of 7 June 1944.
181. DEFE 3/163, KV 5861 of 31 May; DEFE 3/164, KVs 6157 and 6170 of 2 June, 6238 of 3 June; DEFE 3/165, KV 6428 of 5 June 1944.

and CS. By 7 May it had disclosed that 362nd Division, which with 715th Division had borne the brunt of US VI Corps's attack from the beachhead, was being withdrawn into the *Caesar* line and placed under the command of I Parachute Corps.[182] On 30 May it disclosed that on 27 May von Mackensen had reported that both divisions had been severely mauled, losing a considerable proportion of their infantry weapons and much of their artillery, and that there were shortages throughout Fourteenth Army.[183] By 29 May I Parachute Corps had withdrawn 4th Parachute Division, 65th Infantry Divsiion, 3rd PG Division and 362nd Division to specified sectors in the *Caesar* line.[184] On Tenth Army's front 26th Panzer, 15th PG and 5th Mountain Divisions were planning to withdraw before Eighth Army's advance during the night of 27 May.[185] On 2 June LI Mountain Corps reported that 44th Infantry, 5th Mountain and 114th Jäger Divisions were all exhausted and that they had had to give up units to help XIV Panzer Corps.[186] On 4 June LXXVI Panzer Corps reported that the fighting quality of the Hermann Göring Division had fallen very low, and on 5 June 15th PG Division was exhausted and handicapped by lack of fuel and ammunition.[187] On 31 May another decrypt disclosed that as early as 28 May Kesselring had reported that the divisions engaged in the battle had lost 75 per cent of their anti-tank weapons, which he could not replace from existing resources.[188] These are but a few of the decrypts which contributed to the clarity with which the intelligence summaries issued by AFHQ during the Allied advance traced the course of the fighting and, despite its considerable confusion, the enemy's changing order of battle.[189]* On the day-to-day fighting

---

* It is interesting to see from the following telegrams to General Alexander sent on 28 May how closely the Prime Minister was reading the decrypts on the battle: 'We are all delighted to hear your good news. At this distance it seems much more important to cut their line of retreat than anything else. I am sure you will have carefully considered moving more armour by the Appian Way up to the Northernmost spearhead directed against the Valmontone-Frosinone Road. A Cop is much more important than Rome which would anyhow come as its consequence. The Cop is the one thing that matters'. 'I have been looking through the tank strength as we get it from various sources. Boniface [i.e. the Enigma] attributes to you only seven hundred serviceable tanks, but CIGS furnishes me with figures showing you have at least two thousand five hundred serviceable. Surely one half of these could be used and indeed used up in making a scythe movement cutting off the enemy's retreat. 2. I am going to send you and your Armies a public message in a few days and will

182. DEFE 3/161, KVs 5303 of 26 May, 5362 of 27 May 1944.
183. DEFE 3/163, KVs 5761 and 5796 of 30 May 1944.
184. DEFE 3/162, KV 5666 of 29 May 1944.
185. DEFE 3/161, KVs 5462 of 27 May, 5469 and 5471 of 28 May 1944.
186. DEFE 3/164, KV 6175 of 3 June 1944.
187. DEFE 3/165, KV 6463 of 5 June 1944; DEFE 3/166, KV 6583 of 6 June 1944.
188. DEFE 3/163, KV 5916 of 31 May 1944.
189. see, for example, WO 204/969, No 92 of 31 May 1944.

Army Y probably yielded even more intelligence than high-grade Sigint, though it is difficult to identify and assess its contribution to the summaries, and it was no doubt more valuable to the operational authorities because tactical reports in the high-grade traffic were usually decrypted with a delay of about twenty-four hours.

Of the intentions of the GAF's long-range bombers and close support forces, on the other hand, advance notice was often obtained from the Enigma, and this source both underlined the weakness of the enemy's air force and paid tribute to the influence of the Allied air forces on the battle. There were frequent references to enemy requests for air support that could not be met, frequent complaints of the absence of fighter defence, and indications that ground attack aircraft were being operated as fighters.[191] On 1 June a decrypt disclosed that all remaining German fighters were being withdrawn that day to northern Italy.[192] On 27 May a signal from Tenth Army complained that in the absence of fighter defence and of adequate Flak protection Allied fighter-bombers were blocking all traffic, both near the front and in the rear.[193] From a decrypt of 31 May it was known that on 28 May Kesselring reported that on the previous night Allied aircraft had for the first time carried out systematic road patrols using parachute flares, and that they had greatly delayed the movement of reserves and supplies and caused considerable motor transport losses.[194] In a review of Allied battle tactics decrypted at the end of May Kesselring noted that delays of two to three days in re-grouping and bringing up supplies had been imposed on him by the Allied air effort; on one important bridge no less than 100 separate attacks had been made in the space of twenty-four hours.[195]

---

back you up whatever happens, but I should feel myself wanting in comradeship if I did not let you know now that the glory of this battle, already great, will be measured not by the capture of Rome or the juncture with the Bridgehead but by the number of German divisions cut off. I am sure you will have revolved all this in your mind, and perhaps you have already acted in this way. Nevertheless I feel I ought to tell you that, "It is the cop that counts" '.[190]

190. CAB 121/594, telegram 0031/28 May; CAB 120/603, PM registered file 412/34/14, telegram TOO 1905/28 May 1944.
191. DEFE 3/157, KV 4472 of 19 May; DEFE 3/158, KV 4727 of 21 May; DEFE 3/159, KVs 4859 of 22 May, 4961 of 23 May 1944.
192. DEFE 3/163, KV 5971 of 1 June 1944.
193. DEFE 3/161, KV 5525 of 28 May 1944.
194. DEFE 3/163, KV 5917 of 31 May 1944.
195. DEFE 3/163, KV 5825 of 31 May 1944.

PART X

The War at Sea from June 1943 to the
Summer of 1944

CHAPTER 35

U-Boat Warfare

I N May 1943, when Dönitz withdrew the U-boats from the north Atlantic convoy routes, he acknowledged that Germany had suffered a serious defeat, but was confident that the withdrawal need only be temporary. German science, he believed, would soon provide counter-measures against the Allied technical advantages – notably superior radar and the consequent power of surprise air attack – to which he attributed the recent set-backs. Nor did he doubt that, if only to prevent American men and materials from reaching Europe, it was imperative to resume the battle in the north Atlantic. This much the Admiralty knew from the decrypts of his signals to the U-boats,* as also from a German broadcast which publicly admitted that the U-boats had been 'temporarily thwarted' by 'new Allied defensive measures'. From the Enigma the Allies also knew that the size of the U-boat operational fleet remained formidable and was still increasing. On 31 May the Admiralty's Operational Intelligence Centre (OIC) put the number in operational service at 240, an increase of 66 since September 1942 despite the losses inflicted on the U-boats in the interval; in June it calculated that the number was 226 and that almost as many – 208 – were working up in the Baltic.[1] It was accordingly not surprised when, on 10 July 1943, from the decrypt of a telegram from the Japanese Ambassador in Berlin reporting on an interview with Dönitz, it learned that Germany expected to be able to resume 'effective U-boat warfare' at the end of August.

Meanwhile, until the U-boat fleet had been re-equipped with better Flak and an improved search receiver, and issued with the new acoustic torpedo†, the U-boat Command continued its efforts in areas where the U-boats might expect to escape air attack. In the last week of May the sixteen U-boats that remained in the north Atlantic were ordered to form a group 600 miles south-west of the Azores (the *Trutz* group) to operate against convoys on the US–Gibraltar route, while most of the U-boats in the Biscay ports were despatched to more distant waters.

The *Trutz* group had no success. The US authorities sent the escort-carrier *Bogue* to protect two convoys threatened by the new disposition. Despite the fact that there had been uncertainty in

---

* See Volume II, pp 571–572. † See below, p 220 et seq.

1. ADM 223/98, OIC SI 603 of 31 May, 615 of 9 June 1943.

interpreting the signals about the new patrol area, they did not share the OIC's doubts about the area to which the sixteen U-boats had been sent, preferring the alternative south-west of the Azores to that off the Canadian coast.[2] One convoy was successfully diverted whilst the other passed through a gap formed on 4 June, when the *Bogue*'s aircraft, to the surprise of the Germans, attacked three of the waiting U-boats, sinking one.[3] During the next four weeks the group was several times shifted and re-formed but Allied evasive routeing ensured that it found no convoy. At the beginning of July its boats were sent to patrol west of Cape St Vincent, where it lost three more and still failed to make any sightings before being wound up.[4] Nor did the U-boat Command operate another U-boat group against convoys until September 1943.

By then its plan to send most of the U-boats to distant waters had suffered heavily from the stepping up of the Allied offensive against U-boats on passage and in their refuelling areas. The plan depended on the ability to refuel U-boats from supply U-boats (types XIV and X B) at rendez-vous points in mid-Atlantic. Refuelling at sea had enabled U-boats to operate in distant waters since May 1942, and during the winter of 1942–1943 it had contributed heavily to the increase in the scale of the enemy's offensive against the Atlantic convoys. In the twelve months to the end of May 1943 supply U-boats had refuelled 170 U-boats destined for distant areas and 220 of those operating against convoys, and had done so without being disturbed; although three of the refuellers had been sunk, they were all sunk while on passage.[5] At the beginning of June 1943 the U-boat Command still disposed of nine supply U-boats. By the end of the year three further refuellers had become operational. But ten more had been sunk by then, no less than four of them between 13 and 30 July, in an intensive series of attacks by US escort-carrier task forces against the rendez-vous points and by Coastal Command and British surface ships against the U-boats on passage in Biscay and the northern transit area.

During the spring of 1943 the Allies had refrained from attacking the rendez-vous points because they had hesitated to divert forces from convoy protection – and still more because they had been fearful of jeopardising the security of Ultra by arousing the enemy's suspicions.* But in the second week of June aircraft of USS *Bogue*,

---

* See Volume II, p 549 for signals from the First Sea Lord to Admiral King, the US Chief of Naval Operations, in March/April 1943.

2. Op-20-G History, Vol II, p 105.
3. ibid, pp 105–106; ADM 234/68, BR 305 (3), German Naval History Series, *The U-boat War in the Atlantic*, Vol III, p 9.
4. Op-20-G History, Vol II, p 106; ADM 234/68, p 10.
5. ADM 234/68, p 32.

working on clues from the Enigma and on DF bearings, happened to disturb German preparations for a rendez-vous and sink the supply U-boat (U-118). This forced the U-boat Command to take drastic emergency measures which, when they were disclosed by the Enigma after some delay, illustrated for the first time the widespread consequences that might follow if the Allies made the refuelling areas a priority target. Despite the enemy's resort to emergency refuelling after the loss of U-118, some operational U-boats had to be recalled and others were delayed in reaching their distant operational areas, while two were followed from the rendez-vous area and sunk.[6] Together with the discovery that the emergency was in part overcome by U-488, another supply U-boat which refuelled twenty-two U-boats in the middle of June,[7] this evidence no doubt influenced the American decision to exploit the Enigma in an offensive against the German refuelling operations.

It has been argued that the success of the offensive owed little to Sigint.[8] It was certainly the case that the U-boat Enigma (Shark) was sometimes broken with considerable difficulty between June and September 1943; the decrypts for 13–21 June, the first three weeks of July and the first ten days of August were all greatly delayed.[9] To make matters still more difficult, the U-boat Command took special steps to preserve the secrecy of its refuelling arrangements. As well as disguising all grid positions referred to, the signals relating to refuelling were usually encyphered in the Offizier setting; and U-boats in or approaching a rendez-vous area were under strict instructions to keep W/T silence. From 5 June, moreover, as the decrypts revealed, the enemy progressively made these security precautions even more elaborate, and in July the U-boat Command took the further step of introducing modifications to the Enigma machine which completely held up GC and CS for three weeks. But the resulting delays by no means destroyed the operational value of the Shark decrypts. The delays in reading the Enigma were off-set by the fact that the U-boat Command usually issued its orders as much as two weeks ahead of the refuelling date, and even when the decrypts did not yield intelligence about the date and place of the refuelling they provided other intelligence – the identification of the supply U-boats, their departures and movements on passage, the location of favoured refuelling areas – which could be interpreted with sufficient accuracy to warrant the assignment of a task force.[10]

---

6. Op–20–G History, Vol II, pp 134–141, 143.
7. ibid, p 145; ADM 234/68, p 10.
8. Beesly, *Very Special Intelligence* (1977), p 188.
9. ADM 223/98, OIC SI 618 of 21 June, 648 of 26 July, 651 of 2 August, 659 of 9 August and 668 of 16 August 1943.
10. Op–20–G History, Vol II, pp 124–125.

It was on the strength of such evidence that the US escort-carriers *Core* and *Santee* were sent to join the *Bogue* early in July, and that on 13 July aircraft from the *Core* sank the refueller U-487. The Enigma had disclosed that several operational U-boats were outward bound on distant cruises, that they were likely to be refuelled, that the area south-south-west of the Azores was a favoured refuelling area, that U-487 was a supply U-boat and that she had been ordered to head for 36°N, 30°W; and this was sufficient to determine the approximate date and position of the rendez-vous.[11] In the same operation the *Santee* sank an operational U-boat on its way to the rendez-vous.[12] To take another example, USS *Card* was operating in the light of week-old Enigma evidence, though without precise information about the refuelling operation, when she sank U-117 (a type X B supply boat) on 7 August.[13] And when on 27 August she sank U-847*, an operational U-boat which had been ordered to refuel others left stranded by the recent sinkings of supply U-boats, the Enigma had provided details of the rendez-vous several days in advance.[14]

In the months of June, July and August 1943, in addition to three supply U-boats (U-118, U-487 and U-117), eleven operational U-boats were sunk in the American operations against the refuelling points, including U-847:[15] they were operations which benefited from the fact that several U-boats were likely to be found in the refuelling area. In the same way, the British offensive against the northern transit routes and Biscay, especially Biscay, exploited the presence of a large number of U-boats in relatively restricted areas. This offensive had faltered in the autumn of 1942, when the Germans introduced the *Metox* search receiver which could detect the Mark II (metre wave) anti-surface vessel radar (ASV).† In March 1943, however, when Coastal Command began to introduce Mark III (centimetric) ASV, new plans were devised for a system of night and day sweeps which could be switched about and briefed as to methods of attack in the light of Sigint information on U-boat positions and tactics.[16] The number of sightings by Coastal Command at once increased, and the U-boats, which had hitherto generally travelled on the surface by night, were ordered at the end of April to proceed submerged except for short periods by day to charge batteries. As well as slowing down the passage-time of the U-boats, this change of tactics only increased Coastal Command's

---

* See below, pp 216, 218 n‡.   † See Appendix 10.

11. ibid, pp 376–377.   12. ibid, p 378.
13. ibid, pp 183–184.   14. ibid, p 378.
15. ADM 234/68, p 17; Roskill, *The War at Sea*, Vol III Part I (1960), pp 31, 32.
16. ADM 223/88, Colpoys, *Admiralty Use of Special Intelligence in Naval Operations*, pp 289–290.

opportunities. Four U-boats were sunk and three damaged in daylight attacks in the first week of May. The U-boat Command thereupon set about strengthening the Flak armament of the U-boats and from the middle of May introduced further changes of tactics: first deciding that if surprised on the surface, the U-boats were to remain surfaced and fight it out, and then, from the end of May, ordering them to make the passage in groups, submerged at night but proceeding on the surface by day and bringing their combined fire-power to bear on attacking aircraft. The first such orders to an inward-bound group of U-boats were decrypted on 4 June.[17] The fact that most U-boats were proceeding in groups across the Bay, together with details about their speed and instructions as to how they should conduct themselves in their joint cruises, were disclosed by the Enigma on 12 June, on which day Coastal Command first sighted a group, outward-bound.[18] In response to this intelligence Coastal Command changed its own tactics, aiming to hold back as far as possible until it could attack with two or more aircraft, and from 20 June a naval escort group co-operated with its patrols.[19]

These developments coincided with the strengthening of Coastal Command's patrols. At the end of May a few aircraft were diverted from the Atlantic to Biscay; and on 5 June, the Enigma having established that there was no longer any threat on the convoy routes, Coastal Command made a large-scale switch of its forces to the Bay offensive.[20] By 17 June its reinforcement and its new tactics had forced the U-boat Command to cancel U-boat departures and suspend joint cruises until the U-boats had been armed with the new quadruple mounted Flak gun.[21] Group sailings were resumed on 25 June.[22] Of the four U-boats sunk in the Bay in June, two were sunk in the next few days by the surface ships of the Second Escort Group (EG 2) that was co-operating with Coastal Command. They included the Type X B supply U-boat U-119.[23]

From the end of June the pitched battles in Biscay between the U-boats and British forces grew more savage. The German Air Force was drawn in to provide fighter protection for the U-boats and make fighter sweeps against Coastal Command's patrols and, from August, to carry out glider bomb attacks against the British

---

17. ADM 223/182, Ultra signal 2150/4 June 1943.
18. ibid, Ultra signal 1714/12 June 1943.
19. AIR 41/48, *The RAF in Maritime War*, Vol IV, p 114.
20. AIR 41/48, p 105; Roskill, op cit, Vol III Part I, pp 18, 20.
21. ADM 223/182, Ultra signal 1752/19 June 1943.
22. ibid, Ultra signal 1950/25 June 1943.
23. ADM 223/98, OIC SI 622 of 28 June 1943; AIR 41/48, p 115.

surface ships.* On the British side the offensive was extended to the area west of Spain and Portugal when, early in July, the Enigma disclosed that the boats of the *Trutz* group had moved to patrol lines off Cape St Vincent and that six outward-bound U-boats had been sent to join them in operations against convoys on the UK–Gibraltar route.[24] On the strength of this intelligence C-in-C Coastal Command enlisted the help of the RAF at Gibraltar and the USAAF in Morocco; they sank three of the U-boats and damaged several others between 7 and 9 July.[25] In the Bay itself Coastal Command had already sunk four U-boats between 3 and 7 July; no less important, it had also forced the return to base of a supply U-boat (U-462) which had once before been damaged and forced back in June.[26] Between 9 July and 2 August the Biscay patrols and EG 2 sank thirteen more U-boats, including three supply U-boats – U-459, U-462, on her third attempt to make the passage, and U-461.[27] This brought the total number of U-boats sunk in the Bay since the beginning of June to twenty-one, of which four were supply U-boats. Post-war German records show that by 2 August 86 U-boats had attempted the passage of Biscay since 1 July, and that 55 of them had been sighted, seventeen sunk (three of them refuellers) and six forced back to port.[28]

To these figures may be added not only the three U-boats sunk off Portugal by the aircraft operating from Gibraltar and Morocco, but the interruptions and casualties suffered by the U-boats on the northern transit route. On that route the sailing of U-boats in groups had begun on 12 June, but it had been abandoned by the end of June following Coastal Command's success in sinking two of the three U-boats in the first group. During July few U-boats had left the Baltic and PR had noted that an abnormal number had built up in Kiel 'apparently being fitted with the new AA armament'. But U-847, which attempted to evade the air patrols by sailing through the Denmark Strait, struck an iceberg and was forced to return to Bergen. And on 4 August, before group sailings were again suspended, U-489, a supply U-boat which had sailed from Bergen in company with an operational U-boat, was sunk by Coastal Command. At this, sailings on the northern route were again cancelled.[29]

---

* See below, p 339.

24. ADM 223/182, Ultra signals 1543/4 July and 1846/5 July 1943.
25. Roskill, op cit, Vol III Part I, p 24.
26. ibid, p 24; AIR 41/48, p 114.
27. Roskill, op cit, Vol III Part I, pp 27–28; AIR 41/48, pp 128–129; ADM 234/68, p 18.
28. Roskill, op cit, Vol III Part I, p 29.   29. AIR 41/48, p 150.

Early warning of U-boat sailings was usually obtained from the Home Waters Enigma, which was decrypted currently; from time to time, as with U-489,[30] U-boats in the transit areas were also sighted by PR. It is nevertheless difficult to establish the extent to which the Enigma contributed directly to the sinkings of U-boats in the transit areas. If only because the Shark Enigma decrypts were frequently delayed, sightings must have owed much to the skill and patience of Coastal Command's aircrew. But indirectly the Enigma was of enormous value. By means of a daily telephone conference with the Tracking Room, Coastal Command maintained a duplicate of the OIC's U-boat plot, which was largely based on the Enigma, and all urgent intelligence was telephoned to its Senior Naval Liaison Officer from the OIC as it was received. It planned its patrols and strikes on the basis of the OIC's estimates of U-boat movements, as well as on the information obtained from the Enigma about the tactics used by the U-boats when on passage, and it kept aircraft and crews standing by for action in the light of last-minute intelligence. Delays in receiving information from the decrypts were often overcome by the speed and mobility of the aircraft, and although the surface ship groups were more handicapped by these delays, they were still able to operate on the basis of aircraft sightings.[31] To give some examples, Enigma references to the provision of escort for the departure of U-boats on 22 July[32] contributed to the sinking of U-459 on 24 July, while before the sinking of U-461, U-462 and one operational U-boat on 30 July the Enigma had given notice of the fact that they were attempting the passage in company on the surface, had established that two of them were supply U-boats and thus a target of utmost priority, and by indicating their route and estimated progress, had made it possible to concentrate aircraft and EG 2 for the attack.[33]

At the beginning of August the heavy losses sustained on the transit routes forced the U-boat Command to accept another defeat. It dispersed such U-boat groups as were on passage, recalled six U-boats which had just sailed and laid it down that in future the U-boats should make the passage of Biscay along the Spanish coast, making use of territorial waters and remaining submerged by day.[34] On 5 August it suspended sailings by U-boats which had not yet been equipped with the improved Flak and a new radar search

30. ibid, p 148.
31. *The Handling of Naval Special Intelligence*, pp 31, 49.
32. ADM 223/183, Ultra signals 1711/17 July, 2110/21 July and 1446/22 July 1943.
33. ADM 223/88, pp 292–293.
34. ibid, p 293; ADM 234/68, p 14; AIR 41/48, p 133;

receiver (*Hagenuk* or *Wanze*).[35]* By that time, moreover, the successes achieved by the British offensive had, together with those obtained by the US task forces in their attacks on the refuelling operations, dislocated and severely curtailed the U-boat campaign in distant areas. By the end of July, over and above the number of U-boats sunk, seven type IX operational U-boats had had to abandon their cruises and act as emergency refuellers, while six of Type VII, unable to refuel, had been forced to stop short of their planned patrol areas in the Caribbean and operate off Freetown; they had little success there.[36] Nor was this the end of the dislocation from which the campaign suffered. In August, when the U-boat Command realised that three supply U-boats had recently been sunk in Biscay, it made emergency arrangements for U-boats operating off the American coasts in the middle and south Atlantic to be refuelled by U-117 and U-489; off these coasts, particularly off Brazil, the U-boats had chiefly concentrated since the beginning of July and had sunk most of the 37 Allied ships lost during the month, but had themselves already suffered heavy casualties in attacks by shore-based air patrols.[37] And when the Command discovered that U-117 and U-489 had also been sunk, it was forced to recall some operational boats immediately and instruct others to curtail their patrols so as to be able to reach port without replenishment.[38] The orders covered all U-boats except those in, or making for, the Indian Ocean;† and the fate of the project to send an additional force of Type IX U-boats to operate between Bombay and the Persian Gulf (Operation *Monsun*) provides another striking illustration of the scale of the U-boat Command's set-backs. Eleven *Monsun* U-boats sailed at the end of June accompanied by their own supply boat (U-462) and carrying equipment for the construction of a new U-boat base at Penang.[39] Only five got through to the Indian Ocean, and they did not include U-462.‡ At the end of August, to sum up, there were only forty operational U-boats at sea, as compared with

---

* See Appendix 10.   † See below p 228 et seq.

‡ Two were sunk in or near Biscay and a third south of Iceland, while another on passage from the Baltic was forced back and her sailing delayed till the end of July. U-462 was sunk on 30 July on her third attempt to make the Biscay passage. Of the remaining eight operational boats, one was sunk by the USS *Santee* on her way to refuel from U-487; another had to refuel the rest following the sinking of U-487 and then return to Lorient; and a third (U-847) was sunk by USS *Card* after being ordered to refuel other operational U-boats which had been left stranded by the sinking of so many supply U-boats.

35. Roskill, op cit, Vol III Part I, p 88; AIR 41/48, p 135.
36. ADM 234/68, p 17; Roskill, op cit, Vol III Part I, p 31.
37. ADM 234/68, p 18; Roskill, op cit, Vol III Part I, p 31; Op-20-G History, Vol II, pp 162–163.
38. ADM 234/68, p 18; ADM 223/98, OIC SI 668 of 16 August 1943.
39. Roskill, op cit, Vol III Part I, p 219.

seventy-one during July, and most of them were either homeward bound for lack of fuel or outward bound on cruises limited by the impossibility of refuelling them; of the twenty-four that had been in distant areas at the beginning of the month, only three remained on patrol.[40]

The full extent of this enemy reverse was not revealed in all its detail by the Enigma at the time. Gaps and delays in reading the decrypts complicated the analysis and interpretation of the evidence. On some effects of the Allied offensive, particularly the lowering of morale caused by the miseries of crossing the Bay and the anxieties that accompanied emergency refuellings, the decrypts were not explicit.* But except that the clues as to the identity and the destination of the *Monsun* U-boats were still being pieced together in September,[42] the Enigma generally illuminated the immediate consequences of the U-boat casualties – the emergency refuelling arrangements and the progressive reductions in the numbers of U-boats on patrol – within a week.[43] Moreover, the OIC was sometimes able to predict well in advance where U-boats intended to operate. The Admiralty could then economise its overstretched anti-submarine resources by switching from an area not menaced to one that would shortly be threatened. In the Indian Ocean a routine developed by which shipping proceeded with or without escort and in or out of convoy as the U-boat threat advanced or receded.[44] Nor was Sigint the only reliable guide; the amount of Allied shipping sunk by U-boats in all areas fell from 245,000 tons (37 ships) in July to only 86,000 tons (10 ships) in August. It was the Enigma, however, which enabled the OIC to conclude at the end of August that since only two supply U-boats remained afloat, the U-boats would be all the more handicapped when they resumed their attacks on Atlantic convoys.[45]

At the beginning of August, with the decision of the U-boat Command to abandon group sailings, to order the U-boats to hug the Spanish coast and, above all, to require boats to remain submerged to the greatest possible extent, the Biscay offensive was virtually brought to an end. Although Coastal Command continued its patrols until the summer of 1944, the number of U-boats sighted

---

* But an analysis carried out by the OIC in October 1943, of the percentage of U-boats which turned back owing to defects after sailing from a Biscay port, showed that it had risen from 36 per cent in July to 60 per cent in August before dropping to 41 per cent in September.[41]

40. Op-20-G History, Vol II, pp 158–159.
41. ADM 223/170, OIC SI 728 of 9 October 1943.
42. ADM 223/98, OIC SI 688 of 5 September 1943.
43. ibid, OIC SI 668, 673 and 683 of 16, 23 and 30 August 1943.
44. *The Handling of Naval Special Intelligence*, p 51.
45. ADM 223/98, OIC SI 683 of 30 August 1943.

or sunk in Biscay, as on the northern route, slumped after early August 1943. U-boat sailings were soon resumed but while U-boats working to and from southerly latitudes continued to use the Spanish coast route, those crossing the Bay or taking the northern exit route proceeded individually, surfacing at night only to charge batteries.[46] The Enigma disclosed on 18 August that the Spanish route was being used.[47] By 23 August, after other decrypts had provided details about the route and disclosed that seven U-boats had so far used it safely,[48] Coastal Command and C-in-C Plymouth had adjusted their patrols. Coastal Command made a first sighting in the new area on 22 August and sank a U-boat two days later. But on 25 August the GAF obtained a near-miss on HMS *Bideford* with an Hs 293 radio guided rocket missile, and on 27 August in similar attacks it sank HMS *Egret* and damaged HMCS *Athabaskan*.* These attacks forced the surface escort groups to the westward, where they could not operate effectively with the air patrols. They were soon to be withdrawn to the Atlantic: it was clear from the Enigma by mid-September that the U-boat Command was about to resume the campaign against the north Atlantic convoys.

□

Before resuming the attack in the north Atlantic the U-boat Command had equipped the U-boats not only with improved Flak but also, in the belief that the Allied success in detecting the positions of U-boats had rested on the ability to home on radiations emitted by the *Metox* radar receiver, with a new search receiver, the *Hagenuk*.† It also delayed the new offensive until it had begun to take delivery of *Zaunkönig*, the new T 5 acoustic torpedo to be known to the Allies as the *Gnat*. Nine U-boats fitted with all the new equipment sailed from Biscay late in August; eight got safely through the Bay and five were refuelled by U-460 early in September. Early in September thirteen more sailed from Biscay and six from the Baltic, none of them with the *Gnat*. On 15 September twenty-one of these boats were formed into the *Leuthen* group, ordered to take up a patrol line, 350 miles long, well to the south-west of Iceland by the evening of 20 September, and told to expect two westbound convoys shortly. It had been impressed on them that, since secrecy was essential, they must remain submerged, and in the words of the German account of the operation, 'as an additional precaution against treachery, all positions were radioed

---

* See below, p 339.   † See Appendix 10.

46. AIR 41/48, p 214.
47. ADM 223/183, Ultra signal 1106/18 August 1943.
48. ibid, Ultra signal 2102/23 August 1943.

to them in the form of reference points known only to the commanders concerned'.[49]

Some indication of these German preparations and intentions was obtained in the third week of September from decrypts of telegrams from the Japanese Ambassador reporting on a further meeting with Dönitz, held on 22 September. Dönitz explained that he had launched a three-year plan for training 16,000 sea cadets and was still confident that with the aid of German science the U-boats could defeat the Allies; in order to keep pace with Allied counter-measures he had set up a 'Research Council' to supervise a constant improvement of weapons.* Some improvement in guns, torpedoes and, particularly, radio location apparatus had already been made, and he planned to reopen the offensive against convoys in October with new tactics which gave priority to attacks on the escorts.[50] But even before these decrypts were received the U-boat Enigma had enabled the OIC to conclude, after a short period of uncertainty, that a group of U-boats was being formed up in the north Atlantic. On 6 September the OIC reported that 'apart from an indication that another group operation is planned in some area, there is as yet no information about the destinations or intentions of any of the fifteen or sixteen now estimated to be outward bound'.[51] On 12 September, noting that some half-dozen U-boats east of the Azores had been told to avoid detection during 'the waiting period', it suggested that they might be waiting to enter the Mediterranean.[52]† On 13 September its appreciation concluded: 'The greatest problem is the whereabouts and intentions of some 20 U-boats which have recently left Biscay ports. It was intended that a supply U-boat should refuel some of them after 10 September. Various wait areas have been allotted apparently in the same general area as the refuelling position . . . Very strict W/T silence has been ordered . . . If the waiting area is north of the Azores it [the aim] might be a resumption of attacks on convoys, while if the waiting area is close to the islands it may be designed to prevent any move against them [the islands] by the Allies.'[53]‡ On the evening of 18

---

* See Appendix 10, pp516–517 for some of the activities of the new German scientific intelligence department.

† For an account of U-boat operations in the Mediterranean see below, p 232 et seq.

‡ The Allied occupation of the Azores took place on 8 October 1943. Since the previous summer the Allies had known from Axis diplomatic and Abwehr decrypts that Germany and Japan were aware that it was likely; but to the end the enemy had no information about the date.

49. ADM 234/68, pp 23–25.
50. Dir/C Archive, 4484 of 24 September 1943.
51. ADM 223/98, OIC SI 690 of 6 September 1943.
52. ADM 223/184, Ultra signal 1703/12 September 1943.
53. ADM 223/98, OIC SI 697 of 13 September 1943.

September the OIC received the decrypt of the orders to the *Leuthen* group, from which it was able to deduce that there was no threat in the Azores area but unable to decide between two alternative solutions to the reference points that disguised the position in the north Atlantic of the *Leuthen* patrol line.[54] By that time the Enigma had also given details of the instructions sent to the U-boats concerning the use they were to make of *Hagenuk* and the anti-radar decoy balloon *Aphrodite** and had made it clear that they were to resort to a variety of tactics new to boats on the high seas, including shooting back at attacking aircraft. This information was summarised in an Ultra signal on 20 September: the U-boats had been told that when resuming operations in 'the main battle area' they would be engaged in 'the decisive struggle for the German race', that they could expect the Atlantic convoys to be weakly escorted and must exploit the element of surprise, and that they should use their 'new weapons and installations' to 'decimate the escort for moral effect and to denude the convoy'.[55]

On the same day – 20 September – the *Leuthen* group made contact with the west-bound convoy ONS 18; an attempt had been made at the last minute to divert the convoy away from the supposed whereabouts of the group, but the OIC's estimate of the group's position had turned out to be 100 miles south of its actual position.[56] In the next five days, ONS 18 having been merged with a faster west-bound convoy, ON 202, and the escorts reinforced by a support group previously diverted from Biscay, the U-boats sank three escorts and six merchant vessels, and damaged one escort, in exchange for the loss of three of their number and damage to six others. They owed their success to the surprise achieved by the *Gnat* torpedo, to which there had as yet been no precise reference in the Enigma.[57]

The fact that the Germans might develop an acoustic homing torpedo had been mentioned in the Oslo report†. General indications that they were still working on it had been provided by POW and other intelligence sources since the second half of 1941, and the Allies had in any case themselves produced a weapon using the same principle. Work on counter-measures was thus already in hand when in January 1943 an Enigma reference to the zig-zagging (FAT) torpedo, incorrectly taken to stand for Fernakustischtorpedo, led to the decision to give highest priority to the counter-

---

* See Volume II, p 519.   † See Volume I, Appendix 5.

54. ADM 223/184, Ultra signal 2125/18 September 1943.
55. ibid, Ultra signal 1026/20 September 1943.
56. ADM 223/170, OIC SI 713 of 30 September 1943; Beesly, op cit, p 196.
57. ibid, OIC SI 705 of 20 September 1943.

measures trials.* The outcome was that *Foxer*, a towed noise-making device designed to explode the *Gnat* harmlessly, was in use at sea sixteen days after the end of the attack on ONS 18/ON 202.[58] Nor was that all. The U-boat Command, understandably anxious to obtain information without delay about the performance of the torpedo, which had not been tested under operational conditions, requested the U-boats to transmit detailed reports. Within days of the battle the OIC and the Naval Section at GC and CS had prepared an analysis of these reports which, because it could discount the exaggerated claims made by the U-boats, was far more reliable as a guide to the weapon's performance than any that could have been compiled in Germany. In this way the Enigma made an invaluable contribution to the work of perfecting the *Foxer* device.[59] While the number of ships saved by *Foxer* turned out to be not as great as thought at the time, it helped in some measure to reduce sinkings, and its noise put the fear of God into the listening U-boats.

No ship towing *Foxer* was ever hit by an acoustic torpedo.[60] This was but one of several reasons why, although the U-boats continued to hunt convoys for seven months from the end of September 1943, the attack on ONS 18/ON 202 gave them their last substantial success in the Battle of the Atlantic. *Hagenuk*, their new means of defence against radar detection, and *Aphrodite*, their anti-radar decoy balloon, proved to be as ineffective as the *Gnat* torpedo. The sinking of so many supply U-boats severely curtailed the scale of their offensive. Following the occupation of the Azores the Allies could cover the whole of the north Atlantic with shore-based air patrols, while the greater availability of surface escorts and the proliferation of more effective anti-submarine weapons enabled the Allies to intensify the attack on U-boats found near convoys and hunt them to extinction. Not less important, in the intelligence battle between the Allies and the U-boat Command the scales had tilted decisively in the Allies' favour.

From June 1943 the enemy found it increasingly difficult to rely on cryptanalysis as a source of information on convoys, and except for a brief period of limited success at the end of 1943, was effectively deprived of it. He continued to learn from agents and air reconnaissance about the arrival and departure times of some convoys, and from DF and Traffic Analysis he was still able to make some deductions about the position of convoys and the strength of their

---

* In fact FAT stood for Federapparattorpedo; see Volume II, Appendix 10.

58. *The Handling of Naval Special Intelligence*, pp 114–115.
59. ADM 234/68, p 23; ADM 223/170, OIC SI 706A of 27 September, 715 of 14 October and 725 of 10 October 1943; Beesly, op cit, p 198.
60. *The Handling of Naval Special Intelligence*, p 115.

escorts. But as the German history of the Battle of the Atlantic says, he 'knew very little about their routes' because 'never again – not even for the shortest period – did we succeed in re-establishing the same standard of decryption that existed in 1942 and up to May 1943'.[61]* On the other hand, delays in breaking the U-boat Enigma were now all but eliminated; the decrypts were occasionally held up for a few days between September and the beginning of December 1943, but from December the delay was at most 48 hours and rarely more than 24. Nor did another of the many extra precautions taken by the U-boat Command reduce the flow of Sigint. When they resumed the offensive the U-boats were instructed to follow an elaborate procedure for making their own signals on frequencies slightly 'off' their normal ones.[62] This may have enabled them to avoid being DFd by the convoy escorts, but it would not have prevented Allied shore stations from interceptng the transmissions even if the instructions had not been decrypted from the Enigma.

It thus comes as no surprise that between the end of September and the middle of November 1943, when the U-boats were again forced to withdraw from virtually the whole of the north Atlantic, almost every threatened convoy was successfully diverted. The exceptions included SC 143 which, early in October, was the first convoy to have its escort reinforced from an unthreatened convoy before being deliberately routed towards a group of U-boats: this was done to ensure the safe passage of a third convoy, larger and more weakly escorted.[63] As well as being denied contact with convoys the U-boats were overwhelmed in combat with Allied forces. In their vain pursuit of convoys ON 203 and 204 and ONS 19 at the beginning of October they were taken within range of air patrols from Iceland, and lost three of their number as a result of placing too much confidence in their new Flak armament.[64] In their attack on SC 143 three U-boats were sunk for the loss of one merchant ship and one escort.[65] In the middle of October, in an attack on ONS 20, they again suffered heavily from staying on the surface and attempting to repel air attacks with Flak: the convoy lost only one merchant ship but four U-boats were sunk by aircraft and two

---

* See Volume II, Appendix I Part (i).

61. ADM 234/65, pp 9, 27–28.
62. ADM 223/170, OIC SI 745 of 21 October 1943.
63. ibid, OIC SI 732 of 11 October, 735 of 13 October 1943; ADM 223/88, pp 271–272, 275.
64. ADM 223/170, OIC SI 717 of 4 October 1943; Roskill, op cit, Vol III Part I, p 41.
65. ADM 223/170, OIC SI 735 of 13 October 1943.

by the surface escorts.[66] This experience forced the U-boat Command to order a change of tactics. From the end of October the U-boats remained submerged during daytime, thereby still further reducing their chances of finding targets, and were under orders to transmit nothing but important tactical reports.[67] By that date the Enigma had also revealed that since the U-boats were deriving so few opportunities and such poor protection from the new devices – to which were added an attempt to sight convoys with long-range BV 222 flying boats,[68] the equipment of the U-boats with radar against surface targets (*Hohentwiel*),[69]* a new search receiver (*Naxos*)* to give warning against ASV Mark III (10 cm)[70] and the embarkation of B-Dienst detachments which intercepted and took DF bearings on the R/T used by convoys and their escorts[71] – the perplexity of the U-boat Command was beginning to reach neurotic proportions.

Early in November the Command made a still more radical change of tactics by abandoning the long patrol line. A line of more than twenty U-boats had been waiting to the east of Newfoundland since 24 October; despite repeated shifts of position they had failed to contact a convoy and had lost three of their number to air attack. They were now redisposed in five short lines of four U-boats with four single scouting U-boats patrolling ahead, one opposite each major gap.[72] But their fortunes did not improve, and one more U-boat had been sunk when on 8 November they began a gradual withdrawal to the eastward and were dispersed into several small groups between Greenland and the Azores. These decisions were disclosed by the Enigma instructions, which explained to the U-boats that the dispersion had been adopted in order to avoid the premature detection of large patrols by Allied radar.[73] The chief purpose of the dispersion was to improve the prospect of finding convoys, and in this they did not succeed. Partly on this account and partly because the dispersion policy could not be long maintained for lack of supply U-boats – the sinking of U-220 and U-460

---

* See Appendix 10.

66. ibid, OIC SI 745 of 20 October 1943; ADM 234/68, p 31; Roskill, op cit, Vol III Part I, p 45.
67. ADM 223/170, OIC SI 745 of 21 October, 1943; ADM 234/68, p 34.
68. ADM 223/170, OIC SI 726 of 10 October 1943.
69. ibid, OIC SI 745 of 21 October 1943.
70. ADM 223/108, Ultra signal 1317/25 November 1943.
71. ADM 223/184, Ultra signal 1650/10 August; ADM 223/184, Ultra signal 1221/25 September 1943; ADM 223/170, OIC SI 715 of 30 September 1943.
72. ADM 223/170, OIC SI 757 of 1 November, 763 of 8 November; ADM 234/68, pp 32–34.
73. ADM 223/170, OIC SI 771 of 15 November 1943; DEFE 3/724, ZTPGUs 19000 and 19108.

in October had again reduced the number of these to two* – the enemy on 16 November bowed to the need for a second strategic withdrawal and ordered all remaining boats on the northern trans-Atlantic convoy routes to join those operating off the Portuguese coast.[75] In a long signal to all U-boats decrypted on 16 November, the U-boat Command offered 'consolation for the fiasco of the past month': the U-boats were tying down large Allied naval and air forces and preventing them from being used against the homeland; the difficulty of finding convoys would be overcome by increasing long-range air reconnaissance, using the new Ju 290† to supplement the BV 222 and FW 200; and from 13 November He 177s would also be made available for bombing attacks.[76] In its log for 12 November it had summed up in still less confident words: 'The enemy has all the trumps in his hand: long range air reconnaissance constantly covering all areas and using methods of location against which we still have no sure means of warning; as a result, discovery of our U-boats and their dispositions, possibility of diverting and scattering his convoys over a vast sea area. On our side, as yet no air reconnaissance; the U-boat its own scout, with a minimum scouting range; no new means of location. . . . Once more, the imperative demand: long range air reconnaissance of our own, speediest improvement of our own active [radar] and passive [search receiver] devices in the field of location.'[77]

Until the middle of January 1944 U-boats continued to operate in groups in the area off the Portuguese coast, where the U-boat Command had better information about the arrivals and departures of the Gibraltar convoys and could expect assistance from air reconnaissance, and where the U-boats, being closer to their bases, could remain on patrol for longer periods. The U-boat Command had resumed operations there towards the end of October 1943 with eight U-boats. By 13 November, despite sightings by German air

---

* The contribution of the Enigma to the sinking of these U-boats is indicated by exchanges of signals between the First Sea Lord and Admiral King. On 2 October the First Sea Lord asked whether the US Navy could send a task force against a refuelling operation that was to take place north of the Azores; U-460 was sunk in that area on 4 October by aircraft from USS *Card*. The First Sea Lord, on the strength of Enigma evidence that eight or nine U-boats were to be refuelled north-west of the Azores between 11 and 14 October, made a similar request on 9 October. Three US task forces operating in that area made attacks, delaying the refuelling, and eventually sank U-220 on 28 October.[74]

† The Ju 290 was a new type of transport aircraft, adapted for reconnaissance because of the shortage of long-range bomber/reconnaissance aircraft and because of the desperate need for convoy sightings.

74. ADM 234/68, p 33; Roskill, op cit, Vol III Part I, p 43.
75. DEFE 3/724, ZTPGUs 19243, 19265, 19301; ADM 223/88, p 282.
76. ADM 223/186, Ultra signal 1923/16 November 1943.
77. Roskill, op cit, Vol III Part I, p 50.

patrols and thanks to evasive routeing and shore-based air support, three convoys had either avoided the U-boat patrol lines or sailed through them, and had lost only one merchant ship in exchange for the sinking of two U-boats.[78] With the withdrawal on 16 November of the U-boats from the trans-Atlantic routes, however, the number of U-boats in the area was increased to thirty, and plans were made for disposing them in three lines about 150 miles apart on the expected route of a convoy of 67 ships (SL 139/MKS 30) which, as German agents had reported on 13 November, was soon to leave Gibraltar.[79]

The signals containing the preliminary announcement of these intentions and the orders for the formation of the forward line of nine U-boats were decrypted in time to enable the Admiralty to divert the convoy on 16 November. On the next day the convoy was sighted on its new course by enemy air reconnaissance and, too late for further evading action, the OIC learned that the first line of U-boats had been redisposed. During 18 November two U-boats were sunk for the loss of one escort. By then the second line of U-boats had been formed, but no further avoiding action was attempted by the Admiralty. The convoy, reinforced by seven additional escorts from unthreatened areas and provided with constant air support, fought its way through the second U-boat line, and through the third, without loss; one more U-boat was sunk and a U-boat shot down one of the escorting aircraft. On 21 November twenty He 177s attacked the convoy with Hs 293s, sinking a straggler, damaging another ship and losing seven of their number.[80]

Except that this was the last attack with Hs 293 aircraft – they were transferred to the Western Mediterranean until January 1944 – and except that the U-boats, forced to cruise and attack submerged, now concentrated their attacks into a single night, the fighting on the Gibraltar–UK convoy routes continued to follow the same pattern until 28 November. The south-bound convoy OS 39/KMS 30 was safely diverted and its reinforced escorts sank a U-boat on the night of 22–23 November. With the next north-bound convoy, SL 140/MKS 31, evasion was not attempted; it passed unscathed through a group of some twelve U-boats on 27–28 November and its escort, reinforced by three escort-carrier task forces, sank two U-boats and badly damaged two others. It then became clear that the remaining U-boats were moving north-west and the OIC assumed, correctly, that they would join up with newly operational

---

78. ADM 223/88, pp 276–281; Roskill, op cit, Vol III Part I, p 46 et seq.
79. ADM 223/88 pp 281, 282.
80. ADM 223/88, pp 282–283; ADM 223/170, OIC SI 784 of 1 December 1943; ADM 234/68, pp 38–39; Roskill, op cit. Vol III Part I, pp 50–51.

boats from the Baltic which had been building up in the north-west Atlantic.[81]

On 5 December the U-boat Command formed a long patrol line of 25 U-boats in the area south of Iceland and laid on long-range air reconnaissance by Ju 290s. But on 15 December, by which time half a dozen convoys had been routed away from the group, eight of its U-boats were withdrawn to participate in a group of thirteen boats to the west of Biscay. This group (*Borkum*) fought a two-day battle in the last week of December with the escort forces of a convoy, which included the USS *Card*. The convoy was diverted round it; it sank one US and one British destroyer.[82] Between then and the middle of January 1944 when the *Borkum* group was dispersed, evasive routeing denied it any sightings and three or four of its U-boats were sunk or damaged in return for the loss of one more escort vessel.[83]

□

When U-boat operations against the Gibraltar–UK convoys were brought to an end with the dispersal of the *Borkum* group the U-boat effort in more distant waters had already faltered; and except in the Indian Ocean it was never to recover after the beginning of 1944. Following the sinking of U-460 and U-220 in October, the U-boat Command had been forced to confine its forces in the Caribbean and off the Atlantic coasts of north and south America to Type IX boats, and their patrols had had to be shortened to what they could manage without being refuelled. Together with the fact that their endurance was further reduced by their need to proceed submerged, and the fact that so many of them had been lost in recent months, these restraints had during the last three months of 1943 cut the number on patrol at any one time to an average of four. They had still sunk 28 ships for the loss of two U-boats, but they were never again to do so well. In the four months from the beginning of September 1943 to the end of the year the Allies had lost in all areas 370,000 tons of shipping (67 ships) – an average of 92,000 tons (17 ships) per month, or less than one-sixth of the 627,000 tons (108 ships) sunk in March 1943[84] — and a considerable proportion of these casualties had been incurred in the Indian Ocean. But most of them had been inflicted by Japanese submarines; the offensive by German U-boats, which had begun in June 1943, had been blunted temporarily after the end of August.

---

81.   ADM 223/170 OIC SI 776 of 22 November, 782 of 29 November 1943.
82.   ADM 223/171, OIC SI 807 of 27 December 1943.
83.   ibid, OIC SI 814, 823 and 829 of 3, 10 and 17 January 1944.
84.   Roskill, op cit, Vol III Part I, pp 54–55.

In June seven German U-boats had sunk ten ships in an area near the Cape; in July and August, after refuelling from the tanker *Charlotte Schliemann*, they had sunk another twenty-five ships in individual operations off Mozambique, an area hitherto unexplored by the U-boat Command. By the end of August, when one U-boat had been sunk, the remainder had begun their return passage – one of them, the first operational U-boat to do so, making for Penang.[85] They were to have been replaced by the eleven *Monsun* U-boats which had sailed from Europe at the end of June. But there were no offensive U-boat operations in the Indian Ocean in September: only five of the *Monsun* boats had survived* and, as a result of the sinkings of supply U-boats in the Atlantic, they had had to refuel in the Indian Ocean before making their way to the new operational area between Bombay and the Persian Gulf.

In June Sigint had not disclosed the use of the *Charlotte Schliemann* until the U-boats had completed refuelling.[86] In August it had revealed that the Japanese were to supply enough fuel for ten U-boats to a tender called *Brake*,[87] but not until 13 September had it established that the *Brake* had carried out a refuelling operation with the *Monsun* boats from 8 September probably about 450 miles south of Mauritius.[88] On reaching their operational areas, however, the *Monsun* boats had had little success. One was sunk on 16 October in the Gulf of Oman; the remainder had claimed to have sunk only three ships by 25 October, when they began to make for Penang.[89] Nor did the German effort to return to the offensive in the Indian Ocean succeed before the end of the year. Five further U-boats had sailed for the area from Europe in the autumn, but four of them were sunk on passage in the south Atlantic.[90] Of the twenty-one Allied merchant ships lost in the Indian Ocean in the last four months of the year, most were sunk by Japanese submarines.[91]

By January 1944 the U-boats which had reached Penang were back on patrol in the area Ceylon–Gulf of Aden–Mauritius. The twenty-nine Allied ships sunk in this area in January, February and March constituted the highest shipping losses sustained in any theatre of war in that period, and the bulk of them were sunk by these U-boats;[92] given the shortage of escort forces available to C-in-C Eastern Fleet, their successes would have been greater, and

---

* See above p 218.

85.   ibid, pp 219–220.
86.   ADM 223/98, OIC SI of 28 June 1943.
87.   ibid, OIC SI 659 of 9 August 1943.
88.   ibid, OIC SI 697 of 13 September 1943.
89.   ADM 223/170, OIC SI 750 of 25 October, 757 of 1 November 1943.
90.   ADM 234/68, p 48.
91.   Roskill, op cit, Vol III Part I, pp 220–221.   92.   ibid, p 387.

would have lasted longer, but for the fact that the Enigma now made it possible to attack their supply ships.

During January the decrypts disclosed that the *Charlotte Schliemann* was to refuel one U-boat towards the end of the month, but an attempt to intercept her failed for lack of precise information about the rendez-vous area.[93] At the beginning of February the Enigma indicated that she would carry out another refuelling operation on 11 February, and although the German system of disguising positions again made it difficult to choose between three alternative rendez-vous points, she was sighted by Catalina patrols on 11 February and sunk the next day by HMS *Relentless*.[94] When this interception was being planned the Admiralty had insisted that no warship should be within 100 miles of any of the alternative rendez-vous points on the refuelling day. It adopted the same precaution and imposed others when it gave its approval to a further attempt to disturb a refuelling operation. On 23 February the decrypts revealed that the Germans, presuming that the *Charlotte Schliemann* had been sunk, were making emergency arrangements for U-boats to be refuelled by the *Brake* on about 8 March; they later established that the rendez-vous would take place on 11 March at one or another of two positions south of Mauritius. The search for the *Brake* was planned on the understanding that neither aircraft nor surface vessels would appear within 100 miles of either of the rendez-vous positions unless previous contact had been made with the enemy and that surface vessels would not intervene unless DF evidence about the enemy's whereabouts was obtained.[95]

The *Brake* was sighted by aircraft from the escort-carrier *Battler* on 12 March, the day after the rendez-vous, and sunk by the destroyer *Roebuck* 30 miles from the more easterly of the two alternative positions. The next day a signal was decrypted in which one of the U-boats reported that the *Brake* had been sunk and, that U-boat having also been present when the *Schliemann* was sunk, suggested that 'refuellings have been systematically compromised'.[96] The U-boat was not to know that an ex-Italian freight-carrying U-boat had also been sunk on 11 March, by forces under C-in-C South Africa, at a rendez-vous several hundred miles south of the Cape of which details had been obtained from the Enigma.[97] Nor did the U-boat

---

93. ADM 223/179, Ultra signal 1849/9 January; ADM 228/180, Ultra signals 1115/22 January and 0702/31 January 1944.
94. ADM 223/180, Ultra signals 1658/31 January, 2225/4 February, 1245/6 February 1944; ADM 223/88, p 31.
95. ADM 223/181, Ultra signals 1119/29 February, 1645/7 March, 1323/9 March 1944; ADM 223/88, pp 32–35.
96. ADM 223/181, Ultra signal 1730/13 March 1944.
97. ADM 223/88, p 35.

Command wait for evidence of this further loss; on 13 March it brought into force a new emergency procedure for modifying the Enigma settings when compromise was suspected.[98]

The emergency procedure created little difficulty for GC and CS: by 16 March the OIC had received from the decrypt of a signal of 14 March details of two rendez-vous to be made by U-488, the last remaining supply U-boat, on 19 and 23 March in the area west of the Cape Verde islands. The Admiralty sent the information to the operational authorities in West and South Africa and ordered them to keep all their forces clear of the area;[99] and on the following day – 17 March – in a general signal alerting all Ultra recipients in every theatre, thirty-one in all, to the news that the Germans had modified the Enigma, it instructed them to take positive action to ensure that their forces did not make contact at or near any known rendez-vous or in any area where they would not normally be operating.[100] On 16 March, however, aircraft from the US escort-carrier *Block Island* had already sunk a U-boat on its approach to one of the rendez-vous points, and on 19 March the *Block Island* sank a second U-boat. The outcome was an exchange of signals between Admiral King, who had received a copy of the Admiralty's general signal, and the First Sea Lord. Admiral King argued that what had aroused the enemy's suspicions had been the sinking of the *Charlotte Schliemann* and the *Brake*; that it seemed likely that he suspected only the compromise of the current Enigma settings as a result of capture; that the *Block Island* had not appeared at the rendez-vous positions, but was carrying out a general sweep which had done no more than confirm the enemy in his appreciation that the Atlantic was a dangerous area; and that the enemy's suspicions might only be confirmed if the Allies abruptly stopped their attacks on refuelling areas. He added that the practice of consistently diverting convoys away from U-boat concentrations had probably done more than the attacks in the rendez-vous areas to arouse German suspicions. The First Sea Lord agreed that the evidence indicated that the German Navy had not yet concluded that the Enigma was radically insecure, but pointed out that the *Block Island* had been operating near positions given in signals encyphered in the modified settings which it had introduced to counter compromise of the cypher.

Following this exchange a close and anxious eye was kept in Washington and at GC and CS for more basic German security

---

98.   ibid, p 36; ADM 234/68, p 61.
99.   ADM 223/181, Ultra signal 1952/16 March 1944.
100. ADM 223/191, Ultra signal 1839/17 March 1944; ADM 223/171, OIC SI 890 of 20 March 1944.

measures. But none were taken, not even after the US escort-carriers *Croatan* and *Guadalcanal* had in the last week of April, with the help of the Enigma, sunk U-488 and two other U-boats at a rendez-vous point west of the Cape Verdes.[101] The enemy, believing his losses in the central Atlantic to be explained by the fact that, as his U-boats were reporting, the area had been made more dangerous than Biscay, and too dangerous for even occasional refuelling operations, accepted a further restriction on his activities in distant waters. From the spring of 1944 patrols were continued in the Indian Ocean by the U-boats based in Penang and those few reinforcements from Europe which managed to reach the area, but were otherwise virtually confined to those carried out under increasing difficulties on the Arctic routes*, in the Mediterranean and in the north Atlantic.

□

The Allied offensives in the Mediterranean called for a continual increase in follow-up shipping and permitted a continual increase in through-Mediterranean shipping from the middle of 1943; by December of that year the number of sailings in Mediterranean convoys exceeded the number of sailings in Atlantic convoys.[102] Quite apart from the fact that the Mediterranean U-boats had been ineffective against the *Husky* and the *Avalanche* landings,† the enemy thus had every incentive to increase the number of U-boats deployed in the area; and in September 1943, when only thirteen U-boats survived out of the 47 which had passed the Straits of Gibraltar since September 1941, the U-boat Command duly embarked on a series of attempts to reinforce them.[105]

Advance notice of that first attempt was given by Shark decrypts on 19 September in the form of advice to U-boats on how to make the passage.[106] By 29 September Shark decrypts had disclosed that one of the first two U-boats to approach the Straits, after being

---

* See below, p 269 et seq.
    † Six U-boats had operated against *Husky* and two of them had been sunk in exchange for damage to one Allied cruiser.[103] Against the *Avalanche* landings two U-boats operated without success, and one of them beached herself after a bombing attack.[104]

101.   ADM 223/172, OIC SI 922 and 928 of 17 and 24 April, 939 of 1 May 1944.
102.   Roskill, op cit, Vol III Part I, p 210.
103.   ibid, p 138; Molony, *The Mediterranean and Middle East*, Vol V (1973), p 365; AIR 41/54, *The RAF in Maritime War*, Vol VII, Part I, pp 70–71.
104.   Roskill, op cit, Vol III Part I, pp 177, 185; AIR 41/54, p 75; Naval Head-lines, No 800 of 13 September 1943.
105.   Roskill, op cit, Vol III Part I, p 43; Molony, op cit, Vol V, p 363.
106.   Naval Headlines, No 807 of 19 September 1943.

sighted by air reconnaissance, had been forced back by air attacks and that four others had been ordered to abandon the attempt and proceed to the north Atlantic.[107] Between 26 October and 9 November Shark decrypts reported on the attempt to pass another group into the Mediterranean. After one boat had been sunk by air attack, four others were instructed to surface only at night; two of these got through, but two scuttled when attacked by air and surface forces.[108] At the end of November Shark warned that another attempt was due; subsequent decrypts showed that one U-boat had made the passage but was proceeding to Toulon for repairs.[109] Two boats succeeded in making the passage in the first week of January 1944;[110] four did so at the end of January and the beginning of February;[111] three more got through in mid-February.[112] On these occasions, too, the Shark decrypts gave advance general warning that U-boats were approaching the Straits, and 'prior special intelligence'* was a pre-requisite of effective action to stop them.[113] But in view of the difficult Asdic conditions in the Straits, and of the fact – as the Enigma disclosed – that some of the U-boats hugged the Portuguese and Spanish coasts and surfaced only to charge their batteries, it could not be guaranteed that the action would succeed.

By 27 February the decrypts had established that a U-boat bound for the Mediterranean had been sunk on 24 February west of Gibraltar and that two others had left Biscay ports for the same destination.[114] On 6 March, after having been attacked by air, they were ordered to defer their passage of the Straits until about 9 March; and by 27 March it had emerged from the decrypts that one had been forced to return to Biscay and that the second, severely damaged while getting through, was putting in to Toulon.[115] Yet a

---

* 'Special Intelligence' was a term used by the Admiralty when referring to Ultra, ie to the results of high-grade cryptanalysis.

107. Naval Headlines, Nos 814, 816 and 817 of 26, 28 and 29 September 1943; AIR 41/54, p 313.
108. Naval Headlines, Nos 844, 845 and 848 of 26, 27 and 30 October, 850, 853 and 858 of 1, 4 and 9 November 1943; Roskill, op cit, Vol III Part I, p 43.
109. Naval Headlines, Nos 874 of 25 November, 888–891 of 9–12 December; DEFE 3/11 (2), VLs 1505 of 9 December, 1604, 1616, and 1621 of 10 December; DEFE 3/11 (1), VLs 1652 and 1665 of 11 December, 1749 of 12 December 1943.
110. Naval Headlines, Nos 901 of 22 December 1943, 918 of 8 January 1944.
111. Roskill, op cit, Vol III Part I, p 246.
112. Naval Headlines, Nos 950 and 955 of 9 and 14 February 1944.
113. AIR 41/54, p 337.
114. Naval Headlines, No 968 of 27 February 1944.
115. Naval Headlines, Nos 976 of 6 March, 998 of 28 March 1944; DEFE 3/152, VLs 9552 of 17 March, 9610 and 9612 of 28 March; DEFE 3/765, VL 9807 of 30 March 1944.

third U-boat, which had not been referred to in the decrypts, was sunk in the Straits on 16 March.[116] The main reason for the improvement in the Allied performance lay with the arrival at Gibraltar of a US Catalina squadron equipped with the Magnetic Airborne Detector, which enabled a low-flying aircraft to track a submerged U-boat. U-761, the U-boat sunk on 24 February, was the squadron's first victim.[117]

Between the end of March and the middle of May 1944 only three U-boats tried to enter the Mediterranean. Two succeeded, but the third, sunk by the US Catalinas, was the last to make the attempt.[118] Despite Dönitz's efforts to increase it over the previous six months, the number of U-boats in the Mediterranean was then down to eleven, two less than it had been in September 1943. It had never risen above eighteen, the figure at the middle of February 1944,[119] the reinforcements being more than offset by losses. Some of the losses were inflicted by Allied air raids on the Mediterranean U-boat bases at Toulon, Pola and Fiume. The first heavy raid against Toulon was on 24 November. This did so much damage as to enforce a lull in U-boat operations. In later raids Porpoise Enigma decrypts disclosed that one U-boat was sunk in a raid on Pola on 9 January 1944, and another damaged; that in a raid on Toulon on 11 March one was sunk and another burnt out, and three damaged; and that one U-boat was sunk by direct hit in a raid on Toulon on 29 April.[120] In October 1943 the Allied air and surface forces had adopted the 'swamp' method of hunting U-boats, and between then and May 1944 seven were sunk on patrol, four of them in May 1944.[121] The Enigma made little contribution to these successes if only because the four-wheel Enigma key introduced in June 1943 for communications to and from the U-boats themselves (Turtle) was rarely read without delay. But the Porpoise decrypts usually recorded the movements of the U-boats to and from their bases, so that there was little difficulty in deducing how many were operating, and they referred from time to time to the areas in which the boats were operating. At the end of November 1943 it was known that two were on patrol off north Africa and one off Naples; that one was outward-bound from Pola; that several were in port at Toulon, two at Pola and one at Salamis. In the second week of December the

---

116. Roskill, op cit, Vol III Part I, p 246.   117. ibid, p 246.
118. ibid, pp 247, 327.   119. AIR 41/54, Appendix 5.
120. Molony, op cit, Vol V, p 819; Naval Headlines, Nos 920 of 10 January, 982 and 995 of 12 and 25 March, 1030 of 30 April 1944; DEFE 3/19 (2), VL 3609 of 10 January; DEFE 3/147, VL 8259 of 12 March; DEFE 3/151, VL 9352 of 25 March; DEFE 3/44 (2), KV 2369 of 29 April; DEFE 3/44 (1), KV 2438 of 30 April 1944.
121. Molony, op cit, Vol V, p 560; Roskill, op cit, Vol III Part I, pp 208, 326.

Enigma revealed that four were operating between Tangier and Bizerta, where an Allied convoy had been sighted.[122] An appreciation of 12 January 1944, decrypted on the following day, provided a general statement of OKM's policy for the U-boats: no U-boat was then in the eastern Mediterranean, and though two at Pola were due to operate off Palestine, the transfer eastward of others would not be easy given that facilities at Pola and Salamis were limited and that return to the western Mediterranean, a much more profitable area, would be delayed because passage of the Sicilian Channel was now impossible for U-boats exhausted after a patrol.[123]

This statement, as we now know, was provoked by an order from Hitler that U-boats should be transferred to the eastern Mediterranean to counter a threat to that area from a movement eastward by the Royal Navy, which was in fact in process of reinforcing the Fleet in the Far East.[124] If only because it was overtaken by the Allied landings at Anzio, the order was not carried out. On 23 and 24 January the Enigma disclosed that three U-boats had been despatched to the Anzio area, of which one had turned about; and by the end of the month it was known from the decrypts that three U-boats were off the beachhead and that, although a fourth was due to join them from Toulon, no others were available.[125] A boat sank the cruiser *Penelope* off Cape Circe in the middle of February, but the U-boats achieved no other important success against the beachhead or the follow-up convoys.

Against Allied warships the Mediterranean U-boats had few further successes. They sank one destroyer at the end of March and two in May; in the last four months of 1943 they had sunk five destroyers and a minesweeper, and damaged the cruiser *Birmingham*.[126] Their effectiveness against Allied merchant shipping similarly declined. Whereas they had accounted for some 31 ships (136,000 tons) in the second half of 1943, as compared with 41 ships (225,450 tons) to air attack at sea and in harbour, they sank only eight (86,000 tons) in the first five months of 1944, with another seven (44,100 tons) sunk by air attack.* The U-boats sank no ships

---

* For the GAF attack on convoys off the north African coast before its aircraft were withdrawn to meet the invasion threat in north-west Europe see Volume III Part 2.

122.   Naval Headlines, Nos 874 of 25 November, 888–891 of 9–12 December 1943; DEFE 3/11 (2), VLs 1505 of 9 December, 1604, 1616, 1619 and 1621 of 10 December 1943.
123.   Naval Headlines, No 924 of 14 January; DEFE 3/129, VL 3859 of 13 January 1944.
124.   Molony, op cit, Vol V, p 819.
125.   Naval Headlines, Nos 933, 935 and 938 of 23, 25 and 28 January; DEFE 3/132, VLs 4544 of 23 January, 6439 of 24 January 1944.
126.   Roskill, op cit, Vol III Part I, pp 184–185, 208; Molony, op cit, Vol V, pp 559, 560.

after May, the month in which the U-boat Command ceased to reinforce them and in which, with four sunk on patrol, their own casualties became insupportable.[127] By their presence, however, even in small numbers, they had made it impossible for the Allies to reduce the escort forces required for their convoys, and it was because they still constituted a potential threat, particularly to the *Dragoon** convoys planned for August, that the Allies again raided their main base at Toulon on 5 July and 6 August.

After the July raid the Enigma reported that one U-boat had been sunk and that all but one of the other seven in port had been damaged.[128] After the August raid it disclosed that three more had been sunk and one severely damaged.[129] In the event, four of the seven had been sunk, and only one of the remaining three was left fully operational; she sailed on 17 August against the Allied landings in the south of France.[130] On 21 August the Enigma reported that she had grounded and had blown herself up.[131] The last two Toulon boats scuttled on 19 August,[132] leaving only three U-boats in the Mediterranean. The Enigma disclosed in detail the closure of the U-boat base at Toulon and, in July, had already reported that three U-boats, some of them from Pola, were due to take part in anti-invasion exercises in the eastern Mediterranean.[133] In September all three were sunk, one by destroyers and two by US bombers in harbour at Salamis; the Enigma reported the loss of only one of them, but on 28 September it added that the U-boat base at Salamis was being closed down.[134]

□

In the north Atlantic the U-boats, some dozen in number, which had been disposed in a patrol line south of Iceland since mid-December 1943† had meanwhile sighted no convoys by the middle of January 1944. On 22 December, in response to the lack of

---

* The cover-name for the landings in the south of France had been changed from *Anvil* to *Dragoon* at the end of July 1944.

† See above, p 228.

127. Roskill, op cit, Vol III Part 1, pp 106, 210, 327; Molony, op cit, Vol V, p 822; Vol VI Part I (forthcoming), Chapter VII.
128. Naval Headlines, No 1099 of 7 July 1944; DEFE 3/51, XL 954 of 6 July.
129. Naval Headlines, No 1131 of 8 August 1944; DEFE 3/114, XL 5071 of 6 August.
130. Roskill, op cit, Vol III Part II (1961), pp 88, 101.
131. ibid, p 101; DEFE 3/669, ZTPGM 86588.
132. Roskill, op cit, Vol III Part II, p 101.
133. Naval Headlines, Nos 1108 of 16 July, 1131 of 8 August 1944.
134. ibid, Nos 1181 and 1182 of 27 and 28 September 1944; DEFE 3/239, HP 1202 of 25 September; Roskill, op cit, Vol III Part II, p 107.

sightings, they had been broken up into six sub-groups of three U-boats and instructed, after the fashion of U-boats operating in distant waters, to act aggressively on their own initiative. These tactics, first adopted in the north Atlantic in the previous month, gave the need to find targets priority over the advantage of pack attacks. But although the abandonment of the wolf-pack technique made it more difficult for the Allied authorities to carry out evasive routeing, the U-boats continued to be ineffective. In the five weeks between 22 December 1943 and the middle of January 1944 they failed to sight ten convoys which sailed close to them and sank only one merchant ship.[135]

By the end of January some eight of these U-boats, reinforced by twelve which had sailed from the Baltic during that month, were re-formed into two groups, one around Rockall and the other about 300 miles south of Ireland, and the Enigma had meanwhile also reported an increase of the GAF's strength in the Ju 290s which had recently joined the BV 222s for long-range reconnaissance of the Western Approaches. Since groups of U-boats had never before operated so close to the United Kingdom, it seemed obvious that, with additional air reconnaissance, the aim of the U-boat Command was to catch convoys in areas where their room for manoeuvre was restricted.[136] The Allies responded accordingly, reinforcing Coastal Command and moving escort support groups into the threatened convoy lanes; and on 28 January, intensifying their anti-submarine sweeps on the news that the GAF had sighted a convoy on the previous day, they sank two of the U-boats.

The U-boat Command ordered new dispositions in the same areas with an increased number of U-boats early in February.[137] Between 14 and 19 February twenty of these boats, assisted by all available reconnaissance aircraft, failed in their efforts to make contact with convoys ONS 19 and ON 224. By 19 February twelve large convoys had passed safely in and out of the Western Approaches since the middle of January, and in return for the loss of eleven of their number the U-boats had sunk one escort, shot down two aircraft and sunk one straggler.[138]

The attempt to intercept convoys ONS 19 and ON 224 constituted the last centrally directed wolf-pack operation by U-boats in the Second World War. At the end of February sixteen U-boats were ordered to form another group 500 miles north of the Azores,

---

135. ADM 223/171, OIC SI 803, 807, 814 and 823 of 20 and 27 December 1943, 3 and 10 January 1944.
136. ibid, OIC SI 835, 844 of 22 and 31 January 1944.
137. ibid, OIC SI 847 of 7 February 1944.
138. ibid, 861 of 14 February, 865 of 21 February and 874 of 1 March 1944; Roskill, op cit, Vol III Part I, pp 249–254.

but they were disposed over a wide area, each U-boat being allotted an individual patrol zone, and on 22 March, after failing to contact a convoy and losing two of its U-boats in exchange for the sinking of two escorts, the group was disbanded.[139] By that time the number of U-boats available for operations in the Atlantic had been reduced not only by losses but also by diversions to other theatres and by anti-invasion measures. The Arctic flotilla had been increased from 18 to 24 at the end of 1943 and from 24 to 33 on 10 January 1944;* losses in the Mediterranean and the enemy's effort to keep at least twenty U-boats there had necessitated other transfers. The OIC was kept informed by the Enigma of these moves, and at the end of February it knew that the number of U-boats based on Atlantic ports was, at between 110 and 115, lower than at any time since July 1942.[140] From the same source it also knew that since the beginning of 1944, as part of the enemy's anti-invasion precautions, the U-boat Command had posted U-boats in mid-Atlantic solely for the purpose of sending regular weather reports.[141] On 16 February and 22 March respectively, the U-boat Command decided that groups of U-boats were to be held in readiness against invasion in Norwegian and Biscay ports.[142]† From the end of March, again mainly in order to tie down Allied forces that might otherwise be used for the invasion of Europe, such U-boats as remained available for the war against trade were dispersed as widely as their endurance permitted.‡ It was known by then that their numbers were being reduced by a curtailment of the U-boat building programme, and it was soon to be discovered that the enemy was pinning his hopes for a renewal of the Atlantic offensive on the production of new types of U-boat.

□

The Germans had concluded in the summer of 1943 that the existing U-boats which had been designed to carry out a large part

---

* For the operations of the Arctic U-boats see below, p 269 et seq.

† See Volume III Part 2.

‡ In April one of these boats, U-385, fired three torpedoes at a three-funnelled liner and, though the U-boat heard boiler noises, reported that she had continued on her way. This was, as NID commented on 16 April, the *Queen Mary* and it was the only known occasion when one of the 'Queens' was attacked on a troop-carrying mission. When he read about the incident the Prime Minister asked 'which way was she going?' and on being told 'West to East' he asked how many did she have on board. When he received the answer, 11,789 US and 253 British, he told 'C' to inform General Eisenhower.[143]

139.   ADM 223/171, OIC SI 873 of 28 February, 885 of 13 March; Op-20-G History, Vol II, p 184.

140.   ADM 223/171, OIC SI 873 of 28 February 1944.

141.   ibid, 814 of 3 January 1944.   142.   ADM 234/66, p 55.

143.   Naval Headlines, No 1017 of 16 April 1944.

of their operations on the surface, and which were handicapped by blindness, slow speed and poor endurance now that Allied anti-submarine measures were forcing them to spend so much time submerged, must be replaced as a matter of urgency by new types combining high under-water speed with the capacity to spend long periods submerged. Prototype boats incorporating the technology which gave these qualities – the stream-lined hull and the closed-cycle propulsion unit using hydrogen peroxide on which Professor Walter had carried out experiments since the beginning of the war – had been ordered at the end of 1942 as follows: four trial boats of 260 tons; twelve boats of 320 tons with a surface speed of nine knots and a submerged speed of 26 knots (Type XVII) which were to be training boats for a series of 800-ton boats (Type XXVI) to be delivered in the second half of 1945; and two boats (Type XVIII) as prototypes of a series of 1,600-ton boats. At the end of May 1943, however, no longer able to wait for the completion of the development programme for these Walter-boats, the U-boat Command had switched priority to the production of transitional types of U-boat which, while retaining the existing methods of propulsion, used the revolutionary Walter hull, were given greatly increased power and were equipped with many new and formidable aids to navigation and attack. The preliminary design for the larger of these (Type XXI, of 1,600 tons) had been completed in June; on 12 July Hitler had given approval for their production on a large scale as a matter of urgency. About the same time it was decided to produce a similar and smaller boat of 230 tons for work in shallow waters, particularly the Mediterranean and the Black Sea (Type XXIII). Construction had started in December 1943, dispensing with prototypes and using novel methods of pre-fabrication. The Type XXI programme envisaged the completion of three boats in April 1944 out of a total of 238 by February 1945. The Type XXIII programme envisaged the completion of 140 boats between February and October 1944. It was hoped that sufficient Type XXI boats would be operational to permit the resumption of the U-boat campaign in the autumn of 1944.[144] In the event, 61 Type XXIII and 120 Type XXI boats were commissioned by May 1945, but only five Type XXIII boats were operational by the end of the war, and the first Type XXI boat (U-2511) did not leave the Baltic until March 1945.

There had meanwhile been a steady reduction in the output of the old types of U-boat. As from July 1943 no more of these were laid down, the U-boat Command reckoning that the completion of the 250 boats already on the stocks would be sufficient to maintain continuity in the supply of operational U-boats until the new types

144. AIR 41/48, pp 237–239; ADM 234/68, pp 5–7, 83–87.

were available.[145] In the summer of 1943, on the other hand, the Command had also decided to equip the old types with the *Schnorchel*. The *Schnorchel*, an extensible tube which enabled a U-boat to take in oxygen and charge her batteries while remaining at periscope depth and to travel at periscope depth on diesel propulsion, was incorporated in the design of the Walter-boats, which had diesel and electric propulsion as well as the novel closed-cycle propulsion, and it was crucial to the design of the Type XXI and XXIII boats, which depended entirely on diesel and electric propulsion. But it was also the most effective of the various devices designed to prolong the operational life of the old types. By the end of 1943 it had been fitted externally to three of the existing U-boats; and by May 1944 some thirty of these had been equipped with it.[146]

Of all these developments, the first to come to the notice of the NID was the decline in the rate of U-boat construction on which it had reliable evidence from the Enigma, which regularly disclosed the number of U-boats commissioned, and from PR.* At the beginning of August 1943 it had noted that although few newly commissioned boats had entered the Atlantic since the loss of the initiative by the U-boat Command in May, output per month had recently risen to twenty-five, from the previous average of twenty-one.[151] But on 19 October it reported that only sixteen had been completed in September, as compared with twenty-six in August. On 8 November it reported that the number completed in October had climbed back to twenty, and added that it was too soon to reach any firm conclusions. By 29 November it had received various Press and attaché reports that U-boat construction had been curtailed in favour of increased construction of either merchant ships or tanks, but had been told by the Ministry of Economic Warfare that it was unlikely that other production had been increased at the expense of production of U-boats.

By the end of November German public broadcasts had spoken of the intention to introduce new and original methods of U-boat warfare, and the NID had also received POW reports about the existence of U-boats of 250 tons, with a crew of fifteen to twenty,

---

* The accuracy of the intelligence on this subject is shown by the following NID estimates. It estimated that the number of U-boats completed between March 1941 and the end of January 1943 was about 400;[147] the actual number was 417.[148] It estimated that the average monthly construction in 1943 was not more than 25;[149] the actual average was 24.[150]

145. AIR 41/48, p 238.   146. ibid. pp 240–241.
147. ADM 223/107, NID 01730/43 of 15 March 1943
148. ADM 186/802, BR 305(1), Appendix II.
149. JIC (44) 42 of 8 February.   150. ADM 186/802, Appendix II.
151. JIC (43) 282 of 1 August; ADM 223/212, No UT 02/43 of 2 August 1943.

and had linked them with three other items of intelligence – the identification in Kiel by PR in September of two U-boats measuring 110 feet in length; advice from the Naval Attaché Stockholm to the effect that a 'Channel type' U-boat was exercising in Kiel and that a rubber-covered U-boat of 250 tons had been seen in Hamburg; and further information from POW that Germany was developing unconventional methods of propulsion giving higher underwater speeds.[152] It was correct in associating these reports; they all referred to the small prototype Walter-boats, which were 130 feet long and had a crew of nineteen. A month later, however, the NID noted that most of the latest reports of experiments with some novel form of underwater propulsion, other than electric, indicated that the U-boats involved were of 500 tons or over, and suggested that they might include two (U–792 and U–794) which the Enigma had shown to be undergoing trials.[153] In fact, U-792 and U-794 were the first of the Type XVII boats, which had been commissioned in November; the Enigma references to them had thrown no light on the nature of their trials, but had indicated that they were U-boats of an unusual type. At the end of the year the Naval Attaché Stockholm reported that at certain yards the U-boats of the old programme were either being broken up or launched in an incomplete state, the 'building blocks' being re-arranged to take a new type of U-boat.[154]

The first intelligence to the effect that the German experiments were concerned not only with achieving higher under-water speeds, but also with enabling U-boats to cruise submerged for long periods, followed at the beginning of 1944. It included Enigma evidence that a U-boat had carried out submerged tests in the Strander Bucht near Kiel in December 1943 with an unknown and hitherto unheard of device called *Schnorchel*, statements from POW from U-841 in January that a ventilation trunk was being developed and several reports from other POW that the Germans were using closed-circuit engines in experiments with submerged propulsion at high speeds.[155] On this evidence the NID initially assumed that the *Schnorchel* was associated with a programme for developing closed-cycle diesel propulsion; it reported on 24 January that it had received 'indications that Germany intends to improve existing U-boat diesel

152. ADM 223/120, UC report 383 of 23 October, 401 of 26 November 1943; ADM 223/84, History of POW Interrogation, pp 38–39; Naval Historical Branch letter to Cabinet Office Historical Section (D/NHB/3/7/3) of 20 November 1980.

153. ADM 223/120, UC report 413 of 5 January 1944.

154. ADM 223/212, BNA Stockholm War Diary, p 69.

155. Naval Historical Branch to Cabinet Historical Section (D/NHB/3/7/3) of 20 November 1980.

engines to run on a closed exhaust system submerged' and that operational U-boats were 'having preparatory modifications carried out as they come in for refit for conversion to under-water diesel propulsion.[156] But the Naval Section at GC and CS took the view that the *Schnorchel* was no more than a ventilation trunk which enabled the U-boat to charge batteries while submerged, its main argument being that the *Schnorchel* tests in the Strander Bucht, where the depth of water was only eight to ten fathoms, were unlikely to be under-water speed trials. This view was proved correct when, following several other uninformative Enigma references to the *Schnorchel*, signals to U-264, one of the U-boats which searched for convoys ONS 29 and ON 224 in February, revealed that she had been fitted with it and, by instructing her to report her experiences, gave more details about it. She was sunk on 19 February before she could report.[157]

The Admiralty had by then obtained conclusive evidence from PR of the decline in the construction of old-type U-boats. On 10 February, after an interval in which weather had made sorties impossible since the end of September 1943, PR, though still incomplete, had indicated that 201 boats were under construction as compared with 271 in the previous September; and on 20 February, when all the building yards had been covered, the figure of 201 was corrected to 183. On this evidence the NID, arguing that so large a reduction could not be attributed to the effect of Allied bombing, returned to the suggestion that Germany was voluntarily curtailing U-boat building or curtailing it in order to increase the production of merchant ships, locomotives or tanks, and offered that explanation in a report circulated on 1 March.[158]* But by 28 February PR

---

* The report of 1 March provoked the following protest from C-in-C Bomber Command on 7 March: 'I have read your NID UC Report No 435 dated March 1st, 1944, and consider that the general impression which it conveys of the effect which bombing has produced on German U-boat output to be seriously misleading.

The report states that "the fall in numbers is so general that bombing alone cannot be the direct cause of the reduction. It is improbable that it is due to the indirect effect of bombing or to the blockade". It is on this entirely unsupported statement that the conclusion is based that "Germany has deliberately reduced her U-boat building programme". I do not dispute the view that the Germans at this stage in the war have probably decided that their overstrained resources can no longer cope with the production of U-boats on a large scale. It seems to me, however, absurd to suggest that this decision to curtail U-boat building has been voluntarily taken and is not in large measure at least, the result of our bombing and mining policy. Such a suggestion might perhaps be plausible if no account whatever is taken of the known effects of our bombing on supplies of basic products, engines, accumulators and component parts made in industrial centres throughout Germany and if attention is concentrated solely on the damage shown to actual building yards by reconnaissance photographs.

156. ADM 223/119, LC report 892 of 3 February 1944.
157. ADM 223/171, OIC SI 865 of 21 February 1944; Roskill, op cit Vol III Part
      I, pp 253, 258.
158. ADM 223/120, UC Report 435 of 1 March 1944.

had revealed a further reduction to 168 in the number of U-boats under construction, and this prompted the NID to suggest that the decline, if not explained by a switch in the enemy's production priorities or by his conclusion that the number of U-boats built or building was sufficient, might be accounted for by the fact that he had decided to produce new types – small submersibles and/or ocean-going U-boats with an improved performance. In support of this last alternative it noted that there was by now a fair amount of evidence that, in addition to resorting to the *Schnorchel*, Germany was developing both 500-ton U-boats, with closed-cycle propulsion and increased diving depths, and a smaller Walter-boat, described as a submersible E-boat. From NID reports compiled earlier in February it is clear that this evidence had come mainly from U-boat POW, but it included the decrypt of a report from the Japanese Ambassador in Berlin which quoted Hitler as saying that Germany was developing U-boats with increased speeds.

On 28 February the evidence was considered at a meeting of the Naval Staff. The meeting agreed that, in addition to equipping the existing U-boats with *Schnorchel*, the enemy was building small Walter-boats and possibly experimenting with a larger boat which used closed-cycle propulsion and had a higher speed than the existing types. But it devoted most of its time to the threat from the Walter-boat, concluding that it must have been developed as an anti-invasion weapon and, in the absence of intelligence on the point, assuming that a considerable number had already been built. This conclusion was natural enough: the Admiralty was preoccupied with planning for the protection of the *Overlord* convoys, and U-boat POW, still the source of most reports, obscured the difference between the Walter-boat and other new developments by their tendency to associate all innovations with the name of Professor Walter. It was for these reasons, but also because PR, the other chief source of intelligence, could not distinguish between the Walter-boat and the small transitional boat (Type XXIII), that during March and April 1944 the NID, giving no further thought to the possibility that new types of Atlantic boats, some of 500 tons

---

This, however, is obviously an entirely incorrect method of assessment – one which I feel would be adopted only if it were decided deliberately to minimise the efforts of the bombing offensive. It certainly seems to me that a general reduction in activity such as is known to have taken place in U-boat construction is precisely the result which might be expected to follow on the destruction of industrial centres and the disorganisation of German production which has been the avowed aim of strategic bombing to bring about. I note also that no credit is given to Bomber Command for the considerable switch over of resources to shipbuilding which has beyond doubt been forced upon the enemy almost entirely through the destruction caused by the minelaying of this Command . . .'[159]

159. ADM 223/209, C-in-C Bomber Command to DNI, 7 March 1944.

or more, might be being developed, continued to be alarmed by the
threat from the smaller Walter-boats.

In spite of the fact that special PR patrols were flown, only a few
small U-boats were photographed in the Baltic or on the slipways
during those months.[160] By 10 March, on the other hand, the analysis
of PR photographs had established that few if any U-boat hulls of
the old type had been laid down since the previous autumn, and
that some keels on which work had started had been dismantled.[161]
And since MEW was still disinclined to believe that the stop in
building was explained by diversion to other war production, the
mystery remained unsolved until the third week of April. PR
evidence, handicapped hitherto by the novel pre-fabricated methods
adopted for the new U-boats, then detected that the Germans were
building an 'apparently new type of U-boat, 245 foot long', and
were having them 'rapidly assembled in pre-fabricated pressure-
hull sections'. Two had been seen at Danzig, of which one was
already launched, four at Bremen and one at Blohm and Voss in
Hamburg.[162] The NID deduced from the PR evidence that the boat
launched at Danzig could not have been more than six weeks on the
slip, as compared with the minimum of five months taken to build
'a normal U-boat'. The deduction was correct. The pre-fabrication
system adopted for the Type XXI and XXIII boats entailed the
manufacture of parts at 150 factories throughout the Reich, their
incorporation into sections at thirteen shipyards and the transport
of the sections to other yards for final assembly in six weeks.[163]

Of the characteristics of the new types, as of the details of the
pre-fabrication system, nothing was learned for another five weeks.
On 1 May, indeed, the source that was eventually to disclose these
details mentioned Type XXI and Type XXIII U-boats – the first
mention of them to be received – but only heightened the confusion
by referring to them as Walter-boats. This source was the machine
cypher of the Japanese Naval Attaché in Berlin; it had first succumbed to British attack early in 1944 and by April it was producing
results of an unexpectedly high quality on subjects like Germany's
technological developments and anti-invasion preparations on
which the decrypts lost none of their importance from sometimes
being obtained with considerable delay.[164] The reference to Types
XXI and XXIIII received on 1 May was obtained from the
decrypt of a message sent in December 1943. It was followed at the
end of May by the decrypt of a detailed and accurate account of
what NID was soon to call the 'revolution' in U-boat design and

---

160.   AIR 41/7, *Photographic Reconnaissance*, Vol II, p 147.
161.   ADM 223/209, DNI to C-in-C Bomber Command, 10 March 1944.
162.   AIR 41/7, p 147.   163.   AIR 41/48, pp 403–404.
164.   *The Handling of Naval Special Intelligence*, p 117.

construction, as obtained by Vice-Admiral Abe, the Head of the Japanese Naval Mission, in an interview with Dönitz, Meisel (Chief of the Naval Operational Staff) and Fuchs (Chief Constructor for U-boats) on 24 April.*

This decrypt was of inestimable value both negatively and positively. On the negative side, by showing that the propulsion of Types XXI and XXIII was based on established methods, that is on diesels improved by the *Schnorchel* for proceeding at periscope depth and on more powerful electric motors for submerged passage, it established that the Germans had failed to bring to a practical stage the innovation which the Admiralty had most feared – under-water propulsion using a form of closed-cycle engine. On this evidence the Admiralty was able to dismiss the threat to the *Overlord* convoys from Walter-boats. Positively, the decrypt put an end to uncertainty in interpreting the increasing amount of evidence that PR, both by the RAF and the USAAF, was now producing on the German building programme.[165] Nor was it long before other reports from the Japanese Naval Mission were decrypted. By 23 August the NID had the text of a detailed account of the technical specifications of Types XXI and XXIII which had been sent to Tokyo on 13 August. This was followed in the first week of October by two decrypts giving full details of the building programme – the prefabrication system, the final assembly yards and the planned output – as obtained by Vice-Admiral Abe during a visit to the Danzig yard on 29 August.† But already before the end of June a decrypt of a signal from Vice-Admiral Abe had disclosed that because work on the new U-boats had been 'a little retarded' by Allied bombing, the Germans would be unable to have them in service by the autumn, as they had hoped; and on 12 December the Admiralty learned from the decrypt of another of his signals that, on account of the delay imposed by Allied bombing, the new U-boats would not be operational until March 1945.[166]

---

* See Appendix 11 (i) for full text.   † See Appendix 11 (ii).

165. AIR 41/7, p 155.
166. Dir/C Archive, 6897 of 22 June, SJA 385 of 16 June 1944.

CHAPTER 36

The War at Sea: Surface Operations

THE SUCCESSIVE defeats sustained by the U-boats from the summer of 1943 were accompanied by Germany's final abandonment of the attempt to sail blockade-runners to and from the Far East. Her blockade-running programme for the winter of 1943–1944 started in November 1943. By the middle of January 1944 it had run into so much delay and suffered so many losses that she was forced to recognise that the risk of interception had become too high to justify further sailings.

In May and June 1943 Japanese diplomatic decrypts disclosed that, despite the losses incurred in the 1942–1943 season,* the Axis intended to resume blockade-running between Germany and the Far East in the autumn. They stated that seven merchant ships would sail from Europe with 50,000 tons of cargo and that the Germans were also constructing special U-boats in which they hoped to lift 3,000 tons of cargo from Japan during 1943.[1]† During July and August PR of the Biscay ports and SIS reports from the area indicated that sailings for the Far East were being planned, and by 6 September it appeared that seven ships were either ready to sail or making preparations to do so.[2] On 4 October – by which time one of these ships, the *Kulmerland*, had been bombed – the decrypt of a signal from the Japanese Ambassador in Berlin stated that the cargo to be shipped from Biscay in the coming season had been reduced from 50,000 to 35,000 tons by Allied bombing.[3]

This intelligence was followed by the Allied occupation of the Azores on 8 October 1943, which raised the possibility that the enemy would abandon the entire programme.[4] But doubt on this score was removed when on 23 October the Germans brought into force special W/T routines for intercommunication between U-boats and blockade-runners in the Biscay area.[5] At the beginning of November a second suspected blockade-runner, the *Dresden*, was mined. The OIC then estimated that five ships were preparing to

---

* See Volume II, p 540 et seq.
† This was a reference to Type XX which never became operational.

1. ADM 223/98, OIC SI 623 of 28 June 1943.
2. ibid, OIC SI 647 of 26 July, 689 of 6 September 1943.
3. ADM 223/170, OIC SI 731 of 11 October 1943.
4. ibid, OIC SI 741 of 18 October 1943.
5. ADM 223/186, Ultra signal 1322/3 November 1943.

leave Biscay,[6] and it had evidence that at least four ships were loading in the Far East.[7] In the middle of the month the decrypt of a further report from the Japanese Ambassador revealed that the total tonnage to be shifted from Biscay had been reduced to 29,000 tons; it added that he did not know when the ships would leave.[8]

By that time Allied expectations of success against the blockade-runners were high. The Azores were now available as a base for Allied patrols; US naval patrols in the south Atlantic had been strengthened, so had the air and naval forces available to Coastal Command and C-in-C Plymouth for operations in Biscay. At the same time, two intelligence developments promised that operational information about the enemy's movements would be fuller than it had been during the previous winter. The U-boat Enigma was now being decrypted regularly and with less delay; together with the fact that the U-boats were ranging further afield in the south Atlantic and the Indian Ocean, this meant that more frequent orders from the U-boat Command arising from the movement of the blockade-runners were likely to be decrypted promptly. Of no less consequence, GC and CS had in August 1943 broken the Enigma key (which it named Sunfish) used for transmissions to and from the blockade-runners themselves; this yielded decrypts of operational value about the departure of outward-bound ships, on which subject previous intelligence had been poor. Nor were Allied expectations disappointed. Between November 1943 and January 1944, when the Axis abandoned blockade-running, no ship succeeded in getting away from the Biscay ports; and of the five ships which attempted the passage from the Far East, only one succeeded in reaching France. According to MEW's estimates at the time, that ship had brought in 7,500 tons of cargo and the remainder of the total cargo loaded in the Far East (32,815 tons) had been sunk. MEW's estimates compared well with the facts: 33,095 tons were loaded in the Far East of which 6,890 tons were landed in France.[9]

The first evidence that the 1943–1944 programme had begun was received on 16 November from an Enigma decrypt instructing a U-boat not to attack independent ships west of a given line well down in the south Atlantic. Operational authorities were informed that the instruction probably referred to one or more northbound blockade-breakers, and possibly to as many as nine. The four most

---

6. ADM 223/170, OIC SI 762 of 8 November 1943; ADM 223/88, Colpoys, *Admiralty Use of Special Intelligence in Naval Operations*, p 209.
7. ADM 223/170, OIC SI 731 of 11 October, 741 of 18 October 1943.
8. ADM 223/186, Ultra signal 2324/14 November 1943.
9. Roskill, *The War at Sea*, Vol III Part I (1960) p 75.

probable were the *Osorno,* the *Alsterufer* and two others subsequently discovered to have sailed. Five had in fact sailed.[10]

Except that Sigint revealed the names of three blockade-breakers which had sailed or were about to sail from the Far East during November, and of two which had probably sailed, nothing further was heard until 26 November, when the Enigma disclosed the imposition from 1 December of similar restrictions further north, in the south Atlantic 'narrows'.[11] On 5 December further evidence of northerly movement was received when the Enigma revealed the imposition of restrictions in an area extending well north of the Equator from 6 December.[12] The first clue as to which ship, or ships, were affected came when the Enigma gave details of a ship sighted by a U-boat just south of the Equator on 9 December.[13] The NID thought this sounded like the *Osorno* but believed that a further blockade-breaker was likely to be ahead of her.[14] On 12 December, the Admiralty having signalled that it attached great importance to the interception of homeward-bound blockade-breakers, HMS *Glasgow* sailed from the Azores.[15] Patrols made no contact, however. There followed further evidence that one or more ships might be nearing France when, on 18 December, the decrypt of a Sunfish message addressed both to the *Osorno* and the *Alsterufer* on 13 December suggested that the German control was plotting them on jointly;[16] and on 22 December a Shark decrypt revealed the closure of an area west of Biscay.[17] On 23 December U-boats in the Bay were given the rough position of the *Osorno,*[18] and the US escort-carrier *Card,* which was carrying out anti-submarine patrols in the area, sighted an unknown vessel but was unable to maintain touch.[19] On 24 December three cruisers were attempting to intercept and RAF bombers made an unsuccessful attack.[20] But the *Osorno* got through to the Gironde, as emerged from the Enigma on the 25th,[21] and although she struck a wreck and was beached there, the RAF failed in its attempt to prevent the Germans from salvaging her

---

10. ADM 223/88, p 209; Op-20–G History, Vol II, p 330; ADM 223/186, Ultra signal 1132/17 November 1943.
11. Op-20-G History, Vol II, pp 329, 331; ADM 223/170, OIC SI 783 of 29 November 1943.
12. Op-20-G History, Vol II, p 331. 13. ibid, p 332.
14. ADM 223/170, OIC SI 796 of 13 December 1943.
15. ADM 223/88, p 209.
16. ibid, p 211; Op-20-G History, Vol II, pp 332–333; ADM 223/187, Ultra signal 1740/22 December 1943.
17. Op-20-G History, Vol II, p 334.
18. ADM 223/187, Ultra signal 1005/23 December 1943.
19. Op-20-G History, Vol II, p 333; ADM 223/88, p 211.
20. ADM 223/88, pp 211–212. 21. ibid, p 212.

cargo of rubber. It may be that she owed her escape while crossing Biscay to the fact that Allied operations were complicated by the OIC's belief that the Germans would sail outward-bound ships to coincide with her arrival.[22] For this belief the OIC had good evidence as well as the precedents of the previous winter. The decrypts of Sunfish signals to some of the ships waiting to leave Biscay had shown that their departure was imminent, and between 15 and 21 December the Home Waters Enigma had revealed that escorts were being alerted in Biscay.[23] But another of these ships, the *Pietro Orseolo*, had been destroyed by air attack on 18 December and, as the OIC realised by 25 December, the Germans did not attempt to sail any of the four remaining ships at this time.[24]

The Admiralty had meanwhile learned nothing more of the *Alsterufer*, though it was plain that she was one of the blockade-breakers at sea.[25] The first information of her whereabouts came on 25 December, when her position became known through a singular chance. At noon on that day U-305 signalled the position in which, as she thought, she had sighted the *Osorno*. The signal, in Offizier, was read within an hour of transmission. From Control's reply the OIC was able early on 26 December to inform the operational authorities that the ship sighted by U-305 was in fact the *Alsterufer*.[26] Decrypts of early 26 December also disclosed that the fleet destroyers and torpedo-boats which had brought in the *Osorno* would be required again in the very near future.[27] Accordingly HMS *Enterprise* sailed from Plymouth, HMS *Gambia* and the French large destroyer *Le Malin* from the Azores, and HMS *Penelope* and *Ariadne* from Gibraltar. HMS *Mauritius* was placed at the disposal of C-in-C Plymouth and HMS *Glasgow* was still at sea.[28] Also on 26 December the Enigma threw further light on the *Alsterufer*'s movements by revealing that on that day she would be entering a restricted area in outer Biscay.[29] She was sighted by aircraft of Coastal Command and sunk by a Czech-manned RAF Liberator on 27 December.

Meanwhile, early on 27 December, the Enigma had disclosed that, presumably to meet the *Alsterufer*, five German fleet destroyers

---

22. ADM 223/179, Ultra signals 1904/21 December, 1740/22 December, 1620/23 December, 1422/24 December 1943.
23. ADM 223/187, Ultra signals 0040/17 December, 2351/20 December, 1444/21 December, 1740/22 December 1943; ADM 223/88, p 210.
24. ADM 223/187, Ultra signal 0120/25 December 1943; Roskill, op cit, Vol III, Part I, p 74.
25. Op-20-G History, Vol II, pp 333–334.
26. ibid, p 334; ADM 223/88, p 212; ADM 223/188, Ultra signal 0715/26 December 1943.
27. ADM 223/188, Ultra signal 1021/26 December 1943.
28. ADM 223/88, p 213.
29. ADM 223/188, Ultra signal 1140/25 December 1943.

and six fleet torpedo-boats were to sail from various Biscay ports and rendez-vous at a specified, but unidentifiable, position.[30] At 0920 on 28 December, probably with assistance from the decrypts of further signals to it,[31] the German force was sighted by a US Liberator.[32] On the strength of this sighting, C-in-C Plymouth re-directed the cruisers *Glasgow* and *Enterprise,* which had been out after the *Alsterufer.* In the following engagement – which, like that with the *Scharnhorst* that had just been fought,* was made possible only by the fact that the Admiralty was receiving the Enigma decrypts almost as soon as the German addressees – the cruisers sank one enemy destroyer and two torpedo-boats without damage to themselves.[33]†

Within days of this battle the Allies sank the remaining inward-bound ships – they were the last to attempt the passage from the Far East – and within three weeks of it the Germans finally aban-doned the attempt to sail blockade-runners from Biscay. In the case of the inward-bound blockade-runners, the *Weserland,* the *Burgenland* and the *Rio Grande,* their sailing dates from the Far East were known,[34] and it may be safely assumed that it was after these dates had been correlated with various Enigma decrypts instructing U-boats not to attack merchant ships in stated areas at stated times[35] that US forces intercepted all three ships in the south Atlantic between 3 and 5 January 1944.[36] Nine days later Sunfish decrypts disclosed that the Germans, as yet unaware of these losses, ordered two of the ships in Biscay to get ready to sail.[37] But on 21 January the OIC learned from the same source that all four had been ordered to unload as the risk of interception had become too great.[38]

---

* See below, p 263 et seq.

† It was this battle, however, which finally persuaded the Royal Navy that the *Narvik*-class destroyers mounted 6″ guns, see Volume I, p 77.

30.   ibid, Ultra signal 0139/27 December 1943.
31.   ibid, Ultra signals 0445 and 0802/28 December 1943.
32.   Roskill, op cit, Vol III Part I, p 74; AIR 41/48 *The RAF in Maritime War,* Vol IV, p 328.
33.   P Beesly, *Very Special Intelligence* (1977), p 225; J Rohwer, 'Special Intelli-gence' und die Vernichtung der 'Scharnhorst' in *Marine Rundschau,* October 1977, p 56.
34.   ADM 223/170, OIC SI 789 of 6 December 1943.
35.   ADM 223/188, Ultra signal 1531/26 December 1943 summarised these decrypts.
36.   ADM 223/171, OIC SI 822 of 10 January 1944.
37.   ADM 223/188, Ultra signal 1429/14 January 1944.
38.   ADM 223/189, Ultra signal 2235/21 January 1944; ADM 223/171, OIC SI 836 of 24 January 1944.

It learned after the war that Dönitz had proposed the cancellation
to Hitler on 18 January.[39]

□

From the summer of 1943 the Home Fleet, already weakened by
the transfer of many of its destroyers to the Battle of the Atlantic
and the transfers to the Mediterranean of the battleships *King George
V* and *Howe* and of more destroyers, was further weakened by the
need to lend cruisers and destroyers to C-in-C Plymouth for the
protection of Mediterranean-bound convoys against German destroyers based at Bordeaux and, subsequently, for operations against
the blockade-runners. In July it was reinforced by the United States
Navy, which placed two battleships under the command of the
Commander-in-Chief. Together with the battleships *Duke of York*
and *Anson*, these reinforcements provided adequate security against
any attempt by the German Fleet to break out into the Atlantic.
They also enabled the Home Fleet in July to simulate a landing
against Norway in two feints timed to coincide with Operation
Husky against Sicily. But it was accepted that, so long as the *Tirpitz*,
the *Scharnhorst* and the *Lützow* remained operational in north Norway, the sailing of convoys to north Russia, suspended in March,
could not be resumed.

There was considerable uncertainty about what the Germans
intended to do with their surface fleet. Continuing rumours that it
was to be laid up received support from Enigma references to a
drastic comb-out of fleet personnel to meet the need for U-boat
crews, and also for the manning of the new anti-aircraft armament
which was being introduced into U-boats in response to Coastal
Command's anti-U-boat offensive.* But these references clearly did
not apply to the three ships of the Battle Group in north Norway,
which were known to have been carrying out intensive exercises in
Altenfjord for some time past, and the evidence about the ships in
the Baltic was conflicting. The Enigma showed that the *Eugen*, the
Scheer, the *Nürnberg* and the *Emden* were engaged in training U-boat
crews, but it also disclosed that they were carrying out exercises
which included main calibre firing by the *Scheer*.[40] In these circumstances the NID was forced to conclude that it was still Dönitz's
policy to bring the German Fleet '*to a high state of battle efficiency*'† by
intensive exercises. As late as December 1943 NID was anxious
that the *Scheer* might break out.[41]

---

* For this offensive, see above, p 214 et seq.   † Underlining in the original.

39. Roskill, op cit, Vol III Part I, p 75.
40. ADM 223/174, OIC S 628 of 2 July, 638 of 15 July 1943.
41. ADM 223/187, Ultra signals 2130/20 December 1943 and 0130/21 Decem-
     ber 1943.

So far as the Battle Group was concerned, Dönitz's determination to use it seemed to be borne out when the Enigma disclosed that on 10 July he was visiting north Norway[42] and that on 14 July instructions had been issued for an operation (code-named *Wanton* by the OIC) involving the *Lützow*, five U-boats and long-range reconnaissance aircraft. From the fact that the forces to be employed were similar to those accompanying the *Scheer* in August 1942,* and because Fliegerführer North East was also involved, the OIC deduced that the operation would be in the Kara Sea; and from the evidence about the preliminary movements by U-boats it suggested that it would begin before the end of the month.[43] By 15 August, however, there was still no evidence of any move by the *Lützow*, though it was known by then that some U-boats had reached the Kara Sea.[44] Nor did the Germans make any mention of the participation of a surface ship when, on 5 September, the day after GC and CS had decrypted signals from U-boats claiming to have sunk two ships in the Kara Sea, they announced in a radio broadcast that 'the detonation of German torpedoes has made the world conscious of the mouth of the Yenisei'.[45] On 3 September Russian air reconnaissance disclosed that, together with the *Tirpitz* and the *Scharnhorst*, the *Lützow* was still in Altenfjord.[46]

On 6 September the *Tirpitz* and the *Scharnhorst* and ten destroyers sailed from Altenfjord, approached Spitzbergen unobserved and, early on 8 September, bombarded the shore installations of the Allied party which had recently ousted a German meteorological expedition from the area.† Their move was preceded by a GAF

---

* See Volume II, p 223.

† In May 1942, at a time when RAF reconnaissance had failed to establish the presence of Germans there, but when the GAF Enigma had disclosed that the enemy was planning to establish an automatic meteorological station, the British authorities had sent a Norwegian party to Spitzbergen to establish a meteorological base and deny the place to the enemy. The party had been bombed, and it had then been learned from its survivors and from the Enigma that the Germans had all along had a base in Spitzbergen from which they carried out a daily air reconnaissance flight. In July 1942 a stronger Norwegian expedition had been sent, and this had battled with the enemy's party, each side trying inconclusively to destroy the other, until the following November. During this period the Enigma had provided details, often in advance, of the attacks carried out against the Norwegians by the GAF and the occasional U-boat.[47] Thereafter all was quiet until June 1943, when the Norwegian party, recently replenished by cruisers of the Home Fleet, found and put to flight the German party and was itself attacked by a FW 200 aircraft and a U-boat. At the end of June 1943 this U-boat evacuated the German party, as the Enigma disclosed, and a British submarine moved the Norwegians to a safer part of Spitzbergen. But it was clear that the Germans were keeping Spitzbergen under close observation. The Enigma disclosed that a U-boat was ordered to

42. ADM 223/174 OIC S 636 of 12 July 1943.
43. ibid, 639 of 16 July 1943; ADM 223/182, Ultra signal 1234/15 July 1943.
44. ADM 223/174, OIC S 666 of 15 August 1943.
45. ibid, OIC SI 684 of 4 September 1943.
46. ADM 223/88, p 112.
47. See, for example, Naval Headlines No 483 of 30 October 1942.

Enigma decrypt which revealed that at least eight aircraft – an exceptionally large number – would carry out reconnaissance from Lofoten in the areas Narvik-Jan Mayen Spitzbergen-North Cape in connection with another named operation (*Sizilien*); the Home Fleet was so informed at 0808 on 6 September by the OIC, which added that there was no indication of the nature of the operation.[49] Later on 6 September, however, having learned from another decrypt that four aircraft had taken off from north-east Norway early that day in connection with yet a third named operation (*Zitronella*), it advised the Home Fleet that not only these aircraft but also the reconnaissance flights in connection with Operation *Sizilien* were probably associated with the move of the *Lützow* to the Kara Sea.[50] Nor was it until mid-day on 7 September that, despite the use in the decrypts of two code-names in addition to *Wanton*, the OIC realised that at least two separate operations were in progress. This was made clear by the receipt of further decrypts which revealed that the enemy's reconnaissance effort on 6 September had also included eight aircraft flying from Trondheim between Norway and Iceland as far north as North Cape, that for 7 September the enemy had ordered reconnaissance by five aircraft from Trondheim and 'security reconnaissance' by four aircraft from Lofoten in connection with Operation *Sizilien* (to which the OIC gave the name *Sentry*) and 'escort reconnaissance' from Lofoten in connection with Operation *Zitronella* (to which the OIC gave the name *Virtue*). In addition, the Enigma disclosed that during 7 September six aircraft would carry out reconnaissance of the area Narvik-Jan Mayen-Spitzbergen-North Cape. In forwarding this intelligence to the Home Fleet at 1220 on 7 September the OIC commented that operation *Virtue* might refer to the move of the *Lützow* but that 'there is no clue yet to Operation *Sentry*.'[51] This comment failed to do justice to the fact that there had by then been decrypts which showed that the extensive air reconnaissance west and north-west of Norway in connection with Operation *Sentry*[52] greatly exceeded that which was being carried out north-east of Norway in connection with Opera-

---

make a reconnaissance of the fjords from 17 July and that weather-reporting aircraft based at Banak were to be fitted with cameras to enable them to photograph Spitzbergen and Bear Island.[48] During July and August the GAF carried out reconnaissance of the island nearly every day. For German meteorological operations in Greenland 1942–1944 see Appendix 12.

48.   ADM 223/184 OIC S 641 of 18 July, 642 of 19 July 1943.
49.   ADM 223/184, Ultra signal 0808/6 September 1943.
50.   ibid, Ultra signal 1641/6 September, ADM 223/174, OIC S 687 of 7 September 1943.
51.   ADM 223/184, Ultra signal 1220/7 September 1943.
52.   ibid, Ultra signals 0809/29 August, 0126/30 August, 0808/6 September and 1220/7 September 1943.

tion *Virtue*, and that it was in any case most unlikely that reconnaissance on this scale was in preparation for the move of the *Lützow* to the Kara Sea. PR of Altenfjord by RAF Spitfires operating from Russia on 7 September showed that the *Tirpitz* and the *Scharnhorst* had left,[53] but this intelligence did not reach the Admiralty or the Home Fleet till the following morning.

The Home Fleet was thus taken by surprise when, in the morning of 8 September, it learned that Spitzbergen's radio station had reported sighting an enemy force of seven destroyers and three cruisers at 0145 on 8 September[54] and that at 1207 on 7 September the German Battle Group had been sent a weather report for the area between North Cape and Spitzbergen.[55] By the time the C-in-C sailed from Scapa at 1930 on 8 September with the *Duke of York*, the *Anson* and five destroyers a German broadcast had announced that naval forces and an army landing party had destroyed the wireless and meteorological stations at Spitzbergen, together with – an extravagant claim – 'extensive military installations'. While the Home Fleet was preparing to sail, it received the contents of further decrypts which included the news that another weather report for the Spitzbergen area had been sent to the German Battle Group at 1249 on 8 September.[56] In the early hours of 9 September the Enigma revealed that the German ships which had carried out Operation *Sentry* were expected back in Altenfjord some time after 1900 that day.[57] By then it was clear that *Zitronella* was associated with this operation and had nothing to do with the *Lützow*. At 1330 PR showed that the *Lützow* had not left and that the *Tirpitz* and the *Scharnhorst* were still missing; the fact that they had entered Altenfjord at 1400 was disclosed by a decrypt later in the day.[58]

By that time the Home Fleet, clearly in no position to intercept, had begun its return to base. Whether or not it might have been able to intervene effectively if it had been brought to short notice on the morning of 8 September, as it might have been but for the fact that preoccupation in the NID with the expected move of the *Lützow* obscured the possibility that the enemy was contemplating another operation, or even in the afternoon of 7 September, when it became clear that two operations were planned, cannot now be decided. The episode had illustrated once again that Ultra and PR could not always be relied on to give adequate warning of the movements of main units from the Norwegian bases.

---

53. ADM 223/88, p 112.   54. ibid.
55. ADM 223/184, Ultra signal 0801/8 September 1943.
56. ibid, Ultra signals, 1301/1716 and 1840/8 September 1943.
57. ibid, Ultra signal 0143/9 September 1943.
58. ibid, Ultra signal 2255/9 September 1943.

In the last week of September another episode provided further evidence that even if intelligence did give timely warning of an enemy move, it was far from certain that the warning could be put to good account. Between 23 September and 1 October the *Lützow* returned to the Baltic, steaming the entire length of the Norwegian coast without molestation despite the fact that the Enigma and the SIS ship-watching organisation gave early notice of her intentions and unusually precise details about her movements. On 21 September the OIC learned that a Staffel of twin-engined fighters was to operate from Bodö airfield during the next few days, and to keep in close signals contact with Trondheim and Naval Signals HQ in Germany; it at once advised the Home Fleet and (via C-in-C Rosyth) No 18 Group Coastal Command RAF that a main unit was about to move southward from Altenfjord and Narvik.[59] The following day it repeated the warning, commenting in an Ultra signal which reported that destroyers were moving north from Aalesund that their movement was unlikely to be the reason for the transfer of the fighters.[60] On 23 September, when PR from north Russia had shown that the *Lützow* had left her berth and was in mid-fjord,[61] the decrypt of a signal from Admiral Polar Coast disclosed that German naval forces were to be in inshore waters on 23 and 24 September, and on 24 September another decrypt reported the arrival of the fighters at Bodö. The OIC forwarded this intelligence as soon as it was received, and at 1820 on 24 September it commented in another Ultra signal that the evidence was consistent with an impending move by major units.[62] By 25 September the news that twin-engined fighters were moving to Bergen had suggested that the ship or ships would proceed to the Baltic without stopping at Trondheim.[63]* Soon after midnight on 25–26 September the OIC received the decrypt of a request from Admiral Northern Waters for lights as far as Trondheim from 0200 to 2135 on 26 September and, other Enigma signals having by then established that the *Tirpitz* and the *Scharnhorst* were still in Altenfjord,† it advised Ultra recipients that it was the *Lützow* that was on the move.[64] Fúrther Enigma intelligence during 26 September included details

---

* This item does not figure in the Ultra signals issued by the OIC; presumably it was provided by the RAF Y Station at Cheadle.

† See below p 262.

59. ibid, Ultra signal 1625/21 September 1943.
60. ibid, Ultra signal 0948/22 September 1943.
61. ADM 223/88, p 185.
62. ADM 223/184, Ultra signals 1630/23 September, 1537 and 1820/24 September 1943.
63. AIR 41/48, p 355; Roskill op cit, Vol III Part I p 69.
64. ADM 223/184, Ultra signal 0010/26 September 1943.

of the GAF reconnaissance that was being flown to seaward of 'the formation' and details about command arrangements and the disposition of mark-boats, which confirmed that the *Lützow* would proceed south without entering Trondheim.[65] On the same day the Admiralty promulgated an agent's report to the effect that at 0810 on 26 September the *Lützow* and escorting destroyers had passed a point a little to the south of Bodö, moving south.[66].

The official historian of the war at sea expressed surprise that no steps were taken to confirm this last report by air reconnaissance until the morning of 27 September.[67] In the light of the preceding Enigma intelligence, which he could not consult, it seems reasonable to assume that the authorities judged that it was unnecessary to carry out reconnaissance during 26 September. This consideration does not explain why no reconnaissance was flown from 21 to 25 September, when the whereabouts of the *Lützow* remained uncertain. In the subsequent inquiry carried out by Coastal Command and the Home Fleet the C-in-C Coastal Command attributed the omission partly to the fact that it was difficult to provide reconnaissance so far to the north; but he added that, if such reconnaissance had been flown, it might have alerted the enemy and made it more difficult to attack the *Lützow*, and he strongly implied that the available intelligence should in any case have provided sufficient evidence for sailing the Home Fleet's carrier force.[68] In the event, for whatever reason, no preparations for attack were made before 26 September, although clear warning of the impending move had been given as early as 21 September

On 26 September No 18 Group RAF was unable to deliver a strike, and also found that the number of strike aircraft it could make available on the following day would be limited, while the Home Fleet first contemplated sailing the US carrier *Ranger* and then cancelled the move on the ground that she could not be in a position to strike when it was judged that the *Lützow* would be off Stadlandet, the best point of attack, at about 0900 on 27 September. It was then decided that shore-based carrier aircraft should take off from 0830 on 27 September from Sumburgh; but on that morning, after the *Lützow* had been sighted by reconnaissance aircraft 50 miles south of Trondheim, steaming at 25 knots, the order for the take-off was delayed until 1040 by disagreements between No 18 Group and the Home Fleet about escort and other operational arrangements. In a further disagreement as to where the strike

---

65. ibid, Ultra signals 0846, 1355 and 2325/26 September 1943; ADM 223/88, p 187.
66. AIR 41/48, p 335; Roskill, op cit, Vol III Part I, pp 69–70.
67. Roskill, op cit, Vol III Part I, p 70.   68. AIR 41/48. p 361.

should be made, No 18 Group argued for a point south of Stadlandet but the Home Fleet prevailed with a revised estimate of the *Lützow*'s progress. It now calculated that as the *Lützow* would not be able to keep at 25 knots all the way down the Leads, she would probably be off Stadlandet between 1030 and 1500. In the event she passed Stadlandet at 0920, and the strike, making landfall just south of that point between 1300 and 1400, swept northwards without contacting her. She was sighted by reconnaissance aircraft at 1741 on 27 September, too far to the south to permit another strike against her.[69] On 28 September the Enigma established that she was making for Gdynia; it showed that she had arrived there on the following day.[70]

□

During the early stages of Operation *Sentry* the Admiralty had been confused by its belief that the *Lützow* was to leave for the Kara Sea. It may be that when it was receiving the early evidence about the move of the *Lützow* to the Baltic, the Home Fleet was in its turn distracted by its interest in the outcome of Operation *Source*, the attack by midget submarines on the German ships at their berths in Altenfjord which had been scheduled to take place on the morning of 22 September.

The possibility of eliminating the threat from the Battle Group by disabling the ships in harbour had long been under consideration, and a number of methods of attack – heavy bombers, torpedo-bombers, carrier-borne aircraft, conventional submarines and char-iots – had either been rejected or been tried and found to be ineffective. But X-craft (midget submarines) had become opera-tional by the beginning of 1943 and by the summer their attack had been fixed for September. The planning of the operation called for a prolonged effort to gather intelligence about the fjords and about the anti-submarine and anti-torpedo net defences at the berths normally used by the ships, and it had to be made for Narvik and Trondheim, as well as for Altenfjord, since the location of the ships could not be known in advance.[71] Material provided by the Inter-Services Topographical Department (ISTD) proved valuable in this connection.[72] The first PR of Altenfjord for these purposes was carried out by the Russians with the Spitfires left behind by the RAF in 1942.[73]* In August the OIC produced a lengthy study of

---

* See Volume II p 222.

69.   ibid, pp 355–359; Roskill, op cit, Vol III Part I, p 71.
70.   ADM 223/184, Ultra signals 0005 and 1254/29 September 1943.
71.   ADM 234/348, BR 1736 (22) (48), pp 5–6.
72.   D McLachlan, *Room 39* (1968), p 311.
73.   AIR 41/48, p 353; ADM 199/888, SBNO North Russia to Admiralty No 146 of 4 October 1943.

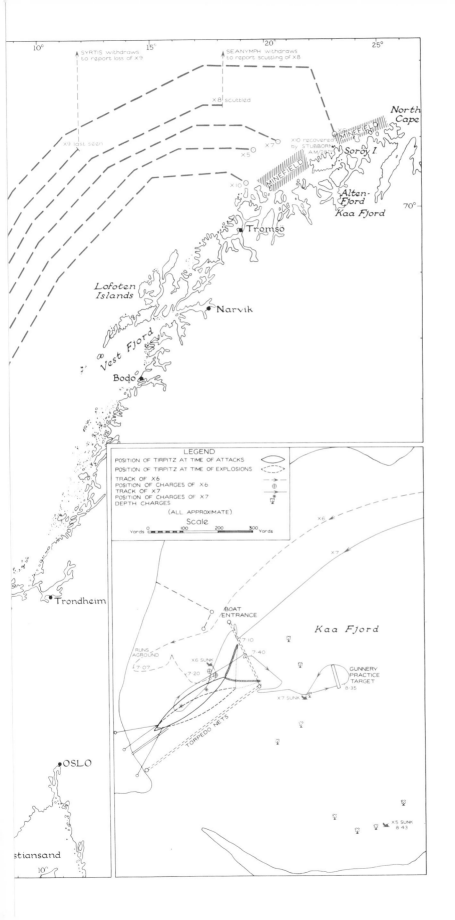

SYRTIS withdraws
to report loss of X9

SEANYMPH withdraws
to report scutting of X8

X8 scuttled

North
Cape

X9 last seen

X10 recovered
by STUBBORN
A.M./29

MINEFIELD

X7

X5

Soröy I.

MINEFIELD

X10

Alten-
Fjord

Kaa Fjord

70°

Tromsö

Lofoten
Islands

Narvik

Vest Fjord

Bodö

LEGEND

POSITION OF TIRPITZ AT TIME OF ATTACKS
POSITION OF TIRPITZ AT TIME OF EXPLOSIONS
TRACK OF X6
POSITION OF CHARGES OF X6
TRACK OF X7
POSITION OF CHARGES OF X7
DEPTH CHARGES

(ALL APPROXIMATE)

Scale

Yards 0   100   200   300 Yards

X6

X7

Kaa Fjord

BOAT
ENTRANCE

7·10

RUNS
AGROUND

X6 SUNK

7·40

7·07

7·20

GUNNERY
PRACTICE
TARGET
8·35

X7 SUNK

Trondheim

TORPEDO NETS

OSLO

X5 SUNK
8·43

stiansand

10°

what was known from Ultra about the net defences at all Norwegian anchorages.[74] While these sources were valuable in checking the information about net defences supplied by SIS agents in Norway and by the British Naval Attaché in Stockholm from Norwegian informants and while the details thus accumulated sufficed for training prupouses, the need for greater precision prompted further measures as the time for the attack approached. Early in August the British took the Russian naval C-in-C in north Russia into their confidence and obtained his approval for the despatch of an RAF PR Spitfire unit to a north Russian base.[75] On 1 September the SIS at last succeeded in its many attempts to establish an agent in the vicinity of the Altenfjord naval anchorage. From 21 August it was arranged that reconnaissance of the anchorage would be carried out by Mosquitoes flying a shuttle service between the United Kingdom and Kola.[76]

In the event, all the Mosquito flights were frustrated by the weather, and the SIS agent, who was to display exceptional bravery in transmitting regular reports from the Altenfjord fleet base until the summer of 1944, was not able to establish himself in time to help with the preparations: the first report from him that can be traced was one in which he related the damage done by the operation. To add to the tension, obstacles and delays were encountered in north Russia in preparing the ground facilities for the RAF Spitfires; they arrived on 3 September but their first successful sortie – that which reported that the *Tirpitz* and the *Scharnhorst* had left Altenfjord* – could not take place until 7 September.[77]

It remained to establish to which base, and to which particular berths, the ships would return; and time was short because the 'convoy' towing the X-craft could not delay its departure beyond 11 or 12 September. But the weather was too bad for flying on 8 September; and on 9 September, while it could be seen that the *Lützow* was at her berth, the rest of Altenfjord was obscured by cloud. In the early hours of 9 September, however, an Enigma decrypt disclosed that the *Tirpitz* and the *Scharnhorst* were expected back there later in the day;† and by 1000 on 10 September another decrypt had established that they had been due to berth there at 1500 on 9 September.[78] Later on 10 September their return was

---

* As it turned out, for Operation *Sentry* – see above p 255.   † See above, p 255.

74. ADM 223/98, OIC SI 655 of 5 August 1943.
75. ADM 199/888, SBNO North Russia No 146 of 4 October 1943.
76. ADM 234/348, p 6.
77. ADM 199/888, SBNO North Russia, No 146 of 4 October 1943.
78. ADM 223/184, Ultra signal 1002/10 September 1943.

confirmed by visual reconnaissance, which gave their exact position.[79] This was the last information given to the X-craft before they left with their towing submarines on 11 and 12 September.[80]

While they were on passage they received on 15 and 17 September the results of further PR of the anchorages and the outlying fjords at Altenfjord. On the basis of this information, which included details about the exact locations and the net defences of the three ships derived from photographs taken on 14 September and flown back to the United Kingdom by Catalina, five X-craft (a sixth had been lost on passage) were allocated to the targets – three to the *Tirpitz* and one each to the *Scharnhorst* and the *Lützow*. No additional intelligence could be sent to them before the deadline fixed for their release – 1500 on 20 September – since no more reconnaissance was possible and the Admiralty could not disclose to them the latest Sigint bearing on the operation. This was an Enigma decrypt received about noon on 20 September which stated that the *Scharnhorst* would carry out firing in Altenfjord between 21 and 23 September, a period covering the planned time of the attack.[81] As it happened, however, the X-craft detailed to attack the *Scharnhorst* encountered so many difficulties after entering Altenfjord that she was unable to reach the *Scharnhorst*'s berth. By 20 September another X-craft had been lost on passage, so that the attack on the *Lützow* was abandoned.

The four remaining X-craft entered Altenfjord on the night of 20–21 September. Two of the three detailed to attack the *Tirpitz* passed through the gate in the anti-submarine net at the mouth of Kaafjord early on 22 September. One of them, X-6, followed a small boat through the gap in *Tirpitz*'s anti-torpedo net enclosure, laid her charges and scuttled, the crew being taken prisoner at about 0730. Another, X-7, getting through the net with difficulty, laid her charges but got entangled in trying to get back through the net;* she appears to have been blown through it at 0812 by the explosion of one or more of the charges laid. She sank at 0832, the commanding officer and all but two of the crew being taken prisoner.[82] The third X-craft, X-5, came under fire from the *Tirpitz*. On 22 October the Germans signalled details of this attack to their naval attachés abroad, claiming that the *Tirpitz* had fired at, and hit at long range, the third midget submarine 'immediately abeam'; the craft was subsequently attacked by depth charges after which knocking noises

---

* See Appendix 13(i).

79.   ADM 199/888, SBNO North Russia, No 146 of 4 October 1943.
80.   ADM 199/888 FO Submarines 2347/SM 04351 of 8 November 1943
81.   ADM 223/184, Ultra signal 1207/20 September 1943.
82.   ADM 234/348, pp 16, 18.

were heard for 24 hours. It was then assumed on board the *Tirpitz* that the craft had been destroyed.[83] Post-war investigations have, however, failed to establish whether X-5 ever reached the anchorage and it may be that the *Tirpitz*'s gunners were mistaken.[84] X-10, which had failed to reach the *Scharnhorst*, was recovered by one of the towing submarines in the approaches to Altenfjord on 28 September.

The first intelligence about the results of the attacks was provided by the Enigma. A series of signals decrypted between 22 September and 3 October* made it clear that complete surprise had been achieved and that, while the *Scharnhorst* and the *Lützow* had not been attacked, the *Tirpitz* had been damaged. It was supplemented by what appears to have been the SIS agent's first report from Altenfjord. Received on 14 October, this said that the *Tirpitz* was down by the bow, badly damaged, after two torpedo hits.[85] Thereafter, although it did not disclose the precise nature and the extent of the damge done to her,† the Enigma gave a general idea of what repairs were necessary and revealed that they were to be carried out in Altenfjord and would not be completed until mid-March 1944. The decrypt of a signal from the German Admiralty of 14 October instructed the Battle Group to explain away the fact that the repairs were being carried out in northern waters by refererence to overcrowding and the danger of air attack at Kiel or Wilhelmshafen and to the strained fuel situation; the Battle Group was also to give it out that 'damage caused by British midget submarines was not the reason'.[87] Together with further decrypts in October and November which disclosed that the *Tirpitz*'s entire ship's company was being granted home leave in three watches, beginning on 1 November, this enabled the OIC at the end of November to discount rumours to the effect that she was to be sent to Kiel. On 2 January 1944 the Enigma disclosed that 15 March had been fixed as the completion date for her hull, engine and electrical repairs. From the middle of October the SIS also supplied some useful

---

* See Appendix 13 (ii).

† It was learned after the war that much damage had been done to the propulsion machinery and the gunnery fire-control systems.[86]

83. ADM 223/170, OIC SI 751 of 26 October 1943.
84. Naval Historical Branch letter to Cabinet Office Historical Section, D/NHB/5/5/4 J of 20 April 1962.
85. ADM 199/888, FO Submarines 2347/SM 04351 of 8 November 1943.
86. ADM 234/348, Appendix C, p 28; D Brown, *Tirpitz: the Floating Fortress* (1977), p 31.
87. ADM 223/185, Ultra signal 1845/15 October 1943.

reports on what could be observed or learnt from the crews about the state of the *Tirpitz*.[88]

□

In the changed situation produced by the disabling of the *Tirpitz* and the departure of the *Lützow* the Home Fleet went briefly over to the offensive, moving close into Bodö in the first week of October 1943 to launch a highly effective strike against coastal shipping.* But the main task of the Home Fleet arose from the resumption of the Arctic convoys. The first homeward-bound convoy left Russia on 1 November and the first eastward-bound convoy sailed on 15 November; and all the convoys had to be provided with substantial covering forces so long as the *Scharnhorst* posed a threat.

On 23 and 26 September the Enigma had indicated that the *Scharnhorst* was to remain at Altenfjord for the winter;[89] on 16 October it added that she and the destroyers were at full war readiness;[90] and from September it showed that she was exercising in Altenfjord with unusual frequency.[91] Nor were these the only grounds for thinking that she might be sent out. The *Tirpitz*'s sortie to Spitzbergen, and the exaggerated language used in German broadcasts about that operation and about the exploits of U-boats in the Kara Sea, had already suggested that the caution with which the enemy had always used his surface ships was having to contend with his anxiety to use them to boost morale by disrupting supplies to the eastern front. Even before the convoys were resumed, moreover, the Enigma had disclosed that the enemy was looking for opportunities to intervene against them. On 29 October the decrypts showed that, following GAF sightings which had been interpreted as indicating a west-bound convoy, an unknown number of German destroyers had left Altenfjord on 27 October and had been recalled from a position off the North Cape on 28 October.[92] The *Scharnhorst* did not sail with them, but this was not confirmed until 1 November, and there was still some anxiety about her until 4 November.[93]

---

* See below, p 278 et seq.

88. ADM 223/87, The *Tirpitz*; Summary of Events.
89. ADM 223/175, OIC SI 705 of 27 September 1943.
90. ibid, OIC S 747 of 12 November 1943.
91. ibid, OIC S 705 of 27 September, 709 of 1 October, 711 of 3 October, 723 of 15 October, 727 of 20 October, 733 of 27 October, 752 of 17 November, 770 of 7 December, 773 of 11 December, 774 of 13 December 1943.
92. ADM 223/185, Ultra signals 2206/27 October, 0010 and 1841/29 October 1943; ADM 223/175, OIC S 735 of 29 October, 736 of 30 October 1943.
93. ADM 223/185, Ultra signals 1232/2 November, 1830/1 November, 1205/4 November 1943.

During the next four weeks the enemy searched actively for the convoys but failed to contact them. On 10 November the Enigma disclosed that the Germans had received an agent's report to the effect that twelve merchant ships were awaiting escort from Scapa Flow to north Russia;[94] this was a week before JW 54A, the first east-bound convoy, was due to sail from Loch Ewe.* JW 54A nevertheless completed its passage unobserved. So did its successor (JW 54B, which sailed on 22 November) and the next west-bound convoy (RA 54B, which sailed on 26 November) despite the fact that the GAF searched for the one on 23 and 24 November[96] and for the other on 2 and 3 December.[97]

For JW 55A, the next Russia-bound convoy, the C-in-C Home Fleet decided for the first time to provide battleship cover right through to Kola, where he stayed in the *Duke of York* from 16 to 18 December. On leaving Kola to return to Iceland he learned from an Enigma decrypt that on 18 December, assuming the approach of a convoy probably with a heavy covering force, the enemy had ordered air reconnaissance, allocated attacking areas to U-boats and brought the Battle Group in Altenfjord to three hours' notice.[98] The Enigma showed that U-boats had sighted the convoy but failed to keep up with it. On 21 December the Enigma added that in the afternoon of that day the Battle Group had reverted to six hours' notice.[99] This experience strengthened Admiral Fraser's belief that the *Scharnhorst* would try to intervene before long.† In his later report of proceedings he wrote that 'with the safe arrival of JW 55A I felt very strongly that *Scharnhorst* would come out and endeavour to

---

* In the last few days of September 1943 the Enigma had disclosed that a U-boat had landed a German agent in Iceland. He had been captured on 29 September [95] but had evidently been replaced (see also below, p 269).

† It has been claimed that the Home Fleet was informed by Ultra signal that on 18 December, during the passage of JW 55A, the German Battle Group had been ordered to take 'preparatory measures so that departure would be possible at any time'.[100] An Offizier message to this effect was indeed decrypted on 20 December.[101] But it was not sent by Ultra, the OIC no doubt considering that it added nothing material to the C-in-C's knowledge that the Battle Group had been brought to three hours' notice.

94. ADM 223/186, Ultra signal 1631/10 November 1943.
95. ADM 223/184, Ultra signals 1122/21 September, 2227/24 September, 0343/27 September.
96. ADM 223/186, Ultra signals 1145/23 November, 0927/24 November 1943.
97. ADM 223/167, Ultra signals 1648/1 December, 1647/2 December, 1040 and 1727/3 December 1943.
98. ibid, Ultra signals 2149/19 December, 0649 and 0752/20 December 1943.
99. ibid, Ultra signal 2330/21 December 1943.
100. Beesly, op cit, p 210; Rohwer and Beesly, 'Special Intelligence' und die Vernichtung der 'Scharnhorst' in *Marine Rundschau*, October 1977.
101. DEFE 3/368, ZTPG 192888 of 18 December 1943; DEFE 3/369, ZTPG 193000 of 21 December 1943.

attack JW 55B'. Before sailing from Iceland to cover that convoy he outlined how he would go about a night action with the *Scharnhorst*, and after sailing on 23 December he held a night encounter exercise.[102] His assessment was correct. We now know that on 19 December, aware that convoys were getting through unmolested and believing that, as a result, the British were relaxing their precautions, Dönitz had obtained Hitler's approval for the use of the *Scharnhorst* against the next convoy to be located, provided the chances of success seemed reasonable.[103]

Convoy JW 55B, which sailed on 20 December, was sighted by a routine meteorological aircraft at 1045 on 22 December.* The sighting, together with the fact that a U-boat had been ordered to operate against the convoy, was disclosed by the Enigma and was reported to the Home Fleet at 0146 on 23 December, and by the early hours of 24 December the Home Fleet learned from the next Enigma decrypts to be received that during 22 December the Battle Group had been brought to three hours' notice, that the Germans had at first suspected that the convoy might be a landing force, and that, when this suspicion was dispelled, eight U-boats had been despatched to form a patrol line south-west of Bear Island.[104] At 0550 on 24 December a further Ultra signal gave the Home Fleet the news that the enemy, appreciating that the convoy was possibly covered by a strong British Battle Group, had ordered air reconnaissance for that day, and that at 2324 on the previous evening, after a further GAF sighting of the convoy on 23 December, the *Scharnhorst* had received a signal advising her that 'German U-boat was not in contact with the convoy'.[105]

At the time he received this first indication that the *Scharnhorst* had already sailed or was about to sail, neither the C-in-C's own Force 2 (the *Duke of York*, the cruiser *Jamaica* and destroyers) nor the cruisers which had sailed from Kola to provide close cover to convoys JW 55B and RA 55A (Force 1, under Vice-Admiral Burnett) were close enough to intervene. Admiral Fraser, approaching from the south-west, increased his own speed to 19 knots and broke wireless silence to order the convoy to back-track for three hours, thus taking the risk of enabling the Germans to confirm their suspicion that the Home Fleet was covering the convoy and to

---

* For this and subsequent Admiralty Ultra signals issued during the battle with the *Scharnhorst*, see Appendix 14.

102. ADM 199/1440, BSR 220A, C-in-C Home Fleet's despatch 147/HF, 1325/101 of 25 January 1944.
103. Beesly, op cit, pp 208–210; Roskill, op cit, Vol III Part I, p 81.
104. ADM 220/187, Ultra signals 0146, 1939 and 2140/23 December, 0140 and 0540/24 December 1943.
105. ibid, Ultra signal 0550/24 December 1943.

obtain DF evidence of its general whereabouts.* At 1025, following this decision, he learned that Admiral Polar Coast had been requested on the afternoon of 22 December to make preparations for the departure of the German Battle Group and that the OIC had had no evidence up to 0740 on 24 December that the Battle Group had sailed.[107] Apart from a signal giving him details of U-boats on passage in the operational area,[108] the OIC had no further intelligence to send him before the GAF sighted the convoy early on Christmas Day.[109]

In addition to the news that the convoy had been sighted, the C-in-C then received details in Ultra signals of the redisposition of the U-boats in consequence of the sighting and of the GAF's intentions for 25 December; the GAF was to regain contact with the convoy and 'to search for what is thought to be a heavy force, approaching from the south-west, which has been DFd. . . .'[110] During the rest of the morning of 25 December current intelligence about the GAF's reconnaissance activity, which was being provided by Cheadle and by RAF shipborne Y parties, was valuable in indicating that the enemy was searching for the east-bound convoy, whereas RA 55A, the west-bound convoy, had escaped detection and would soon be clear of danger. On this evidence the C-in-C, again breaking W/T silence, ordered four fleet destroyers from RA 55A to join JW 55B and diverted JW 55B further to the north so as to delay the *Scharnhorst*'s attack and give the Home Fleet more time to come up with her.[111] He then received Ultra signals informing him that at 0901 that morning a U-boat had made contact with JW 55B and that seven other U-boats had been ordered to follow up the contact.[112] The next Enigma intelligence was issued by the OIC at 2142; at 1158 an R-boat had been ordered to proceed to the *Scharnhorst* in Langfjord and told that she would receive further orders there.[113] After the receipt of this intelligence, which had

---

* The German Admiralty has been criticised for paying too little attention to what has been assumed to be the DF fix for this transmission.[106] Leaving aside the question whether they did or did not DF this transmission, the operational authorities in north Norway had concluded by early on 25 December from DF evidence that a heavy force was approaching from the south-west, as we record in the next paragraph.

106. Beesly, op cit, p 212. See also Rohwer in *Wilhelmshafener Zeitung* of 9 May 1958.
107. ADM 223/187, Ultra signal 1025/24 December 1943.
108. ibid, Ultra signals 1312/24 December, 0215/25 December 1943.
109. ibid, Ultra signals 0210/25 December, 1943.
110. ibid, Ultra signals 0210 and 0550/25 December 1943.
111. Roskill, op cit, Vol III Part I, p 80; A R Wells, *Studies in British Naval Intelligence 1880–1945* (Unpublished thesis, University of London 1972.)
112. ADM 223/188, Ultra signals 1350 and 1557/25 December 1943.
113. ibid, Ultra signal 2142/25 December 1943.

reached the OIC at 2050, there was a short delay before GC and CS broke the Enigma setting which had come into force at midday on 25 December. But among the first of the new series of decrypts was one which, reaching the OIC at 0025 on 26 December, disclosed that the Battle Group had at 1530 on 25 December been given the executive command '*Ostfront* 1700/25/12'.[114] At 0130 the OIC issued this information in an Ultra signal, adding the comment that the meaning of *Epilepsy* (the British substitute for the codeword *Ostfront*) was not yet evident, and that while Ultra information would be available with a delay of some hours until noon, it would not necessarily be complete for the north Norway area.[115]* However, at 0217 the OIC was able to issue an emergency Ultra signal – 'Emergency: *Scharnhorst* probably sailed 1800 25 December' – and at 0218 it followed this up by notifying Ultra recipients that the *Scharnhorst* had informed a patrol vessel in the Altenfjord area that she would be passing outward-bound from 1800 on 25 December.[118] For the benefit of the convoy's escort and other ships not in receipt of Ultra, it also broadcast at 0339 the general message: 'Admiralty appreciates *Scharnhorst* at sea'.[119]

At 0401, when Force 1 and Force 2 were both steering courses to intercept the *Scharnhorst*, the C-in-C again broke wireless silence to announce his own position and order Force 1 and the convoy's escort to give theirs.[120] The OIC had informed him at 0230 that his own force had apparently not yet been sighted by the enemy,[121] and his RAF Y party had no evidence to the contrary. His plot showed him that the prospects of cutting off the *Scharnhorst* were good unless she sheered off on learning his whereabouts. It may therefore be

---

* The despatch of this Ultra signal was followed from 0150 by the receipt of several Offizier signals, some of them from the Battle Group. British forces had made contact with the *Scharnhorst* before the full texts of these signals were decrypted. The earliest full text was sent to the OIC at 0916 on 26 December; it was a signal from the Battle Group reporting that it was ready for sea by 1630 on 25 December.[116] In addition to Offizier signals, twelve messages that were completely indecypherable were intercepted between 2130 on 25 December and 1344 on 26 December; GC and CS judged that these were encyphered in the special key reserved for Fleet operations (Barracuda).[117]

114. ADM 223/36, Signals concerning the sinking of the *Scharnhorst*, ZTPG 194876, TOO 1527/25 December, T/Pd to OIC at 0025 26 December.
115. ADM 223/188, Ultra signal 0130/26 December 1943.
116. ADM 223/36, ZTPG 195049, TOO 1516/25 December, T/Pd to OIC at 0916/26 December.
117. ADM 223/36, ZIP/ZZG/692; Rohwer and Beesly, 'Special Intelligence' une die Vernichtung der 'Scharnhorst', *Marine Rundschau*, Oct 1977, p 563.
118. ADM 223/188, Ultra signals 0217 and 0218/26 December 1943.
119. Roskill, op cit, Vol III Part I, p 81.
120. ibid, p 83.
121. ADM 223/188, Ultra signal 0230/26 December 1943.

presumed that in breaking wireless silence he had decided that the risk of alerting the enemy must be accepted in the interest of saving the convoy; and it was no doubt for this reason that at 0628 he ordered the convoy to alter course to the north and told Force 1 to close in to support.[122] GAF contact with Force 2 followed about 1000, when the Cheadle party in the *Duke of York* reported powerful signals from a reconnaissance aircraft; thereafter Force 2 was shadowed by three aircraft, one of which made W/T reports and was in radar contact for nearly three hours.[123]

Whether or not the interception and DF-ing of the C-in-C's latest transmissions had assisted the GAF to contact the C-in-C's force is a moot point. The GAF had already been searching on 25 December for what the enemy thought, on DF evidence, to be a heavy British force approaching from the south-west; it might well have found the C-in-C's force on 26 December even if he had not transmitted again or if his transmissions had been missed. More important is the fact that, despite this earlier appreciation, the Germans now attached no significance to the GAF's sighting reports. It later transpired that at 1012 on 26 December the aircraft had reported locating 'five warships, one apparently a big one' by radar, but Fliegerführer Lofoten omitted the reference to a big ship when passing the report to the naval authorities, which he did at 1306.[124] The naval shore authorities appear to have assumed that the aircraft had sighted the *Scharnhorst*'s destroyers returning to base. The *Scharnhorst*, on receiving Fliegerführer Lofoten's signal in the mid-afternoon would have known that it was not her own destroyers that had been sighted, and that some other force was at sea, but by then it was too late.* Another oversight on the part of the Germans may have helped to seal the *Scharnhorst*'s fate. From 0936 on 26 December the German B-Dienst knew that a second British authority was in the battle area, in communication with the Cruiser Admiral, but it has been claimed that the naval authorities took no steps to inform the *Scharnhorst*.[126]† In assessing the part played by intelligence in

---

* The *Scharnhorst* may have intercepted the aircraft's report of 1012, as did the *Duke of York*; if so, nothing is known of what she made of it. The signal in which Fliegerführer Lofoten re-broadcast the sighting report of 1012 on 26 December was decrypted by GC and CS but, like certain other signals concerning the battle, was not sent by the OIC to C-in-C Home Fleet because it was received too late to influence events.[125]

† But this conclusion may overlook the Barracuda signals referred to in the footnote on p 266; of these, eleven were transmittted to the *Scharnhorst* and one from her.

122. Roskill, op cit, Vol III Part I, p 83.
123. ADM 199/1440, C-in-C Home Fleet's despatch 147/HF of 28 January 1944.
124. DEFE 3/371, ZTPG 195239 of 26 December 1943.
125. ADM 223/171, OIC SI 816 of 3 January 1944.
126. Beesly, op cit, pp 216–217; McLachlan, op cit, p 37; Rohwer and Beesly in *Marine Rundschau*, October 1977.

bringing about her destruction, however, it is not wise to dwell too much on the failings of the Germans. These would not have been crucial unless the British forces had been in a position to take advantage of them; and the fact that the British forces were so placed was due to the high quality of British intelligence. It was a tribute in particular to the value of the Sigint, the only source which had contributed;* and if it was also a tribute to the C-in-C's imaginative and decisive use of the Enigma, that owed much to the confidence he knew he could place in it.

Even the Enigma ceased to be useful after it had disclosed that the *Scharnhorst* had sailed. By 1000 on 26 December it had revealed that during 25 December the GAF had sighted no support forces within 50 miles of the convoy, and that at 2100 on 25 December the *Scharnhorst* had signalled that the weather in the operational area was likely to hamper operations by her destroyers.[127]† At 1215 the C-in-C learned that the northernmost U-boat in the enemy's patrol line had sighted the convoy at 0945 that morning.[128] In the afternoon the OIC sent him the contents of two decrypts which showed that at 0043 on 26 December the U-boats had been informed that the *Scharnhorst* and five destroyers had passed through the northern exit from Altenfjord at 2300 on 25 December with the intention of attacking the convoy at about 0900 on 26 December, and that at 1021 on 26 December the U-boats had been ordered to operate against the convoy themselves.[129]‡ But before he received the first of these signals the C-in-C had heard that Force 1 had picked up the *Scharnhorst* by radar at 0840, had sighted her at 0921, and had opened fire at 0929. All now depended on whether contact with the *Scharnhorst* could be maintained.

At 1000 Force 1 lost contact, the *Scharnhorst* using her superior speed to draw away to the north-east; and at 1100 the C-in-C signalled that 'unless touch can be regained there is no chance of

---

* The SIS agent in Altenfjord had not reported the *Scharnhorst*'s departure; his base opposite Kaafjord was a long way from her berth in Langfjord.

† This and some of the other Ultra signals quoted in this paragraph were based on the Offizier decrypts referred to in the footnote on p 266.

‡ This order was issued after the *Scharnhorst* had withdrawn from her first attempt to approach the convoy; she had perhaps reported her withdrawal in the Barracuda key since an indecypherable ship-transmission was intercepted at 0938/26 December (see footnote on p 266). No further signal from her was intercepted until 1609, when she had been engaged by the Home Fleet, but at 1355 Captain U-boats Norway informed the U-boats that she had signalled at 1240, that is during her second attempt on the convoy, that she was in action with several enemy ships.[130] This signal was decrypted after she had been sunk, as were her own transmissions during the engagement with the Home Fleet.

127.   ADM 223/188, Ultra signal 1000/26 December 1943;
128.   ibid, Ultra signal 1215/26 December 1943;
129.   ibid, Ultra signals 1304 and 1317/26 December 1943;
130.   DEFE 3/371, ZTPG 195200 of 26 December 1943.

my finding the enemy'. Touch was regained shortly after 1200, Force 1 having correctly appreciated that the *Scharnhorst* would make a second attempt on the convoy from the north. After a further exchange of fire she again broke off and started on a southerly course for home at maximum speed shortly before 1300, some three hours after she could have learned that the GAF had located Admiral Fraser's Force 2. Thanks to this delay, and helped by the fact that Force 1 managed to shadow her by radar, the *Duke of York* opened fire at a range of 12,000 yards. Three hours later the *Scharnhorst*, damaged and slowed by gunfire, was sunk by torpedoes from the Home Fleet's destroyers.

□

For three months following the sinking of the *Scharnhorst* the Admiralty was able to dispense with battleship cover for the Arctic convoys; it took the opportunity to reinforce the Eastern Fleet from which, thanks to the battle of Midway, another Allied victory that owed much to Sigint, it had been able to transfer ships to the Mediterranean Fleet in 1942.[131] But the convoys continued to need cruiser support against possible attack by the German destroyers – a threat which did not materialise – * and the U-boat effort against them continued, indeed increased.

In their attack on the first east-bound convoy of 1944, JW 56A, the U-boats, which had now been equipped with Gnat torpedoes,† achieved their first success since the convoys had been resumed in the previous November. They sank three merchant ships on 25 January, and this despite the fact that the Enigma had disclosed the positions of their patrol line on 8 January and gave notice on the morning of their attack that on the strength of an agent's report from Iceland[133] they had been told to expect the convoy.[134] On the night of 27–28 January, when the C-in-C Home Fleet learned from the Enigma that U-boats had been sent against the next east-bound convoy, JW 56B,[135] he postponed the sailing of the west-bound convoy and ordered its escort to reinforce JW 56B. In the resulting battle the enemy sank one destroyer and damaged another for the loss of one U-boat, but the convoy got through unscathed.[136].

---

* On 1 February 1944, however, the Enigma showed that the 4th Destroyer Flotilla in Altenfjord had been brought to two hours' notice on 30 January during the passage of convoy JW 56B, and had remained at that readiness until late on 31 January.[132]

† See above, p 220 et seq.

131. Roskill, op cit, Vol II (1957), p 67; Vol III Part I, p 267.
132. ADM 223/189, Ultra signals 0025 and 1308/1 February 1944.
133. Roskill, op cit, Vol III Part I, p 268.
134. ADM 223/188, Ultra signals 1859/8 January, 0905/25 January 1944;
135. ADM 223/189, Ultra signals 2240/27 January, 0431/28 January 1944.
136. ADM 223/171, OIC SI 850 of 8 February 1944.

In the light of these incidents the C-in-C, drawing on the experience that had been gained of the use of the Enigma in the offensive against the U-boats in the Atlantic, abandoned the practice of sailing the Arctic convoys in two sections and asked for the loan of escort-carriers and support groups from the Western Approaches. When JW 57 sailed on 23 February the Enigma had revealed in advance the positions of the patrol lines in which all the northern operational U-boats, fourteen in number, were searching for it;[137] but the convoy was protected by the escort-carrier *Chaser* and no fewer than seventeen destroyers, as well as other escorts. The escorts sank two U-boats for the loss of one destroyer, and the convoy sustained no damage. The corresponding west-bound convoy, RA 57, which sailed on 2 March, fared even better; three U-boats were sunk and two damaged for the loss of one merchantman. The convoy had been ordered to make a large detour to the east on leaving Kola, the Enigma having shown before it sailed that the U-boats had been deployed on a line to the north-west of the inlet;[138] but while this tactic delayed the U-boat attack, it could not avert it. The Enigma was more valuable in enabling the OIC to analyse the attacks on RA 57 and JW 57 in great detail. The analysis confirmed the extent of the enemy's losses and showed that the escort had been effective in deterring the U-boats.[139]

The next east-bound convoy, JW 58, was accompanied by a still more formidable escorting force. It included two escort-carriers, equipped with fighters to suppress gunfire from the U-boats* as well as with aircraft armed with rockets and depth charges, and two experienced support groups from the Western Approaches. Another powerful Home Fleet force, which included two fleet-carriers and further escort-carriers, was in the vicinity at the same time because the launching of an attack on the *Tirpitz* with carrier-borne aircraft (Operation *Tungsten*)† was timed to coincide with the convoy's transit. Before the convoy sailed the Enigma established that for his part, too, the enemy was preparing to make a special effort against it. A decrypt of 20 March informed the U-boats that another east-bound convoy was expected which would be 'decisive for the war in the east'; it also instructed them to remain submerged by day and to concentrate their attack on the first night – a tactic long resorted to in the Atlantic but now adopted for the first time in the

---

* For the development of U-boat Flak see above, p 215, 216, 224.
† See below, p 273 et seq.

137. ADM 223/190, Ultra signals 2025/14 February, 1315/22 February 1944.
138. ADM 223/191, Ultra signals 0416 and 1304/29 February, 1216/1 March 1944.
139. ADM 223/171, OIC SI 882 of 11 March, 893 of 21 March 1944.

Arctic.[140] By 26 March it was clear from the Enigma that despite recent losses the number of U-boats in the Arctic had been increased to sixteen at sea and thirteen in port.[141] And on the evening of 30 March, when the convoy was sighted by the GAF, all the U-boats at sea were sent at top speed to a patrol line in the Bear Island passage and ordered to attack on the night of 31 March – 1 April.[142] In the battle which followed, the escort sank three U-boats – it had already sunk one on 29 March – and its aircraft shot down no less than six of the enemy's shadowing aircraft; and except that one merchant ship was damaged by ice, there were no British casualties. JW 58 was the last east-bound convoy before the invasion of Normandy, but towards the end of April, after RA 58 had been sailed without loss, a similar success was scored with the last west-bound convoy. RA 59 lost one merchant ship in exchange for three U-boats sunk.

□

The Home Fleet had meanwhile delivered another attack on the *Tirpitz* – this time a dive-bombing attack on her while she was in her berth in Kaafjord by aircraft from the carriers *Victorious* and *Furious*. Preparations for the attack had begun early in January, as soon as the Enigma indicated that repairs to the *Tirpitz* would be completed by 15 March.* Not only because of what was known about the state of the *Tirpitz*, but also because Traffic Analysis during February had pointed to a build-up of the Japanese Fleet at Singapore and made it a matter of some urgency that the *Victorious* should return to the Far East as soon as her refit was completed, every effort had been made to prepare the attack for the beginning of March. When it had to be postponed beyond that date, on account of delays in the refit and working-up of the *Victorious*, the Admiralty was at first afraid that it might have to abandon the operation, but eventually prevailed on the US Navy to lend an aircraft carrier to the Eastern Fleet on the ground that, if the attack were delayed beyond early April, it would be necessary to delay it until the end of the summer period of almost total daylight in the north, and thus to postpone for months the ability to redeploy the heavy ships of the Home Fleet.[143] Delay until early April, on the

---

* See above, p 261.

140.   ADM 223/191, Ultra signal 1849/20 March 1944.
141.   ADM 223/192, Ultra signal 1426/26 March 1944.
142.   ibid, Ultra signals 0418 and 0536/31 March 1944.
143.   ADM 223/190, Ultra signal 1242/24 February 1944; Roskill, op cit, Vol III Part I, p 348.

other hand, incurred the risk that the *Tirpitz* would no longer be in Altenfjord.

At the end of January the OIC, summarising all the evidence about the repairs to the *Tirpitz*, had reported that while her hull, engineering and electrical repairs would be completed by 15 March, her gunnery repairs were likely to be delayed beyond that date, and that even then she would not be operationally effective as she had not docked for two and a half years.* During February the SIS reported that continuous work was in progress on the *Tirpitz* and one report, dated 10 February but received only on 10 March, quoted a good source as saying that she would leave during March.[144] In the light of this intelligence it had to be assumed that she would be seaworthy by mid-March and the possibility that before she could be attacked she would move, perhaps to Germany, was strengthened in the next two weeks. The SIS agent reported on 3 March that she had fired her guns; on 11 March that she was ready to sail; and on 15 March that she had sailed. On 12 March Coastal Command ordered emergency deployments for her interception;[145] but on receiving the last of the SIS agent's reports the OIC advised the Home Fleet that there was no Enigma evidence to suggest that she was moving from Altenfjord, and later on 13 March the Enigma indicated that she was still there.[146] By 14 March the fact that she had returned to her berth was confirmed both by the SIS agent and by a British PR flight from north Russia.[147] But on 15 March the Enigma revealed that the *Tirpitz* would be at sea in Altenfjord for trials on 15 and 16 March,[148] and on the following day it added the news that her Commanding Officer was to command the Battle Group and that the staffs of Admiral Commanding Northern Waters and Captain (U-boats) Norway were to be amalgamated in a single operational staff.[149] The OIC warned that 'the significance of the new organisation in relation to the *Tirpitz*'s future movements cannot be appreciated'. It had already testified to the acute anxiety that now existed by informing the Home Fleet that the GAF Enigma had been read up to 0001 on 16 March and the naval Enigma up to 1200 on 16 March and that there were as yet 'no indications of any immediate intentions of the *Tirpitz* to leave Altenfjord.'[150]

---

* See Appendix 13 (iii).

144. ADM 223/87, *Tirpitz* summary.   145. AIR 41/48, p 367.
146. ADM 223/191, Ultra signals 1314 and 1515/13 March 1944.
147. ADM 199/941, SBNO North Russia 146/1 of 6 April 1944.
148. ADM 223/191, Ultra signal 1819/15 March 1944.
149. ibid, Ultra signal 1954/16 March 1944.
150. ibid, Ultra signal 1920/16 March 1944.

The uncertainty was not cleared up when, on 18 March, the Enigma provided the *Tirpitz*'s report on her trials. The OIC concluded from this that, although her repairs were evidently nearly complete, there was no sign that she was preparing immediately to move south.[151] On 21 March it suggested that, because of the great importance they were attaching to the disruption of supplies to Russia, the Germans might take more than the normal risks with her and sail her against a convoy if they were sure that she would not have to contend with heavy ships or a carrier, and the Admiralty accordingly instructed the C-in-C Home Fleet to provide battleship cover for convoy JW 58.[152] In the same signal, however, the C-in-C was informed that the Enigma had disclosed that the *Tirpitz* was sending a cruiser motor turbine to Mannheim by air on 2 April. There was this much indication that she would be in Altenfjord up to and probably beyond that date when the C-in-C arranged at the end of March to combine the carrier attack on her (Operation *Tungsten*) with the provision of battleship cover for the convoy.

Like the X-craft attack on the *Tirpitz*, Operation *Tungsten* depended on the collection of topographical intelligence about the target area – and this was necessary for Narvik and Trondheim as well as for Altenfjord, in case she should move from there – but its success also demanded accurate advance information about the enemy's anti-aircraft defence of the anchorage and its surroundings to which the attacking aircraft would be particularly vulnerable when used for bombing rather than when they were making torpedo attacks. This meant that a large number of fighter aircraft had to be used to suppress the German Flak and they could be effective only if they had accurate knowledge of the anti-aircraft positions on shore, on the *Tirpitz* and on the other enemy ships. From the end of January all the intelligence obtained on these subjects from PR, from plans of the *Bismark* and from the SIS agent near Altenfjord and other SIS agents was checked against what was provided by the Enigma – which was now disclosing details about the emergency measures the Germans were taking to strengthen their defences against a possible incursion by battleships into Altenfjord – [153] and incorporated into the construction of an exercise range on Loch Eriboll, which most nearly resembled Kaafjord, and into a model of Kaafjord made by the ISTD. According to the reports on Operation *Tungsten* the exercise and the briefings carried out in February and March in the light of this intelligence were of 'inestimable value' in giving the aircrew who took part in the attack the

---

151.   ibid, Ultra signal 1246/18 March 1944.
152.   ibid, Ultra 0027/21 March 1944.
153.   ADM 223/171, OIC SI 839 of 27 January 1944.

feeling that it was 'almost an exercise which they had frequently carried out before'.[154] This was all the more the case because visibility over Kaafjord was excellent at the time of the attack. But despite all the preparations the effectiveness of the attack depended in the end on finding the *Tirpitz* at her berth in Kaafjord.

Whether this would be so remained uncertain until the last minute. The British PR detachment, which had supplied the bulk of the intelligence about topography and the fixed defences, had been taken to north Russia at the end of February.[155] From 11 March, when the SIS agent and the Enigma began to report movement by the *Tirpitz*, this detachment made every effort to fly frequent sorties for intelligence about her latest whereabouts. After 31 March, however, when PR showed that she was in her usual position, reconnaissance from north Russia proved impossible until 6 April.[156] For the C-in-C Home Fleet and the *Tungsten* force, which was approaching the fly-off area on 1 April, much accordingly depended on whether the SIS agent or Sigint would yield any later news than the PR report of 31 March, which had confirmed what they had already learned from the Enigma – that the *Tirpitz* had reported earlier that day that she was at anchor in Altenfjord and was intending to return to her net enclosure.[157]

Because so much depended on good weather over the target, the SIS agent had been instructed to make two-hourly weather reports from the anchorage area; he had nothing to report until the first of these was received at 1700 on 2 April. But in the forenoon of 1 April, by great good fortune, an Enigma decrypt disclosed that the *Tirpitz* had postponed for 48 hours the continuation of her speed trials and would probably sail for them on the morning of 3 April. When sending this information out the OIC pointed out that she had been away from Kaafjord on trials between 1000 and 2359 on 15 March and between 0730 and 1700 on 16 March; it added that on those earlier occasions the SIS agent had reported her departure and her return within five hours and that while further Enigma might become available its receipt could not be guaranteed.[158] In the light of this intelligence the C-in-C Home Fleet, in order to increase the chances of finding her in her berth, at once advanced the planned time of the attack and ordered it for 0530 on 3 April. His three escort-carriers – the *Emperor*, the *Searcher* and the *Pursuer* – were then

---

154. ADM 199/941, VA 2's report 2BS/128/026 of 10 April 1944; HMS *Searcher's* report of 6 April 1944.
155. Roskill, op cit, Vol III Part I, p 274.
156. ADM 199/941, SBNO North Russia 146/1 of 6 April 1944.
157. ADM 223/192, Ultra signal 2028/31 March 1944.
158. ibid, Ultra signal 1140/1 April 1944.

at some distance from the main force; in order to reach the rendez-vous position by the afternoon of 2 April they had to maintain maximum speed for more than twenty-four hours. Early on 3 April another decrypt disclosed that the *Tirpitz* would sail at 0530 that day, but this cannot have influenced the time of the attack. The information was sent out by the OIC at 0435,[159] but zero hour for flying-off had by then been fixed for 0415 and by 0437 the first wave of the attack had formed up in the air.[160] At 0530 the first wave of the attack caught the *Tirpitz* as she was weighing anchor to proceed on her trials.[161] It achieved complete surprise. An hour later the second and final wave encountered a smoke screen over the ship, but was not greatly impeded by it.

The attack put the *Tirpitz* out of action for three months. An initial estimate that she had sustained far more serious damage, which was based on study of the action photographs in the *Victorious*, had helped to persuade VA 2, in command of the *Tungsten* force, not to repeat the attack on 4 April.[162] This estimate was soon scaled down by the Admiralty. After considering the action photographs, PR evidence and reports from the SIS agent, it warned on 11 April that no reliable assessment of the damage would be possible for some time, and pressed the C-in-C Home Fleet to make another attack.[163] On 18 April, the Enigma having disclosed nothing on the subject of damage, it had to rely on further reports from the SIS agent and it would only say that it was unlikely that her repairs would be completed before three months or that she would be available for offensive operations within five months.[164] The C-in-C had meanwhile agreed to repeat the operation; it was planned for 24 April but had to be called off on account of the weather. In two further attempts against the *Tirpitz* with carrier aircraft, in the middle of May and at the end of that month, no attack was made for the same reason.

In the middle of May the Admiralty still felt that it would be five months before the *Tirpitz* was fully effective, and that she would be out of action for three months, but it had by then received only two useful additions to the initial reports on the *Tungsten* attack – a report from the Naval Attaché Stockholm to the effect that it would take eight weeks from the time of the attack to repair the under-water damage caused by a near miss, and a report from the SIS

---

159.   ibid, Ultra signal 0435/3 April 1944.
160.   Roskill, op cit, Vol III Part I, p 275.   161.   ibid, p 276.
162.   ADM 199/941, VA 2's report 2BS/128/026 of 10 April 1944, *Victorious* to VA 2 1737/3 April, and *Victorious*'s report 0137/6206 of 5 April 1944.
163.   ibid, AM 231 of 11 April 1944.
164.   ibid, AM 1413 of 18 April 1944.

agent that her engines had received no damage. The Enigma, which had been so informative after the X-craft attack on the ships, disclosed nothing between the day of the *Tungsten* attack, when the *Tirpitz* herself had reported that she had received several hits,[165] and the beginning of June, when another decrypt indicated that casualties had been severe.

At the end of May intelligence suffered the loss of the SIS agent's services; he had stayed on at Kaafjord to make weather reports during the May attempts, but at the end of May intensified German security measures forced him to flee across the mountains into Sweden. But another agent had begun reporting from a position some 30 miles north of Kaafjord during April, and it was presumably he who provided the information which reached the Admiralty on 4 July to the effect that the *Tirpitz* was exercising in Altenfjord. As this information conformed to the Admiralty's estimate as to when her repairs would be completed, and as the Admiralty was then considering the resumption of the Arctic convoys, the decision had already been taken to make a further attempt on her with the new aircraft carriers *Indefatigable* and *Formidable* when Enigma decrypts provided confirmation of the agent's report. On 9 July they disclosed that a large bomber force was moving to Norway; on 11 July they added that Me 110s were also on the move and carried an instruction to the Battle Group to 'report the date for the start 8 days in advance'. From this the OIC concluded that the *Tirpitz* would be moving south, but not before 16 July.[166] The *Indefatigable* and the *Formidable* sailed on 14 July with the *Duke of York*, the *Furious*, three cruisers and twelve destroyers. Their first attack was thwarted in the early hours of 17 July by dense smoke, the enemy having received warning of the approach,* and a second attack failed on account of fog. Intelligence from the Enigma and the SIS established that the *Tirpitz* had sustained no important damage.[168]

PR carried out after the attacks of 17 July showed that the *Tirpitz* had a caisson alongside, a fact which, taken together with the failure of the attacks, suggested that her trials had established that she needed further repairs before she moved. On 28 July an SIS agent reported that she had been under way in the fjord,[169] and at the

---

* After the attack of 24 April the Admiralty had suspected that the Germans had been alerted by intercepts of VA 2's Special W/T and during the attack made in the middle of May the Enigma had disclosed that they had been alerted by intercepts of British carrier R/T on 13 May.[167]

165. ADM 223/192, Ultra signal 1211/3 April 1944.
166. ADM 223/198, Ultra signals 1659/9 July, 1223/11 July 1944.
167. ADM 223/194, Ultra signal 0810/14 May 1944.
168. ADM 223/87, *Tirpitz* summary of events.
169. ADM 223/87, loc cit item 222.

beginning of August, when it seemed probable that she had com-pleted her temporary repairs, it was decided that another attack should be made to coincide with the sailing of the first of the new cycle of Arctic convoys, for which it was felt that battleship cover had in any case to be provided. But despite taking special measures, including W/T deception, to avoid detection, the large force which sailed on 18 August failed to obtain surprise; it flew several strikes against the *Tirpitz* on 22 and 24 August but all were handicapped by smoke and fog. The Enigma, which disclosed that the enemy had been alerted by intercepts of carrier R/T as early as 21 August,[170] later reported that no hits had been made on 22 August and that the results of the strikes of 24 August had been 'insignificant'.[171]*

After the August attack, in the course of which an unsuspected U-boat sank the frigate *Bickerton* and seriously damaged the escort-carrier *Nabob*, it was finally recognised that carrier attacks were inadequate for the task, and plans were laid for an attack by RAF Lancaster bombers operating from northern Russia. This attack, using mainly 12,000 pound MC bombs (the standard 'Tall-boy'), was carried out on 15 September. Although it did not achieve complete surprise, and encountered some smoke, it had what an Enigma decrypt of 16 September described as 'serious consequences'.[174] By 25 September the decrypt of a signal to all German attachés added the information that the *Tirpitz* had been hit by a heavy bomb but that, as the attacking aircraft had not seen the results, only slight damage was being admitted. By 21 September PR also had shown that she had received serious damage and reports to the same effect were received between 23 September and 2 October from SIS sources.[175] On 29 September the Admiralty received the decrypt of a message to all U-boats from Dönitz which said: 'After successfully defending herself against many heavy air attacks the *Tirpitz* has now sustained a bomb hit, but by holding out in the operational area the ship will continue to tie down enemy forces and by her presence confound the enemy's intentions'.[176]

The *Tirpitz* had indeed performed most effectively in this role for many months; and in her last days she briefly excelled in it. On 16

---

* The decrypts of 24 August included one of a signal from the *Tirpitz*[172] urgently requesting the help of a GAF party in rendering a bomb safe; not until after the war was it learned that one 1,600 pound bomb had penetrated her main armour and eight decks but failed to explode.[173]

170. ADM 223/202, Ultra signal 1659/21 August 1944.
171. ADM 223/203, Ultra signals 1664/23 August, 0339/25 August 1944.
172. ibid, Ultra signal 0339/25 August 1944.
173. Roskill, op cit, Vol III Part II (1961), p 160.
174. ADM 223/205, Ultra signal 1408/16 September 1944.
175. ADM 223/87, loc cit.
176. ADM 223/205, Ultra signal 1603/29 September 1944.

October the Enigma disclosed that she had sailed at 1200 on the previous day, anchored off Tromsö and taken over 'new tasks'.[177] Although the agent at Altenfjord then reported that she had made the passage under tow, the OIC concluded that, as she had made good 7 knots, she must have moved under her own steam with the assistance of tugs. Her movement nevertheless caused so much alarm that the Home Fleet, temporarily without a modern battleship while the *Duke of York* was in dock, was reinforced by the *King George V*, which was ordered to move at maximum speed to Scapa from Devonport, where she was about to leave for the Far East.[178] Furthermore, the aircraft-carrier HMS *Implacable* had sailed on 16 October, as a precaution, to attack only if the *Tirpitz* remained at sea. On 18 October her aircraft provided the first confirmation that the battleship was settled in a new protected anchorage near Tromsö.[179] It subsequently emerged that the *Tirpitz*'s move had been made in connection with the German decision to evacuate part of north Norway: on 30 October the Enigma showed that the Germans feared that the Russians would try to break through to Narvik, thus cutting off Altenfjord, while the British occupied some of the offshore islands, and on 12 November it showed that evacuation had begun.[180] But the transfer to Tromsö had brought the ship within the range of Bomber Command's operations from the United Kingdom. She was attacked by Lancasters on 29 October; the Enigma disclosed that they scored only a near miss which, however, admitted 800 tons of water. On 12 November she was sunk in a second Lancaster raid, as the Enigma confirmed in the early hours of the following day.[181] The Enigma also showed that the *Tirpitz* requested air protection before this final attack, but none appeared.[182].

□

Although it was the lack of firm intelligence about the state of the *Tirpitz* which persuaded the Admiralty to continue the attacks on her, the Home Fleet's strikes against her could without great difficulty be fitted into its general programme of raids against the Norwegian coast. This programme had a dual objective – that of

---

177. ADM 223/206, Ultra signals 0251, 0401, 1140, 1228, 1732 and 2227/16 October 1944.
178. ADM 199/2303, Admiralty War Diary for 14 and 16 October 1944; ADM 199/1440, Despatch of C-in-C Home Fleet No 2300/HF 1326 of 22 December 1944.
179. ADM 199/2303 and 1440, loc cit.
180. ADM 223/207, Ultra signal 1541/30 October; ADM 223/208 Ultra signal 1958/12 November 1944.
181. ADM 223/208, Ultra signal 0059/13 November 1944.
182. ADM 223/212, OIC study, '*Tirpitz*; March 1941 – November 1944', p 16.

persuading the enemy that Norway was the destination of the invasion forces that were building up in the United Kingdom,* and that of dislocating the enemy's coastal shipping.

The attack on coastal shipping had been steadily increased since the middle of 1943, when Enemy Branch of MEW, which had earlier calculated that Germany's merchant shipping would be insufficient for her military needs and her priority economic cargoes by the end of the year unless she replaced losses at the expense of other war production,† recognised that the measures introduced by the Reichskommissar für die Seeschiffahrt were bringing about some improvement. The amount of merchant shipping under construction was increasing. Stronger escorts with better weapons and trained anti-aircraft parties were being provided for coastal convoys. In particular, although the enemy was now abandoning the use of Rotterdam, by far the most economical port for supplying the Ruhr with iron ore, and was discharging the ore at Emden apparently because of the refusal of insurers to cover the risks of sending Swedish ships further west, more shipping had been allocated to the Norwegian trade. It was calculated that iron ore imports from Norway and Sweden had risen to three and a half million tons in the first half of 1943 as compared with one and a half during the first half of 1942; shipments from Narvik had increased from 95,000 tons in January 1942 to 234,000 tons in May 1943.[183] But if these signs of improvement provided an additional incentive for increasing the British resources devoted to the attack on coastal shipping, the offensive was also sustained by the knowledge that partly as a result of the losses it was inflicting, and partly because of other set-backs, the Germans were encountering mounting difficulties.

At the end of June 1943 MEW estimated that although new construction had been increased, it remained 'negligible compared with current losses', and that Germany's total merchant shipping in the Baltic and North Sea was 300,000 tons less than she needed for her essential military and economic purposes. In August it learned that, except for the movement of oil, Sweden had cancelled the agreement under which Germany had been allowed to transit troops and military cargoes to Norway and Finland; oil was included in the ban from 1 October, by which time the movement of German shipping between German and Danish ports and Oslo, normally not within striking distance of the United Kingdom, was increasing. By the beginning of November it was observed that the enemy was

---

* See Volume III Part 2.   † See Volume II, pp 188–189.

183. AIR 41/48, pp 243–244 (quoting MEW monthly and six-monthly reports), 265–267; Roskill, op cit, Vol III Part I, p 92.

withdrawing shipping, particularly large diesel vessels suitable for military cargoes and troop-carrying, from Biscay and the Channel to the North Sea and the Baltic, where it was presumed that shortages caused by the ending of the Swedish transit traffic were being compounded by losses, by dislocation following the RAF's bombing of Hamburg in July and the USAAF's bombing of Emden at the end of September, and by the need to build up a reserve of shipping to deal with the uncertain situation that was developing on the Russian front and in Scandinavia.[184]* At the end of 1943 MEW reported that neither the economies and improvisations introduced by the German shipping administration nor such new construction as was being undertaken had, or was likely to, offset the growing weight of the Allied anti-shipping offensive.[185] Since April 1943 the RAF had in fact sunk 75,000 tons of merchant shipping – more than three times that completed in 1943 by the German emergency shipbuilding programme.[186]

Tactical intelligence about the movements of coastal shipping had meanwhile continued to improve. Derived mainly from the study by the OIC and GC and CS of references in the Enigma to navigational and other arrangements for convoy movements, it provided a reliable picture of the enemy's routines – showing which swept channels the convoys normally used, where they spent the night, the times at which they made and left harbour, and when and where they met their escorts – and thus a means of detecting those divergencies from routine which indicated that especially important convoys were to be expected.[187] Even so, the immediate results of the various methods adopted for the direct attack on shipping remained disappointing in the second half of 1943.

The Beaufighter Strike Wing of No 16 Group Coastal Command, firing torpedoes and (from the end of June) rocket projectiles, obtained only modest results off the Dutch coast and in the Bight, where the intelligence was most complete. Immediately after resuming operations, in April 1943, it had obtained a number of successes up to 13 June;† but between then and the end of July, when 55 convoys were sighted between the Elbe and the Hook of Holland,

---

* See above, p 18.　　　　　　　† See Volume II, p 537.

184.　AIR 41/48, pp 243, 263.
185.　FO 837/19, MEW Weekly Intelligence Report No 108 of 29 February 1944 (Survey of Economic Developments in German Europe in the six months ending 31 December 1943).
186.　AIR 41/48, pp 295–296.
187.　ADM 223/209, 'Receipt of Special Intelligence in Admiralty and its dissemination in German Surface Units Section'.

only nine were attacked – and that without important results.[188]* Nor did its performance improve during the remainder of 1943.[190] No 18 Group Coastal Command, operating against the Norwegian coast from Scottish bases, did no better despite the fact that it was reinforced by a special Beaufighter unit from July; and Fighter Command, operating with fighter-bombers against the shipping that was moving from Biscay and the Channel ports, had few successes before the end of the year.

The operations of the RAF off the Dutch and French coasts were supplemented by the activities of a large force of motor torpedo-boats and motor gun-boats under the Channel and East Coast Commands and by destroyer sweeps from Portsmouth and Plymouth. Off the Norwegian coast the 30th Norwegian MTB Flotilla increased its activities, and there was an unsuccessful attempt to penetrate Bergen harbour with one-man midget submarines. These operations, too, were planned with help from Enigma intelligence about the enemy's convoy routines and, in the case of the destroyer sweeps, on the receipt of advance warning from Enigma of shipping movements. They added considerably to the strain on the enemy's thinly-stretched defence forces, but did no great damage to shipping. In the Channel they involved continuous but mostly inconclusive fighting with German E-boats; about 50 of these were operating[191] and, as before, the Enigma rarely gave advance notice of their sorties. On the night of 22–23 October, in one of the destroyer sweeps, the British lost the cruiser *Charybdis*. During 20 and 21 October the Enigma disclosed that five Elbing-class fleet torpedo-boats had been ordered to proceed to Brest for escort duties,[192] and on the evening of 22 October C-in-C Plymouth sailed six destroyers, covered by the *Charybdis*, against the expected convoy. The cruiser and the destroyer *Limbourne* were sunk by the torpedo-boats while sweeping west off the Brittany coast.[193] There had been warning of the enemy's proximity from R/T intercepts and radar contacts, but no further Enigma intelligence was received.

---

† This disappointing performance led the RAF to question whether the Strike Wing should continue to operate. MEW pleaded for its retention on the grounds that its activities complemented those of the Nore Flotilla, by forcing enemy convoys to move at night, and were part of an integrated campaign, involving mining, daylight bombing of ports and night bombing by Bomber Command, of which cumulative effects were more important than direct successes.[189]

188. Roskill, op cit, Vol III Part I, p 92.
189. AIR 41/48, p 269; Roskill, op cit, Vol III Part I, p 92.
190. AIR 41/48, pp 269–270.
191. ADM 223/98, OIC SI No 685 of 1 September 1943.
192. ADM 223/185, Ultra signals 1726/20 October, 2305/21 October 1943.
193. Roskill, op cit, Vol III Part I pp 99–100.

The only striking British success in direct action against coastal shipping in the second half of 1943 was obtained by the carrier aircraft of the Home Fleet. As soon as it was clear that the *Tirpitz* had been disabled by the X-craft attack in September 1943, the C-in-C Home Fleet took the US carrier *Ranger* close into Bodö, where her dive-bombers and torpedo aircraft sank five ships totalling 20,750 tons, including a loaded troop-transport, and damaged seven other ships. The strike made use of recent Enigma intelligence about shipping movements in the area[194] – one of the damaged ships was a large tanker which was known to be taking oil to Altenfjord[195] – and of the analyses that were regularly provided by the OIC on such matters as traffic in Norwegian waters and GAF dispositions in Norway. It profited from the fact that the GAF could no longer deploy bomber or torpedo forces on the Norwegian coast, and also from the fact that carrier strikes could reach areas beyond the range of Coastal Command's routine operations, and could thus hope to achieve surprise and to find shipping proceeding in daytime. MEW estimated that largely as a result of this operation ore exports from Narvik declined by 58 per cent in October compared with the previous month, and were lower than in any month since May 1942.[196]

The attack on shipping in Norwegian waters was intensified from the beginning of 1944. By May 1944 when the lengthening hours of daylight put a stop to their campaign until the autumn, the Home Fleet's submarines, hitherto mainly deployed against the German fleet units, accounted for fifteen merchant ships, totalling about 56,000 tons.[197]* Anti-shipping strikes by the Home Fleet's carriers became more frequent from early February and were often combined with other fleet operations such as attacks on the *Tirpitz*;† they sank eight merchant ships totalling 30,000 tons and damaged eleven, totalling 33,500 tons. Coastal Command's No 18 Group, now armed with two Strike Wings, sank nine ships totalling 21,000 tons between January and the beginning of April, when the Strike Wings were transferred to the Channel area to provide flank protection for the invasion of Normandy. By the end of March, according to MEW's calculations, the sinkings off Norway from all causes

---

* In addition the submarine *Sceptre* towed over an X-craft which penetrated Bergen harbour and sank a 7,500 ton merchant ship on 14 April.

† See above, p 271 et seq.

194. ADM 223/185, Ultra signal 2231/3 October 1943.
195. ibid, Ultra signals 0941/2 October, 1032/7 October 1943.
196. AIR 41/48, p 286; FO 837/18, MEW Weekly Intelligence Report No 93 of 25 November 1943.
197. Roskill, op cit, Vol II Part I, pp 229, 285.

since January represented a quarter of the total tonnage plying between Norway and the German North Sea ports.[198] The Enigma provided prompt details of the damage and sinkings caused by these operations and showed their wider effect in disrupting enemy coastal traffic. By the end of January, for example, it showed that No 18 Group's activities had forced the Germans to order convoys to proceed only at night between Stavanger and Christiansand.[199] For the planning of the operations the chief value of Sigint continued to reside in the contribution it made to the long-term analysis of the enemy's shipping routines, though it frequently gave information about movements in progress.[200] The SIS's coastal reporting network remained in operation and reports from it increasingly supplemented the Enigma decrypts in both of these directions during 1944.[201]

Further south, the Strike Wings of No 16 Group Coastal Command found few targets off the German and Dutch coasts during the first half of 1944 even though they occasionally contrived to strike east of the Ems and had at least one success there.[202] But this was because very little enemy shipping was now going west of the Ems for fear of attack. Early in March the Admiralty learned that the German rail system was under greatly increased strain because the Swedes had refused to resume sailings to Rotterdam. In the eastern Channel, for the same reason, the Air Defence of Great Britain's (ADGB) anti-shipping successes were not significant, but the Dover batteries, relying on radar and visual observation, sank two large ships and damaged a third.[203] In Biscay the iron ore traffic from Bilbao to Bayonne had become more important to the enemy as that from Sweden came under attack; from March the Enigma and other sources revealed a large rise in its volume and provided some guide to the frequency and routes of the convoys. In May the submarine *Sceptre* sank two of the few ships available for this traffic, which dropped back to its previous proportions.[204]

Total losses sustained by enemy shipping from direct attack in the first half of 1944 in European waters (other than the Mediterranean) amounted to 46 ships (140,000 tons) and 18 more ships

---

198.　FO 837/20, MEW Weekly Intelligence Report No 134 of 31 August 1944 (Survey of Economic Developments in the German Economy in the six months ending 30 June 1944).
199.　ADM 223/190, Ultra signal 1228/1 February 1944.
200.　eg ADM 223/190, Ultra signals 1926/7 February, 1906/9 February 1944.
201.　ADM 223/87, loc cit.
202.　ADM 223/191, Ultra signal 1156/6 March 1944.
203.　AIR 41/48, p 511; Roskill, op cit, Vol III Part I, p 291.
204.　ADM 223/172, OIC SI 929 of 24 April 1944; AIR 41/48, p 520; Roskill, op cit, Vol III Part I, p 287.

(63,000 tons) were damaged.[205] To these casualties must be added the dislocation caused by the bombing of German ports, though the raids destroyed few ships, and by the sinking and dislocation produced by Allied minelaying. In the second half of 1943 the minelaying, carried out mainly by Bomber Command, had been concentrated in Biscay, as part of the anti-U-boat offensive, and off the Dutch and German North Sea coasts. Except for one operation off Gdynia at the end of September, in an unsuccessful attempt to catch the *Lützow*, and occasional operations in the Baltic approaches against the increased traffic between Oslo and Germany following the cancellation of the Swedish-German transit agreement, the Baltic had been neglected, not least as a result of the great strengthening of the air defences of north-west Germany. RAF minelaying sank 69 ships (totalling 25,750 tons) and damaged 13 (36,925 tons) during this period – a lower rate of success than had been achieved in 1942.[206] From the beginning of 1944, however, Bomber Command again extended its operations to the Baltic with the aim of dislocating U-boat training as well as of destroying shipping.[207]* At the same time it introduced important technical improvements, using the bomber navigational aid H2S from February to raise from 6,000 to 15,000 feet the height from which mines were dropped, and increasing the frequency with which it introduced new types of mine and new mine circuits.[208] Combined with the higher monthly rate of minelaying, these developments, which gave the minelayers better protection against Flak and enabled them to concentrate against more important and more heavily defended areas, produced both a decline in British casualties – 48 aircraft in the five months to May 1944 compared with 53 aircraft in fewer sorties in the second half of 1943 – and an increase in the enemy's shipping losses. RAF minelaying sank 79 ships (61,500 tons) in this period and damaged 15 ships (28,000 tons).[209] It also added greatly to the strain on Germany's minesweeping, defence and escort forces, and contributed to a slump in Sweden's exports to Germany. In May 1944 it was estimated that some 40 per cent of the total personnel of the German Navy was engaged in the clearance of shipping routes or in minefield escort duties;[210] and it

---

* See Volume III Part 2.

205. Roskill, op cit, Vol III Part I, pp 279, 287–288.
206. ibid, p 94.
207. Naval Historical Branch, BR 1736 (56) (1), p 477.
208. ibid, pp 477, 478, 481.
209. Roskill, op cit, Vol III Part I, p 289.
210. ADM 223/209, 'The Role of Special Intelligence in Bomber Command's Minelaying Campaign in the Baltic', p 14.

was later to emerge that the number of vessels used for minesweeping, guard and escort duties in the Baltic alone increased to 440 by April 1944, as compared with 340 at the end of 1942 and 420 at the end of 1943.[211] On 12–13 May Mosquitoes carried out a specialised operation to mine the Kiel Canal which had long been advocated by MEW; the Enigma, PR and information from the Naval Attaché Stockholm revealed great congestion at both ends of the canal which had still not been cleared by the end of the month. In June MEW estimated that in May the export of Swedish iron ore had fallen to 420,000 tons, as compared with 1,307,000 tons in May 1943, and that, mainly because of the mining of the Kiel Canal, Sweden's exports of iron ore to Germany during the five months January to May were nearly 1½ million tons less than in the corresponding part of 1943.[212]

As opposed to general estimates of this kind, which could not be checked until after the war, the results, direct and indirect, of individual minelaying sorties were commonly obtained without delay from the Enigma decrypts. In the case of direct casualties the decrypts usually established the name, type and tonnage of the vessel, whether it was sunk or damaged, and the time and exact position of the incident. Apart from their value for the assessment of enemy shipping losses, they thus indicated the areas in which future operations would be most productive. The Enigma was also the source from which the OIC derived its ever growing familiarity with the swept routes used by the different types of enemy shipping, with the numbers, types and dispositions of his mine-clearing craft, with the extent to which the enemy was using different ports, with the areas and harbours that were closed by mining at any one time and with those in which, at any one time, he was suffering from the greatest disorganisation or devoting his greatest mine-clearing efforts. Its contribution to the detailed planning of the minelaying campaign had always been important. But its value increased from the beginning of 1944, when it more than off-set the continual expansion of Germany's mine-clearing forces by enabling the OIC and Bomber Command, working in close collaboration, to maximise the demoralising effect of the campaign by selecting for most sorties the times and locations at which mining was likely to produce the greatest dislocation.[213] To an increasing extent the decrypts also disclosed what changes the enemy was making to his mine-clearing methods as he encountered new and modified types of Allied mines, and although no detailed record remains of the use that was made

211. BR 1736 (56) (1), pp 490, 491, 494.
212. FO 837/19, MEW Weekly Intelligence Report No 125 of 29 June 1944.
213. ADM 223/209, 'The Role of Special Intelligence in Bomber Command's Minelaying Campaign in the Baltic', pp 8–14.

of this intelligence, it is clear that the Admiralty put it to good use in its design programme.[214]

All aerial minelaying was carried out by Bomber Command, but motor torpedo-boats, motor-gunboats and other small ships in the Nore and Dover Commands regularly laid mines in the course of their operations against coastal shipping off the Dutch coast and in the Channel. Like the RAF's mining campaign, and like the activities of other forces engaged in direct attacks on shipping, these operations made use of the intelligence about the German shipping which the OIC derived in part from PR, POW interrogation, agents' reports and captured documents. Like those of the Norwegian motor torpedo-boats which raided the Norwegian coast from a base in the Shetlands, they helped to tie down the enemy's escort and defence forces. But it was not possible to assess the effectiveness of their minelaying and despite the many claims made for that of their direct attacks, the Enigma showed that they sank few, if any, merchant ships. The operations continued to take the form of skirmishing with German escort vessels and E-boats in which, as the Enigma disclosed, the enemy escort was occasionally sunk,[215] but in which the E-boats kept the upper hand.

It was known from the Enigma that some 50 E-boats were still operating from Ijmuiden, the Hook of Holland, Boulogne and Cherbourg;[216] and the same source established that, except that two E-boats were sunk, their activities were unaffected by a raid by 358 aircraft on the new concrete E-boat shelters at Ijmuiden on 26 March.[217] The Enigma regularly gave details of the frequent sorties they made for torpedo attacks, minelaying or anti-invasion reconnaissance off the English coast. But the decrypts were obtained with an average delay of fifteen hours after the E-boats had left port, and were of no operational value. Nor could anything useful be derived from analysing them after the event; there was no regular pattern in the timing, the direction, the targets or the scale of the E-boat attacks, and from mid-April to 31 May,[218] in response to the growing seriousness of the threat, the OIC could do no more than issue a new series of reports on E-boat operations during the previous week.* The E-boats' greatest success was the sinking, with

---

* See Appendix 16. This is an example of the statistical analyses prepared in the OIC, mostly on subjects connected with U-boats, by a civilian scientiest lent to the OIC by the Chief of the Admiralty Operational Research Branch in 1943 (Professor Blackett).

214.   *The Handling of Naval Special Intelligence*, pp 115–116.
215.   eg ADM 223/191, Ultra signal 1658/6 March 1944.
216.   ADM 223/172, OIC SI 906 of 5 April, 969 of 2 June 1944.
217.   ADM 223/192, Ultra signals 2330/27 March, 0140/4 April 1944.
218.   Beginning with ADM 223/172, OIC SI 914 of 12 April 1944.

the loss of over 700 American soldiers, of one landing craft and the damaging of two others in an unforeseen attack on an invasion rehearsal convoy off Lyme Regis at the end of April.* From then on the decrypts showed that they devoted more of their time to anti-invasion reconnaissance,[219] and their movements were increasingly circumscribed by Allied aircraft, which attacked them as soon as they left harbour.[220]

Few E-boats were sunk by these attacks, but some were damaged, and the enemy had meanwhile lost a fleet torpedo-boat and some smaller war vessels to the destroyers of Plymouth Command which, often with the support of a light cruiser, continued to operate along the French coast. With the assistance of advance notice of German movements from the Enigma, these ships scored successes on 5 February, 26 April and 28 April,[221] and though on the last of these dates the Canadian destroyer *Athabaskan* was sunk in exchange for the destruction of the torpedo-boat, their activities contributed to the steady attrition of the serviceable warships the Germans had at their disposal against the Allied cross-Channel invasion. At the end of May, in the last assessment it made on the subject before D-day, the OIC knew that in Ostend and all ports west of Calais these had been reduced to four destroyers, one Elbing-class fleet torpedo-boat, three small torpedo-boats and 30 E-boats excluding those based at Ijmuiden, together with 178 minesweepers and mine-clearers and a number of minor escort vessels[222] – by no means so great a threat to the huge invasion fleet the Allies were assembling as would be presented, or so it seemed, by the German Air Force and the U-boats.

---

* See Volume III Part 2.

219. eg ADM 223/193, Ultra signal 2001/28 April 1944.
220. AIR 41/48, p 523; Roskill, op cit, Vol III Part I, p 294.
221. ADM 223/189, Ultra signal 1000/4 February; ADM 223/192, Ultra signal 2151/23 April; ADM 223/193, Ultra signals 1116/27 April, 1940 and 2355/28 April 1944.
222. ADM 223/172, OIC SI Nos 967 of 30 May, 969 of 1 June 1944.

PART XI

The Air War from June 1943 to the Summer of 1944

CHAPTER 37

The Allied Air Offensive

AT THE Washington conference in May 1943, at a time when Bomber Command in the Battle of the Ruhr and US Eighth Air Force in its daylight precision attacks on selected military and industrial targets were both suffering severe casualties,* the Combined Chiefs of Staff had concluded that 'if the German fighters are materially increased in numbers it is quite conceivable that this would make our daylight bombing unprofitable and perhaps our night bombing too'.[1] The outcome of their discussions was a new directive to the Allied air forces. Issued on 10 June, it ordered Eighth Air Force to give priority to reducing the German fighter force, as a preliminary to attacking targets which sustained Germany's capacity for armed resistance, and instructed Bomber Command to design its operations 'as far as practicable to be complementary to the operations of the Eighth Air Force'.[2] The directive led to the formation of the 'Jockey Committee', which met weekly from June 1943 till the end of the war to lay down priorities for the offensive against German fighter production. It comprised representatives of AI 2 and AI 3, RAF and USAAF commands.[3]†

The Eighth Air Force responded to the directive by trying to concentrate its efforts against the aircraft production industry and the German day-fighters. But Bomber Command, its freedom of action unaffected by the wording of the directive,‡ made no departure from the aims and principles that had governed its area bombing policy since 1942. On the contrary, encouraged by developments which promised a rapid increase in its own strength and effectiveness – by the fact that Lancasters were coming forward in large numbers and the versatile Mosquito was joining them; that

---

* See Volume II, p 519, et seq.
† See Appendix 1, p 471.
‡ An early draft of the directive had explicitly associated Bomber Command with the decision to give priority to the reduction of German fighter strength.[4] Had this wording survived, the directive would have required Bomber Command to direct its area bombing against aircraft production centres, that is to follow what was later to be called a policy of selective area bombing.

1. Webster and Frankland, *The Strategic Air Offensive against Germany*, Vol II (1961), p 24.
2. ibid, p 29.
3. Air Historical Branch, *Air Ministry Intelligence*, pp 23, 237–238, 246.
4. Webster and Frankland, op cit, Vol II, pp 27–28.

RAF Jamming Device

'Oboe'* and H2S* were improving navigation and bombing accuracy; that 'Window'† was now available against the enemy's defences and other radio counter-measures were being produced – it embarked on another stage of the area bombing offensive in the belief that not least by its effect on German civilian morale it 'would presently and decisively bring the war to a successful conclusion'.[5]

believed they could end the war

Between 24 July and 1 August, in four raids on Hamburg and in single raids on Essen and Remscheid, the offensive achieved an unprecedented degree of concentration and intensity, and it seemed for a time that Bomber Command's expectations might be well-founded. Thanks to the introduction of 'Window', British casualties were well below the insupportable level they had reached during the Battle of the Ruhr,[6] and this could be contrasted with the experience of Eighth Air Force, which was being forced by continuing heavy losses to diversify its offensive.‡ At the same time, intelligence left little doubt that the raids had produced devastation on a scale never before known. PR showed that Hamburg had been all but destroyed.[7] The secret sources, while not disclosing the first reactions of Speer and Milch, who feared that a few more raids on the same scale would reduce the Reich to impotence,[8] confirmed that the damage done was unusually severe. On 2 August the Enigma reported that all Service leave to the Hamburg area had been stopped; on 10 August it showed that the ban was still in force.[9] By the end of the first week of August decrypts of a report from the Japanese Vice-Consul in Hamburg and of a circular issued by the German Foreign Ministry had added that the damage was appalling, 80 per cent of the heart of the city having been destroyed, and that casualties were 'extremely high'; other decrypts of Axis diplomatic telegrams had reported that anxiety about the raids was lowering morale in the armed forces and in Berlin, where schools, hospitals, archives and government departments were being evacuated and the population was queueing to leave by train; and Abwehr decrypts had referred to German plans for dispersing war production and putting it under ground.[10] We need not doubt, moreover, that reports of this kind sustained the hopes that had accompanied the intensification of the bombing.

---

* For details of 'Oboe' and H2S see Webster and Frankland, *The Strategic Air Offensive against Germany* (1961), Vol IV, Annex I.

† For details of 'Window' see Volume II, pp 517–519.   ‡ See below, p 296.

5. ibid, p 25.   6. ibid, pp 155–158.   7. ibid, pp 154 (n), 224.
8. ibid, p 211; Irving, *The Rise and Fall of the Luftwaffe* (1973), p 229.
9. CX/MSS/2993/T11, 3036/T31.
10. Dir/C Archive, 4074 of 3 August, 4099 of 5 August 1943, 4109 of 7 August 1943.

The optimism was not confined to Bomber Command. In Whitehall expectations were all the higher because other decrypts had recently suggested that the bombing of northern Italy by Bomber Command and of targets in central and southern Italy by US bombers operating from Mediterranean bases had contributed to the collapse of Mussolini's regime at the end of July. AI 3(b)'s reaction to the fact that the Germans had used day-fighters against the raids was that it was a sign of 'weakness'* and the section attributed the reduction in Bomber Command's losses, which was due to 'Window', to 'severe strain' and 'less determined . . . opposition' on the part of the German aircrew.[11] On 2 August a commentary prepared for the DNI suggested that the German authorities might be discussing the dispersal of war production from the need to persuade the population that Germany's capacity to sustain bomb damage was greater than it was in fact; and on 6 August the NID thought it possible that they might declare Berlin an open city. On 15 August the Chief of the Air Staff believed that 'attacks on Berlin on anything like the Hamburg scale must have an enormous effect on Germany as a whole.'[12]

From the beginning of August, however, until the third week of November, when it launched the Battle of Berlin, Bomber Command did not again achieve the concentration of attack it had briefly delivered against Hamburg. This was reflected in the fact that Sigint produced few reports on the immediate effects of the major raids it now carried out against widely separated cities including Berlin; and these made it clear that the raids were producing much less damage than that inflicted on Hamburg. Of the three raids that proved most costly to Bomber Command, those made on Berlin on 24 and 31 August and 3 September, only the first was referred to by Sigint; a single decrypt reported 'considerable damage'.[13] But the night photography evidence indicated that only 27 of the 1,729 sorties despatched had dropped their bombs within three miles of the aiming point.[14]† The only other decrypts were those reporting that the raid on Frankfurt on 4 October had caused slight production

---

* This development was in fact part of a fundamental change in German night-fighter methods which was before long to create grave difficulties for Bomber Command. See below, p 303 et seq.

† For the use of night photography as a means of assessing the accuracy of Bomber Command's raids see Volume II, p 260. The number of night films taken increased from 1,000 a month in 1942 to 4,000 a month in 1943.[15]

11.   Air Sunsets 83 of 1 August, 85 of 9 August 1943.
12.   Webster and Frankland, op cit, Vol II, p 31 fn.
13.   CX/MSS/3113/T34.
14.   Webster and Frankland, op cit. Vol II, p 163.
15.   AIR 41/7, *Photographic Reconnaissance*, Vol II, p 43.

losses, and that 100,000 had been made homeless, 3,000 killed and many arms factories hit in Hanover on 9 October.[16] At the same time, Bomber Command's casualties began to return to the disturbing level reached during the Battle of the Ruhr.[17] They did so despite the lengthening nights, despite the introduction of further radio counter-measures in succession to 'Window' and despite the resort to extensive tactical counter-measures from September; and the immediate explanation was not in doubt. Whatever else might account for this disappointing outcome, the intelligence sources disclosed a continuing increase in the GAF's front-line fighter strength in Germany.

It had been clear from the Enigma before the beginning of August that the GAF was making no attempt to replace on other fronts the immense losses it had incurred in the summer, especially in the Kursk battle and in Sicily, but was on the contrary progressively withdrawing fighter units from Russia and the Mediterranean for the defence of the Reich. As early as 2 August, in the light of the Air Ministry's knowledge of the enemy's order of battle, the GAF section in the Admiralty's OIC had remarked that 'unless the increase in German fighter strength is checked it will eventually make the bombing of Germany impracticable'; and a fortnight later it had noted that 'the defence of the Reich . . . is now regarded as of such supreme importance that its [the Reich's] present fighter strength is almost equal to that of the eastern and the Mediterranean fronts combined.[18] At the Quebec conference in the same month it had been reported that the total German fighter force had increased by 22 per cent since the beginning of the year, but that its strength in western Europe had doubled.[19] On 21 September the Air Ministry calculated that fighter strength in the Reich, at 780 single-engined (day) and 740 twin-engined (night) fighters, had come to constitute 60 per cent of Germany's total fighter forces, the further increase being partly accounted for by the rapid reinforcement of the defences in south Germany and Austria following the first USAAF raid on Wiener Neustadt from Mediterranean bases on 13 August.[20] Still more significant, on 20 August the decrypt of a report from the Japanese Ambassador in Berlin had disclosed that Milch planned to double military aircraft production, at present 2,700 planes a month, over the next fifteen months, and was giving priority to

---

16.   CX/MSS/3323/T38, 3410/T26 and 30.
17.   Webster and Frankland, op cit, Vol II, pp 146–148.
18.   ADM 223/98, OIC SI 663 of 15 August 1943.
19.   Webster and Frankland, op cit, Vol II, p 31.
20.   Air Sunsets 95 of 8 September, 102 of 19 September, 103 of 21 September 1943.

fighters over bombers.* This appears to have been the first firm indication that Germany was giving priority to fighter production; it was confirmed at the end of October, when the Enigma showed that one-third of her long-range bomber Gruppen were to be disbanded.[21]†

On 27 September, in the light of Bomber Command's disappointing performance and of this intelligence, the Deputy Chief of the Air Staff returned to the argument which the Combined Chiefs of Staff had voiced for the first time at the Washington conference.[23]‡ Pointing out that the continuing increase in enemy fighter strength made it evident that the Germans had decided to accept 'very serious military handicaps in Russia and the Mediterranean rather than reduce their fighter defences in West Germany', and emphasising that 'the winning of air superiority is the decisive battle', he warned the Chief of the Air Staff that 'at present we are not progressing with measures to overcome the German night air defences, especially measures against their night fighters. The approved radio counter-measures may go a considerable way towards defeating them but the strength of the night fighters continues to increase, and we feel that unless we can stop their numbers increasing or else introduce some effective measures of combatting them, we may find that either we are unable to maintain the night offensive against Germany or that the Germans can sustain the intensity of attack which we can develop'. He added that, notwithstanding the directive of 10 June, Bomber Command had done little to further the objective of reducing German fighter strength, in that it had not yet attacked any town associated with fighter production, and urged that it should now be instructed to give higher priority to such targets.[24]§

The Deputy Chief's démarche failed to produce a review of Bomber Command's priorities. So did the fact that in the next few

---

* See appendix 16.

† Milch's reforms had in fact produced a great increase in output by July 1943 but he was unable to complete the switch of priority from bombers to fighters till towards the end of the year. As late as April 1944 the Japanese diplomatic decrypts reported Milch as saying that fighter production had not exceeded 1,400 per month in February, but that it would increase soon as important factories were being placed underground.[22]

‡ See above, p 291.

§ He further added that failure against the night-fighters 'may also result in the failure to demonstrate the power of the strategic air offensive with consequent and dangerous repercussions upon post-war policy.'

21. Air Sunset 113 of 25 October 1943.
22. AIR 41/10, *The Rise and Fall of the German Air Force*, pp 289, 306; SJA 29 of 7 April 1944.
23. Webster and Frankland, op cit, Vol II, p 24.
24. ibid, p 34; AIR 41/43, *The RAF in the Bombing Offensive against Germany*, Vol 5, p 159.

weeks intelligence established that Eighth Air Force's offensive was failing to prevent a continuing increase in the front-line strength of the German fighters on the western front. By the end of October the Air Ministry judged that the number of single-engined fighters had risen from 740 at 1 July to 800 at 1 October (when the actual figure was 964) and that the number of twin-engined fighters had jumped during the same period from 470 to 725 (actual figure, 682); and in a minute giving these figures to the Chief of the Air Staff on 3 November ACAS(I) predicted that they would continue to rise, to 800 and 760 on 1 December 1943 and to 880 and 830 on 1 April 1944, even if the USAAF persevered with the daylight offensive.[25]

This prediction was disturbing enough: in June 1943, when the Combined Chiefs of Staff issued the current directive on strategic bombing, the Allies had hoped that the total enemy fighter force in the west would be reduced to 650 aircraft by 1 April 1944.[26] But still more disquieting was the realisation, which soon followed, that the enemy had forced the USAAF to accept temporary defeat. During September the Enigma and the German fighter R/T traffic had indicated that the GAF was giving highest priority to defence against the daylight raids; it was not only strengthening the fighter force in south Germany and Bavaria, but also diverting twin-engined fighters to day-fighting and equipping them with a rocket projectile adapted from the Army's 21 cm mortar, a weapon which, first referred to in the Enigma in August, proved to be formidably effective against the US bombers. Against the US raid on Schweinfurt on 14 October the intelligence sources revealed that the GAF had used not only every available single-engined and twin-engined day-fighter unit, including four Gruppen equipped with the 21 cm rocket projectile, but also almost all its night-fighter units.[27] And it had done so to good effect: Eighth Air Force's losses were so heavy that after Schweinfurt it abandoned its deep-penetration raids until it could protect its bombers with long-range fighters, which would not be available until the new year.

Together with the knowledge that the German fighter force was still growing and the fact that the USAAF also sustained severe casualties in raids on Wiener Neustadt from the south on 1 and 24 October and 2 November,* this set-back sharpened American criticism of Bomber Command's total concentration on area bomb-

---

* The day after the formation of US Fifteenth Air Force in the Mediterranean theatre of operations.

25. Webster and Frankland, op cit, Vol II, pp 45–46.
26. ibid, p 46.
27. Air Sunsets 89 of 21 August, 95 of 8 September, 105 of 28 September, 115 of 31 October 1943.

ing.[28] At Bomber Command, however, it strengthened the case for another phase of intense area bombing, this time primarily against Berlin, and even prompted the suggestion that the USAAF should take part in it. On 3 November Air Chief Marshal Harris, AOC-in-C Bomber Command, put this plan to the Prime Minister in a personal minute. Harris supported his proposal with PR evidence of damage already done to housing – it showed that 19 towns had been 'virtually destroyed', 19 seriously damaged and 9 damaged – and also with the claim that 'what actually occurs is much more than can be seen in any photograph'. He was convinced that 'Germany must collapse before this programme, which is more than half complete already, has proceeded much further'. The destruction of Berlin would be the turning-point. 'We can wreck Berlin from end to end if the USAF will come in on it. It will cost between 400 and 500 aircraft. It will cost Germany the war'.[29]

The proposal met with a mixed reception in Whitehall. ACAS(I) supported it in a minute of 5 November. He made allowance for the fact that the AOC-in-C, a man who believed that the war could be won 'by immediate offensive action long before our defensive plan has come near to completion', was given to making exaggerated claims. But he was convinced that the morale of the population was 'the joint in the German armour', that Bomber Command's attacks were 'doing more towards shortening the war than any other offensive' and that the AOC-in-C was justified in asking for American participation.[30] 'Embroiled as we are with *Overlord* and consequently with the necessity of lowering German fighter strength and production, we are apt, perhaps, to overlook the fact that the war can be won in the face of or in spite of an increasing air defence'.[31] The Deputy Chief of the Air Staff, continuing to resist 'the temptation to believe that Germany could not long endure the scale of attack which Bomber Command had been bringing to bear since March 1943',[32] stated on 12 November that the proposed assault on Berlin was unlikely to end the war even if it achieved damage comparable to that done in Hamburg.[33] In a minute of the same date the Director of Bomber Operations was no less sceptical; indeed, he argued that to choose to attack Berlin in preference to targets having a bearing on Germany's fighter strength would be as great a mistake as that made by the GAF when, on the point of

---

28. Webster and Frankland, op cit, Vol II, p 42; M Hastings, *Bomber Command* (1981), pp 306–309.
29. Webster and Frankland, op cit, Vol II, pp 47–48.
30. ibid, p 49.   31. AIR 41/43, p 122.
32. Webster and Frankland, op cit, Vol II, p 34.
33. ibid, p 50.

defeating 'the famous few', it had switched its attack to London in the Battle of Britain.[34]

The official history of Bomber Command's operations has pointed out, however, that this analogy was false in one important respect; unlike Fighter Command's in 1940, Germany's fighter strength was growing in 1943.[35] Far from preventing its growth, moreover, Eighth Air Force had failed in its daylight precision attacks against aircraft production and had recently been forced to accept temporary defeat. It must also be remembered that, unlike Eighth Air Force, Bomber Command was not yet trained for attack on precise targets such as aircraft factories and their aircraft parks. In all these circumstances it can cause no surprise that Bomber Command's belief in the power of an independent strategic air offensive and the effectiveness of area bombing again prevailed against the mounting scepticism, to be put to one more test in the Battle of Berlin.

□

When such basic considerations, operational and psychological, conspired to produce this decision, so that firm intelligence about the growing strength of German fighter defences could be ignored or deliberately set aside, intelligence that told equally firmly against the more sanguine estimates of the invisible effects of area bombing on Germany's war production and civilian morale could alone, perhaps, have altered the outcome. But these were subjects on which a body of indisputable or unambiguous evidence did not exist.

It is true that in the summer and autumn of 1943 the Ministry of Economic Warfare was providing cautious and by no means optimistic assessments of the effects of area bombing on the German economy. In July 1943, in the first of a series of quarterly reports commissioned by the Chief of the Air Staff on the subject, the JIC, which relied for its evidence on MEW and also took US opinion into account, conceded that only a small proportion of the enemy's production capacity had yet been destroyed. But it noted that there would be a time-lag before the effects were fully felt, since the industries which had sustained most damage were those producing for other industries. It also argued that there was no simple yardstick by which these effects could be measured; a nation's economic and industrial structure formed an organic whole with the endurance and capacity of its population, so that injury caused by bombing could not be assessed 'by counting houses and factories'.[36] The

---

34. ibid, pp 36, 41.   35. ibid, p 45.
36. JIC (43) 294 of 22 July.

JIC's second report, issued on 12 November and covering the third quarter of the year, again pointed to the importance of morale; it set MEW's estimate, to the effect that by September bombing had reduced armaments production and total industrial production to between 85 and 90 per cent of the January 1943 level, in the context of increasing damage to civilian conditions of life, with between 5 and 6 million people homeless and a shortage of consumer goods so severe that the needs of air raid victims could not be met.[37] But if damage to the economy could not be considered without reference to damage to morale, the evidence for the effects of the bombing on morale, such as it was, was resistant to objective assessment or at any rate to measurement.

The Japanese diplomatic decrypts, the Sigint source that referred most frequently to the impact of the bombing on morale, had assessed the situation in grave terms during August. A report by the Japanese Ambassador in Berlin on 4 August, decrypted on 13 August, had said that while the German authorities were naturally gloomy about the intensification of the bombing offensive, they felt 'no cause for anxiety over morale'.[38] In a report of 11 August, however, decrypted on 23 August, a representative of the Japanese Home Office had admitted that the Hamburg raids had caused panic in Berlin and that there was 'as yet no split between the Führer and the people but things are tending that way: the future behaviour of the people will be governed by the intensity of the raids as well as by developments at the fronts'. On 20 August the decrypt of the Ambassador's report on his interview with Milch,* which had taken place on 17 August, had been reassuring about the effects on industry, but had not mentioned the effects on morale. Milch had admitted that 'the raids had been very violent and that the damage to production plants in the Ruhr area and elsewhere was not to be dismissed lightly'; he had added that since 'British and American bombing consisted largely of the bombing of towns', and since damage to factories was less than that to dwelling houses, the resultant reduction of production potential was not more than 10 per cent, and the government would quickly redistribute work to other factories. After the end of August, however, the Japanese decrypts had not referred to the subject again until the first half of October; and the Japanese Ambassador had then assured his government that while there were ups and downs in the level of German morale, 'there will be no internal collapse as a result of the war not

* See Appendix 16 and above, pp 294–295.

37. JIC (43) 458 of 12 November.
38. Dir/C Archive, 4160 of 14 August 1943.

going well, or of the intense air raids', that the raids were not having a long-term effect on morale and that the German authorities were now intensifying the air defences.[39]

Not unnaturally – and all the more so because the Ambassador had stressed in his October report the difficulty of investigating the effects of the bombing – the authorities in Whitehall were disposed to regard such Japanese testimony as subjective or tainted* and to place more reliance on the only other available sources – SIS reports; POW interrogations; German newspaper and radio information and propaganda, analysed by the Political Warfare Executive (PWE); such assessments by the representatives of neutral governments as reached the Foreign Office through the diplomatic missions; and (though these were rarely revealing before 1944) decrypts of German police signals. The Foreign Office assessed the evidence from these sources in regular reports for the War Cabinet incorporating 'the agreed views of the various Departments concerned', including the Service departments.† There is no reason to think that the sources were at fault in pointing to a decline in German morale when Germany's prospects of victory were so obviously diminishing, or, when Allied bombing was causing so much physical and visible damage, in indicating that the deterioration was more pronounced on the home front than among the armed forces. But they could not provide evidence as to whether and, if so, when and in what ways deterioration would turn into collapse. Nor did the compilers of the assessments attempt to remedy this deficiency. In relation to morale in the Services, indeed, there was sufficient evidence from the fronts to make them cautious; the conclusion that morale in the armed forces was higher than at home was supported by the argument that 'if it were not, it is hard to see how the German Army could continue to fight so well'.[40] In the attempt to discover how much lower was the morale of the civilian population the compilers puzzled over the failure of the sources to report any signs of serious political opposition and

---

* On a later report in May 1944 NID 12 commented: 'This is almost the first time the Japanese Ambassador has given his own impressions instead of relying entirely on German statements (which he invariably swallows whole). This may have been caused by the fact that he says he has found it difficult to get information about the results of air raids from the Germans, although he still swallows whole those that he does get.'

† Responsibility for assessing the evidence on the state of German morale, a task which had earlier been attempted by the JIC (see Volume II, pp 7–8), had passed to the Foreign Office after October 1942; it made regular reports to the War Cabinet from that date. But from the end of 1943 the JIC was also reporting regularly on the subject to the Chiefs of Staff and for the Combined Intelligence Committee in connection with Operation *Rankin* (see above, p 44 et seq).

39.   ibid, 13 October 1943.
40.   CAB 66/43, WP (43) 527 of 22 November.

consoled themselves with the argument that 'the steady weakening of the nation's willpower as exemplified by increased apathy . . . and general physical exhaustion is in many ways more dangerous than organised opposition, since it is more insidious and more difficult to combat'.[41] But as to when apathy and exhaustion would reach the dimensions of a collapse that would end Germany's ability to continue the war, they confined themselves to the unexceptionable conclusion that this might happen at any time, and must happen in the long run, if the Allies kept up the pressure.

These assessments were not calculated to discourage the decision to launch the Battle of Berlin. But it can hardly be held that they justified the stronger claims which preceded the decision and which continued to be made for some weeks after the battle began on the night of 18–19 November. AOC-in-C Bomber Command had insisted in advance that 'Germany must collapse before this programme, which is more than half complete already, has proceeded much further'*; on 7 December he assured the Air Staff that provided priority was given to Lancaster production, and provided there was no further increase in its casualties, Bomber Command could by itself bring about the surrender of Germany by 1 April 1944.[42] On 12 November, stressing the effects of the raids on Hamburg, the JIC felt that 'the discipline of the people now shows signs of considerable weakening'.[43] The CAS believed on 22 November that 'social disruption threatened the structure of the entire home front';[44] and on 3 December he had 'no shadow of doubt' that German morale was at an extremely low ebb and thought that Bomber Command might be 'at least half-way along the road of industrial devastation towards the point where Germany will become unable to continue the war'.[45]† A report by Bomber Command's intelligence staff of 17 December, written after the first PR sortie of Berlin since the assault had begun, was entitled *Götterdämmerung*; it asserted that 'the administrative machine of the Nazis, their military and industrial organisation and above all their morale, have by these attacks suffered a deadly wound from which they cannot recover'.[47] It is indeed clear that such claims did not reflect the intelligence assessments, for what they were worth, so

---

* See above, p 297.

† This statement reproduced the sense of a report prepared by the Air Intelligence Branch and PWE which had said that 'the favourable climatic conditions of the last three months were one of the factors why there had been no general break in morale'.[46]

41. CAB 66/40, WP (43) 396 of 14 September.
42. Webster and Frankland, op cit, Vol II, p 55–58.
43. JIC (43) 458 of 12 November.
44. Webster and Frankland, op cit, Vol II, p 255.
45. ibid, p 51.   46. AIR 41/43, p 160.   47. ibid, p 125.

much as express the high hopes which were necessarily invested in the outcome of the battle.

Before the end of December the Air Staff was nevertheless coming to accept that the area bombing offensive was again failing to fulfil the hopes that had been placed in it. Its retreat may have been partly caused by the fact that, whereas it had hoped for evidence of a dramatic deterioration in Germany, such slight evidence as had been received had been by no means encouraging. The only Sigint evidence, a single decrypt of a telegram from the Japanese Ambassador at the end of November, had remarked on Berlin's methodical rescue services and reported that the population remained 'surprisingly calm'.[48] By 23 December POW interrogations had corroborated earlier intelligence to the effect that 'whereas the German people feared the night attacks, Hitler and the German High Command feared the daylight precision attacks on individual factories'.[49] The Air Staff forwarded this last item of intelligence to Bomber Command to support the argument that selective area bombing – attacks on cities selected for their association with aircraft production – would be more effective than the continuation of the Battle of Berlin; on 17 December, indeed, the Air Staff had already urged Bomber Command to give priority to an attack on Schweinfurt.[50]* But it is clear that the Air Staff was also influenced by Bomber Command's casualty rate and Sigint evidence of the continuing resilience of the enemy's fighter forces. Bomber Command's losses, surprisingly low in the first two weeks of the Battle of Berlin, rose appreciably in December.[51] Sigint disclosed that while fewer fighter Gruppen were now being transferred to Germany from other fronts – there were fewer to transfer – new Gruppen were still being formed.[52] At the end of December the Air Ministry estimated that the front-line strength in the west was 865 single-engined fighters (as compared with 800 on 1 October) and 750 twin-engined fighters (as compared with 725 on 1 October) out of a total front-line strength that had increased to 1,710 single-engined fighters and 1,100 twin-engined (as compared with 1,430 and 920 on 1 October).[53]

---

* See Appendix 17 for the importance of Schweinfurt as the centre for ball-bearing production.

48. Dir/C Archive, 7 December 1943.
49. Webster and Frankland, op cit, Vol II, p 60.
50. ibid, pp 61, 65.   51. ibid, p 204.
52. ADM 223/170, OIC SI 761, 779 and 786 of 6 and 27 November, and 5 December; ADM 223/171, OIC SI 804 of 26 December 1943.
53. Air Sunset 136 of 10 January 1944; AIR 40/2393, DDI 3 Appreciations file, Part 2.

In January 1944 these trends became more pronounced. Bomber Command's casualty rate worsened.[54] German fighter strength continued to increase, and although it was noticeable that the single-engined fighter force was now expanding faster than twin-engined fighters, it was known that in consequence of a radical change in her air defence tactics Germany was using both single-engined and twin-engined fighters against Bomber Command's raids.* At the end of January the Air Ministry estimated that the single-engined force had risen from 865 to 900 since the beginning of the month, whereas the twin-engined force had declined from 750 to 650.[55]

As well as protesting against the diversion of some of his effort into attacks on the V-weapons launching sites,† AOC-in-C Bomber Command had hitherto resisted the Air Staff's recommendation that he should attack Schweinfurt. But on 14 January the Air Staff ordered him to bomb Schweinfurt and over-ruled his protests. Bomber Command's attack on Schweinfurt did not take place until 24 February. By that date, as we can now see, Germany had won the Battle of Berlin: after bombing Berlin at short intervals on the nights of 27, 28 and 30 January and making further raids on Berlin on 15 February and Leipzig on 19 February, Bomber Command, unable to sustain the casualties it was incurring on the northern routes, switched a large proportion of its effort into less concentrated raids against south Germany. Nor was it long before it accepted the necessity for a more lasting change in its bombing tactics. On 24 March it returned to Berlin for the last time, and again suffered heavy casualties. On 30 March, the day before SHAEF was by previous arrangement to assume general direction of its operations,‡ it carried out a raid on Nuremberg, which was a still more costly failure, casualties amounting to well over 10 per cent and few of the bombers reaching the target.§ This was the last raid of the war in which all available bombers, up to 800 in number, attacked in a single bomber stream.

The Battle of Berlin had been fought against a back-drop of somewhat dispiriting conclusions about the impact of the bombing on Germany's economic performance. The quarterly report on this subject, issued by the JIC on 4 March, recorded that in MEW's view the impact had been less impressive in the last quarter of 1943 than in the two previous quarters; industrial production had not recovered from the damage previously inflicted, but the rate of

---

* See below, p 309 et seq.   † See below, p 416, 435.
‡ See Volume III Part 2.   § See Appendix 21 (ii).

54. Webster and Frankland, op cit, Vol II, pp 204–205.
55. AIR 40/2393.

decline had slowed down.[56]* And during the first quarter of 1944, as the JIC noted in its next report in June, MEW had been still more modest in its claims. It had not only been unable to detect any decline in the level of output since the summer of 1943, but except in relation to the machine tool industry, where it thought a loss of production of about 10 per cent attributable to the air offensive was beginning to have serious effects on armament production, had also found it impossible to establish how far the lack of recovery was due to bombing and how far to other factors.[58] These assessments, however, reflected as much on the effectiveness of the US daylight offensive against precision targets as they did on that of area bombing, particularly as the daylight offensive had given high priority to attacks on ball-bearing factories since August 1943 in an effort to disrupt Germany's war industry;† and if only for that reason Bomber Command's turning away from Berlin was not accompanied by any immediate retreat from its belief that German morale would disintegrate before D-day. But that belief had faded by the spring.

It had remained high at the end of January 1944, the authorities in Whitehall being undeterred by the optimistic tone of the decrypts from the Japanese embassy in Berlin. In two reports at the end of December 1943 the embassy admitted that the raids in November had caused severe damage, but stressed that electricity and water supplies had quickly been restored and claimed that the popular resolve to continue the war was not faltering. In January the Japanese Ambassador repeated this claim: 'Internal collapse will certainly not be brought about by means of air raids; the vicissitudes of the war situation as a whole will constitute spiritually, as well as otherwise, the most important factor'.[59] On receiving this last decrypt AI was finally moved to comment on 26 January that the Ambassador's view was in direct conflict with a substantial body of evidence from competent first-hand observers in Berlin and else-

---

* See above, pp 298–299, for the assessments for the first half of 1943. The assessments for the last quarter were not dissimilar to those given in the decrypted telegrams of the Japanese embassy in Berlin. In October 1943 the Ambassador claimed that the bombing was not obstructing munitions production. Early in January 1944, in a review of bomb damage for the period from 22 November to mid-December, he repeated that the munitions industry had not been seriously disturbed. Early in February 1944 he was more positive: despite the raids, Germany's war potential was expanding, especially the production of aircraft, tanks and 'other important weapons', though it was difficult to estimate the extent of the expansion'.[57]

† See Appendix 17.

56. JIC (44) 80 of 4 March.
57. Dir/C Archive, 5592 of 5 February 1944.
58. JIC (44) 241 of 13 June.
59. Dir/C Archive, 5470 of 26 January 1944.

where'.* It was no doubt referring in particular to reports received from such sources as foreigners with contacts in Germany and German businessmen visiting neutral capitals, which the SIS had begun to circulate in a new series to the Service ministries, the Foreign Office and other departments at the beginning of the year.† But the most recent of these reports, circulated on 21 January, had been open to different interpretations. It had claimed that morale was bad, without any signs of improvement; but had also admitted that the German authorities were making some impact with propaganda stressing the horrors that would follow if Germany capitulated, and that the SS's surveillance ruled out any question of revolt.[61] Nor did the SIS's informants become less equivocal after the end of January.

A collection of reports circulated on 22 February included one from a visitor to Berlin who had witnessed in January instances of shaken morale bordering on panic, but another observer, while contrasting the growth of anti-Nazi feeling in Berlin with the pro-Nazi sentiment of the provinces, added that unrest in Berlin was usually a short-lived reaction to a raid.[62] On 24 February the SIS reported a German businessman as saying that morale in Berlin had been badly shaken by the January raids but quoted a Finnish businessman as believing that the situation there was best described as one of apathy.[63] The word 'apathy' had already appeared in a Foreign Office report on German morale of 8 February; this had concluded that if no threat to the Nazi regime had yet emerged, it was because the population was in such a state of physical, mental and nervous exhaustion that it could envisage no alternative to the present government.[64]

On 25 February the AOC-in-C Bomber Command protested to the Air Staff against the growing use of the term 'apathy' as a description of the average German's reaction to heavy bombing. The Deputy Chief of the Air Staff replied on 29 March: 'The word

---

* The decrypt and this comment are attached to a minute of 26 January from D of I (O) instructing the Air Intelligence Branch to send the gist of such decrypts together with its own comments to the Chief Intelligence Officer at Bomber Command. At this stage the hopes of Bomber Command were clearly shared in many departments in the Air Ministry.[60]

† The only copy of reports in this series which we have been able to find is in the Dir/C Archive, which contains only such of them as were brought to the attention of the Prime Minister.

60. Air Historical Branch, II G/142/1/54/2, Minute from D of I (0) to A1, 26 January 1944.
61. Dir/C Archive, 5740, No 22 of 21 January 1944.
62. ibid, 5713, No 56 of 22 February 1944.
63. ibid, 5834, No 57 of 24 February 1944.
64. CAB 66/46, WP (44) 93 of 8 February.

"apathy" is used by so many independent witnesses that we must tend to accept it as a fair description of the general state of mind'; on the other hand, 'apathy created in ever-widening circles, and on a continuing downward trend, is likely to be fatal to the German war effort, and therefore apathy as a term should not in itself be regarded as derogatory to the effects of air bombardment'.[65] The term had meanwhile been repeated on 4 March in the JIC's next quarterly summary of intelligence on the effects of the bombing offensive. This argued that although the offensive had 'deepened apathy' throughout Germany and 'spread various forms of defeatism' in raided areas, 'the security services are still strong enough to suppress any serious disturbances'.[66] The word 'apathetic' had been used again in a report from the SIS representative in Switzerland, circulated on 7 March. But he had gone on to say that since the middle of February there was less evidence of open unrest; morale had improved since the news of Anzio, and the German authorities had had some success with propaganda to the effect that they were confident of repelling the Anglo-American invasion attempt.[67] And on 14 March the SIS had issued a report from a reliable source in touch with the German Chamber of Commerce in Stockholm which claimed that the bombing was seriously disrupting the administrative apparatus of government and private firms, but had had little effect on morale.[68]

It does not seem unreasonable to infer from these reports that by the middle of February the bombing had brought Germany to a crisis of morale which she had barely survived, and she might well have succumbed to it if Bomber Command had not then been forced to disperse its efforts. This was clearly implied in the decrypts of two telegrams sent from Berlin by the Japanese Naval Attaché at the end of March and the Japanese Ambassador at the end of April. According to the Attaché, the situation would certainly have been alarming and critical if the bombing had been intensified until it outstripped the defences, but in the event 'the apparent self-confidence of the German leader, the thoroughness of air raid precautions, and the immediate use of troops and SS detachments in the industrial cities after Allied air attacks have sufficed to maintain German morale and to surmount for the time being the crisis brought on by the social unrest caused by the bombing of towns and cities'.[69] According to the Ambassador, morale in Berlin had

---

65.   Air Historical Branch, II G/142/2/5/1, Letter from DCAS to ACM Harris, 29 March 1944.
66.   JIC (44) 80 of 4 March.
67.   Dir/C Archive, 5945, No 69 of 7 March 1944.
68.   ibid, 6008, No 74 of 14 March 1944.   69.   SJA 116.

been at its lowest ebb in January and February but, because the government had used its enormous power and influence well, the fighting spirit of the people had been intensified 'to the pitch of seeing no course but to fight to the finish'. But these telegrams were not decrypted till the beginning of May, by which time the JIC had concluded on 10 April and again on 1 May that a collapse of German resistance before D-day for *Overlord* was most improbable.*

The SIS had meanwhile circulated on 16 April a report by an informant in Berlin; apathy continued, with indifference to the loss of territory on the eastern front and to propaganda efforts to increase anti-western sentiment, but so did fear of the consequences of capitulation, and there was no sign of organised opposition.[70] On 20 May the same source repeated that the SS was penetrating every institution, and added that political instruction and a concealed system of political control by commissars were being introduced into the armed forces, and that the government's propaganda was emphasising that if Germany could prolong the war by repelling the Allied invasion 'some unforeseen stroke of luck' might enable her to conclude a satisfactory peace.[71] The JIC incorporated his views on 3 June in its next survey of intelligence on the effects of the Allied bombing. Remarking on the 'fairly successful' efforts of the German propaganda and security sevices to maintain morale on the home front, this concluded: 'Though the eventual success of their efforts depends on a successful repulse of the Allied invasion of the west, and though they have for some time been unable to arrest the steady decline in the over-all war effort of the civilian population, these two influences remain strong enough to preserve order and prevent a breakdown in the administration of the country or the rise of organised opposition to the regime. While, therefore, we cannot rule out the possibility of a collapse occurring suddenly, especially if Allied military successes in the east and in the west transform the present anxiety into something approaching panic, there is no evidence to suggest that the Allied bombing may shortly foment any effective opposition to the regime, or that the stamina and discipline of the German people have deteriorated to such an extent that a collapse may be considered likely within the next month or so'.[72]

□

---

* See above, pp 43, 46.

70. Dir/C Archive, 6273, No 105 of 16 April 1944.
71. ibid, 6337, No 140 of 20 May 1944.
72. JIC (44) 228 (o) of 3 June.

The AOC-in-C Bomber Command had meanwhile acknowledged that his hopes had been frustrated by the German night-
fighters. On 7 April, pleading for long-range fighter protection for
the bombers, he told the Air Ministry that he had 'long foreseen
. . . that the strength of the German air defences would eventually
reach a point at which night bombing with existing methods and
types of heavy bomber would produce percentage casualty rates
which could not in the long run be sustained'. He felt that 'we have
not yet reached this point' but went on to say that 'tactical innovations which have so far postponed it are now practically exhausted'.[73] This was indeed the case, but not only on account of the
inability of the Allies to prevent the increase in German fighter
production. The success of the night-fighters had also rested on the
development by the German Air Force of new and unsuspected air
defence techniques. Bomber Command's doctrine of area bombing
was bound up with the belief that though its bombers were big,
vulnerable, lightly-armed and unescorted, they could in hours of
darkness rely for survival on evasion. The German night-fighter
force had confounded this belief by introducing since the autumn of
1943 new methods of interception which, circumventing the
counter-measures which the British had introduced against its
previous methods of interception, enabled it to inflict increasing
casualties on the bombers.

For general early warning of raids the Germans relied on their
radars, notably the long-range *Freya*. The British had successfully
jammed *Freya* for a brief period from the end of 1942 with 'Mandrel',
but for over a year from the spring of 1943 the Germans defeated
'Mandrel' by pushing up the frequency of *Freya* until it was out of
reach.[74] 'Window', the next important British counter-measure, was
introduced in July 1943 with the aim of jamming the main elements
in the German defence system – the Ground Controlled Interception
(GCI) *Würzburg* radars of the Kammhuber line, which vectored
the night-fighters on to individual bombers until they were close
enough to locate the bombers by Air Interception apparatus (AI);
the AI apparatus (*Lichtenstein*) used by the night-fighters; and the
gun-laying *Würzburg* radars used by the enemy's Flak and searchlight batteries.* In the bombing raids on Hamburg and the Ruhr
between 24 July and 1 August the Enigma decrypts and Kingsdown's R/T intercepts showed that 'Window''s success was respon-

---

* See Volume II pp 252 et seq, 517 et seq.

73. Webster and Frankland, op cit, Vol III (1961), p 147.
74. *Bomber Command Counter-Measures*, p 41; AIR 20/1683, ASI Interim Report
on the Effect of 'Window' on German Night Defences of 4 October 1943;
Price, *Instruments of Darkness* (1967), p 129.

sible for Bomber Command's initially low rate of casualties.* But the British were disappointed in their hope that the Germans would take between six months and a year to overcome 'Window'. By the end of July, while it was clear from the Enigma that the enemy Flak had been forced to go over to pre-radar methods of barrage fire and sound ranging,† the Enigma and the R/T had also disclosed that some night-fighters, their box controls disrupted,‡ were being told to freelance, that freelancing single-engined day-fighters were also operating above the bomber streams, and that ground stations were broadcasting on R/T a running commentary on the movements of the bombers.[75]

The Enigma had previously shown that the Germans had been experimenting in recent weeks with two new methods of ground-controlled fighting which would enable the controller to locate a fighter and direct it to a bomber stream without interruption from 'Window': one used the *Freya-AN* and the other (called *Benito* by the British) the *Y-Gerät* system.§ Together with indications from the Enigma that the *Würzburgs* were still finding some gaps in the 'Window' cloud, that *Lichtenstein*, though greatly disturbed by 'Window', was still being used, and that night-fighters controlled by *Benito* were still operating in the box system, this intelligence at first encouraged the hope in Whitehall that radar ground-control rather than the new freelance visual tactics, which could not be disrupted by interference with the enemy's radars, would continue to be the backbone of the German night-fighter organisation.[76] At the beginning of August, however, in view of the fact that the defences had also been experimenting 'for the last few weeks' with the freelance operation of both night-fighters and single-engined fighters, ADI (Sc) warned that they might 'permanently adopt this tactic when possible' unless they could be discouraged by such measures as an increase in the RAF's intruder patrols.[77] But intruder patrols were unable to counter the freelance system, which enabled the German fighters to fall back to bases beyond the range of Fighter Command's Beaufighters, and during the next few weeks it became all too plain

---

* An agent at a German night-fighter station also reported on 'Window''s success, using the pigeon service operated by the RAF and the SIS to do so; his report made it possible to circulate the news to Bomber Command's crews.

† For 'Window''s success against the enemy's Flak defences, see Appendix 18.

‡ For the box control system see Volume II, pp 255–256.

§ For the *Y-Gerät* system see Volume I, p 559 et seq.

75. AIR 20/1661, ASI Report No IV of 3 August 1943; *Bomber Command Counter-Measures*, p 51; *Air Ministry Intelligence*, pp 163, 310; RV Jones, *Most Secret War* (1978), pp 279, 300–301, 305; Price, op cit, p 141.

76. AIR 20/1661.   77. ibid.

that the Germans were making extensive use of the new tactics and had 'discarded almost entirely their box-control system'.[78]

Without foreknowledge that the British were preparing to resort to 'Window', the Germans had paved the way for their prompt response to that development by experimenting since the early summer with new methods of operating their night-fighters. In the first place, utilising the fact that most of the fighters were by then equipped with AI (*Lichtenstein*), they had reduced the rigidity of the box system of control in the Kammhuber line by operating several fighters simultaneously, one fighter being under control and the others freelancing. At the same time – and this represented a bigger step towards independence from ground control – they had tested a system called *Wilde Sau* in which single-engined day-fighters sought out the bombers over their targets and attacked them from above. To begin with, the fighters, making frequent landings for refuelling and rearming, had relied on the light of the fires and Pathfinder flares in the target area, but after achieving some success over Cologne on 3 July they had co-operated with Flak and search-lights over Hamburg to still greater effect at the end of that month. From that point *Wilde Sau* underwent rapid development. By the time of the raid on Peenemünde on 17 August*, against which it was used on a large scale, the Germans had begun to expand the number of single-engined fighters available for night-fighting, had decreed that all twin-engined fighter squadrons were to resort to *Wilde Sau* when they could not use other methods of interception, and had further improved the system by installing beacons, first visual and then radio, around which the fighters could congregate until they received on the R/T running commentary such information about the imminence of a raid and about its likely target as was obtained from early-warning radar and the visual and aural observations of the Observer Corps (the Flugmeldedienst).[79] And by the end of September the new system, which so effectively circumvented 'Window', had become established as the standard night-fighter procedure.

Although *Wilde Sau* effectively circumvented 'Window', and was proof against any other counter-radar measures that might be developed, it was vulnerable to tactical counter-measures. Since it was used to summon fighters from all over the Reich to the assembly beacons selected by the controllers in the light of their plots of impending raids,[80] the running commentary was broadcast on

* See below, p 382.

78. AIR 20/1683.
79. AIR 41/10, pp 276–277; Price, op cit, pp 145–147, 167.
80. AIR 41/10, pp 277–278; Price, op cit, p 168.

high-powered transmitters.* Intercepted regularly by Kingsdown from the middle of August, this soon disclosed that the forecasts of the likely targets made by the *Wilde Sau* controllers were sometimes inaccurate. During the Peenemünde raid the intercepts showed that, because the controllers first thought that the target was to be Berlin, the fighters had arrived late; but that they had nevertheless inflicted heavy casualties. In the three deep penetration raids against Berlin between 23 August and 3 September, the R/T showed that *Wilde Sau* had worked to great effect, fighters being drawn in from as far afield as northern Denmark and central France, and that Bomber Command's casualties, higher than it could afford for long, would have been still higher if the controllers had not been mistaken in calculating the return route chosen for the bombers after the second raid. During a raid on Mannheim on 5 September it became clear from the commentary that bomber losses were kept down because the controller made the mistake of first sending the fighters to Nuremberg.[82] It was as a result of these experiences that Bomber Command, whose first response to the introduction of *Wilde Sau* had been to try to jam the running commentary,† brought into force from the night of 22–23 September, with what ADI(Sc) was later to criticise as undue delay, those tactical counter-measures – deceptive routeing and diversionary raids to confuse and mislead the German controllers – which down to the end of the war were to be of some assistance in reducing its casualties.[83]

Bomber Command's operations staff was guided in its use of these counter-measures mainly by the intelligence obtained from Kingsdown's interception of the R/T running commentary, which was prolific and uninhibited, the Germans paying no regard to radio security. The staff received the intelligence both in the form of current information, teleprinted from Kingsdown, and in the daily analyses of the enemy's activities in the previous twenty-four hours (the BMPs) which the Air Section at GC and CS produced

---

* It also called for a higher level of control, the controllers of the individual GCI boxes being replaced by control from the HQs of Germany's five Jagd divisions. The subordination of most night-fighter units to the Jagd divisions and their deployment were known from the Enigma; this showed that a large reorganisation took place at the end of October, when Fliegerkorps XII became Jagdkorps I and its subordinate Jagd divisions were re-numbered. Early in 1944 it disclosed the creation of two further Jagdkorps and the subordination of the Jagdkorps to a new Luftflotte Reich.[81]

† See Appendix 19 for details of the jamming efforts.

81. Air Sunsets 115 of 31 October 1943, 464 of 6 February 1944.
82. *Bomber Command Counter-Measures*, p 67; Webster and Frankland, op cit, Vol II, pp 159, 164–165; Price, op cit, pp 168–169, 171.
83. *Bomber Command Counter-Measures*, pp 58, 69; Webster and Frankland, op cit, Vol II, p 202.

after interpreting the R/T in the light of intelligence obtained from the Enigma and such low-grade codes as those which transmitted radar plots and the reports of the enemy Observer Corps.* Once the positions of all the German assembly beacons had been located – a piece of research that was accomplished during September and October, partly by comparing bomber crew reports and DF bearings with the running commentary, but primarily with the aid of documents seized by a Belgian agent of the SIS from the pilot of a crashed night-fighter[84] – Bomber Command appears normally to have made efficient use of the intelligence when planning routes and diversionary raids.† Certainly the R/T commentary disclosed that on many nights the deception measures had been of some value in containing Bomber Command's losses.[86] But from the beginning of December, when the losses began to rise to the prohibitive level which was to force Bomber Command to withdraw from the Battle of Berlin, it became clear that further major changes in Germany's night-fighter system were making the deception tactics progressively less effective.[87]

One of the improvements the Germans introduced had been foreseen by ADI(Sc) in October.[88] He had then concluded that if

---

* These GAF low-grade codes were now exploited at GC and CS, and not at Cheadle, because work on them interlocked with work on the Enigma; but Cheadle continued to contribute by working on other low-grade traffic, notably that of the W/T Safety Service which transmitted reports of night-fighter landings and threw much light on fighter movements.

† There were occasions when Bomber Command's planning was criticised, particularly for routeing bombers close to the fighter beacons (as, for example, in the costly raid on Nuremberg on 30–31 March 1944).[85] It is difficult to be sure whether the criticisms were justified. It was not easy to avoid both the beacons and the Flak-defended areas. On the other hand, there is some evidence that maximum use was not made of the conclusions built up by the BMPs. The Air Section at GC and CS complained that Bomber Command regarded the daily BMP narratives as too academic, and that although GC and CS produced from November 1943, at the suggestion of Group Captain Winterbotham, a quicker and briefer version of the daily BMP and longer term analyses of the R/T traffic over two monthly periods, the Air Ministry did not allow these papers (as opposed to the daily BMP narrative) to go to Bomber Command until February 1944 when, following a visit to GC and CS from the Deputy C-in-C of Bomber Command, arrangements were made to send the brief daily report to Bomber Command by despatch rider and a GC and CS representative was attached to Bomber Command so that it could be given the main details of the enemy's reactions to raids by telephone. GC and CS also criticised Bomber Command's earlier reliance on Kingsdown's teleprinter reports on the R/T intercepts which, it claimed, contained 'startling inaccuracies of interpretation'. But GC and CS may not have made enough allowance for the difficulties encountered by operational staff in operational conditions.

---

84. *Bomber Command Counter-Measures*, p 54 (n); *Air Ministry Intelligence*, p 311; Jones, op cit, p 383.

85. *Bomber Command Counter-Measures*, pp 54, 69; Webster and Frankland, op cit, Vol II, pp 164, 208–209.

86. AIR 41/43, p 125 and Appendix X, p 48; Webster and Frankland, op cit, Vol II, pp 199–299, 203.

87. Webster and Frankland, op cit, Vol II, p 204.   88. AIR 20/1683.

the present counter-measures – deceptive routeing and diversionary raids; the jamming of the R/T – succeeded in hampering the defences, the enemy would try to reduce the scope for evasive routeing and increase the time available to the fighters by intercepting the bombers at points farther away from their targets and nearer to their bases. This was, indeed, one feature of the new system, called *Zahme Sau* by the night-fighters, which had largely supplanted *Wilde Sau* by the late autumn of 1943; by February 1944 the fighters were sometimes flying out to meet the bombers over the North Sea.[89] ADI(Sc) had at the same time believed that such tactics would not greatly profit the defences 'as long as we can keep the German detection equipment neutralised . . .'. But it was another feature of *Zahme Sau* that, after obtaining early warning of raids from the plots of the long-range radars and information about the course of the bomber streams from the Observer Corps, the controller inserted into the stream a night-fighter controlled by *Benito* (and, after February 1944, by *Egon*).* This fighter enabled the controller to direct other fighters to the stream, either by emitting a DF note for other fighters to home on to[90] or by announcing that it was in contact so that the controller, knowing its position from *Benito* or *Egon*, could inform the waiting fighters by R/T.

Even more important, the fighter was helped in making and retaining contact by a new AI set, SN2,† which was immune from 'Window'. SN2 was the prerequisite for the introduction of *Zahme Sau*, and the key to its success, in that it made interception possible even though it was now taking place in darkness, away from the illumination provided by flares, searchlights and fires at the bombers' target. And before long the new system incorporated yet a third advance. For early warning of raids and plots of the bomber streams the Germans had hitherto relied mainly on their long-range radars, *Freya*, *Mammut* and *Wassermann*‡, whose frequencies had been moved out of reach of jamming by the summer of 1943, and on the sound locators and visual range-finders of the Observer Corps.§ They now introduced into service new detection devices which picked up the radiations emitted by the equipment used by the

---

* See Appendix 23.   † See Appendix 20.
‡ See Volume II, pp 251–252.
§ They were also alerted frequently by interception of the tuning signals which the bombers made before take-off, and sometimes by interception of the J-beams which Bomber Command switched on before a raid as a means of concealing the 'Gee' navigation system from the Germans,[91] (see Volume II, pp 266–268).

89. Webster and Frankland, op cit, Vol II, p 205, Vol III, p 129.
90. Air Sunset 135 of 4 January 1944.
91. AIR 41/10, p 27; Irving, op cit, p 229; Price, op cit, p 179.

bombers for the purposes of protection, navigation and communication – their Identification Friend or Foe equipment (IFF); their H2S centimetric ground-scanning radar; 'Oboe', their precision-navigation and bomb-aiming aid; and 'Monica', which gave them radar warning of fighters approaching from astern. Together with SN2, these passive radar devices, which could not be intercepted and jammed, were the essential basis of *Zahme Sau*, the method of route-interception which constituted 'the ultimate counter to the bomber tactics' and was to remain so 'as long as the German fighter force lasted as an effective operational weapon'.[92]

The date at which the Germans brought SN2 into force is stated by different accounts to have been August, September or October 1943.[93] Not until February 1944, however, did it become clear from occasional references by the intelligence sources to new equipment that *Lichtenstein* was being replaced by a new AI set, and that this must go some way to account for the increase in British bomber losses. The search for the frequency of the new set was then begun but it met with no success until July 1944, when an SN2 set was recovered from a German night-fighter which landed intact and by mistake in East Anglia. SN2 had by then operated without interference and to great effect for some nine months. Various radiation detection devices, the earliest of which were ground-based, for exploiting the Allied bombers' radar emissions were also coming into use by October 1943. In that month the Germans began to create a tracking organisation in which the plots obtained by the new devices were at first collated by a selected GCI station in the area of each Jagd division.[94] This organisation, which was eventually amalgamated with the Observer Corps into a single service called the Flugwegverfolgung (route-tracking) service, enabled the Germans to replace the *Wilde Sau* system with the *Zahme Sau* system before the end of the year. But the existence of this service was apparently not suspected by British intelligence until the summer of 1944, when, on the basis of Enigma decrypts, ADI(Sc) recorded that the Germans had formed a widespread raid-tracking organisation thought to be following H2S and H2X.[95]*

---

* H2X, the next advance on H2S, worked on a wavelength of 3 cm and was used by the USAAF. (For details of H2S see Volume II, p 513, and Webster and Frankland, op cit, Vol IV, Annex I.)

92.   Webster and Frankland, op cit, Vol III, p 129.
93.   AIR 41/10, p 27; Jones, op cit, p 393; Price, op cit, pp 179, 195; Irving, op cit, p 229.
94.   *Bomber Command Counter-Measures*, pp 55–57; Price, op cit, p 175; Irving, op cit, p 239.
95.   AIR 20/1652, ASI Report No 73 of 13 July 1944.

The scale on which Germany had developed radiation detection devices, both airborne and ground, had meanwhile also gone largely unsuspected. Enigma decrypts of some unidentifiable plot reports began to be received in October 1943. In December ADI(Sc), who had already recognised some of these as plots of Mark I (non-centimetric) 'Oboe', deduced that the others were plots of the transmissions of the bombers' IFF sets; and in January he warned that the Germans would 'probably try other radiations should we now thwart them on IFF and we shall therefore need to be even more circumspect than before in our use of all radio equipment which involves continual transmissions from our aircraft'.[96] Later in January 1944, when the Germans' exploitation of IFF had been confirmed by a proving flight, Bomber Command forbade the use of IFF over enemy territory; at the same time it brought into force Mark II (centimetric) 'Oboe'. But the bombers did not entirely relinquish the use of IFF over Germany until March, and, despite ADI(Sc)'s January observation, it was not until May that Bomber Command could be given definite proof that its bombers were being tracked with plots obtained from their 'Oboe', H2S and other transmissions.[97] This discovery, made on the basis of Enigma fragments, was confirmed in detail by documents captured in Normandy in June; in July, when the recovery of equipment from a night-fighter had provided further evidence, ADI(Sc) reported that the enemy was plotting no less than eight different types of transmissions from the bombers, including W/T and R/T as well as centimetric radar.[98]*

This delay owed something to the fact that, while it was accepted that the Germans could listen to centimetric radar, having recovered the apparatus from the many bombers that had crashed, the British technical experts were reluctant to acknowledge that they could, within a few months, have learned to exploit the centimetric transmissions for plotting and homing.† But it must also be stressed that it was extremely difficult to obtain firm intelligence about the enemy's detection devices. The devices were passive radar receivers, not active radar transmitters working on frequencies that might have been intercepted. No relevant documents were captured before June 1944. No equipment could be recovered in the United Kingdom until the night-fighter landed there in error in July 1944. POW

---

* See Appendix (21) 1 for further details.

† As late as April 1944 RAF night-fighters equipped with a centimetric AI homing device, were forbidden to operate over enemy territory.

96. AIR 20/1668, ASI Report No VI of 8 January 1944; *Air Ministry Intelligence*, P 334.
97. AIR 20/5804, ADI (Sc) Minute to Bomber Command, 4 May 1944.
98. AIR 20/1652.

and agents' reports, mostly vague or wild on such matters as radar, were unhelpful unless they could be assessed and corrected in the light of more reliable sources; and Sigint, the only reliable source in the absence of captured material, was sparse and difficult to understand. On the other hand, so great was Bomber Command's reliance on radar and jamming for reducing its casualties, and for accuracy in navigation and bombing, that it could not curtail or abandon the use of them without firm evidence that they were as much a liability as they were an asset. It was not for nothing that the scientific and technical intelligence authorities preferred to pronounce 'only . . . when a reasonably complete or important picture is obtained' and regarded this as 'the best way of stimulating action'.[99]

The discovery at the end of June that the German defences were making effective use of a wide range of detection devices, and that 'the only way to deny this information to the enemy is to stop all transmissions from our aircraft',[100] did, indeed, present Bomber Command with a dilemma. At the end of February it had briefly reduced its casualties by diverting much of its effort to less well defended target areas well south of Berlin, but the German night-fighters had quickly filled the vacuum there. In March Bomber Command had again obtained temporary relief while some of its operations were directed against *Overlord* targets in France; but before long the night-fighters had begun to intercept over France. During April, May and June, when it was in any case increasingly engaged in shallow-penetration raids in support of *Overlord*, it had kept its casualty rate down. But it had done so by departing from the aims and tactics it had adopted since early in 1942, and at the expense of reduced pressure on Germany. Only 25 per cent of its sorties were over Germany in May, only 10 per cent in June, as compared with 40 per cent in April. From the end of June it knew that, if it was to avoid heavy casualties in the absence of any effective means of countering the night-fighters, it had either to abandon the concentrated area bombing offensive altogether or stultify it by denying the bombers the assistance of their indispensable radar aids.

This dilemma was short-lived. In August 1944, not long after it was recognised, the problem was resolved by other developments. After devoting much of its effort to daylight bombing in June and July* despite its inexperience in this type of operation, Bomber Command was then able to return to large-scale night-bombing – and, more than that, to establish night-time air superiority over

---

* See Volume III Part 2.

99. *Air Ministry Intelligence*, p 308.   100. AIR 20/1652

Germany and make full use of the capacity for accurate night-bombing which it had been developing since the end of 1943 – primarily because the German night-fighter defences were collapsing as a result of inadequate training of pilots and shortage of fuel, as well as from the loss of their network of early warning ground radars to the advance of the Allied armies.

□

Indications to the effect that deficiencies in the training of pilots and a shortage of fuel were handicapping the German Air Force, if not as yet its night-fighter operations in defence of the Reich, had appeared in the intelligence sources before the end of 1943. These earlier indications – which included the fact that reconnaissance flights had been reduced[101] and the disclosure that test-pilots and ferry-pilots were being called on to operate fighters against the USAAF's daytime raids[102] – had been followed in January 1944 by the news, disclosed by the Enigma, that Hitler had ordered a cutback in the meteorological service and a reduction in the period of recuperation allowed to the wounded. Thereafter, while the Enigma showed that the Germans were combing-out GAF non-combatants, in an effort to provide more fighter pilots as well as to meet the needs of their land forces,[103] the USAAF had exploited and intensified the GAF's deficiencies so effectively, and particularly its shortage of trained pilots, that by the beginning of April it had established daytime air superiority over western Europe.

The USAAF had resumed its deep-penetration raids in the second week of January, and had extended them as its long-range Mustang fighters became available in increasing numbers. By the middle of February the Enigma had shown that its raids were imposing a high wastage rate on the German single-engined fighters and that in combat with its P 51 Mustangs the enemy's twin-engined rocket firing aircraft were having to be escorted by single-engined fighters.[104] During 'Big Week', a programme of accurate precision attacks on an unparalleled scale on which the USAAF embarked on 20 February, it claimed to have destroyed 600 fighters. The claim was greatly exaggerated,* but that German losses were

---

* One authority states that Luftflotte Reich lost 225 fighters in daylight operations in February, 236 in March and 343 in April. In addition, Luftflotte 3 in France and the Low Countries lost 338 fighters between the beginning of February and the end of May.[105]

101. CX/MSS/T44/38, T60/55; *Air Ministry Intelligence*, p 77.
102. Air Sunset 119 of 14 November 1943.
103. Air Sunset 142 of 6 February 1944.
104. Air Sunset 146 of 18 February 1944.
105. AIR 41/49, *The Air Defence of Great Britain*, Vol V, pp 295, 297.

rising was so clear, from Sigint as well as from combat reports, that the USAAF decided to give greater priority to the destruction of German fighters in direct combat. Beginning with a major attack on Berlin on 4 March, it suspended attacks on the aircraft production industry, ceased to route its raids with a view to avoiding the defences, and chose targets and routes with the aim of forcing the enemy fighters to do battle.

In the next four weeks it was estimated that the Germans lost at least 10 per cent of the fighters they committed against the USAAF's attacks, and that the wastage sometimes rose to 40 per cent. It also became clear that, though still offering determined opposition from time to time, the enemy's fighters were abstaining from all-out combat,[106] and the Enigma confirmed that this policy of conservation was being imposed by a critical shortage of fighter pilots; it referred to 'the present lack of men and material' and showed that bomber and transport pilots were being transferred to fighter units as a matter of emergency.[107] On 6 June the Japanese Naval Attaché, summing up the recent daylight attacks, reported that they had achieved considerable success: daylight attacks on Berlin indicated that the Germans were 'being crushed by overwhelming superiority'; the wastage of German fighters was 10 per cent of those engaged; mass German counter-attacks had been greatly reduced by the scale of the American attack; Allied claims that 20 per cent of German fighter production had been destroyed by the end of April were reasonably accurate.[108] By the beginning of April the USAAF had established that daytime air superiority over western Europe, including the Reich itself, which the Allies were to retain for the remainder of the war.

In the course of gaining this victory, which has been accounted 'one of the most decisive in the war in the air',[109] the USAAF commands were assisted by three types of intelligence from which, on account of the different nature of its operations, Bomber Command derived little benefit.

For help in studying and identifying their targets they relied on the target intelligence organisation under AI 3(c) at Hughenden Manor near High Wycombe, whose 'integrated' staff of 80 officers and 300 clerical assistants included US officers. It collated the product of research in the Service departments and MEW with all the information that it could collect from other sources – ISTD,

---

106.   W Craven and J Cate, *The Army Air Forces in World War II*, Vol III (Chicago 1951), pp 46–48.
107.   Air Sunsets 156 of 30 March, 165 of 24 April 1944.
108.   SJA 287 of 10 June 1944.
109.   Webster and Frankland, op cit Vol III, p 131.

CIU, POW, refugees, learned societies and professional associations, technical journals, insurance companies and other private firms – and carried out the elaborate process of turning the results of its labours into target maps and target illustrations for distribution to briefing officers and bomber crews.[110]* Its work did not influence the selection of targets, which was settled by the planning and intelligence staffs at the commands in the light of priorities laid down by Whitehall and the US authorities in London.[111] But it ensured that, whatever targets were selected for attack, Bomber Command, Eighth Air Force and Fifteenth Air Force (to which AI 3(c) sent its material by air) could be provided at short notice with the means of recognising and locating them. This kind of assistance was of far greater value to the USAAF's daylight precision raids than it was to Bomber Command's area bombing.†

In selecting their targets and planning their raids the commands found that, though it was supplemented by others, notably excellent PR, the GAF Enigma was the most important source of intelligence. The US Strategic Air Force, which was set up at the beginning of 1944 to command both the Eighth and Fifteenth Air Forces, recorded after the war that it was 'the root of our target intelligence' while the primary object was to destroy the GAF and establish air supremacy, in that it provided invaluable information on the enemy's order of battle, dispositions, production, wastage, casualties, serviceability and reserves.[112]‡ The Enigma also regularly supplied reliable weather reports for the European area, the value of which to the planning of operations may be judged from the fact that the

---

* The scale of its activities may be judged from the fact that for each of over 3,000 individual strategic targets 7,000 sets of material had to be made available for distribution to bomber crews and 1,500 sets for distribution to briefing officers, and that all the material had to be kept up to date by amendments. The production and distribution of material on tactical targets was an even more complex operation.

† But Bomber Command, whose selection of targets was made in the light of operational considerations rather than of MEW's priorities, took detailed target intelligence into account when selecting the bomb-aiming points within its targets; and it relied on it as heavily as did the USAAF when it was required to operate against such special targets as Peenemünde, the *Tirpitz*, the *Crossbow* sites, the Ruhr dams, U-boats pens and the communications network in France.

‡ Until the beginning of 1944 the US Strategic Air Force had received the Enigma only in the form of appreciations from the Air Ministry. Thereafter, having moved its HQ to the SHAEF building at Bushy Park, it received the decrypts direct from GC and CS, though it continued to assess them in close consultation with the specialist sections of the Intelligence Branch in the Air Ministry.

110.   *Air Ministry Intelligence*, p 242 et seq.
111.   W Rostow, *Eisenhower's Pre-Invasion Bombing Strategy* (1981), Chapter 1.
112.   R Lewin, *Ultra Goes to War* (1978), p 297.

forecast of a few days of suitable weather entirely determined the time chosen for the launching of 'Big Week' in February.[113]*

The Enigma was especially valuable to the USAAF's offensive against aircraft on the ground, at airfields, depots and training stations, which was perhaps even more important than the attempt to reduce the German fighter force by direct combat. The intelligence that was most useful in combat, on the other hand, as distinct from that which helped in the selection of targets and planning of raids, came from the R/T of the German day-fighters. The potential value of this traffic for the information it provided on such matters as the take-off times of the fighters, the routes they followed when assembling, their intentions to intercept and their tactics in combat was established by GC and CS's daily BMPs. Eighth Air Force's Fighter Command had received these since April 1943; its Bomber Command had received them from a still earlier date. In the summer of 1943, after much trial and error following the first attempt to turn the intelligence to operational account during the Dieppe raid,† the Kingsdown Hook-up had been set up. This met a need which did not exist for Bomber Command but which was of great importance for the American fighter-escorted daylight operations – the need to pass the intelligence to the fighters while they were airborne.‡ During 1943 Eighth Air Force had derived only limited operational benefit from the Hook-up and the BMP analyses of the R/T traffic. It had made use of the R/T intelligence about the rendez-vous points used by the German fighters to develop a relay-escort procedure which prolonged the length of time its bombers would be given fighter protection. This had been of some value in countering the practice by which the German fighters normally held back from attacking the deep-penetration raids until the short-range US fighters had come to the end of their endurance and the US bombers were without fighter protection. But it had not enabled the USAAF to avoid the heavy losses which forced it to

---

* The Enigma was by no means the only source of weather intelligence. The Meteorological Section at GC and CS derived its weather forecasts from a wide range of Sigint sources; and weather reports were received regularly from the Polish resistance.[114] But some of the best reports, such as those covering the whole of Europe that the SS regularly issued from Cracow, came from Enigma decrypts.[115]

† See Volume II, pp 273, 695–704.

‡ The Hook-up used four inter-communicating telephone circuits to co-ordinate the work of the R/T intercept stations, to assemble their intercepts and DF bearings at Kingsdown, to discuss the interpretation of this raw material and to pass considered operational assessments as fast as possible to the controllers at the HQs of Eighth Air Force and other users – some Fighter Command Groups, Coastal Command and, from December 1943, Bomber Command's No 100 Group. (For the establishment of No 100 Group RAF see Appendix 19.)

113.   Craven and Gate, op cit, Vol III, pp 31–32.
114.   Lewin, op cit, p 295.
115.   ibid, p 384.

abandon deep-penetration raids and confine itself to attacks in north-west Germany from October 1943.* From that date, however, the USAAF planned for the resumption of deep-penetration raids from the beginning of 1944, when its long-range Mustang fighters would become available, in close consultation with the BMP party in the Air Section at GC and CS; and at the same time GC and CS and the Air Ministry took measures to improve the service given to Eighth Air Force through the BMPs and the Hook-up. In November GC and CS's analyses of the activity of the German day-fighters, as of the night-fighters, were tightened up, the daily BMP being supplemented by a special bulletin after each major operation and by condensed surveys of the latest developments which were tele-printed to Eighth Air Force HQ and all its fighter formations after every six operations.[116] In December the head of GC and CS's day-fighter section was transferred to Kingsdown to be the chief intelligence officer of the Hook-up.

These improvements bore fruit when the US deep-penetration raids were resumed in earnest with the Mustang fighters in February 1944. Everything that was known from the BMPs about the procedures and probable reactions of the German fighter controllers was applied to the planning of the operations carried out in 'Big Week'. On 24 February, for example, Eighth Air Force used the intelligence in its plan for co-ordinating major attacks in Poland, on Gotha and on Schweinfurt with raids against Dutch airfields, timed to hit the German fighters when they were preparing to intercept, and with a diversionary and costly raid by Fifteenth Air Force against the important ball-bearing factory at Steyr in Austria.[117] From the beginning of March the German defences testified to the efficiency of Eighth Air Force's use of this intelligence by ceasing to use R/T when assembling their fighters; but the intelligence parties at GC and CS and Kingsdown worked out a new method of timing the Mustang sweeps which enabled them to catch the German fighters as they were assembling, and which contributed a good deal to Eighth Air Force's success in its policy of deliberately seeking out the German fighters and forcing them to accept combat.[118]

By the end of March, in the course of winning daylight air superiority, Eighth Air Force had driven the enemy fighters from bases that were within R/T range of the United Kingdom. It is further evidence of the importance the US controllers attached to the R/T intelligence that steps were at once taken to meet this loss.

---

* See above p 296 and Volume II, pp 520.

116. *Air Ministry Intelligence*, pp 91, 93.
117. Craven and Gate, op cit, Vol III, pp 32, 52.
118. *Air Ministry Intelligence*, pp 92–93.

From April airborne R/T operators – German-speaking Americans –
were flying with the American raids to intercept raw material for
analysis at GC and CS and Kingsdown,* and preparations were
made for establishing an advanced Y centre on the continent, staffed
from Kingsdown, after the Allied armies had landed in France.†
But the US Strategic Air Force was deprived of tactical intelligence
between April and the Normandy landings – when most of its
operations were concentrated against *Overlord* targets and, from 15
May, against Germany's synthetic oil production.‡

---

* US Fifteenth Air Force, which could not profit at its bases in Italy from the Kingsdown
Hook-up and the BMP service, had made use of airborne operators since the previous
February. Nevertheless Fifteenth Air Force was able to analyse the nature and scale of
German resistance – sometimes extremely fierce – from pilots' reports, airborne R/T, PR
and Ultra signals from GC and CS.

† Though make-shift arrangements were made from November 1944, this centre did not
function until March 1945.[119]

‡ See Volume III Part 2.

119.   *Air Ministry Intelligence*, p 93.

CHAPTER 38

The German Air Offensive against the United Kingdom January to June 1944

BETWEEN April 1944, when the Allies achieved daylight air superiority over Germany, and August 1944, when they finally established virtually total control of the air, by night as well as by day, the German Air Force had withdrawn from what was to be its last bombing offensive against the United Kingdom. It embarked on this offensive with about 500 bombers and fighter-bombers, a scale of attack much larger than any it had attempted since 1941, in January 1944. But the last raid of the war against London with piloted aircraft took place on the night of 18–19 April; and except for a few intruder raids in East Anglia in March 1945, an intruder raid against East Anglian airfields on the night of 27–28 June 1944 was the last major piloted attack of the war against the United Kingdom.

German daylight bombing of the United Kingdom had virtually come to an end after the transfer to the Mediterranean in June 1943 of 60 per cent of Fliegerkorps IX's fighter-bombers and 50 per cent of the long-range bombers.[1]* It had ceased altogether before the end of the year. Small-scale night raids by fighter-bombers and bombers, including the new high speed Me 410 in its fighter-bomber role,† had continued against coastal towns, against London and against Allied air bases in East Anglia – indeed, they had increased

---

* See Volume II, pp 510–511.

† The Me 410 was a development of the Me 110 which had been the GAF's basic twin-engined fighter since 1939. AI 2(g) first reported on it in May 1943, shortly before it entered service, having obtained details of some of its outstanding characteristics from POW interrogation.[2] AI 2(g) expected it to be a fast day-fighter, but when it first appeared over the United Kingdom – in July 1943 – it was as a fighter-bomber[3]. Its use in this role had been foreshadowed in decrypts from the Enigma which disclosed at the beginning of that month that the Me 410 was likely to supplement other fighter-bombers in night operations and intruder raids over eastern England.[4] When a Me 410 was captured intact in Sicily AI 2(g) was able to report several characteristics hitherto unknown.[5] Enigma decrypts later disclosed that, with the Me 110, it was being used, armed with the 21 cm rocket projectile, against American bomber formations.[6]

1. Air Sunset 70 of 20 June 1943.
2. AIR 20/2166, AI 2(g) Report No 2175 of 20 May 1943.
3. AIR 41/49, *The Air Defence of Great Britain*, Vol V, p 205.
4. Air Sunset 73 of 5 July 1943.
5. *Air Ministry Intelligence*, p 362
6. Air Sunset 93 of 3 August 1943.

somewhat in frequency after the end of August, when the Enigma had disclosed that Peltz, the Commander of Fliegerkorps IX, had returned to Brussels to take up his old post as Angriffsführer England.[7] But they had done little damage and Peltz's small force had suffered heavy casualties.

The first sign that Peltz might be receiving reinforcements was given by the Enigma in the middle of December 1943; the decrypts on the subject stressed the necessity of keeping the movement absolutely secret[8] and were followed by elaborate W/T measures to simulate long-range bomber activity in northern Italy. They revealed, however, that four bomber Gruppen, two-thirds of the total bomber force in the northern Italy theatre, had been withdrawn to Germany with all their aircraft.[9] By 10 January 1944, when Enigma decrypts had established that all six of the bomber Gruppen in Italy had been withdrawn early in December and that another Gruppe had more recently moved from Germany to the Brussels area, the Air Ministry surmised that 'the GAF may intend retaliatory bombing of this country in the immediate future',[10] and it expected the bombing to take place mostly at night against London. The first of the GAF's large-scale raids on the United Kingdom followed on the night of 21–22 January. The enemy had intended to begin the offensive at the end of December, but had been delayed by the bad weather.[11]

Before the opening of the offensive the Air Ministry had estimated that the reinforcements would bring Peltz's force to about 500 aircraft – the actual figure was 524 – and would make possible a maximum effort of up to 350 sorties in one raid, an intensive effort of up to 200 sorties on two or three nights a week and a sustained effort of no more than 75 sorties a night.[12] This scale of attack was far larger than any delivered against the United Kingdom since 1941, and far larger than the Air Ministry had bargained for before receiving the unexpected news that bombers were being removed from Italy. In July 1943 it had assumed that the German bomber effort would not again rise above 150 bombers and a maximum of between 75 and 100 sorties. Moreover, as the CAS explained to the Prime Minister in a long and somewhat defensive memorandum on 3 January 1944, counter-measures which the Air Ministry had decided on in July 1943 against the possible resort by the GAF to 'Window' in operations over the United Kingdom had fallen behind

7. Air Sunset 70 of 20 June 1943; CX/MSS/3043/T32, 3105/T29, 3108/T8.
8. Air Sunset 129 of 13 December 1943. 9. ibid.
10. Air Sunsets 131 of 20 December 1943, 136 of 10 January 1944.
11. AIR 41/49, p 212.
12. ibid, p 209; Air Sunset 131 of 20 December 1943.

schedule, and would not be completed before March 1944*. But the CAS was nevertheless able to be reassuring because the GAF had been using 'Window' (which the Germans called *Düppel*) without great effect since October; and because he felt that the augmented German bomber force was unlikely to make effective attacks, the fighter squadrons allotted to the air defence of Great Britain, which had been halved in November 1943 by transfers to the commands that were preparing for *Overlord*, were not strengthened. The Air Ministry knew that the German bomber force had long neglected training for accurate bombing against defended targets, a fact that had been reflected in its poor performance over the United Kingdom in the small-scale raids in recent months, and it judged that the attacks would not be pressed home. It also knew that, in addition to resorting to 'Window' during its raids since October, the GAF had equipped its bombers with a backward-looking warning radar (*Neptun*) to warn against the approach of night-fighters, had carried out Pathfinder and flare-dropping experiments over the United Kingdom and had expanded and modified its radio aids to navigation and bombing accuracy.† But the use of *Düppel* had done little to increase the efficiency of the enemy's raids or reduce his casualties, and the counter-measures authorities were confident that they could neutralise the other developments.[13]

These estimates and expectations were largely borne out by events. *Düppel* and *Neptun* did not help the GAF to avoid heavy casualties; in the five months to the end of June, when the offensive was called off, the defences shot down 10 per cent of the bombers sent against the United Kingdom, and the GAF incurred other losses from accidents due to bad weather, inexperience and lack of training. Mainly for the same reasons, but also in some measure as a result of the work of the counter-measures authorities, the German bombers derived no great benefit, either, from the Pathfinder tactics and the radio aids on which they relied. In the initial raid aimed at London on 21–22 January – employing 447 aircraft, it was also the heaviest – they failed completely. Because the Germans had concentrated the bombers in conditions of strict W/T silence at the last possible moment, intelligence gave no tactical warning; but the bombing was wildly inaccurate – only half of the bombs fell on land and only 30 tons on London itself. The GAF's performance against London improved during the remainder of the offensive, and in two of the five raids carried out at the end of February the bombing

---

* See Appendix 22.　　　　　† See Appendix 23.

13.　AIR 41/49, pp 201, 209; Collier, *The Defence of the United Kingdom* (1957), pp 323–326.

reached a high standard of accuracy. But elsewhere the Pathfinders dropped their flares miles from the target areas and, as well as being off target, the follow-up bombing was widely scattered.[14]

After increasing during February despite the withdrawal of two of Peltz's bomber Gruppen for operations against Anzio* – a movement that was disclosed by the Enigma at the end of January[15] – the scale and tempo of the offensive declined from the beginning of March. At the same time, the GAF diverted some of its effort away from London to Bristol and Hull in the belief that they harboured invasion shipping.† And after the night of 18–19 April, when piloted aircraft carried out their last raid of the war against London, it devoted almost all its remaining effort to ineffective attacks against the ports where shipping was collecting for *Overlord*. On 25–26 April all Peltz's available bombers were thrown into two attacks on Portsmouth. Four further raids on Portsmouth followed before the end of the month. On 29–30 April 100 bombers, twelve of them carrying the FX bomb,‡ attacked a concentration of ships, including the battleship *King George V*, at Plymouth. In all these attacks the bombing was widely scattered and did little damage. In May, despite a change in the GAF's Pathfinding techniques, two large raids – against Bristol on 14–15 May and against Portsmouth on the following night – failed to reach the target, and smaller raids against other south coast ports did little damage in return for heavy losses. In June – following the Normandy landings – the GAF confined its operations over the United Kingdom to intruder raids against East Anglian airfields. Except that it briefly returned to such attacks in March 1945, an intruder raid on the night of 27–28 June was the last major attack of the war on the United Kingdom by piloted aircraft.[17]

The Enigma, which had given warning of the imminence of the offensive and accurate information about the size of the forces that the GAF planned to devote to it, provided little intelligence about the offensive once it had begun. It occasionally confirmed that the GAF's radio aids had been rendered ineffective by jamming. Before the FX raid of 29–30 April it disclosed that FX bombs had been brought into Bordeaux and that the GAF had knowledge of battleships in Plymouth. After the event it showed that FX-carrying Do

---

* See above, p 187.

† A GAF Enigma signal decrypted on 23 February reported the receipt of information to the effect that Bristol was full of important invasion shipping.[16]

‡ See below, p 337 et seq.

14. AIR 41/46, No 80 Wing RAF Historical Report, p 55; AIR 41/49, p 209.
15. Air Sunset 140 of 28 January 1944.
16. CX/MSS/T102/51.
17. AIR 41/49, pp 212–215, 222–223.

217s of III/KG 100 from the south of France had participated in the attack – knowledge that was corroborated by POW and captured documents.[18] But a good deal was learned about the performance of the enemy's radio aids and the effects of British jamming from POW interrogations,* and a variety of other sources frequently gave the defences notice of a raid one or two hours before the early-warning radar could do so. Kingsdown obtained such warnings from its interception and DF-ing of the bombers' R/T. Cheadle got them from its interception of signals in which the GAF notified Flak units in the Channel Islands and ships and naval stations between Dinard and Nantes that its bombers would be passing over, and also of signals (which Cheadle named 'Xylophone') in which in advance of a raid the Safety Service in France requested the activation of beacons and other navigational aids. The counter-measures authorities got them from their monitoring of transmissions from equipment in the bombers, the *Neptun* set and a radio altimeter (FuGe 214), and from their ability to detect that the bombers had switched from the *Sonne* to the *Elektra* system of beacons,† a procedure which the bombers used in conjunction with *Knickebein*† in an attempt to avoid jamming.[19]

It may be assumed that great efforts were made to take advantage of this tactical intelligence; that its value was recognised is confirmed by a general order for the conduct of British night-fighter operations which specified that standing patrols were to be mounted at strategic points 'when weather conditions are favourable and intelligence reports indicated that enemy activity is likely.'[20] But the surviving records suggest that tactical intelligence had little impact on operations, the weakness of the German offensive being largely due to lack of experience, poor training and limited resources. The burden of the offensive was borne by bombers designed before 1939 – the Ju 88, the He 111 and the Do 217 – with assistance from only a few of the new sub-stratospheric bombers – the Ju 188 and the He 177 – which Germany had deployed to squadrons in October 1943. As we shall now see, she had neglected the development of new aircraft until her requirements forced her to devote to the modernisation of her fighter and fighter-bomber arms such resources as were left over from the development of the V-weapons, the retaliatory programme

---

* See Appendix 23.

† See Appendix 23 for details of *Sonne* and *Elektra*. For *Knickebein* see Volume I, Appendix 11(ii).

18. Air Sunset 168 of 5 May 1944.
19. AIR 41/46, p 66; AIR 41/49, pp 199–200, 210; *Air Ministry Intelligence*, p 86; Cheadle Abridged War Diary, pp 10–11.
20. AIR 41/49, Appendix 26, p 1.

to which she had given first priority; and it was mainly because she was unable to launch the V-weapon offensive by the beginning of 1944 that she committed her inadequate bombers against the United Kingdom.

CHAPTER 39

Intelligence on Germany's New Aircraft and Aerial Weapons

L OOKING back at the end of the war, the intelligence branch at the Air Ministry considered that next only to providing intelligence about the order of battle and the operational intentions of enemy air forces, its main task had been 'to ensure that the enemy should not spring a surprise through some secret weapons or new type of aircraft or armament'.[1] The task grew enormously in importance, and in complexity, from the middle of the war, and especially from the middle of 1943.

In the first two years of the war the technical section of AI which carried it out (AI 1(g)) was fully occupied in examining the many enemy aircraft that crashed in the United Kingdom and other theatres of war. It was on this evidence above all that it based the standard books on the enemy's aircraft, aero-engines and air armament which, together with other recognition material, it produced for circulation to the front line air forces. Nor did it have any great incentive to pay much attention to information from the other sources – attachés, POW, agents, neutral observers, PR, captured documents, postal censorship, patent specifications – on which it was later to rely.[2] Until the end of 1941 the German Air Force, expecting to win the war with them, confined itself to bringing in modifications to the aircraft designed before 1939 – the Me 109 and 110, the Ju 87 and 88, the He 111 – and AI 1(g) felt confident that its inspection of crashed aircraft was keeping it sufficiently informed of the modifications.

It was the shock administered at the end of 1941 by the unheralded appearance of a new German aircraft, the FW 190, that forced AI to give more attention to the need for obtaining advance intelligence about new technical developments in the German Air Force. As a history of its technical section records, the introduction of the FW 190 'achieved considerable notoriety' in Whitehall because it 'imposed a temporary check on Allied technical superiority'; and it was all the more a 'disturbing debut' because the qualities of the aircraft, high performance combined with heavy armour and armament, were not fully appreciated until a FW 190 force-landed

---

1. *Air Ministry Intelligence*, pp 2–4, 484.
2. *Technical Intelligence Sources*, p 3; *Air Ministry Intelligence*, p 354 and Appendix B.

in Wales in June 1942.[3] But by the beginning of 1942, in response to this salutary experience, AI 1(g) had developed into AI 2(g), and whereas AI 1(g) had been content merely to collect and distribute the latest information about enemy aircraft types, AI 2(g) was a research section under the Director of Intelligence (Operations). The dissemination of reports to the commands on the characteristics of German aircraft and the preparation of recognition material for Allied aircrews continued to be an important part of its work; and the examination of crashed, surrendered or captured aircraft, for which it now set up inspection teams in all theatres of war whose activities it controlled from a central operations room in the Air Ministry, remained one of its chief sources of information.[4] But increasingly from that date it assumed responsibility for scrutinising and assessing intelligence from all sources on possible new developments in the German Air Force with a view to providing advance warning to the Air Staff and the Whitehall departments of the emergence of new types or sub-types of aircraft, new aero-engines and new armament, radar and other equipment.

The task of foreseeing innovations in these fields was not made easier by the fact that in 1942, when Germany at last gave high priority to bringing forward new aircraft, including jet aircraft, and to improving her existing types, the German Air Ministry still exercised only a loose control over the many German private aircraft and aero-engine companies which, in the hope of catching the eye of Hitler or Göring, worked on a large number of new developments simultaneously. Early in 1942 no fewer than forty different aircraft types were under development, and about 200 aircraft types and sub-types (which amounted to as many as twenty for a versatile aircraft) were in simultaneous production as late as March 1944.[5] From the spring of 1944 the Germans were finally forced to rationalise this situation because, on the one hand, the Allied air offensive began to overwhelm the German aircraft industry and, on the other, because they began to invest their hopes increasingly in jet fighters and the V-weapons.* Until then, however, AI 2(g)'s sources abounded with references to new developments of which few – which could not be known in advance – would culminate in any practical achievement. Some of its reports, moreover, were necessarily based on somewhat insubstantial evidence from agents, journalists and other observers not always blessed with technical

---

* See below, Chapter 41.

3. *Technical Intelligence Sources*, pp 2, 11.
4. *Air Ministry Intelligence*, pp 354–355 and Appendix C.
5. AIR 41/10, *The Rise and Fall of the German Air Force*, p 309; Irving, *The Rise and Fall of the Luftwaffe* (1973) p 130.

understanding, who submitted any rumours that might conceivably be of interest. Nor could it wait on the receipt of more reliable evidence from high-grade Sigint and PR if it was to give the requisite early notice of new developments. At some point in the first half of 1942 the senior members of AI 2(g) began to receive the Enigma and other decrypts, especially the Japanese diplomatic decrypts, that were essential to it in its new role as a research section. But these sources did not begin to refer to new German aircraft until the beginning of 1944, and even then the Enigma usually provided information on them only when they were about to be deployed to squadrons. PR was valuable in that it detected new aircraft at an earlier stage in their development, but it could not do so until they had reached the test airfields.

From the middle of 1943 AI nevertheless benefited from a notable increase in the amount of intelligence about innovations in German aircraft design from POW, agents and captured documents and, as was to be seen when PR and the high-grade Sigint eventually confirmed its reliability, much of it was of high quality despite the technical character of its subject matter. The growing frequency of reports from these sources was in large measure explained by the fact that it was at that time that the first of the new German aircraft, passing beyond the design stage, began to arrive at the test stations and to go into production. But the accuracy of the detailed information which some of them provided was due to other developments. As a result of the shortages of manpower in the GAF, men previously engaged in maintenance, repair and other necessary work were now being drafted as aircrew. When taken prisoner such men not only possessed greater technical expertise than the average aircrew; from professional interest, and perhaps out of resentment at being taken out of the jobs for which they had been trained, they were prepared to divulge and discuss their knowledge. In the same way, in an attempt to redress her growing shortage of skilled and semi-skilled labour, Germany was calling on highly skilled men from the occupied territories and setting them to work in aircraft factories and even in research establishments like those at Peenemünde. If only a few such men succeeded in relaying the fruits of their experience to the Allied espionage networks the outcome was nevertheless reflected, as we shall see, in agents' reports of exceptional value and obvious authenticity.

With these circumstances working in AI 2(g)'s favour, it turned out that while its zeal in investigating every rumour tempted it to pursue some false trails, and while it sometimes caused premature or unnecessary alarm in its anxiety to give the earliest possible warning of innovations which might be countered only if long notice was provided, it largely succeeded in the last two years of the war in discharging its responsibility of ensuring that the German Air

Force 'should not spring a surprise through some secret weapon or new type of aircraft or armament.' Ultimate responsibility for investigating the threat from Germany's most important secret weapons, the V-weapons, passed from AI 2(g) to other hands in the spring of 1943* After that date it was taken entirely by surprise when the first radio guided rocket missile (the Hs 293) and the first radio controlled bomb (the FX 1400) became operational in the German Air Force;† and it long remained unaware that German fighters had been equipped with upward firing cannon (*Schräge Musik*).‡ But it detected in good time each of the significant new departures in aircraft and aero-engine design and production on which Germany embarked from 1942.

□

The earliest of those new departures, and potentially the most important, was Germany's decision in early 1942 to give high priority to the production of jet propelled aircraft.

The world's first pure jet aircraft – Germany's Heinkel 178 – made its first flight in August 1939. The outcome of work done on gas turbines in several countries since the 1920s, it incorporated the centrifugal compressor, as did the He 180 and the He 280, subsequent experimental aircraft which contributed to the operational appearance at the end of 1944 of the single-engined jet fighter, the He 162.[6] Meanwhile, in 1939, the German Air Ministry had placed the contract for the first Junkers jet engine, the Jumo 004, which incorporated the axial-flow in preference to the centrifugal compressor. This engine was mated to the Me 262, an aircraft designed in 1940, and this combination was preferred to the He 280 in 1942, when Germany first gave high priority to gas turbine development. The Me 262 made its first successful flight with jet engines in July 1943 and went on to become the world's first operational jet propelled military aircraft.[7]

Partly as a result of the Allied bombing offensive, which made it necessary to evacuate the factory producing the Jumo 004, the plan to have the first hundred Me 262s operational by May 1944 was delayed from October 1943. A more important cause of the delay was Hitler's decision that the aircraft should be developed as a light bomber and held back for its shock effect on the beaches against the

---

* See below, pp 364–365.　　　　　† See below, p 337 et seq.
‡ See below, p 345 n and, Appendix 21 (ii), pp 567–568.

6.　M M Postan, D Hay and J D Scott, *Design and Development of Weapons* (1964), p 188; Irving, op cit, pp 75, 78, 83.
7.　Postan, op cit, pp 210–211; Irving, op cit, pp 218–219; Webster and Frankland, *The Strategic Air Offensive against Germany* (1961), Vol III, p 262.

Allied invasion of western Europe. The GAF authorities had intended to introduce it as the replacement for the Me 109 fighter in the belief that, being faster than any Allied fighter, and heavily armed, it would completely alter the balance of force in the air war over Germany; and they did indeed ignore Hitler's wishes to the extent of building up an 'experimental squadron' of Me 262 fighters which numbered 52 by October 1944.[8] As a result of having to convert it for carrying bombs, and of having to divert manufacturing capacity for the development of an alternative new fighter, the Me 209, Germany was unable to start production of the Me 262 till March 1944 and by May had produced only thirteen.[9] The delay frustrated Hitler's own immediate purpose; although eight more Me 262s were produced in June and 59 in July, none appeared over the Normandy beaches. By July Hitler's more general determination to give the GAF and German aircraft production a more offensive character, and to incorporate jet bombers with the V-weapons and the new U-boats in a renewed offensive strategy, was being undermined by the Allied strategic air offensive. But no fewer than nine heavy bomber units were converting to the Me 262 as late as October, and it was not until November that Hitler permitted the re-conversion of the Me 262 to the fighter role.[10]

The aircraft with which the GAF itself hoped to recover its offensive capacity was the twin-engined Ar 234. Powered by the BMW 003 gas turbine axial-flow engine, and developed as a light bomber and armed reconnaissance aircraft, this went into series production in the winter of 1942–1943. It turned out to have a remarkable performance – a top speed of 500 mph and a range of 1,000 miles – but the need to evacuate the Arado factory in October 1943, when only five had been assembled, delayed its series production until September 1944. The GAF had taken delivery of only 200 by the end of the war. In the autumn of 1944, however, Ar 234s contributed to the Allied alarm about German jet developments by making a number of sensational reconnaissance flights over the United Kingdom.[11]

Another new aircraft was rocket propelled. Germany had begun to experiment with rocket propelled aircraft before 1939, when the first such aircraft to fly, the interceptor He 176, was demonstrated at the GAF's development establishment at Rechlin on 3 July.[12] She

---

8.   Webster and Frankland, op cit, Vol III, p 272; Irving, op cit, p 289.

9.   Webster and Frankland, op cit, Vol III, p 272; Irving, op cit, pp 231, 232, 237, 249, 252, 254.

10. AIR 41/10, pp 313–314; Webster and Frankland, op cit, Vol III, p 272.

11. AIR 41/10, pp 368–369; Webster and Frankland, op cit, Vol III, p 273; Irving, op cit, pp 159, 253, 257.

12. Irving, op cit, p 73; Kens and Nowarra, *Die deutschen Flugzeuge 1933–45* (Munich, nd) pp 288–290.

subsequently developed the Me 163 as an interceptor to counter the USAAF's high-flying daylight bombers. Propelled by two rocket motors which used the same fuels as the A-4 rocket,* it was designed with a very short fuselage, so that it was often called 'a flying wing', with a very rapid rate of climb to a high altitude and with a very high speed over a short period. It was under development during 1943 and went into service with operational units from June 1944. But from the end of 1944, when only 45 had become operational, it was to be superseded by the He 162, an interceptor with superior qualities.[13]†

Little or nothing was learned in London about the early stages of these developments until 1943. At the end of 1939 'an escapee from the Heinkel factory' alerted the Air Ministry to the fact that Germany was carrying out research in jet propulsion and assisted take-off (ATO) rockets, and supplied some details about the He 280 and other Heinkel aircraft, but not, apparently, about the He 178.[14] In April 1940 AI received reports, source unspecified, that the He 280 was a development of the He 180, was being test-flown and was capable of a speed of 495 mph.[15] There is no evidence that this intelligence had any influence on the British decision in the same month to order the building of the first Whittle engines and arrange for the Gloster firm to design a fighter, later to be called the Meteor, around them.[16] In May 1942 two PR photographs of the Heinkel factory airfield at Rostock revealed an aircraft which fitted the earlier description of the He 280. In November 1942 there was a report that Heinkel and Messerschmitt were concerned with rocket aircraft with a speed of about 435 mph which should go into production in 1944; it added that Heinkel, the more advanced firm, had flown its first jet aircraft.[17] No doubt because they did not indicate that Germany was at last giving the high priority to jet propulsion which it had received in 1940–1941 in the United Kingdom, where it was now being developed at a more leisurely pace, these scraps of information received no special attention until July 1943, when AI included them with more recent intelligence in its first comprehensive report on German jet propelled aircraft.

This report, dated 19 July 1943, had clearly been under preparation for some time following an increase in the number of intelligence reports about jet propelled aircraft from the spring of that year, but its circulation was no doubt prompted by the detection by PR at

---

* See below, p 371 and Chapter 42.   † See Volume III Part 2.

13. AIR 41/10, p 314; *Technical Intelligence Sources*, p 25.
14. *Air Ministry Intelligence*, p 354; *Technical Intelligence Sources*, pp 2, 27.
15. AIR 20/2690, D of I (O) Report No 3004 of 19 July 1943.
16. Postan, op cit, pp 194–195.
17. AIR 20/2690, No 3004 of 19 July 1943.

Peenemünde on 23 June of four small tailless aircraft, named P 30 by the CIU, and the fact that similar objects were then identified in earlier but poorer photographs going back to April.[18] It appears that it was the report of these objects, which AI 2(g) took to be jet propelled piloted aircraft, which led the Defence Committee on 29 June to ask for a report on the state of development of 'pilot-less and/or jet propelled aircraft in Germany.'[19]

AI drew attention in its report to the fact that PR of the Heinkel works at Vienna-Schwechat had identified an aircraft similar to that seen in Rostock; that the British Air Attaché in Berne had reported that an aircraft called the He 280 was powered by two BMW 003 turbo-jets; and that a POW had reported that in a lecture at Caen shortly before June 1943 General Galland, the GAF's Inspector of Fighter Aircraft, had assured fighter pilots that a Heinkel jet would be in mass production in 1944. AI assumed that these items all referred to the He 280 and concluded that it would be operational in limited numbers in 1944, with a few appearing for trials or propaganda purposes in the autumn of 1943. By May, however, the Air Attaché Berne had heard of two other new aircraft; one was the Me 163 which was thought to be powered by a combination of jet propulsion and internal combustion, the other was the Me 262 which was fitted with two Jumo 004 engines and had a speed of 527 mph and a rate of climb of 2,600 feet per minute; and in July a POW had mentioned that a Me turbo-jet with a speed of 600 mph, which AI took to be the Me 262, was being developed at the Messserschmitt factory at Augsburg. AI assumed that the Me 262 and the He 280 were being developed in parallel. The same POW had added that a Me rocket driven fighter was also under development; AI was uncertain whether this was the aircraft another POW had seen at Rechlin earlier in 1943, which was towed or catapulted into the air, or the apparently tailless aircraft which had been photographed by PR at Peenemünde, but it believed it was in any case the Me 'rocket-propelled flying-wing' to which, in addition to the He 280, Galland was said to have referred in his Caen lecture. Some further twenty items of intelligence in the report dealt with a variety of experiments with other forms of propulsion – turbo-prop, rocket boosted and jet boosted conventional aircraft – and included a rumour about a plan to build a long-range, rocket propelled bomber with a speed of 800–1,120 mph that was capable of reaching New York.* AI summed up by

---

* This was a pointer to the development of the Ju 287. The first prototype of this bomber did not fly until the summer of 1944 and no further intelligence about it was received before then. See Volume III Part 2.

18. *Air Ministry Intelligence*, p 375; AIR 20/2690.
19. CAB 121/211, SIC file B/Defence/2, Vol I, DO (43) 5th Meeting, 29 June.

stressing that in addition to doing a considerable amount of work on combined power plants, Germany was now pushing along fast with jet propulsion, so fast that at least one jet propelled aircraft would appear in service in 1944, and was experimenting with rocket powered aircraft which, dependent on the production of novel fuels, might 'outclass and render practically obsolete all aircraft with gas-turbine engines or combined power units'.[20]

Because it put together 'the first definite intelligence' that Germany was developing new types of manned aircraft, AI's July report 'caused some alarm to the Cabinet'.[21] Its immediate result was to revive the demand for a fast jet propelled, short-range interceptor fighter, which had declined with the great reduction of air attacks on the United Kingdom from the beginning of 1942. 'By directive of the Prime Minister . . . an order for 120 Meteors was given'.[22]* On more than one occasion in the remaining months of 1943 the Prime Minister was prompted by intelligence reports to express his anxiety about British progress in jet aircraft development. On 31 July 1943 he minuted the Ministry of Aircraft Production: 'I am concerned that you hold out such slender hopes of our getting jet propelled aircraft, and we cannot afford to be left behind'.[23] And on 6 October 1943 he minuted the Chief of Air Staff; 'recent evidence shows that the Germans are working hard on jet propelled aircraft, and accentuates the need for the utmost pressure to be put on their development here'.[24]

The more profound impact of AI's report may be seen in the fact that in the United Kingdom 'it is from this moment that we can trace the first serious attempts to tackle the aerodynamic problems of supersonic flight – problems which had to be resolved before the unconventional power plant could be fully exploited'.[25] The report had a further consequence on the administrative level. In April 1943, as a result of a growing number of intelligence reports to the effect that Germany was developing a long-range rocket, Mr Duncan Sandys had been charged with responsibility for co-ordinating the assessment of intelligence and the development of counter-measures in relation to that threat. Pointing out at the beginning of

---

* It is of considerable interest that the Meteor and the Me 262 became operational in the same month, July 1944. In the event, while Germany was prevented by formidable difficulties – particularly by the impossibility of undertaking any serious training – from obtaining any important advantage from her new aircraft, the Gloster Meteor, the production of which was accelerated by the discovery that German aircraft were being developed, was to have considerable success against the VI flying bomb over southern England from July 1944.

20. AIR 20/2690, No 3004 of 19 July 1943.
21. Postan, op cit, p 221.   22. ibid, p 224.
23. Churchill, *The Second World War*, Vol V (1952), p 579.
24. ibid, p 588.   25. Postan, op cit, p 221.

September that his responsibility had now been extended beyond the long-range rocket, long-range guns and other novel projectiles to jet propelled aircraft, jet propelled or gliding bombs and pilotless aircraft, he proposed after discussion with the Air Staff that the Air Ministry should become wholly responsible for jet propelled aircraft. The Chiefs of Staff approved the proposal on 10 September.[26]

On the following day, by way of terminating his responsibility for that subject, Sandys submitted a summary of AI's latest assessment of the intelligence on jet propelled aircraft to the Defence Committee. It added nothing to what AI's July report had said about fighter aircraft powered exclusively by jet propulsion or bomber aircraft driven by a combination of jet propulsion and internal combustion power, but said that the latter were unlikely to be operational before the autumn of 1944. It further stated that while it had clearly emerged that Germany had made considerable progress in experiments with aircraft powered by rocket motors, many problems remained to be solved before such aircraft could become 'a serious operational threat'.[27]

□

When proposing early in September 1943 that the Air Ministry should assume responsibility for intelligence on jet aircraft, Sandys also proposed a different arrangement for pilotless aircraft and jet propelled or gliding bombs: the Air Ministry should be responsible for them, too, but since they were being developed at Peenemünde alongside the long-range rocket, and were frequently confused with the rocket in intelligence reports, its assessments should be sent to him for submission to the Defence Committee.[28]* A week earlier British ships in Biscay had been taken by surprise by the first successful German attacks with the Hs 293, a radio guided rocket missile which was guided to its target by the launching aircraft. A few days later the Allies were again surprised – indeed profoundly shocked – when, following the announcement of the Italian armistice, the GAF, in successful attacks on the Italian Fleet, sank the new battleship *Roma*. They were soon to learn from the Enigma that the *Roma* had been sunk with the PC 1400 FX high altitude free-fall bomb, an armour-piercing (AP) weapon whose fall could be corrected by radio beam from the aircraft launching it.

---

* See below, p 392.

26. CAB 121/211, COS (43) 520) (0) of 7 September, COS (43) 212nd (0) Meeting, 10 September.
27. ibid, DO (43) 18 of 11 September.
28. ibid, COS (43) 520 (0) of 7 September.

There had been occasional references in 1941 and 1942 by POW and agents to the fact that the Germans were experimenting with radio controlled bombs.[29] These had caused no surprise, if only because similar experiments were taking place in the United States, and it is unlikely that they were associated at the time with the Oslo Report of 1939 which had mentioned that the German Navy was developing remote controlled gliders about three metres long and three metres in span (an accurate general description of the future Hs 293) for use against ships.* They had also aroused little attention because the British scientific community had believed that the Germans were unlikely to overcome the practical difficulties in perfecting guided weapons. Nor did the receipt of the first Enigma decrypt on the subject greatly change the situation. Received at the end of May 1943, the decrypt was an order from the C-in-C of the German Air Force to an unidentified authority, thought to be in the Mediterranean theatre, to the effect that 'objects Hs 293 and FX' were to be taken out of store and given, as new weapons, very special protection against espionage and sabotage.[30] The NID noted that although there had been no previous reference to these weapons, another decrypt had already disclosed that a weapon called *Feuerteufel*, surrounded by the same security precautions, was being dropped experimentally by Do 217 aircraft at Banak in north Norway. But it did not relate the decrypts to the earlier references to radio controlled bombs, and thus failed to recognise that here was the first evidence that the first ever guided missiles were about to become operational.

At the end of July 1943 further Enigma decrypts revealed that KG 100 with all its personnel and equipment was to move from Italy to Istres, near Marseilles, having been recently equipped with over 50 special Do 217 aircraft; that it was divided into two groups, II/KG 100 with Do 217 E 5 (He† 293) aircraft and III/KG 100 with Do 217 K 2 (FX) aircraft; and that operations by II/KG 100 both by day and night were now permitted.[31] This intelligence was forwarded to the Mediterranean authorities; but no alert was issued to Allied ships, either in the Mediterranean or more generally, partly because the decrypt contained no technical details. By the time the decrypt was received III/KG 100 had already begun

---

*   See Volume I p 508.
†   By July 1943 GC and CS had wrongly concluded that the earlier reference to 'Hs' was a corruption of 'He'. This belief persisted for some time as is reflected in the quotations made below.

29.   *Air Ministry Intelligence*, pp 378.
30.   CX/MSS/2641/T18.
31.   CX/MSS/2980/T14, 2984/T16, 2993/T14.

operations with the FX in July against ships off Malta and Sicily, but because it scored no hits the crews of the ships attacked did not realise that unusual weapons were being used against them. This was the situation when the aircrew of a Do 217, shot down over the Mediterranean early in August, claimed that they had been taking part in the first 'service test' operations with a new radio controlled bomb.[32]

There was further delay before Whitehall learned about this report by the aircrew. The news that Do 217s had begun carrying out experimental attacks on Allied cruisers in the Mediterranean was first given wide circulation in a signal from the Air Ministry on 21 August.[33] It seems probable that the NID had not learned of the report by 19 August, for on that day it submitted the Enigma evidence to the Admiralty's Directorate of Scientific Research, the members of which were not indoctrinated and were thus allowed to see only bowdlerised versions of high-grade decrypts, as 'indications from Most Secret Sources of the nature of a new GAF weapon which is likely to come into force in the very near future against warships in the Mediterranean'. Although it did not know the meaning of He and FX, it suggested that 'He 293 is a type of glider-bomb produced by Heinkel and that FX stands for Funk X-Gerät (Radio Apparatus X) which would accord with the dropping of a glider-bomb by one aircraft to be controlled by another.' Nor was it until 27 August that the full text of the report on the interrogation of the Mediterranean POW was distributed in Whitehall. This made it clear that two different weapons had been developed. The POW stated that their own unit, III/KG 100, which was using FX in the Mediterranean attacks, and another unit, II/KG 100, which had carried out experiments with a different type of radio controlled bomb fitted with wings, had both moved initially to Istres, but that II/KG 100 had later been transferred to Cognac.[34]

On the same day, 27 August, the Germans carried out the first successful attacks with the Hs 293. He 177s of II/KG 100, operating from Cognac, had obtained a near miss on HMS *Bideford* in Biscay on 25 August, and on 27 August they damaged HMCS *Athabaskan* and sank HMS *Egret* in the same area.* There is no evidence to suggest that either the Enigma or RAF Y† gave advance warning of these attacks, let alone of the fact that they were to be of a special

---

* See above, p 220.
† The RAF Y party embarked in the *Egret* were killed.

32. *Air Ministry Intelligence*, p 378.
33. Air Sunset 89 of 21 August 1943.
34. AIR 20/3283, ADI (K) No 360/1943.

character, and it is perhaps a tribute to the reliance it had come to place on having good forward intelligence that the Admiralty experienced considerable disquiet at the fact that it had not given all ships a general warning against glider bombs before the attacks occurred. The Germans again achieved surprise in their first successful operation with the FX on 8 September, when they attacked the Italian Fleet on the announcement of the Italian armistice, sinking the *Roma* and damaging the *Italia*.* The Italians reported that the ships had been attacked by Ju 88s using armour-piercing rocket propelled bombs of a type that had been in use for some time. But the decrypts of KG 100's report on the operation established that it had been carried out by Do 217s using both Hs 293 and the FX, and fragments obtained from the Italians subsequently confirmed that the hits had been made with the FX[35].

Writing after the event NID 12 noted that the new weapons had 'arrived virtually out of the blue as far as ships at sea were concerned, although the heads of the appropriate divisions had been kept informed and some Ultra messages were sent in spite of the scepticism of some authorities . . . '. It attributed the oversight to the inefficient handling within the Admiralty of high-grade decrypts containing items of scientific intelligence that might be of interest to the Navy. The system adopted when Ultra first became available, and still in force, was one by which NID 12 bowdlerised such decrypts and circulated them to the technical divisions of the Admiralty as information received from a reliable and highly-placed source; and it had two defects which, in NID 12's view, 'became absolutely obvious . . . with the advent of the Hs 293 glider-bomb'. NID 12 recognised that it was not itself competent to select and paraphrase this kind of intelligence, and it suspected that the recipients of its memoranda dismissed them as being 'reports that we get from NID that might eventually turn out to be correct, but probably would not . . .' The outcome was that in the autumn of 1943 NID established a Scientific Intelligence Section (NID 7S).† At the end of August 1943, in the absence of such a section in the Admiralty, the work of visiting all ships attacked by the new weapons, interrogating the crews, inspecting the damage and examining such fragments of the weapons as could be recovered was centralised in the Air Ministry's Technical Intelligence section (AI 2(g)), which reported to the Royal Aircraft Establishment at Farnborough (RAE) and to a committee in the Admiralty.[36]

---

* See above, p 337.   † See Appendix 1, p 470.

35. *Air Ministry Intelligence*, pp 382–383.
36. ibid, p 379, 380.

On 3 September, following the first investigations of the attacks on HMS *Bideford* and HMCS *Athabaskan*, the Admiralty was able to describe to ships at sea the main external characteristics of Hs 293, including the fact that it was radio controlled by the aircraft which delivered it.[37] The examination of German aircraft abandoned when the Allies entered Foggia later in the autumn of 1943 disclosed the frequency used for the radio control of Hs 293 and the FX, which had basically similar systems, and radio counter-measures were then put in hand.[38]

Thereafter, little difficulty was encountered in reconstructing the design and performance of the FX to the extent that ships could be advised on the evasive and anti-aircraft tactics they should adopt against it. Study in the United Kingdom of fragments collected at Foggia made it possible to calculate the amount of control that an aircraft could apply to the bomb after its release and POW interrogations made it clear that after releasing the FX the aircraft had to reduce speed and continue in its line of flight, thus becoming vulnerable to anti-aircraft fire while guiding the bomb to its target.[39] But understanding of the design and performance of Hs 293 was still not complete when, in the spring of 1944, the British broke the cypher of the Japanese Naval Attaché in Berlin and obtained from one of the early decrypts a detailed specification of the weapon.[40]*

Even then there remained some uncertaintly about the thrust of its rocket motor, and thus of its performance. This could not be determined without identifying the fuels used. Farnborough had established as early as 10 September 1943 that the Hs 293 was rocket propelled by liquid fuel, but because in rocket propulsion with liquid fuels the enemy was ahead of the Allies the fuels could not be identified.[41] The interrogation of POW had soon disclosed that the Germans called the fuels T-Stoff and Z-Stoff. Examination of fragments of the weapon had then shown that one of the fuels was sodium permanganate, and this was seen to be Z-Stoff, but intelligence had failed to throw any light on the nature of T-Stoff. It was eventually concluded in technical experiments that T-Stoff must be concentrated hydrogen peroxide.† But no stores of this substance were available in the United Kingdom, and since the attempt to locate the enemy's storage points and recover samples

---

* For further details about this cypher see above p 244.　　　† See below, pp 418, 428.

37.　ibid, p 380; AIR 20/3283, AI 2(g) Reports 3007 of 31 August, 3010 of 2 September 1943.
38.　*Air Ministry Intelligence*, p 381.
39.　ibid, p 383.
40.　*Admiralty Handling of Special Intelligence*, p 117.
41.　*Air Ministry Intelligence*, p 380; CAB 121/211, COS (43) 530 (o) of 13 September, paras 16–20.

came to nothing, the experimental deduction was not finally confirmed until a large underground store was over-run in France after the invasion of Normandy.[42]

□

Germany's introduction of novel airborne weapons, notably the world's first rocket propelled guided missile in the form of the Hs 293, was followed by further evidence that she not only hoped to have jet aircraft in service before long, but was also developing rocket propelled aircraft and long-range jet and rocket propelled unmanned missiles. But the second half of 1943 was the stage of the war in which the development of the conventional piston-engined aircraft reached its apogee. In the twelve months beginning in the summer of 1943 AI was heavily occupied in sifting a mass of intelligence relating to Germany's efforts to improve her existing fighters and bombers and introduce new conventional types. Not unnaturally at a time when the GAF was having to give priority to fighter defences, most of the evidence encountered by AI concerned the development of fighter or fighter-related aircraft.

By July 1943 AI knew from the examination of crashed or captured aircraft in Africa that the latest sub-type of the Me 109 single-engined night-fighter – the Me 109G – had the improved DB 605 engine;[43] and by October it had discovered that it used GM (nitrous oxide) injection to give it extra speed and altitude.[44] In October it had reason to believe that another sub-type of the Me 109, with either a special version of the DB 605 engine or a new engine, would soon be in service; that the Me 209, a more heavily armed development of the Me 109, was probably already in service in small numbers; but that another project, the Me 309, had already been cancelled as inferior to the 209.[45] In fact the GAF had cancelled both the Me 209 and the Me 309 in April in favour of the Me 262, the first jet to go into production, but had had to restore production of the Me 209 after Hitler had decided in August that the Me 262 should be developed as a bomber.*

In October 1943 AI also knew a good deal about the latest development of the FW 190. It then circulated a detailed report on the FW 190D, the sub-type which had received the BMW radial engine and GM injection, and expressed the belief that the FW 190

---

* See above, pp 332–333.

42.   *Air Ministry Intelligence*, pp 381–382.
43.   AIR 40/2166, AI 2(g)Report No 2185 of 7 July 1943.
44.   ibid, Report No 220 of 22 October 1943.
45.   ibid, loc cit.

was already being tested with liquid-cooled engines, among others the Jumo 213 and DB 628, which would greatly improve its performance.[46] At the beginning of December this expectation was confirmed by a captured document dated November 1942 which gave the specifications for current and projected versions of the aircraft; this showed that a new model was being developed with a DB 603 in-line engine.[47] This model – the long-nosed FW 190* – did not enter squadron service till late in 1944, as AI learned from captured photographs and a solitary R/T intercept; when one crashed and was examined in January 1945 it was found to have the Jumo 213 engine.[48]

The circulation to Allied aircrew of the news that up-dated versions of the Me 109 and FW 190 were to be expected prompted in the last three months of 1943 many false claims about encounters with fighters of improved performance, with speeds between 400 and 445 mph and altitudes up to 35,000 feet, and AI was disposed to credit them.[49] But in January 1944 the British Air Attaché in Berne acquired copies of notes, taken from communications aircraft and dated January 1943, for a series of lectures by General Galland to German pilots.† Two of the lectures, one dealing with the development of day-fighters and the other with the development of aircraft armament, made it clear that until the jets came forward in large numbers at the end of 1944 the GAF intended to rely on the Me 109 and FW 190 in the belief that their high-altitude capability could be improved by the provision of more powerful engines, new propeller designs, and various forms of super-charger and GM injection. More particularly, the notes referred to the introduction of the DB 605 engine and GM injection into the Me 109 and to radial engines (but not in-line engines) for the FW 190. They added that the FW 190 was to be given a formidable increase in fire-power, including two 30 mm guns.[50] This enabled AI to narrow down the range of new developments that were likely to affect the German single-engined fighters, and its confidence that the enemy was giving priority to improving the Me 109 and FW 190, rather than to bringing forward new types of conventional aircraft, was increased by the lack of any references in intelligence to the Me 209 and 309 after the beginning of 1944.

---

* Radial engines were air-cooled. In liquid-cooled engines the cylinders were arranged in line and engines with a large number of cylinders required a long-nosed aircraft.

† Not to be confused with Galland's lecture at Caen in June 1943, see above, p 335.

46. ibid, loc cit.
47. ibid, Nos 2205 and 2210 of 6 and 13 December 1943.
48. *Technical Intelligence Sources*, pp 13, 28–29.
49. ibid, p 13; AIR 40/2166, No 2217 of 29 December 1943.
50. ibid, No 2218 of 7 January 1944; *Technical Intelligence Sources*, pp 17, 22.

Galland's notes of January 1943 also stated that 'a version of the FW 154 night-fighter with two Jumo 213 engines must be developed for long-range day fighting duties.' AI had known for some months that the GAF was improving the engines and armament of its existing twin-engined fighters – the Me 110, Me 410* and Ju 88 – and increasingly using them for night operations as well as by day, and the FW 154 was one of three new high performance twin-engined fighters about which intelligence had been obtained since the middle of 1943. The first reference to the aircraft, in a letter from a factory worker in Germany to a German soldier, was intercepted by the censorship authorities; referring to it as the TA 154, the letter said the first model had 'just come off the production line', but did not mention that it was powered by a conventional piston engine.[51] In June 1943 this was followed by an agent's report to the effect that a twin-engined fighter unit was to be equipped with the TA 154 in the autumn of 1944, and in the belief that T stood for 'turbo' AI assumed that it was powered by both jet and conventional power units.[52] In fact the Germans used the TA designation for aircraft designed by Kurt Tank, the FW company's chief designer, and from December 1943, having discovered its mistake, AI called the aircraft the FW 154[53] Nothing more was heard of it until the middle of 1944, when it was located by PR. In September 1944 AI, assuming it was about to become operational, issued a full description of it, including the information derived from POW that it was called the German Mosquito.[54] It was made of glued plywood sections in imitation of the Mosquito. AI appears never to have learned that its production had been abandoned in the first half of 1944 following the destruction by bombing of the only factory capable of making the glue for binding its plywood sections.[55]

The GAF had meanwhile developed the twin-engined He 219 as a night-fighter that might challenge the Mosquito. When the Enigma disclosed early in 1944 that one Gruppe (about 30 aircraft) of He 219s had become operational with a night-fighter unit at Venlo in Holland, AI had received so much information about this aircraft since early 1943, from agents, POW and PR of the GAF's development establishment at Rechlin, that it was able to issue a comprehensive report on its performance and characteristics. The report showed that the He 219's speed exceeded that of the Me 410

---

* See above, p 323 n†.

51.   *Technical Intelligence Sources*, p 20.
52.   AIR 20/2690, No 3004 of 19 July 1943.
53.   AIR 40/2166, No 2213 of 20 December 1943.
54.   ibid, No 2263 of 5 September 1944.
55.   AIR 41/10, p 310; Webster and Frankland, op cit, Vol III, p 271.

– so far, Germany's fastest fighter.[56] A fuller report issued on 28 April added that an agent had recently described a He 219 which had an added turbo-booster to give it jet assistance, and AI commented that this refinement would not only greatly increase its normal long-range performance as a night-fighter but also give it the capability of engaging day-bombers and their escorts.[57]* It seems probable that this intelligence prompted Eighth Air Force's first raid on Vienna-Schwechat at the end of April; by July, in any event, AI reported that repeated bombing at Schwechat had dislocated He 219 production.[59] The lack of references to the aircraft in subsequent intelligence reports indicated that no more were employed after that date.

The third new twin-engined fighter, the Do 335, had both engines in tandem inside the aircraft, one driving a forward and the other a rear propeller. It developed into one of the fastest ever propeller driven aircraft, a prototype reaching 400 mph at ground level and 500 mph at its proper altitude on its first flight towards the end of 1944. It could be used as a bomber as well as a day-fighter, and in May 1944 Hitler was looking to it to join the Me 262 jet aircraft in opposition to the coming Allied invasion. In March and April 1944, however, Allied raids on the Dornier plant destroyed all the Do 335's production tools, so that only a few of the aircraft were built by the end of the war and none became operational.[60] The first reference to it, in an agent's report, reached AI sometime before February 1944. The report described a new light bomber with a speed of 450–500 mph, a 1,800 lb bomb-load and high fuel consumption, calling it the Do 235.[61] That this was a precursor of the new aircraft emerged when, on 22 February, the Enigma decrypt of a circular from the GAF's Inspector of Reconnaissance Aircraft was circulated. This showed that the Germans were seeking pilots with the highest qualifications for training with the Ar 234, Do 335 and Me 262, and, because the Me 262 had by then been so identified,

---

* The circulation of this report was followed by many claims by RAF crew that they had encountered the He 219 equipped with an auxilliary turbo-jet unit. In fact only one jet-assisted He 219 was built and it was not used operationally.[58] On the other hand, the report also discussed the armament of the He 219 in detail, but was not aware that the aircraft was fitted with the 20 mm upward-firing cannon (*Schräge Musik*). This weapon was not described by AI 2(g) until September 1944. (See Appendix 21 (ii), pp 567–568).

56. AIR 40/2166, No 2223 of 26 January 1944.
57. ibid, No 2235 of 28 April 1944; *Technical Intelligence Sources*, p 5.
58. *Air Ministry Intelligence*, p 390.
59. AIR 40/2393 AI 2(a) Report of 12 July 1944.
60. AIR 41/10, p 310; Webster and Frankland, op cit, Vol III, p 271; Irving, op cit, pp 179, 261, 284.
61. AIR 40/2166, No 2231 of 28 March 1944; *Air Ministry Intelligence*, p 374.

the Do 335 was assumed by AI to be a jet aircraft.[62] Early in May PR photographs of the Dornier airfield at Löwenthal disclosed an unidentified aircraft similar in lay-out to the Me 262 but rather larger; although the photographs detected no sign of jet engines, AI assumed that the aircraft was the Do 335.[63] Not until the autumn of 1944 did it become clear that the aircraft was propeller driven. A sketch of its unconventional engine disposition provided at that time by a deported French workman reminded an officer in AI 2(g) that he had seen a similar drawing in connection with a Dornier patent, and investigation in the Patent Office showed that the Do 335 derived from this patent, which had been renewed in 1942.[64] In October 1944, when AI issued a detailed report on the aircraft, it remained unaware that its production had been interrupted;[65] indeed, it had recently been led to expect it to go into quantity production by an Enigma decrypt which stated that orders for dummy aircraft – for the purpose of deceiving the Allies – would in future be restricted to the following types of aircraft: FW 190, Me 109, Ju 88 and Do 335.[66] An otherwise valuable guide to German aircraft production policy, this decrypt was misleading about the Do 335, perhaps because it reflected the anxiety of the GAF to have the aircraft, and AI continued till the end of the war to expect it to appear in squadron service.[67]

Soon after the beginning of 1944, on the other hand, AI gave up the suspicion that Germany would bring new bombers into service. During the last few months of 1943 it had given increasing attention to this threat, for which there was little supporting intelligence, in the belief that Germany's interest in retaliating against the Allied strategic bombing offensive and her need for long-range reconnaissance in the Battle of the Atlantic – a need she could meet with the same types of aircraft – would force her for the first time in the war to develop high-altitude and multi-engined bombers. By October 1943 the intelligence sources had mentioned several such aircraft. They included the Ju 86, an aircraft of pre-war design which was known to have carried out high-level reconnaissance over the Nile delta in 1942. A captured handbook had shown that it had a small bomb-load and AI thought it was unlikely to go into production. No more was heard of it. The same was true of the Ju 288, which had been cancelled in 1942; AI rightly concluded that it had no future. Of other aircraft that had been referred to, AI believed that

---

62. *Air Ministry Intelligence*, p 374; CX/MSS/T102/104.
63. AIR 40/2166, No 2236 of 4 May 1944.
64. *Air Ministry Intelligence*, p 374; *Technical Intelligence Sources*, p 28.
65. AIR 40/2166, No 2279 of 30 October 1944.
66. *Ultra Material as a source of Technical Intelligence*, p 2.
67. *Air Ministry Intelligence*, pp 351, 374.

the He 178 might be a four-engined bomber derived from the He 177; in fact the He 178 was a jet fighter* and the bomber which was under development, but which the Germans did not proceed with, was the He 277. Apart from the He 277, only one of the bombers considered by AI was receiving serious attention in Germany. This was the Me 264. Designed in 1940 with a trans-Atlantic capacity, the production of this bomber was briefly contemplated by the GAF in 1943 – a fact reflected in September and October in Japanese diplomatic decrypts in which it was reported that the aircraft was capable of reaching New York. To the Me 264, however, as to the other high performance bombers discussed by AI in the closing months of 1943, there was no further reference by the intelligence sources after the end of that year.[68]

The new sub-stratopheric bombers which Germany deployed to squadrons in October 1943 – the He 177 and the Ju 188 – were thus the first and the last new German bombers of the war. The four-engined He 177 had been ordered in 1938 and test-flown in 1941. It was introduced on the Russian front in 1942, but the Enigma had shown that it was quickly withdrawn as unsatisfactory: it had a large bomb-load, but poor speed, altitude and manoeuvrability. When it reappeared in service in October 1943 AI believed that its shortcomings had not been corrected, and this assumption was borne out when a few He 177s reached London during the German offensive at the beginning of 1944.[69] Of the Ju 188, little had been heard before it took part in small-scale raids against the United Kingdom in the late summer of 1943. But the examination of one that then crashed in Yorkshire showed that it had a small bomb-load, and AI assumed that it was intended for anti-shipping operations, possibly with the Hs 293 and the FX 1400, as much as for bombing. The Ju 188 continued to be used as a bomber against the United Kingdom in the winter of 1943–1944, when it emerged from another crash inspection that it had been equipped with the Jumo 213 engine, but only small numbers were available and few of them survived.[70]

It remained possible that the Ju 88, the Do 217 and the He 111 – the older bombers which, together with the Ju 188 and the He 177, bore the brunt of the bombing offensive against the United

---

* See above, p 332.

68. AIR 40/2166, Nos 2201 of 25 October, 2208 and 2215 of 23 and 24 December 1943; Irving, op cit, pp 151, 245, 280.
69. Air Sunset 113 of 25 October 1943; AIR 40/2166, Nos 2201 of 18 October 1943, 2240 of 18 May 1944; *Technical Intelligence Sources*, pp 12–13.
70. Air Sunset 113 of 25 October 1943; AIR 40/2166, Nos 2201 of 18 October 1945, 2240 of 18 May 1944; *Technical Intelligence Sources*, pp 12–13.

Kingdom in the winter of 1943–1944 – would be equipped with improved piston engines or boosted for extra speed and altitude by turbo-superchargers or GM injection. In the event, however, only the Ju 188 underwent this development before the offensive was brought to a close.

□

Although the GAF's bombing of the United Kingdom had faded out by the time of the Normandy landings in June 1944, there still remained some anxiety at that point not only about the GAF's anti-shipping aircraft, including those equipped with the Hs 293 and FX 1400, but also about the danger of intervention by German jet and rocket propelled aircraft.

In contrast to the intelligence about German bombers, which strongly suggested after the end of 1943 that new high performance aircraft were unlikely to come into service, the intelligence about German fighters left little doubt that the German Air Force was continuing to give high priority to the production of jet aircraft; and at the beginning of 1944 it finally established that one of the fighters under active development, the Me 163, was rocket powered.

By December 1943 AI had learned little for several months about the He 280 jet fighter. Though it still believed that this aircraft had successfully passed its tests, AI was forced to assume that its production had been delayed.[71] By then, on the other hand, AI had acquired so much intelligence about the Me 262 that it assumed that the aircraft was already in series production and felt able to rate it as superior to the He 280. It knew that it was powered by two Jumo 004 axial-flow engines which gave it a maximum speed of 550–560 mph and a ceiling of 46,000 feet; that because of its high speed it incorporated a novel feature, the ejector seat; and that one of its shortcomings was that its speed and heavy take-off weight necessitated an extra-long runway.* AI was also well informed about the Me 262's formidable armament, putting it at three 20 mm and two 30 mm guns (in fact, it was four 30 mm guns). This intelligence had been supplied by POW and agents. Late in 1943 an agent who must have been in contact with a knowledgeable jet technician provided a further illustrated report on the Jumo 004 engine which gave valuable details about the mountings, composition, shaping and manufacture of the turbine blades.[73]

---

* This was soon recognised by AI's airfield section which was accordingly able to predict from what area jet aircraft might operate.[72]

71.   AIR 40/2166, No 2214 of 1 December 1943.
72.   AIR 40/2393, AI 2(b)Report of 13 August 1944.
73.   AIR 40/2166, No 2216 of 24 December 1943; *Technical Intelligence Sources*, p 6.

In January 1944, through the capture of the notes for lectures by General Galland*, AI knew that the Me 262 had by January 1943 reached 527 mph in tests, that it was comparable in performance with the He 280, which was powered by two BMW 003 engines, and that the GAF claimed it could manage with various up-dated marks of the Me 109 and the FW 190 until these jet aircraft came into service.[74] This reference to the He 280 prolonged the belief that the aircraft would soon go into service. At the beginning of March 1944 AI believed that it would be encountered operationally in small numbers in the next six months.[75] Nor was it until October 1944 that the Japanese diplomatic decrypts – by then a prolific source of accurate intelligence on Germany's jet aircraft – disclosed that the He 280 was not going into production.[76]

Galland's notes also gave details about the Me 163: its role was that of an 'alarm fighter'. for home defence, its speed was greater than that of any existing aircraft, but its endurance at full throttle was no more than eight minutes. The notes did not clear up continuing uncertainty as to whether it was powered by jet or rocket engines; they made a reference to cold and hot units, which were later seen to apply to rocket fuels, but AI 2(g) could make nothing of this information at the time.[77] This problem was solved later in January 1944 by interrogation of POW who had been GAF mechanics at Peenemünde and by a report from a French engineer who had also been employed there. They provided a wealth of accurate detail about the Me 163's propulsion, as well as more information about its performance, controls and armour protection, and revealed that there were plans to fit it with heavy armament.[78] At the beginning of March AI described it as powered by a liquid rocket engine supplied by Walter of Kiel and issued a full report on its high speed, its rapid rate of climb and its limited endurance.[79] In the light of this intelligence it was no longer confident, as Sandys had reported it to be in September 1943, that many problems remained to be solved before rocket propelled aircraft became a serious operational threat.† It continued to call the Me 163 the 'mystery' plane,[80] but only because the Allies had no experience of their own with rocket propelled, as opposed to jet propelled aircraft.

---

* See above, p 343.   † See above, p 337.

74. ibid, No 2218 of 7 January 1944.
75. ibid, No 2226 of 1 March 1944.
76. SJA 1038 of 24 October 1944.
77. AIR 40/2166, No 2218 of 7 January 1944.
78. *Air Ministry Intelligence*, p 376.
79. AIR 40/2166, No 2225 of 1 March 1944.
80. ibid, No 2233 of 20 April 1944.

At the end of January 1944 PR identified the Me 262 for the first time; one was photographed at the airfield of the Messerschmitt factory at Augsburg and another at the nearby airfield at Lechfeld.[81] And on 7 February, in its first reference to any of the jet propelled aircraft, the Enigma disclosed that Army specialists were being transferred from the Balkans to Germany for employment in the production of the Me 262.[82] At the beginning of March AI 2(g) issued full details of the aircraft's appearance, performance, power unit and ejector seat, and announced that it would be the first German jet propelled fighter to go into service, probably within six months.[83]

Meanwhile, on 22 February, another Enigma decrypt had stated that the GAF's Inspector of Reconnaissance Aircraft was seeking highly qualified pilots for training with the new aircraft Ar 234, Do 335 and Me 262.* This was the first evidence the Allies had received of the existence of the Ar 234 and the first reliable evidence of the Do 335. As we have seen, it took AI several months to establish that, unlike the Me 262, the Do 335 was not a jet aircraft. By March, on the other hand, AI had satisfied itself that there was no evidence that either of these aircraft had reached the stage of series production.[84] But in the spring of 1944 the Allied authorities, already apprehensive at the prospect that the Germans had developed three aircraft superior to the Allied fighters, and formidably armed, of which two – the He 280 and the Me 262 – would soon be in service, were given more urgent grounds for further alarm by the news that the third aircraft – the rocket driven Me 163 – might soon be operational. In March two Me 163s, which had hitherto been detected only at Peenemünde, were photographed by PR at Bad Zwischenahn. On 18 April this first intimation that the aircraft had gone into production was confirmed by the Enigma: a signal from Galland's Director of Equipment, after referring to the intention to speed up 'the bringing of the Me 163 into service', discussed the training of Me 163 mechanics at Walterwerke Kiel, mentioned a test unit at Zwischenahn and implied that ten Staffeln of twelve aircraft each were to be created.[85] In a long and detailed account of all that was known about the aircraft, AI 2(g), which was now able in the light of the decrypt to confirm that the Me 163 was intended for the interceptor role, noted on 20 April that 'its performance will

---

* See above, p 345.

81.   *Technical Intelligence Sources*, p 20.
82.   CX/MSS/T99/127.
83.   AIR 40/2166, No 2224 of 1 March 1944.
84.   AIR 40/2166, No 2231 of 28 March 1944.
85.   DEFE 3/140, KV 1417 of 18 April 1944.

undoubtedly be startling, but its very unconventionality prohibits any reliable assessment of its fighting potentialities'*

The release to RAF crews of the intelligence about the Me 163 and Me 262 prompted many false 'sighting reports' of the aircraft in advance of any evidence that they had flown operationally.[86]† This was obtained when a Me 163 attacked a PR Spitfire at the end of May and a Me 262 challenged a PR Mosquito in July.[88] From April, however, PR, visiting Lechfeld every few days, had photographed an increasing number of both aircraft.[89] And during May and June the Enigma indicated that their entry into squadron service was imminent. In June the Enigma disclosed that a unit at Leipheim near Augsburg was re-equipping with the Me 163.[90] In May it reported the existence of 'Experimental Unit 262' at Lechfeld, and in June another decrypt, the reply to an enquiry from Luftflotte 3 in Paris, listed the fuel capacity and the overall measurements of the Me 262 and stated that it needed a runway 4,500 feet long. This news, coinciding with the launching of *Overlord*, was the more disturbing in that there was considerable uncertainty about the role intended for the aircraft.[91] During May and June several Enigma decrypts suggested that it was to be used for reconnaissance, but in June a POW claimed that it was to be used as a bomber.[92]

In the event, the Me 163 and 262 did not enter squadron service till August 1944, the delay being to some extent due to the fact that the Allied air forces had frequently bombed Lechfeld, Leipheim and Augsburg between April and July. In the case of the Me 163, advance warning that it was to become operational was obtained from an Enigma decrypt of 26 July which informed 7th Jagd Division that Me 163s would operate with immediate effect round Leipzig in defence of the Leuna hydrogenation plant.[93] A further decrypt in August established that the Me 262 had entered squadron service as a bomber.[94]‡ But if the Allies obtained some relief from

---

* See Appendix 24.

† From this point on, the Enigma having made it suspicious of pilots' reports, AI 2(g) preferred to rely on combat film for proof that a new aircraft had become operational.[87]

‡ It was not until September that the Enigma disclosed that Experimental Unit 262 remained in existence at Lechfeld under Galland with twelve aircraft and seventeen pilots,[95] but the next month would see the first of many Enigma references to the transfer of Me 262 units from the bomber to the fighter role (see Volume III Part 2).

86. *Technical Intelligence Sources*, p 24.   87. ibid, p 26.
88. ibid, pp 25–26; AIR 40/2166, No 2252 of 29 July 1944.
89. AIR 40/2393, AI 2(b)Report of 13 August 1944.
90. CX/MSS/T212/10.
91. CX/MSS/T188/59, T248/83.
92. CX/MSS/T171/77, T189/4, T220/59.
93. CX/MSS/T261/125.
94. CX/MSS/T317/50.
95. CX/MSS/T327/91.

this delay, they benefited still more after September, when Germany was increasingly unable either to maintain the production of the latest aircraft or to carry out the training of pilots.

The Allies had learned in July from the decrypt of a signal from the Japanese Naval Mission in Berlin that, although the GAF then had fewer than 100 jet aircraft, it would have 300 by September and would be receiving them at the rate of 1,000 a month by January 1945;[96] and as late as November the same source reported in a decrypt circulated on 2 December that the production of Me 163s would be 100 a month by the end of the year, by which time the number produced would have reached 500.[97] It was no doubt in the light of the first of these two items of intelligence that in September the USAAF, which did not expect to receive jets of its own till October 1945, gave high priority, second only to the oil target, to the attack on plants producing jet air-frames and engines,[98] and at the end of September AI learned that the Me 262 production programme had been set back by damage to the Jumo factory at Dessau.[99] It was not solely on this account, however, that neither that aircraft nor the Me 163 ever appeared in large numbers. In the case of the Me 163 the Japanese Naval Mission in November attributed the failure to Germany's inability to produce more than a tenth of the planned amount of one of the components (brom-acetone) of the fuel used by the aircraft,[100] and the accuracy of this explanation was to be confirmed at the end of the year. In December the Enigma disclosed that Germany was faced with still another difficulty; it reported in that month that the number of Me 163 pilots completing their training, which had been 38 in October, had dropped to nil.[101]

These difficulties, brought about by the Allied air offensive against German communications by area bombing and by the attack on oil targets as much as by attacks on air-frame and aero-engine factories, also prevented the Ar 234 from becoming a serious menace. In September 1944, when nothing definite had been learned of this aircraft since the previous February, the Enigma established that it was being used for strategic reconnaissance.[102] Beginning in September, it carried out high-speed reconnaissance over the United Kingdom on several occasions.[103] In October, however, the Enigma

---

96. SJA 579 of 23 July 1944.
97. SJA 1233 of 2 December 1944.
98. Craven and Cate, *The Army Air Forces in World War II*, Vol III (1951), p 659.
99. AIR 40/2393, AI 2(a) Report of 29 September 1944.
100. SJA 1233 of 2 December 1944.
101. CX/MSS/T407/43.
102. CX/MSS/T327/91.
103. Webster and Frankland, op cit, Vol III, p 273; SJA 995 of 4 October 1944.

gave what turned out to be a month's notice that it was to become operational as a bomber, and in the same month the decrypt of a signal from the Japanese Naval Mission provided a lengthy account of its impressive characteristics.[104] This intelligence precipitated some alarm as to the number of Ar 234s that Germany might produce in 1945, though AI insisted – rightly, as we shall see – that they would not appear in numbers sufficient to justify real anxiety.*

---

* See Volume III Part 2.

104. CX/MSS/T336/93, T365/31, T366/66, T369/75.

PART XII

The V-Weapons

CHAPTER 40

The V-Weapons during 1943

THE GERMAN liquid fuel rocket programme started in the early 1930s.[1] Experiments and static firings were carried out from 1932 at a site at the Army's artillery testing ground at Kummersdorf, near Berlin. A series of rockets were designed thereafter, from A-1 through A-5, of which the A-4, which also later went under the name of V-weapon,* was to become an operational weapon weighing 12 tons, with a warhead of about one ton and a speed of nearly 4,000 mph. The first successful launchings were of two A-2s from a site at Borkum in December 1934. Fifteen months later General von Fritsch, the C-in-C of the German Army, inspected the programme and encouraged Dornberger, who was in charge, to design a weapon for operational use, with a warhead of about a ton (1,000 kg) and a range of about 150 miles. Peenemünde, on the island of Usedom near Swinemünde and about 50 miles from Stettin, was to be the new Army development station. By the end of 1937 the next rocket in the series, the A-3, was fired from a launch point on Greifswalder Oie, not far from Peenemünde. Two rockets were fired, but the results were somewhat disappointing, and indicated that problems of control had yet to be solved. This caused some delay to work on the A-4, while the A-5 was introduced as a test vehicle. Hitler visited Kummersdorf in the spring of 1939 and witnessed a combustion test, but was not convinced that a large rocket would become an important weapon.

By the spring of 1942 the first experimental A-4s were nearing completion; the first static firing took place on 18 March. Trial launchings began at Peenemünde in June 1942. On 13 June one was fired only to return to earth about a mile away; control troubles continued to be the difficulty. On 3 October, six years after the weapon had been conceived, an A-4 achieved accuracy over a range of about 120 miles. Three more were launched before the end of the year. None was as successful as the October firing, but Speer was

---

* A = Aggregat, a non-committal cover-name meaning 'unit' or 'series'. V initially stood for Versuchsmuster (experimental type) but later came to be used by the Germans as the equivalent to Vergeltungswaffe = reprisal weapon.

1. W Dornberger, *V2*, (English edition 1954); B Collier, *The Defence of the United Kingdom* (1957), Chapter XXII; D Irving, *The Mare's Nest* (1964), Parts I and II.

impressed. At the end of 1942 he issued a decree for the weapon's production.

At that time Hitler was supporting the project. In March 1943 his interest declined: he is said to have had a dream that the A-4 would not reach England. In July 1943, however, he was shown a film of the October 1942 launching, and the status of the programme was described to him by Dornberger and von Braun, the designer; and on 25 July he decreed that 'the successful prosecution of the war against England requires the maximum output of A-4 weapons in the shortest time'.[2] Priority was then given to a programme for raising the production of the A-4 to 900 a month by the end of the year; with final assembly at Peenemünde, Friedrichshafen and Wiener Neustadt.[3] The weapon's designers were still proposing a warhead of about one ton and a range of about 150 miles.

By that time the GAF's programme for the development of a pilotless aircraft had also reached the point at which decisions had to be made about production. Shortly before the outbreak of war the firm of Argus had been invited to submit plans for a pilotless missile with a range of 350 miles incorporating the firm's experiments with a pulse-jet. Since the pulse-jet had proved unsuitable for such a range, and since the radio devices necessary to control the projectile over that range had been in short supply, the project had been dropped. In the spring of 1942, when Hitler ordered reprisals after the bombing of Lübeck, the GAF had revived it. Since it could now be fired from northern France, a missile with a much shorter range was specified which could use the pulse-jet and dispense with radio control, and it would carry a warhead roughly the same as the rocket's. In June 1942 the Air Ministry had given the revised project, officially known as FZG 76 to conceal its true purpose,* the highest priority; in December the first launching of the missile from a catapult had satisfied the test conditions by flying about 3,000 yards. By the middle of 1943 some 50 launchings had been made and, although there had been many failures, one at least had fulfilled expectations; a range of about 150 miles and a speed of 375 mph had been shown to be possible. At that point Göring ordered production plans to be made.[4] The target was set at 60 per month in September 1943, 300 in October and 5,000 by the end of 1943. But production at Fallersleben began only late in September.[5]

---

* FZG = Flakzielgerät = Anti-aircraft target apparatus. As the air-frame was manufactured by the firm of Gerhard Fieseler, while the firm of Argus produced the propulsion unit, the weapon was sometimes also called the Fieseler 103.

2. Collier, op cit, p 339.
3. Ehrman, *Grand Strategy*, Vol V (1956), p 306.
4. Collier, op cit, pp 338–339, 353–355; Irving, op cit, pp 72–73, 91.
5. Ehrman, op cit, Vol V, p 306.

For the development and testing of the pilotless aircraft the GAF had set up an experimental site and airfield at Peenemünde, alongside the Army's research station. At first co-operation between the two projects, the Army's A-4, which also became known as the V 2, and the FZG 76, which became known as the V 1, had been close and mutually beneficial. As they developed, however, and necessarily diverged, they began to compete with each other, and by 1943 the rivalry was acute.[6]

□

Although long-range weapons had been studied theoretically in England, where the pioneer work with liquid fuel rockets carried out in the 1920s by Goddard in the USA and by Oberth in Germany was well known, no immediately practicable suggestions for long-range weapons had been made before the outbreak of war; and there was no suspicion that Germany was engaged in developing such weapons.

In the autumn of 1939, after a scrutiny of past SIS reports in an effort to throw light on Hitler's 'secret weapon' speech*, the Air Ministry's Scientific Intelligence Officer noted that, while there was no justification for thinking that the Führer had been referring to gliding bombs, a number of reports had mentioned a small pilotless aircraft and a long-range gun. He concluded that they were probably under development in Germany. He also noted that, apart from one recent reference to work on a 'rocket shell', no evidence was available about the development of long-range rockets.[7] In another report on new German weapons, compiled in May 1940, he did not mention these weapons;[8] there had clearly been no further information indicating that they were under active development.

In the same month there appears to have been a report to the effect that the German Army was experimenting with a 30 ton rocket at a site near Stettin;[9] and in August 1940 the SIS in Switzerland obtained from a source in contact with Admiral Canaris the information that 'guns of exceptionally long range' were being tested at Peenemünde. These items did not find their way into reports made by the Service intelligence branches in Whitehall – a good indication that their association with the information given in

---

* See Volume I, p 99.

6. Collier, op cit, pp 335–338, 357; Dornberger, op cit, pp 94–97.
7. AIR 20/8535, ASI Report, No 1, of 11 November 1939; R V Jones, *Most Secret War* (1978) pp 65–66.
8. AIR 20/1622, ASI Report No 5 of 23 May 1940.
9. Iriving, op cit, p 33.

the Oslo Report of November 1939 went unnoticed. The Oslo Report* had stated that Peenemünde was the site of the testing ground for remote control glider rockets propelled after launch from aircraft, and that the Germans were developing rocket propelled remote controlled shells. In October 1940 the SIS reported that a 'fairly good source' had said that a number of rockets with gas filling and a range of 100 km were being prepared on the French Channel coast.[10] This report aroused little attention before the spring of 1943, and it was the last information about long-range weapons to be received for over two years. But at the end of 1942 the SIS and POW began to provide a series of more detailed reports from which a considerable body of imprecise and conflicting evidence was built up during the next three months.

The first of these reports, dated 18 December 1942, was received by the SIS from a chemical engineer who was travelling extensively on his firm's business. He related a conversation in a Berlin restaurant between a Professor Fauner (a Professer Forner was known to exist) of the Berlin Technische Hochschule and an engineer, Stefan Szenassy. They had mentioned a rocket containing five tons of explosive, having a maximum range of 200 km and being capable of doing damage over an area of ten km square. Pressed for more information, this source produced two more reports. In one, dated 1 January 1943, he added that the rocket's course and range were directed by a metal body, inserted into the projectile before firing and working automatically when the rocket reached its zenith, and that the rocket then flew horizontally before turning over on to its target. In the other, dated 31 March 1943, he reported that its blast effect was considerable and that a large area was cleared when it was first tried out between 30 November and 2 December 1942. It was manufactured at the Opel works in Rüsselsheim and was known to have been tried out near Swinemünde.[11] This source was a new one, but other information he provided on aircraft factories helped to establish his reliability.

Another SIS source, 'undoubtedly reliable and well practised in examining his informants and sifting their information', reported on 17 January and 8 February 1943 that a new factory had been built at Peenemünde where a new weapon was being manufactured. It was a rocket which had been fired from a testing ground. He added that it had previously been tested in Latin America – a statement which may well have tended to reduce the value of the

---

* See Volume I, pp 100, 508–512.

10.	CAB 121/211, SIC file B/Defence/2, Vol I, COS (43) 342 (o) of 27 June 1943, (A) (i).
11.	ibid, (A) (iv).

rest of his information. He also reported that a large aerodrome was being constructed on Usedom and that one of the rockets fired there had been seen to rise vertically and suddenly to disappear in a horizontal direction.[12]

A third source, a neutral, reported to the SIS on 14 February 1943 that at a big factory in Peenemünde experiments were being carried out with a new rocket which contained ten tons of explosive and had a range of 100 km. The source's informant was said to have given the information from his personal observation, and to have added that the rockets were shortly to be used on the French coast against England.[13] Similar information from a neutral source, reporting at second or third hand, was received on 7 March 1943. This stated that Krupp was mass-producing rocket guns with a range of 120 km; they were being placed on the Channel coast and were to be brought into action during the middle of March.[14]

By 30 March 1943 the SIS had acquired a much more detailed report from 'a most reliable and expert source which has provided most valuable information over a long period'. He was indebted for his evidence to Luxembourgers who had been pressed into service for construction work at Peenemünde, and the contents suggest that it came from more than one informant. It reported that experiments were being made with rockets which could carry explosives up to 250 kg (ie about ¼ ton) and that one out of every sixteen experiments appeared to be successful. The experiments were said to be under the direction of the inventor, a French engineer. A rocket 17–18 metres long, 4–5 metres in diameter was mentioned. It was intended to fire this to a very long range by means of an extremely powerful explosive, and to direct it in flight by radio control. The filling of the head was compressed air and it would be able to destroy houses over a big area. Trial results were not up to expectations. During the period 10 October to 30 December 1942 three trials were held; the first projectile fell in the sea about level with the bay of Danzig; the second travelled only some eighteen miles; the third was a bad 'tipper' due to the failure of a radio control valve. Moreover, a propellant had not yet been found good enough to get ranges of hundreds of kilometres. 'Incidentally', the source added, 'it is during one of these trials that General Udet is said to have been killed'.* The report went on to describe other rocket experiments: the development of rocket assisted take-off (ATO) for fighters; the rocket propulsion of an air-launched torpedo; a high speed fighter aircraft. All this was going on at Peenemünde, where there was a test pit for each type of experiment to a

---

* General Udet committed suicide on 17 November 1941, see Volume II, p 145.

12.   ibid, (A) (ii).   13.   ibid, (A) (iii).   14.   ibid, (A) (v).

number of 12 or 16; the rocket trials were carried out in pit number 7.[15]

These reports agreed with each other in referring to long-range rocket development and in stating where the development was taking place. But the possibility that they were supplying 'planted' information could not be ruled out; it was still being borne in mind in September 1943[16] and was to bedevil the intelligence investigations for weeks afterwards. The reports were inconsistent, moreover, in what they said about the rocket and its performance; and especially when taken together with such impossible claims as that made for the destruction power of compressed air, the mention by some of them of a weapon with a danger area of ten km square seemed 'too far fetched to be completely reliable'.[17]

Like that received from the SIS, technical information provided by POW engendered uncertainty and scepticism. The first POW to refer to rocket development had done so on 24 January 1943. He had said that ranges up to six km had been obtained, and that ranges of 60 or even 100 km were hoped for, and had remarked that it was incredible how large the rocket was – 'as large as a motor car'.[18] Another prisoner, a technical officer attached to a Panzer regiment in north Africa whose technical ability was not in doubt, had produced reliable information on tanks, but had obviously relied to some extent on his imagination when talking about rockets. He had spoken of one having a weight of 120 tons, a weight of explosive of 60 to 80 tons, a range of 1,500 to 1,800 km, and a blast sufficient to 'wipe out' everything within a radius of 30 km. This was on 29 March 1943.[19] A little earlier he had referred to 'those 50 to 100 ton things which travel 60 to 70 km'.[20] By the end of March, however, CSDIC had at least produced dependable evidence that long-range rocket experiments had been taking place for some time and that, despite their discrepancy and exaggeration, there was some substance in the SIS and POW reports.

On 22 March 1943 General Crüwell, captured in north Africa in May 1942, and General von Thoma, captured in November, were brought together for the first time in a room which had been 'bugged'. General von Thoma was heard to say:

' . . . but no progress whatsoever can have been made in this rocket business. I saw it once with Feldmarschall Brauchitsch, there is a special

---

15.   ibid, (A) (vi).
16.   CAB 121/211, COS (43) 592 (o) of 29 September 1943.
17.   R V Jones, Broadcast on BBC Radio 4, *The Rocket's Red Glare*, 1 August 1974.
18.   CAB 120/748, PM registered file, 413/4, JIC/492/43 of 21 April 1943.
19.   ibid.
20.   ibid.

ground near Kunersdorf*. . . . They've got these huge things which they've brought up here. . . . They've always said they would go 15 km into the atmosphere and then. . . . You only aim at an area. . . . If one was to . . . every few days . . . frightful. . . . The Major there was full of hope, he said "Wait until next year and then the fun will start". . . . There's no limit. . . .'[21]

As General Von Thoma had clearly seen something of experimental long-range rocket development, and as it was known from his other conversations that he had very good technical knowledge, his overheard remarks at last convinced many in Whitehall that the German rocket development programme had to be taken seriously.

☐

In January 1943, after the SIS reports had begun to come in, the PRU was asked to photograph Peenemünde. The area had previously been covered only once, in May 1942. A PRU Spitfire had then obtained photographs which showed considerable constructional activity, including three large unusual circular emplacements, but they had attracted little attention.[22] On 19 January 1943 and again on 1 March new photographs revealed that more construction, including many large buildings and a power house, had taken place. In itself, however, this information could neither confirm nor contradict the existence of a long-range rocket programme.[23]

In January 1943 MI took the further step of warning the CIU that there was some indication that the Germans were developing long-range rocket projectors, capable of firing weapons to the United Kingdom from the French coast, and asked it to keep a close watch for the erection of rails, scaffolding and unusual constructions in the area.[24]

At the end of March, after considering the other evidence in the light of the report on von Thoma's conversation, MI decided to alert operational staffs to the possibility that a grave threat from rockets was developing. On 11 April, after consultation with the Scientific Adviser to the Army Council (SAAC) and the Controller of Projectile Development (CPD) in the Ministry of Supply, the VCIGS circulated for consideration by the Vice-Chiefs of Staff a paper on 'German Long-Range Rocket Development'. The paper

---

* Thought at the time, correctly, to be Kummersdorf.

21. CAB 121/211, COS (43) 592 (o) of 29 September 1943, para 4.
22. AIR 41/7, *Photographic Reconnaissance*, Vol II, pp 110, 127; C Babington Smith, *Evidence in Camera* (1958), pp 200–201.
23. CAB 121/211, COS (43) 342 (o), (D) (i); AIR 34/196, CIU Interpretation Report DS 1 of 29 April 1943.
24. Babington Smith, op cit, p 202.

accepted that, though still unconfirmed, the evidence obtained since the beginning of the year strongly suggested that the Germans had been doing considerable development work on long-range rockets. It quoted from the evidence one set of figures: 5 tons of explosive, and 130 miles (200 km) range. It offered a technical opinion that it was possible to attain that range with a multi-stage rocket whose weight would be of the order of 9½ tons, having a warhead of 1¼ tons containing 1,600 lbs of explosive. 'Such a rocket', it said, 'would have a diameter of about 30 inches and a length of about 95 feet. The projector would have to be some 100 yards long, unless an extremely accurate method of directional control has in fact been developed'. It explained that 'while the exact form of this projectile is not known . . . the estimations are based on one particular possibility which has been studied in some detail in CPD. . . .' It offered three alternatives as to how the projector, a main disadvantage, might be constructed.[25]

On 12 April the Vice-Chiefs of Staff agreed that the evidence summarised in the paper necessitated a report to the Prime Minister and, 'in view of the powerful moral and surprise effect of such a weapon', a warning to the Minister of Home Security.[26] Their minute to the Prime Minister, agreed on 15 April, said: 'The Chiefs of Staff feel that you should be made aware of reports of German experiments with long-range rockets. The fact that five reports have been received since the end of 1942 indicates a foundation of fact even if details are inaccurate. . . . The Chiefs of Staff are of the opinion that no time should be lost in establishing the facts. . . . They therefore suggest that you should appoint an individual who should be charged with the task forthwith. They suggest for your consideration the name of Mr Duncan Sandys. . . .'[27] The appointment of Mr Duncan Sandys, Joint Parliamentary Secretary to the Ministry of Supply, followed on 20 April.[28] His terms of reference for his investigation, which was later to be given the code-name *Bodyline*, required him first of all to establish whether the intelligence which pointed to the development of long-range rockets was reliable; if satisfied that it was, he was both to investigate ways and means of acquiring precise intelligence about the weapon's form and projector, and about the state of its development, and to draw up a programme of counter-measures.

The appointment at this juncture of an investigator with ministerial powers and these terms of reference has been criticised since

25. CAB 121/211, COS (43) 184 (0) of 11 April 1943.
26. ibid, COS (43) 90th Meeting 12 April 1943.
27. W S Churchill, *The Second World War*, Vol VI (1952), pp 201–202.
28. CAB 121/211, COS (43) 203 (0) of 19 April 1943.

the end of the war. The war-time ADI (Sc) has argued that it would have been better if the intelligence authorities had been allowed to establish the reliability of the evidence and determine the characteristics of the weapon before counter-measures were considered. MI, he wrote, 'while correctly interpreting the early intelligence reports as indicating a long-range rocket, nevertheless caused unending trouble by barking too soon. . . . We [ADI (Sc)] . . . had raised no alarm at all . . . because we did not know enough and certainly no one else knew enough, to take any counter-measures'.[29] But it must be remembered that the War Office was bound to be reluctant to leave responsibility for the intelligence work entirely to the Air Ministry. At the time, moreover, it could not be overlooked that if delay in preparing counter-measures was accepted, intelligence might still fail to establish such vital facts as the range of the weapon and the weight of its warhead before the threat materialised. This consideration apart, it may be argued that against even the possibility of so great a threat it was imperative to avoid delay in taking steps to reduce it, and that, like civil defence preparations, those steps, probably bombing of essential facilities, would be essentially the same whatever the nature of the weapon.

A second criticism has been expressed by the official historian in the following terms: 'An investigator accustomed to found his conclusions on evidence from the enemy's camp would be more likely . . . to establish the nature of the new weapon than someone used to working on a wider field and therefore more apt to be influenced by the views of British experts as to what was feasible'.[30] We shall see that the assumptions of the British rocket experts did indeed have unfortunate consequences for the collection and interpretation of the intelligence. We shall also see, however, that this was practically unavoidable in view of the novelty of the V-weapons, the paucity of intelligence about their performance and technical characteristics while they remained in the research and development stage and – not least because these were subjects on which Sigint was throwing no light and with which the SIS agents had no familiarity – the difficulty of distinguishing what was reliable from what was not in the intelligence that was coming in.

□

Immediately on his appointment Mr Duncan Sandys encouraged the SIS and CSDIC to collect further intelligence, asked for more photographic reconnaissance of Peenemünde, and requested from

29. RUSI Journal, August 1947, pp 361–362, Lecture given by R V Jones on 19 February 1947.
30. Collier, op cit, p 342.

the JIC its considered opinion as to the reliability of the reports circulated with the VCIGS's paper of 11 April and of any additional reports the JIC may have had relating to the development of German long-range rockets and to the development of exceptionally long range artillery. He also asked the JIC specific questions arising out of the reports. What information was there of special activities at Opel and Krupp? Had tests of rockets been made in Latin America? As to PR, what were the strange circular constructions at Peenemünde? What were the structures which had been discovered by photographs of the Fécamp area, and at Cap Gris Nez, which had not yet been explained?

The JIC replied on 25 April. There was good evidence that experiments were being carried out at Peenemünde in rocket development. That the Germans were developing anti-aircraft and field rockets should be accepted. The evidence that long-range rockets carrying heavy quantities of high explosive were being developed was less convincing, but it would be reasonable to deduce from the SIS and POW reports that some attention was being paid to the possibility. However, the JIC felt reasonably confident that if experiments of this nature were being carried out, they must still be some way from the operational stage.[31] In answer to Mr Duncan Sandys's specific requests for further information, it could provide none except that one report received early in 1942, while making no reference to rockets, had said that the firm of Opel had produced a new liquid propellant and had claimed that this solved the problem of a rocket propelled aircraft.[32]

On 29 April, by which time it had been instructed to give highest priority to the search for evidence of new weapons, the CIU issued a detailed interpretation of the facilities photographed at Peenemünde.[33] The report compared the results of a fourth sortie, carried out on 22 April, with earlier photographs. It drew attention to five major features: a factory area; two large high buildings; a power house; an elliptical embankment with associated buildings; and three circular emplacements. The general appearance of the factory suggested that it might be for the manufacture of explosives because it had extensive steam piping; some of its buildings had been there since May 1942, some were new, and clearances indicated that more were to be erected. Two buildings, whose construction had been in an early stage in May, were unusually large, one 670 feet by 318, the other 810 feet by 400; they, too, were thought to be concerned with production of explosives. It was noted that the power house

31. JIC (43) 188 (o) of 25 April 1943.
32. ibid, Annex B.
33. AIR 34/196, CIU Report DS No 1 of 29 April 1943.

and its chimneys were not smoking. (It was working; but the Germans had taken steps to suppress smoke). Near the seashore at the northern tip of the area was an elliptic embankment. Its major and minor axes were 670 feet and 470 feet respectively; it was served by rail; and it had a deep trench with vertical walls and shelving ends. A travelling crane spanned the trench, in which there was an unidentified tall object. A number of buildings were associated with the emplacement, as well as some unexplained tower-like structures; one of the structures had moved between photographic frames. On some of the photographs a large cloud of white smoke could be seen drifting across the area. On one photograph an object 25 feet long was seen projecting from one end of one of the service buildings: on the next frame, four seconds later, this too had disappeared. The three circular emplacements, well away from the factory area, were as they had been at the time of the first reconnaissance. 525 feet in diameter, two had earth embankments; they were 620 and 650 yards apart but only in the centre one were there signs of any structures.*

Although there was nothing in this evidence which pointed decisively to experimental work with rockets, it strengthened the opinion that the most unusual features, the ellipse and the circles, indicated a research establishment which, because of the mounded emplacements, might have something to do with propellants, explosives or projectiles. It was this evidence from the CIU that convinced Mr Duncan Sandys that the whole Peenemünde site was an experimental station and that its elliptic and circular earthworks were probably for the testing of explosives and projectiles.[34] It was mainly on the strength of the CIU's interpretation that he produced an interim report for the Chiefs of Staff on 17 May 1943, which concluded that the Germans had been engaged on the development of a long-range rocket for some time and that 'such scant evidence as exists suggests that it may be far advanced'.[35] The report also revised upwards the likely size of the rocket† and, since it might take a long time to obtain conclusive evidence, listed possible counter-measures and civil preparations and recommended that they should be studied while more intelligence was being sought. The Vice-Chiefs of Staff approved this recommendation on 20 May.[36]

□

---

* See map facing this page.   † See below, p 372.

34. Babington Smith, op cit, pp 203–204.
35. CAB 121/211, COS (43) 259 (0) of 17 May 1943.
36. ibid, COS (4) 107th Meeting, 20 May 1943.

Between the end of May and the end of June the search for further intelligence produced some general warnings from POW and the SIS about the preparation of a long-range weapon for reprisals against the United Kingdom. The weapon was being called 'a rocket weapon for the Channel'. The bombardment of southern England with guns having a range of 120 miles was to be expected shortly. According to other warnings, experiments with a new gun 'on the rocket principle', with a range of several hundred kilometres, were finished, and the weapon would be ready by the autumn; guns with a range up to 250 km were a constant topic in military circles; and it had been learned from high official circles in Germany that large rocket-type projectors might be used against London at any time.[37] One POW said that his commanding officer had been told during a recent visit to Hitler and Göring that a rocket bomb or rocket ammunition was to be used against the United Kingdom soon.[38] But the new developments at this time were the arrival of references to a new fuel and the confirmation by photographic reconnaissance that a rocket did indeed exist at Peenemünde.

The POW from the Panzer regiment was re-interrogated. He now stated that Germany's rocket research incorporated a new method of propulsion, called an 'athodyd' by the interrogators, and a new fuel which could also be used as an explosive.[39] It was clear that the athodyd could have nothing to do with a rocket.* For the new fuel the POW claimed an impossibly large specific heat. When the PRU on 20 June photographed a launching site in the Black Forest that he claimed to have visited in 1942 it failed to find anything,[40] and his credibility took another knock.

Another POW, a general, was questioned about the athodyd. He had no recent knowledge but confirmed that it existed, and also vouched for the development of a liquid propellant projectile which could travel 200 km. He stated his belief that the fuel was pure alcohol and burned with a steely blue flame. He had been present at experiments on the Greifswalder Oie in which at least one such projectile was fired as far as Bornholm† It was about six metres long and contained 140 kg of explosive. Unlike the other POW he though that difficulties with the materials required for fuel containers, jets and burners would hold up the mass production of the projectiles.[41]

---

* An acronym from Aerodynamic-Thermodynamic-Duct; the modern term is ram-jet. In fact, the athodyd was used to power the flying bomb, see below, p 429.
† This was presumably the A-3.

37.   ibid, COS (43) 342 (o), (A) (viii), (ix), (xi), (xii), (xiii).
38.   ibid, (B) (iii).   39.   ibid, (B) (i).
40.   AIR 34/196, CIU Report DS No 11 of 21 June 1943.
41.   CAB 121/211, COS (43) 342 (o), (B) (ii).

The first confirmation that a large rocket existed was meanwhile being provided by photographic reconnaissance of Peenemünde. By the end of May the CIU had reported two new features on the basis of the fifth PRU flight over Peenemünde, carried out on 14 May. The first was that a fan-shaped area was being prepared on the foreshore on the eastward side of the ellipse. The second was that the photographs of 14 May and, on further investigation, those of 22 April showed that road vehicles and railway trucks inside and near the ellipse were carrying unidentifiable cylindrical objects measuring 38 feet by eight.[42] The next photographs, taken on 20 May, had also revealed a cylindrical object, 40 feet by eight, on a transverser carriage; the CIU report had added that although the station appeared to be very active, the power house still gave no sign of being in use.[43] The next CIU report, interpreting photographs taken on 12 June, noted that a 'thick vertical column about 40 feet high and 4 feet thick' had appeared on the foreshore.[44] On seeing these latest photographs ADI (Sc) drew Sandys's attention to the appearance on them of another object, about 35 feet long, which he believed to be a rocket.[45] In an addendum to its report the CIU announced that 'this object is 35 feet long and appears to have a blunt point. For 25 feet of its length the diameter is about 8 feet. The appearance . . . is not incompatible with it being a cylinder tapered at one end and provided with 3 radial fins at the other'.[46] The CIU also said that the object had a definite resemblance to those revealed in the earlier photographs.

On 23 June the next cover of Peenemünde, the best to date, confirmed and amplified this description. Excellent photographs clearly revealed two identical 'torpedo-like' objects within the ellipse. They were 38 feet long, 6 feet in diameter, with a tail of three fins which started 25 feet from the nose and was 12 feet wide. This evidence of the activities at Peenemünde proved to be a critical point in the investigation.[47]

Since 11 June, when a reconnaissance programme had been agreed between Sandys and the Air Ministry, the PRU, in addition to Peenemünde, had photographed Lettstadter Höhe, Greifswalder Oie, Rügen, Bornholm and Holzkirchen, but without producing any firm intelligence on weapons or their testing.[48] On 24

---

42. AIR 34/196, CIU Report DS 3 of 24 May 1943.
43. ibid, DS 4 of 26 May, DS 5 of 27 May 1943.
44. ibid, DS 9 of 16 June 1943.
45. Jones, *Most Secret War*, p 340.
46. AIR 34/196, CIU Report DS 9 Addendum, undated, June 1943.
47. ibid, DS 16 of 28 June 1943.
48. CAB 101/90, VCAS Minutes to Sandys 4 and 10 June 1943, Sandys Minute to ACAS (o) 11 June 1943.

June the Adam Opel AG at Rüsselsheim had also been photographed and some new construction was noticed, but it was impossible to judge its extent or purpose.[49]

The PRU had also been photographing as much as possible of the area of France within 130 miles of London: nothing suspicious was detected except in the Inghem-Wissant area near Cap Gris Nez, where a large concrete emplacement was seen under construction on 13 June.[50]* At three or four other places in northern France earlier photographs had shown some unexplained construction work; but on 27 June nothing had been observed there which anybody could definitely associate with rockets or projectors.[52]

Mr Duncan Sandys reviewed the latest intelligence in a third report on 28 June (his second report of 17 June[53] had been confined to suggestions for tracking the missile by radar, put forward by an expert committee). 'The German long-range rocket has undoubtedly reached an advanced state of development. . . . Experimental work in connection with this project is going on at high pressure on the island of Peenemünde . . . where frequent firings are taking place'. POW and SIS reports indicated that the range of the weapon might be up to 130 miles. As to the imminence of the threat, evidence remained scanty and what little there was was contradictory. If a range of 130 miles was accepted, the rocket was most likely to be fired from the Pas de Calais; but the programme of obtaining photographic cover of all northern France within 130 miles of London, though not yet completed, had so far detected construction work of a suspicious character only at Wissant. Another consideration was the suggestion in some of the SIS and POW evidence that 'important technical troubles are still being experienced which . . . seriously affect the accuracy of the weapon'. As against that, some of this same evidence indicated 'that Hitler sees in the long-range rocket a means of retaliating against England for the bombing of the Ruhr and that he is pressing for it to be brought into action as quickly as possible, without awaiting the completion of development'. On the state of readiness of the rocket the report concluded that 'should it be decided . . . to accept a considerable loss in accuracy and efficiency, it is probable that the development of the weapon is sufficiently advanced for it to be put into operational use

---

* The SIS organised an investigation of this site, but three of the agents sent there were unable to get into the area, which was heavily guarded, and a fourth was arrested.[51]

49. AIR 34/196, CIU Report DS 15 of 28 June 1943.
50. ibid, DS 6 of 31 May, DS 13 of 27 June 1943.
51. CAB 121/211, COS (43) 342 (0), (A) (xvi).
52. AIR 34/196, CIU Report DS 8 of 15 June, DS 13 of 27 June 1943.
53. CAB 121/211, COS (43) 312 (0) of 17 June 1943.

at a very early date'.[54] On the evidence of the Peenemünde photographs of 23 June Sandys also gave a new assessment of the rocket's characteristics.

□

In the light of the evidence they had seen up to the end of June 1943, few of those concerned in the investigation disagreed with these conclusions. There was a very considerable difference, however, between the status of the evidence pointing to the probability that a long-range rocket was being developed and that of the information which described the rocket's technical features. The latter contained on the one hand so many gaps and inconsistencies and, on the other hand, so few clues as to which of the conflicting reports should be trusted, that the estimate of the rocket's characteristics and performance had perforce to be made by British rocket experts with assumptions made on the basis of their own technical knowledge. But some of their assumptions were incorrect.

The first wrong assumption, that the rocket used solid propellant when it in fact used liquid oxygen and alcohol, arose simply from British lack of experience with liquid fuelled rockets except in one limited application. The second arose because the first estimate of the weight of the warhead was increased – and greatly exaggerated – in the light of the claims made by many of the intelligence reports. The third concerned the method of launching. Since British rockets were uncontrolled once they had left their projectors, there was no reason for thinking that, as was the case, the German long-range rocket was controlled during its burning by vanes in its jet to give it initial stability and improve accuracy, and could thus be launched vertically from a simple apparatus. As a result, the references in the intelligence reports to rocket shells or rocket guns were taken to be descriptions of the rocket which supported the assumption that it must be fired from a long projector, which might be enclosed in a tunnel or a tube. Once made, these assumptions exerted an effect on the collection of further intelligence; in particular, they led to a search for large projectors which did not exist but which had been given prominence in the first estimate, that contained in the paper circulated by the VCIGS on 11 April.* Equally important, they prevented the correct interpretation of such accurate intelligence as was coming in about some features of the rocket.

The estimate in the paper of 11 April was merely a feasibility study which showed that a range of 130 miles could be attained by

---

* See above, pp 363–364.

54. ibid, COS (43) 349 (o) of 28 June 1943.

a two-stage rocket using solid propellant, 95 feet long and 30 inches in diameter, and carrying a warhead of 1¼ tons. It can be faulted only if undue reliance is placed on hindsight; those who have criticised it since the war for assuming the use of solid propellant[55] have overlooked in their turn that the intelligence reports had not then thrown up anything that clashed with this assumption.

This was not quite the case when the Sandys report on 17 May offered a new estimate, saying that it was 'likely that the weapon . . . is a multi-staged rocket propelled projectile 20 feet in length and 10 feet in diameter', with a solid propellant and a total weight of 70 tons – including a warhead of 10 tons – and launched from a projector.[56] The white clouds noted on the photographs taken of Peenemünde on 22 April were either the vapour caused by the filling of a rocket with liquid oxygen or smoke from other rocket tests. But the fact that nothing had yet suggested liquid fuel goes some way to excuse the failure to grasp this. Moreover, the assumption of a multi-staged rocket avoided the necessity of assuming that a liquid propellant was required if the reported range was to be achieved. The serious mistake, apart from technical criticism, in this second assessment was its acceptance of the intelligence reports which claimed that the warhead weighed as much as ten tons.

The Sandys report of 28 June offered a third assessment of the rocket's characteristics. In the light of the photographic evidence from Peenemünde of 12 June that it was 38 feet in length and 7 feet in diameter, and on the continuing assumption that it used solid fuel, the total weight was now judged to be between 60 and 100 tons, and the weight of the warhead two to eight tons, and it was thought possible that the tower-like structures photographed at Peenemünde were the launching or projector apparatus. The assessment thus continued to overlook the possibility that the rocket used liquid fuel, and did not have to be multi-staged to reach the required performance, even though the intelligence reports had at last made several references to the use of liquid fuel. In addition, the appearance on the photographs of 12 June of a 'thick vertical column' on the foreshore at Peenemünde had been noted but not commented on.

At the same time, study of the photographs of the Peenemünde objects had raised several questions which the estimates left unanswered. The shape of the nose of the object was not compatible with it being a projectile of high performance. The large fins pointed to severe problems in attaining stability and accuracy at launch, for the fact that the rocket was subject to jet control had still not been

---

55. Collier, op cit, p 241; Irving, op cit, p 37.
56. CAB 121/211, COS (43) 259 (o) of 17 May, para 6.

suspected. And were the objects indeed multi-staged? It was these questions which induced a few people, notably Lord Cherwell, to question even whether a large rocket was being developed. Sceptical to begin with, they had become even more so as they considered the various estimates proposed for the weight and performance of the weapon.

When the third estimate was issued Lord Cherwell had already challenged those of 11 April and 17 May. On 22 April in a letter to the Prime Minister he had doubted whether the Germans had solved the technical problems connected with firing a long-range rocket from a projector, and had also been sceptical because nothing had been seen in the Calais area, where the launching sites would have to be placed.[57] After studying the report of 17 May he had become convinced that a rocket of 70 tons could not be fired and that the Germans could not establish the necessary installations in the Calais area unobserved, and had told the Prime Minister that he did 'not favour directing any considerable effort to cope with what seems to me to be a remote contingency'. An un-manned radio directed aeroplane would be more feasible.[58] Nor did he relent when he read the assessment given in the Sandys report of 28 June, which had also quoted an estimate by the Ministry of Home Security of the damage the rocket might do – an estimate that each rocket would kill 600 people, seriously injure 1,200 and slightly injure 2,400, and that rockets might be fired at the rate of one an hour over an extended period.[59] On 29 June, when the Defence Committee met to consider the threat, he developed the argument that the rocket story was a well-designed German cover plan to conceal some other development, perhaps a pilotless jet propelled aircraft.[60]

A number of considerations led him to believe that the Germans could not have solved the technical problems of firing such a large rocket. The firing of the rocket would give rise to a terrific flash of light; if firings had taken place it was extraordinary that no flashes had been reported by Swedish fishermen. As to the evidence that had come in, there was a natural tendency to fasten on the reports which fitted in with one's assumptions; but there were many reports that did not fit in. Some, moreover, were highly questionable on scientific grounds. At this point Lord Cherwell emphasised the unreliability of the Panzer regiment POW. If a rocket indeed existed, the assessment of the damage it would do had been exaggerated. The rocket seen in the photographs was clearly a single-stage rocket which would have a maximum range of 40 miles; if a

---

57. PREM 3/110.   58. ibid.
59. CAB 121/211, COS (43) 349 (o).
60. ibid, DO (43) 5th Meeting, 29 June 1943.

double-stage rocket were to be developed, it would have a much smaller projector.

Asked for his opinion, ADI (Sc) rejected the idea of a cover plan and agreed with the intelligence assessment in the Sandys report. The photographs had conclusively proved that a rocket existed; although it was likely that the German experts would prefer to perfect it, there was a chance that Hitler would insist on using it at the earliest possible moment. ADI (Sc) had already circulated these conclusions in a paper dated 26 June. In this paper he had also more or less accepted the Sandys assessment of the weight of the rocket. The paper had stressed that the total weight, like the weight of explosive, remained conjectural, but ADI (Sc), at first inclined to suggest 20 to 40 tons given the photographed dimensions, had settled on 40 to 80 tons after discussion with Sandys's technical advisers.[61]

Sandys and ADI (Sc) had further agreed that, while the study of other counter-measures must continue, 'the most effective way to prevent the use of this weapon is to destroy or disorganise by bombing attack the experimental establishments and factories connected with its development and production'. Nor did Lord Cherwell object to the proposal that Peenemünde should be bombed. This, the main recommendation of the third Sandys report, was accepted by the Defence Committee on 29 June, when the Committee decided that Bomber Command should make the heaviest possible attack on the first occasion when conditions were suitable. The Committee's other decisions were that aerial reconnaissance of Peenemünde should be restricted until the attack was made; that the Air Ministry should consider the bombing of IG Farben factories at Leuna and Ludwigshafen, which had been associated in one report with the production of a new fuel for rockets; that plans should be made for air attack on rocket firing points in France as soon as they were located, but that the bombing of the Wissant construction should be delayed so that its development could be watched; that the RAF should continue the rigorous reconnaissance of the area of northern France within a radius of 130 miles of London; and that the manufacture and installation of radar equipment should be pressed on with.

On the day these decisions were reached in Whitehall Himmler was at Peenemünde to see the firing of two of the A-4 rockets. One of them achieved a range of 145 miles; the other firing was a catastrophic failure. Although unexpected failures were still occurring, about 40 rockets had by then been fired with some degree of

---

61. AIR 20/1681, ASI Interim Report, 'German Long Range Rockets', of 26 June 1943.

success, and Speer had called for a report on the programme and for a comparison between it and other projects – the V 1, the Me 163 rocket aircraft,* the *Wasserfall* anti-aircraft rocket – which competed with it for development and production priorities. In the light of the report it was decided to make no change to the production programme for the V 2 laid down in April 1943 – this had called for the production of 3,080 rockets by December 1944 at a rate rising to 950 a month by the end of the period – and 1 November 1943 remained the date on which the Germans hoped to begin firing rockets operationally from an underground bunker that was being prepared near Watten in the Artois.[62]

□

The Germans intended to use the V-weapons principally against the London area, with a secondary group of targets in the south and south-west including Plymouth, Southampton, Winchester, Aldershot and Bristol. For the offensive against London launching sites were to be situated in and near the Pas de Calais; for the targets in the south and south-west the sites were established further west, many in the Cherbourg peninsula. But while the launching areas were the same for both weapons, installations for the A-4 and the FZG 76 were quite different. A-4 needed a small mobile structure with a clear line of fire towards the target, a clear path from the firing point to its equipment and advanced stores and testing stations at points which had their own communications both with the mobile firing sites and with the rear. FZG 76 needed a more elaborate site consisting of two long inclined rails, bedded at the inner end in a concrete emplacement and pointing in the direction of the target, and stores, testing facilities and accommodation in advanced centres; both sites and centres needing communication with each other and with the rear. For the A-4 sites work began in the spring of 1943 on a plan for 45 sites of simple construction between the Pas de Calais and Cherbourg, with a main forward base at Watten, near St Omer in the Pas de Calais, which was due for completion in mid-October 1943. In May 1943 work was begun on two other A-4 sites near Cherbourg, one of which was converted before completion to a site for the FZG 76. For the FZG sites work only began in August to a plan for 64 main sites, with another 32 in reserve, situated in a belt from Cherbourg to St Omer, and eight protected stores each holding 250 weapons. The firing sites were

---

* See above, p 334.

62.   Collier, op cit, p 339; Irving op cit, pp 28–29, 73–74, 83.

due for completion by 1 November, the supply sites by mid-December 1943.[63]

Early in July intelligence drew attention to the fact that unusual construction work was going on at sites in France, especially at Watten, but in the next six weeks, while the raid on Peenemünde was being planned, it failed to establish any firm connection between the sites and new weapons. Moreover, uncertainty prevailed about the nature, the imminence and the size of the threat, as no further information was obtained about either the characteristics of the rocket or the stage reached in the German development programme, and intelligence could do nothing to allay the growing anxiety.

The SIS issued on 4 July a recent report about Watten, together with some information about the site that had come in in April.[64] In April the source had said that a railway to the site was nearly completed and that great trenches were being dug there. In June he reported that one of the trenches was 80 metres deep, and had a reinforced concrete floor, and that there was also a large oval excavation 30 metres across. This prompted Sandys to alert the PRU which, in sorties made on 14, 15, 17 and 26 July, established that a number of buildings were nearing completion in a deep excavation which measured 460 feet by 330.[65] On 27 July an 'excellent' SIS source said that Watten had extensive railway lines and employed 6,000 men, but he did not know what the site was for.[66] On 15 August a further PRU sortie showed that the buildings were far from complete but could throw no light on their purpose.[67]

Except at Watten, photographic reconnaissance discovered nothing new in northern France. However, two other SIS reports from the area dealt once more with Wissant. On 9 July a 'new and very reliable' source reported that very large guns were in place under eight metres of concrete between Wissant and Ardres and were to bombard London within a few days.[68] On 19 July Wissant was mentioned by another source as a site for long-range rockets.[69] In August the SIS heard that a very large gun had been seen at Valenciennes; the place was visited by the PRU on 14 August and three objects which might be gun barrels were detected.[70]

The PRU had covered Peenemünde again on 27 June but during the next month it visited the place only twice – on 22 and 26 July.

---

63. Ehrman, op cit, Vol V, p 307.
64. CAB 121/211, COS (43) 448 (o) of 7 August, (A) (xxii) and (xxxii).
65. AIR 34/196, CIU Reports DS 18, 19, 23 of 19, 20 and 29 July 1943.
66. CAB 121/211, COS (43) 483 (o) of 21 August 1943, (A) (xliii).
67. AIR 34/196, CIU Report DS 28 of 17 August 1943.
68. CAB 121/211, COS (43) 448 (o), (A) (xxv).
69. ibid, (A) (xxxi).
70. CAB 121/211, COS (43) 483 (o), (D) (ix).

From these sorties something was learned about the firing procedure. On 27 June the 'torpedo' seen on 23 June had gone and its place had been taken by a transporter cradle; it was deduced, correctly, that each projectile was transported in a separate cradle from the factory to the firing point.[71] The photographs of 22 July disclosed seven cradles in all; there were no torpedoes in or near the ellipse; but an object similar to a torpedo was identified in the factory area.[72] On 26 July no torpedoes were seen but the photographs revealed for the first time an object at the bottom of the trench inside the ellipse: it was 35 feet long and fitted the width of the trench.[73] This last sortie also provided excellent coverage of the coast at Peenemünde from which the CIU was able to identify seven other test sites; they were being used for static testing and for the development of smaller missiles including the *Wasserfall*, though this could not be established at the time.[74] One of them resembled a site at Kummersdorf which had been photographed in May, and a similar site was observed at Friedrichshafen when this was reconnoitred on 15 July, but no information was obtained about what was taking place at these sites.[75]

The remaining SIS reports at this time gave seemingly precise but conflicting details about new weapons and the likely date of their operational use. One stated on 29 June that the Germans were putting the finishing touches to guns which had been installed on the Dutch, Belgian and French coasts and which had a range of 230 miles. On 6 July another said that 24 guns with a range of 260 miles would be ready by the end of the month. Yet another quoted the director of the U-boat works at Bordeaux: he had witnessed the firing of a rocket which weighed 20 tons, carried 12 tons of explosive and would annihilate everything within a range of 150–200 km. Another source had heard from a journalist that the rocket weighed 2 tons and was 3 to 4 metres long, and that, although August was talked about, October was the most likely operational date. On 10 July a 'very well informed and reliable' source reported that the rocket weighed 5 tons and had a range of between 200 and 300 km; that it was fired from light mobile steel mountings; that it would destroy everything within 500 metres; that serial production was hoped for from September 1943; and that Hitler planned to start the bombardment of London with 500 of the weapons in the autumn. Having also mentioned that Brown-Boveri at Mannheim was one

---

71. AIR 34–196, CIU Report, DS 17 of 2 July 1943.
72. ibid, DS 21 of 25 July 1943.
73. ibid, DS 22 of 28 July 1943.
74. ibid, DS 24 of 31 July 1943.
75. ibid, DS 20 of 22 July, DS 26 and 29 of 5 and 20 August 1943.

of several plants involved in the production, the same source added on 19 July that Peenemünde was the main research centre, that the facilities there were continually being extended, that they were under the direction of Hans von Braun* and a man named Trele or Trede, that the rocket's range was between 400 and 500 km, and that experiments and the construction of underground plans for serial production at Friedrichshafen were nearing completion.[76] At the end of July another source said the rocket weighed 40 tons, was about 20 metres long, had reached a range of 270 km – but 500 km was hoped for – and was being produced at Usedom, Bremen, Friedrichshafen and Vienna;† one million were being produced and they would be operational by 1 September.[77]

There were several more general SIS reports of rumours circulating in Berlin and other cities to the effect that Germany was planning early reprisals with a variety of weapons. The weapons mentioned, all devastating, including big guns with very long muzzles, phosphorus bombs dropped by thousands of light aircraft, 'Queen Bee' (pilotless) aircraft, liquid air bombs, gliders loaded with explosives or very large bombs, and guns with rocket missiles. Some of the reports said the attacks were to begin in August, others gave September or October, others claimed that the offensive should have taken place a few months ago but had been delayed by the RAF's bombing of airfields.[78] Another agent mentioned that Peenemünde was the centre for experiments with long-range guns, but added that the project was by no means close to completion – his informant had said it might be ready for the next war – but the SIS rated him as 'not invariably reliable'. Yet another, also rated as not very reliable,‡ quoted a highly placed official of the Waffenamt (the Army's weapons office) saying that there were no secret weapons; it might be different in two years' time but so far, in spite of intensive experiments, nothing had been perfected.[79]

The POW reports obtained during July and August 1943 added nothing to the SIS evidence.[80] Nor did the few warnings that now came in from the diplomatic posts[81] – though one of these, dated 25

---

* This appears to have been the earliest reference in the intelligence reports to Wernher von Braun, who developed the V 2 but was not director of the establishment.

† It is likely that this was a natural mistake for Wiener Neustadt.

‡ But see below, pp 385–386.

76. CAB 121/211, COS (43) 448 (o), (A) (xvii), (xx), (xxiv), (xxvii), (xxx), (xxxiii).

77. CAB 121/211, COS (43) 483 (o), (A) (xli).

78. CAB 121/211, COS (43) 448 (o), (A) (xxxiv), (xxxvi); COS (43) 483 (o), (A) (xlix), (l), (lii), (lvi).

79. CAB 121/211, COS (43) 448 (o), (A) (xxviii), (xxi).

80. CAB 121/211, COS (43) 448 (o) (B); COS (43) 483 (o), (B).

81. CAB 121/211 COS (43) 448 (o), (C); COS (43) 483 (o), (C).

July, is of interest in that it stated explicitly for the first time that two weapons were being developed, a rocket as well as a pilotless aircraft of the 'Queen Bee' type.[82] The same was true of the first contributions made by Sigint to the investigation. These were decrypts of two diplomatic telegrams, one from the German Foreign Ministry to Buenos Aires, obtained on 10 August, which asked that propaganda should begin to stress the severity of the reprisals that Germany was preparing against the United Kingdom, the other, on 13 August, repeating rumours that Germany was ready to deploy hundreds of big guns.[83]

Approaches were made to the USA and Russia at this stage, but they failed to produce anything of value. The reply of the American intelligence authorities to a request for information was received early in July; its evidence added nothing to what was already in British hands and differed only in giving emphasis to the fact that 'numerous indications point to Germany's use of gas in conjunction with a secret weapon'.[84] By 24 July the British Military Mission in Moscow had replied that nothing could be learned from the Russians.[85] At the end of July Whitehall received the answers to a questionnaire that it had asked the American authorities to put to von Opel, who had been interned in the USA. He said he had had no interest in rockets since 1937, and had heard nothing of subsequent developments, but that he did not think it practicable to develop a rocket for long-range bombardment. Asked about projectors, he thought the best form would be a trench mortar. He had experimented with liquid fuels with no great success, but thought aircraft propulsion possible either with solid fuel or with a liquid fuel.[86]

From the end of June Sandys and his advisers were assessing this intelligence, and summarising the work that was proceeding on counter-measures and civil defence preparations, at roughly weekly intervals in reports to the Defence Committee. In his assessment of the intelligence Sandys gave prominence to the construction that was being detected at sites in northern France, concentrating more and more with the passing of time on the importance of Watten. On 9 July he noted that the work going on at Watten, at Wissant and also at Bruneval near Fécamp was far from complete.[87] On the following day Sir Stafford Cripps, Minister of Aircraft Production, proposed that these sites should be bombed at once, and every day,

---

82. CAB 121/211, COS (43) 448 (o), (C) (ix).
83. CAB 120/748, PM 413/4 Vol I, Annex.
84. CAB 121/211, JIC 955/43 of 2 July 1943.
85. CAB 120/748, JIC 1085/43 of 24 July 1943.
86. ibid, JIC 1118/43 of 29 July 1943.
87. CAB 121/211, COS (43) 369 (o) of 9 July.

but on 13 July the Chiefs of Staff decided that the evidence about the purpose of the sites was too inconclusive to justify a diversion of the bombing programme; instead they asked for close-up air photography and for the Chief of Combined Operations to investigate the possibility of making a sea and airborne attack on a coastal projector site to obtain more information.[88] In his report of 19 July Sandys emphasised that there was still no definite evidence associating the long-range rocket with the northern French sites – he now mentioned three more of these, at Noires Bernes, Wambringue and Marquise.[89] In his report of 25 July he noted that the work at Watten was proceeding rapidly, but was unlikely to be completed before the end of August, and that no further suspicious constructions had been observed in France.[90] On 29 July the Chief of Combined Operations reported that a seaborne operation against Wissant or Bruneval had little chance of success, but that he had prepared a plan for dropping airborne troops on Wissant; the successful withdrawal of the force was extremely unlikely.[91] On 2 August the Chiefs of Staff decided that the mounting of a raid would not be justified.[92]

In his report of 6 August Sandys recommended that the bombing of Watten should be considered at an early date, but thought it safe to delay for about a fortnight. The rapid progress of the work there indicated the importance the Germans attached to the site, though there was still no evidence about its purpose.[93] On 9 August the Chiefs of Staff accepted the proposed delay, but noted that a daylight attack on Watten and Wissant by the USAAF was being prepared and invited the CAS to circulate details as soon as possible.[94] By 13 August, however, the Air Staff was doubtful whether the Watten site had anything to do with rockets – it might be a protected operations room.[95] This led Sandys to consider the possibility of bombarding Wissant with heavy guns in the Dover area, but his next report on 14 August stressed that air attack on the north French sites was much more likely to obtain results.[96] On 17 August the Air Staff, still reluctant to divert effort from the bombing of Germany, produced a paper in which it stressed the problems

---

88. ibid, COS (43) 372 (o) of 11 July; COS (43) 156th and 157th (o) Meetings, 13 and 14 July 1943.
89. ibid, COS (43) 388 (o) of 19 July.
90. ibid, COS (43) 402 (o) of 25 July.
91. ibid, COS (43) 418 (o) of 29 July.
92. ibid, COS (43) 178th (o) Meeting, 2 August 1943.
93. ibid, COS (43) 447 (o) of 6 August 1943.
94. ibid, COS (43) 183rd (o) Meeting, 9 August 1943.
95. ibid, COS (43) 187th (o) Meeting, 13 August 1943.
96. ibid, COS (43) 457 (o) of 14 August 1943.

associated with air attacks on these sites. It agreed that conditions were now right for the attack on Peenemünde and that the IG Farben plants at Leuna and Ludwigshafen would be bombed as soon as circumstances permitted; but in relation to the French sites it asked that a decision should be deferred until Sandys had produced more information on the purpose of the sites, the nature of the firing points and the date at which firings might start.[97]

As for the imminence of the threat, far from being able to add anything to the evidence of the progress at Watten which he had given in his assessment at the end of June, Sandys had begun to have doubts. On 9 July he had confessed that it was impossible to assess the reliability of the SIS and diplomatic reports that Germany intended to unleash a massive attack on the United Kingdom with guns, rockets or pilotless aircraft, from a variety of different dates.[98] On 13 July, with more reports of this type available, he had asked the JIC for an opinion on whether their frequency was consistent with the fact that the Germans might be expected to shroud such an intention in complete secrecy. On behalf of the JIC a Committee of Experts, which presumably included representatives from the Political Warfare Executive,* had replied on 24 July that although German propaganda was referring to terrible reprisals with a long-range gun, it was possible that talk of a gun was cover for the rocket. It was also possible, however, that the purpose of the propaganda was solely to raise morale – in which case it might be mentioning a new weapon either because the experiments with the rocket were having no success or because the propaganda authorities did not know that a long-range rocket was being developed. The JIC had concluded:

'There are some signs that we are receiving too much information about a rocket or a long-range weapon and there are, therefore, grounds for hope that German experiments in this direction are proving unfruitful. On the other hand there are, for the most part, not unreasonable explanations why we should be receiving so much information; and therefore we would not be justified in relaxing any precautions and must still be prepared for the possibility that the Germans will use the long-range rocket.'[99]†

After considering the Sandys report of 6 August the Chiefs of Staff had not been inclined to be as sceptical as the JIC. On 9 August,

---

* See below, pp 406, 418, 430.

† Also in July the Committee controlling the operation of double agents was asked to get those agents to make enquiries of Germany as to when rocket attacks might be expected. No response was received till September, see below, p 406 n*.

97. ibid, COS (43) 369 (o) of 17 August 1943.
98. ibid, COS (43) 369 (o) of 9 July.
99. CAB 120/748, JIC 1085/43.

when they learned that the attack on Peenemünde should be possible before the end of the month, they had agreed that, for all the contradictions they contained, the reports that were coming in indicated that a threat was likely to materialise in September or October.[100] On 13 August the Vice-Chiefs had decided to reconsider the date at which the rocket was likely to become operational as soon as Sandys produced his next progress report.[101] But his ninth interim report of 14 August had added nothing on this subject.

The ninth report revealed growing uncertainty, also, about the nature of the rocket. It concentrated on the possibility that, in view of recent reports about guns, the threat might come not only from a rocket of the type envisaged so far, but also from gunfire with a smaller projectile which might not be able to be tracked by radar. It accordingly recommended that sound ranging and flash spotting units should be set up on the coast to locate the gun positions.[102] On 16 August the Chiefs of Staff asked the War Office to implement this recommendation.[103]

□

The raid on Peenemünde was carried out on the night of 17–18 August.[104] Peenemünde was bombed not as a general area but as a collection of precise targets,* selected priority being made possible by study of the excellent PR evidence, and with the particular objectives of killing or injuring technical personnel and damaging the factory area and many of the installations.[105] From photographic reconnaissance on the following day, it was clear that damage to buildings had been severe[106] – so severe that the Air Staff asked the USAAF to defer its planned follow-up daylight attack on Peenemünde until there had been a detailed assessment of the damage and Sandys had produced his next report.[107]

In this, a comprehensive review dated 21 August 1943,[108] Sandys felt that the evidence still tended to confirm his earlier conclusions. But the photographic evidence from Peenemünde continued to be

---

* See map facing, p 367.

100.   CAB 121/211, COS (43) 183rd (o) Meeting, 9 August 1943.
101.   ibid, COS (43) 187th (o) Meeting, 13 August 1943.
102.   ibid, COS (43) 467 (o).
103.   ibid, COS(43) 189th (o) Meeting, 16 August 1943.
104.   AIR 41/43, *The RAF in the Bombing Offensive against Germany*, Vol V, pp 101–103; Collier, op cit, p 346.
105.   AIR 40/1884, Enclosures 7 and 8 of 25 June 1943.
106.   CAB 121/211, COS (43) 192nd (o) Meeting, 19 August 1943.
107.   ibid.
108.   CAB 121/211, COS (43) 481 (o) of 21 August 1943.

the only firm information underlying them, and that evidence was conclusive only about the linear dimensions of the rocket. In a re-examination of this evidence recently carried out by the CIU the best estimate of its size was a length of 38½ feet, diameter about 6 feet, tail length about 12 feet and tail width about 8 feet.[109] Sandys, pointing out that such a rocket would need a propellant much more powerful than any produced in the United Kingdom, now drew attention to the intelligence items which suggested that Germany had developed a new fuel. Most of the intelligence reports put the range of the rocket at over 100 miles; a range of 200 miles or more would not be impossible if a new fuel had been developed. At the same time, he thought, the possibility could not be excluded that Germany was also developing a long-range rocket that was con-siderably smaller in size than that which had hitherto been described.

The latest SIS reports had mentioned other weapons beside the large rocket, notably pilotless and jet propelled aircraft on which Sandys promised a separate assessment, and reports continued on long-range guns in spite of the fact that experts had advised that no gun could fire a projectile more than about 100 miles unless the projectile was self-propelled for part of its flight. There had also been recent references to Germany's development of new explosives based on liquid oxygen or atomic energy and to her possible use of gas, but there was no evidence on which to base any assessment of their reliability.

The report then reviewed the evidence for the date at which the rocket would become operational. On this question it suggested that the evidence still supported the earlier view: while the Germans were experiencing technical difficulties, the rocket had reached an advanced stage of development and might be put into service before it had been perfected. This conclusion hinged partly on a study of such evidence as seemed to have been put out by the German government to raise morale, and partly on a study of some of the constructions seen in northern France. In the spring and early summer some of the reports received had seemed to reflect a wish to encourage the German people to expect a new weapon in reply to the bombing of Germany. During the past six weeks such reports had appeared to avoid any promise of early retaliation. Experts in the PWE believed that the propaganda campaign had initially had some solid basis in fact, and was conducted in the belief that action would follow in the near future, but that more recently, from a date before the Peenemünde raid, the propaganda evidence suggested

---

109. AIR 34/196, CIU Report DS 27 of 16 August 1943.

that the introduction of the new weapon, though still planned, had been delayed.

For the view that its introduction was nevertheless still planned, possibly before development was complete, the report quoted two pieces of evidence. First, it seemed likely that production of the weapon at Peenemünde had been at the rate of at least one a day up to the time of the RAF attack, so that a stock of weapons could have been built up. Secondly, there were the developments at Watten. At the other sites in France nothing had yet been discovered which suggested that they were connected with the rocket programme. Watten was different. After studying the photographs and a model made from them by the CIU the experts had dismissed the idea that the construction was merely an operations room; it was being built for some purpose which involved bringing in large and heavy objects for processing and, as it had the appearance of being designed to handle large quantities of liquids, it was a reasonable assumption that it was being built for an offensive with rockets that had to be filled with a volatile liquid fuel. On this assumption the threat would not materialise before the site at Watten could be used and the photographs showed that it would not be completed before the middle of September.

The report ended by advising that absolute reliance could not be placed on any of its deductions: the range of the rocket might be greater than had been assumed; Watten might not be associated with it; there might be other sources of manufacture than Peenemünde. For a firm appreciation of when and where it might be launched, and in what numbers, the intelligence was still inadequate. But it was a reasonable conjecture that Watten was part of the programme, and as the threat might be delayed indefinitely if Watten was put out of action, Sandys recommended that the site should be bombed as soon as possible, before its concrete roof was completed.

As it happened, the report was correct not only in identifying Watten as a rocket bunker but also in judging that the rocket programme was still going forward. On 8 July Hitler had been shown the film of a successful A-4 launch and a model of Watten and, finally convinced that it would be a decisive weapon, he had ordered that its production be given the highest priority. As a result Speer had rescinded a draft Führer decree authorising increased tank production and had replaced it by a decree ordering accelerated production of the rocket.[110] The raid on Peenemünde had followed on 17–18 August, killing many scientists and engineers as well as damaging important buildings and delaying the A-4 programme for

110.   Collier, op cit, p 339; Irving, op cit, p 85.

about two months.[111] By the end of August plans had been made to replace the A-4 programme at Peenemünde by moving development work to a cavern at Traunsee, near Salzburg, by transferring the main rocket assembly works to an underground factory in the Harz mountains and by creating a new overland firing range at Blizna, near Debica in Poland; and at the beginning of September 1943 von Braun considered that, in spite of set-backs, the development of the A-4 was practically complete and that firings with live warheads would be possible by mid-November.[112]

☐

The Vice-Chiefs of Staff considered the Sandys report of 21 August, together with a summary of the intelligence received up to 20 August, on 23 August.[113] They accepted the recommendation that Watten should be attacked. The attack was carried out by the USAAF on 27 August. On 30 August PRU photographs of the site showed that two very heavy concentrations of bombs had burst directly on the target. The raid nevertheless did not completely destroy the site, and further photographs on 2 September showed that the Germans had increased the Flak defences. A second raid was accordingly made on 7 September. The PRU evidence after the second attack showed that the site had been reduced to 'a desolate heap' and suggested that 'the simplest method for the enemy to adopt would be to start again from the level of the foundations'.[114] The Germans did, indeed, abandon Watten and begin to develop a new site at Wizernes, where they had intended to build an underground depot for rockets.

On 31 August a ministerial meeting, summoned to consider the next Sandys report, dated 27 August,[115] was able to do so in the light of more intelligence recently received from the SIS source who was in touch with a senior member of the Waffenamt. According to the source, his informant had stated that two different rocket weapons were under construction – a pilotless aircraft officially known as PHI 7* and a rocket projectile officially known as A-4.

---

* PHI = Fi = Fieseler, the firm which manufactured the air-frame of the pilotless aircraft.

111. Dornberger, op cit, pp 163–164.
112. Collier, op cit, pp 347–348; Irving, op cit, pp 123, 135.
113. CAB 121/211, COS (43) 195th (o) Meeting, 23 August 1943; COS (43) 481 (o) of 21 August 1943; COS (43) 483 of 21 August 1943.
114. AIR 41/43, pp 106–107; Collier, op cit, p 348, Craven and Cate, *The Army Air Forces in World War II*, Vol II (1949), p 687; CAB 121/211, COS (43) 580 (o) of 25 September 1943, (D) (xvi).
115. CAB 121/211, COS (43) 202nd (o) Meeting, 31 August 1943; COS (43) 493 (o) of 27 August 1943.

Except that it was launched by catapult, he could give no details about the PHI 7, as the Waffenamt was not connected with its development. On the A-4 he provided a good deal of information. This was accurate as to the length, though not as to the diameter, but it did not quote the total weight and it much exaggerated the effect of the explosive charge. On the launch, flight and range it was largely correct, and it gave another reference to the possibility of mobile projectors. Even more important was his evidence that 100 A-4 projectiles had been fired and a further 100 were in hand. His information on impending operations was no less noteworthy. Hitler had set 30 October 1943 as zero day for the beginning of rocket attacks on England and had ordered the production by then of 30,000 rockets; although this rate of production was beyond the bounds of possibility, first priority was being given to the production of both weapons.*

In a separate assessment of this intelligence of 27 August Sandys had noted that the distinction it made between the two weapons made it easier to understand some of the earlier SIS reports.[116] At the ministerial meeting he urged that the intelligence confirmed his own previous conclusions, though it failed to put an end to uncertainty about the rocket's range and accuracy. On the other hand, he now felt it unlikely that attacks with the weapons would take place on any appreciable scale before the end of 1943. But Lord Cherwell remained as sceptical as before. He again argued that many of the reports that had been received were inconsistent, that some were scientifically inaccurate, and that none had referred to rocket flashes. He felt that the latest report, from the man in the Waffenamt, might be one of the many spurious answers that one was bound to get if one put out through a large number of channels definite questions about any technical subject. 'C', who attended the meeting, admitted that this hazard existed but stressed that the latest report was from a source who was known to be in a position to obtain reliable information. The CAS, recalling Lord Cherwell's earlier suggestion that the Germans might be using reports about a long-range rocket to camouflage some other development, was impressed by what the report said about a pilotless aircraft, especially as a rocket propelled bomb fitted with wings had been seen on Bornholm coming from the direction of Peenemünde.† The meeting agreed that every effort should be made to discover more about the development of this weapon. The ministers then turned to their main business, the discussion of civil defence measures.

---

* See Appendix 25.   † See below, p 390.

116.   ibid, COS (43) 493 (o).

These included the provision of shelters, preparations for the evacuation of priority classes from London, Southampton, Portsmouth and Gosport, and the possible revival of plans for moving the government from London.[117]

Civil defence preparations and counter-measures were further considered on 7 September, when the Chiefs of Staff approved arrangements made by the Air Ministry for issuing warnings of rocket firings, for computing the firing points from radar data and for making attacks on the firing points.[118] On 14 September the Chiefs of Staff agreed that the possibility of making a second attack on Peenemünde should be studied[119] and the Defence Committee, rejecting the idea of reviving plans for removing the government from London, authorised the preparation of additional civil defence preparations.[120] But the Defence Committee was on this occasion concerned mainly with the intelligence assessment in the latest Sandys report, which had been issued on the previous day.[121]

The final conclusion of this report was that it now seemed that the German rocket would not be fully fit for operational use before the end of the year. This conclusion was based mainly on the fact that there had been no evidence of further construction in France that could be associated with rockets and on reports of the damage in Peenemünde. PRU sorties to Peenemünde on 18 and 20 August had shown that the northern works area, the southern labour camp and the Karlshagen camp had been very heavily damaged and that one of the large buildings in the southern works area had been hit.[122] SIS reports received during September on the Peenemünde raid had been mixed; one, received on 11 September, had claimed that it had caused a delay of only one to two months in the assembly work, and that much remained undamaged,[123] but the majority had indicated considerable dislocation.[124] In view of the warnings to the effect that the Germans had developed a new fuel, the report gave a brief account of the scientific possibilities; it also noted that examination of fragments of a radio-guided rocket missile (the Hs 293)* suggested that its fuel was novel, but confessed that nothing

---

* See above, p 341.

117. ibid, COS (43) 202nd (o) Meeting.
118. ibid, COS (43) 512 (o) of 5 September 1943; COS (43) 209th (o) Meeting, 7 September 1943.
119. ibid, COS (43) 216th (o) Meeting, 14 September 1943.
120. ibid, DO (43) 8th Meeting, 14 September 1943.
121. ibid, COS (43) 530 (o) of 13 September 1943.
122. ibid, COS (43) 580 (o), (D) (xv); AIR 34/196, CIU Report DS 34 of 4 September
123. CAB 121/211, COS (43) 580 (o), (A) (lxxxxi).
124. ibid, (A) (lxix), (lxxv), (lxxxviii), (lxxxxviii).

was known of it.[125] As for the method of projection of the rocket, it stated that further examination of the Peenemünde photographs indicated that the barrel need not be so conspicuous as the towers that had earlier been assumed to be projectors: cordite or compressed air could be used to expel the rocket from a simple form of mortar. With regard to the rocket's accuracy, two reports had given estimates: one that it was between 10 and 15 miles at 120 miles range; the other, deduced from information referring to range closure, that it had an accuracy of 28 miles in range and 6 miles in line.[126] The Sandys report consequently confined itself to the general conclusion that the range was at least 100 miles, that the accuracy was adequate for a target the size of London and that against such a target the weapon would undoubtedly cause heavy loss of life and extensive dislocation and destruction.[127] As for the production of the weapon, reports had been received from numerous agents and POW of large-scale production at places other than Peenemünde which could manufacture in excess of what might be required for experiment. The report gave a list of possible firms.[128]

At the Defence Committe on 14 September Mr Duncan Sandys withdrew the paragraphs of the report relating to fuel: he had set up a more thorough scientific investigation into this part of the problem. But others wanted the problem as a whole to be re-investigated. Lord Cherwell asked that the estimate of casualties and damage made by the Ministry of Home Security should be re-examined. The Minister of Home Security suggested that a panel of scientists should answer a number of specific questions and be asked to commit themselves to a firm statement as to whether or not the rocket was scientifically practicable. Although Sandys explained that the evidence had already been examined by scientists, including the majority of scientific advisers at the ministries, and that not one of these was prepared to say that the weapon was not possible, the Defence Committee adopted the suggestion, appointing the Minister of Home Security, Lord Cherwell and Mr Duncan Sandys to prepare a questionnaire and select the panel of scientists. It also instructed Sandys to obtain a statement from 'C' about the reliability of the intelligence that had been received so far.[129]

The selection of the panel of scientists – the *Bodyline* Scientific Co-ordinating Committee – and the composition of the questionnaire were completed, largely by Lord Cherwell, on 29 September.

---

125.   CAB 121/211, COS (43) 530 (o), Annex A para 16–20.
126.   ibid, paras 14–16, 27–29.
127.   ibid, Conclusions (e), (f), (r).
128.   ibid, Annex A, para 21–23.
129.   CAB 121/211, DO (43) 8th Meeting, 14 September.

On the same day the Defence Committee received 'C's' assessment of the reliability of the intelligence about the rocket threat.[130] Written for 'C' by ADI (Sc) on 25 September, this review concurred in the interpretation which the periodic Sandys reports had put on the key items of evidence – the Oslo Report; the conversation between von Thoma and Crüwell; the PRU photographs of Peenemünde, the various reports obtained by the SIS in Switzerland from foreign workers employed at Peenemünde; the reports from the SIS's contact in the Waffenamt – and did so either because some external check suggested that the source was reliable or because the details of the evidence itself, or the circumstances in which it was obtained, were inconsistent with the supposition that it had been planted and was part of a complete hoax or of a cover plan. More particularly, it rejected the suggestion that the rocket study was a cover for the development of pilotless aircraft on the ground that the intelligence reports were now talking of both; moreover, since the reports were claiming that both were being developed at Peenemünde, the Germans could hardly be hoping to protect the one from bombing by drawing attention to the other. The first of ADI (Sc)'s conclusions was thus that:

'Allowing for inaccuracies which often occur in individual accounts, they [the intelligence reports] form a coherent picture which, despite the bewildering effect of the propaganda, has but one explanation; the Germans have been conducting an extensive research into long-range rockets at Peenemünde. Their experiments have naturally encountered difficulties which may still be holding up production, although Hitler would press the rockets into service at the earliest possible moment; the moment is probably still some months ahead. It would be unfortunate if, because our sources had given us a longer warning than was at first appreciated, we should at this stage discredit their account'.

His second conclusion summed up what his report said about the assessments of the technical characteristics of the rocket which had aroused so much of the scepticism. In the report he avoided a discussion of the speculations that had been advanced on this subject and was content to say that 'if the torpedo-shaped objects are not the long-range rocket, implied by so many sources, it is hard to find an alternative'. In the conclusion he said:

'There are obvious technical objections which, based on our own experience, can be raised against the prospect of successful rockets, but it is not without precedent for the Germans to have succeeded while we doubted. The beams are a sufficient example'.*

---

* For the beams see Volume I, p 323 et seq, and its Appendix 11.

130.   ibid, COS (43) 592 (o) of 29 September.

In his third conclusion he dealt with the evidence which at last suggested that in addition to a long-range rocket the Germans were developing pilotless aircraft.

☐

Until the end of August the scattered hints in the intelligence about pilotless aircraft had done more to confuse the attempt to establish the characteristics of the long-range rocket than to prompt the conclusion that the Germans were developing two separate weapons for the bombardment of England.

The first report that there was 'a bomb with wings' at Peenemünde reached the SIS in April 1943 from the Polish intelligence network in the Paris area.[131] The text of this report has not survived; it was not taken up by those inquiring into the V-weapons, presumably because they believed that Peenemünde was concerned only with rockets.* A report which, as we can now see, described the V1 was received by the SIS on 23 June from one of the Luxembourgers at Peenemünde. It described a cigar-shaped missile fired from a cubical contrivance, gave its range as 150 km for certain but believed 250 km was possible, and mentioned that gas bottles used in the firing were manufactured in a wood beside the rocket factory.[133]† This was the earliest report on the V1 to be noted by the investigators. But it was taken both by Mr Duncan Sandys[134] and by ADI (Sc)[135] to be a further and different description of the rocket. Sandys is said to have asked the CIU at the outset of his inquiry in April to search for 'remotely controlled pilotless aircraft',[136] but the Defence Committee did not ask him to include pilotless aircraft in his

---

* The intelligence surveys similarly made no reference to a report said to have been received in May by the double agent Tricycle to the effect that his German informant had found no evidence for the existence of a monster weapon of 70 tons, but had heard that a new weapon was being developed by two firms, Argus and Fieseler (in Kassel) which specialised in light aircraft.[132] Whereas we know that the April report was circulated in Whitehall we have no evidence that this May report was circulated, or indeed received, and this fact is not the only evidence that Tricycle's testimony is not always to be relied upon.

† Either with the report or a week or two later, the SIS also received 'a very dirty ragged sketch plan' of the launching of a pilotless aircraft which the Luxembourger, who had escaped from forced labour at Peenemünde, had sent by messenger to Switzerland. The SIS later informed its office in Switzerland that the sketch had been invaluable for the light it threw on what was going on at Peenemünde.

131. J Beevor, *SOE: Recollections and Reflections 1940–45* (1981), p 208.
132. N Longmate, *The Doodlebugs* (1980), p 33 quoting Popov, *Spy Counter-Spy* (1974), pp 213–214.
133. CAB 121/211, COS (43) 342 (o); COS (43) 592 (o), para 6.
134. COS (43) 349 (o) of 28 June, para 18.
135. AIR 20/1681, ASI Interim Report, Section 6.
136. Babington-Smith, op cit, p 204.

investigation until 29 June, and it took this step because of Lord Cherwell's insistence that a pilotless aircraft was more practicable than a rocket, not because the intelligence had already suggested that such a weapon was being developed.* By then, it is true, the SIS had reported that, as well as an Army research station, there existed in the Peenemünde area a GAF research station that was connected with the main research establishment at Rechlin and that was involved in testing Flak material, new shells and aircraft armament. It had also reported that Peenemünde was connected with secret radio or radar work by the GAF on Bornholm.[137] The PRU photographs of Peenemünde on 23 June had indeed disclosed that there were four small tailless aircraft on the airfield, and similar objects were then identified in earlier but poorer photographs; but the CIU and AI had agreed that these experimental machines (christened P 30) were not pilotless aircraft. This interpretation was later shown to be correct: they were the Me 163.[138]

From the end of July the intelligence sources began to refer more frequently and more distinctly to pilotless aircraft. The diplomatic report of 25 July which first clearly stated that a pilotless aircraft and a rocket were both being developed has already been noticed.† On 1 August a SIS source regarded 'as usually sound' said that self-propelling bombs, stabilised by gyroscopes and probably remote controlled, were being prepared for delivery in August: they were being designed by the Argus firm and were part torpedo and part pilotless aircraft.[139] On 7 August a 'fairly good source' reported that the rocket aeroplane was showing serious deficiencies and that serial production at the intended rate had proved impossible: in July Hitler had said that the weapon was to be used in 1943 but he had now ordered that production should be increased by the spring of 1944.[140] A few days later another SIS report claimed that a new type of aerial torpedo, which was given an initial propulsion by catapult and further speed and range by rocket, would be brought into position in August or September: the width of the wings was seven metres and the rocket engine was being made in the Argus factories.[141] But it was not until they received the report from the SIS's contact in the Waffenamt, to which Sandys drew attention on 27 August,‡ that the intelligence authorities were finally convinced

---

* See above, p 322.   † See above, p 379.   ‡ See above, p 386.

137. CAB 121/211, COS (43) 448 (0) of 7 August, (A) (xviii); AIR 20/1681, Section 7.
138. *Air Ministry Intelligence*, p 375; AIR 41/7, p 128; Babington Smith, op cit, pp 205–206.
139. CAB 121/211, COS (43) 483 (0) of 21 August, (A) (xlviii).
140. ibid, (A) (li).   141. ibid, (A) (liv).

that the Germans were developing a pilotless aircraft as well as a rocket.

After considering this report with the Air Staff, Sandys obtained a revision of his responsibilities. On 6 September, pointing out that these now included jet propelled or gliding bombs, pilotless aircraft and jet propelled aircraft as well as long-range rockets, long-range guns and other novel types of projectiles, he proposed that the Air Ministry should become wholly responsible for jet propelled aircraft, that he should remain responsible for long-range rockets, long-range guns and other projectiles, and that special arrangements should be introduced for jet propelled bombs and pilotless aircraft. For them, the Air Ministry should assume responsibility; but since, like the rockets, they were being developed at Peenemünde and were frequently confused with the rocket in the intelligence reports, the Air Ministry should furnish him with periodic assessments for inclusion in his regular reports to the Defence Committee and he should continue to receive the intelligence reports on all the weapons. The Chiefs of Staff approved of this reorganisation on 10 September.[142]

In accordance with these arrangements Mr Duncan Sandys met the request made by the Defence Committee at the end of June for a report on jet propelled aircraft by issuing on 11 September a summary of AI's assessment of the evidence,* and in his periodic report of 13 September he incorporated another AI assessment of pilotless aircraft. The second of these reports mentioned that unconfirmed intelligence reports had suggested that two types of pilotless aircraft were being developed; light aircraft carrying incendiary bombs and an aircraft produced by the Fieseler firm which was launched by catapult and propelled thereafter by rocket. The report had added that the latter aircraft was controlled automatically, not by radio; if this were to be the case the weapon could not be jammed. Sandys added the comment that pilotless aircraft could be dealt with by fighter and anti-aircraft defences if their heights and speeds were not exceptional, but that otherwise they might demand the same counter-measures as the rocket – the bombing of the production plants and of the launching sites.[143]

The intelligence reports mentioned in the paper of 13 September have not been identified. Presumably they included the sketch sent by the Luxembourger,† and several other items had by then come in which clearly referred to aircraft even when they confused descriptions of aircraft with descriptions of the rocket. A SIS report of

---

* See above, p 337.   † See above, p 390 n†.

142. CAB 121/211, COS (43) 520 (o) of 7 September; COS (43) 212nd (o) Meeting, 10 September.

143. ibid, COS (43) 530 (o), Annex B, summarising AI Report 3006 of 11 September.

20 August, from a new French source in touch with an informant attached to Peenemünde, described the firing of the rocket but also claimed that KG 100 was carrying out trials with radio controlled bombs; it also said that after experiments with radio controlled bombs under the direction of a Colonel Wachtel a GAF Flak Regiment, to be known as 155 W, was to be deployed in France about the beginning of November, with HQ at Amiens and batteries of catapults at Amiens, Abbeville and Dunkirk. To begin with, the regiment was to have 108 catapults capable of launching a projectile every twenty minutes, and it would ultimately have 400 deployed from Brittany to Holland.[144] On 27 August some not very clear photographs, said to be of a 'new rocket propelled glider bomb' that had landed on Bornholm, were received from SIS Stockholm.[145] The British Military Attaché in Stockholm had reported that guns were to be set up on the French coast to fire a new remote controlled aerial torpedo; this was hardly believable, but he added, correctly, that the torpedo was fired initially by catapult and then propelled by an engine made by the Argus factory in Berlin.[146]

It was on the strength of some of these reports that ADI(Sc) argued in his report of 25 September that the fact that the evidence for the rocket was reliable did not preclude the conclusion that Germany was also developing pilotless aircraft. But what had chiefly convinced him that this was so was the fact that two Enigma signals, dated 7 September, had made the first Sigint references to Flak-zielgerät (Flak target apparatus) 76. In one of the decrypts Luft-flotte 3 had urgently requested Flak protection for the ground organisation of Flakzielgerät 76 following the capture of a British agent who had had the task of establishing at all costs the position of the new German rocket weapon, and in view of the fact that five 'reception stations' had already been attacked, some of them re-peatedly, by the Allied air forces. The second decrypt had laid it down that Luftflotte 3 itself was solely responsible to the operational staff of the C-in-C of the GAF for the Flak protection of this ground organisation in the area of Luftgau Belgium – North France. On 14 September ADI (Sc) had deduced from this evidence that Flak-zielgerät was a code-name for a rocket driven weapon intended, probably, for long-range bombardment of England; that the weapon was much more likely to be a pilotless aircraft than the long-range rocket (this second conclusion being based largely on the Oslo Report, which had associated FZ development numbers with glider bombs and pilotless aircraft); and that while the decrypts added

---

144.   ibid, COS (43) 580 (o), (A) (lxx).
145.   ibid, (A) (lxxx); Jones broadcast of 1 August 1974.
146.   CAB 121/211, COS (43) 580 (o), (C) (xv).

credibility to other reports which had claimed that both weapons existed, the development of the pilotless aircraft might be ahead of that of the rocket and its use might be 'fairly imminent'.* In his paper of 25 September, which could not quote the Enigma evidence, he repeated these arguments and ended as follows:

'In fact, much of the critical evidence points to both weapons and it is at least plausible that while the German Army is developing the one, there is keen rivalry with the Air Force developing the other. Moreover, none of the technical difficulties of the rocket stands in the way of the pilotless aircraft, and so it would not be surprising if the latter were used first, or even if suitable emplacements were now being built in northern France.'[148]

At the time this report was written the production of the V 1 was just beginning at the Volkswagen factory at Fallersleben. It was now less than three months before the date, December 1943, which the Germans had fixed in June for the opening of the V 1 campaign, but design changes and, to a smaller extent, delays in the development programme following damage to the Fieseler factory during an RAF raid on Kassel had held up the start of production.[149]

□

When the panel of scientists began their deliberations on the rocket at the end of September, intelligence had amounted since December 1942 to 159 reports from SIS, 35 from POW and 37 from diplomatic posts,[150] but it had provided little new information during the previous month. The SIS and PR had established that construction had been suspended at Watten[151] but had reported new construction at other places, including Wizernes which the SIS said resembled Watten.[152] There had been one or two references in reports from the SIS and the diplomatic missions to factories

---

* See Appendix 26. Neither in this memorandum of 14 September nor in the paper of 25 September did ADI(Sc) refer to a report, said to have been received in September from Tricycle, which claimed that his source in Germany, though still unable to find any trace of a 70-ton weapon, had informed him that the weapon being developed by Argus and Fieseler was a pilotless machine known as FZG 76; it carried a bomb of about one ton and was now in mass-production at Fallersleben.[147] As with Tricycle's first report (see above, p 390 n*), we have been unable to establish whether this report was circulated in Whitehall or indeed received. The only record that survives with reference to this agent at the relevant time is the warning he received of rocket attacks from the French coast (see below, p 406).

147. Longmate, op cit, p 49 quoting Popov, op cit, pp 213–214.
148. CAB 121/211, COS (43) 592 (o), Section 14.
149. Collier, op cit, p 356.
150. CAB 121/211, COS (43) 682 (o) of 3 November.
151. ibid, COS (43) 600 (o) of 2 October, (A) (cix), (D) (xviii); COS (43) 654 (o) of 24 October, (A) (cxxvii), (cxxviii), (D) (xx).
152. ibid, COS (43) 654 (o), (A) (cxxx); COS (43) 682 (o), (A) (cxlv).

involved in making parts or fuel for the rocket.[153] But as to when the weapon would be ready the latest evidence had been scanty and conflicting. Of twelve new POW interrogated, three high ranking officers had doubted the existence of a secret weapon, and one of these had dismissed talk of a very long range rocket as bluff.[154] But other POW had referred to a variety of new weapons. In addition the German public was still being encouraged to expect them: Hitler had referred in a recent speech to 'technical and organisational preparations . . . which will enable us not only to break his [the Allied] terror tactics, but also by other and more effective means to retaliate'.[155] There had been more diplomatic decrypts – one in which Ribbentrop had informed German missions abroad on 24 August that the Allied bombing would diminish 'when the measures we have in hand are completed'; others in which the Japanese ambassadors in Berlin and Rome had said that new German methods of retaliation would be introduced before the winter in spite of slight delays inflicted by the bombing of Peenemünde and Friedrichshafen – names which the ambassador in Berlin begged Tokyo to keep secret.[156] Among the diplomatic reports, one from Berne conveyed the rumour that raids would start in September.[157] On the other hand, the British Military Attaché in Berne had reported on 14 September that the air attacks on Peenemünde and other places of production, including Friedrichshafen, had delayed 'Gerät A-4', the new weapon which Germany had hoped to have operational by the autumn of 1943.[158] On 7 October a telegram from the Japanese Ambassador in Berlin was decrypted giving information dated 30 September. This said that experiments had shown the possibility of 'fairly accurate shooting up to a range of about 400 kms by some form of artillery bombardment'. The weapon would be used with good effect 'not only against London but also against the manufacturing towns in its vicinity' and would be operational 'by the middle of December at latest'. The Prime Minister personally ensured that Sandys knew of this decrypt.[159]

The reports on the weapon's characteristics and performance had been equally inconsistent, giving references to weights of from 10 to 80 tons, to bomb loads of 2 and 4 tons, to ranges of between 220 and

---

153. ibid, COS (43) 600 (o), (A) (cvii), (C) (xxiv); COS (43) 682 (o), (A) (clvi), (clviii).
154. ibid, COS (43) 580 (o), (B) (xviii) – (xxv).
155. COS (43) 530 (o), Annex A, para 43.
156. CAB 120/748; PM file 413/4, Annex; Dir/C Archive, 4394 of 18 September 1943.
157. CAB 121/211, COS (43) 580 (o), (C) (xxi).
158. ibid, (C) (xxiii).
159. CAB 120/748, Annex; Dir/C Archive, 4561 of 7 October 1943.

500 kilometres and to warheads carrying unspecified materials or gas or 'bacteriological germs'.[160] A SIS report of 25 August had said that the weapon would destroy all buildings within 2½ kilometres; another, received in September, had announced that an area 50 × 10 nautical miles had been closed to shipping off Stolpemünde;[161] a third had referred to bombs and shells that did not depend on the laws of ballistics and to projectiles that were fired through the stratosphere.[162] There had been a POW reference to 'liquid air bombs on the rocket principle'.[163] Other reports had mentioned that the rocket was remote controlled and given details about the method of control, the firing of the propellant charges and the rocket's exhausts, but little could be made of them. One of them might have pointed to the fact that one of the propellants was liquid oxygen; in fact, however, it said that the explosive material was liquid air.[164] Another claimed that the rocket when fired was said 'to rise very slowly from the ground, making a considerable noise'; but this only perplexed the rocket experts, whose picture of the launching arrangements did not allow for that type of initial flight.[165]

In the absence of firm information about the range of the rocket, the weight of its warhead, its fuel and the method used to launch it, the efforts by the rocket experts and scientists to determine the scientific possibilities and the technical probabilities produced both indecision and acrimonious disagreements. The fuel panel of the Sandys' *Bodyline* Committee, set the task of deciding what fuels were necessary to achieve the rocket's performance, was led instead to consider whether the specified rocket was a reasonable engineering proposition when its attention was drawn to the fact that to attain the range required the amount of fuel carried by the rocket was more important than any assumption of a new and more powerful propellant. Dr Crow, the Controller of Projectile Development (CPD), recognising that the high ratio of the weight of the fuel to the total weight of the rocket* needed for the range could not be

---

* The ratio of the fuel weight to the total weight of the rocket is usually known as α. In elementary rocket theory, ie ignoring air resistance and second order terms, the maximum velocity V attained when the propellants have been all burnt is given by

$$V = \omega \log_e \{ 1/(1 - \alpha) \}$$

and the maximum theoretical range by

$$R = V^2/g.$$ *(cont. on p 397)*

160. CAB 121/211, COS (43) 600 (o), (A) (cii) (ciii), (cxviii); COS (43) 682 (o), (B) (xxxiii).
161. ibid, COS (43) 580 (o), (A) (lxiii), (lxxxi).
162. ibid, (A) (lxx).   163. ibid, (B) (xiv).
164. CAB 121/211, COS (43) 654 (o), (A) (cxxxii); COS (43) (o), (A) (cl).
165. ibid, COS (43) 654 (o), (B) (xxiii).

achieved using a solid propellant, maintained his view that a single-stage rocket could not attain the range specified in the Sandys assessments. Influenced by preliminary information about liquid fuel rocket development in the USA, and now realising that previously known liquid fuels might be employed to solve the range problems, the remainder of the fuel panel came to believe during September that the construction of a rocket with a range of 100 miles or more, and an explosive warhead of one ton or more, was indeed a reasonable proposition. But they felt that it was most improbable that Germany had yet developed such a weapon. On 11 October, however, asked to pass judgment on the 'torpedo' photographed at Peenemünde, a majority of the fuel panel conceded, against the opposition of Lord Cherwell who attended the meeting, that 'it may be a rocket'.[166]

The previous day, Mr I Lubbock, the chief engineer of the Asiatic Petroleum Company who was developing a petrol/liquid oxygen ATO rocket for the CPD, returned from a visit to the USA and was immediately asked by Sandys to attempt a design for a long-range rocket of the size shown in the Peenemünde photographs. Choosing nitric acid and aniline as the liquid fuels, and assuming a selection of warhead weights, his study was completed in time for its discussion by the full *Bodyline* Scientific Committee on 22 October.[167] It did not gain universal approval, mainly on account of the engineering assumptions Lubbock had had to make – it was to be severely criticised by Lord Cherwell. It nevertheless established that high values of the critical ratio of the fuel weight to the total weight could be obtained, and that long ranges could be attained, and on 22 October the *Bodyline* Committee, with only one dissentient voice, reported to the Defence Committee that a rocket with a warhead of 10 to 20 tons and a range of 130 miles was scientifically possible, that ranges up to 300 miles would be possible with smaller warheads, and that a rocket possessing such performances 'could have the dimensions of the object seen at Peenemünde'. At this point the smaller panel of scientists nominated by Lord Cherwell had not yet given an answer to the questionnaire.

In his next periodic report, dated 24 October, Mr Duncan Sandys recapitulated this scientific opinion and repeated his earlier assessments of the intelligence: although the prolonged full-scale bom-

---

Here ω is the exit velocity of the gases from the rocket, and since this is directly proportional to the specific impulse produced by the chemical energy released in combustion, it will be seen that changes in α will be more important than changes in the chemical energy.

The value of α for the A-4 was 0.64, for the American development at that time, about 0.52, for British cordite rockets less than 0.3.

166. Irving, op cit, p 155.
167. CAB 121/211, DO (43) of 25 October, Annex B and C.

bardment that had been planned by Germany was unlikely before early in 1944, the long-range rocket development had reached the stage at which it could be used operationally; production, though delayed by the raid on Peenemünde and other places, might have been as much as 200 a month since September; apart from Watten, which looked more and more to have been a rocket emplacement, unexplained construction was taking place in the St Omer, St Pol and Dieppe areas. The problem of how the rocket was launched remained unsolved but it was probable that it was fired from a tube 60 to 100 feet long emplaced in a tunnel or bomb-proof structure. His conclusion was that with perhaps 500 projectiles ready for firing, and as many as six projectors capable of firing one an hour over several days, 'we must . . . reckon with the possibility that the equivalent of some 2,500 to 10,000 tons might be delivered on London during the course of a single week in November or December, unless successful offensive action is taken to prevent it'.[168]

On 25 October the Defence Committee considered this paper, together with the pronouncement from the *Bodyline* Scientific Committee, 'C's' report on the reliability of the intelligence about the rocket, and a summary of the intelligence reports received since its last discussion. It was informed that the JIC, although in agreement with Sandys's other assessments, felt that he had over-estimated the probability of an early attack. Lord Cherwell agreed with the JIC – whatever the weapon was, it could not be brought into operation for some time as the Sandys assessment was making insufficient allowance for the gap between experiment and operational readiness. He still doubted, moreover, whether the weapon was a rocket: the Peenemünde objects could not possibly be rockets with the characteristics that were being attributed to them, and he scathingly criticised Mr Lubbock's design. He felt that 'at the end of the war, when we know the full story, we shall find that the rocket was a mare's nest'. ADI (Sc) said that the objects were too large for aircraft torpedoes and that the only reasonable deduction was that they were rockets. He also spoke against the suggestion of a hoax: it was impossible to say what degree of success the Germans had achieved with rockets, but there was no doubt that they had put a great deal of effort into their development. Mr Lubbock explained the great strides in rocket development in the US and defended his design, in which he was supported by the Chief Engineer in the Armament Design Department (CEADD). The Scientific Adviser to the Army Council (SAAC) felt that the American information 'completely altered the picture', but Sir Robert Watson-Watt of the Ministry of Aircraft Production thought that a pilotless aircraft was

---

168.   ibid, COS (43) 652 (o) of 24 October.

a better engineering project than the rocket. While admitting that the Germans had put out some false information, 'C' defended the reliability of the intelligence which pointed to the existence of a large rocket, but added that there was some evidence that the Germans were also developing a pilotless aircraft. On the other hand, he was less disposed now to agree with Lord Cherwell in doubting the existence of a large rocket; but there were unresolved problems, including the fact that the shape of the Peenemünde objects did not fit the type of weapon that might be expected. The CIGS thought that a long-range rocket existed.[169]

The Prime Minister and the ministers present at the meeting agreed with the CIGS and, accepting the Sandys recommendations, reiterated that the highest priority should be given to measures against the threat – the bombing of suspected projector sites and of the factories believed to be engaged in the project; intensive reconnaissance of northern France for other sites; further steps to obtain accurate intelligence. In addition they ordered the Chiefs of Staff to consider the use of gas against the sites and the advisability of a warning to Germany that Great Britain would retaliate with gas against rocket attack on her civilian population.* As a further indication of the anxiety that now developed, the Prime Minister informed President Roosevelt after the meeting in a personal telegram that he was sending him by courier the latest report on the intelligence that had accumulated in the past six months about the nature and timing of the threat.[171]†

---

* This suggestion was examined by the JIC, which reported on 11 November on the probable reactions of Germany and of neutral countries to the use of gas.[170]

† Compare the statement (Craven and Cate, *The Army Air Force in World War II* (1951) Vol III, pp 95–96) that 'not until December 1943 had the British conveyed to their American allies the full measure of their alarm . . .' The Prime Minister's telegram was followed by a fuller exchange of intelligence. On 29 October, at the suggestion of the JIC, the Chiefs of Staff agreed that in future the latest intelligence about the rocket should be passed verbally, under strict security conditions, to the United States authorites at ETOUSA and COSSAC and in Washington. Enquiries had been made of the Americans in July (see above, p 379) and discussions had subsequently taken place between British and American rocket experts (see above, p 397), but hitherto the Americans had been given no intelligence on the rocket apart from what had appeared in general intelligence reports and POW interrogations, which they received as a matter of course.[172] On 2 November the JIC agreed to allow MEW to discuss intelligence about the rocket with the United States authorities.[173] Replying to the Prime Minister's telegram on 9 November, the President said that the United States had received many reports on rocket activity, but that he had no recent intelligence of any value apart from indications that production factories existed at Berlin, Schweinfurt, Wiener Neustadt and near Vienna.[174]

169. ibid, DO (43) 10th Meeting, 25 October.
170. ibid, JIC (43) 449 (o) of 11 November.
171. ibid, T1727/3 of 25 October 1943.
172. ibid, JIC (43) 432 (o) of 26 October; COS (43) 263rd (o) Meeting, 29 October.
173. JIC (43) 56th (o) Meeting, 2 November.
174. CAB 121/211, T1903/3 of 9 November 1943.

At a meeting of scientists on 28 October Lord Cherwell defined his position. He was not saying that Germany could not or had not designed a long-range rocket, but only that he did not see how the characteristics of a long-range rocket could be incorporated in the objects photographed at Peenemünde. The CPD repeated his conviction that a rocket of that size was quite impossible on a solid fuel basis: the problem resolved itself into whether it was possible to have such a rocket with liquid fuel and a sufficiently light structure. After much debate on the engineering problems stemming from these two propositions three of the scientists present at the meeting, all of whom had endorsed the pronouncement of 22 October, withdrew their endorsement to the extent of agreeing that there were formidable difficulties in accepting that the Peenemünde objects were rockets. However, they did not depart from the view that a rocket was theoretically feasible and the meeting therefore decided that no firm pronouncement was possible until the difficulties were solved.[175]

Later on 28 October, when they met the Prime Minister, some of his ministerial colleagues and Mr Duncan Sandys, it emerged that the scientists were far from being in agreement about whether the Germans were making progress with a long-range rocket. As well as repeating his conclusion that the objects were not long-range rockets, Lord Cherwell now returned to the argument that in view of the difficulties involved in producing a rocket with the characteristics that had been attributed to it in the Lubbock design, it would be very much easier for the enemy to make pilotless aircraft. But after listening to the discussion Sir Stafford Cripps pointed out that Lord Cherwell's objections – as he had himself admitted – were directed to showing that the Peenemünde object could not be a rocket and that he had not established that the Germans could not produce a rocket.[176] And the next day, when the meeting was continued under his chairmanship, Cripps concentrated the discussion on this wider subject and obtained general agreement to the conclusion that 'although the difficulties were formidable, there was nothing which from a scientific point of view rendered impracticable the production of a long-range rocket with the range and the performance postulated'.[177]

On 2 November this conclusion was reported in a paper to the Prime Minister. The paper registered the uncertainty about what interpretation to put on the photographic evidence from Peenemünde and admitted that some of the objections raised by Lord

---

175.   ibid, DO (43) 26 of 28 October.
176.   ibid, DO (43) 11th Meeting, 28 October.
177.   ibid, DO (43) 12th Meeting, 29 October.

Cherwell could not be completely resolved. But it insisted that these difficulties did not rule out the possibility of developing a liquid fuel rocket of the necessary performance. 'There is nothing impossible in designing a rocket of 60–70 tons to operate with a 10 ton warhead at a range of 130 miles'. The paper added that, while this was 'on the whole . . . a unanimous opinion', 'there would be many difficulties to overcome which would at best occupy a number of years in research and development.'[178] But it did something to offset its caution – a caution which is understandable when it is remembered that the scientists were discussing estimates of total weight and weight of warhead that were far in excess of the truth, and that they still had no intelligence about the method of launch – by remarking that, since the Germans had embarked on preparations in northern France for the operational use of a rocket, it must be assumed either that they were satisfied that they had overcome the difficulties or that they expected that any remaining problems would soon be solved.

Lord Cherwell's objections were not stilled by this paper. On 9 November, in reply to the Prime Minister's request for his views on it, he observed that Sir Stafford Cripps had overlooked the difference between what was scientifically possible and what was technically practicable and, 'in order to sort out this confusion', selected fifteen passages in the paper which failed, he felt, to come to grips with either the scientific possibility of designing a rocket of the range envisaged or the difficulty of reconciling the design requirements with the rockets that had been photographed. His criticisms were all cogent points, given the assumption that the German rocket and particularly its warhead weighed very much more than was in fact the case. But in view of the continuing lack of intelligence about the design of the rocket they were necessarily couched in the form of objections to the view that the Germans could have surmounted the difficulties, and Lord Cherwell voiced these objections all the more strongly because he continued to believe that the Germans would have found it more practicable to develop the pilotless aircraft. He ended his comments by saying:

'Naturally I do not argue against reasonable precautions, but I am anxious lest concentration on this particular weapon [the rocket] should distract us from preparing counter-measures against other forms of bombardment which I consider much more likely, since they involve no serious difficultes and are in line with the proved course of German development.'[179]

□

---

178.   ibid, DO (43) 27 of 2 November.
179.   PREM 3/110.

The point that a German programme for the bombardment of London ought logically to rest on pilotless aircraft, which presented no insuperable difficulties, rather than on rockets, was meanwhile being strengthened by GC and CS. At the end of October it had begun to produce the Sigint evidence which finally confirmed that the Germans were experimenting with pilotless aircraft.

From an early stage in the search for intelligence about the rocket GC and CS had kept a special watch for activity by 14th and 15th Companies of the GAF Signals Experimental Regiment, the units which had been associated with the development of the navigational beams and might now be using radar to plot the rocket's flight.[180] In April 1943 the Enigma, in its first reference to Peenemünde, had indicated that the GAF had an experimental radar station there.[181] By the end of June it had added that 14th GAF Signals Experimental Company had detachments specialising in radar on Bornholm and at Stolpemünde.[182] There had been no further decrypts until October, but the GAF Enigma then disclosed that two groups of plotting stations were at work. One – Group Wachtel – was carrying out firing experiments and tests of explosives with a battery located at Zempin. The other – the 'Insect' Group – was experimenting with catapults at Zempin and Peenemünde; it had a control station, possibly at Greifswalder Oie, and a series of out-stations equipped with radar and engaged in plotting objects fired from Zempin and Peenemünde in a north-easterly direction. In addition to the Enigma decrypts, which left it unclear whether the two groups were connected, a series of plot reports from the stations themselves in a simple code was intercepted from 12 October. These were clearly related to trials with an aircraft and not a rocket – the plots gave range and bearing, but not heights – and from the evident interest in its impact point it was clear that the object was a weapon and not a new manned aircraft. By the end of November it had been established from the decrypts of the traffic of 14th Company that the speed of the missile was between 216 and 300 mph, and once 420 mph, that the rate of its fall was 2,000 metres in 40 seconds, thus implying that the missile had wings, and that the maximum range might be 120 miles.[183]

Possibly prompted by inquiries arising out of the Enigma evidence, the CIU, continuing its search for small aircraft, found on 13 November on photographs of Peenemünde an aircraft smaller

---

180.   AIR 20/1681, ASI Interim Report, of 26 June 1943, Section 6.
181.   ibid; CX/MSS/2435/T17, 2438/T16.
182.   CX/MSS/J 1 of 26 June 1943.
183.   CX/MSS/J 3, 5, 7, 9, 12, 15 of 29 October, 3, 8, 12, 19, 25 November 1943; CAB 121/211, COS (43) 715 (0) of 17 November, Appendix III; JIC (43) 483 (0) of 24 November, para 13.

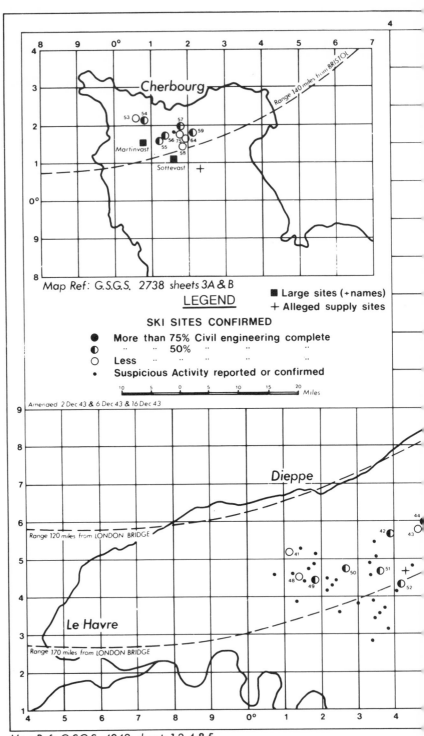

Map Ref: G.S.G.S. 2738 sheets 3A & B

LEGEND

■ Large sites (+names)
+ Alleged supply sites

SKI SITES CONFIRMED

● More than 75% Civil engineering complete
◐ " " 50% " " " "
○ Less " " " " "
• Suspicious Activity reported or confirmed

Amended 2 Dec 43 & 6 Dec 43 & 16 Dec 43

Map Ref: G.S.G.S. 4042 sheets 1,2,4 & 5

than the P 30 which had been observed in the photographs of 23 June. Photographs taken on 22 July and 30 September were then re-examined, and they disclosed a similar object – named P 20 – which appeared to have a span of about 20 feet and to be propelled by some type of jet. The size was judged to be suitable for an expendable pilotless aircraft and the object was located near the airfield, outside what was thought to be a test house, and not near the rocket test site.[184]

While evidence from GC and CS and the CIU was thus pointing unmistakably to experiments with pilotless aircraft, the SIS and photographic reconnaissance were together uncovering new material in France. Some time before the end of October* London had learned from one of its French networks that since August six sites in northern France had been found, each having a strip of concrete and some a line of posts that were aligned on London.[188] The PRU Spitfires began to photograph these sites on 3 November. The PRU had already noticed that new construction was taking place in the Pas de Calais area and on 24 September had shown that at one site, Bois d'Esquerdes, there was considerable activity. Its reconnaissance of the six sites reported by the SIS found that they were similar to that at Bois d'Esquerdes and that that at Bois Carré was the most advanced.[189] By 10 November the number of sites reported had grown to 26. By 24 November 38 had been confirmed by the PRU and as many as 60 reported by the SIS; all were set back up to 20 km from the coast in a corridor 200 miles long by 30 miles wide in Seine-Inférieure and the Pas de Calais.[190] By the end of the month 75 sites had been located in that area and seven in the Cherbourg peninsula,[191] and analysis of them had established that those in the Pas de Calais-Dieppe area were aligned within $\pm 7°$ of London, and were within 140 miles of Bristol and 100 miles of Portsmouth and Southampton.[192]† By the same date the SIS had provided a detailed drawing of one of the sites – it had a ramp 150

---

* The RAF's PR Narrative says soon after 24 September.[185] A report by Sir Stafford Cripps of 17 November says 'only very recently'.[186] A report by the JIC of 24 November says 'after . . . 24 October'.[187] In view of the fact that the PRU began its search on 3 November the report was probably received towards the end of October.

† See map facing p 403.

184. JIC (43) 483 (o), paras 14, 15; Babington Smith, op cit, pp 218–219.
185. AIR 41/7, p 128.
186. CAB 121/211, COS (43) 715 (o), Appendix I para (b) (iv).
187. JIC (43) 483 (o), para 3.
188. G Martelli, *Agent Extraordinary* (1966) p 154.
189. AIR 41/7, p 128.
190. ibid, op 129; JIC (43) 483 (o); Martelli, op cit, p 164.
191. AIR 41/7, p 129.
192. ibid; CAB 121/211, COS (43) 715 (o), Appendix I.

feet long, inclined at $15°$[193] – and the photographs had shown that each site had three long narrow buildings, each with a gently curving end rather like a ski lying on its side, and a flat platform, and that on an extension of the platform there was a series of studs, possibly for the installation of a ramp.[194]

☐

Sir Stafford Cripps's report of 2 November on the outcome of the scientific deliberations had meanwhile prompted the Prime Minister on 4 November to ask him to conduct another inquiry, this time into the intelligence bearing on the long-range rocket, the pilotless aircraft and glider bombs. With two members of the Ministry of Aircraft Production acting as assessors, he was invited to establish, after consultation with Mr Duncan Sandys and Lord Cherwell and the relevant intelligence bodies, what was known of the characteristics of the weapons, of their production and of preparations for their use. In addition, presumably at the instigation of Lord Cherwell, he was asked to consider, with reference to the rocket, whether the evidence was merely the product of German propaganda, whether it was being planted to conceal some other development, whether the French sites might in reality be intended for some quite different purpose, and whether the Germans had yet succeeded in overcoming the technical difficulties.[195]

By 12 November, following a series of meetings on 8 and 10 November, Sir Stafford Cripps had completed his intelligence inquiry and was writing his report in the light of the discussions and with the aid of memoranda submitted by various bodies. His report, issued on 17 November, marshalled the latest intelligence assessments in six appendices, ordered mainly according to the intelligence sources.[196]

The first appendix, on photographic reconnaissance, dealt with Peenemünde and the French sites. It showed that considerable progress had been made by the CIU and the Sandys organisation in the interpretation of the activities at the Peenemünde site and the functioning of the entire area. The factory area was clearly identified, and believed to have been substantially complete by April 1943, but in the absence of any direct association of the A-4 with the factory there was doubt as to whether this was the place of the rockets' manufacture or assembly. In the research establishment a number of test sites were seen, but only one, the large elliptical emplacement, was used for the firing of large rockets. There the

---

193. Martelli, op cit, p 175.
194. CAB 121/211, COS (43) 715 (0) Appendix I.
195. ibid, COS Minute of 4 November.   196. ibid, COS (43) 715 (0).

tower-like structures were identified as cranes and it had been deduced that they were used for taking the rockets off their trucks for filling before firing. The latest estimate had suggested that the rockets weighed about 12 tons empty and that they could be carried on the trucks seen around the test site; a study of these trucks indicated that about seven rockets a week might have been fired during June and July. Other trucks had been seen between the site and the foreshore, and on one occasion a rocket was seen being recovered from the sea. In addition to the trucks, ordinary tankers had been seen and some of the installations at the site could be asociated with liquid fuels.* The elliptical emplacement remained the only place where evidence of long-range rocket activity could be obtained, and there was no sign in the Peenemünde area of any operational prototype site of the kinds seen in France, either of the Watten type or of the ski sites.

In France the CIU had established that construction had been discontinued at Watten, but two similar sites had been identified on the Cherbourg peninsula and the existence of a third was suspected. Between these sites, including Watten, and the A-4 no obvious association had been established. The same was true of another type of site, the turn-table site, of which 30 to 40 had been in existence for two years. Of a third type of site, incorporating a tunnel, only one had been located, at Mimoyecques Marquise; nothing was known of its purpose.† In recent weeks, on the other hand, no less than 30 sites of yet another type (the ski sites) had been photographed. The appendix gave the details about these, and added that there was no evidence to connect them with the A-4.

The second appendix, summarising the SIS evidence, noted that agents had reported as many as 70 or 80 ski sites, but had provided no evidence which enabled them to be associated with the A-4 or any other known weapon. On the SIS reports about activity at Peenemünde it felt that they provided reliable evidence that experiments had been carried out with rockets up to the size of A-4. The SIS information contained no evidence, however, that successful final trials had been carried out, either at Peenemünde or elsewhere. Commenting on the more general SIS reports about the rocket, the appendix noted that they had increased rapidly in volume once the SIS had begun to make inquiries; this might be because the Germans, suspecting that the British had learned about the rocket, had turned this set-back to their advantage.

---

* But this could not have led the interpreters to think of liquid oxygen, and the significance of the vapour clouds as well as the column on the foreshore had still not been commented on.

† It was intended for a long-range multi-barrelled rocket firing gun of revolutionary design (the Hochdruckpumpe), though what this was remained unknown until the site was overrun.

Other aspects of German propaganda were dealt with in the fourth appendix. This summarised papers submitted to the inquiry by the PWE and the Air Ministry. The PWE paper had brought up to date its analysis of German propaganda items referring to secret weapons, of which it had collected 115 for either home or foreign consumption since March. As in earlier analyses done for the Sandys investigation, it had judged that the items established beyond reasonable doubt that the Germans possessed a weapon which they believed to be unknown to the Allies and with which they expected to obtain striking results, but that they also indicated that something had happened about the middle of August and again between 3 and 10 September which had led the German leaders to believe that D-day for the introduction of the weapon would be delayed beyond the date they had been working to. In June the propaganda had suggested a D-day in mid-September; from early September it had suggested a D-day at the beginning of December. On the basis of the subsequent evidence it was 'tentatively estimated that the German leaders expect this offensive weapon to come into use not before the middle of January 1944 and not later than the middle of April'.[197] But PWE added: 'There is unlikely to be an error of more than a month each way in the first of these estimated dates, but there might well be an error of two months either way in the latter'. Since the beginning of September there had indeed been a marked decline in the number of propaganda items and of 'scare' warnings received via the SIS, and they had changed their tone; one of the latter, received in September, had claimed that Hitler hoped to start bombarding England within three or four months.[198] The paper from the Air Intelligence Branch had scrutinised the diplomatic decrypts which referred to the weapon – of which it had singled out seven. It had noted that information about rocket projectiles was being used to reassure the Japanese about Germany's military position, and that threats of reprisals against the United Kingdom were being circulated in neutral countries for the same purpose, but had emphasised that the references 'are related to the general exigencies of the war situation and do not give reliable indications of German intentions to use the weapon or to the time at which its employment may become a practical possibility'.[199]*

---

* The attempt to acquire intelligence about the timing of the threat by another method, getting double agents to make enquiries of their German contacts, had produced no useful information. In September one double agent had received a warning against continuing to live in London, which was a likely target for rockets sited on the French coast. On 18 November, however, another was told that he and his family had no cause for alarm about the rocket gun.[200] These enquiries were to continue until May 1944. See below, p 426.

197.   CAB 120/748, Annex, PWE note of 8 November 1943.
198.   CAB 121/211, COS (43) 600 (o), (A) (cii).
199.   CAB 120/748, Annex, AI 3a (2) note of 10 November 1943.
200.   J C Masterman, The Double Cross System (1972), p 178.

Cripps's fifth appendix, on what was known about Germany's manufacturing resources and what could be deduced about the production of long-range weapons, repeated and endorsed the findings of a paper that had been drawn up by MEW. MEW had assumed that three types of weapon might be under development – a small one, of just sufficient range to reach London, which was either an enlarged version of the Hs 293 or some other form of glider bomb; a medium-sized rocket of the Peenemünde type, identifiable as the A-4 but with less destructive effect and of smaller size than the estimates of the A-4 had so far suggested;* and a very much larger version of the A-4. As for quantity production, the evidence, such as it was, suggested that 'it is not yet concerned with the larger types', though the small weapon might have been in quantity production for some months. Many types of rockets and projectors for tactical use were already being produced in quantity, and the intelligence sources were probably often referring to these 'in all good faith' when purporting to be reporting on *Bodyline* weapons. Moreover, 'during the frequent interrogation of POW, a good deal of intelligence has been manufactured by ourselves and is being repeated back to us'. If the larger types were indeed in series production, MEW would have expected more frequent mention of heavy engineering firms and some evidence of assembly at other locations than Peenemünde and Friedrichshafen. At the firms which had been mentioned as being involved in the manufacture of *Bodyline* weapons it was in MEW's opinion doubtful whether the resources were adequate for the series production of the A-4. The intelligence sources had produced no clear evidence of the manufacture of the special fuels, though they had mentioned activity at, and extensions to, a number of chemical factories.[201] After summarising this paper the fifth appendix stressed that, if the empty weight of the A-4 was indeed 10 to 12 tons, it could be made only in small quantities, but that the firms mentioned in the intelligence could turn out large quantities in series production if the size of the rocket had been exaggerated.

In a sixth appendix the Cripps report dealt with the intelligence about pilotless aircraft. The appendix began by saying that 'there is no direct evidence of any preparations for the use of this weapon. This does not, however, necessarily determine the matter, since they could be launched from any ordinary aerodrome in north

---

* See above, p 383, for the reference made by Sandys on 21 August to the possibility of a smaller rocket. It is not clear in the records whether MEW supposed the existence of a small rocket under the influence of this earlier report or deduced it from its study of the factories involved.

201. CAB 120/748, MEW note of 10 November.

France'. There was, it added, no evidence of the volume of production but reliable reports supported the conclusion that this method of attack had reached an advanced stage of development, and the 'Most Secret' intelligence already summarised in the third appendix might well refer to pilotless aircraft.

As well as summarising what had been learned from the Sigint from Zempin and Peenemünde – noting the fact that the missile had wings and the associated SIS information to the effect that Wachtel, in command of Flak Regiment 155 (W), was to have his HQ in the Abbeville-Amiens area* – the third appendix wrestled with the two GAF Enigma references to Flakzielgerät 76 which had been decrypted in September. ADI(Sc)'s interpretation of the references, as of the plot reports, had been brought to Cripps's notice, but he and others to whom he had turned for advice were obviously not persuaded that Zielgerät 76 was the pilotless aircraft.† Noting that it was impossible to identify the five 'reception stations', which, as the decrypts had stated, had been subjected to Allied air attack, or otherwise to explain what the reception stations were, Cripps agreed that Zielgerät 76 might be a weapon, but allowed that it could be a pilotless aircraft or a rocket or a bomb. Less understandably, in view of the fact that it was known that the rocket was an Army project while GAF Flak Regiment 155 (W) had been connected with Wachtel by the SIS‡ and Wachtel had been connected with experiments with the pilotless aircraft in the GC and CS evidence,§ he suggested that the W might stand for 'Werfer' and denote connection with rocket apparatus. The third appendix concluded by saying that 'beyond the above, there is no indication of any connection of A-4 with any of the sites in north France'.

In the summary of his conclusions Sir Stafford Cripps accepted that the rocket story was 'not a pure hoax, though it has no doubt been exaggerated'.[202] 'There is no doubt that the Germans are doing their utmost to perfect some long-range weapon, and the new unexplained structures in northern France are certainly most suspicious'.[203] As for the weapon, he suggested that, in order of probability, four long-range weapons had to be allowed for: (i) a larger Hs 293; (ii) pilotless aircraft; (iii) a long-range rocket smaller than A-4; (iv) the A-4 rocket.[204] That the next step after the Hs 293 would logically be a larger and longer range weapon of the same kind 'would fit in with the most secret information set out in Appendix

---

* See above, p 393.   † See above, pp 393–394 and Appendix 26.
‡ See above, p 393.   § See above, p 402.

202. CAB 121/211, COS (43) 715 (o), Appendix G, Conclusion 15.
203. ibid, Conclusion 24.   204. ibid, Conclusion 19.

(iii), which indicates the testing of a long-range weapon with wings. This might equally well be a pilotless aircraft. . . .'[205] However, glider bombs and pilotless aircraft 'would not require any special apparatus for launching beyond what could be put on to an ordinary airfield', whereas the rockets 'would require special apparatus both for launching, servicing and handling especially in view of the sort of fuel they would have to employ';[206] and this prompted the feeling that the French sites, although apparently connected with the GAF,[207] were nevertheless being developed for rockets. 'There is no reliable evidence apart from that in Appendix (iii) to connect the sites mentioned in 8 [Watten type sites] or 9 [the ski sites] above with a long-range rocket or with any other long-range weapon. . . .'[208] 'It is not possible to say that the sites could not be used for launching rockets such as the A-4 but there is at present no sign of any launching apparatus on or in connection with them'.[209] On the other hand, these sites 'could in all probability be so used if and when they are fitted with launching and handling apparatus'.[210] More particularly, 'the possibility of some smaller rocket [than the A-4] must not be overlooked in connection, especially, with the ski sites'.[211]

Sir Stafford Cripps appears to have made this suggestion as a means of reconciling MEW's lack of evidence for the large-scale production of large rockets with his belief that other evidence established that rockets were being developed. Another of his conclusions reads: 'Although there is a considerable volume of evidence tending to show manufacture of a rocket of the A-4 type, this is not such as to indicate any large-scale production. On the other hand, if this evidence were taken to refer to a smaller and lighter type of long distance rocket then it would be consistent with a very considerable flow of continuous production'.[212] But it will be apparent that, given the unquestionable existence of the ski sites, another consideration bulked large in his chain of reasoning – the mistaken assumption, which was due to the lack of intelligence about the nature and design of the V 1, that the pilotless aircraft required no special launch apparatus. It was on this assumption that his report, setting aside not only the earlier correct assumption that Watten was associated with rockets but also the Sigint and SIS evidence that the GAF was experimenting with pilotless aircraft and was associated with the ski sites, failed to connect these sites with the pilotless aircraft. In view of the scepticism about the estimated

---

205. ibid, Conclusions 16 and 17.

207. ibid, Conclusions 10 and 14.

209. ibid, Conclusion 13.

211. ibid, Conclusion 18.

206. ibid, Conclusion 20.

208. ibid, Conclusion 12.

210. ibid, Conclusion 21.

212. ibid, Conclusion 23.

weight of the A-4 and earlier speculation about the existence of a smaller rocket,* it was then an easy step to the suggestion that the ski sites were being developed for a rocket smaller than the A-4.

Even so, the suggestion ran contrary to the advice given to Cripps by the assessors to his inquiry. In addition to voicing doubts occasioned by discrepancies between the supposed characteristics of the A-4 rocket and the Peenemünde evidence, they had argued that the enemy was more likely to be developing a pilotless aircraft; had emphasised that there was no similarity between the sites seen in France and any of the constructions seen in the Peenemünde area, and had noted that there was no reliable evidence pointing to the existence of rockets smaller than the A-4.[213] In reaching his conclusions Cripps had also been unconvinced by a memorandum submitted to him at the outset of the inquiry by Sandys, and presumably prepared in collaboration with ADI (Sc). This had noted that the latest intelligence gave some support to ADI (Sc)'s suggestion of 25 September that the pilotless aircraft might be operational before the rocket and to the view that it might be associated with the ski sites. It had argued that although there was increasing evidence that the Germans were continuing their experiments with rockets – evidence which could not be explained away by the hypothesis of an elaborate German hoax – the evidence that the ski sites were for rockets might be the product of a German cover plan to divert attention from the fact that the pilotless aircraft was more advanced than the rocket. 'It largely emanates from bona fide informants who are unlikely to have expert knowledge and who, on the other hand, are likely to have been influenced by the extensive circulation of the rocket story'. And it had added that 'nothing in the evidence nor in the construction of the emplacements [the ski sites] themselves is incompatible with the theory that a pilotless aircraft is their raison d'être. There is indeed, certain [i.e. some] evidence that this is the case'.[214]

This essentially correct conclusion was soon to prevail over the findings of the Cripps inquiry. But it did not do so before those findings had prompted other responses. On 24 November, commenting on the inquiry at the Prime Minister's invitation, Lord Cherwell complained that it had not faced up to the question of whether the rocket, even if scientifically possible, was technically practicable. He maintained his long-established conviction that the evidence for the large rocket was being planted by the Germans,

---

* See above p 383.

213.   CAB 120/748, Annex, Stanier and Merton minutes to Cripps of 9 November, notes of meeting 10 November 1943.

214.   ibid, Annex, unsigned note 4 November 1943.

who had been careful to provide no advance information on 'their real new weapons'. As to what the real new weapon might be, he gave no consideration to the suggestion that a smaller rocket existed but argued that Zielgerät stood for a predictor and that the pilotless aircraft was a development of the Hs 293: 'if a secret weapon exists at all, some form of pilotless aircraft or glider bomb – which is the same thing – is by far the most likely. But I should be surprised if the scale of attack were serious'. His argument thus made no attempt to account for the ski sites, on which he was content to agree with Cripps that they did not seem suitable for a large rocket.[215] In this respect, as in others, it was totally at variance with the comments on the Cripps inquiry which were issued on the same day, 24 November, by the new *Crossbow* Sub-Committee of the JIC in its first report.* This discounted the hypothesis that the GAF

---

* The JIC's *Crossbow* Sub-Committee, with representatives from the Air Ministry, the War Office, the Admiralty, MEW, 21st Army Group and COSSAC, was set up when responsibility for investigating the V-weapons was transferred from the Sandys Committee to the Air Ministry in the middle of November. The JIC had expressed uneasiness about the responsibility for assessing *Bodyline* intelligence as early as August 1943, and in October it asked for a ruling on whether or not the responsibility belonged exclusively to the Sandys Committee.[216] The COS decided that the JIC should in future comment on the Sandys reports submitted to the Defence Committee other than those which were purely scientific.[217] At the end of October the JIC had not overcome its suspicions that neither it nor the Service departments were receiving all the available evidence and it set up its own small sub-committee of experts to sift SIS, diplomatic, consular and POW reports on the long-range rocket.[218] On 11 November Sandys suggested to the COS that the new arrangements would produce unnecessary duplication between his committee and the JIC; either the JIC should take over his responsibility or be placed at his disposal. The COS adopted the first alternative on several grounds. The intelligence was dealing to an increasing extent with pilotless aircraft and glider bombs, as well as with rockets, but the Sandys Committee had been set up to investigate only the rocket. The most important intelligence was now coming from 'Most Secret Sources', 'the knowledge of which it is undesirable to extend to a wider circle than that of the regular inteligence organisations'. Finally the problem had reached the stage at which it required day-to-day attention by the regular intelligence organisations and the operational staffs.[219] The outcome was that from 16 November the responsibilities of the Sandys Committee were taken over by the Air Ministry, assisted by a new sub-committee of the JIC for the collection of all intelligence concerning the V-weapons, and supervised by an *ad hoc* inter-departmental committee chaired by the DCAS on which were represented the JIC, the Air Ministry, the Ministry of Home Security and the Home Defence Executive. Within the Air Ministry a new Directorate of Operations (Special Operations) was formed to handle operational and defensive counter-measures and its head became chairman of the new JIC Sub-Committee in order to facilitate co-ordination between the intelligence and operational staffs. On 15 November *Bodyline* was replaced by *Crossbow* as the code-name for the enemy's long-range weapons.[220]   *(cont on p 412)*

215. PREM 3/110.
216. JIC (43) 42nd (o) Meeting, 17 August, 49th (o) and 50th (o) Meetings, 5 and 12 October; CAB 121/211, JIC/1599/43 of 12 October 1943.
217. CAB 121/211, COS (43) 253rd (o) Meeting, 19 October.
218. JIC (43) 53rd (o) Meeting, 26 October.
219. CAB 121/211, COS (43) 276th (o) Meeting, 11 November; CAB 120/748, Jacob minute to PM 11 November, JIC/1828/43 of 15 November 1943.
220. CAB 121/211 JIC (43) 468 (o) of 23 November; COS (43) 739 (o) of 29 November; *Air Ministry Intelligence*, p 13.

trials with pilotless aircraft involved merely a controlled glider bomb carried on aircraft, or a towed glider bomb, and made no reference to the suggestion that a rocket smaller than A-4 might exist. But it also emphasised that there was no evidence that a pilotless aircraft was yet in quantity production; and it was presumably on this ground that, despite recognising that the sites were designed for use by the GAF, it concluded that 'a number of reliable reports concerning the activity of Col Wachtel link the ski sites beyond reasonable doubt with some weapon, probably a large rocket, designed for long-range attack against this country'.[222]

When the Chiefs of Staff considered the JIC's first *Crossbow* report, together with the conclusions of the Cripps inquiry, on 30 November the view that the ski sites, the pilotless aircraft and Zielgerät 76 were all associated with each other was gaining ground. On 18 November the DCAS had told the Defence Committee that although there was no evidence that a pilotless aircraft was yet in production, it might not be the case that the ski sites were intended for rockets.[223] On 30 November ACAS(I) advised the Chiefs of Staff that, on the contrary, 'at present the balance of opinion is inclined to interpret these sites as intended for pilotless aircraft'.[224] Nor was it long before the CIU virtually established that this was the correct conclusion. On 1 December two members of the CIU met the JIC *Crossbow* Committee to report on the fuller study of photographs of the French sites, and on a PRU sortie over the Peenemünde airfield at Zempin which had taken place on 28 November. They had come to the conclusion that the sites were for pilotless aircraft and had developed some theories as to the method that was to be used for supplying and using the sites. That same night the interpreters at the CIU located in recent photographs a ramp at Peenemünde West and examination of the photographs disclosed on the ramp 'a tiny cruciform shape set exactly on the lower end of the inclined rails – a midget aircraft actually in the position for launching'. This led to a re-examination of earlier photographs, which established that the ramp had been built late in 1942, and of the recent photographs at Zempin, where the interpreters now found a launching position with ramp foundations resembling those located at the

---

Such was the anxiety with which the JIC approached its new responsibilities that it refused the request of the COSSAC representative on its *Crossbow* Sub-Committee to attend meetings only once a week, sending a deputy on other occasions. In doing so the JIC agreed that *Crossbow* was of such importance that it must take precedence even over the officer's very important duties at COSSAC's Theatre Intelligence Section.[221]

221.　JIC (43) 63rd (o) Meeting, 14 December.
222.　JIC (43) 483 (o) of 24 November.
223.　CAB 121/211, DO (43) 13th Meeting, 18 November.
224.　ibid, COS (43) 293rd (o) Meeting, 30 November.

French sites.[225] The CIU summed up its findings in a report to the JIC which concluded that:

(i)   Bois Carré type sites are designed for the projection of glider bombs of the Peenemünde type (wing span approximately 19–20 feet, length 19 feet);

(ii) the site at Zinnowitz [Zempin] confirms that the body of the bomb must pass through the larger rectangular building;

(iii) the absence of the skis at Zinnowitz tends to confirm that these are for storage;

(iv) the firing points in northern France are being developed on similar lines to the early stages of construction of the prototype firing ramps at Peenemünde airfield, and it seems probable that they will follow the same later stages until reaching the final form seen both at Peenemünde and Zinnowitz'.[226]

□

On 4 December the *Crossbow* Sub-Committee of the JIC, in its second report, accepted the CIU's findings, concluding that 'evidence is accumulating that the ski sites are designed to launch pilotless aircraft'.[227] If this wording suggested that it still had some reservations, none was intended: when the Chiefs of Staff received the second report on 7 December their discussion of possible counter-measures envisaged an aircraft-type missile, not a rocket. It was felt that, as jamming, balloons and anti-aircraft fire might not be very effective, priority must be given to the bombing of the sites.[228] By 14 December plans had been drawn up for attacks on 27 of the sites;[229] they began on 18 December.

If only because of the existence of the larger sites, however, the rocket threat was not overlooked. On 7 December the Chairman of the JIC *Crossbow* Sub-Committee reported that although the evidence remained slender, the larger sites might be intended for rockets,[230] and in its next report, issued on 11 December, the Sub-Committee noted that seven had now been identified by PR and agents' reports – Watten, Mimoyecques, Wizernes (all three of which had already been bombed), and Sottevast, Siracourt, Lottinghem and Martinvast (where work had started with the construction of two trenches over 500 feet long, and with their long axes orientated at right angles to the line to London or Bristol). The Sub-Committee confessed that their purpose was still a mystery.[231]

225.   AIR 41/7, p 129; Babington Smith, op cit, pp 219–224.
226.   AIR 41/7, p 130.
227.   CAB 121/211, JIC (43) 501 (o) of 4 December.
228.   ibid, COS (43) 298th (o) Meeting, 7 December.
229.   ibid, COS (43) 760 (o) of 14 December.
230.   ibid, COS (43) 298th (o) Meeting, 7 December.
231.   ibid, JIC (43) 508 (o) of 11 December.

In his first *Crossbow* progress report to the Chiefs of Staff on 14 December, which dealt mainly with the pilotless aircraft, the DCAS recapitulated the latest evidence about the larger sites and repeated that their purpose was unknown.[232] But he added that 'there is reliable evidence that the enemy is developing a long-range rocket in addition to a pilotless aircraft for use against the United Kingdom'. There had been a recent report from SIS's long-standing contact in France, Colonel Bertrand,* that two weapons existed, but there can be no doubt that the DCAS was really influenced by a new GAF Enigma decrypt.

In a signal intercepted on 26 November and decrypted on 10 December two of the observation posts in the 'Insect' group in the Baltic had been informed that 'you will be used now and again for measuring the A-4 from Ost. You need merely attempt to pick up the ascent vertically and to hold it as long as possible. W/T as for 76.'[233] As the JIC Sub-Committee noted in its next report on 18 December, though without referring explicitly to the decrypt, this first Sigint reference to the A-4 confirmed that it was a weapon undergoing trials in the Baltic and left little doubt that it was a high altitude rocket.[234]

---

* See Volume I, Appendix 1 and Volume II, p 18.

232.   ibid, COS (43) 760 (o) of 14 December.
233.   CX/MSS/J 20 of 10 December 1943.
234.   CAB 121/211, JIC (43) 516 (o) of 18 December.

CHAPTER 41

The Flying Bomb from December 1943 to June 1944

BY THE beginning of December 1943 the intelligence authorities had established that Germany was developing both a pilotless aircraft and a long-range rocket, had correctly associated the pilotless aircraft with the ski sites in France, and were concluding, equally correctly, that while the rocket might be the more formidable of the two weapons, the pilotless aircraft constituted the more imminent threat.

With regard to the pilotless aircraft, soon to be called the V 1, they knew the size of the missile from PR and had made accurate estimates of its current performance – its speed, range and accuracy – from the decrypts of the plot reports from the test stations in the Baltic.* With this intelligence it was possible to begin the development of appropriate defensive counter-measures seven months before the V 1 in fact became operational.† But neither from it nor from what they knew about the state of the ski sites had they yet been able to estimate when an offensive might be launched against the United Kingdom. Moreover, because they knew little about the design and the physical features of the missile, particularly its propulsion unit, they could only guess at the weight of the warhead; and they knew nothing about Germany's programme for its production – another consideration that would determine the scale on which an offensive against the United Kingdom could be sustained.

---

* See above, p 402.

† As early as 22 December 1943 the Defence Committee, on the advice of the Chiefs of Staff, had rejected the Prime Minister's initial suggestion that it should denounce the use of V-weapons as indiscriminate warfare and prepare for retaliation by gas attack.[1] By the same date preliminary plans had been drawn up for defensive measures in the knowledge, clearly established by analysis of the Baltic plots, that the V 1 was an aircraft which, unlike a rocket, might be dealt with by RAF fighters and anti-aircraft guns, with the assistance of radar. The plans made use of the indications that had been received from the Baltic intercepts about the missile's height and speed, though it had already been noted that the flying bomb had been detected flying at up to 420 miles an hour, and that this might be too fast for fighters and would make the weapon a difficult target for the guns. Early in the New Year a more detailed plan was prepared by which fighters, guns and balloons would be deployed in zones which avoided mutual interference.[2]

1. CAB 121/212, SIC file B/Defence/2, Vol 2, DO (43) 14th Meeting, 22 December.
2. Collier, *The Defence of the United Kingdom* (1957), pp 362–364, 373; AIR 41/55, *The Air Defence of Great Britain* Vol VI, p 47.

The only evidence for the weapon's design was the photographs taken of the P 20 at Peenemünde, which indicated its approximate wing-span and overall weight. This set limits for the weight of the warhead, but the limits were wide; according to contemporary calculations, the weight could be half a ton if the missile was rocket propelled but could be two tons if the propulsion system was turbo-jet. The only sources of information on the German production programme were agents' reports to the SIS; they left little doubt that production had been widely dispersed, but this meant that their varying estimates of the rate of production could not be checked by PR. Explicit reference by the agents to the timing of the threat, equally discordant, had been supplemented only by occasional diplomatic decrypts. As we have seen, in September 1943 the Japanese Ambassador in Berlin had reported that despite the raids on Peenemünde and Friedrichshafen Germany would introduce 'new and more effective measures of retaliation . . . before the winter' and later decrypts had indicated that threats of reprisal weapons were being used to reassure the Japanese about Germany's military position.* But these decrypts had not given reliable indications of the time at which their employment might become a practicable possibility. Nor were later diplomatic decrypts from the same source any more precise. For example, after talks with his German contacts late in December, the Japanese Ambassador could only tell Tokyo that the delay in launching retaliatory weapons against Britain was not because preparations were incomplete but because Germany was awaiting a suitable moment to act from both the military and political points of view.

In the absence of reliable evidence about when the offensive would come, an intensive attack was mounted against the ski sites as soon as their association with the flying bomb was established early in December. In the first instance 2nd Tactical Air Force and US Ninth Air Force diverted against them all the medium and fighter-bombers that were being assembled for *Overlord*. When it emerged that they were achieving poor results, in part because of adverse weather conditions, the heavy bombers and Mosquitoes of Bomber Command were called in from the middle of the month and Eighth Air Force was asked to give overriding priority to the ski sites as targets for its daylight bombers.[3] The urgency underlying the bombing campaign was sustained when the JIC's *Crossbow* Sub-Committee, asked to estimate the earliest date at which the threat might materialise, reported on 18 December that pilotless

---

* See above, pp 395, 406.

3. Craven and Cate, *The Army Air Forces in World War II*, Vol III (1951), pp 93–95.

aircraft could drop 300 tons on Greater London in eight hours from mid-January and that the scale of attack might rise to 1,000 tons in eight hours during February.[4] By 20 December COSSAC had been advised that the threat was so serious that he should consider the need for *Overlord* bases outside the range of the flying bomb, as alternatives to Portsmouth, Southampton and Plymouth.*

In its assessment of the threat the JIC's *Crossbow* Sub-Committee had taken into account the number of ski sites identified by PR – this rose from 70 at the beginning of December to 87 by the end of the month – and it had made allowance for the continuing inaccuracy of the flying bomb, as indicated by the low-grade Sigint traffic from the Baltic plotting stations on its range, height and speed.† As for the weight of the warhead, it had accepted that in the light of the estimated size of the missile this might be either one or two tons, according to whether the missile was rocket propelled or used a turbo-jet system of propulsion, and had assumed the latter to be more likely. On 21 December the Chiefs of Staff were sceptical of the argument that the weapon remained inaccurate: 'the enemy might have perfected an original model' and it could not be ruled out that 'the bad results which had been remarked in the Baltic were due to the fact that experiments were proceeding on an advanced type of long-range weapon'.[5] At the Defence Committee on the following day, on the other hand, Lord Cherwell argued that the JIC's *Crossbow* Sub-Committee's assessment of the threat was exaggerated. He felt that the warhead probably weighed only half a ton, since references to the use of two types of fuel had suggested that the missile was rocket propelled, and pointed out that the sites were capable of housing at most twenty missiles each, and probably no more than ten or twelve. He also doubted whether Germany was capable of producing more than 650 automatic pilots a month.[6] And on 23 December some of these arguments were set out at greater length by ADI (Sc) in a report which provided a lower estimate of the threat. It concluded that Germany was unlikely to be able to mount an offensive before March, that the maximum load she could then deliver within ten miles of Charing Cross would be 40 tons an hour, or 320 tons in an eight-hour raid, and that she would be unable to sustain that scale of effort so that 'it would take a long time to achieve serious damage to London.'[7]

ADI (Sc) rested this conclusion in the first place on the belief that the accuracy of the flying bomb was of the order indicated by

---

* See above, pp 47–48.   † See below, p 418.

4. CAB 121/211, SIC file B/Defence/2, Vol 1, JIC (43) 516 (o) of 18 December.
5. ibid, COS (43) 311th (o) Meeting, 21 December.
6. CAB 121/212, DO (43) 14th Meeting, 22 December.
7. AIR 20/1667, ASI Report No V of 23 December 1943.

the plot reports of the Baltic stations. Since the beginning of December a further 60 of these reports, as well as providing more information on the missile's performance by indicating that its speed was 1,400 metres in ten seconds, that its range was 200 kilometres (but 240 km had been attained on one occasion) and that it flew at a height of 2,000 or 2,200 metres,[8] had revealed that a large number of the missiles had failed at or immediately after launch. For some of the firings, moreover, signals to the stations had given the intended direction of the flight, and for a few they had announced the expected range; and comparison of these intentions with the plots given by the stations for actual flights gave a rough indication of the missile's present performance. The analysis suggested that in an attack on Greater London a third of the missiles would fail at start and only between eleven and fifteen per cent would hit the target.

Assuming that one in five of missiles fired would fall within ten miles of Charing Cross, that the Germans would have 100 sites by February and that each site was capable of firing no more than two missiles an hour, ADI (Sc) argued that London would be hit by a maximum of 400 tons of bombs in a ten-hour raid and that such raids could not be repeated every day. As can be seen, this calculation depended on the further assumption that the warhead probably weighed one ton. ADI (Sc)'s arguments for this were that, aside from the fact that there were no pointers to jet propulsion, there were three pieces of evidence for propulsion by a bi-liquid rocket. Containers for the two fuels used by the Hs 293 – hydrogen peroxide (T-Stoff) and sodium permanganate (Z-Stoff) – had been seen at Peenemünde; the Enigma had revealed that the Wachtel organisation had absorbed a military unit known to be involved in servicing those fuels; and the facilities at the ski sites included provision for the separate storage of two fuels.[9]

On 1 January 1944, in a revised assessment of the threat, the JIC's *Crossbow* Sub-Committee took some account of the views expressed by Lord Cherwell and ADI (Sc), and it also took note that a review by PWE of German propaganda up to that date did not indicate that the enemy expected to launch a V-weapons offensive with any sensational results in January.* But it was uncon-

---

* By early March SIS had evidence of a further down-grading of the V-weapons threat in German propaganda. It had received reports about the issue of confidential instructions to Nazi officials to stop referring to vengeance weapons in their propaganda; other reports pointed to the weapons being regarded as a joke among the population in southern Germany.[10]

8. CX/MSS/J 17, 20, 22, 24, 28 and 30 of 2, 10, 14, 19, 24 and 30 December 1943.
9. AIR 20/1667.
10. Dir/C Archive, 5945, No 69 of 7 March 1944.

vinced by the arguments in favour of rocket propulsion – arguments which indeed turned out to be incorrect – and remained cautious about the weight of the warhead. This might be half a ton if the missile was rocket propelled, but could be 1.8 tons if the propulsion system was turbo-jet. According to which view was taken about the warhead, the Sub-Committee calculated that the Germans would be able to deliver in a ten-hour attack on London either 215 or 700 tons from 75 sites by late February and either 430 or 1,540 tons from 150 sites by late March if no allowance was made for the effects of the Allied bombing offensive against the sites. By this time, however, 50 of the sites had been attacked and preliminary interpretation of the PR photographs of the bomb damage had indicated direct hits on essential elements at thirteen of them.[11] The Sub-Committee accordingly offset its estimates of the theoretical scale of the threat with the calculation that 142 of the then expected total of 150 sites might be neutralised during January and February; if this calculation proved to be correct, the threat would be reduced to nil by the end of February, but the enemy might be able to start an offensive on the scale of between 85 and 300 tons of bombs over a ten-hour period at the end of March.[12]*

□

* This was the last report of the JIC's *Crossbow* Sub-Committee. Early in January 1944 the JIC believed that the sub-committee had outlived its purpose and that the stage had been reached when intelligence could best be handled on the orthodox lines of delegating responsibility to the Service intelligence organisations. The COS agreed that the JIC's *Crossbow* Sub-Committee should be disbanded, but rejected the JIC's recommendation that the long-range rocket should now be studied in the War Office, while the flying bomb became the Air Ministry's responsibility. The JIC had felt that given the good liaison that existed between AI and MI there ought not to be a great overlap of work and that the division of responsibilities between the two intelligence sections might even be fruitful. The COS, however, accepting the CAS's opinion that rocket weapons and pilotless aircraft were 'inextricably mixed', made the Air Ministry responsible for both weapons. Within the Air Ministry the head of the Directorate of Operations (SO), the operational authority for counter-measures to *Crossbow*, became responsible for also co-ordinating intelligence on both weapons.[13] While the operations staff continued to issue the weekly reports on the progress of counter-measures which had been introduced by the COS before the disbandment of the JIC's *Crossbow* Sub-Committee, ACAS (I) took over from the sub-committee the submission of regular reports on *Crossbow* intelligence to the COS: these were issued weekly during January and February 1944, thereafter at fortnightly intervals. By an arrangement with the Director of Operations (SO) the evaluation of the radar plots was left in the hands of ADI (Sc).[14] In February 1944 the work on *Crossbow* being carried out by the Theatre Intelligence Section (now a part of SHAEF) was also transferred to the Air Ministry.[15] For the further reorganisation of *Crossbow* intelligence in the Air Ministry in the summer of 1944 see below, p 455.

11. CAB 121/212, COS (43) 792 (o) of 27 December, para 3.
12. ibid, JIC (44) 531 (o) of 1 January 1944.
13. ibid, COS (44) 5 (o) of 3 January, COS (44) 2nd (o) Meeting, 4 January.
14. CAB 121/211, COS (43) 306th (o) Meeting, 16 December; Jones, *Most Secret War* (1978), p 413.
15. CAB 121/212, COS (44) 38th (o) Meeting, 8 January.

After the beginning of January 1944, when the initial alarm had subsided, further attempts were made to estimate the timing and the scale of the threat.[16] They were used on 2 February in the first formal assessment drawn up by the Chiefs of Staff for the Defence Committee; this assumed that the warhead weighed one ton and concluded that there might by mid-March be an initial *Blitz* on the scale of 400 tons over ten hours (approximately the scale of the GAF's bomber raids of April and May 1941); that two further attacks on the same scale might follow at 48-hour intervals; and that thereafter the offensive might continue at the rate of 600 tons a month.[17] When the Defence Committee considered this statement on 3 February, however, it emerged that there were still no firm pointers to the weight of the warhead and no evidence at all about the German production programme for the weapon. The Prime Minister summed up the discussion by saying that while it was important not to exaggerate the danger, it remained impossible to assess the scale of it.[18]

The assessment had in any case made no allowance for the Allied air offensive against the launching sites, and in the next few weeks, as the bombing was intensified and as PR evidence accumulated about its effect, opinion about the extent and the date of the threat became optimistic.* By the first week of March, when it was still

---

* At the end of February, in consequence of the Allies' destructive attacks on the ski sites, the defence plan referred to above (p 420 n†) was scaled down to correspond to what was thought to be the threat from those of the ski sites which had been left intact or were likely to survive further attack. The number of guns for the protection of London was reduced from 746 to 438. Already on 21 February the DCAS had advised that the special radar watch for the rocket which had been instituted in the autumn could be discontinued; the threat was no longer thought to be imminent. No change was made after the discovery of the modified sites (see below, p 423 et seq). Indeed, a further 50 guns were withdrawn by D-day. After the start of the V 1 offensive it took a fortnight, during which London was heavily bombarded from the modified sites, to restore to its defence the number of guns originally envisaged.[19]

AI, however, remained unwilling early in March to guarantee to give a month's notice of the initiation of *Crossbow* attacks and the COS asked if transmission of ground reports could be accelerated.[20] It was difficult for agents to operate in the heavily defended areas of France where the V-weapon sites were located and where the Gestapo was specially watchful. But in addition to the activities of SIS agents SOE had by now established a section working with the Polish community round Lille and elsewhere in northern France from which reports of locations of V 1 sites, and their development, were being received.[21] A hazardous method of obtaining quick information about the sites, involving special duty flights to carry out voice conversations with agents by very short range VHF R/T, was also in use by this time.[22]

---

16.   ibid, COS (44) 19 (o) of 8 January, 25 (o) of 10 January, COS (44) 14th (o) Meeting, 18 January.   17.   ibid, COS (44) 46 (o) of 2 February.
18.   ibid, DO (44) 4th Meeting, 3 February.
19.   ibid, COS (44) 182 (o) of 21 February; COS (44) 57th (o) Meeting, 23 February; Collier, op cit, pp 362–364 AIR 41/56, p 47.
20.   CAB 121/212, COS (44) 77th (o) Meeting, 7 March.
21.   Beevor, *SOE: Recollections and Reflections 1940–45* (1981), p 211.
22.   M R D Foot, *Resistance; an Analysis of European Resistance to Nazism 1940–1945* (1976), p 103.

thought possible that some sites had not been identified and that the planned total might be 120,[23] PR showed that 54 sites out of the total of 96 that had by then been identified had received major damage, that nine of them were under repair but that at 31 of the others there were no signs of repair work. On 16 March, when no further sites had been located and the planned total was judged to be 100, the Air Ministry gave the Chiefs of Staff a revised estimate of the time and scale of the enemy offensive. It calculated that if the bombing programme continued, the number of sites completed and intact in the first week of April was likely to be eight; at the worst the number would be reduced to ten by 15 April. In the first fifteen days of an offensive beginning at the end of March the enemy would be able to deliver only five attacks equivalent to 160 tons of bombs in ten to twelve hours at 48-hour intervals, and in the next fifteen days his offensive would be reduced to five further attacks of half that intensity. Moreover, if he could not be ready to begin the offensive by late March or early April the scale of his attack would be progressively reduced to very small proportions by Allied bombing.[24] The Chiefs of Staff thereupon informed the Defence Committee that the maximum scale of attack would not exceed between one-third and one-half of the estimate provided at the beginning of February, and that if the sources of Allied bombing continued at its existing level all the sites would have been neutralised by the end of April.[25]

As well as making the worst assumption about the weight of the warhead, this assessment took into account the fact that, on the evidence of the plots transmitted by the Baltic stations, the Germans had greatly improved the performance of the missile since the end of 1943. Analysis of the signals had disclosed that they had almost wholly resolved in the course of a single week in January 1944 the difficulties that had previously caused a large number of flying bombs to fail at or immediately after launch; and by the middle of March it had shown that they had so improved the accuracy of the weapon that 40 per cent of those fired against London would hit the target area. The number of firings in the Baltic had meanwhile steadily increased, from two and a half a day in December 1943 to four and a half in March 1944.[26]

By the end of March the signals indicated that the improvement in accuracy was continuing; it was then calculated that 60 per cent

---

23. CAB 121/212, COS (44) 77th (o) Meeting, 7 March.
24. ibid, COS (44) 261 (o) of 16 March.
25. ibid, COS (44) 87th (o) Meeting, 18 March.
26. ibid, COS (44) 266 (o) of 18 March.

of the missiles fired might fall in the target area.[27]* By the same
date the Air Ministry had detected what appeared to be an improvement in the enemy's ability to repair damage to the ski sites. PR
coverage of the sites had earlier indicated that the enemy's repair
rate had dropped by the end of January to about a quarter of what
it had been at the end of 1943, and the drop had been attributed to
the fact that the scale of Allied bombing had taken the enemy by
surprise and had induced his work-force (mainly local labour, POW
and Spanish workers) to desert or to refuse their services. From the
middle of March a falling off in the Allied air attacks was followed
by a noticeable increase in the enemy's repair rate.[28] Inevitably this
fact, together with some doubt as to the extent of the damage caused
by the air raids, even when the damage could be classified as being
heavy, led to uncertainties in the assessment of the number of sites
to be regarded as operational, or potentially so. In the middle of
March AI estimated that ten sites could be regarded as operational
but that, as the enemy might operate from sites that were not
complete, he might have twenty sites operational by the end of the
month if that figure was not reduced by further bombing.[29] At the
end of March, however, the number of sites which might be capable
of operations had risen to 41; twenty of these were thought to be 80
per cent complete and the other 21 were undergoing repair or were
under construction.[30] When AI reconsidered the estimates on 15
April the number of sites regarded as operational was 25.[31]

On 17 April, in the light of these developments, the War Cabinet
pressed for an intensification of the attack on the sites and on 18
April the Chiefs of Staff agreed that it had become a matter of
urgency to neutralise the threat at once so as to avoid the need to
divert forces during operation *Overlord*, when the situation might be
more critical.[32] There followed a series of heavy raids, accompanied
by harassing attacks by RAF fighters to prevent repairs, which
reduced the number of ski sites that were thought to be capable of
being brought into operation from 45 on 27 April to 25 to 7 June.
But no sooner had the level of the Allied assaults been raised than

---

* It was recognised that there was an element of uncertainty in these calculations. The
signals to the plotting stations, though often giving the aiming points of individual firings,
did not divulge the purpose of the test, so that what might have been special tests were
included in the analysis of the accuracy of the weapon's flight. But it was later to be noted of
the flying bombs launched against London that the percentage reaching the target was in
fact 40.

27. ibid, COS (44) 340 (o) of 4 April.
28. AIR 40/1777, AI 2 report 207 of 23 October 1944, p 10.
29. CAB 121/212, COS (44) 261 (o) of 16 March.
30. ibid, COS (44) 306 (o) of 31 March.
31. ibid, COS (44) 344 (o) of 15 April.
32. ibid, WM (44) 51 of 17 April; COS (44) 125th (o) Meeting, 18 April.

the authorities were confronted with a new situation as a result of the discovery by the CIU, on 27 April, of the first of a series of new and hitherto unsuspected launching sites.

□

When the Allies opened their offensive against the ski sites in December 1943 the hope was already fast receding in Germany that the V 1 would be available in sufficient numbers for a full-scale offensive by January or February 1944. By mid-December 1943, when LXV Army Corps was formed for the control of all secret weapon formations, design changes and technical modifications introduced in the course of the development trials had set back the production of the first prototype series and seriously complicated the transfer from prototype manufacture to mass production. Whereas the initial production plan of June 1943 had called for an output of 1,500 missiles in November 1943, rising to 5,000 a month by May 1944, the programme was revised in December 1943 to yield 1,200 missiles in February 1944 and 4,000 a month by May. But in February it was calculated that production might not even reach 1,000 a month by the following July, and already at the end of December General Heinemann, commander of LXV Army Corps, had cut through considerable confusion – and considerable reluctance to report the facts to an impatient Hitler – by announcing that the flying bomb offensive could not start before May or June 1944.[33]

Before making this report Heinemann had toured the ski sites in France and had found them to be unnecessarily elaborate and too distinctive and vulnerable. From the beginning of January 1944, while continuing construction and repair of the ski sites for deception purposes, he had seized upon the delay in the V 1 production programme as an opportunity to replace them with about 150 new sites that were less easily visible, less elaborate, and capable of rapid construction from pre-fabricated parts. At the same time he had decided to abandon the original supply sites, of which eight had been planned, and to use instead underground caves and tunnels for storing the flying bombs.* He had also imposed rigorous security measures to safeguard the locations and the functions of the new

---

* The largest of the new underground storage depots was at St Leu d'Esserent in the Oise valley. In March 1944 an agent of SOE accidentally came by information about this site which, he reported, contained 2,000 flying bombs ready to fire.[34]

33. Collier, op cit, pp 356–357, 359; Irving, *The Mare's Nest* (1964), pp 178–183, 200, 205.
34. M R D Foot, *SOE in France* (1966), pp 369–370; Churchill, *The Second World War* Vol V (1952), p 40.

installations and of the HQ of Wachtel's Flak Regiment 155 (W), which remained in operational charge.

Despite these precautions, by far the largest proportion of the ground reports received by the SIS from its agents in France were from as early as February giving warning of suspicious construction activity at places other than the existing ski sites, and some of the reports were stating that the new sites were of a different type; and the SIS also obtained a general warning that 120 sites, different from though in purpose similar to the ski sites, were under construction and would be ready at the end of May.[35] Despite these warnings, on the other hand, the German deception measures achieved a considerable degree of success. It was not until 27 April that the PRU and the CIU succeeded in identifying the first of the new sites; by that date, at an enormous cost in aircraft, the Allied bombing had delivered over 20,000 tons of bombs against the ski sites.[36]

The new site, with its construction well advanced, was discovered at Belhamelin in the Cherbourg peninsula, an area where previous PR cover had revealed nothing at the end of March and only some scarrings on 6 April.[37] These circumstances provide much support for the conclusion, advanced by AI in the autumn of 1944, that 'it is reasonable to suppose that the enemy surveyed these [new] sites as early as February and that the sources were reporting [only] an intention to build'.[38] It must be repeated that the new sites were well hidden and possessed no distinctive characteristic, as the ski sites had done. And certainly no energy had been spared in following up the SIS reports. On 18 March AI reported that:

'in order to check some 150 reports by agents of suspicious activity a special photographic reconnaissance was ordered of the ski site areas between Calais and Le Havre and in the Cherbourg peninsula. Since the beginning of March 90 per cent of the Calais-Le Havre and 60 per cent of the Cherbourg areas have been covered by photographs of good quality. The great majority of the 150 "suspected" pinpoints have also been covered.'[39]

At the same time, there must be more than a suspicion that there was some delay in finding the first of the new sites because the interpretation of the PRU photographs had been influenced by the

35. AIR 40/1777, p 15.
36. See progress reports by the DCAS in CAB 121/212 and 213, COS (44) 4 (o), 22 (o), 38 (o), 67 (o), 107 (o), 138 (o), 160 (o), 182 (o), 228 (o) 271 (o), 313 (o), 344 (o) and 360 (o) of 3, 9, 17 and 24 January, 2, 7, 14 and 21 February, 5 and 19 March, 2, 16, and 30 April 1944.
37. AIR 40/1777, p 15; AIR 41/7, *Photographic Reconnaissance* Vol II, p 140.
38. AIR 40/1777, p 15.
39. CAB 121/212, COS (44) 266 (o) of 18 March.

understandable concentration of AI and the CIU on the search for additional ski sites and on the study of the damage and the repair work done at the sites already known.

Ironically, the Prime Minister had suggested, as early as the end of 1943, that many of the ski sites might be dummies.[40] AI had advised the Chiefs of Staff at that time that there was no evidence to support this idea.[41] On 18 January 1944, puzzled as to why the Germans were constructing so many sites, Lord Cherwell had returned to the possibility; however, dummy sites, of which the number would have to be large if a decoy policy was to be effective, had seemed to him to be only one possible explanation – it might as easily be the case that the enemy planned a huge initial attack, or that the rate of fire from the sites was lower than the British authorities had calculated – and AI had remained unconvinced that any of the sites were dummies.[42] On 22 January and again on 5 February AI had produced what it took to be good evidence that all the sites were genuine: SIS reports and PR indicated that work on them was indeed being abandoned when damage was very heavy, and that the enemy was increasingly giving camouflage priority over repair, but they also left little doubt that the sites were being abandoned only when repairs were impossible, and there had been some reports to the effect that craters were being left unfilled to give the impression that sites had been abandoned when in fact their launching areas were being repaired.[43] Thereafter, the suspicion that at least some of the ski sites might be dummies was abandoned, and the enemy's policy of carrying out superficial repairs at those sites, and particularly of intensifying this repair programme from the end of March, by which time the construction of the new sites had been in progress for some weeks, succeeded in misdirecting the Allied bombing programme for over four months and in delaying the discovery of the new sites for about a month.

As soon as the first of the new sites had been identified, the PRU, in a huge effort involving No 106 Squadron RAF at Benson, the Tactical Reconnaissance Squadron of the 2nd TAF, the Strategical squadrons of the American 7th Photo Group and the Tactical Reconnaissance squadrons of Ninth Air Force, once again set about covering the whole of northern France within range of London and the area of the Cherbourg peninsula within range of Bristol.[44] By 2 May the CIU had identified five of the new sites, of which three

40.   ibid, Frozen telegram 1011 of 31 December 1945.
41.   ibid, CAS telegram, Grabd 1120 of 3 January 1944.
42.   ibid, COS (44) 14th (o) Meeting, 18 January.
43.   ibid, COS (44) 59 (o) of 22 January, COS (44) 130 (o) of 5 February; AIR 41/7, p 140.
44.   AIR 40/1777, p 16; AIR 41/7, p 141.

were in the Cherbourg peninsula,[45] and between then and 7 June it had located as many as 61 – thirty-eight north of the Somme, twenty in the Cherbourg peninsula and three in Calvados.[46] Nor was the contribution of the SIS reports to the work of the PRU and the CIU any less valuable than it had been in relation to the ski sites. Before the flying bomb campaign was finally launched on 13 June from the modified sites, 'ground agents had reported 110 locations from which launching was to take place. Of these, 31 were confirmed by subsequent photography'.[47] Thereafter the SIS reports continued to guide the effort to identify more sites. In October 1944 AI reported that:

'In all, nearly 500 different places have been reported as being launching sites, of which the greater proportion have been examined by interpreters at CIU. Out of a total of 165 sites known to have been constructed, 76 of them have been constructed at places indicated by ground sources. One agent alone reported 37 sites.'[48]

The discovery of the new sites undermined previous assessments of the scale and timing of the threat. The PRU and the CIU quickly established that ski buildings were not being built at the new sites; as early as 2 May this fact had led Lord Cherwell to conclude that the enemy had decided to abandon the ski sites and that the lack of skis at the new sites meant that he had given up the hope of being able to deliver the pilotless aircraft in a concentrated attack.[49] But AI could not be certain that the ski sites had been wholly abandoned, and by the first week of June the discovery of some 60 new sites had still not put an end to its uncertainty on that point. Furthermore, there was still no evidence from other directions as to when the offensive might start.*

By 14 May the PRU and the CIU had shown that the new sites consisted of a launching point and a square building, but as none of the sites was then complete, their final form remained uncertain.[50]

---

* In the middle of December one of the double agents who was being used in an effort to acquire information about the timing of the threat (see above, pp 381, 406) had been told to move outside London and have a reserve radio transmitter built. In February 1944, however, he was told that probably no warning could be given. In May the Germans made arrangements for him to receive special questionnaires to which he was to reply, urgently, both to Berlin and to Arras which was at that time the HQ of the Abwehr Kommandos with the Field Army. SIS pointed out that it was from Arras that the flying bomb offensive might be directed. But the double agent appears to have supplied no subsequent information about the imminence of the threat.

45. CAB 121/212, COS (44) 141st (o) Meeting, 2 May.
46. AIR 40/1777, Appendix X.
47. ibid, p 15.   48. ibid, p 15.
49. CAB 121/213 SIC file B/Defence/2 Vol 3; COS (44) 141st (o) Meeting, 2 May.
50. ibid, COS (44) 419 (o) of 13 May.

On 26 May AI was still unable to judge from PR and agents' reports whether the new sites were designed to be self-contained units, like the ski sites, or whether the enemy intended to use them only as firing points, carrying out the preparation of the missiles at the supply sites.[51] Of the eight supply sites planned by the Germans, PR had identified seven by the middle of March when six of them were judged to be complete.[52]* On 1 June the COS were informed that 84 of the 96 ski sites had suffered heavy damage but that 52 new sites had been identified and eight more were suspected.[54] On the previous day they had been advised that as yet the Germans appeared to be completing only the foundations of the new sites, the presumption being that they would erect pre-fabricated buildings at a later stage in their preparations.[55] This presumption was soon confirmed by the CIU's study of the latest photographs from Zempin. These had shown how a site of the modified type was being constructed there by fitting together and erecting six metre lengths of rail and by assembling pre-fabricated parts for the square building on the spot. This intelligence, together with the deduction that the modified sites, and perhaps some of the ski sites, could be made ready for use in a matter of 48 hours, was conveyed to AI at a meeting on 5 June.[56]†

□

Meanwhile no intelligence of value had been obtained by the beginning of June about the design and the detailed characteristics of the flying bomb.

During February and March several SS Enigma (Quince) decrypts had confirmed that, as had already been reported by the Polish underground,‡ the Germans were carrying out V 1 trials at 'Heidelager', which was already known to be the code-name for a camp at Blizna in Poland. The decrypts had referred to the completion of a firing site associated with catapults. They had also

---

* There were no Allied attacks on the supply sites until after the start of the V 1 offensive on 13 June, because there was no further evidence associating them with either the ski sites or the modified sites. By the time the attack on them began the Germans had already ceased to use them and were instead using underground caves and tunnels for storage[53] (see above, p 423). For further information see Volume III Part 2.

† No official record of this meeting has been found, but there is no reason to doubt that it took place.

‡ See below, pp 437–438.

51.   ibid, COS (44) 461 of 26 May.
52.   ibid, COS (44) 261 (o) of 16 March.
53.   Collier, op cit, pp 361–362.
54.   CAB 121/213, COS (44) 177th (o) Meeting, 1 June.
55.   ibid, COS (44) 175th (o) Meeting, 30 May.
56.   Babington Smith, *Evidence in Camera* (1958), p 227; Irving, op cit, p 226.

mentioned the existence of a T-Stoff depot and of Z-Stoff, and had associated with the missile a fuel called E 1 which later turned out to be a low-grade aviation fuel.[57] It was subsequently to emerge that E 1 was the low-grade aviation fuel which fuelled the V 1, and that while T-Stoff (hydrogen peroxide) was used for the launching of the flying bomb, the references to Z-Stoff (sodium permanganate) were explained by the fact that the A-4 rocket was also undergoing trials at Blizna. At the time, however, these references were associated with the V 1 and, in view of the fact that the Enigma had previously mentioned T-Stoff and Z-Stoff in connection with Hs 293*, they perpetuated the erroneous supposition that, like the Hs 293, the flying bomb was rocket propelled. In April AI believed that 'while there is still a little doubt as to whether T-Stoff is used as the main propellant for the FZG 76, there is no doubt that it plays an important part either in the launching or the propulsion of this missile.'[58]

The first report to be received of a sighting of the V 1 in flight had proved to be equally inconclusive. This report was obtained by NID from the British Naval Attaché Stockholm on 16 April. He had learned that on 15 March the master of a freighter had seen two large rocket projectiles at a height of 300 m in position 54°10′N, 13°46′ E; they had been fired in succession from a shore installation ten miles away, were the size of a small fighter, had short camouflaged wings and were 'propelled at very high speed by a rocket tube which gave approximately 300 detonations a minute.' 'Each detonation appeared to give two flashes in the form of a ring'. The report prompted a series of questions to the Naval Attaché: what had been the interval between the two firings; did the projectile have a cylindrical or cigar-shaped object slung under the body; was the tube in the tail or fitted as a separate unit; was there any sign of wires trailing from the projectile; could the source confirm the number of detonations? The Attaché provided answers on 24 April. There had been half an hour between the sightings; a cylinder was fixed above the body as a separate unit; there were no wires; the detonations had been counted by the Master's watch. On the same day he was asked to confirm that the noise had been a series of explosions, and not a rumbling noise.[59] That the source had correctly

---

* See above, p 341.

57. CX/MSS/J 56 of 14 March, 58 of 21 March, 61 of 30 March 1944; CAB 121/ 212, COS (44) 308 (o) of 31 March.
58. CAB 121/212, COS (44) 340 (o) of 14 April, Appendix E.
59. ibid, NA Stockholm telegram to DNI 151723 of 16 April 1944, Admiralty to NA Stockholm 201536 of 20 April, NA Stockholm to Admiralty 241103 of 24 April, Admiralty to NA Stockholm of 24 April.

described the appearance of the flying bomb and the noise of its flight was to be obvious when the V 1 campaign began, but at the time nothing could be made of his information and nothing further was learned about the design of the weapon until it became possible to subject a V 1 to physical examination.

The opportunity to do this had arisen at the end of May, when British experts were allowed to examine the wreckage of two pilotless aircraft in Sweden; one of them had been recovered from the sea by the Swedish Navy, the other had crashed in Sweden on 13 May. The findings from this inspection, and from information provided by the Swedish authorities about two other crashed missiles, were that the missile, mainly of steel and designed to be mass produced, was a mid-wing monoplane with a span of 16 feet, powered by an athodyd* which used low-grade aviation petrol. It was controlled by a rudder and two elevators, but little could be learned about the control mechanism beyond the fact that it involved three gyroscopes, one of which was monitored by a compass. It appeared to have no radio equipment. Although they provided no direct information about the warhead, both projectiles having had dummy warheads, these findings bore on that problem by quite destroying the assumption that the propulsion unit was a rocket fuelled by hydrogen peroxide. They were available in the Air Ministry by 8 June and were reported to the Chiefs of Staff on 9 June.[61].†

□

In the report of 9 June AI also advised the Chiefs of Staff that while the construction of the new sites, of which 61 had then been identified and another eight were suspected, was still not far advanced, the resort to pre-fabrication 'might result in their early completion', and that it was apparent 'that these sites are self-contained after the manner of the ski sites'. In the same report, after noting that there was nothing in PWE's study of the latest German

---

* See above, p 368. The athodyd had previously been described as a ram-jet. In the case of the missile which crashed in Sweden the propulsion unit was found not to be a ram-jet but a pulse-jet. This was discovered by AI 2(g) on 13 June when the first V 1 that landed in the United Kingdom was examined.[60]

† A more detailed report of the Swedish wreckage together with information derived from operational wreckage in England was not issued until 16 June.[62]

60. AIR 40/2166, AI 2(g) report No 2242 of 13 June 1944.
61. AIR 40/2452, AI 2(g) Minute to DDI 2 of 6 June 1944; CAB 121/213, COS (44) 509 (0) of 9 June.
62. AIR 40/2166, Report No 2243 of 16 June 1944.

propaganda to indicate that a large-scale offensive was imminent,* AI concluded that 'while the possibility of the modified . . . sites being brought to a state of readiness at short notice cannot be ruled out, the general inference is that a large-scale attack on this country with *Crossbow* weapons is unlikely to take place in the next fortnight'.[64]

At the time of this assessment PR sorties over the sites had been suspended since 4 June, partly as a result of bad weather and partly on account of the opening of Operation *Overlord* on 6 June. But when PR of the sites was resumed on 11 June the CIU at once detected evidence of activity at some of the nine sites, all in the Pas de Calais area, that were photographed; it informed AI that evening that the square building was complete at six sites and that at four of them rails had been laid on ramps.[65] At about the same time AI received from the SIS, from 'a usually reliable source', a report to the effect that on 9–10 June a train of 33 wagons each loaded with three 'rockets' had passed through Ghent to Tourcoing, and that further trains were expected. AI advised the Chiefs of Staff of these intelligence developments on the morning of 12 June. It added that at least twenty of the 42 sites located in the Pas de Calais area might be structurally ready, since it was known that the foundations had been completed at twenty of them. And it concluded that 'the indications are that the Germans are making energetic preparations to bring the pilotless aircraft sites into operation at an early date.'[66] An estimate of the scale of the threat, drawn up the same morning, judged that 400 tons of high explosive might be delivered from the modified sites in the first ten hours; this assumed the firing of one missile every half-hour from twenty sites.[67]

In the event the Germans opened the V 1 offensive with a far smaller attack. Hitler had decided on 16 May that the bombardment of London must begin in mid-June, and the Allied landings in Normandy on 6 June had reinforced his determination to permit no delay. But the systematic Allied bombing of the French communications that was carried out in connection with the landings disrupted the enemy's preparations for last-minute distribution of

---

* This indicated that up to 24 May while the enemy had not abandoned the expectation of being able to launch *Crossbow* on a large scale, a large-scale offensive was not planned for the near future, and certainly not before the start of *Overlord* in early June; but there was nothing either to confirm or refute the possibility that a small-scale offensive might be launched as a counter-invasion measure.[63]

63.   CAB 121/213, COS (44) 471 of 28 May, Appendix C.
64.   ibid, COS (44) 509 (0) of 9 June.
65.   Babington Smith, op cit, pp 227–228.
66.   CAB 121/213, COS (44) 517 (0) of 12 June.
67.   Collier, op cit, p 368.

pre-fabricated parts, equipment and missiles to the sites. On 11 June, when Wachtel's preparations should have been completed, none of the sites was fully operational. By the evening of 11 June he had had catapults fitted to 54 or 55 of the 64 available sites, but two-thirds of them had not yet been tested and on account of lack of equipment the essential pre-firing safeguards had not been taken. Wachtel's original order called for two salvoes, at 2340 on 12 June and 0040 on 13 June. Fifteen minutes before the time for the first salvo he was told that in the absence of safety equipment no site was in a state to fire. He obtained permission to postpone the attack briefly, and ordered the sites to fire at 0330, but not earlier. They could barely meet the new schedule. In an initial offensive that had been planned to deliver some 500 of the missiles, only ten flying bombs were launched and only four reached England, five having crashed immediately. A raid on London by bombers of Fliegerkorps IX, which was to have accompanied the offensive, was cancelled.[68]

After holding an enquiry into the fiasco of the night of 12–13 June the Germans resumed the V 1 offensive on the night of 15–16 June. By noon of 16 June, from 55 of the modified sites, 244 flying bombs had been fired, of which 144 crossed the English coast and 73 reached London.[69] On 17 June, to permit the maximum production of flying bombs, Hitler ordered a reduction in the production of the A-4 rockets. He rescinded this decision in August, when all the launching sites were in danger of being over-run and the rocket offensive was about to begin.

---

68. ibid, pp 368–370; Irving, pp 229–233.
69. Collier, op cit, pp 368, 370, 371 and Appendix XIV; AIR 41/56, p 86; Irving, op cit, pp 234, 237.

CHAPTER 42

The V 2 Rocket from December 1943 to July 1944

AFTER the raid on Peenemünde in August 1943 the Germans had continued to carry out some work on the rocket there, particularly testing of the weapon's flight, but they had transferred the testing of its warhead, in flight tests with live warheads, to the overland range at Blizna where they subsequently carried out the field trials of the rocket, as of the V 1 and other rocket weapons, with the units who were to fire them operationally. The first A-4 launch at Blizna had been attempted on 5 November; it had failed on account of the faulty emplacement of the firing platform. The rocket programme thereafter fell steadily behind schedule, the delays being mainly due to design and development problems, which were far greater than those associated with the V 1, and to the decision to embark on mass production before those problems had been solved. In the autumn of 1943 an order had been placed for the production of 12,000 rockets at the rate of 900 a month at an underground Volkswagen factory near Nordhausen in the Harz region; but after rising from 50 in January 1944 to 437 in May, monthly production fell back to 374 in August. Only then, when some 65,000 modifications had been made to its basic design, was the rocket cleared for full production. These delays increased, and were themselves compounded by, the anxiety of the German authorities to avoid interference with the V 1 production programme. In March 1944 Hitler insisted that the Nordhausen factory should produce the V 1 as well as the V 2; at the same time he called for another close enquiry into the progress of the V 2 programme.[1]

Further problems had meanwhile been created by the heavy Allied bombing of the large protected sites that the Germans were constructing in France for the firing of the rocket. By the beginning of 1944 the Germans had decided to abandon work at such of those sites as could not be completed before the following autumn. But before coming to this decision they had established that the rockets could be launched no less effectively with simple mobile ground

---

1. Dornberger, *V 2* (English edn 1954), pp 204–217; Collier, *The Defence of the United Kingdom* (1957), pp 347–348, 399–400; Irving, *The Mare's Nest* (1964), pp 141, 145, 182, 221–223.

equipment than from a bunker; and they had made plans for the formation of two mobile units and an independent SS Werfer Batterie in addition to a bunker unit.[2]

□

Beyond the fact that the Germans were constructing large sites in France, the British authorities knew little about these developments at the beginning of 1944. The PR photographs taken over Peenemünde since the August raid were reviewed at the end of 1943, when the Enigma had finally established that the A-4 was undergoing trials there;* the review confirmed that while no attempt had been made to repair the damage done, activity involving torpedo-like objects, about 38 feet long, was continuing.[3] By the same date a few Enigma signals announcing the intention to fire A-4s in the Peenemünde area had been intercepted, and the Baltic plotting stations had occasionally reported attempts to track A-4s in the low-grade code;[4]† the Chiefs of Staff were informed in January that 'during December we heard of five or perhaps six attempts to fire A-4 projectiles, although we only have positive evidence that the projectile flew on one occasion, and that it failed to start on another occasion'.[5] In the case of the rocket, as in the case of the pilotless aircraft, there was no evidence of the state or location of production. MEW had in December listed five firms that might be concerned with the rocket – two in Friedrichshafen, one in Frankenthal, one in Berlin and one in Wiener Neustadt (the Raxwerke) – but in January the Air Ministry advised the Chiefs of Staff that the failure of agents to distinguish in their reports between the rocket and the pilotless aircraft and 'the lack of definite corroboration . . . by photography or other means' made it impossible to reach firm conclusions about the places and rates of production of either weapon.[6]

In these circumstances attention not unnaturally focused on the large sites under construction in France. On 22 January 1944, after sifting once again all the evidence from PR and the SIS, the Air Ministry recognised that there was still no positive proof that the

---

* See above, p 414.   † See above, p 402.

2. ibid.
3. AIR 34/197, CIU Report DS 47 of 29 December 1943; CAB 121/212, SIC file B/Defence/2, Vol 2, JIC (43) 531 (o) of 1 January 1944.
4. CX/MSS/J 32 of 5 January 1944.
5. CAB 121/212, COS (44) 31(o) of 15 January.
6. CAB 121/211, SIC file B/Defence/2, Vol 1, COS (43) 760 (o) of 14 December; CAB 121/212, COS (44) 94 (o) of 28 January.

sites were associated with the rocket.* But it noted that they did not appear to have any industrial or defensive function; that all were within 150 miles of London and had a system of trenches which in most cases lay at right angles to a line extending through London or Bristol; and that in the reports received from agents they had invariably been associated with rockets or rocket guns. Its report concluded by recommending an intensive bombing campaign against the sites.[8]† At the end of January the Chiefs of Staff accepted this recommendation and ordered the campaign to begin as soon as possible; they were reminded that there was no definite evidence that the sites were for rockets and informed that the Sigint from the Baltic plotting stations indicated that the rocket was still undergoing trials, but they felt that preparations for launching rockets from France might well be in train.[9]

On 19 March, by which time nearly 2,500 tons of bombs had been dropped in thirty raids against the large sites,[10] the progress of the campaign was considered in the light of the PR evidence. It was estimated that at Martinvast it would take three months to repair the damage done, and further attacks were suspended. At Lottinghem repairs would take between one and a half and three months; at Siracourt and Sottevast they would take between two and six weeks. No serious damage had been done at Watten, Wizernes and Mimoyecques. By that time PR had also disclosed that Mimoyecques was being developed on different lines from the other sites, with emphasis on the construction of two tunnels, and an agent had reported that a concrete chamber was to be built near one of the tunnels for the installation of a tube, 40 to 50 metres long, which he referred to as 'a rocket launching cannon'. The agent's report was correct; as we have seen, Mimoyecques was being developed for the Hochdruckpumpe and not for the V 2. But since other agents had often referred to guns and cannon in their reports about the rocket,

---

* Of the seven sites, Watten was the first to be developed for launching the A-4; it had a store for rockets and liquid oxygen, an oxygen liquifaction plant and a place for testing, fuelling and servicing the rockets. When Watten was damaged (see above, p 385) it was retained only as a liquifaction plant, and Wizernes, originally intended to be only a store, was developed into an A-4 launching site. Sottevast and Martinvast were also A-4 sites but Martinvast subsequently converted into a V1 site. Siracourt and Lottinghem were designed as V 1 launching sites but Mimoyecques was designed for the installation of the revolutionary gun called the Hochdruckpumpe[7] (see above, p 405)

† The report gave details of what was known of the construction of the sites, of the strength of their Flak defences and of the effects of the Allied bombing raids already carried out. These are given in Appendix 27, together with the further evidence that accumulated up to the end of March.

7.   Collier, op cit, pp 348, 360.
8.   CAB 121/212, COS (44) 59 (o) of 22 January.
9.   ibid, COS (44) 23rd (o) Meeting, 25 January, 38th (o) Meeting, 25 January.
10.   ibid, COS (44) 271 (o) of 19 March.

and since the British continued to assume that the A-4 would have to be launched from some kind of tube or projector, the effect of this evidence was to strengthen or revive doubts as to whether the other large sites were associated with the rocket. On 18 March ACAS (I), in one of his regular reports on *Crossbow* intelligence, sent the PR information about Mimoyecques to the Chiefs of Staff with the comment that 'the nature of the works supports the statement put forward in a recent intelligence report that they may be intended for the launching of a large rocket'.[11] At a meeting of the Chiefs of Staff on 21 March the shortage of information about the sites was discussed, Mr Duncan Sandys pressing for special efforts to acquire intelligence and ADI (Sc) conceding that although they were already a top priority target, intelligence was scarce because the Germans were not making use of foreign labour in their construction.* In the end, however, the Chiefs of Staff resolved to inform the USAAF that they attached great importance to all the large sites and hoped it would give priority to attacks on them.[13]

In the last ten days of March, by which time the Germans had little interest in continuing the development of the large sites except for the purpose of deception,† the USAAF and the RAF carried out nine more heavy attacks on Mimoyecques, Watten, Wizernes and Siracourt, inflicting damage which it was estimated would take between one and a half and three months to repair at Wizernes and between two and six weeks at Mimoyecques and Watten.[14]

□

Neither PR of Peenemünde nor the coded traffic of the Baltic plotting stations had in the meanwhile produced any intelligence about the characteristics, the performance or the state of development of the rocket. Warnings to the stations to expect rocket flights were intercepted six times in January, three times in February and

---

* Sandys had already suggested at the end of January that the SOE might undertake a special operation to capture a German technician as a means of acquiring information about the large sites. The Chiefs of Staff had approved the idea of 8 February, and AI had subsequently briefed SOE on five Germans who might be appropriate targets. A SOE agent began his search for these men on 19 March, located one of them at the end of April, but did not succeed in making a capture.[12]
† See above, pp 423–424.

11.   ibid, COS (44) 255 (o) of 18 March.
12.   ibid, COS (44) 23rd (o) Meeting, 25 January, 30th (o) and 38th (o) Meetings, 1 and 8 February, 141st (o) and 175th (o) Meetings, 2 and 30 May; COS (44) 131 (o) of 5 February, 271 (o) of 19 March; Foot, *SOE in France* (1966), p 368.
13.   CAB 121/212, COS (44) 93rd (o) Meeting, 21 March.
14.   CAB 121/212, COS (44) 313 (o) of 2 April.

three times in March,[15] but on the performance of the rocket, as opposed to that of the pilotless aircraft, the stations' own signals were uninformative. Nothing could be made of the one new feature disclosed in the PR sorties to Peenemünde – the appearance in photographs taken on 5 and 7 January of three columns about 45 feet tall standing in a triangle on the foreshore.[16] But by February 1944 it was recognised that a new and more valuable source on these aspects of the rocket problem had been opened up by the Poles.

The SIS had been receiving Polish reports from the Blizna area since October 1943. The earliest reports, which showed that the Germans were evacuating villages in the area and building a new railway to Lemberg (Lwow), had included references to rockets, and three with December dates had given details of the range of the missiles, and been accompanied by a photograph of a rocket in flight over trees. Their texts have not been preserved; perhaps because they referred or were taken, reasonably enough, to be referring to the flying bomb, the *Crossbow* investigators did not single them out from many other agents' reports on the V 1. In February 1944, however, two further Polish reports were regarded as being of more than usual interest; they quoted missile dimensions that were close to those of the 'torpedoes' observed at Peenemünde but mentioned missile weights that were considerably lighter than those given in most earlier agents' descriptions of rockets. The first, dated 15 February, said the rocket was fourteen metres long with a weight of seven tons, including a warhead of one ton. The second, dated 22 February, quoted a length of twelve metres, a diameter of one and a half metres and a weight of eleven to twelve tons, including eight tons of fuel and a warhead of two tons.[17]*

At the end of March the Poles submitted an account of the trials of missiles at Blizna which they had observed between 29 November 1943 and 17 January 1944, some of which, at least, appeared to refer to rockets. They had seen five firings at a distance of one and a half kilometres from the 'projector'; one had annihilated two farms, another had made a crater about 50 metres in diameter and

---

* Similar dimensions and weights were given in a report received from Norway on 9 March. It claimed that the rocket was cigar-shaped, twelve metres long and one to one and a half metres in diameter, that it weighed eleven to twelve tons, including eight tons of 'oxygen alcohol' propulsion fuel and two tons of explosive, and that its maximum range was 250 km[18]

15.   CX/MSS/J 121 of 22 June 1944; AIR 20/1688, ASI Report on the A-4 of 26 August 1944.
16.   AIR 34/197, DS 50 of 12 January 1944.
17.   AIR 20/1688. Appendix D.
18.   ADI(K) 107A/1944 of 9 March.

fifteen metres deep, and a third had not exploded. The firings, which they had heard over distances of about ten kilometres, had been accompanied by a strong flash, without any detonation, and had been followed by a loud roar, a stream of smoke when the missile reached a height of about 300 metres and a bright light when it reached 500 metres. At about 1,000 metres the trajectory had changed and the missile had ceased to go up. The 'projectors' incorporated special rails mounted on a lattice construction at an angle of 45°. The report added that on railway wagons in the area observers had seen tubes six metres long, cylinders 1.2 metres in diameter and a tank which, according to railway workers, contained the special mixture used for ejecting the rockets; a cold, odourless, bluish gas was evaporating from the taps of the tank, and it was suggested that this indicated 'liquid air'.[19]*

The interest now shown in the Polish reports was all the greater because Blizna had by then been associated with A-4 trials, as well as with the flying bomb programme, in the decrypts obtained from the SS Enigma key (Quince). In addition to making several references to the flying bomb,† these decrypts included two, both obtained in March, which discussed the fact that the construction of facilities at 'Heidelager' was being delayed by the Army's 'secret command project'; they were exchanged between Peenemünde and 'Heidelager' with copies to Berlin for a Dr Kammler, who was believed, correctly, to be Chief Engineer of the Waffen SS.[21] Beyond the conjecture that the Army's 'secret command project' was the A-4 programme, and that it was interfering with the flying bomb trials at Blizna, not much could be made of these somewhat cryptic references, but together with the indications from the low-grade Sigint of the Baltic plotting stations that A-4 firings at Peenemünde remained infrequent, they strongly suggested that the rocket programme was still at the experimental stage.

□

There was some reduction in the Allied bombing of the French sites after the end of March, but no relaxation in the PR coverage of the effects of the bombing raids on their development. At the end

---

* By as early as January a number of agents had mentioned German measures to increase the supply of liquid oxygen and had associated the expansion with 'secret weapons' without specifying how the oxygen was used.[20]

† See above, pp 427–428.

19.   AIR 41/55, *The Air Defence of Great Britain*, Vol VI, p 190; R V Jones, *Most Secret War* (1978) p 430.
20.   CAB 121/212, COS (44) 31(0) of 15 January, Annex para 8.
21.   CX/MSS/J 55–59 issued between 10 and 23 March 1944.

of April the PR evidence showed that construction was continuing at Sottevast, Siracourt and Mimoyecques, but that work appeared to have been abandoned at Martinvast and Lottinghem. At Watten repairs were not being made to buildings damaged by the Allied raids, but a new large building was nearing completion, as was a large dome-like structure at Wizernes.[22] A fortnight later the Air Ministry reported that further raids had set back construction at Sottevast, Mimoyecques and Wizernes, but that good progress was still being made at Siracourt and Watten; from the fact that the anti-aircraft defences had been increased at all the large sites it also judged that the Germans continued to attach great importance to them.[23] At the end of May the PR evidence indicated that, while work had still not resumed at Martinvast and Lottinghem, military equipment was still being delivered to the other sites; it also suggested that at these sites (except Sottevast) the Germans had probably made the structures impervious to ordinary bombing. The Chiefs of Staff at once requested heavy raids on Siracourt, Mimoyecques, Watten and Wizernes at the first favourable opportunity.[24] On 11 June they were informed that in raids against Siracourt and Watten hits had been made at Siracourt without causing appreciable damage.[25]

On the night of 12–13 June the Germans opened the V 1 offensive, and from the night of 15–16 June the attack was carried out on a scale which temporarily overwhelmed the defences. This development, which may of itself have aroused apprehension about the threat from rockets, was accompanied by others which heightened the tension. On 14 June the British Air Attaché in Stockholm reported that a rocket had crashed in Sweden, at a place about 200 miles from Peenemünde, and had made a crater several metres wide and one and a half metres deep.[26] And on 18 June the three Directors of Intelligence produced for the Chiefs of Staff a joint memorandum in which they reviewed the most recent PR intelligence of the large sites in France in the light of an agent's report dated 16 June to the effect that 'Watten will by now be ready to function'. They noted that the sites at Watten and Wizernes were more advanced than those at Siracourt and Mimoyecques, and urged that certainly at Watten, and possibly at Wizernes, the evidence indicated that civil engineering work was completed and

22. CAB 121/212, COS (44) 308 (0) and 375 (0) of 14 and 28 April.
23. ibid, COS (44) 344 (0) and 380 (0) of 16 and 30 April, 427 (0) of 14 May.
24. CAB 121/213, SIC file B/Defence/2, Vol 3, COS (44) 471 (0) of 28 May, COS (44) 175th (0) Meeting, 30 May.
25. ibid, COS (44) 513 (0) of 11 June.
26. AIR 40/2452, Telegram A 351 to Air Ministry, 14 June 1944; Jones, op cit, p 431.

that military construction had begun. They added that, as the agent was thought to be normally reliable, and as it was known that the large sites were not associated with the V 1 offensive, it would be unwise to ignore his statement. They therefore recommended that Watten should be attacked again at the very first opportunity.[27] The Chiefs of Staff, meeting with the Prime Minister in the chair, responded at once by ordering a daylight raid with Tallboy bombs against Watten as soon as weather conditions were favourable, to be followed by attacks on the other large sites.[28] At the same time, but mainly to deal with the V 1 offensive, the Prime Minister set up a Cabinet *Crossbow* Committee to meet daily with himself as chairman; but on 20 June he relinquished the chairmanship to Mr Duncan Sandys, who was instructed to keep under review the threat from both the flying bomb and the rocket and the progress of counter-measures against them.[29]

At its first meeting under Sandys's chairmanship on 22 June the committee noted that the highest priority was being given to heavy raids with Tallboy bombs on the four protected sites in the Pas de Calais but that there was some doubt whether the bombs would penetrate the main structures. At the same meeting the committee was reminded that the association of the large sites with the rocket still rested almost wholly on negative evidence – on the fact that no other use for them could be suggested, and on the fact that it was beyond question that the Germans had developed a rocket – but was informed that Sottevast, the large site in the Cherbourg area, had been overrun by the Allied armies and was being inspected.[30]*

The next fortnightly *Crossbow* report from ACAS (I) to the Chiefs of Staff followed on 26 June. It drew attention to agents' reports that rockets were being transported to the Pas de Calais, particularly to Watten, and to warnings from a variety of sources that preparations were being made for a rocket offensive. The other warnings presumably included that obtained from a Japanese diplomatic decrypt to which 'C' had drawn the Prime Minister's attention on 22 June; in it the Japanese Ambassador in Berlin had said that he had recently learned that 'other secret weapons with which Germany would bomb England were even more effective [than the V 1]', and that he was confident that they 'could deal with England'.[31] ACAS (I)'s report concluded that, unless it was averted

---

* See below, p 446.

27.   CAB 121/213, COS 1029/4 of 18 June 1944.
28.   ibid, COS (44) 199th (o) meeting, 18 June.
29.   ibid, CBC (44) 1st Meeting, 19 June, CBC (44) 1 of 20 June.
30.   ibid, CBC (44) 2nd Meeting, 22 June.
31.   Dir/C Archive, 6890 of 22 June 1944.

by air raid damage to the launching sites, there was no reason to suppose that the offensive would not begin in the comparatively near future.[32]

□

Anxiety about the rocket threat at the end of June was all the greater, as was the concentration of attention on the French sites, because intelligence about the development, the performance and the production of the weapon was still scanty.

On the network used by the plotting stations in the Peenemünde area, intercepts reporting A-4 firings had remained infrequent. In April only one probable firing was recorded, in May none at all, in June three certain and six probable. Nor did the firings increase in July, when the score was two certain and three probable. This evidence reflected an actual low rate of firings, resulting from the severe development difficulties the Germans were encountering; but, the more so because nothing was known of these difficulties from other sources, it could not be relied on as an accurate guide at the time.* The signals to the stations included cancellations as well as notices of firings, and it could not be assumed that the stations were notified of all firings. There were still no plot reports from the stations on the flight of the A-4 of the kind that had earlier thrown so much light on the probable range and accuracy of the V 1[35]†

The Poles had continued to report regularly from Blizna, where they had organised search teams to pick up fragments and take photographs at the sites of explosions. They had observed nine firings in February, eighteen in March, still more in April (when eleven or twelve missiles had been launched in a day on at least

---

* In fact the low-grade decrypts were a reasonably reliable guide. A document captured in 1945 disclosed that between 14 January and 12 September 1944 57 firings took place, excluding faulty shots. In the same period the number of firings registered by the intercepts was 50, including possible as well as certain and probable firings.[33] The number of firings detected increased in August to ten certain and ten possible from Peenemünde and five certain and two possible from Greifswalder Oie[34]. The decrypts continued to record firings at this rate until the network closed down in February 1945.

† It was not until September 1944 that the signals disclosed some information about the performance of the A-4. They then showed that there were two kinds of firing, one to a range of 20 to 30 km and the other to a range of 200 km. In November this latter range was increased to 300 km; thereafter half the tests were fired to 200 km and half to between 300 and 330 km.[36]

32. CAB 121/213, COS (44) 573 (0) of 26 June.
33. CX/MSS/SJ 45 of 29 July 1945.
34. CX/MSS/SJ 11 of 6 September 1944.
35. CX/MSS/SJ 3 of 29 July 1944.
36. CX/MSS/SJ 16, 22 and 26 of 2 October, 6 November and 4 December 1944, 28 of 6 January 1945.

four occasions) and twenty in May; and they had noted that some of the missiles had exploded prematurely, high in the air. But their reports had suggested that they had not realised for some time that the Germans were testing both the V 1 and the rocket, and as late as June those which clearly referred to the rocket, while still agreeing that it was about 40 feet long and six feet in diameter, and had a range of 250 km, remained contradictory or imprecise in other respects. Some had said that it was launched from rails, others that the launcher was in the form of a tube. Some had given the altitude of its flight as 6,000 metres, others as 10,000 metres. The Poles had also found pieces of radio equipment including a transmitter and receiver and had analysed some fuel in the area and found it to be hydrogen peroxide.[37]* A PR sortie had been flown over Blizna from Italy in mid-April; the photographs had identified a flying bomb ramp, but had detected no sign of the larger installations seen on photographs of Peenemünde and thought to be associated with the launching of the rocket. Nor had photographs taken during a second sortie on 5 May as yet provided any useful information.

Further evidence on the rocket was obtained at the end of May when a German chemical warfare instructor who had attended a rocket course in Peenemünde in August 1943 was captured in Italy. He said that the missile contained two chambers, one filled with 96 per cent ethyl alcohol and the other with liquid oxygen (for which he substituted liquid air when interrogated a second time); that it carried about one ton of explosive, which could be increased to one and a half tons; and that its range was between 300 and 350 km. On being fired, it went up at 2° to an altitude of 10,000 metres, after which it was steered by wireless from a control station, and its nose housed a very secret and complicated steering capsule (Steuerspitze). It was fired from a metal base or frame between one and one and a half metres high to which it was transported on a trolley; the trolley elevated it until it could be slid off into a vertical firing position. He added that one type of rocket was mobile and required no fixed frame for firing;[38] this was perhaps a reference to the Army's short-range rocket launcher, the Nebelwerfer.

---

* The reports were now made direct to London by radio. At the end of July, however, one agent from Blizna flew to London with recovered fragments and documents, after cycling 200 miles to a landing strip. A good deal had by then been learned about the rocket from other sources; but his evidence showed that the Poles at Blizna had analysed and submitted their observations with great care, and he helped to establish that the performance of the A-4 was still imperfect by enlarging on the reports they had made about premature explosions.

37.   AIR 41/55 p 192; AIR 20/1688, pp 7, 9; Collier, op cit, p 401.
38.   CSDIC/CMF/M 148, Report of Interrogation 22–26 May and ADI (K) Minute of 9 June 1944.

In a telegram to Tokyo decrypted in the middle of June the Japanese Naval Attaché described the A-4 as 'a kind of rocket glider with a total weight of about twenty tons and an explosive charge weighing about eight tons'. He added that it was fired by a special charge, driven by the explosion of a rocket propellant and controlled during its flight by wireless from two ground stations; that three large railway wagons were needed to carry the firing charge and the propellant for a single rocket; and that because the Allies were bombing the launching points on the French coast and the railways leading to them, the Germans were making plans for transporting building materials and the rocket fuels by road.[39] A further message from the Attaché, decrypted on 20 June, provided some remarks on the V 1 offensive which indicated that he was having difficulty in obtaining reliable information, but added that at least one A-4 had crashed in Sweden because 'rather too much range' had been used during tests.[40]

In the middle of May GC and CS's routine inspection of unreadable Enigma traffic for signs of careless German encypherment enabled it to break a new and little used Army Enigma Key (Corncrake). The decrypts turned out to be signals between Peenemünde and Blizna, and by the end of June – though only by giving it highest priority at the expense of work on other keys – GC and CS had read the traffic for sixteen days in the period from the end of March, when it was first intercepted, to 8 June.[41] The decrypts named General Dornberger and Professor von Braun and provided some technical details about the A-4 by referring to a radio control system; to 'pressure bottle installation'; to the transfer from Peenemünde to 'Heidelager' of A-Stoff and B-Stoff trucks, Z-Stoff canisters, non-operational warheads (Blinde Spitzen) and sets of a jet-rudder (Strahlruder); to a fourth fuel, C-Stoff; and to a firing platform. One decrypt listed data about what appeared to be eight missiles, some of which were given serial numbers and all of which were given another number indicating a form of colour code; other signals quoted serial numbers within a series running from 17053 to 17767 for objects that were being transferred from Blizna to Peenemünde.* These signals suggested that the colour code numbers were associated with 'frequency inserts'. They also identified

---

* After the end of June the traffic was broken for a few more days within the period up to 23 July, when it died out following Germany's evacuation of Blizna. In one of these later decrypts, obtained on 14 July, the serial numbers rose to 18036.[42]

39. Dir/C Archive, 6897 of 22 June; SJA 385 of 16 June 1944.
40. SJA 394 of 20 June 1944.
41. CX/MSS/J 131 of 29 June 1944.
42. AIR 20/1711, *Crossbow* Weekly Intelligence Summary No 1 of 30 July 1944.

the units engaged in the trials at Blizna. Although this could not be foreseen at the time, the units identified were later to appear in an operational role in the west.[43]

Like the technical intelligence which, such as it was, had been obtained from the other sources since the end of March, the contents of these decrypts had not been passed to the Chiefs of Staff by the time the Prime Minister set up the Cabinet *Crossbow* Committee in the third week of June. On 22 June that committee was informed that, as was indeed the case, intelligence about the production of the rocket was non-existent and intelligence about the weapon itself was still slight; apart from the bombing of the French sites, the only action so far prompted by intelligence was a recent decision to place hydrogen peroxide plants in Germany on the list of priority bombing targets.[44]* In his regular fortnightly report to the Chiefs of Staff of 26 June ACAS (I) dwelt on the intelligence which recorded activity at the French sites; he added only that it was reasonably certain that the main fuel of the rocket's bi-liquid propellant was concentrated hydrogen peroxide, and that a number of POW had calculated the weight of the rocket to be between fifteen and twenty tons.[47]

This was the situation when, on 6 July, at the suggestion of ACAS (I), ADI (Sc) was made responsible for assessing and distributing intelligence on the rocket. The change was made because the double task of carrying out counter-measures against the V 1 offensive and of co-ordinating *Crossbow* intelligence was becoming too great a burden on the operational staff at the Air Ministry.[48]† But it was no doubt influenced by the fact that, at a time when knowledge of the rocket remained so scanty, the prospects

---

* But a Japanese diplomatic decrypt claimed at the beginning of May that the Raxwerke factory producing the A-4 had been moved in great secrecy from Wiener Neustadt to a remote village and that the factory at the new site had subsequently been destroyed by Allied bombing, the Allies having learned about the new location.[45] PR sorties against factories reported by agents to be associated with rockets and liquid fuels, or thought to be capable of producing hydrogen peroxide, had been carried out since the end of April. They had produced no positive results by the end of June.[46]

† For the assumption of this dual responsibility by the operations staff in January 1944 see above, p 419 n*.

43.   AIR 20/1688, p 5; CX/MSS/J 91, 96, 101, 103, 117, 121, 122, 131, 134, 143, 146, 147 of 16, 20 and 26 May, 1, 3, 8, 19, 22, 23 and 29 June, 2 and 17 July 1944.
44.   CAB 121/213, CBC (44) 2nd Meeting, 22 June.
45.   Dir/C Archive, 3 May 1944.
46.   AIR 34/197 DS reports 58, 59, 60, 63 and 64 of 20 and 29 April, 1, 13 and 16 May, 66–70, issued between 2 and 24 June 1944.
47.   CAB 121/213 COS (44) 573 (o) of 26 June.
48.   AIR 40/2452, Minutes of Meeting in Air Ministry, 6 July 1944; Jones, op cit, p 425.

that the Enigma might make crucial disclosures about it were rapidly improving.

□

Meanwhile, arrangements had been made to obtain information about the missile that had crashed in Sweden. On 22 June the British Air Attaché in Stockholm had reported that it was different from other weapons that had previously landed in Sweden, and was equipped with a 'turbo-compressor', and on this evidence that it was not a V 1 the Air Ministry had obtained permission to send two experts to inspect it.[49] On 7 July the experts reported that it was much larger than a V 1; rocket propelled, without wings, with directional control apparently exercised by vanes and by radio control similar to that used in the Hs 293, it was six feet in diameter and they guessed that 'the weight of the war-head would not be less than 10,000 pounds [five tons] and might be considerably more'.[50]* On 9 July ACAS (I) incorporated this information in his next report to the Chiefs of Staff, together with selections from the less recent intelligence. These included the statement that the Polish evidence about the trials at Blizna strongly suggested that the A-4 was a large radio controlled rocket with a range of 200 miles or more using hydrogen peroxide fuel, the statement that the traffic of the Baltic plotting stations had shown that at least seven missiles had been fired between 7 and 30 June, and the statement that when they had recently been re-examined a large rocket had been identified on the PR photographs taken on 5 May over Blizna.† The report concluded that a few rockets could be fired against the United Kingdom at any time, provided firing bases in France were completed.[53]

---

* Unfortunately, the missile was not typical of the A-4s that were later used operationally. Only 20 per cent of these were radio controlled. It subsequently turned out to be an experimental hybrid consisting of a genuine A-4 rocket fitted with an extremely elaborate radio guidance system primarily designed for the small rocket known as *Wasserfall* which was being developed for anti-aircraft purposes.[51]

† This discovery had presumably just been made, though a full report on the re-examination of the photographs, showing that the rocket had four fins and was moved by trailers of a special design, was not made until later. The re-examination had also disclosed a large crater which, in the opinion of the explosive experts, must have been made by a warhead weighing about five tons; ADI (Sc) took account of this further information in his report of 16 July, see below, p 447).[52]

49.   ibid, telegrams between Air Ministry and Air Attaché Stockholm, A 370 and 372 of 22 and 23 June, AX 189 of 23 June 1944.
50.   ibid, A 391, 395, 401 and 409 of 7, 8, 11 and 13 July 1944.
51.   Jones, op cit, pp 431, 452.
52.   AIR 34/134 Interpretation Report BS 780 of 4 August 1944.
53.   CAB 121/213, COS (44) 611 (o) of 9 July.

ACAS (I)'s report also stated that the examination of the cap-tured site at Sottevast* had produced no firm evidence that the large sites were in fact 'rocket projectors'; but it seemed probable that they were intended for the bulk storage of rockets. The report issued by Mr Duncan Sandys for the information of the *Crossbow* Committeee on 10 July noted that attacks on these sites would continue and that, as it was vital to delay the development of the rocket and of improved flying bombs, Peenemünde was going to be heavily raided.[54] On the following day the Chiefs of Staff advised the Prime Minister that he should take steps to get the remains of the missile from Sweden and obtain permission for a mission to be sent to inspect Blizna when the Soviets occupied the area.† In the course of their discussion Lord Cherwell, though no longer express-ing disbelief in the existence of a rocket, doubted whether the French sites were associated with rockets, rather than with the V 1, and Mr Duncan Sandys disagreed with him.[56] It was presumably on this account that later on 11 July the Prime Minister took the chair at a meeting of the *Crossbow* Committee summoned to discuss 'conflict-ing intelligence' about the rocket. At that meeting the CAS insisted that there was no doubt that a rocket existed.[57] On 12 July censorship and deception plans, drawn up with a view to denying Germany information about the impact made by the rocket if it was launched against the United Kingdom, were submitted to the COS.[58]

On 13 July GC and CS issued an Enigma decrypt containing a reference by the Abwehr representative at LXV Corps HQ at Arras to the imminence of 'bombardments'.[59] On seeing his copy the Prime Minister feared that it might refer to the rocket and asked for 'C''s comments. 'C' answered on 14 July in a memorandum pre-pared in consultation with ADI (Sc); they believed that the decrypt was referring to the V1, but could not exclude the possibility that the rocket would be used at an early date.[60] It was presumably on this account that, as the *Crossbow* Committee was informed on the same day, ADI (Sc) was ordered to prepare a report on the state of

---

* See above, p 440.

† The Prime Minister had kept Stalin informed about the V 1 attacks in a series of telegrams since the middle of June. On 13 July he asked Stalin to preserve whatever might be found at Blizna until British experts had examined it.[55] They were not to do so till September 1944, about two months after the Russians overran the site.

54.   ibid, CBC (44) 17 of 10 July.
55.   ibid, CBC (44) 6th Meeting, 14 July.
56.   ibid, COS (44) 230th (o) Meeting, 11 July.
57.   ibid, CBC (44) 5th Meeting, 11 July.
58.   ibid, COS (44) 621 (o) of 12 July.
59.   Dir/C Archive, 7084 of 13 July 1944.
60.   ibid, 7093 of 14 July 1944.

the intelligence about the rocket.[61] On the following day the alert was maintained by the receipt of a Japanese diplomatic decrypt in which the Ambassador in Berlin repeated that Germany would be employing a weapon, or weapons, even more devastating than the flying bomb.[62]

ADI (Sc)'s report, issued on 16 July,[63] described itself as an 'interim summary statement of the broad lines of our knowledge and ignorance'.* But it assembled a good deal of evidence in support of the conclusion that the Germans had brought a technically impressive rocket missile to a stage of development at which it was 'good enough at least for a desultory bombardment of London'. The evidence it used was as follows. The Poles at Blizna had claimed that the missile had a range of about 185 miles (and the weapon recovered in Sweden had crashed 200 miles from Peenemünde) and that the Germans had improved its accuracy to the point that half the shots were falling into a circle of twenty miles. Its overall weight was not known, but the craters seen on PR photographs of Peenemünde and Blizna indicated that the warhead weighed between three and seven tons.† There was no reliable information about its production; but one report had claimed that production had been resumed after being interrupted in March to give priority to the fighter aircraft programme, and the Swedish rocket showed signs of series production. The Poles had reported that nineteen rockets had been fired from Blizna between 30 April and 7 May and that the launchings were continuing in June, in which month the decrypts of the plot reports had disclosed that probably a dozen had taken place at Peenemünde. It seemed likely that, altogether, the Germans had fired between thirty and forty in June. Provided they had launching sites ready in France, they could fire a number against the United Kingdom, but there were no pointers as to when an attack could be expected. Observation of the large French sites showed that none could be ready for some time. On the other hand, only two of these sites appeared to be intended as launching points; and one of the gravest gaps in the intelligence about the rocket concerned the methods used in firing it.‡ It had to be borne in

---

* Professor Jones has recorded that he protested that the demand for a report was premature, the evidence being still so incomplete that conclusions drawn from it might be seriously misleading.[64]

† This, a serious over-estimate, was one of the two chief errors in the report. The other was the conclusion that the main fuel was hydrogen peroxide. See below p 454 and Volume III Part 2 for the subsequent correction of these deductions.

‡ See below p 449 et seq for further details.

61. CAB 121/213, CBC (44) 6th Meeting, 14 July.
62. Dir/C Archive, 7110 of 15 July 1944.
63. CAB 121/213, CBC (44) 24 of 16 July.
64. Jones, op cit, p 434.

mind, moreover, that, as had been the case with the V1, the advance of the Allied armies might produce a demand for the use of the rocket against the United Kingdom at an early date even if the production programme had been delayed and the weapon's performance was not yet wholly satisfactory. This was all the more likely because it could be assumed that an A-4 campaign, being more spectacular than the V1 bombardment, would be nearer to the Führer's heart.

When the Chiefs of Staff considered this paper on 18 July the CAS thought it significant that following the suggestion that A-4 production has been interrupted in March, there had been firings in May and June; and Lord Cherwell conceded that 'if . . . the enemy has seen fit to divert so much of his resources to produce a long-range weapon, the threat cannot be altogether disregarded'. Remarking that he had not seen all the evidence, Cherwell added that, as the engineering problems were formidable, the results of a rocket attack were unlikely to be very serious.[65]* And on the evening of 18 July, taking the chair at a meeting of the *Crossbow* Committee, the Prime Minister, who was presumably somewhat shaken by the alarms of the past few days, pursued the point that Cherwell had not seen all the evidence. He criticised the Air Ministry for keeping back the developments summarised in ADI (Sc)'s report of 16 July instead of advising all concerned as and when they had occurred; and the minutes duly record that he 'directed that Dr Jones [ADI (Sc)] should keep Lord Cherwell fully informed of all aspects of intelligence on the long-range rocket'.[67] He became still more disturbed, moreover, when new items of intelligence, additional to those summarised in the paper of 16 July, were reported to the meeting.

According to one personal account of what was clearly a stormy discussion, he exclaimed 'We have been caught napping' when he was given more details about the rocket that had crashed in Sweden.[68] Another says that he thumped the table and uttered this exclamation when he was told that the Germans had so far fired about 150 rockets experimentally, and had produced about 1,000; it adds that ADI (Sc) explained that he had been able to make this last calculation only in the past few days, and pointed out that, even if the warhead weighed five tons, the Germans were in a position to

---

* After the meeting the CIGS noted in his diary that 'the rocket is becoming a more likely starter'.[66]

65. CAB 121/213, COS (44) 239th (o) Meeting, 18 July.
66. Quoted in Irving, op cit, p 267.
67. CAB 121/213, CBC (44) 8th Meeting, 18 July.
68. Irving, op cit, pp 267–268, quoting Cherwell's account of the meeting.

drop only 5,000 tons of explosive on London, little more than Bomber Command had dropped on Berlin in a single night.[69] It appears that these comments failed to reassure the Prime Minister. The minutes of the meeting of 18 July record that in summing up the discussion he said he was prepared after consultation with the United States and the USSR to threaten the Germans with large scale gas attacks if they resorted to a rocket bombardment.[70] At a later *Crossbow* meeting on 25 July he complained that on 18 July he had been surprised to learn of two developments about which he felt he should have been kept more fully informed: it had suddenly been brought to light not only that the Germans had made 1,000 rockets, but also that the rocket could be fired with a mobile mechanism from a simple concrete bed and did not need a bulky launching edifice.[71]

□

ADI (Sc) had arrived at the figure of 1,000 rockets after concluding that the serial numbers given in the Enigma decrypts about movements from Blizna to Peenemünde must be production numbers for rockets; and it is clear that he could not have arrived at it before 14 July, the date on which the decrypts took the series from 17053 to 18036. But when did he conclude that the numbers were production numbers? There is no difficulty in accepting that he came to this conclusion, also, only a few days before the meeting. With hindsight, and bearing in mind that the decrypts had disclosed by the end of June that the serials had already risen to 17767 by 8 June,* we might argue that he could have done so earlier – on 9 July, when a rocket was identified on the Blizna photographs,† or even when the serial numbers began to appear in the decrypts in June, by which time there was little doubt that rockets were being fired at Blizna.‡ But even when it had become clear that rockets were being fired at Blizna it may have remained difficult to reach the conclusion that the numbers referred to rockets that were being sent back from Blizna to Peenemünde for inspection after they had been fired.[72]

The second criticism, that there had been undue delay in distributing the evidence which showed that the rocket was fired from a simple concrete platform, was, strictly speaking, equally unfounded.

---

* See above, p 443.   † See above, p 445.   ‡ See above, p 443 n*.

69.   Jones, op cit, pp 437–439.
70.   CAB 121/213, CBC (44) 8th Meeting, 18 July.
71.   ibid, CBC (44) 9th Meeting, 25 July.
72.   AIR 20/1711, No 1 of 30 July 1944; Jones, op cit, pp 435–436.

Valuable, not to say decisive, information to this effect had been obtained from POW at the end of June, and this had been mentioned to the Chiefs of Staff and the *Crossbow* Committee by 11 July. On the other hand, there is no doubt that ADI (Sc) had not sufficiently stressed the significance of the POW evidence before the meeting of 18 July, and it was on this account that he then produced consternation by announcing that he had identified a concrete platform on the Blizna photographs on the previous day.

On 20 and 29 June CSDIC had circulated reports on the inter-rogation of the POW recently captured from Sonderstab Beger, a unit which they said was engaged in selecting, surveying and constructing rocket installations in France under the control of LXV Army Corps; they added that this had been set up in January 1944 and had the same relationship to the rocket as Flak Regiment 155 Wachtel had to the flying bomb. The POW listed fourteen areas in which some 24 firing sites and at least four supply dumps had been projected or under construction by January 1944 in a rushed building programme that was to be completed by June or July. They made sketches of most of the firing sites; one of these, at Bernesy, had been completed by January and another, at Bray, had been far advanced. Each site consisted of three rectangular plat-forms of different depths of reinforced concrete, so built that they would be scarcely distinguishable from the nearby road; the rocket was to be fired on the platforms from a metal tripod. At the supply dumps the rockets were to be stored in tunnels from which they would be taken first to an assembly shed and then to the firing site. One of the dumps was in a quarry. At another, at La Meauffe in the Bois de Baugy, the tunnels were being dug in an embankment, and a narrow gauge railway leading from them passed through three sheds; the bed of the railway had been laid to carry a maximum weight of nine tons.[73]

In his regular report of 9 July to the Chiefs of Staff, ACAS (I) had mentioned this evidence, pointing out that 'a report from a prisoner indicates that the launching mechanism may be much simpler than was formerly thought'.[74] Perhaps because it was pre-occupied with the news that the examination of Sottevast had apparently confirmed the association of the large sites with the rocket, the Cabinet *Crossbow* Committee had not discussed this suggestion when it considered the report on the following day*. On 11 July the attention of the Chiefs of Staff had been drawn to ACAS (I)'s reference to the POW evidence, but except indirectly, in the

---

* See above, p 446.

73.   CSDIC(UK) SIR 395 and 469 of 20 and 29 June 1944.
74.   CAB 121/213, COS (44) 611 (0) of 9 July.

dispute between Lord Cherwell and Mr Duncan Sandys as to whether the large sites were associated with the rocket, the subject had not been discussed.*

It may seem strange that these meetings devoted such scant attention to the POW evidence, but it must be emphasised that it was by no means easy to come to terms with it. A succession of agents' reports had stated that the rocket was launched at high speed from a gun or a projector of considerable size. British scientists had assumed that a large launching apparatus would be needed to keep the missile stable during the initial stage of its flight. The large tower-like structures seen on the many PR photographs of Peenemünde had conformed to this assumption, and the large sites in France had seemed to be consistent with it. A brief reference to the possibility that, on the evidence of a POW, the launching system might be much simpler was thus unlikely to attract notice from the Chiefs of Staff and the *Crossbow* Committee. But the idea was presented to them in this tentative form at this stage because ADI (Sc) had not yet been persuaded that the POW reports were either conclusive in themselves or adequately supported by other information.

There were those who thought otherwise. On 3 July, in a report for circulation in the War Office, MI 14 had pointed out that there was other evidence to support the conclusion that the rocket was launched from simple concrete platforms. MI 14 singled out three early SIS reports. One of 10 July 1943 had said that the rocket would be fired from mobile steel mountings which, owing to their light construction, could be placed in any position and the position changed rapidly, if found necessary.† Another was the report from the source in touch with the Waffenamt, dated 12 August 1943, which had provided the first indication that two V-weapons existed; this described the A-4's launching projections as of simple construction, which could be placed in open fields if necessary.‡ Thirdly, there was the original SIS report on Wachtel of 20 August 1943, which had mentioned 400 catapults as the ultimate total to be deployed from Brittany to Holland.§‡ In MI 14's view there was support, too, from the Corncrake Enigma decrypts; although their evidence was not conclusive, they had referred to special vehicles, trailers and firing platforms (Abschussplatforme). The information obtained from the POW from Sonderstab Beger had thus to be taken seriously. Unless it was pure invention, the report went on, which was most unlikely, it pointed to the fact that a large special organisation – referred to by the POW as an Army Corps – was

---

* See above, p 446.   † See above, p 377.

‡ See above, pp 385–386 and Appendix 25. MI 14 was of course in error in using this V 1 information as evidence.

§ See above, p 393.

constructing rocket launching sites in northern France which intelligence had failed to identify; and it suggested that the sites were designed to achieve a high rate of fire by enabling the projectiles to be brought forward from a nearby supply base three at a time and fired at short intervals. MI 14 conceded that it was somewhat surprising that no 'simplified' sites had been identified, but it pointed out that they might be difficult to locate from the air and that, as the A-4 apparently had a greater range than the flying bomb, some of them might lie outside the much-examined ski site belt. It added that PR had identified what appeared to be eleven railway turntables of unusual construction, and suggested that they might be rail-mounted A-4 projectors.[75]

ADI (Sc) had not been convinced by the MI 14 report. On it he commented: 'The A-4 would want a bigger site and should therefore be more conspicuous'. In the note of 14 July which he helped 'C' to draft for the Prime Minister he stated that no V 2 launching site had yet been definitely identified, but that it might be easier to know what to look for after obtaining further PR of Blizna, which was to take place when the weather improved.* And in the report he issued on 16 July he was still arguing that speculation was not justified until more definite information was available.† The report quoted the POW claim that the rocket was fired from a concrete pad; but it pointed out that whereas one of the sites they had mentioned had been investigated in liberated Normandy, as yet without result, a Polish witness at Blizna had said that the launching ramp was a lattice construction at an angle of 45°.

ADI (Sc) was cautious not only towards the POW reports, but also about the negative evidence that the May photographs of Blizna had failed to discover large installations there of the kind seen at Peenemünde. In August he was to concede that this had made it a reasonable assumption that the rocket's launching point was a much simpler platform[76] but in his report of 16 July he argued that speculation was premature until, among other things, further PR of Blizna became available. It seems clear that he was concentrating all his efforts on establishing positively that there were no substantial structures at Blizna and, if possible, on clinching the matter by locating a concrete platform.

He succeeded in doing this on 17 July. Re-examining once again the earlier Blizna photographs, he then noticed on them a patch of concrete about 35 feet square which, as he reported to the *Crossbow*

---

* See above, p 446.   † See above, p 447–448.

75.   WO 208/4116, MI 14 Report 35/94/44 of 3 July 1944.
76.   AIR 20/1688, p 16.

Committee on the following day, he identified as a rocket launching pad.[77]

□

In the next regular report from ACAS (I) to the Chiefs of Staff, dated 22 July, ADI (Sc) remarked that the identification of the concrete patch as a launching pad had not yet been confirmed.[78] By then, however, the Air Ministry had received a report on the examination of some sites listed by the POW from Sonderstab Beger as rocket launching points; dated 17 July, this showed that platforms and two camouflaged terraces parallel to and on either side of the road had been found at one of the sites near Château Molay, west of Bayeux.[79] By then, also, earlier but hitherto unsuspected clues to the nature of the launching system were beginning to fall into place. Once it was accepted that the rocket was fired without a complex launching mechanism, it could be seen that the 40-foot columns disclosed by the Peenemünde photographs were rockets standing vertically at their firing points, and that the jet rudders mentioned in the Enigma decrypts and the small flaps discovered on the fins of the rocket salvaged in Sweden kept the rocket stable during the initial stage of its flight.

At the next meeting of the Chiefs of Staff on 25 July Mr Duncan Sandys returned to the charges that had been made on 18 July. Asserting that his scientific sub-committee had worked out from first principles that the rocket could be launched from a simple site, exactly as had now been suggested by the intelligence authorities, he complained that the intelligence authorities had wasted the time of the scientists by holding back a considerable volume of evidence for several weeks. He protested that he could not discharge his responsibility if he was furnished only with periodic digests of the available intelligence instead of with the intelligence raw material as and when it was obtained; the Air Staff should not permit AI to delay circulating information until it was absolutely certain of the complete reliability of its conclusions on every point.[80] On the same day, at the meeting of the *Crossbow* Committee, Mr Herbert Morrison, the Home Secretary, who had taken no part in discussions about the rocket threat until 18 July, echoed Sandy's complaint: he was sure that any information on such developments should be

---

77. Jones, op cit, pp 436–437.
78. CAB 121/213, COS (44) 245 (o) of 22 July.
79. AIR 40/2452, Air Technical Intelligence, HQ 2nd TAF, Report No INT/
     C/167 of 17 July 1944; Jones, op cit, pp 432–433.
80. CAB 121/213, COS (44) 247th (o) Meeting, 25 July.

circulated rapidly. As already noted, the Prime Minister sympath-
ised with it.* The Secretary of State for Air defended AI by arguing
that much of the important intelligence had been obtained only
after the rocket had crashed in Sweden; but the Prime Minister
insisted that a great mass of evidence had been available earlier,
and Sandys claimed that this was particularly the case with the
discovery that the rocket was launched from mobile firing points†
and that it was also true of the discovery that the rocket was fuelled
by liquid oxygen.[82]

There was no justification for the second of these charges. One of
ADI (Sc)'s staff had had discussions with the officers who had
investigated the rocket in Sweden as soon as they returned to the
United Kingdom. He was immediately reminded by what they said
about the pump that fed the fuel into the rocket's combustion
chamber that one kind of pump used in the process of liquefying air
was lubricated by the fuel itself; this established that the rocket's
main fuel must be liquid oxygen, not hydrogen peroxide as hitherto
believed. But the discussions did not take place until 23 July.[83] The
complaint that there had been unnecessary delay in circulating the
intelligence which had established that the rocket was fired from
concrete launching pads was better founded. Although the first
positive evidence to this effect, that obtained from the POW at the
end of June, was circulated earlier than Sandys claimed, it was
circulated only on 9 July, and neither then nor after 17 July, when
its accuracy had been confirmed by the location of a concrete
platform at Blizna, had ADI (Sc) attached to it the importance it
clearly deserved. But the complaint made no allowance for the
possibility that such errors of judgment would sometimes be made
by those responsible for assessing and interpreting the intelligence
on so novel and complex a problem as the rocket.

Whatever the rights and wrongs might be, the dispute was
provoked by discontent, on the part of those who were charged with
supervising counter-measures against the V-weapons and of those

---

* See above p 448.

† Sandys had already put details of this complaint in a minute to the Chief of the Air Staff.
The POW reports of 20 and 29 June about concrete firing points in Normandy had not
reached him till 21 July, after he had heard of them indirectly. Confirmation of the existence
of a firing site near Château du Molay had been obtained by 14 July, but he had not been
informed until he had made enquiries on 22 July. The identification of a concrete platform
at Blizna had not been brought to his notice till 19 July. He had still received no report on
the discovery that an organisation connected with that conducting the trials at Peenemünde
and Blizna had been at work in Normandy, by which he presumably meant the POW
evidence that their unit was working under LXV Army Corps.[81]

81.   AIR 40/2452, Undated Sandys Minute to CAS c 25 July 1944.
82.   CAB 121/213, CBC (44) 9th Meeting, 25 July.
83.   Jones, op cit, pp 434–435.

charged with providing the intelligence that bore on the threat, with all efforts to demarcate their responsibilities for assessing the intelligence. That the issue was a long-standing one may be judged from the many readjustments of responsibility and procedure that had been adopted since the threat was first perceived. And that it was perhaps insoluble is suggested by the further change in responsibilities adopted in response to Sandys's protest. His demand that he and his advisers should be shown the intelligence raw material as and when it was obtained could not be granted. It took no account of the hesitations and uncertainties involved in the assessment of intelligence, or of the danger of reaching premature conclusions, or of the rules which restricted the circulation and discussion of such of the intelligence as was derived from high-grade Sigint. He was not refused, however, when he insisted that the responsibility for distributing *Crossbow* intelligence must be transferred to other hands, on the ground that ADI (Sc), the intelligence adviser on the *Crossbow* Committee, had shown a disinclination to circulate and discuss intelligence until he was sure of the accuracy of his conclusions and had thus taken no account of his (Sandys's) understandable anxiety, as the committee's chairman, to be abreast of the state of appraisal. At the end of the meeting of 25 July Cherwell defended ADI (Sc) in a minute to the Prime Minister, and on the following day ADI (Sc) rebutted Sandys's charges in a minute to the Chief of the Air Staff.[84] But these steps failed to avert the removal from ADI (Sc) of the responsibility for co-ordinating all *Crossbow* intelligence.* He continued to be a member of the *Crossbow* Committee, but on 30 July ACAS (I) appointed the Director of Intelligence (Research) (an RAF Group Captain) to be responsible for co-ordinating the work of all sections of AI engaged on *Crossbow* intelligence and for providing all other agencies with the intelligence they required.[85]

---

* For ADI(Sc)'s recent assumption of these responsibilities see above, p 444.

84. AIR 40/2452, ADI (Sc) Minute to CAS 26 July 1944; Irving op cit, p 270.
85. *Air Ministry Intelligence*, p 13.

APPENDICES

The Organisation of Intelligence from June 1943 to June 1944

By the summer of 1943 the intelligence bodies and the network of relations between them had essentially acquired the form they were to retain till the end of the war. Except for those specially introduced in preparation for Operation *Overlord*, which will be dealt with in the next volume, the changes that occurred in the twelve months ending June 1944 may thus be summarised briefly:

A. THE PROCUREMENT OF INTELLIGENCE

1. *The Sigint Board and GC and CS*

The Y Board and the Y Committee (See Volume I, pp 23, 271–272) remained responsible for policy at all British Sigint centres, under the authority of the Chiefs of Staff, until October 1943. The Board, its name changed to the Signal Intelligence Board, was then given a new Charter by the Chiefs of Staff in which Sigint was defined as comprising interception, cryptanalysis, traffic analysis (TA) and the 'Special Intelligence' that resulted from these processes. It was at this point that, as noted earlier (Volume I, p 21 fn), the term 'Signal Intelligence' finally superseded the term Y, Y being subsequently limited to the process of interception, including DF, and the breaking of low-grade codes for tactical intelligence purposes. At the same time, the Y Committee was absorbed into the Board, which set up sub-committees to supervise the more technical activities for which it had been responsible. Among the last of the tasks carried out by the Y Committee was the negotiation of a new interception plan in the Mediterranean following the capture of Tunisia, with a view to ensuring that Enigma intercepts got back from the Mediterranean to GC and CS without delay.

After October 1943 the Signal Intelligence Board met only at long intervals. It had come to be accepted by then that the main Sigint production centre, GC and CS, should not only formulate policy decisions for the Board's approval after consultation with the three Services, but also carry out without reference to the Board the day-to-day work of reconciling the interests of the Services, supervising the programme of the British Sigint centres throughout the world and settling the issues which arose from the ever-expanding collaboration between the British and the American Sigint authorities.

The extent of GC and CS's supervision of British Sigint overseas varied according to circumstances. It naturally became most complete in relation to the Mediterranean commands, British and Anglo-American. Even there, however, it was exercised informally. Unlike the London Y Committee, the Middle East Y Committee in Cairo and the North American Y Committee, which had been set up as an Anglo-American co-ordinating body in December 1942, continued in existence (though changing their names to Signal Intelligence Committees). But after the capture of Tunisia the Committees left Sigint policy and planning almost entirely in the hands of the Service Sigint officers in the two theatres; those officers worked in close consultation with GC and CS, and the rapid increase in their contacts with GC and CS after the middle of 1943, by signal and through the increase of personal visits which had hitherto been unavoidably infrequent, made it unnecessary to take the formal step of appointing a representative of the Signal Intelligence Board or of GC and CS to each command to oversee Sigint planning. On the contrary, it was the growth of these informal exchanges, together with the declining importance of Cairo as the war moved away from the Middle East, which led to the decision to close down the Combined Bureau Middle East (CBME) in March 1944.

Once the two countries had entered into the formal agreements of the spring of 1943 (see Volume II, pp 56–58) Anglo-American collaboration in the production and distribution of Sigint was similarly developed by informal arrangements between GC and CS and its opposite numbers in the US Navy and War Departments. Existing liaison parties were expanded as a result of the formal agreements and additional ones were established, but in practice the US delegations at GC and CS became completely integrated with GC and CS's staff. In the case of the Navy Department the collaboration was almost entirely confined to the cryptanalytic field; there was little need to arrange for the exchange of decrypts because the Navy Department itself intercepted all enemy Atlantic traffic (the assessment of which it discussed with the Tracking Room in the Admiralty on a direct link) and was content to receive via the Admiralty summaries of GC and CS's decrypts for other theatres including the Mediterranean. The War Department maintained at GC and CS both a technical party, for liaison in cryptanalysis and interception, and an intelligence mission; the latter had the double task of ensuring that the War Department received as much as it needed of the Sigint that GC and CS was transmitting to US commanders in Europe and of maintaining close contact with those commanders through Ultra liaison officers attached to them.*

GC and CS itself had already undergone its most rapid war-time expansion in the year ending in the summer of 1943, when the total staff had increased from 2,095 to 5,052. In the year ending June 1944 the staff increased from 5,052 to 7,723 (of which 3,371 were civilians and 4,352 from the three Services); it was to reach its war-time peak, a total of 8,995, in January 1945. Its output also continued to expand. The number of groups encyphered by its Cypher Office increased from 2 million a month in the summer of 1943 to 3 million in the autumn of 1944, the war-time peak in this respect (3,400,000 groups) being reached in April 1945. To take another rough criterion, it broke over fifty new Enigma keys in the year June 1943 to June 1944 (See Appendix 3) as compared with twenty-seven in the previous twelve months (See Volume II, Appendix 4) – and this despite the fact that from the summer of 1943 German measures to safeguard the security of the Enigma were presenting it with increasingly serious problems.

In February 1944, to take account of the expansion of the organisation, 'C', hitherto Director of GC and CS, became Director General and his deputy in charge at Bletchley (Commander E W Travis) was promoted from Deputy Director (S) to be Director of GC and CS, Commander A G Denniston remaining head of the Diplomatic and Commercial Sections as DD (C).

2. *The SIS and SOE*

In the summer of 1943 new procedures were introduced for channelling via IS (O) (for which see Vol. II p 10 et seq) the requests of the Service departments and force commanders for intelligence from the SIS; while the SIS continued to make direct contact with its customers when it needed guidance on the degree of priority they attached to their requirements, it had become essential to reduce the pressure on SIS HQ arising from the increasing demand for SIS's services.[1]

The increasing pressure was mainly the result of the intensification of planning for Allied operations, notably *Overlord*, and the emergence of new intelligence targets, notably the V-weapons, which set up a heavy demand for information from northern France; this was an area where the strength of the SIS's resources and the efficiency of its communications enabled it to make a contribution of great value, and one that could not at this stage be supplied by the other intelligence sources. But the pressure also reflected the

---

* These arrangements covering the European theatre were complemented by others made for the war in the Far East.

1. JIC (43) 269 (o) of 26 June.

fact that in close collaboration with its counterparts in Europe, most notably the Polish Secret Service, the SIS was improving its organisation and performance throughout Europe. Expansion and improvement were most marked in Italy, where it established itself following the Allied landings (see above, p 178), in Switzerland, where it took over the assets of the Italian Secret Service after the Italian armistice, and in Sweden, where it obtained an increasing amount of intelligence from Germany itself. In Western Europe the Netherlands was the only area which saw no improvement; because from the summer of 1943 it was known that the Germans had penetrated the SOE's Dutch network since March 1942, the SIS got no support in Whitehall for its plans to increase its operations there until after the Normandy landings. From eastern Europe the SIS now succeeded in obtaining from Romania and Hungary, and to a lesser extent Bulgaria, a considerable if irregular supply of information on army identifications, troop movements, airfields and oil.

In the wake of its improved performance and particularly as a result of the importance they attached to its contribution to the *Overlord* preparations and the stock of intelligence on the V-weapons, the Service departments became less critical of the SIS. At the end of 1943 the experiment by which the three Service representatives at SIS HQ had been appointed Deputy Directors (see Volume II, p 18) was abandoned by mutual agreement. The Service officers continued to represent their intelligence branches at SIS, but SIS HQ was again organised under SIS officers acting as regional controllers.

Between the SIS and the SOE, on the other hand, friction continued to break out at intervals. In August 1943, after investigating the inability of the two bodies to co-ordinate their activities in France, the JIC suggested, to no avail, that SOE might for the present reduce operations there.[2] In the autumn their competing requirements for aircraft generated a quarrel as to whether SOE should be permitted to resume operations in the Netherlands. During 1944 SOE complained of the efforts of the SIS to increase its coverage of Denmark.

Two developments appear to have sustained the mutual hostility of the SIS and SOE and to have ensured that no settlement of their quarrels would be other than temporary. The SOE, though continuing to be primarily an operational force, was acquiring increasing importance as a source of tactical operational intelligence. The SIS

---

2. CAB 79/63, COS (43) 173rd (o) Meeting, 29 July, 178th (o) Meeting, 2 August, 180th (o) Meeting, 4 August; CAB 69/5, DO (43) 7th Meeting, 2 August; JIC (43) 325 (o) of 1 August.

recognised this in October 1943, when it agreed that SOE, which had hitherto passed its intelligence to Allied commands on SIS links, must be free to pass it to the commands direct on its own channels.[3] But it made this concession reluctantly, and still hoped to exercise some check on the reliability and significance attached to SOE intelligence by the commands. For its part, SOE resented any attempt by the SIS to put a check on its activities because its autonomy as an operational force was under attack from other quarters. In the autumn of 1943 the Middle East Defence Committee all but abolished SOE Cairo; it survived only at the expense of having its activities placed under the control of the Cs-in-C. SOE in London regarded this set-back in Cairo as a threat to the future of its organisation in all theatres, the more so as it followed so soon after the temporary suspension of its operations in Europe following the discovery that the Germans had penetrated its organisation in the Netherlands. But as Allied forces moved forward in Italy and prepared to land in France it had to reconcile itself to increasing supervision of its activities by the military commands. In March 1944 SOE Cairo's responsibilities were limited to Greece, Bulgaria and Romania, its forces in Italy, Yugoslavia and Albania being placed under a military organisation, Special Operations Mediterranean HQ (SOM HQ), which was made responsible to SACMED. In May 1944 its forces in western Europe were brought into a similar organisation, Special Force HQ, which was part of SHAEF.[4]

In that part of its activities which corresponded to those of SOE, the American Office of Strategic Services (OSS) was similarly subjected to closer supervision by the military commands. On that account, and especially when the commands were Anglo-US commands, SOE and OSS worked closely together and maintained good relations. In the Middle East, a purely British theatre, relations were strained for a time from the summer of 1943 when, as well as imposing close supervision on SOE, the Cs-in-C resisted the attempts of the OSS to develop independent field organisations in the Balkans, but the two bodies enjoyed an easy collaboration in that area from the beginning of 1944 despite complaints by OSS that it was being 'tightly controlled by the British Services'.[5] In Italy their activities were closely co-ordinated, especially after the establishment of SOM HQ, though the CCS's directive to SACMED to amalgamate both organisations in SOM HQ was not put into effect because OSS was unwilling to participate. In January 1944, however, in the light of experience gained in the Mediterranean, both

3. JIC (43) 52nd (o) Meeting, 19 October.
4. L F Ellis, *Victory in the West*, Vol 1 (1962), p 123.
5. US War Department, *Report on OSS*, Vol II (New York 1976), p 207.

bodies formed a single organisation at SOE HQ in London, with a director from SOE and a deputy director from OSS, to co-ordinate their operations in western Europe. This body developed into Special Force HQ, which was made responsible to SHAEF on 1 May 1944.[6]

Between the SIS and the OSS relations were more troubled than they were between the SOE and OSS. This was not solely because they ran into the problems which underlay the rivalry between the SIS and the SOE, whose function the OSS combined with that of the SIS in a single organisation. In addition, while the two bodies freely exchanged intelligence between their HQs in London, the OSS had early decided that it did not wish to co-ordinate, let alone to merge, its intelligence gathering activities in the field with those of SIS.[7] For operations carried out in the Middle East from Cairo it was agreed between the SIS and the OSS that each would operate independently and relations between the two HQs there were friendly. For operations into southern France the two bodies agreed in July 1943 that the plans of their HQs in Algiers should be concerted locally and submitted to London for joint American and British approval before being implemented; but this understanding was rarely observed.[8] For operations from the United Kingdom into Europe, however, the SIS insisted that the OSS should carry out no such operations without full consultation, was reluctant to provide aircraft for OSS operations unless it was satisfied with the trustworthiness and the training of the OSS agents, and continued to resist – as it had done in 1942* – OSS's desire to establish liaison with foreign intelligence services in London.[9] SIS was perhaps jealous of its prerogatives, but its attitude stemmed from its fear of confusion and duplication of effort in intelligence reporting. To the OSS this attitude smacked of a desire to hamper its development and it resented the attempt to control its activities as a means of maintaining the SIS's monopoly in a crucial theatre, pleading that it was 'dangeous to the ultimate interests of both countries'.[10] In the autumn of 1943 the American Chiefs of Staff gave the OSS qualified authority to conduct intelligence operations in Europe, but they do not appear to have protested when, the JIC having upheld the SIS's position, the US theatre command (ETOUSA) accepted it.[11]

---

* See Volume II, pp 52–53.

6. ibid, pp 144, 191; J G Beevor, *SOE: Recollections and Reflections 1940–45* (1981), p 85.
7. US War Department, op cit, Vol II, p 207.
8. ibid, pp 141, 225–226, 236.
9. JIC (43) 379 (o) of 13 September.
10. US War Department, op cit, Vol II, pp 5–6.
11. ibid, pp 5–6; JIC (43) 379 (o) of 13 September.

3. Photographic Reconnaissance and Interpretation

Following the arrangements made for operation *Husky* (see above, p 83) there was a temporary departure in the Mediterranean theatre from the merger of British and American PR resources that had been achieved in the western Mediterranean during the campaign in Tunisia. In October and November 1943 the RAF and the USAAF formed separate PR Wing HQs to control their PR squadrons in Italy: the RAF Wing HQ had moved from Tunis to the Foggia area by the end of 1943. With the amalgamation of the Allied air forces into Mediterranean Allied Air Forces (MAAF) in January 1944 integration was restored and expanded. The North African PR Wing (see Volume II p 757 fn) was re-named Mediterranean Allied PR Command and given control under an American commander of the operations of the separate PR Wings. An inter-Allied Mediterranean Photographic Intelligence Centre was established to co-ordinate and settle the priority of demands made on the PR Command and photographic interpretation was as far as possible centralised by the formation of the Mediterranean Army Interpretation Unit (MAIU) with an eastern and a western component. The eastern component comprised the remnants of the Army Air Photographic Interpretation Unit from the Middle East (see Volume II, p 289). The western component was responsible under the direct control of the PR Command for meeting the needs of the Italian front, including those of Eighth Army; it maintained interpretation sections at Corps and Divisional HQs.[12]

The integration of British and American PR resources in the United Kingdom was already far advanced by the middle of 1943. In June 1943 No 106 PR Wing RAF was formed to take operational control of all British PR units in the United Kingdom (other than those of the Allied Expeditionary Air Force, including 2nd Tactical Air Force which was working with 21st Army Group in preparation for *Overlord*) under the operational direction of ACAS (I). It worked closely with the 7th Photo Group of US Eighth Air Force, which was represented on its staff, and as far as possible met such American requirements as could not be carried out by the Photo Group. The CIU at Medmenham continued, under the operational control of ACAS (I), to process and interpret the results of all sorties for the benefit of both air forces. By the end of 1943 the number of American officers at CIU was 60.[13] But in January 1944 Eighth Air Force, discontented with the procedure by which its requests for PR, by 7th Photo Group as well as by No 106 Wing, had to be submitted

---

12. AIR 41/7, *Photographic Reconnaissance*, Vol II, pp 66–67; Mockler-Ferryman, *Military Intelligence Organisation*, pp 191–192.
13. AIR 41/7, pp 9–11, 79–80.

to ADI (Ph) at the Air Ministry, proposed to withdraw the American staff from the CIU and set up a separate US PR/Photographic Interpretation organisation.

The costliness of such duplication, not to speak of the dislocation it would produce during the run-up to *Overlord*, eventually produced an agreement in favour of the complete merger, from 15 May 1944, of all British and American activities in the United Kingdom that were devoted to strategic PR. No 106 Wing became No 106 Recce Group RAF, which was made responsible for co-ordinating all photographic intelligence activities in the United Kingdom (other than those undertaken by the Allied Expeditionary Air Force). It comprised four RAF PR squadrons of Spitfires and Mosquitoes and, with USAAF officers on its staff, co-ordinated their operations with those of the American 8th Recce Wing to carry out a single PR programme; this was drawn up by a new inter-Allied and inter-Service Joint Photographic Reconnaissance Committee (JPRC) which took over under the JIC the functions of ADI (Ph) and worked at the chief PR base at Benson. No 106 Group also took over control of the CIU, re-named Allied Central Interpretation Unit (ACIU); with an American chairman and reinforced by additional American personnel, this carried out all strategic photographic interpretaton (other than that associated with US bomber strikes) for British and US forces in Europe for the rest of the war.[14]

No such merger and centralisation was adopted for the PR requirements of the Allied Expeditionary Air Force. It was accepted that 2nd Tactical Air Force should fulfil its own requirements with two squadrons at its HQ alongside 21st Army Group, one squadron attached to Second British Army and one attached to First Canadian Army. The squadrons were operational from southern England by February 1944, photographing invasion targets and V-weapons sites. Subsequently the need to make these formations mobile and self-contained led to the establishment of an Army Group Photographic Interpretation Unit at 21st Army Group and of an Army Photographic Interpretation section with each of the Armies.[15] The Americans established PR units and interpretation teams with Ninth Air Force and 12th US Army Group. The American and British systems operated independently of each other, and there was considerable duplication and waste of effort, as there was within each system.

Over and above the PR forces allotted to 2nd Tactical Air Force (four squadrons, each of 18 aircraft, by March 1944, to which a fifth squadron was added on the day before D-day), the combined

---

14.   ibid, pp 9, 11–14, 44–45, 80; *Air Ministry Intelligence*, pp 57, 333; JIC (44) 16th, 20th and 22nd (o) Meetings, 11 April, 9 and 23 May.

15.   AIR 41/7, pp 20, 50, 53; Mockler-Ferryman, op cit, pp 61, 147.

strength of the RAF PR forces in the United Kingdom was set at 80 aircraft in four squadrons by the end of 1943. From the beginning of 1944 they were being re-equipped with the latest Mosquito (the Mosquito XVI) which had a range of 2,090 miles at 30,000 feet when fitted with drop tanks; their other aircraft was the Spitfire XI, which had a range of 1,290 miles without drop tanks. From the end of 1943 the establishments in the Mediterranean were 36 Spitfire XIs in three RAF squadrons and 8 Mosquito XIs with a South African squadron.[16]

Apart from improvements in aircraft performance, the main technical developments after the middle of 1943 were associated with the need to facilitate, in poor weather and against enemy opposition, the low-level sorties which provided the large-scale, low-angled photographs that yielded the maximum intelligence. For this purpose forward-facing oblique cameras were fitted into the wing bulges and drop tanks of the aircraft, and later into the nose of the Mosquitoes, and improved cameras were developed (the F 52 and F 643) which compensated for the great speed at which the aircraft flew across the target.[17]

Another technique, PR by night (as distinct from the use of night photography to assess the effects of bomb damage; see Volume II, p 38) remained in an experimental stage. A safe flash was developed by April 1944, but the results obtained with it were on too small a scale for accurate interpretation; and because the demand for day-time PR was so great, and the supply of PR Mosquitoes so limited, No 106 Group suspended work on night-time strategic PR. The USAAF equipped one Mosquito XIV squadron with night cameras and adequate radar, but made little use of it. There was some use of night PR for tactical purposes after D-day, but its development was slow.[18]

4. POW

In the RAF all interrogation, other than that of Japanese POW, was centralised in September 1943 under ADI (K), who took control of the detailed interrogation centres at Cairo and Algiers and of forward units in Sicily, Italy and, later, north-west Europe.[19]

Until the summer of 1944 a British naval interrogator was attached to the US POW centre in Washington and an American naval interrogator worked at CSDIC (UK), each being treated as belonging to the country in which he was working.[20]

---

16. AIR 41/7, pp 20–21, 51, 65.
17. ibid, pp 23–24. 18. ibid, pp 26–29.
19. *Air Ministry Intelligence*, pp 13, 101 and Appendix D.
20. ADM 223/84, History of POW Interrogation, p 53.

In preparation for *Overlord*, arrangements were made by which the facilities of CSDIC (UK) would be at the disposal of the large number of American Army interrogators who would be working in the UK and on the continent.[21]

5. *No 30 Commando (No 30 Assault Unit)*

The idea of having an assault commando to land with the first wave of Allied invading forces in order to seize urgently needed enemy documents or equipment originated in the example set by an Abwehr detachment during the German invasion of the Balkans in 1941. On that occasion decrypts of Abwehr signals disclosed that an 'intelligence commando' under the leadership of Kapitän Leutnant Obladen entered Athens with the first German troops, put its radio links at the Army's disposal when the Army's broke down, and proceeded immediately to British Army HQ where it seized documents which included staff maps of Libya. Other comparable activities were also disclosed by decrypts.*

NID had proposed the formation of a British commando with similar objectives in March 1942, but No 30 Commando was not operational until the Allies landed in north Africa in November of that year.† Until the end of 1943 the Commando operated in Tunisia, Sicily, Italy and elsewhere in the Mediterranean, where it captured documents and equipment of considerable value relating to enemy W/T, cyphers, radar and weapons. Sigint material featured among the selected targets all the more because the importance of capturing such material was increased during this period as it was then that the Germans began to introduce new and more complex encypherment and signals procedures designed to improve the security of the Enigma cyphers.

The following are examples of the more important captures, as recorded by NID. In north Africa, a new high-grade Abwehr machine cypher, hitherto unbroken, with the immediate result that six weeks' traffic on the link could be read.[22] During the *Husky* landings, a complete set of Italian Air Force cyphers for homing beacons, which enabled the Allied Tactical Air Force to fly on to targets in northern Italy guided by Italian beacons.[23] During the

---

* NID described Obladen as 'very efficient': in early 1944 the Abwehr signals revealed him as one of the German officers who trained the German Navy in the techniques used by the Italians in their underwater anti-shipping activities, (see above, p 195).

† See Volume II, Appendix 13 for the temporary arrangements made for the capture of documents and equipment during the Dieppe raid.

21.   Mockler-Ferryman, op cit, pp 53, 147.

22.   ADM 223/213, History of Sigint Operations undertaken by 30 Commando/ 30 AU, para 4.

23.   ibid, para 5.

landings on the west coast of Sicily, a *Wassermann* radar installation at Cape Passero with some W/T equipment and a mobile VHF set of novel design; but at Porto Palo material of 'extreme importance' was missed – for example, when radar sets were searched but no attempt was made to trace the location of the related filter.[24] At Catania, a new anti-aircraft predictor of Italian make at an AA battery; but a small *Würzburg* radar apparatus had probably been at the site and was missed.[25] At Trapani, an 'extremely rich harvest' from the naval stores including hitherto unknown mining and minesweeping equipment.[26] During the German evacuation from Cape Peloro, full working drawings of the Gamma system of remote power control for AA guns; but there is no evidence that these ever reached the Admiralty.[27] At Messina, from the wreckage from a raid on a mobile Y station, a code book compiled by German book breakers and notebooks relating to British and American codes and cyphers.[28] In the early stages of the campaign in Italy, a Y station on Capri was captured more or less intact, with documents on enemy work on Allied codes and cyphers; but a plan to capture the centre of the German Y service in Italy could not be carried out because SOE was unable to provide the necessary air lift.[29] In the Baia area, annotated maps were captured showing locations of all German units in the area – which were said to have been well received by British X Corps.[30] In the same area, material and documents of 'considerable value' were taken from the Ansaldo armament works at Pozzuoli and the Ivra steelyard at Bagna which showed damage inflicted in Allied air raids.[31]

The Commando returned to the United Kingdom at the end of 1943 to prepare itself for *Overlord*, and was renamed No 30 Assault Unit. Its Army troop was, however, sent back to Italy at the request of 15th Army Group, leaving the naval troop to select *Overlord* targets and collect intelligence about them under the supervision of the DNI.[32] By that time it was felt that 'a reasonably satisfactory system of operating had been evolved by trial and error', but that there was a need for better intelligence briefing in advance of operations.[33] To meet this need the DNI set up NID 30 in January

---

24. ADM 223/214, History of 30 Commando (latterly called 30 Assault Unit and 30 Advanced Unit), Chapter V, paras 2, 6.
25. ibid, Chapter V, para 60.   26. ibid, Chapter V, para 64.
27. ibid, Chapter V, para 85.   28. ADM 223/213, loc cit, para 6.
29. ibid, para 7, 8.
30. ADM 223/214, loc cit, Chapter VI, para 73.
31. ibid, Chapter VI, paras 81, 83, 84.
32. ibid, Chapter X, paras 1–4.
33. ibid, Chapter V, para 96, Chapter IX, para 21; Part II Section; ADM 223/213, loc cit, para 3.

1944. With assistance from a representative of the ISTD, NID 30 drew on a wide variety of sources for briefing the Assault Unit on *Overlord* targets. Among the most useful sources were captured documents and POW.[34] The sources did not include Sigint. But the Enigma machine and other Sigint material featured among the selected targets, which also included Germany's developments in torpedoes, mines and minesweeping, centimetric radar, and the plans she had made for obstructing ports and harbours through demolitions and other means.[35]

B. THE SERVICE INTELLIGENCE BRANCHES

1. *The Naval Intelligence Division*

The only changes of any importance were the creation of NID 7S and NID 30.

NID 7S was established within NID 7 (the technical section) as a sub-section for scientific intelligence in the autumn of 1943, after the Germans had achieved surprise with the introduction into service of the Hs 293 and the FX 1400; this had shown the need for more efficient handling within the Admiralty of high-grade decrypts containing items of scientific intelligence (see above, p 340). Its terms of reference were to provide expert opinion on scientific intelligence from all sources and to ensure that the Admiralty authorities responsible for such matters as weapons, research and development of torpedoes and mines were supplied with all available intelligence on enemy developments in their fields.[36]

It is interesting to note that the German Admiralty established a scientific intelligence department at about the same time (see Appendix 10, p 516).

NID 30 was formed on 1 February 1944 to plan the seizure by the naval section of No 30 Assault Unit (see above p 468 et seq) of all types of enemy naval documents and other material.[37]

2. *M I, War Office*

An additional Deputy Director, DDMI (Planning), was appointed in April 1944 to ease the burden on DDMI (Intelligence). He took

---

34. ADM 223/214, loc cit, Chapter X, paras 11–14; Part II Section 3.
35. ibid, Chapter X, para 31; ADM 223/213, loc cit, para 9.
36. ADM 223/107, Development and Organisation of the NID September 1939–April 1944, pp 16, 34.
37. ibid, pp 48–49.

over responsibility for the secretariat section (MI 17), whose work came to include relations with the JIC, the IS (O) and the Joint Planning Staff. Two further new Deputy Directors were to be appointed in September 1944; DDMI (Germany), to take charge of MI 14 and MI 15 the anti-aircraft section, and DDMI (Censorship).[38]

The Anglo-American Military Intelligence Research Section (MIRS), formed under MI 14 in 1943 to co-ordinate British and American intelligence from captured documents on the German Army (see Volume II, p 49), trained from the end of 1943 the staff for a SHAEF Document Section, which crossed to the continent in August 1944.[39]

3. AI, Air Ministry

Apart from the creation of the Directorate of Intelligence (Research) in April 1944 (see Volume II, p 653) and the centralisation of POW intelligence under ADI(K) (see above, p 467), the only important changes were those made in the attempt to improve the selection of targets and the assessment of bomb damage for the strategic bomber forces.

In the summer of 1943, when German fighter production became a priority target for the strategic bombing forces, the Jockey Committee was set up to bring together all concerned in the selection of targets. Comprising representatives from AI 2, AI 3, the RAF commands, the Tactical Air Force, and Eighth and Ninth US Army Air Forces, it met weekly from June 1943 to April 1945.[40]

Early in 1944 Bomber Command's need for more detailed bomb damage assessments led to proposals for introducing statisticians and industrial experts into AI 3, but in the event, it was decided that the work of AI's bomb damage sub-section, AI 3(c)2, should be taken over by the section in MEW which already assessed the effects of bomb damage on German industry.[41]

The establishment of the Jockey Committee did not replace the system by which USAAF officers served as members of AI's sections. Representatives from the operational and intelligence staffs of the Eighth, Ninth and Fifteenth Air Forces continued to be appointed to work in AI 2 and AI 3.[42]

---

38. JIC (44) 8th (o) Meeting, 25 April; Mockler-Ferryman, op cit, pp 17, 26, 28.
39. Mockler-Ferryman, op cit, pp 28, 66 et seq.
40. *Air Ministry Intelligence*, pp 23, 237–238, 246.
41. ibid, pp 13, 275–276 and Appendix D.
42. ibid, pp 23–24, 214, 238.

C. THE JIC AND ASSOCIATED INTER-DEPARTMENTAL BODIES

1. *The JIC*

The structure of the JIC and its components remained unchanged between the spring of 1943 and June 1944 except for the addition of two new sub-committees for which the JIC was responsible: the Joint Photographic Reconnaissance Committee (see above, p 466) and the Special Sub-Committee on Intelligence Priorities.* The latter was formed in May 1944 following a suggestion, made originally by PWE and taken up by MEW, that special steps should be taken to collect intelligence on the rise of Nazi Germany and her speedy build-up of strength after Hitler came to power. Its task was to draw up lists of 'targets' for such intelligence for the guidance of SHAEF and SACMED in the assault phases of the re-occupation of Europe and before an enemy collapse.[43] Neither the SIS (which made its own arrangements with SHAEF) nor the Security Service were represented on this new committee and its Foreign Office member did not attend its meetings regularly; otherwise its composition was that of its parent committee.

The formation of the Special Sub-Committee on Intelligence Priorities was part of a process whereby the JIC gave increasing attention to the supply of information needed for the study of post-war problems in Europe. It accepted these new responsibilities reluctantly because the authorities who needed the information were primarily civilian, whereas the JIC existed largely to meet military requirements, but did so in order to avoid the establishment of individual and overlapping intelligence sections in civilian ministries.[44]

The demands of the military authorities on the JIC increased as preparations for the invasion of Europe progressed, first after the formation of COSSAC in the spring of 1943 and then of SHAEF in January 1944.* The continued existence of a joint secretariat with the Planning Staff (see Volume II, p 6), and the close relations between intelligence and planning officers which had resulted, had reduced the once considerable flow of *ad hoc* operational questions

---

* For the JIC's role in relation to the V-weapons see above, p 411 n*. For its role in the intelligence preparations for *Overlord* see Volume III Part 2.

43. JIC (43) 57th (o) Meeting, 9 November; JIC (44) 2nd (o) Meeting, 11 January, 18th (o) Meeting, 25 April, 20th (o) Meeting, 9 May, 21st (o) Meeting, 16 May, 22nd (o) Meeting, 23 May; JIC (44) 224 of 30 May.
44. JIC (43) 27th (o) Meeting, 25 May, 35th Meeting, 9 July, 36th (o) Meeting, 13 July, 37th (o) Meeting, 20 July.

submitted to the Joint Intelligence Staff, leaving it freer for the compilation of longer term strategic appreciations, but the number of regular progress reports that had to be prepared continued to grow. The *Rankin* reports on the possibility of a German collapse were started in the autumn of 1943 (see above, p 45 et seq). The quarterly series on the effects of the strategic bombing offensive against Germany was supplemented by monthly reports from March 1944.[45] And by April the JIS was producing a weekly situation report on the bombing of the Balkans.[46]

For the preparation of the Rankin series of reports the JIC evolved a complicated system for the briefing of the Combined Intelligence Committee in Washington, which was responsible for writing the reports, and the JIC London also found it necessary to supply the JIC (Washington) with more detailed background intelligence briefs to assist it in drafting the *Rankin* series.[47] In the spring of 1944 the JIC considered that the working of the JIC (W) both for the compilation of the *Rankin* reports and in the fulfilment of its tasks generally was satisfactory.[48] The US JIC, with whom the London JIC's relations seem to have been harmonious, concurred.[49] In London regular meetings of American intelligence officers with the JIC's subordinate country sections had been discontinued in the autumn of 1943: they had become superfluous with the growth of close contacts between the Americans and the Service intelligence departments.[50]

2. *The Intelligence Section (Operations)*

The burden on the IS (O) of meeting requests from AFHQ for operational intelligence in connection with the planning of Mediterranean operations greatly increased from the middle of 1943; and in the autumn of 1943 the IS (O) and AFHQ reached agreement on a division of labour and introduced new procedures to reduce the load on the IS (O).[51]

In the early months of 1944 the IS (O) became less involved in supplying static intelligence on such matters as beaches, ports and defences, this work being undertaken by the Theatre Intelligence Section of SHAEF for the authorities planning the re-entry into

---

45. JIC (44) 95 (o) of 11 March; CAB 79/71, COS (44) 80 (o) of 9 March.
46. JIC (44) 131 (o) of 3 April.
47. JIC (43) 47th (o) Meeting; 21 September, 53rd (o) Meeting, 26 October, 63rd (o) Meeting, 14 December; JIC (43) 440 (o) of 28 October, 510 (o) of 14 December.
48. JIC (44) 14th (o) Meeting, 28 March.
49. JIC (44) 16th (o) Meeting, 11 April.
50. JIC (43) 47th (o) Meeting, 21 September.
51. JIC (43) 62nd (o) Meeting, 7 December.

Europe (see Volume III Part 2). But the IS (O) began to canalise demands for intelligence on police and para-military organisations in Europe and for collating information on the main German administrative machine. Before the end of 1943 the IS (O) had also assumed responsibility for the co-ordination of demands on the ISTD on behalf of the Inter-Service Topographical Sub-Committee (see Volume I, pp 161, 162, Volume II, p 9).[52]

3. *The Inter-Services Topographical Department*

An inquiry into the work of the ISTD was carried out in the summer of 1943, following a joint appeal to the Chiefs of Staff by the JIC and the Joint Planners that it should be given more staff. In September 1943, after initially questioning whether the ISTD's work was valuable for operational planning purposes, the COS accepted that it was, and that its customers were at fault in putting to it many unnecessary demands.[53] The outcome was that the JIC introduced a new procedure to ensure that requests for information from the ISTD were strictly confined to topographical questions and, in the event of excessive requests or conflicts of priority, were rationed by the IS (O).[54]

In the summer of 1943 Dutch nationals, because of their knowledge of the Far East, were added to the Americans and Norwegians already serving on the ISTD's staff.[55] In the autumn of 1943 a visit to Washington of an ISTD mission demonstrated that collaboration in the production of topographical reports was close.[56]

4. *The JIC (Middle East) in Cairo and the JIC (Allied Forces) in Algiers*

In February 1944 the hitherto informal JIC (ME) at Cairo (see Volume II, p 360 n) became an official body on the lines of its counterpart in London. This came about after protracted discussion during the previous autumn about the best way to reorganise the intelligence system in the Middle East following the transfer of the main theatre of operations to the central Mediterranean. It was finally decided that, as the informal JIC had not exercised supervision over the authorities responsible for non-operational intelligence, it should be replaced by a formally constituted JIC which

---

52. JIC (43) 64th (o) Meeting, 24 December.
53. JIC (43) 33rd (o) Meeting, 29 June, 35th Meeting, 9 July, 38th Meeting, 27 July; CAB 84/55, JP (43) 287 of 5 August (which is also JIC (43) 332); CAB 79/27, COS (43) 124th Meeting, 10 August, 141st Meeting, 3 September; CAB 80/41, COS (43) 246 of 30 August.
54. JIC (43) 47th (o) Meeting, 21 September; JIC (43) 390 of 19 September.
55. JIC (43) 32nd Meeting, 25 June.
56. JIC (43) 60th (o) Meeting, 23 November; ADM 223/90, Hippisley Coxe and Barrett, *NID 21; Contacts*, p 4.

was expanded to include representatives of those authorities – MEW, the Political Intelligence Committee, Middle East (PICME) and Security Intelligence, Middle East (SIME). At the same time, however, in view of the reorganisation of the Allied Command structure which made GHQ, ME subordinate to AFHQ in January 1944, the JIC (ME) was made responsible to the JIC (AF) at Algiers.[57]

JIC (Allied Forces) had been established at Algiers as an Anglo-American inter-Service organisation since April 1943 (see above, p 80). In January 1944 it, too, was expanded to include representatives of the authorities responsible for political and economic intelligence, but unlike JIC (ME) and the JIC in London, which had Foreign Office chairmen, it remained under Army chairmanship. In February, with a view to minimising duplication between the two bodies, it was laid down that the JIC (ME) would be responsible for intelligence on southern Russia, the Balkans (except for the Adriatic coast) and Turkey, and that its appreciations would be forwarded to London and Washington by the JIC (AF) with the JIC (AF)'s comments.[58]

From the beginning of 1944 senior members of the JIC (AF) were being withdrawn to the United Kingdom to form the nucleus of SHAEF's intelligence staff and in the summer of 1944 a JIC (SHAEF) was established within this HQ (see Volume III Part 2).

---

57. Mockler-Ferryman, op cit, pp 160–162; JIC (44) 35 (o) of 27 January, 111 (o) of 19 March; JIC (44) 5th (o) Meeting, 1 February.
58. Mockler-Ferryman, op cit, pp 171–172; JIC (44) 8th (o) Meeting, 22 February; JIC (44) 77 (o) of 25 February, 118 of 23 March.

APPENDIX 2

Geheimschreiber (Fish)

From as early as 1932 the Metropolitan Police wireless organisation at Denmark Hill and the GPO Y station at St Albans, both working on behalf of the Foreign Office's interception programme, detected German experiments in transmitting non-morse teleprinter impulses by radio. The pre-war intercepts were apparently unencyphered. The first encyphered non-morse transmissions to be intercepted were found in the second half of 1940; later named Fish at GC and CS on the strength of an Enigma reference to the fact that one non-morse encyphered system, properly named Geheimschreiber, was being called Sägefisch, they remained intermittent until the middle of 1941. It was clear by then, however, that Germany was developing on-line cypher machines to provide simultaneous encypherment and transmission and simultaneous reception and decypherment on radio, and probably also on land-line, teleprinter links of messages based on the impulses of the international five-unit teleprinter code.

In the middle of 1941 regular operational non-morse encyphered transmissions began to be intercepted on an experimental German Army link between Vienna and Athens which used a cypher machine later named Tunny by GC and CS. This was the Schlüsselzusatz 40 (SZ 40) made by Lorenz; the name Tunny was retained for later developments, the SZ 42 in several lettered versions. Fish names were also given to the individual links using Fish cyphers (but some fish names, like Shark, denoted naval Enigma complexes). During the next twelve months it was established that another machine, in fact Siemens T52 (called Sturgeon by GC and CS), was coming into widespread use in the GAF and that some Fish traffic was being passed by the German naval authorities and the SS.

At the end of 1941, in view of the fact that the Enigma was providing so much intelligence about the GAF and given the growing need for more intelligence about the German Army, the decision was taken to concentrate the Fish programme of the intercept stations against the Army traffic which used the Tunny machine. Thereafter only occasional watch was kept on the GAF links and little naval Fish traffic was intercepted, while another Army Fish machine that was introduced on a Wehrkreis link (Thrasher) remained unbreakable. Nevertheless, if it had become essential to devote more interception and cryptanalytic resources to exploiting Fish cyphers – for example, as a result of a reduction of GC and CS's ability to read Enigma traffic or its replacement on some networks – effort could to some extent have been re-deployed in an attempt to increase the volume of high-grade Sigint from Fish. The German Army network that used the Tunny machine developed steadily from the middle of 1942. By 1944 it had two main exchanges – Straussberg near Berlin as the terminus for western stations and Königsberg as the terminus for eastern stations – and had developed 26 links.* During the experimental period these transmissions were by Hellschreiber, a form of facsimile, which enabled GC and CS to intercept the texts in an accurate form.

By January 1942 GC and CS understood the design and method of operation of the Tunny machine, and by the summer of the same year was in the same position for the Sturgeon machine. The charting of these links, on which many messages went over the air for only part of their journey, finishing or starting by land-line or submarine cable, and identification of their users, which after a while were designated by call-signs in the encyphered texts of the messages, were complicated tasks. They were undertaken by the section at GC and CS which specialised in applying Traffic Analysis to the German Army and Air Force Enigma networks. From the beginning of 1944 the familiarity of this section (SIXTA) with the external behaviour of the Fish links was rendering invaluable assistance to those who wrestled with the interception and decryption of the Fish traffic. For interception a new station was established at Knockholt from the end of 1942, to replace Denmark Hill and St Albans; thereafter, as the German links proliferated, Knockholt expanded steadily and more and more staff (reaching about 600 persons) was trained in the skills for the many processes which proved necessary. Formidable difficulties were encountered, since beaming of the signal as well as the greater distance from the transmission site meant that the signal reaching Knockholt was generally much poorer than that received by the other end of the German link. Transmissions were often very lengthy, as the Germans found it convenient to send several messages in one transmission; a message as long as 60,000 characters was observed. The portions sent in auto-mode were at high speed. The transmissions consisted of an unbroken stream of elements (mark or space) and very accurate timing was required to divide it correctly into these units. For most of the time laborious hand processing was necessary, reading the teleprinter characters from the undulator tape produced by the intercept equipment, ie a tracing of the elements. This hand-written copy was then converted to the master perforated

---

* See chart facing p 482 below.

tape. The intercept equipment could also produce a perforated tape, and this raw version was sometimes adequate. Perforated tapes could be used as input to the teleprinter links from Knockholt to GC and CS, but the hand-written version and the master tape reached GC and CS by despatch rider, and this allowed further checking where necessary. At GC and CS new methods were called for to exploit the Tunny traffic. But even when the details of the wheels and the setting letters were known, decryption was normally too laborious to be undertaken by hand and the first stage of mechanisation was the provision of a decyphering machine, delivered early in June 1942.

A new Fish section was formed in July 1942 and with the assistance of decyphering machines it read many of the transmissions on the Vienna–Athens link until the link ceased operation at the end of October. This was to be the last time, as well as the first, that Fish traffic was read nearly currently. With subsequent improvements in German cypher security it became clear that existing methods of breaking the individual settings would only serve for a small proportion of cases and that new cryptanalytic methods would have to be devised.

A research party at GC and CS investigated the problem of solving Fish settings not susceptible to the previous special methods; and in December 1942 concluded that a new approach should be employed, using high-speed machinery designed for the purpose. The prototype machine was something of a lash-up and so was named '(Heath) Robinson'. This became available in May 1943 and proved sufficiently satisfactory to justify the decision to order 24 copies of it. The Research Station of the GPO at Dollis Hill gave the highest priority to this programme, on instructions issued by the Prime Minister in February 1943 at the instance of the Director of GC and CS. In fact, only two other Robinsons were delivered, each incorporating improvements. Later the mechanisation effort was largely diverted to the design and construction of a faster and more flexible machine, Colossus (Mark I). Both Robinson and Colossus examined binary data, but whereas Robinson read from a loop of 5-level paper tape, Colossus generated data electronically. The development of Colossus necessitated close collaboration between GC and CS and the Research Station of the GPO at Dollis Hill. Collosus I used 1,500 valves, far exceeding the number in any previous electronic device: the first Robinson, for example, had fewer than 100 valves. Colossus Mark I began work at Bletchley Park in February 1944. Experience of this machine soon led to ideas for improvement; they were implemented in Colossus Mark II, which used 2,400 valves and was faster and more versatile. By the end of the war ten Colossi were in service in the Fish Machine Section, into which the research party referred to above developed.

Colossus has been justly claimed as a pioneer programmable electronic digital computer. Although itself fairly specialised, it was important in the British development of general-purpose computers, amongst other things because it had demonstrated that components of sufficient speed and reliability were available. The circuit elements of Colossus included binary adders, binary and decade counters, AND, OR, NAND (ie mod 2 add) and NOR logic gates, and short registers. The sequence of operations was determined mainly by setting of external switches and by plug-boards, but in Mark II some conditional branching could be determined by data generated and stored in the machine. Other decisions, in the light of the latest printed results, were taken by the Wren operators who were given a 'tree' of instructions. The internal memory was of very limited capacity, the main data – the long cypher texts – being read photo-electrically from a loop of perforated tape. The tape drive was purely frictional; whereas on Robinson the tape drive worked on the sprocket holes, on Colossus these were only read to control the timing. The basic speed of circuit operation was 5,000 tape positions per second, but with parallel processing the bit-processing rate could be five times this.

Up to May 1943 solution of the limited number of Fish settings in use could only be tackled by special methods; thereafter, while some continued to be soluble this way, most of the solved settings on the increasing number of links coming into use were obtained either by machine or by a combination of methods. The delay in decryption was in sharp contrast to the position on Enigma traffic, where the whole of a day's traffic on any one key could in general be easily decrypted. With Fish the basic setting was in force for a month, but considerable further work was needed on each transmission before it could be decrypted. Even after new machinery had been successfully developed to undertake this work there was always delay in decrypting Fish signals.

German measures to improve security included an operating change in August 1942 and modifications to the Tunny machine, the first of these being in February 1943. Some of these measures had a serious effect for a time, but in general it is true that improved methods, supplemented by the use of machines from the middle of 1943, kept GC and CS abreast of the new problems and the proliferation of Fish links even before the completion of Colossus Mark I in February 1944.

Expansion of the Fish sections at GC and CS was not, of course, restricted to the acquisition of additional major machines. The Fish Machine Section operated a considerable number of minor machines of varying complexity down to simple hand counters; in one of the Fish sections half the staff were engineers and operators of the decoding machines. The total staff in the two sections reached a figure of over 425, over half of whom were Wrens. There was a stimulating rivalry between the cryptanalytic staff in the two sections, as parts of the task could be tackled by different methods. From June 1944 daily meetings took place to co-ordinate the work of Knockholt and the Fish sections, in accordance with the intelligence priorities, while a committee met weekly to deal with more general matters of planning and co-ordination.

Success against Fish resulted from a combination of events, including mistakes,* but the delay in producing Fish decrypts was offset by the high quality of the intelligence which they yielded. The average delay was three days in 1943 and 1945, and during 1944 it was as much as seven days. The German Army, as was made clear by the Fish decrypts from August 1942, and no doubt also the other Services, used the Fish links for communications at the highest level (ie Army Groups and OKH).†

The Fish traffic thus complemented the Enigma, which was used mainly within Armies, occasionally between Armies, but very rarely above Army level; and because its contents were less operational and tactical than the Enigma's in character, the decrypts, especially those containing orders and appreciations from the highest authorities, were often more important and less liable to suffer in value from delay in decryption. From the end of 1942, on the other hand, the number of Fish links increased steadily, and GC and CS's success soon banished its initial fear that new Army links would use a different machine from the Tunny machine, instead of different settings of the same machine as proved to be the case.

On 1 November 1942, upon the disappearance of the Vienna–Athens link, a new link had been established between Straussberg (Berlin) and Army Group E in the Balkans, and another between Königsberg and Seventeenth Army in the Crimea. In December 1942 yet another link opened up between Army Group C (Italy and north Africa) and von Arnim's Fifth Panzer Army in Tunisia. By July 1943 six links were known to be in operation; and the number had grown to ten by the following autumn, the majority of them on the Russian front.

In February 1944 the Germans brought into general use an additional cryptanalytic security device for Fish transmissions. This device was first used for a brief period in March and April 1943 on

---

* Notably by a 'depth' resulting from the re-use of key to encypher more than one message, which was broken by the late Brigadier John Tiltman.

† It has been claimed that the extension of Fish down to divisional level was considered by the Army in 1943. In the event this step was not taken, perhaps because the use of Geheimschreiber, a much larger and more complicated machine than Enigma, would have been impracticable and risky from the security point of view in many circumstances at the lower levels.

the Tunis link. In December 1943 it was introduced on the links between OKH and Army Groups C and E and by February 1944 it had come into practically universal use for the Fish traffic. This threw the task almost entirely on to GC and CS machine resources, and there was a marked drop in the number solved. In February the number of decrypts totalled less than half that achieved in the previous month. The experience gained in operating Colossus Mark I led to the specification of the Mark II version in March 1944. This required extensive re-design, but the GPO team undertook to try to complete the first copy within the given time limit, which was less than three months. To save time, they assembled it at GC and CS and by a special effort made it operational in the early hours of 1 June 1944, just in time to make an invaluable intelligence contribution to the success of Operation *Overlord*.

GC and CS's recovery from the set-back of February 1944 began well before delivery of Colossus Mark II. One of the first results of the improved co-ordination between the various disciplines was the solution in March 1944 of the Fish settings on a new link (Jellyfish) between Straussberg and Paris, first intercepted at the beginning of the year. The link proved to be that between OKH and C-in-C West and in the month before the Normandy landings its decrypts were to be of the greatest value. From the point of view of its operational importance GC and CS regarded the solution of Jellyfish as its most significant cryptanalytic achievement during 1944.

From mid-June 1944 the Fish programme continued to be handicapped by the steady spread of the use of the new device (and by further major improvements in German operating procedures). From September, however, the device began to fall into disuse – it had caused difficulties for the Germans – and since both the number of Fish links and the number of Colossus Mark II machines in operation continued to increase there was a rise in the output of decrypts, one which continued almost without check till the end of the war. GC and CS decrypted more Fish transmissions between October 1944 and May 1945 than it had done between November 1942 and September 1944.

APPENDIX 3

Enigma Keys Attacked by GC and CS between June 1943 and June 1944

Part 1
The German Air Force

GC and CS Name	Date Broken	Date Identified by GC and CS and Duration	Remarks
Lion	14.6.43	June 1942 (to end of war)	Luftflotte 5 (later Luftwaffenkdo Norway).
Mayfly	30.6.43	June 1943 (to January 1945)	Fliegerkorps XIV (Mediterranean).
Squirrel	3.7.43	July 1943 (to November 1943)	Luftflotte 2 (Italy) long-range bombers.
Puma	1.8.43	August 1943 (to end of war)	Luftflotte 2 Flivo key with AOK 10 (Tenth Army)
Poppy	13.9.43	September 1943 (to April 1944)	Luftgau XII/XIII.
Gorse	20.9.43	March 1943 (to November 1944)	Luftgau XXVI (USSR). Called Foxglove IV (see Volume II p 661) till April 1943.
Indigo	3.10.43	October 1943 (to end of war)	General distribution key of high authority.
Yak	22.10.43	October 1943 (to ?)	Fliegerführer Croatia.
Leopard	5.2.44	February 1944 (to end of war)	Luftflotte 2 (later Komm. Gen. Italy.)
Lama	9.2.44	December 1943 (to September 1944)	Fliegerführer Albania.
Jaguar	11.2.44	December 1943 (to end of war)	Luftflotte 3 (later Luftwaffenkdo West).
Puce	Never broken	February 1944 (to October 1944)	Luftflotte 4 (USSR)

Part 1
The German Air Force

GC and CS Name	Date Broken	Date Identified by GC and CS and Duration	Remarks
Hyena	March 1944	February 1944 (to end of war)	Luftflotte Reich.
Cricket	24.4.44	December 1943 (to November 1944)	Jagdkorps II, NW Europe.
Gnat	1.5.44	May 1944 (to August 1944)	Fliegerkorps X.
Ocelot	31.5.44	May 1944 (to end of war)	Luftflotte 3 (Western Front) Flivo key.

Part 2
The German Army

GC and CS Name	Date Broken	Date Identified by GC and CS and Duration	Remarks
Merlin	February 1943	July 1942 (to November 1943)	Staff key, Balkans.
Albatross	2.6.43	May 1943 (to April 1945)	Tenth Army, Italy. Read 50 per cent of time.
Puffin	23.7.43	July 1943 (to May 1945)	OKH/Sicily/Italy.
Shrike	23.8.43	August 1943 (to April 1944)	Fourteenth Army, Italy.
Peregrine	24.8.43	June 1943 (to September 1943)	V SS Panzer Corps, Yugoslavia. Not regularly broken.
Wryneck I	18.9.43	August 1943 (to March 1945	Second Panzer Army, Yugoslavia.

Part 2
The German Army

GC and CS Name	Date Broken	Date Identified by GC and CS and Duration	Remarks
Wryneck II	31.1.44	? (to late 1944)	Second Panzer Army Staff key.
Woodpecker	16.11.43	October 1943 (to March 1945)	SE Europe.
Toucan	?	November 1943 (to March 1944)	Supply key, Italy.
Magpie	29.11.43	October 1943 (to January 1944)	Dodecanese.
Bullfinch*	15.12.43	December 1943 (to February 1944)	Tenth Army, Italy.
Owl	14.2.44	November 1943 (to March 1944)	Seventeeth Army, Crimea.
Chicken	27.2.44	April 1943 (to April 1945)	Supply key, Fifteenth Army, France.
Bantam	1.3.44	April 1943 (to May 1945)	Western Front operational key.
Nightjar	17.3.44	February 1944 (to August 1944)	Military occupation authorities, France.
Pelican	27.3.44	March 1944 (to June 1944)	First Panzer Army, USSR.
Moorhen	?	April 1944 (to May 1944)	Supply key, Italy.
Corncrake	13.5.44	March 1944 (to July 1944)	Between Peenemünde and Blizna for units connected with V-weapon experiments. Broken by chance.
Kingfisher	30.5.44	May 1944 (to April 1945)	Fourteenth Army, Italy.
Duck	9.6.44	April 1943 (to May 1945)	Seventh Army, France.
Pullet	11.6.44	August 1942 (to March 1945)	Y key for C-in-C West.

* See Volume II, p 666 for Bullfinch in Tunisia.

Part 3
The German Navy

GC and CS Name	Period of Use by German Navy	Date Broken	Remarks
Seahorse	1940 to May 1945	September 1943	Used between Berlin and German Naval Attaché Tokyo. Called Bertok by Germans. Offizier Barnacle.
Plaice	June to November 1941; May 1942 to January 1943; April 1943 to May 1945	1 January 1944	Eastern Baltic, but reverting to Dolphin (see Volume II, pp 663–664) during gaps noted in column 2. Replaced Dolphin in western Baltic early 1944. Extended to the Belt, Sound, Skagerrak and part of North Sea April 1944. Called Potsdam by Germans. Offizier Whelk, usually read.
Sunfish	September 1941 to May 1945	August 1943	Supply ships and U-boats, Far East. Intermittently broken. Called Tibet by Germans.
Freya	10.2.43 to May 1945	June 1944	B-Dienst.
Turtle	June 1943 to October 1944	June 1943	U-boats Mediterranean. Called Medusa by Germans. Offizier Cockle.
Grampus	October 1943 to August 1944	October 1943	Black Sea, including U-boats. Called Poseidon by Germans. Offizier Clam.
Porpoise*	October 1943 to May 1945	October 1943	Surface ships and shore authorities Mediterranean. Called Hermes by Germans.

* See Volume II, p 667.

Part 3
The German Navy

GC and CS Name	Period of Use by German Navy	Date Broken	Remarks
Trumpeter	October 1943 to April 1945	April 1944	OKM/ Mediterranean. Called Uranus by Germans.
Bonito	March 1944 to May 1945	May 1944	Small Battle Units Command (KDK), to operational staffs. Read fairly completely from July 1944. Called Eichendorff by Germans. Offizier Cowrie, usually read.
Narwhal	25.6.44 to May 1945	September 1944	U-boats Northern Waters. Called Niobe by Germans. Offizier Mussel, usually read.

Part 4
Non-Service Keys

GC and CS Name	Date Broken	Date Identified by GC and CS and Duration	Remarks
?	28.8.43	27.7.43 (to February 1944)	Sicherheitsdienst Rome/Berlin.
Roulette	10.2.44	February 1944 (to May 1945)	Senior Police Officers, ocupied Europe.
Pumpkin	1.4.44	April 1944 (to April 1945)	SS propaganda key, Rome/Berlin.
Grapefruit	21.8.44 (read on this day only)	May 1944 (to April 1945)	SS key used in connection with concentration camps.
Medlar	29.5.44	May 1944 (to May 1945)	SS key for W/T cross-working. Rarely broken.

APPENDIX 4

Intelligence Estimates and German Statistics on the German War Economy

(a) MEW Estimates of raw materials in German Europe*
(000) metric tons)

	Stocks at 1 Jan	1942 Current Supplies	Consumption	Stocks at 1 Jan	1943 Current Supplies	Consumption	Stocks at 1 Jan	1944 Current Supplies	Consumption	Stocks at 1 July 44
Chrome ore (all grades)	50	140	190	NIL	175	175	NIL	100	100	NIL
Molybdenum (Metal)	1.8	0.5	2.0	0.3	0.4	0.7	NIL	0.3	0.3	NIL
Wolfram	2.8	3.4	5.8	0.4	3.7	4.1	NIL	1.5	1.5	NIL
Manganese (50% Mn. Ore)	95	316	380	31	300	350	60	90	135	15
Copper	100	250	275	75	215	200	90	100	100	90
Nickel (metal)	6.4	3.5	9.0	0.9	7.5	8.4	NIL	5.5	4.5	1.0
Tin (metal)	41.1	5.3	12.0	7.4	5.1	8.5	7.0	1.3	4.0	4.3
Bauxite	1,400	1,200	1,500	1,100	1,500	1,600	2,750	1,075	1,130	2,695
Alumina	(b)	575(a)	575	(b)	625(a)	625	90	360	450	—
Aluminium(c)	(d)	460(a)	460	(d)	500(a)	500	(c)	300	300	—

(a) includes production lost and imports less exports.
(b) very small.
(c) primary and secondary metal.
(d) impossible to estimate but probably 50–100,000 tons mainly circulating scrap.
* Compiled from FO 837/19, MEW WIR No 108 of 29 February 1944, FO 837/20, MEW WIR, No 134 of 31 August 1944.

(b) *Official German Statistics showing stocks of raw materials 1943 and 1944**
(000 metric tons)

	Stocks at 1.1.43	1943 Current supplies	Consumption	Stocks at 1.1.44	1944 Current Supplies	Consumption	Stocks
Chrome ore	22.6	30.8	38.7	18.7	61.5	42.4	29.8
Molybdenum	0.6	0.5	0.8	0.4	0.8	0.7	0.4
Wolfram	1.6	1.8	2.2	1.5	1.5	1.5	1.3
Manganese ore	54.0	198.3	178.5	110.7	n.a.	n.a	n.a.
Copper	265.0	314.0	221.0	373.0	226.0	219.0	452.0
Nickel	10.4	7.6	9.4	8.6	10.9	9.5	7.9
Tin	16.7	8.3	9.5	15.6	11.7	7.7	20.1
Bauxite	213.8	n.a.	n.a.	n.a.	n.a.	n.a.	n.a.
Aluminium	90.8	382.1	384.0	6.5	437.6		

* Source: US Strategic Bombing Survey, Synoptic Volume, Table 83, pp 263–264.

(c) *MEW Estimates of German acquisition of natural rubber*

1941 until 21 June, 31,000 tons (12,000 tons via Trans-Siberian Railway, plus 19,000 tons by blockade-running)
1942 49,000 tons by blockade-running
1943 8,000 tons by blockade-running
1944 5,000 tons by blockade-running
Source: German Handbook, Economic Survey Section P, p 3.

MEW May 1944 Estimates of:

(1) *German annual output of synthetic rubber* (000 tons)

1939	22
1940	54
1941	70
1942	76
1943	74
1944	104

Source: MEW German Handbook, Economic Survey, Section P, Table 1, facing p 36.

(2) *German total supply of rubber* (000 tons)

End of 1939	128
End of 1940	128
End of 1941	160
End of 1942	175
End of 1943	140
End of 1944	168

Source: MEW German Handbook, Economic Survey, Section P, Table 2, p 3

(d) *German Statistics of the actual annual output of synthetic rubber*
(000 tons metric)

1939	22
1940	39
1941	71
1942	101
1943	119
1944	93

Source: Alan S Milward, *War, Economy and Society 1939–1945* (English ed 1977), p 79.

(e) *MEW Estimate of the distribution of working population of Greater Germany as at September 1943*

Total population Greater Germany (a) May 1939		79.38m
Total civilian population October 1943 (including working and non-working foreigners and POW)		c75 m
Distribution of Working Population (b)	1939 in 1000's	September 1943(c) in 1000's
I Metals, engineering and chemicals	5,430	6,829
II Agriculture, forestry and fishing	10,878	11,100
Mining	796	800
National & local government & public utilities	2,345	2,470
Transport	1,685	1,630
Food, drinks & tobacco	1,655	1,200
TOTAL GROUP II	17,309	17,200
III Distribution services, trade, banking etc – Other services & professions	7,724	5,860
Other industries	8,403	5,831
Total Group III	16,127	11,691
IV Civilian employees of the Wehrmacht	502	(d)
V Full-time defence and allied services	—	1,000 approx
Total working population	39,368	36,720(e)

a. Area as it was in May 1939.
b. Working population covers all those gainfully employed, with the exception of members of the armed forces and of the Air Defence of the Reich.
c. Figures for September 1943 are estimates only, subject to revision.
d. It has not been thought feasible to separate civilian employees of Wehrmacht undertakings from the general industrial distribution in the 1943 estimates.
e. Including approximately 6.5m foreign workers and working POW.
Source: FO 837/19, MEW WIR No 108 of 29 February 1944.

Appendix 4

(f) *German tank production*

| | Anglo-American Estimates* | | Actual Output† | |
	Total	Monthly average	Total	Monthly average
1939	1680	140	—	—
1940	2030	170	1459	121
1941	2925	240	3245	270
1942	3920	330	4137	345
1943	5750	480	5996	500
1944	–	775(a)	8344	695
		(in June 1944)		

(a) as deduced from general evidence the monthly rate of output of tanks in *June* 1944 is
    estimated at

Pzkw IV	350
Panthers	325
Tigers	100
	775

The last intelligence estimate of the German output of the main types of tanks for 1943 was
issued in May 1945. It was close to actuality:

Estimates of Tank production in 1943 *		*Actual output†*	
Pzkw IV	2700	Pzkw IV	3073
Tiger	650	Tiger I	647
Panther	1900–2000	Panther	1850

Sources: * German Handbook, Economic Survey Section K.
        †US Strategic Bombing Survey, Synoptic Volume, Table 104, p 278.

(g) AI 2(a) Estimates of German aircraft production (operational types) February 1943 – April 1944

	SEF	TEF	(Total Fighters)	L R Bombers	Misc	All Op Types
1943						
Jan	470	130	600	460	240	1,300
Feb[a]	550	160	600	420	270	1,350
March[a]	610	170	780	435	215	1,430
April	635	185	820	435	210	1,465
May	590	175	765	420	215	1,400
June	680	200	880	440	205	1,525
July	770	210	980	455	205	1,640
Aug	810	210	1,020	435	210(?)	1,665(?)
Sept	665	215	880	435	180	1,515
Oct	600	275	875	440	175	1,490
Nov	600	270	880	385	160	1,425(?)
Dec	600	270	870	315	150	1,335
1944						
Jan	650	190	840	315	130	1,285
Feb	600	200	800	300	125	1,225
March[b]	400	95	450	295	110	855
April[c]	355	90	445	285	105	835
May	(d)					
June	(d)					

(a) Revised June 43 (AI 2(a) 9/43 of 19.6.43)
(b) Revised May 44 (JIC(44) 177(o) of 1.5.44)
(c) Estimate JIC(44) 177(o)
(d) No estimates made

Sources: Statistics collated from all contemporary intelligence documents in which estimates of production appear. The two principal sources are (a) AI 2(a) monthly reports in AIR 19/543; (b) JIC reports containing average production figures supplied by AI 2(a).

(h) *Estimated monthly averages of German aircraft production*
September 1939–June 1944

	Sept–Dec 1939	Jan–June 1940	Jul–Dec 1940	Jan–June 1941	Jul–Dec 1941	Jan–June 1942	Jul–Dec 1942	Jan–June 1943	Jul–Dec 1943	Jan–June 1944
S E FIGHTER	205	280	300	325	360	410	435	595	645	655
T E FIGHTER	75	100	120	110	130	130	120	175	255	250
DIVE–BOMBERS	80	80	80	70	85	100	100	95	90	55
L R BOMBERS AND BOMBER RECCE AIRCRAFT	365	320	365	370	425	435	465	430	450	290
ARMY CO-OPERATION, COASTAL AND MISC AIRCRAFT	120	145	150	160	150	155	160	120	95	60
TOTAL OPERATIONAL TYPES	845	925	1015	1035	1150	1230	1280	1415	1490	1310
TRANSPORT AIRCRAFT	50	55	60	65	75	70	65	80	80	60
LIGHT TRANSPORT AIRCRAFT AND TRAINERS	280	360	420	475	500	520	535	535	545	500
TOTAL ALL TYPES	1175	1340	1495	1575	1725	1820	1880	2030	2115	1870

* Source: German Handbook, Economic Survey Section **K**, Appendix 1, p 100.

(i) *Actual aircraft production 1943-44*

Year and Month	Fighters	Bombers	Tpts	Trainers	Others	Total
1943						
Jan	512	674	128	125	86	1,525
Feb	858	781	130	125	110	2,004
March	962	757	173	156	118	2,166
April	936	735	172	145	112	2,100
May	1,013	718	178	179	108	2,196
June	1,134	710	178	194	100	2,316
July	1,263	743	191	190	88	2,475
Aug	1,135	710	201	174	117	2,337
Sept	1,072	678	201	201	62	2,214
Oct	1,181	738	184	200	46	2,349
Nov	985	702	171	183	70	2,111
Dec	687	643	126	204	74	1,734
1944						
Jan	1,555	522	141	160	67	2,445
Feb	1,104	567	112	170	62	2,015
March	1,638	605	139	243	47	2,672
April	2,021	680	134	154	45	3,034
May	2,212	648	133	226	29	3,248
June	2,449	703	104	331	39	3,626
July	2,954	767	136	325	37	4,219

Source: US Strategic Bombing Survey, Table 102, p 277

APPENDIX 5

GAF Operations during Operation
Avalanche

The GAF reacted vigorously to *Avalanche*, and Enigma decrypts yielded good intelligence throughout the battle. They showed that some 170 sorties of close support forces were flown on 8 September by II and III/SKG 10, I/JG 77, IV/JG 5 and I, II and III/JG 53.[1] Fliegerkorps II's intentions for 9 September, sent to the Mediterranean by GC and CS at 2159 on 8 September, were for reconnaissance and operations with all forces against Allied landings in the area Salerno-Naples.[2] Orders to II and III/SKG 10, decrypted very early on 9 September, were to take off as early as possible for attacks on the Allied landing fleet, with troop transports, merchant ships and landing craft as priority targets.[3] On that day, 82 fighter and 26 ground attack sorties were flown. At 0344 on 10 September Mediterranean commands were informed of orders to JG 53 for operations that day to freelance over the Gulf of Salerno and make low level attacks on landing craft.[4] All rocket firing aircraft,* which were said to have had splendid successes the previous day, were to be employed against transports and landing craft. Attacks by these aircraft on gun positions in the beachhead, disembarkation points and landing craft were ordered for 11 September, but the main fighter effort was to be on the defensive front south of Salerno with fighter patrols over German motorised movements between Castro Villari and Polla.[5] This was, no doubt, for the protection of the reinforcements for the Salerno front which were being withdrawn from Calabria. The information was not available until late on 11 September. On 12 September operations were concentrated in support of the German offensive against the beachhead; Fliegerkorps II flew 122 fighter, 8 rocket and 15 ground attack sorties.[6] On 14 September the figures were 69 fighter and 37

---

* The rocket projectile was adapted from the German Army's 21 cm mortar.

1. eg CX/MSS/3181/T15, 37, 40 and 60; AIR 41/10 *The Rise and Fall of the German Air Force*, p 262.
2. DEFE 3/878, JP 3708 of 8 September 1943.
3. ibid, JP 3731 of 9 September 1947.
4. ibid, JP 3869 of 10 September 1943.
5. DEFE 3/879, JP 4083 of 11 September 1943.
6. ibid, JP 4350 of 13 September 1943.

ground attack sorties and 44 and 35 on 15 September.[7] Fliegerkorps
II's intentions for 16, 17 and 18 September were to continue attacks
by ground attack aircraft with fighter escort on shipping in the Gulf
of Salerno and to protect supply routes in the area of LXXVI
Panzer Corps.[8] On 16 September 62 fighter and 31 ground attack
sorties were flown,[9] amd 49 fighter and 16 ground attack sorties on
17 September.[10] On 19 September Fliegerkorps II's effort fell to 39
fighter and 9 ground attack sorties,[11] reflecting the withdrawal
northwards of the greatly overmatched close support forces which
had begun on 16 September when II and III/JG 53 moved to the
Rome area. They were immediately bombed out and retreated to
Lucca on 21 September.[12] The outcome of the adjustments made –
which was duly revealed in the Enigma decrypts – was that by 23
September only exiguous forces (I/JG 53, II/JG 77 and II/SKG
10) remained to provide close support for the Army and fighter
escort for the rare bomber attacks. Moreover, from 27 September
this force had also to cover the evacuation of Corsica.[13]

The bomber forces in Italy comprised I and II/JG 1, II/KG 30,
III/KG 54, I and II/KG 76, III/KG 100 equipped with the new
FX 1400 bomb, II/LG 1 at Foggia and I and III/KG 30 at
Viterbo. There were also anti-shipping units of KG 26 and KG 100
at Istres in southern France; the transfer there from Atlantic bases
of II/KG 100, the group which had been using the new Hs 293
missile, was reported in the Enigma on 7 September.[14] The bomber
effort against the Salerno landings was stronger than any attempted
in the Mediterranean for some time. During the night 8–9 September
158 sorties were made against the landing fleet, 18 aircraft being
lost.[15] At 0034 on 9 September GC and CS warned the Mediterranean
authorities that III/KG 100 had been ordered to carry out an
attack as early as possible on 9 September; all serviceable fighters
from Naples and Foggia were to provide escort.[16] Another decrypt,
sent to the Mediterranean authorities at 0608, gave the target as
cruisers and battleships in the probable area of landing.[17] Around
noon GC and CS sent out three decrypts: a report from the German
Chief of Staff at Genoa that Italian warships had sailed and that an

---

7.   DEFE 3/880, JP 4510 of 15 September 1943.
8.   ibid, JPs 4617 and 4618 of 17 September, 4730 of 18 September 1943.
9.   ibid, JP 4679 of 17 September 1943.
10. ibid, JP 4754 of 18 September 1943.
11. ibid, JP 4947 of 20 September 1943.
12. DEFE 3/881, JP 5021 of 21 September 1943.
13. CX/MSS/3265/T28, 3270/T8;
14. DEFE 3/878, JP 3575 of 7 September 1943.
15. CX/MSS/3185/T40.
16. ibid, JP 3727 of 9 September 1943.
17. ibid, JP 3758 of 9 September 1943.

attempt to seize the Italian Fleet had failed;[18] a report by Flieger-korps II that III/KG 100 had 8 aircraft ready to take off to attack 6 battleships, 6 cruisers and 6 destroyers if reconnaissance confirmed that these were Italian;[19] and a message to KG 100 at 1000 hours authorising an attack on unspecified units.[20] An Italian report that the battleship *Roma* had been sunk at 1420 on 9 September by a bomb from a German aircraft was signalled by GC and CS early on 10 September.[21]

A signal from Luftflotte 2, available at midday on 10 September, ordered that Foggia, Viterbo and Grosseto were to remain as operational bases as long as possible but elements not required were to be sent back to the Po valley and the south of France.[22] His orders at 1300 for operations against shipping in the Naples–Salerno area during the night 10–11 September were sent to the Mediterranean commands by GC and CS at 2202; attacks were to be made at 2045 and 0300, but as German ground forces would be counter-attacking near Salerno early on 11 September the second raid was to be confined to battleships, aircraft carriers and cruisers.[23] During 11 September heavy bombers made daylight attacks on shipping. The USS *Savannah* was heavily damaged by an Hs 293 bomb, and HMS *Uganda* was also disabled.[24] Orders for a single concentrated attack on ships off Salerno between 0100 and 0115 on the night 11–12 September were sent out by GC and CS in the early evening of 11 September,[25] and four decrypts containing orders for a similar attack during the night 12–13 September had been sent by 0214 on 13 September.[26] However, the intended timing of the attack – 0230 on 13 September – was not known until later.[27] In a message of 1335 on 13 September GC and CS warned Mediterranean authorities that orders had been issued at 1015 to III/KG 100 to make a daylight attack on large naval units including two battleships in Salerno bay which were considerably hampering the German counter-attack.[28] Fighter protection was to be provided from Foggia and on the return trip aircraft were to refuel at Ciampino.

A message from GC and CS at 1456 on 14 September carried the news that III/KG 100 had again been ordered at 1100 to attack

---

18. ibid, JP 3780 of 9 September 1943.
19. ibid, JP 3789 of 9 September 1943.
20. ibid, JP 3788 of 9 September 1943.
21. ibid, JP 3884 of 10 September 1943.
22. ibid, JP 3901 of 10 September 1943.
23. ibid, JPs 3955 and 3976 of 10 September 1943.
24. AIR 41/34. *The Italian Campaign*, Vol I, pp 134–136.
25. DEFE 3/879, JP 4072 of 11 September 1943.
26. ibid, JPs 4200, 4204, 4206 of 12 September, 4265 of 13 September 1943.
27. ibid, JP 4268 of 13 September 1943.
28. ibid, JP 4303 of 13 September 1943.

two battleships in Salerno Bay that day.[29] The immediately following message added that fighter escorts would be arranged and the timing of the attack would be at the discretion of KG 100 which was to carry out the operation independently in the light of its tactical experience.[30] For the night 15–16 September advance notice was given that weak forces were to attack shipping at Salerno in three phases; the remaining bomber forces were to rest.[31] No warning could be given of the attack on 16 September when an FX 1400 bomb disabled HMS *Warspite*. Orders for the nights 16–17 and 17–18 September for attacks on the transport fleet at Salerno came to hand too late.

Orders to the bombers at Foggia to begin withdrawal were decrypted very early on 19 September.[32] Their evacuation to locations in northern Italy and southern France, revealed in the Enigma decrypts, was complete by 25 September.[33] Disorganisation resulting from these moves rendered the GAF's long-range bomber effort in Italy negligible throughout October.

---

29.   ibid, JP 4405 of 14 September 1943.
30.   ibid, JP 4406 of 14 September 1943;
31.   DEFE 3/880, JPs 4505 and 4516 of 15 September 1943.
32.   ibid, JP 4810 of 19 September 1943.
33.   CX/MSS/3235/T32, 3268/T11, 3271/T17, 3276/T1.

APPENDIX 6

The Sources of Sigint on the Situation in the Balkans*

Before the spring of 1942 such Sigint as was available was almost all obtained from the GAF general key (Red). Some of the medium-grade and low-grade hand cyphers used by the Germans in the area were read at GC and CS; but as most of the traffic was intercepted only in the Middle East and had to be sent back to the United Kingdom for decryption, it was decrypted at GC and CS with considerable delay and provided little intelligence of any value.

From the spring of 1942 GAF Red decrypts were supplemented by the traffic on the non-morse link between Vienna and Athens (Tunny), the first of the Fish links to be broken at GC and CS; this was frequently read currently till it disappeared in the autumn.† From the same date GC and CS broke the Army Enigma key used by Twelfth Army and later by Army Group E at Salonika (Raven) and two GAF Enigma keys that were used in the Balkans (Primrose and Foxglove),‡ but could not yet give much priority to exploiting them; until the end of 1942 the Raven settings were not broken regularly and Primrose and Foxglove were generally decrypted with a delay of between ten days and three weeks.

In the autumn of 1942 the Vienna–Athens Fish link was replaced by a non-morse link between Straussberg and Salonika (Codfish); GC and CS broke it with little delay and a good deal of the traffic was read currently. By then intelligence of some interest was beginning to be obtained both from the Enigma key used by the Abwehr in the area and from the hand cyphers used locally by the Abwehr and other authorities. GC and CS was given permission in July 1942 to incorporate this Enigma intelligence in its SCU/SLU signals to the Mediterranean HQs, but it did not find that any of the material was worthy of dissemination before the autumn.

---

* This appendix deals for the most part with the Sigint relating to Yugoslavia. In comparison with the plethora on Yugoslavia, the Sigint on Greece was sparse, the keys in use by formations there proving harder to break than those in Yugoslavia. But it is doubtful that much of value to Allied planning was lost because the Germans indulged in far less planned activity in Greece than in Yugoslavia and it is obvious that more Sigint would be produced by purposive warfare than by warfare consisting chiefly of passive waiting for the isolated guerrilla raid.

† See Appendix 2, pp 477, 481.   ‡ See Volume II, Appendix 4.

From the middle of 1942 the SIS agreed to permit exploitation of the hand cyphers at Cairo, whose intercept stations took most of the traffic; hitherto SIS had had no section in Cairo to undertake security control and the interpretation of the decrypts.* From the autumn the volume of CBME's decrypts, about thirty a month to begin with, steadily increased.† Most of the decrypts came from cyphers used by the Police and the Abwehr, with occasional signals from the Sicherheitsdienst. By no means all the traffic passed in the cyphers was decrypted, or even intercepted. Police decrypts, for example, were available from Serbia after September 1942, but from Slovenia only a few were obtained in September and October 1942 and then no more until March 1943, and there were none from Croatia until April 1943. Interception improved rapidly from the summer of 1943, when stations were set up at Derna and Benghazi and elsewhere in the central Mediterranean, and from the time of the Italian capitulation the cyphers produced a wealth of information on the political situation in Yugoslavia and on Abwehr and Police collaboration with the Army in counter-guerrilla operations. By then, however, the Germans had begun to improve the security of these hand cyphers. GC and CS still managed to read the Abwehr ones with assistance from the Abwehr Enigma, until that was tightened up in January 1944. But without this assistance decryption of the cyphers in Cairo became progressively more difficult before ceasing altogether in January 1944.

Meanwhile, greater German activity had combined with the growth of GC and CS's resources to produce a marked increase in the volume and scope of Enigma decrypts from the beginning of 1943, and particularly from the summer of that year when Germany reorganised her forces in anticipation of Italy's defection.‡ The Raven key was read continuously from January; another Army key which carried information on German/Italian relations (Merlin) was broken in February; the key used by the German Army in Albania (Buzzard) was read from time to time between May and June; and the key allotted to Second Panzer Army after the German reorganisation (Wryneck) was broken regularly almost from the time it appeared. With the introduction of Wryneck, the Raven traffic declined in importance, eventually becoming confined to matters of mainly local interest in Greece. The same happened to the Codfish traffic to and from Army Group E when, also in the summer, Army Group F at Belgrade acquired its own Fish link

---

* See above, p 141.
    † For examples of the use made of this material in Cairo from January 1943 see above, pp 141, 150, 154, 160.
    ‡ For the details of GC and CS's attack on the Enigma keys see Appendix 3, and Volume II, Appendix 4.

(Gurnard); but this link was, like Wryneck, broken as soon as it was introduced. By that time the SS general Enigma key (Quince) had been read for some months; its short-lived subsidiary key (Peregrine) used by V SS Mountain Corps to communicate with its 7th SS Mountain Division, was also being read, as were several Abwehr cyphers, but the SS and Abwehr decrypts had not yet produced intelligence of any great interest.

Following the Italian collapse in the autumn of 1943 the existing Enigma keys and Fish links all carried more traffic, more new keys were introduced and GC and CS's capacity to break the daily settings increased – so much so, that from then until the end of the war it found the volume of high-grade German decrypts somewhat overwhelming. The result was that it could process as a matter of urgency only the decrypts in those keys which had a bearing on operations in which Allied forces were directly involved – these included the naval key (Porpoise), which became the chief source of intelligence about the fighting on the Yugoslav coast and islands, and Gadfly, the key for Luftwaffenkommando Süd Ost which was now read currently as a valuable source of information for the planning and the effects of Allied air raids – and that those covering the fighting inland were still decrypted and translated with some delay and sent out to the commands in the form of periodic summaries of what they had disclosed about the enemy's intentions and the general progress of his operations.

Gadfly was read currently until the middle of 1944, when the introduction of a new wheel for GAF keys made it unprofitable for GC and CS to work on it – and also reduced, at last, the value of the GAF general key (Red). The other new GAF keys were that for Fliegerführer Croatia (Yak), which was broken in October 1943, and that for Fliegerführer Albania (Llama), which was read between February and September 1944; neither produced much valuable intelligence. As for the Army, the key for Rommel's Army Group B (Shrike) was broken in October 1943, and another new key was read from January 1944; this (Wryneck II) was at first used mainly for the traffic of the German Army's intelligence authorities.

From October 1943 an additional source of intelligence became available in the shape of decrypts of Croatian codes and cyphers. Exploited by the Army Y organisation in Italy as well as at GC and CS, some 25 of these were identified; mostly low-grade, they threw some light on the poor equipment and morale of the Croatian Army, on the location of German troops and on the confused and confusing state of relations between Germans, Cetniks and Partisans.

APPENDIX 7

Appreciation for Operation *Shingle*

Special Unnumbered Signal of 7 January 1944 from 15th Army Group at Bari on SLU channels via London to General Alexander on a visit to AFHQ Algiers.

Build up appreciation for operation SHINGLE complicated by change German dispositions as follows:
(a) Relief of Hermann Goering Division by 114 Jaeger Division.
(b) Moves of part or whole of 3 P.G. and 90 P.G. Divisions.
(c) Relief of 29 P. G. Divison.

A.   On 30th December according to ULTRA, Kesselring stated that H.G. Division was being transferred to France and that 114 Jaeger Division was to take its place. Latter last located area Sibenik–Split and on 24th December Y shows its elements were still widely dispersed. Calculate on basis of present communications capabilities of Division could be complete Frosinone area about last week January. H.G. Division is to start moving away before complete arrival of 114 Jaeger so that strength in vital area should not increase and may decrease. On 5th January, P.G.R. 1 H.G. was still ?there as it was put in line to meet attack along road 6. 114 Jaeger Division may have 3 infantry regiments but no tank and no S.P. gun battalion. Training and morale certainly inferior to H.G. Division. All horse drawn. H.G. will take away with it 40 tanks, 14 assault guns, 18 S.P. anti-tank guns and 55–60 field, medium and anti-aircraft guns which must be subtracted from total to meet SHINGLE landings. 114 Jaeger probably comparatively weak in artillery.

B.   On 4th January Y showed 103 recce unit of 3 P.G. Division reconnoitred road Rome–Avezzano–Chieti and unit headquarters moved to Chieti. Still in Chieti on 6 January and joined in same area by other elements unidentified of 3 P.G. Division. Also 6th January 26 Panzer Division in message referring to billets in area Moscufo C 0425 was informed that although 90 P.G. Division was withdrawing from sector billets were nevertheless not to be occupied by 26 Panzer Division. From this can deduce fact that 90 P. G. and at least some of 3 P.G. Divisions are moving. Possible explanations.

1. 90 moving to west coast and 3 to east coast as former, though weakened by losses, the better division.
2. 90 P.G. Division leaving theatre altogether and being replaced by 3 P.G.
3. Either 3 or 90 P.G. intends to relieve 26 Panzer Division from 76 ?Corps to allow its transfer to 14 Corps to fill gap made by imminent departure of H.G., only other armoured division. Armoured formation probably considered essential in Frosinone plain.
4. 3 P.G. to reinforce 76 Corps sector in view of apprehension loudly expressed by 26 Panzer Division last few days of imminent allied attack this sector. Impossible on present evidence to decide between above. Do not consider likely Germans will keep both 3 and 90 P.G. Divisions in reserve on 76 Corps front as 14 Corps front much more vital. Note that part at least of 8 P.G.R. of 3 P.G. Division was in CIVITA VECCHIA on 2nd January and consider Germans will have to continue to protect this vital port.

C. 29 P.G. Division now withdrawn from line. 1 battalion arrived area 11 Fliegerkorps 23rd December. We appreciate whole Division will remain in 11 Fliegerkorps area south of Rome responsible for coast from Terracina to Tiber. Probably now no elements of 3 P.G. Division south of Tiber and see paragraph B above. Conclusions for SHINGLE build up. H hours 2 RCT* 29 P.G. Division. H plus 6 add 3 parachute battalions (note: may be less than 3 available). H plus 22 add 1 RCT 114 Jaeger division unless motorised ad hoc in which case H plus 10. H plus 24 add S 1 RCT 90 P.G. Division. H plus 36 add possibly 1 RCT 3 P.G. Division from CIVITA VECCHIA provided enemy expects no threat there. H plus 48 add 1 infantry regiment from Lucca (35 SS P.G.R.). H plus 60 (or later depending on state of road) add 1 RCT from 76 Corps. H. plus 72 add 1 further RCT from 76 Corps. Note that considerable element of uncertainty still present as have no indication of intended employment of 114 Jaeger division which might be used to release from line last mobile division still committed in south viz: 15 P.G. If so relief would probably be in progress on D day.

---

* ie Regimental Combat Team.

APPENDIX 8

Intelligence on the German Army's Order of Battle in Italy, January 1944

Allied coverage of Tenth Army's order of battle, mainly from high-grade Sigint, had been excellent throughout the autumn campaign. At the turn of the year 1943–1944 it was known that the German line was held from left to right by LXXVI Panzer Corps with 1st Parachute, 26th Panzer and 334th Infantry Divisions; Corps Group Hauck with 305th Infantry Division and two or three independent Alpine battalions; and XIV Panzer Corps with 5th Mountain, 44th Infantry and 29th Panzer Grenadier Divisions, a battle group of the Hermann Göring Division, 15th Panzer Grenadier Divison and 94th Infantry Division. 90th Panzer Grenadier Division and the bulk of the Hermann Göring Division were in immediate reserve, the former in the Pescara area, the latter behind the right wing of XIV Panzer Corps. It was also known from Sigint that the Germans intended to withdraw 29th Panzer Division into XIV Panzer Corps reserve, a process which continued well into January. Close at hand in the area of Rome were 3rd Panzer Grenadier Division and a new parachute division which was in process of formation; both were under command of Fliegerkorps II which was responsible for the coastal sector from Terracina to Grosseto. 65th Infantry Division, which had been very recently relieved in the front line by 334th Infantry Division, was on its way to Genoa to join Fourteenth Army.[1]

Information about the German order of battle in central and northern Italy under Fourteenth Army was less precise. 336th Infantry Division and a regiment of the Brigade Reichsführer SS were in the Leghorn area; the latter formation was being expanded to form 16th SS Panzer Grenadier Division and the main body was collecting at Ljubljana. 362nd Infantry Division was forming at Rimini; a division (later identified as 278th Infantry Division) was at Bologna; there were mountain troops at Belluno and Bolzano;

---

1. CAB 121/592 SIC file F/Italy/6/1, Vol 1, JIC (44) 4 (0) of 4 January; WO 204/968, AFHQ Weekly Intelligence Summary No 71 of 1 January 1944; DEFE 3/13(2), VL 2006 of 16 December; DEFE 3/14 (1) VL 2434 of 22 December; DEFE 3/15 (1), VL 2734 of 27 December; DEFE 3/16 (2) VL 2758 of 27 December; DEFE 3/16 (1), VLs 2936 and 2939 of 30 December 1943.

71st Infantry Division was at Fiume; and 162nd Infantry Division was in Slovenia.[2]

The already copious flow of Ultra was augmented in January by the breaking of the key (known to GC and CS as Bullfinch) used for Tenth Army's day reports to OKH, and throughout the month the Allies were extremely well informed about the enemy position. We may preface an account of what intelligence revealed about German reactions to Fifth Army's offensive up to the landing at Anzio with some examples of other information about German dispositions and capabilities which became available during this period. A decrypt of 6 January yielded orders from Kesselring that 114th Jäger Division was to be brought from Slovenia to replace the Hermann Göring Division which was to be transferred to C-in-C West.[3]* Later decrypts disclosed that the loading of 114th Jäger Division was to begin on 20 January, the same day as the Hermann Göring Division was due to be released, but that the former's move to the entraining point was being obstructed by Partisan activities.[4] From decrypts between 9 and 13 January it became clear that 3rd PG Division in the Rome area and 90th PG Division in LXXVI Corps reserve near Pescara were changing places.[5] Information that 71st Infantry Division in Istria was on the move came to hand on 12, 14 and 15 January;[6] on 16 January a decrypt disclosed that the first elements of this division had arrived in the XIV Panzer Corps sector on 13 January[7] and further arrivals were reported in decrypts on 17, 18 and 19 January.[8] On 18 January it was learnt that Kesselring had issued instructions on 7 January for seven Ost battalions to be brought up to Frosinone and Pescara for work on the Führer's switch-line and the Foro position as ordered by Hitler.[9] The replacement of Fliegerkorps II, which had been responsible for the coastal sector Terracina–Grosseto and had administered formations in the Rome area, by a new 1 Parachute

---

* See Appendix 7.

2. WO 204/968, No 71 of 4 January 1944; DEFE 3/14(2), VL 2307 of 20 December; DEFE 3/16 (1) VLs 2961 and 2995 of 31 December 1943.
3. DEFE 3/18(2, VL 3361 of 6 January 1944.
4. DEFE 3/129, VLs 3797 of 12 January, 3998 of 15 January; DEFE 3/130, VL 4217 of 18 January; DEFE 3/131, VL 4340 of 20 January 1944.
5. DEFE 3/19(2) VLs 3539 of 9 January, 3616 of 10 January; DEFE 3/19(1), VLs 3658 of 10 January, 3723 of 11 January; DEFE 3/129, VL 3825 of 13 January 1944.
6. DEFE 3/129, VLs 3765 of 12 January, 3895 of 14 January, 3996 of 15 January 1944.
7. DEFE 3/130, VL 4033 of 16 January 1944.
8. DEFE 3/130, VLs 4093 of 17 January, 4189 of 18 January; DEFE 3/131, VL 4308 of 19 January.
9. DEFE 3/130, VL 4186 of 18 January 1944.

Corps was revealed by a decrypt on 12 January;[10] another on 14 January placed the headquarters of 1 Parachute Corps at Frascati.[11] On 18 January a decrypt showed that the headquarters of Fliegerkorps II, which had not been mentioned in Italy since 22 December, was at Compiègne.[12]

C-in-C South West's supply return for 29 December (decrypted on 7 January) described Tenth Army's transport situation as extraordinarily acute.[13] The main railway line had been cut at Chiusi and would be interrupted for eight to fourteen days. Guerrillas had blown up a bridge near Modane on the Mont Cenis–Turin line and interrupted the crossing for a considerable period. The review for 5 January (decrypted on 12 January) reported that the transport situation in Tenth Army's area had improved, though the arrival of trains was not satisfactory yet.[14] By 10 January (a decrypt of 18 January) train arrivals from the Reich were described as adequate; communications in central Italy had improved and Tenth Army's supply situation was assured.[15] However, on 16 January (decrypted on 23 January) C-in-C South West referred to delay in bringing up 71st Infantry Division because of railway disruption.[16] No returns of armoured fighting vehicles had been decrypted since the end of November and none became available during the first three weeks of January.

The brunt of the attack by US II Corps in the Cassino sector in the second week of January fell on 44th Infantry Division. Tenth Army's report for 7 January, decrypted on 9 January, spoke of very severe fighting along the division's whole front and heavy casualties.[17] Next day the division was reported to be taking up a new line.[18] Reports of ceaseless Allied attacks on 10 January and some Allied penetration of the new defence line on 10 January were decrypted on the following day.[19] On 12 January, when the French Expeditionary Corps opened its offensive, there were reports (decrypted on 15 January) of penetrations in the sector of 5th Mountain Division while the Allies were following up withdrawals in the sector of 44th Division.[20] A message at 1530 on 13 January, signalled by GC and CS at 2248, reported that 5th Mountain Division's greatly

10. DEFE 3/129, VL 3774 of 12 January 1944.
11. DEFE 3/129, VL 3931 of 14 January 1944.
12. DEFE 3/130, VL 4194 of 18 January 1944.
13. DEFE 3/18(1), VL 3397 of 7 January 1944.
14. DEFE 3/129, VL 3754 of 12 January 1944.
15. DEFE 3/130, VL 4235 of 18 January 1944.
16. DEFE 3/132, VL 4545 of 23 January 1944.
17. DEFE 3/19(2) VL 3552 of 9 January 1944.
18. DEFE 3/19(1), VL 3661 of 10 January 1944.
19. DEFE 3/19(1) VL 3715 of 11 January 1944.
20. DEFE 3/129, VL 3827 of 13 January 1944.

weakened units were unable to offer effective resistance and were forming a new defence line.[21] Decrypts of 16 January showed that on the previous day 44th Infantry Division rear guards in the Cervaro area had been forced to withdraw, while 5th Mountain Division had been subjected to renewed heavy Allied attacks on a wide front and suffered considerable losses.[22] Tenth Army reported on 15 January (decrypted on 17 January) that the left wing of 44th Infantry Division and the right wing of 5th Mountain Division would be withdrawn during the night and that a regiment of 3rd PG Division (which it will be remembered had recently moved to LXXVI Panzer Corps from reserve) was being brought up for employment in 5th Mountain Division's sector.[23] On 17 January, a GAF liaison officer's message at 0900, signalled by GC and CS at 1759, disclosed that 3rd PG Division was transferring into the southern area.[24] On 18 January the decrypt of Tenth Army's day report for 16 January confirmed that 26th Panzer Division had taken over 3rd PG Division's sector of the front held by LXXVI Panzer Corps.[25]

From another decrypt of 18 January it was learned that the GAF liaison officers on XIV Panzer Corps's right wing had reported on 17 January that the Allies had moved up to the Garigliano on a broad front.[26] Tenth Army's appreciation on the evening of 17 January (signalled by GC and CS at 2012 on 18 January) was that Allied reinforcements of the Gari in 15th Panzer Division's sector left open the possibility that this new concentration represented the main Allied effort.[27] US X Corps crossed the river in the Minturno sector during the night 17–18 January and broke into the main defences held by 94th Infantry Division. During the next few days, while Army Y rejoiced in the volubility on VHF of regimental and battalion commanders of 94th Infantry Division who provided (and throughout the Garigliano battle continued to provide) a detailed account of the action,[28] the Enigma laid bare the broader German reactions. At 1904 on 19 January GC and CS signalled extracts from Tenth Army's report for the previous day disclosing that elements of 29th Panzer Division, which had been in XIV Panzer Corps reserve, were moving and the intention to concentrate all available reserves to strengthen the defensive front of 94th Infantry

---

21.   DEFE 3/129, VL 3886 of 13 January 1944.
22.   DEFE 3/130, VL 4070 of 16 January 1944.
23.   DEFE 3/130, VL 4093 of 17 January 1944.
24.   DEFE 3/130, VL 4141 of 17 January 1944.
25.   DEFE 3/130, VL 4189 of 18 January 1944.
26.   DEFE 3/130, VL 4204 of 18 January 1944.
27.   DEFE 3/130, VL 4228 of 18 January 1944.
28.   *History of Sigint in the Field*, pp 116, 118.

Division.[29] Later instalments of this report, signalled at 2135 on 19 January and 0201 on 20 January, contained Tenth Army's (very accurate) appreciation that the Allies were using at least two divisions in this sector and would continue their attack in order to force an entry into the Cassino valley, and that the main attack by US II Corps on 25th PG Division's front must be expected soon. A diversionary attack by the French on 5th Mountain Division's front was also thought possible.[30]

On 20 and 21 January a stream of high priority signals flowed from GC and CS to the Allied commanders. One sent at 0304 on 20 January disclosed that 29th PG Division had taken over part of 94th Infantry Division's sector.[31] Fliegerführer Luftflotte 2's intentions for the day followed at 0346 and his picture of the situation at 0405. The Allies, he said, had made some penetrations in the centre of 94th Division; 5th British Division, which had been withdrawn a fortnight earlier from LXXVI Panzer Corps front, had appeared in the Ausente valley; the Allies were presumably continuing to concentrate in front of 44th Infantry Division for their main attack; the occurrence of the strongest attacks yet launched by the Allied heavy bombers against German airfields suggested that large scale operations were in hand.[32] At 0423 on 20 January GC and CS signalled that 29th PG Division was to move in that day for a counter-attack in the Ausente valley to restore the main defence line.[33] Signals sent at 0650 and 0654 reported the operation of the German close support air forces the previous day. Fighters on freelance patrol over XIV Panzer Corps front had had to be diverted to defend German airfields against massive attacks by bombers and fighter-bombers with fighter escort, reckoned to be at least ten times as numerous as the defending fighters; German close support operations had been curtailed because aircraft had had to use alternative airfields.[34] At 0103 on 21 January GC and CS signalled extracts from Tenth Army's report for 19 January.[35] Intentions for 20 January had also included the employment of elements of the Hermann Göring Division in a counter-attack in 94th Infantry Division's sector and the formation of a battle group consisting of 94th Infantry and 29th PG Divisions; elements of 3rd PG Division were again on the move. Orders for close support aircraft operations on 21 January

---

29. DEFE 3/131, VL 4302 of 19 January 1944.
30. DEFE 3/131, VLs 4308 of 19 January, 4324 of 20 January 1944.
31. DEFE 3/131, VL 4331 of 20 January 1944.
32. DEFE 3/131, VLs 4334 and 4335 of 20 January 1944.
33. DEFE 3/131, VL 4337 of 20 January 1944.
34. DEFE 3/131, VLs 4341 and 4342 of 20 January 1944.
35. DEFE 3/131, VL 4391 of 21 January 1944.

were signalled by GC and CS at 0124[36] and the information that
94th Infantry Division intended to try to close the gap in the main
defence line went out at 0359.[37] Decrypts of Tenth Army's report at
1800 on 20 January were signalled at 0757 and 1237 on 21 January.
The first decrypt showed XIV Panzer Corps under considerable
strain. In the Minturno area the Allies were threatening Santa
Maria Infante; a counter-thrust had been initiated. Allied pressure
was continuing in the Ausente valley and communications with that
area had been cut. 29th PG Division had recovered some ground.
Elements of the Hermann Göring Division were engaged in bitter
defensive fighting around Castelforte.[38] The second instalment reported 15th PG Division's successful repulse of the attempted
crossing of the Garigliano by US X Corps at San Ambrogio.[39]

In a signal sent with the highest priority at 0159 on 22 January
GC and CS told Allied commanders that Tenth Army's day report
for 20 January had disclosed that at 0900 on 21 January 1 Parachute
Corps was to take over operational command of the German Front
on the right of 15th PG Division. Its task was to regain the old main
defence line and for this purpose 90th PG Division would be under
its command. 3rd PG Division, less elements already committed
(in 5th Mountain Division's sector), was in Army reserve with a
view to operations in and south of the Cassino area.[40] A decrypt
sent at 1802 on 22 January confirmed that at 1300 on 21 January I
Parachute Corps was under Tenth Army and in command of 94th
Infantry, 29th and 90th PG Division.[41] But by now US VI Corps
was ashore at Anzio.

---

36. DEFE 3/131, VL 4393 of 21 January 1944.
37. DEFE 3/131, VL 4404 of 21 January 1944.
38. DEFE 3/131, VL 4422 of 21 January 1944.
39. DEFE 3/131, VL 4431 of 21 January 1944.
40. DEFE 3/131, VL 4464 of 22 January 1944.
41. DEFE 3/132, VL 4506 of 22 January 1944.

APPENDIX 9

Intelligence on GAF Bombing Operations at Anzio, January 1944

The intelligence yield for 24 January 1944 included Enigma decrypts about intended bomber operations at Anzio. A German naval message, sent out by GC and CS at 1514,[1] stated that fairly large formations of various types would fly low that afternoon and towards evening from Marseilles to Leghorn and on to Nettuno, via Siena if the weather was cloudless, and via Elba and Civitavecchia if it was overcast. A decrypt sent at 2047 added that activity would continue into the night 24–25 January; the last aircraft would be returning about 2200.[2] A message, sent by GC and CS soon after midnight, indicated another attack by Ju 88s overland to Nettuno from 2200 onwards.[3] Another German naval signal on 26 January referred to two waves of bombers routed via Ancona–Benedetto–east of Rome and returning via Grosseto.[4] This decrypt, sent out at 2353, was several hours later than the timing given for the first wave but preceded that given for the second wave. A report that the landing fleet and unloading operations had been attacked by 107 heavy bombers on the night 26–27 January was decrypted on 28 January.[5]

With these exceptions no warnings were received from high-grade Sigint about German bomber attacks, which were frequent but not particularly successful. AFHQ's intelligence summary issued on 11 April noted that little or no part had been played by the bomber forces in north Italy, probably as a result of damage inflicted in attacks on airfields by the Allied strategic bombing offensive at the end of January.[6] By 15 February London had appreciated that the enemy bomber effort in the preceding week had been confined to small first and last-light operations against shipping: some thirty aircraft had operated in the evening of 12 February. The Ju 88s in north Italy had been remarkably inactive, perhaps because inadequately trained crews were unable to cope with bad weather.

---

1. DEFE 3/132, VL 4650 of 24 January 1944.
2. DEFE 3/132, VL 4675 of 24 January 1944.
3. DEFE 3/132, VL 4699 of 26 January 1944.
4. DEFE 3/135, VL 4879 of 26 January 1944.
5. DEFE 3/133, VL 4999 of 28 January 1944.
6. WO 204/968, AFHQ Intelligence Summary No 85 of 11 April 1944.

Assessments of the strength of the GAF close support forces changed only marginally between the landing at Anzio on 22 January and the start of the major German counter-offensive on 16 February. These forces included 33–35 fighter-bombers and, although the total of single-engined fighters in Italy declined from 200 to 175, numbers in central Italy were maintained at around 100.[7] Apart from reconnaissance, and with rare exceptions as on 3 February when fighter-bombers and fighters were diverted to supplying Army elements west of Cassino with ammunition, and on 6 February when most sorties were again in the Cassino sector, the close support forces devoted their efforts to the beachhead front.[8] Their intentions were often known in advance from the Enigma,[9] but were in any case easily predictable.

---

7. WO 204/968, Nos 74–77 of 24 January, 1, 8 and 15 February 1944.
8. DEFE 3/135, VL 5493 of 4 February 1944.
9. eg DEFE 3/133, VL 4971 of 28 January; DEFE 3/134, VLs 5041 of 29 January, 5120 and 5175 of 30 January; DEFE 3/135, VLs 5430 and 5438 of 3 February; DEFE 3/138, VLs 6083 of 12 February, 6156 of 13 February; DEFE 3/139, VL 6299 of 15 February 1944.

APPENDIX 10

German Anxieties about Allied Ability to Locate U-boats

At the time the U-boats were withdrawn from the north Atlantic in May 1943 the U-boat Command was uncertain whether the ability of the Allies to locate the U-boats and divert the convoys was the result of treachery, the compromise of the Enigma or of some mysterious airborne radar which was proof against the *Metox* radar receiver it had distributed to U-boats in the autumn of 1942.[1] The last of these explanations had been supported in March 1943 by the GAF's discovery that the H2S ground-scanning radar of a crashed RAF bomber worked on 9.7 cm – a discovery which probably accounts for the fact that in June the British authorities learned from an Abwehr decrypt that the Abwehr's agents had been asked to find out how Allied aircraft used 10 cm transmissions against the U-boats. For some time however the U-boat Command was unconvinced by this evidence; its scientists assured it that the Allies could not have overcome the difficulties involved in operating centimetric ASV for U-boat location,[2] and they had themselves developed a device which, if fitted to the *Metox* receiver, enabled it to give warning of ASV transmissions that it could not otherwise detect.[3] By the end of April the U-boat Command's faith in this device, which had meanwhile been fitted in all U-boats, had been shattered by the continued successes of the Allies with evasive routeing and the many night locations of U-boats in Biscay that had followed Coastal Command's adoption of Mark III (centimetric) ASV at the beginning of March. In May, unable to explain the mystery, it ordered all possible precautions.[4] The precautions included the introduction of a new fourth wheel for the Shark Enigma; this was brought into force on 1 July.

During June and July 1943 the mystery remained unsolved, but a report from the Japanese Ambassador in Berlin, decrypted at GC and CS on 10 July and summarising an interview with Dönitz, stated that the Germans believed that the causes of the Allied successes were ' a new direction finder' and the resort to 'auxiliary aircraft carriers'. The report added that no method of countering

---

1. AIR 41/48, *The RAF in Maritime* War, Vol IV, pp 169–171.
2. Roskill, *The War at Sea*, Vol III Part I (1960), p 16.
3. AIR 41/48, pp 170–171.   4. ibid, p 171.

the direction finder (ie the location device) had yet been devised. At the end of July, however, the German investigations established that the *Metox* receiver emitted radiations, and the U-boat Command seized on this as the explanation it had been looking for: Allied aircraft were homing on to the radiations. The use of *Metox* was forbidden in dangerous areas, a ban which deprived the U-boats, except those with radar, of their best means of warning against attack, and priority was given to the development of a non-radiating search receiver – the *Hagenuk*.[5]*

The *Metox* explanation fitted with the continuing belief of Dönitz's technical advisers that 10 cm ASV was impracticable; and early in August it appeared to be borne out by a RAF POW who claimed that the Allies were able to home on to the radiations. By that time, moreover, suspicion had been deflected from cypher insecurity as the explanation by the fact that the new Enigma fourth wheel had not led to any reduction in the effectiveness of the Allied attacks on U-boats in Biscay or in the refuelling areas. And so much so that, when continuing Allied successes also undermined the argument that the *Metox* radiations had been the explanation, the U-boat Command became more and more convinced that the key to the problem must lie with Allied radar. During the autumn of 1943, as it reflected on the loss of so many of the *Monsun* U-boats† to attacks by carrier-borne aircraft, it judged that they had been victims of the 'age of radar' and concluded that the Allies 'had a system of plotting the boats as they moved southwards, occasionally checking their positions by radar and then awaiting favourable conditions of cloud and sun to carry out a decisive attack without using radar'.[7] And towards the end of 1943, following the establishment of a scientific intelligence department in OKM in September, it finally accepted that its troubles must be due to the fact that the Allies had developed centimetric ASV for use against the U-boats.[8]

At the end of October 1943 the U-boat Command began to equip the U-boats with the *Naxos* search receiver, a rudimentary device for giving warning of the proximity of aircraft using 10 cm ASV,

---

* Or *Wanze*. *Hagenuk* was the firm's name. *Wanze* was an abbreviation of Wellenanzeiger (frequency indicator). The Germans wasted precious time not only in developing a non-radiating search receiver but also in devising means against detection by infra red. The Allies knew of this preoccupation with infra red from the naval Enigma and played upon it by spreading reports through double agents that they were in fact achieving success by this means. This helped to delay the enemy's realisation that the U-boats were being detected by centimetric radar.[6]

† See above, pp 218, 229 et seq.

5.   ibid, pp 172–174; ADM 234/68, BR 305 (3), German Naval History Series, *The U-boat War in the Atlantic*, Vol III, p 54.
6.   *The Handling of Naval Special Intelligence*, pp 95–96.
7.   ADM 234/68, p 48.   8.   AIR 41/48, pp 174–175.

and with a radar set for detecting the aircraft itself, adapted from the GAF's ASV set (*Hohentwiel*). From the beginning of 1944, when Dönitz told Hitler that 'all our previous ideas about British location were wrong: it was 10 cm radar ... which had caused all the German losses',[9] a great effort was made to develop better search receivers. *Naxos* was gradually replaced first by the *Fliege* receiver, which was much more sensitive against 10 cm transmissions, and then by *Mücke*, a receiver developed to counter the next Allied advance, 3 cm ASV.[10] These innovations became known from the Enigma. The Admiralty first learned of *Naxos* in November 1943 when it informed the operational authorities that there were 'strong indications' that it was capable of detecting radar transmissions in the 10 cm band: at least eight boats were so fitted.[11] At the beginning of 1944 Enigma decrypts showed that the enemy had acquired full details of Allied use of centimetric ASV from aircrew of a crashed anti-submarine aircraft. On 3 January the Admiralty confirmed that *Naxos* covered the 10 cm band and told the operational authorities what tactics U-boats had been ordered to adopt when warning was received. The Admiralty added that all boats were probably now fitted, except for those in the Indian Ocean, and that the receiver could not be counted on to give useful warning.[12] A Shark decrypt disclosed that on 2 January Hitler had sent an order of the day to U-boat crews telling them that the ebb in their fortunes could be ascribed entirely to a 'single technical invention of our enemies'.[13] In February there was evidence that Germany's introduction of technical innovations had been accompanied by intensive research into further radar counter-measures: the Allies found that one of the U-boats sunk near the convoys ONS 29 and ON 224 in February had embarked a party of scientists to investigate radar and anti-radar techniques in operational conditions.[14] When captured, these scientists provided valuable information about the state of German technical counter-measures. Other developments followed from April 1944, including the introduction of a new radar decoy device (*Thetis*). By then, however, the enemy had accepted that the old-type U-boats were inadequate for operations in the Atlantic and, pending the delivery of new U-boats, was concentrating his efforts on equipping the old boats with *Schnorchel* to enable them to operate submerged. From June 1944 no U-boat was sent to sea unless it was equipped with both *Schnorchel* and *Hohentwiel*.[15]

---

9. ADM 234/68, p 53.   10. ibid, p 57.

11. ADM 223/186, Ultra signal 1317/25 November 1943; Naval Headlines No 865 of 16 November 1943.

12. ADM 223/188, Ultra signal 0317/3 January 1944.

13. DEFE 3/725, ZTPGU 20744.

14. Roskill, op cit, Vol III Part I, p 253.

15. ADM 234/68, pp 57, 61.

Intelligence on New U-boats from Japanese Diplomatic Decrypts

(i) NID 12/SI/Tech/003 of 30 May 1944
U-boat policy, as disclosed by Admiral Doenitz

On the 24th April [1944] Vice Admiral Abe (Head of Japanese Naval Mission in Berlin) and the Japanese Naval Attaché, Berlin, visited Admiral Doenitz. The latter had invited them in order to answer Admiral Abe's request for information about the German high speed U/boats. Among others present at the meeting were the Chief of German Naval Operations, Meisel, and 'the Chief Constructor', Fuchs.

1. The Germans started with what may be described as a 'pep talk' about the war situation and pointed out that the failure of any invasion on the Western front was inevitable and that the war would therefore go on for some time so that Allied dissensions would turn the situation to Germany's advantage.

2. The Germans had therefore decided to resume the U/boat offensive with two new types of U/boat with high underwater speed, operating mainly underwater. Work was going ahead and new boats should be ready by the autumn of 1944. The earlier types had proved incapable of achieving success against Allied radar and aircraft.

3. Both types had a fish-shaped hull; battery-power three times that of the old type; and an extensible ventilating shaft (presumably SCHNORKEL)* for charging batteries submerged.

4. The larger type was intended for Atlantic operations; the smaller type for Mediterranean operations. The smaller type could be transported overland.

5. Particulars were given as follows –

   (i) *Larger type*
      About 1,600 tons
      Armament: 6 torpedo tubes and 14 reserve torpedoes
                  Four 3 cm machine guns.

---

* This anglicisation of *Schnorchel* was universally used in intelligence documents.

Speed: 18 knots (surface)
            15.6 knots (submerged)
Endurance: Surface – 15,500 miles at 10 knots
                      28,500 miles at 6 knots
            Submerged – 24 miles at 17 knots
                         450 miles at 3 knots
(Comment: It is noted that the maximum submerged speed figures are inconsistent.)

(ii) *Smaller type*
     About 250 tons
     Armament: 2 torpedo tubes (no reserve torpedoes)
               No guns
     Speed: 13 knots (surface)
               13.1 knots (submerged)
     Endurance: Surface – 1,350 miles at 9.7 knots
                Submerged – 300 miles at 3 knots.

6. Experiments to test the likely effect of Allied counter-measures had been carried out in local waters, which had proved that the new types were hard to locate by radar and could easily evade depth-charge attack by reason of their high underwater speed and an increase in their permissible depth to 135 metres. The Germans thought that, until the Allies had had time to develop counter-measures, they would be able to do nothing about the new types. The Germans considered existing Allied sound and electro-magnetic detectors inadequate. For these reasons the Germans were particularly anxious to keep the new developments secret.

7. The Germans then said that the Japanese had not been told of these U/boats before as the experiments were incomplete, and to inform them of matters on which experiments were in progress would only lead to confusion; it was hoped that details of a new torpedo with which the Germans were experimenting might be given in about a fortnight.

8. Admiral Abe further reported that he had thanked Doenitz for this close co-operation and he pointed out to Tokyo that while co-operation between the Germans and the Japanese Navy had always been good, it was now improving steadily owing to the war situation having grown more acute for both Japan and Germany and the fact that the Japanese Navy had always been frank and revealing to the Germans. The Naval Attaché would telegraph the details of the U/boats to Tokyo.

Comment:

(1) The larger type is believed to be identical with a new prefabricated 245 ft type of U/boat recently seen by air reconnaissance in German yards. 9 examples have been seen building and

2 have already been launched after not more than 6 weeks assembling on the slips.

(2) The smaller type may, though evidence is inconclusive, be identical with a type of small U/boat, 100 ft long, recently seen by air reconnaissance in German yards. 7 examples have been seen under construction and 2 have already been launched.

(3) 'Experiments in local waters' probably refers to U/boat exercises and experiments frequently reported since Autumn 1943 in the Sonderborg (Denmark) and Kiel Bay areas.

(4) It is noteworthy that the propulsion of both types is a development of the established method, ie, diesels (apparently with addition of extensible air intake – SCHNORKEL) for surface and periscope-depth passage and improved electric motors for submerged passage. By negative implication it appears that underwater propulsion by a form of closed-cycle engine, which is believed to have been the subject of German experiments in 1943, has not been brought to a practical stage by German U/boat designers.

(ii) NID 12/SI/Tech/005 of 8 October 1944 1,600 Ton Type XXI U-Boat – Production Methods and Technical Details

On 29 August 1944 Vice Admiral Abe (Head of the Japanese Naval Mission in Berlin) and the Japanese Naval Attaché, Berlin, accompanied by German technical officials, visited Danzig to inspect the large-scale production of the 1,600 ton Type XXI U/boat. The Naval Attaché reported on the visit to Tokyo on 12th September, and he supplemented his report on 13th September by his personal observations. The following is a summary of the information contained in his two reports.

Method of Construction

(i) The hull consists of 8 round sections, which are made separately at the Schichau yard, Danzig, and the three shipyards at Gdynia. These sections are then joined together at the Schichau yard, Danzig, where the launching takes place.

(ii) Each of the sections is carried around the factory or the stocks on a huge wagon in a 3 or 4 day cycle, during which time the outer casing, inboard and outboard pipes, electric leads, main engines, auxiliary engines and propeller shafts are fitted. The result is that each section is separately completed (except for the fitting of the batteries), including armament and all equipment, even down to the loading of ballast and painting. The maximum weight of the heaviest section – the one containing the control room – is 170 tons.

(iii) The final assembly takes place in the Schichau yard. The several sections are hoisted up on to the stocks, the hull is joined up by welding, and the various pipes and electric leads are connected up. The vessel is then launched.

(iv) Vice Admiral Abe and the Naval Attaché were also informed that the Type XXI was constructed by a similar method at Bremen (where the final assembly was done at the Deschimag yard) and at Hamburg (where the final assembly was done at the Blohm and Voss yard).

Comment: This description of the method of constructing the Type XXI is amply corroborated by evidence of aerial reconnaissance, secret reports and captured documents.

The process of construction falls into four distinct phases:

(a)   Manufacture of basic castings and individual parts at dispersed factories, mostly inland; numerous factories have been reported.

(b)   Complete assembly of separate sections and conning towers at shipyards; the following yards are seen to be engaged in this stage of construction:

Deschimag, Bremen; Danzigerwerft, Danzig: Blohm and Voss, Hamburg; Howaldt, Hamburg; Deutsche Werke, Kiel; Germania, Kiel; Howaldt, Kiel; Flenderwerke, Luebeck; Vulkanwerft, Vegesack; Kriegsmarinewerft, Wilhemshaven.

(c)   Transport of finished sections by land or sea to three yards (at present) for final assembly:

Schichau, Danzig; Deschimag, Bremen; Blohm and Voss, Hamburg.

(d)   Launching and fitting out alongside.

2. *Construction Time*

(i) Excluding the time taken to make the inner hull parts, which are separately sub-contracted to inland iron works, the time taken in constructing the different parts (Comment: Assembly of separate sections is probably meant) varies from 3–6 weeks according to the difficulties peculiar to each.

(ii) The final assembly on the slips is planned to take 6 weeks.

(iii) Fitting out between launch and commissioning is planned to take 3 weeks.

(iv) Production is at present only just getting started, and the above progress has not yet been achieved in practice. Work on the first U/Boat was begun about mid-March, 1944, and the boat was commissioned on 19th July, 1944.

Comment: At Schichau, Danzig, where, on 15th September, 1944, 12 boats were assembling on the slips, 3 were fitting out alongside, and one or two had already commissioned, the time on the slips has varied between about 6 weeks and about 11 weeks, and the fitting out period has varied between about 7½ weeks and about 9 weeks.

The first Type XXI U/Boat observed assembling at Schichau, Danzig, was seen to be laid down between 8th March and 14th April, and to have been launched between 14th and 19th April.

3. *Planned Output Programme*
   (i) The planned monthly output is 8 U/Boats at Schichau, Danzig; 11 U/Boats at Deschimag, Bremen; and 11 U/Boats at Blohm and Voss, Hamburg: ie. 30 U/Boats monthly. (48,000 tons.)
   (ii) Speer, Minister of Munitions, previously mentioned to the Japanese Ambassador, Berlin, Oshima, that the Germans planned to reach a monthly output of 58,000 tons by December 1944.

Comment: The present situation, including all three yards, as far as it is known from aerial reconnaissance and Special Intelligence, is as follows:–

On Slips	*Fitting Out*	*Commissioned*
37 U/Boats	13 U/boats	11 U/Boats

It is estimated on present reconnaissance evidence and on the probably minimum assumption that the production rate will remain the same as in September 1944, that the monthly output by December will be over 4 at Hamburg, 6 at Bremen and 7 at Danzig, ie. over 16 monthly (over 23,500 tons). The Germans may therefore have given the Japanese an exaggerated figure, but evidence is not sufficient to discredit the figure with assurance.

4. *Performance and Technical Details*
   On 29th August four Type XXI U/Boats were undergoing official tests at the Acceptance Trials. In addition Vice Admiral Abe and the Naval Attaché saw 7 or 8 others fitting out after launching, and inspected one of them.

Comment: It is estimated that, by 29th August, 4 Type XXI U/boats had commissioned and 6 were fitting out at Hamburg; 1 or two had commissioned and 4 were fitting out at Bremen; and 2 had completed (though possibly not commissioned) and 3 were fitting out at Danzig.

Tests in many different conditions were necessary, but, as tests were not complete, the true performance of the Type XXI was not known. The Naval Attaché, however, was given the following results of trials to date:

(a) *Underwater Speed*: 16 knots (the Germans expected to increase it to 17 or 18 knots).

(b) *Underwater Manoeuvrability*: Remains good at all speeds. Retractable diving rudder not needed at above 4 or 5 knots. At high speed, also, automatic control is used. Alteration of course by means of separate hand-operated steering gear is said to be easy.

Comment: 'Diving rudder' probably means forward hydroplane.

(c) *Minimum underwater speed*: Lowest possible speed on cruising motor is *0.5–1 Knot*: in this case, with a view to silent submerged passage, reduction is by driving the propeller shaft by 12 V-shaped rubber belts. When the main motor is used, however, this is done by reduction gearing.

(d) *Turning Circle*: Turning circles are large, *875 yards (800 metres) surfaced and 437 yards (400 metres) submerged*, and present a problem.

(e) *Diving*: The boat has 5 main tanks. No Kingstons. Experiments being made to alter the area of the flooding inlets. The Germans appear to be trying to reduce the time taken to submerge completely. The Naval Attaché was told that the time between opening vents and complete submergence was *15 seconds*.

(f) *Torpedo Tubes*: No pistons, inboard venting being used.

(g) *Guns*:	One twin 20mm M.G. forward and another aft on the bridge. To lessen water-resistance when submerged the guns are mounted inside what are really streamlined turrets. The Naval Attaché was told that the 20mm guns would eventually be replaced by 30mm ones.
(h) *Schnorkel*:	Fitted.

5. *Japanese Naval Attaché's Personal Observations*

(i) Construction on this system is characterized by specialization. As the workmen do the same job over and over again in the 3 or 4 day cycle there is no need for them to be skilled men. The fact that the same components are always fitted into the same places makes remarkable efficiency possible. Since the fitting of all armament and equipment is carried out separately before final assembly, the work is simple and easy.

Thus the system has the great advantage of permitting a rapid increase in production rate. From his observations at Danzig the Naval Attaché considered that, as far as the technical side of the matter is concerned, the planned output of 30 U/Boats a month should be reached before very long.

The chief disadvantage of the system, however, is the fact that, if one of the construction places is damaged, the whole work will be held up. Since 'enemy' air raids are likely to get heavier and heavier, while German AA defence is inadequate, there is room for considerable doubt as to whether construction will in fact progress according to plan.

(ii) Change-over from the old to the new system necessitates a large amount of reconstruction of factories and slips. This requires large quantities of steel and heavily draws on skilled labour; an even greater disadvantage is that the work precludes the building of ships. The Naval Attaché was told that the work of reconstruction was begun in the shipyard at Danzig in October, 1943, and took 2,500 tons of steel. The Naval Attaché expressed his admiration to the Germans for the way in which they had determinedly gone ahead in spite of the difficulties mentioned above; and he lays emphasis on the fact that the change-over has caused a suspension for nearly a year of U/Boat building, while at this most crucial stage of the war the new U/Boats have not yet been able to join battle.

Comment: It is not clear whether the Naval Attaché wishes by his last observation to underline the determination of the Germans to carry their programme through despite difficulty and delay, or to suggest that the Germans have left it too late and lost the gamble.

(iii) With regard to the tactical value of the new U/Boats, the Naval Attaché states that he and Vice Admiral Abe have only inspected one of them at its moorings, and that they have only heard a general description of its performance in the official trials, many experiments being still incomplete. They therefore cannot reach definite conclusions. But it would seem at first glance that the Type XXI is an epoch-making U/Boat, to the construction of which the Germans have devoted every possible effort and made use of practical fighting experience as well as the cream of scientific knowledge. Though the boat will no doubt need certain improvements the Naval Attaché felt that its tactical value would be very great.

He thinks that, as it is intended for exclusively underwater operation, it should as a rule be used in harbours or at frequent points on shipping routes, and that if employed in the open sea the co-operation of aircraft will be essential. (He notes finally, that it has no anchor and no deck railings.)

Comment: The Japanese have since been told by Doenitz that some of the Type XXI U/Boats will be sent to the Indian Ocean area at some unspecified date in the near future.

APPENDIX 12

German Meteorological Operations in Greenland from 1942–1944

In August 1942 the *Sachsen*, one of the trawlers which had patrolled as floating stations for the German Navy in 1940 and 1941, succeeded in landing her party in Greenland; neither the Enigma nor any other source gave warning of her departure from Tromsö. Moreover, although she was sighted in the ice off Greenland by the US Coastguard Service ship *Northland's* aircraft soon after her arrival,[1] no other intelligence about the expedition was received until April 1943, when the naval Enigma disclosed that Gruppe Nord was anxious that the land party should continue reporting in spite of the fact that its whereabouts had been detected – it had been surprised by a US sledge patrol in March 1943 – and that a relief expedition was being prepared. Towards the end of May, after this intelligence had been passed to the US authorities,[2] the party was bombed by the USAAF. The GAF Enigma then disclosed that a FW 200 had dropped supplies for the party on 26 May and in June it emerged from the naval Enigma that no less an authority than OKM was anxious about the threat to the station, but no further information was obtained before the expedition was evacuated by air on 17 June.[3]

At that time, the German parties in Spitzbergen having also suffered a series of setbacks*, the German authorities decided that in future meteorological expeditions must be sent to areas that were even more inaccessible to the Allies and must be able to defend themselves. But such was their need for weather reports that the next expedition for Greenland left Narvik in the trawler *Coburg* in the middle of August 1943; she was to have been escorted by a U-boat but in bad weather it had failed to pick her up.[4] By the end of August, at about the time of her arrival, the Enigma had disclosed that she had sailed. But no further intelligence was obtained until November 1943, when the Enigma reported that the GAF had

---

* See above, p 253 n†.

1. *The Polar Record* (Scott Polar Research Institute, Cambridge). Vol 6, No 42, July 1951, p 199.
2. ADM 223/117, Ultra signal 1431/16 May 1943.
3. *Polar Record*, Vol 6, No 42, p 201.　　　　4. ibid, p 208 et seq.

dropped supplies to the *Coburg* and that she was having difficulties in the ice. Working sometimes on land and sometimes in the ice, the party continued its transmissions until 22 April 1944, when its camp was attacked by an Allied ground patrol.[5] Thereafter it was kept under observation by Allied ground and air forces until it was evacuated by air on 3 June.[6] On 27 May the Enigma had already disclosed that the ship and the station's long-wave transmitter had been destroyed. Two days after the evacuation an Enigma signal was decrypted in which Captain U/Boats Norway thanked the party for the effective support it had given him and congratulated it on its safe return.

The next expedition, which left Tromsö for Greenland at the end of August 1944, was less successful. On reaching Greenland in the trawler *Kehdingen* under U/boat escort on 1 September, it was met by the *Northland*, which forced the trawler to scuttle and captured her passengers. On the same day the decrypt of the Enigma signal from the U/boat disclosed this misfortune, adding that the U/boat had unsuccessfully fired a torpedo at the *Northland*. There is no evidence, however, that the *Northland*'s success owed anything to advance intelligence about this expedition, and this is also true of the further success of the US Coastguard Service in intercepting an expedition in October 1944. This final enemy attempt to land a party in Greenland followed on the news of the loss of the *Kehdingen*, when the Germans diverted to Greenland an expedition that was being prepared for Franz Josef's Land. It reached Greenland in the trawler *Externsteine*, again under U/boat escort, at the end of September, but was sighted by air patrols on 2 and 3 October, and on 4 October the party was captured and the trawler caught by the US Coast Guard ships *Eastwind* and *Southwind*.[7] The NID had at that time received no intelligence about the expedition; it heard of its capture from Washington on 9 October.

---

5. ibid, p 210.   6. ibid, p 211.   7. ibid, p 216.

APPENDIX 13

Intelligence Reports Relating to Attacks on the *Tirpitz*

(i) Tirpitz's anti-torpedo net enclosure

After the war a myth grew up that correct intelligence of the triple anti-torpedo net enclosure surrounding the *Tirpitz* was available but had not been passed on to the X-craft. It is claimed that the British Naval Attaché Stockholm was incensed because the crews had not been briefed about the existence of a double AT net round the *Tirpitz* of which he had provided details and a sketch map. This, he said, he had obtained, in response to specific requests from the Admiralty, from young Norwegian 'resistance men'.[1] This is consistent with NID's claim that it provided details of the mesh and dimensions of the torpedo nets round the *Tirpitz*.[2]

The story appears to be garbled. PR had established that the *Tirpitz* was surrounded by close nets which consisted of three lines and were for AT protection. What could not be established by PR was the depth to which these nets extended. FO Submarine's report on the operation of February 1944 says 'It was considered unlikely* that they would reach the bottom in water 20 fathoms deep'; they would extend down only 50 ft.[3] This is confirmed in an account of X-7's operation written in 1953, which states that X-7 chose to try to go underneath the net at 75 ft which should have been well below the maximum depth of such nets.[4]†

This suggests that the 50 ft depth of net was an arbitrary assumption imposed on the photographs by experts. Moreover, the

---

* Presumably by the boom defence experts at the Admiralty.

† This account implies that while in the end X-7 was able to deliver her attack she would have been able to do so more efficiently if she had not had the preliminary struggle to get through the nets.[5] As we have seen above, p 260, she did so by only what FO Submarines later called 'some extraordinarily lucky chance'.[6] In his report of 2 February 1944, he specifically said that X-7's struggle with the AT net on her way in interfered with her attack.[7]

1. McLachlan, *Room 39*, (1968), p 211; ADM 223/210, BNA's War Diary, p 72.
2. McLachlan, op cit, p 355.
3. ADM 199/888, FOSM's report of 2 February 1944.
4. Warren and Benson, *Above the Waves* (1953), p 130.
5. ibid, p 132.
6. ADM 199/888, FOSM's final report, 26 July 1945.
7. ibid, FOSM's report of 2 February 1944.

possibility that NID was originally correct*, but overruled by experts, is suggested in Admiralty comment after the war on FO Submarine's final report of July 1945, drawn up in the light of the return of the X-craft captains from captivity. The Director of Boom Defence stated: 'The original opinion of German multiple line nets was that they were "staggered" or "stepped" to cover the full depth and this was reported in [a minute by NID] dated 1.1.43'. The DBD added:

> 'Records recently obtained from Germany refer to a triple line of nets around the anchorage, two lines described as "Torpedoschutznetze 18 × 18 m" (A/T nets, 58 ft × 58 ft) and the third line as "Tiefenschutz bis 36m", corrected in pencil to 45 m (deep defence to 117 ft or 146 ft).'[8]

(ii) *Enigma decrypts on Operation* Source

OIC/SI 724†
8 October 1943

From	*Too* *22 Sept*	*Purport*
Battlegroup	0831A	Midget S/M destroyed inside 'TIRPITZ' net barrage at 0830A. 4 Englishmen taken prisoner.
Battlegroup	1009A	S/M Alarm in KAA Fjord. 'SCHARNHORST' to send an A/C to Kaafjord.
Battlegroup	1032A	'SCHARNHORST' A/C is to return to ship forthwith.
Battlegroup	1048A	Send Power ship 'WATT' to 'TIRPITZ' forthwith. (*Note*: 'WATT' is reported to be used to charge U/boat accumulators, and to be capable of electric welding.)

* It is not known how the Norwegian resistance obtained the information; it is unlikely that it could have been by visual observation.
† Reproduced from ADM 223/170.

8. ibid, DBD minute of 6 September 1945.

(ii)   *Enigma decrypts on Operation* Source

Battlegroup (Via STEINBRINK)	105?A (sic)	Heavy explosion 60 metres to port of 'TIRPITZ' at 0912A. (Submarine destroyed by time bombs.) 500 cubic metres (of water in the ship).
		A second S/M (was destroyed by time bombs) 300 metres (on ship's starboard bow) at 0935A. Commanding Officer was taken prisoner.
		A third (S/M) was fired on when 600 metres distant, on the starboard beam, several hits being observed.
		(*Note*: Portions in brackets were corrupt but it is thought that their sense is conveyed correctly.)
Battlegroup (to 'SCHARN-HORST')	1056A	Break off firing (exercises). Keep on the move.
FL/Lofoten	1209A	One BV 138 due to take off at 1215A to search area radius of 100 miles from 70 deg 37½'N, 22 deg 15'S for possible launching vessel.
FL/Lofoten	1250A	1 BV 138 up at 1241 with radar.
Adm Northern Waters	1259A	3 A/S vessels to report to battlegroup for employment. Lofoten to fly inshore water recce as far as 100 miles in coastal area and then A/S hunt in Altenfjord and approach route. (5 A/S vessels left Honningsvaag at 1400A for Altenfjord.)
Battlegroup	13–6A (sic)	'SCHARNHORST' is to go into net enclosure at Sopnes. 'LUTZOW' to anchor in Langfjord at her own discretion. 'SCHARNHORST' to detach destroyer to Kaafjord.

(ii)   *Enigma decrypts on Operation* Source

Battlegroup	1621A	Keep S/M alarm in Kaafjord absolutely secret.
'SCHARN-HORST'	1632A	Anchored provisionally in Langfjord Botn 1600A.
FL/Lofoten	1903A	1 BV 138 down at 1816 without enemy sighting; area covered exhaustively.
'SCHARN-HORST'	2046A	Owing to weather, lateness of tugs and darkness setting in, intend to enter net enclosure AM 23 September.
Battlegroup	2105A	'LUTZOW' is anchored at Tappeluft. No T/P connection.
SO Harbour Defence Flotilla	2216A	Fishing smack traffic prohibited Vargsund–Stjernsund–(?) Kaafjord.

23 Sept

Battlegroup	1541A	Short report on Submarine attack of 22 Sept was sent by T/P via Tromsö at 0100, 23 Sept.
Battlegroup	1936A	(? Recommendations:) a. Improvement in net protection of Kaafjord and Langfjord. b. Electrical warning device in circuit (portion missed). (Appreciation:) In our view repetition of S/M operation in this form in the near future improbable as the advantage of surprise is gone.
Gruppe Nord-Fleet	2139A	Enquiry whether submarines came through opened boom gaps or through the nets.
'SCHARN-HORST'	2048	1. Judging by conditions last winter, do not consider berthing in Bogen Bay net enclosures advisable when strong Westerly winds are prevailing.

(ii) Enigma decrypts on Operation Source

2. Consider Langfjord to be a suitable winter berth for the following reasons:
a. Narrow long entrance. . . .
b. Langfjord is more difficult to see into by air reconnaissance than Kaafjord. Owing to the narrowness of the fjord, attacks by A/S Torpedo offer little prospect of success.
c. Stocks of nets at Sopnes and Rivabukta permit nets to be laid in two main directions.
d. Should weather force vessel(s) to leave the net enclosure they can anchor temporarily in Langfjord Botn where there is magnificent holding ground. This can easily be enclosed by anti-torpedo protection.

25 Sept.

Battlegroup	0717A	Increased alertness against sabotage danger.
Sea Defence Commandant, Trondheim	1805A	Warning to Listening Stations and Look-out posts against English midget submarines.

3 Oct

Operation Division (to FO Cruisers)	0756A	Report at once whether gate to Barbrudalen net enclosure was closed on night before midget submarine attack and during the forenoon.
Battlegroup	1028A	1. The boom gap of the Barbrudalen net enclosure was open during the night prior to the attack, 21–22 Sept, and in the forenoon, owing to continuous boat traffic with Bossekop T/P Station.

(ii)   Enigma decrypts on Operation Source

		2. During the hours of darkness it is guarded by a fog cutter, manned by personnel from 'TIRPITZ'.
		3. 'TIRPITZ's' listening post was manned until o6oo (full daylight).
Naval Chief Command, Norway	0735A	Where is A/T net with depth protection being laid in Langfjord? Lay out net so that it is impossible to dive underneath.
Netlayer 2	1059A	Fourfold Anti-Torpedo Defence with depth protection closes off Langford – Botn about one mile WSW of VARDEKEI (?) Light. According to barrage plan and by soundings it has been ensured that depth protection rests on bottom everywhere. Diving under it is impossible.

(iii)   'TIRPITZ' – State of Readiness

OIC/SI 840*
27 January 1944

1. Prior to the 22nd September [1943], permission had been given for 'Tirpitz' to undergo a longish period not at war readiness and extensive granting of leave whilst in Northern Norway.

2. On 22nd September 'Tirpitz', then in Kaafjord was damaged in an attack carried out on her by British midget submarines. Her initial report, one and half hours after the attack, reported 500 tons of water inboard. A Commission was appointed to investigate the damage; the preliminary results of the examination were to be teleprinted to Germany on 14 October and the Commission left for Germany by air on 16 October. In the meantime a foreman fitter from Brown, Boveri and Co, makers of electrical appliances and diesels, had visited the ship and a report was called for on 3rd

---

* Reproduced from ADM 223/171.

October as to whether the requirements of fitters and spare parts had been agreed with him.

3. On 15 October it was reported that the power installation of the ship was unserviceable, but the protection of the ship was guaranteed. Possibly only one dynamo room would be serviceable for a period of the refit, but it would be adequate for the protection of the ship and to keep the guns at readiness. The primary and secondary armaments would each have one forward turret ready for action at all times and 50 per cent of the flak would be ready. Agreement had been reached for personnel to proceed on leave in three batches of 600 each, beginning on 1 November 1943.

4. On 17th October 'Tirpitz' requested 3 power ships for use of 'Tirpitz' and 'Scharnhorst' as 'Tirpitz' had only one electric motor fit to be operated for a short time only.

5. It is known by PRU that the repair ship 'Neumark' was in Altenfjord at the time of the attack and had moved alongside 'Tirpitz' by 23rd September. It was evidently intended that the repair ship, 'Huascaran' in Narvik should move round to Kaafjord at the end of October, but her departure was delayed owing to emergency repairs including under-water welding, which had to be carried out to the tanker 'Schleswig', damaged during air attack off Bodo on 4th October. The 'Huascaran' eventually arrived Altenfjord about 26th November.

6. The 'Monterosa' (14,000 GRT) formerly employed transporting troops between Germany and Oslo, proceeded to Altenfjord about 28th November, carrying workmen and special equipment for repairing 'Tirpitz'.

7. On 19th December, in a message to Kiel Dockyard, requesting the despatch of gunnery materials, 'Tirpitz' asked that they should be sent 'independently of the caisson (or cofferdam)' and that the latter should be sent up to Altenfjord in sections where it could be welded together.

8. Since the beginning of October 'Tirpitz' has sent many messages to Kiel requesting supplies of various descriptions for carrying out repairs, these included 20 tons of carbide for acetylene welding.

9. In a message dated 30th December, 'Tirpitz' expressed grave concern at the inability of the 100 ton crane, which had sailed from Trondheim on 25 December, to reach Altenfjord. It was pointed out that even if the available labour were organised in the most efficient manner possible, the punctual execution of the necessary gunnery repairs entirely depended upon the provision in good time of a crane with adequate lifting capacity, and that without such a

crane the gunnery programme could not even progress according to plan.

10. The 15th March had apparently been mentioned in correspondence as the anticipated completion date of all the work being carried out at Altenfjord, and it was pointed out that, as far as gunnery repairs were concerned, this date could only be adhered to if a 100 ton crane were to arrive by 10th January at the latest. It was urged that, in the absence of a large crane, one of 20 tons capacity should be provided, in order to cut down to a minimum 'the stoppage of gunnery repairs which are of life-and-death importance'.

11. It was added that these circumstances in no way affected the completion of 'ship construction, engine construction and electrical engineering work' by 15th March.

12. A 20 ton crane from Narvik arrived Altenfjord at the beginning of January but the 100 ton crane was completely wrecked shortly after leaving Trondheim and the crane pontoon with wreckage of the crane returned to Trondheim about the middle of January.

Conclusion

Hull, engineering and electrical repairs to 'Tirpitz' are expected to be completed on 15 March, but completion of gunnery repairs is likely to be delayed for some time after that date, and until then 'Tirpitz' will not be operationally fit for sea. Even when all these repairs have been completed, 'Tirpitz' cannot be considered as operationally effective for prolonged periods at sea, as she has not docked for two and a half years.

APPENDIX 14

Admiralty Ultra Signals Concerning the Sinking of the *Scharnhorst*, 11 to 27 December 1943*

(The times of origin of all Admiralty signals were in 'A' time ie GMT plus 1 hour.)

TOO of
Admiralty
Ultra Signal

11 December

1052   On 9 December SCHARNHORST announced intentions to carry out exercises in Altenfjord on 14 December.

15 December

1816   At 0800A/15 December a vessel presumed to be a destroyer reported to SCHARNHORST and 4th Destroyer Flotilla that she had left Kaafjord, speed 29 knots. *Comment.* Purpose not known but there is no reason to believe SCHARN-HORST has left Altenfjord area.

17 December

0110   SCHARNHORST and destroyer Z29 left a place presumed to be Kaafjord or Langfjord at 0830A/15 December. *Comment.* It appears possible that exercises referred to in AM 111052 may have been delayed. There is no indication that any main unit has left Altenfjord area.

19 December

2149   On 19 December air reconnaissance from North Norway for presumed convoy was intended. *Comment.* No details of reconnaissance received.

20 December

0649   [This signal stated that at 1645/18 December two of four U/boats at sea sighted a presumed convoy between North Norway and Bear Island but that no contact ensued. Attacking areas were allocated to the four U/boats at 0412/19 December. JW55A was in the vicinity at the time.]

---

* Compiled from signals in ADM 223/186.

TOO of
Admiralty
Ultra Signal

0752   At 1823/18 December Battle Group was put to three hours
        notice. Reconnaissance from Lofotens against convoy which
        was certainly to be assumed, and heavy forces probably at
        sea was cancelled at 1025/19 owing to weather.

21 December
2330   Battle Group reverted to 6 hours notice at 1645A/21
        December.

22 December
2158   [This signal showed latest U/boat dispositions in the oper-
        ational area and disclosed that further boats were being
        allocated to the Arctic force making 20 in all.]

23 December
0146   Convoy JW 55B was sighted by German aircraft at 1045A/
        22 December. At 1925A a U/boat was ordered to operate
        against convoy if situation was favourable. *Comment.* Position
        of U/boat not known.

1939   At 1300A 22 December Battle Group was brought to 3 hours
        notice again.

2140   AM 230146. Enemy appreciation from this sighting was that
        convoy was steering 045 degrees at 10 knots from latitude 63
        degs 50' N, longitude 04 degs 50' W. [U/boats] C and E
        were thereupon ordered to proceed at top speed to area
        between latitude 66 degs 20' N, and 67 degs 10' N and
        longitudes 09 degs 30' E and 11 degs 45' E.
        2. AM 23 December [U/boat] A was proceeding via
        approximate position latitude 68 degs 30' N, longitude 10
        degs 30' E to area between latitudes 72 degs 36' N, and 73
        degs 30' N and longitudes 20 degs 00' East and 23 degs 00'
        East.
        3. [U/boat] N was ordered to report ice limit to northward
        of his patrol area.
        4. [U/boat] U was to leave Narvik pm 22 December to
        northward.
        Comment to para 1. The enemy A/C had reported 40
        transports.   .

TOO of
Admiralty
Ultra Signal

24 December

0140   [Contained instructions issued 1735/22 December to two U/
boats to occupy patrol areas south west of Bear Island.]

0540   [Revised instructions to two U/boats in 0140 and six others
to form extended patrol line south-west of Bear Island and
to expect GAF reconnaissance on 24 December.]

0550   Consequent upon sighting of convoy JW 55B on 23 December Germans appreciate that convoy is making for Bear
Island area possibly covered by a strong battle group.
2. GAF intentions for 24 December from Lofoten area include recce with four BV 138s with Radar in the area Bodo
– latitude 72 degs, 45' N, longitude 04 degs, 00' E – latitude
70 degs, 00' N, longitude 00 degs 00' E – Tromso. Turning
point at 1130A.
3. At 2324A 23 December SCHARNHORST was informed
that German U/boat was not in contact with convoy bound
for North Russia.

1025   At 1342A 22 December Admiral Northern Waters requested
Admiral Polar Coast to make preparations for departure of
battle group.
Comment. Up to 0700A/24th there have been no signs that
battle group has left Alten Fiord.

1312   [Estimated positions of U/boats on passage in the operational area.]

25 December

0210   German aircraft from Lofoten area reported convoy in latitude 70 degs, 27' N, longitude 03 degs, 25' N at 1220A 24
December, course 30 degs, speed 8 knots.

0215   [Revised patrol areas for 8 U/boats south-west of Bear Island
ordered at 1423/24 December.]

0550   GAF reconnaissance intentions for 25 December from Lofoten area include
a. Convoy recce by 3 BV 38 aircraft with radar in area
Tromso – latitude 70 degs 37' North, longitude 20 degs 45'
East – latitude 74 degs 07' North, longitude 12 degs 05' East
– latitude 72 degs 52' North, longitude 07 degs 15' East –
Tromso.

TOO of
Admiralty
Ultra Signal

b. Search for what is thought to be a heavy force approaching from the Southwest which has been D/F'd, to be carried out by 1 aircraft with radar and 2 without radar in area Tromso – latitude 69 degs 52′ North, longitude 17 degs 15′ East – latitude 72 degs 42′ North, longitude 06 degs 55′ East – latitude 70 degs 52′ North, latitude 00 15′ East – 69 degs 52′ North, longitude 17 degs 15′ East – Tromso.

1350   U/boat W reported at 0901A 25 December that convoy steering 060 degs had passed over him in approximately latitude 72 deg 25′ North, longitude 12 degs 30′ East.

1557   AM 251350. At 1045A 25 December the other 7 U/boats were ordered to operate on the basis of report from W.

W was still in contact with destroyers and unidentified vessels on North Easterly course in latitude 73 degs, 33′ North, longitude 12 degs 30′ East at 1102A 25 December. Those U/boats will be known as Group E.

2142   At 1158A 25 December an R Boat was ordered to proceed to SCHARNHORST in Langfjord, where she was to receive further orders.

26 December

0130   At 1530A 25 December Admiral Commanding Northern Waters informed Battle Group and Admiral Polar Coast "Codeword EPILEPSY 1700A/25 December". *Comment.* Meaning not yet evident. ULTRA information will be available with a delay of some hours until 1200A/26 December but will not necessarily be complete for the North Norway area.

0132   [Two U/boats reported indecisive contact with convoy pm 26 December. Group E to assume convoy steering 070 deg.]

0217   EMERGENCY
SCHARNHORST probably sailed 1800A/25 December.

0218   AM 260130. A patrol vessel presumably in the Altenfjord area was informed at 1715 that SCHARNHORST would pass outward bound from 1800A/25 December.
2. AM 250550. 5 of these aircraft landed between 1300 and 1600A/25 December without having made any sightings.

TOO of
Admiralty
Ultra Signal

The sixth aircraft is overdue but an aircraft reported convoy in latitude 72 degs 52′ North, longitude 13 degs 15′ East, 20 miles away at 1413/25.

0230   Force 2 does not repeat not yet appear to have been sighted.

0316   [One U/boat of Group E returning damaged. Remaining seven to steer for new patrol line at highest possible speed.]

1000   At 2100A 25 December Battle Group informed German Admiralty that anticipated weather conditions in the operational area greatly impaired offensive action by destroyers owing to weather restricting speed. Aircraft which shadowed convoy pm 25 December sighted no repetition no support group within 50 miles of convoy.
Comment. It would appear that no repetition no cruiser or above has been sighted since at least am 23 December.

1215   The most northerly U/boat of Group E reported convoy at 0943A 26 December in latitude 73 degs, 57′ North, longitude 19 degs, 30′ East.

1304   AM 261215A. As a result of this report Group E were ordered at 1021A 26 December to operate against the convoy.

1317   At 0043A 26th U/boats were informed SCHARNHORST and 5 destroyers left Lopphavet at 2550A/25 and intended attacking convoy at about 0900A/26th.

27 December
0625   1. Group E were ordered at 2247A 28 December to search for survivors of SCHARNHORST in a 70 mile sweep on course 140 degrees commencing from position line latitude 72 degrees 57′ North, longitude 18 degrees 30′ East to approximately latitude 72 degrees 39′ North, longitude 26 degrees 50′ East in order A, C, B, W, J, N, E.
2. They were to report position of sinking immediately, as it was only assumed that it was in area latitude 72 degrees 00′ North, to 72 degrees 18′ North, longitude 29 degrees 00′ East, to 30 degrees 00' East.
3. Attacks on warships are permitted and the presence of Russian submarines in the search area is possible.

APPENDIX 15

Note of E-Boat Operations in the English Channel from January–May 1944

OIC SI 974A*
During the period 1st January to 24th May, the number of E-boats based on the Channel ports increased from 18 to 24; the average number on strength was 16. The scale of activity of these craft is broadly summarised in Tables I and II.

Table I – E-Boat Operations in the Channel 1st Jan–24th May 1944

Number of operations undertaken	36
Number of E-boat sorties	315
Average number of operations per month	7.4
Average number of sorties per month per E-boat on strength	3.8
Average number of E-boats engaged in an operation	8.8

Thus over half (8.8 out of 16) of the E-boats available take part when an operation occurs.

The operations undertaken are subdivided in the following table.

Table II –	*Type of Operation*	*Probable number*
	Torpedo operation	15
	Minelaying	10
	Defensive	2
	Uncertain	9
		36

In addition, intended operations were cancelled on 12 occasions. The reasons are unknown except in one case (cancellation because of moonlight) but were probably not connected with weather.

---

* Reproduced from ADM 223/172.

Results of Operations

The results achieved in the operations detailed in section I are summarised below.

Table III – E-Boat Operations, 1st Jan – 24th May 1944

Convoys attacked	5		E-boats intercepted on 12 occasions
Ships torpedoed.	11	sunk	E-boats sunk 2
	1	damaged	E-boats damaged 2 or 3 (probably)
	12	in 4 convoys	
Ships mined*	possibly 1.		

(* During the period considered, one ship only – a minesweeper – was sunk in the Channel by a mine. It is not known if the mine was laid by an E-boat.)

The following points may be noted –

i. The 'exchange rate' for the operations was 5½ or 6 ships sunk per E-boat.

ii. The chance that an E-boat would fail to return from a sortie was much less than 1 per cent (2 were sunk in 815 sorties). Taken in conjunction with the level of activity shown in Table I this implies that the average lifetime of an E-boat would be of the order of 3 years.

iii The number of ships hit per convoy attacked was rather high (2.4 casualties). The E-boats were thus limited mainly by the difficulty in contacting convoys. Of the specifically anti-convoy operations, between 65 per cent and 75 per cent failed to locate a target.

2. Our forces attempted to intercept the enemy, so far as is known, on all but one occasion. Since the E-boats when at sea are normally split up into several groups of 2 or 3 members, it is unusual for our forces to contact all the E-boats engaged on a particular operation. Very roughly, some 50 E-boats were probably engaged by our forces in the course of the 12 interceptions listed in Table III. We thus have the following estimates –

i. The chance that some part of the E-boat force would be intercepted was about 1 in 3. Alternatively, in 2 out of every 3 E-boat operations, our forces failed to intercept.

ii. Of those E-boats contracted by our forces, about 4 per cent were sunk (2 out of approximately 50) and probably an equal proportion was damaged.

Of the 12 interceptions, 5 were due to light coastal forces, 4 to destroyers and 3 to combined forces. Destroyers were responsible for both E-boat sinkings.

3. *Effect of Moon*

The extent to which E-boats avoid operating by moonlight is shown by the following figures –

Table IV

Phase of Moon	Number of nights between 1/1/44 and 24/5/44	Number of Operations	Average number of operations per 30 days
Crescent	67	25	11
Between quarter and full	78	11	4

No operations were carried out within any one of the weeks centred around full moon. In the 4 nights after the first quarter and those 4 preceding the last quarter, the level of activity (averaging about 8 operations per 30 days) was not markedly less than during the crescent moon periods.

3.i. *Effect of Wind*

It is to be expected that E-boat sorties would not normally be made when the wind was force 7 or more. The available data do not, unfortunately, provide any statistical confirmation or contradiction of this statement. They do however indicate that when the wind force was 6 or less there was no tendency for operations to occur in lower rather than in higher winds, and vice versa.

4. *Enemy Effort Month by Month*

Table V shows the number of operations and of sorties carried out each month.

Table V

Month (1944)	Average number of E-boats on strength	Number of Operations	Sorties	Average number of sorties per 30 days per E-boat on strength
January	12	6	40	3.2
February	16	5	46	3.0
March	17	8	74	4.2
April	17	9	98	5.7
May 1st-24th	19	8	57	3.8
		36	315	

The enemy thus appears to have increased the scale of effort of *each* E-boat in March and April 1944, with the primary object of achieving more operations per month (though the average number of boats employed in each operation also increased slightly).

4.i. *Operations on Consecutive Nights*

On occasion, a series of operations has been carried out on consecutive nights, or with only one blank night. The details are summarised below ;

Table VI

Series of Operations	No of Occasions		No of Operations
4 operations on 4 successive nights ?	0	} 2	8
4 operations within 5 nights	2		
3 operations on 3 successive nights	2	} 3	9
3 operations within 4 nights	1		
2 operations on 2 successive nights	2	} 6	12
2 operations within 3 nights	4		
Single operations	7		7
			36

The evidence does not indicate whether (apart from the effect of moonlight) a long series of (3 or 4) operations is followed by a long blank period.

APPENDIX 16

Decrypt of the Japanese Ambassador's Report to the Foreign Ministry Tokyo of his Interview with Field Marshal Milch in Berlin, 17 August 1943

My interview with Field Marshal Milch lasted for about an hour and a half. I feel that Milch in this conversation expressed his views especially candidly to Japan as an Ally. Much of what he said is related to military secrets and, as Milch himself expressed a wish to this effect, I should be grateful if particular care may be taken in the way in which the information is handled.

1. I said that there had recently been extraordinary activity on the part of the British and American air forces and that the Field Marshal had told me some time ago that Germany was carrying out a great expansion of the Luftwaffe to counter this activity. I had myself visited two or three factories and knew the general situation; but how long would it take, I asked, to bring the Luftwaffe up to a point where it could offer effective resistance. Milch showed me figures and plans for the increased production of planes and speaking very frankly said that to tell the truth the Luftwaffe was in considerable difficulties since America was at present sending the greater part of the planes which she was producing in large quantities to Europe. A strong air force was absolutely essential to victory and accordingly Germany was doing her utmost to increase production. At present the monthly output of first-class fighting planes was 2,700 a month (this figure is particularly confidential) and in about 15 months time it would be double. These plans were proceeding smoothly and production during the last four months had been 170 more than anticipated, so that he expected the plans to be carried out earlier than originally thought. Against this the enemy's monthly production was estimated to be:–

America, about 5,000; England and Canada combined, about 2,000; and the USSR, about 2,000. But these figures included training planes, transport planes and other kinds and he did not think that any further great increase in production was possible, while there had recently been a great falling off in the efficiency of Soviet planes so that he was confident that with the progress made in the plans for the extension of the Luftwaffe which he had mentioned it would be able to cope with the situation.

2.   I then asked whether the recent British and American air raids had not affected the plans for the expansion of the Luftwaffe. Milch replied that the raids had been very violent and that the damage inflicted upon production plants in the Ruhr area and elsewhere was not lightly to be dismissed. Germany was doing her best in the way of defence by installing a greater number of AA guns and she was trying to increase the number of fighters. But the area to be defended was extensive and it was no easy matter. On the 13th [August] American planes from Benghazi had visited Wiener Neustadt, had bombed the factories making fighter-planes and had caused considerable damage. No fighter squadrons had, however, been assigned to that district, so that the fighters just completed in the factories had been unable to put up a fight. For these reasons the production of bombers was not being given priority at present and first place was being given to fighters and destroyer-planes [Zerstörer], while the defences were being strengthened. Looking at the situation as a whole, however, since the production of munitions was entirely under the control of the government so that they could give orders quickly as regards the distribution and allocation of work to factories, since the British and American bombing consisted largely in the bombing of towns, and since the reconstruction of damaged factories was proceeding satisfactorily, the damage done to production establishments was very small as compared with the damage done to ordinary houses and was not more than 10% of Germany's total productive potential.

3.   Judging from these remarks made by Milch it is plain that at the moment the German Air Force is very inferior [to that of the United Nations] and that even now it has to make a big effort merely in the matter of defence. Then there is the Soviet offensive and the political change in Italy so that for the present Germany has no option but to adopt a defensive action. As, moreover, conditions are not likely to improve quickly we must recognise that for the time being the conduct of the war by Germany will continue to be difficult.

APPENDIX 17

The Air Offensive Against the German Ball-Bearing Industry

The German ball-bearing industry was known to be heavily concentrated in the Stuttgart area, in factories at Schweinfurt and Bad
Constatt; and in November 1942, estimating that two-thirds of
production went to the armaments industries, MEW had argued
that the importance of Schweinfurt alone presented 'an opportunity
to strike a blow at German war industry which is not shared, or
even approached, by another town or industrial target in Axis
Europe'.[1] In March 1943 the Committee of Operations Analysis,
recently set up to select targets for the US air offensive, accepted
the industry as a priority target.[2] Schweinfurt was raided in August
1943, and again on 14 October, and the attack, resumed in February
1944 with raids by the USAAF and Bomber Command on Schweinfurt, Steyr, Constatt and Eckner, was kept up until April of that
year. MEW then estimated on PR evidence that the offensive had
by March 1944 reduced the total production in Axis Europe to 53
per cent of the mid-1943 level; but it recognised that damage had
never been so severe as to cause a complete temporary stoppage of
output, and it was unable to link known shortages of equipment in
the German armed forces with the shortage of ball-bearings.[3] By
June it had received a number of reports suggesting that the shortage
was affecting the production of tanks, aircraft and motor transport.[4]
Reassessing the effects of the raids up to April, it then judged that
they had reduced Axis production to 45.5 per cent of the mid-1943
output, and concluded that this reduction, together with cuts in
Swedish exports of ball-bearings to Germany which had just been
negotiated, and together with renewed attacks on the enemy factories, 'might well eventually have an effect on Germany's military
capabilities.[5]*

* The German official figures show that production in Germany, which constituted 73 per
cent of total Axis production in mid-1943, was down to 64 per cent of the mid-1943 level by
March 1944 and to 49 per cent of it by April 1944. It recovered to 64 per cent in May and 84
per cent in June 1944.[6] Production of medium sized bearings was more seriously affected.[7]

1. Webster and Frankland, *The Strategic Air Offensive against Germany*, Vol IV
   (1961), p 246.   2. ibid, p 269.
3. ibid, p 506, reproducing Table 19 from US Strategic Bombing Survey, Synoptic Volume.
4. JIC (44) 177 (o) of 1 May; JIC (44) 228 (o) of 3 June; JIC (44) 241 of 13 June.
5. FO 837/19, MEW Weekly Intelligence Report 124 of 22 June 1944.
6. Webster and Frankland, op cit, Vol IV, p 506.   7. ibid.

AOC-in-C Bomber Command seized on this conclusion to complain of MEW's earlier assertion that the industry was vital to the German war effort; had that been correct, a reduction of output of over 50 per cent would have been a fatal blow to the enemy, and MEW should 'be called upon to account for their overweening enthusiasm over the enemy's ball-bearing position'.[8] MEW replied in July that it had never claimed more than that an offensive against the industry was the best practical way 'directly to impair the enemy's ability to fight' and that the results obtained had had that effect – though 'whether fatally or not, would of course depend on the military situation, whilst the speed with which it would be felt at the front would depend on the rate of wastage'.[9]

In the next three months evidence obtained from POW who had worked in the industry, from an important refugee from Aachen, from German records captured in Paris and from records and statements of French manufacturers supported the conclusion that reduced output of ball-bearings remained 'a strongly limiting factor' in Germany's production of war equipment.[10] This was despite the fact that the decline in the weight of attack on the industry since the spring had permitted the repair of damaged works and the opening of new factories. Commenting on this at his interrogation and in his memoirs, Speer claimed that 'the Allies threw away success when it was already in their hands. Had they continued the attacks of March and April [1944] with the same energy we would quickly have been at our last gasp. As it was, not a tank, plane or other piece of weaponry failed to be produced because of lack of ball-bearings even though such production had been increased by 19 per cent from July 1943'.[11] He thought the Allies had failed to press home the attacks because they had either assumed the industry had been dispersed or had overrated the effects of the damage they had achieved.[12] In fact, MEW had correctly assumed that dispersal would have done little to off-set the damage done to the industry,[13] and its estimates of that damage were near the mark, but it could not even attempt to assess the effects of the reduction of the output of ball-bearings on Germany's industrial production.

8. ibid, p 253.   9. ibid, pp 253–256.
10. AIR 20/5815, Report of 24 October 1944.
11. Webster and Frankland, op cit, Vol IV, p 374; Speer, *Inside the Third Reich* (Sphere books 1971), p 392.
12. Speer, op cit, p 392.
13. FO 837/20, MEW Weekly Intelligence Report 134 of 31 August 1944.

APPENDIX 18

The German Flak Defences

The introduction of 'Window' in July 1943 forced the German Flak and searchlight organisation to revert in the first instance to box barrages in which the guns and searchlights were guided by aural and visual observations. By making modifications to the gun-laying *Würzburg* radars and developing an improved radar ranging set called the *Mannheimgerät*, and by increasing resort to alternative frequencies, the Germans subsequently overcame the effects of the jamming to the extent that some batteries were again able to fire with considerable accuracy. But the night Flak defences as a whole never regained their earlier technical efficiency.[1]

Germany compensated for this decline by increasing the number of guns and searchlights deployed in the Reich. During 1942 a great deal of Flak had been sent to other fronts, much of it to Italy, but from the end of that year the intensification of Bomber Command's offensive and the greater concentration of its raids had been countered by a reversal of this trend. After the introduction of 'Window' still greater priority was given to the reinforcement of the Reich. This development was reflected in a contemporary intelligence estimate which gives the following figures:[2]

January 1943	*Flak guns*	*Searchlights*
Germany and Western front	14,949	3,726
Other fronts	8,030	660
January 1944		
Germany and Western front	20,625	6,880
Other fronts	9,569	960

Bomber Command felt the effect of these reinforcements from the beginning of 1944, when exceptionally heavy gun and searchlight defences combined with the night-fighters to prevent it from achieving against Berlin the concentration of attack that it had achieved against Hamburg in the previous summer.[3] From the same date the

---

1. AIR 20/1656, ASI Report No 101 of 6 March 1944; AIR 20/1657, ASI Report No 103 of 25 April 1944; AIR, 41/10, *The Rise and Fall of the German Air Force*, *p 285;* AIR 40/2392, MI 15 Periodical Intelligence Summary No 12 of 24 May 1944.
2. Webster and Frankland, *The Strategic Air Offensive against Germany*, Vol II (1961, pp 295–296 (n).
3. ibid, pp 195, 204, 207, 210, 211.

USAAF also encountered heavier and more accurate Flak. From the spring of 1944 Flak accounted for more American losses than did the German fighters.[4]

Against the Flak concentrated in their target areas the Allied bombers had no assistance except what 'Window' could provide.* But the proliferation of the German defences and the need to avoid Flak whenever possible meant that intelligence about the deployment and performance of the German guns and searchlights acquired increasing importance as a factor determining the routeing of the Allies' raids. The intelligence was collated by MI 15, an inter-Service and inter-Allied body in which US officers worked alongside staff drawn initially from the RAF and later mainly from the anti-aircraft branch of the Royal Artillery, and was distributed directly to the Commands, which used it for planning purposes and the preparation of Flak maps for bomber aircrew. The sources included PR, operational reports from the Allied bombers themselves, and the GAF Enigma – both the mainly static Flak for the defence of the Reich and the mobile Flak provided for the German Army came under GAF control.[6] In the autumn of 1943 GC and CS set up a new section to make a special study of Flak 'in view of its increased importance'. It has left no record of its researches, which were presumably incorporated in MI 15's periodical summaries.

---

* When the US bombers operated in clear weather, as they tried to do, the Flak could be ranged against them visually, but when they were bombing in cloud conditions, as they were often forced to do, they encountered *Würzburg* – controlled Flak. Against this, they made use of 'Window' and also of an American jamming device called 'Carpet' from the autumn of 1943.[5]

4. Craven and Cate, *The Army Air Forces in World War II*. Vol III (1951), p 56.
5. Price, *Instruments of Darkness* (1967), pp 243–244.
6. Mockler-Ferryman, *Military Intelligence Organisation*, p 26.

APPENDIX 19

Intruder Operations and Radio Counter-Measures against the German Night-Fighters

Against the German night defences Bomber Command relied mainly on tactical counter-measures (evasive or deceptive routeing and diversionary raids). It derived some, though less, benefit from the only other measures available to it, intruder operations and radio counter-measures.

Intruder operations were resumed in the spring of 1943, for the first time since 1940, Fighter Command planning them with the help of intelligence from Cheadle's W/T intercepts about the bases, movements and landing-times of the fighters and from Kingsdown's R/T intercepts about their routes and times of take-off.[1] From June 1943 Fighter Command's operations were also assisted by an airborne device ('Serrate') which was designed to enable its fighters to home on to the *Lichtenstein* AI of the German fighters. The operations did not meet with much success, and in September, when the enemy fighters were adopting the *Wilde Sau* system of interception and withdrawing to bases beyond the range of Fighter Command's Beaufighters, they were suspended.[2]

At the end of September the realisation that in the form of *Wilde Sau* the Germans had developed an effective system of defence against Bomber Command's concentrated raids prompted the decision to establish No 100 Group RAF, a special formation incorporating No 80 Wing and other units, to be responsible under Bomber Command for investigating further enemy radar developments and co-ordinating the application of all possible radio and tactical counter-measures against them, including intruder operations.[3] No 100 Group became operational in December 1943 and received some of the resources of Air Defence of Great Britain (ADGB), as Fighter Command was called for almost a year from October 1943.[4] Together with aircraft of that command, it carried

---

1. *Bomber Command Counter-Measures*, p 43.
2. Webster and Frankland, *The Strategic Air Offensive against Germany*, Vol II (1961), pp 140–151; Price, *Instruments of Darkness* (1967), p 170; Jones, *Most Secret War* (1978), p 384; AIR 41/46, No 80 Wing RAF Historical Report, pp 92–93, 113.
3. *Bomber Command Counter-Measures*, pp 59–60.
4. Webster and Frankland, op cit, Vol III, pp 145–146.

out offensive patrols against enemy night-fighters over north-west Germany, northern France and the Low Countries on the nights of Bomber Command's raids. No 100 Group's patrols with 'Serrate' Mosquitoes were directed mainly against night-fighters round their assembly beacons and Bomber Command's target areas, while those of ADGB were aimed principally at night-fighter bases and training schools.[5] Both types of operation depended on the supply of operational and background intelligence from GC and CS, the RAF Y organisation, ADI (Sc) and other Air Ministry intelligence sections. Together they destroyed about 70 aircraft on the ground and in the air, mostly night-fighters, in the first five months of 1944.[6] Bomber Command regarded operations on this scale as having little more than a nuisance value.[7] This limited result – though recent evidence suggests that the nuisance value was considerable –[8] sprang from material shortcomings and, to a less extent, from inexperience of enemy night-fighter tactics. More particularly – since everything depended on interception of the enemy – the 'Serrate' patrols, of which well over 500 were carried out between January and May 1944,[9] met with decreasing success from the autumn of 1943 when the Germans began to equip their fighters with the new AI set, SN 2,* with a maximum range of four miles, double that of its predecessor.[10]

With the introduction of *Wilde Sau* the attempt to interfere with the system's running commentary had in any case been given priority over the value of its tactical intelligence for operational purposes. Under the system the German fighters could adopt freelance tactics only after the controller had informed them by R/T of the position, course and probable target of the bomber stream; for this purpose he used a high-powered transmitter on HF with a frequency which was changed daily. Airborne and ground-station jamming of his transmissions began at the end of August 1943.

The airborne jamming was done by the bombers with a device called 'Special Tinsel'†, which they resorted to on being informed

---

* See Appendix 20.

† This was a variant of 'Tinsel' which had been developed as an airborne device for jamming the HF R/T ground-to-air instructions of the Kammhuber box system. At the end of 1942 VHF had replaced HF in that system and a new airborne jammer, 'Cigar', had been developed against the VHF transmissions. After the introduction of *Wilde Sau* the Germans continued to use VHF for directing the *Benito*-controlled night-fighters to the bomber stream, and 'Cigar' continued to be used in the bombers against the *Benito*-controlled fighters.[11]

5. AIR 41/49, *The Air Defence of Great Britain*, Vol V, p 315.
6. ibid, p 320; AIR 41/56, *The RAF in the Bombing Offensive against Germany*, Vol VI, p 30, fn 2.
7. Webster and Frankland, op cit, Vol III, p 147.
8. Gebhard Aders, *History of the German Nightfighter Force* (1979), p 202.
9. AIR 41/56, p 30.   10. Price, op cit, pp 69, 179.
11. *Bomber Command Counter-Measures*, p 49; AIR 41/46, pp 94–95, 98.

that Kingsdown had identified the day's frequency. The Germans responded by introducing more frequent and more irregular changes of frequency and by using multiple transmissions. Bomber Command responded in its turn by equipping specialised bombers with a higher-powered jamming device; known as 'Jostle', this came into service in 1944.[12]

Ground-station jamming of the running commentary with high-powered transmitters, under a system called 'Corona', was combined with attempts to confuse the German pilots by inserting bogus instructions and false weather reports into the running commentary. Initially these surprised the enemy who took various steps to counteract them, but their effect was wearing off by December 1943.[13] By then, moreover, in their efforts to counteract the jamming, the Germans were taking advantage of the replacement of *Wilde Sau* by *Zahme Sau*, under which it was necessary to transmit to their fighters only the course and height of the British bombers and the code-name of the chosen fighter assembly beacon, to abbreviate the running commentary. For a few days early in December they used a high-powered public radio transmitter at Stuttgart to broadcast short messages to the fighters. When these broadcasts were jammed, the British using a high-powered Foreign Office transmitter ('Aspidistra') for the purpose, the Germans resorted to a system by which what purported to be a German Forces Programme, *Anne Marie*, issued the fighters' instructions by broadcasting dance music; the Reich having been divided into eight zones, the types of orchestra or of popular music relayed indicated in which zone the fighters had to assemble, and the other information they required was included in coded form in the radio announcer's introductions. It was quickly realised that *Anne Marie* was broadcast only at night, and only when Bomber Command was operating, but because legal objections were raised against the jamming of this kind of programme, the Germans were able to use it with little or no interference from the middle of December 1943 until it was superseded in the middle of February 1944.[14]

By the middle of February 1944 the Germans had completed their preparations for transmitting instructions to the fighters in morse by W/T, a form of transmission that was more difficult to jam than R/T. The W/T commentary was monitored and jammed from Cheadle with such success, however, that from February the Germans were forced to broadcast their orders simultaneously on a number of channels. Eventually they were using both R/T and

12.   Webster and Frankland, op cit, Vol III, p 23.
13.   ibid, Vol II, p 202; *Bomber Command Counter-Measures*, p 63.
14.   *Bomber Command Counter-Measures*, pp 63–65; Price, op cit, p 188.

W/T and transmitting the W/T on medium, high and very high frequencies.[15]

From their efforts to counter the jamming of their communications it is clear that the German night defences were inconvenienced by it, but there is no reason to believe that Bomber Command's casualties were greatly reduced by the confusion and delay that the jamming may have caused.[16] A GAF authority has said that although the jamming created problems, the gist of the commentary always got through.[17] Moreover, while the intercepted running commentary commonly disclosed that the tactical counter-measures had delayed the enemy by keeping him guessing about Bomber Command's targets, neither it nor any other intelligence source ever disclosed that the enemy's fighter reactions were delayed by successful jamming. Nor is this surprising when it is recalled that the German fighters needed only brief instructions to tell them where to assemble and that from before the end of 1943 they could increasingly rely on their radar and radar-detection sets to find their way to a bomber stream once they had received some indication of its approximate position and course.

Against the airborne and ground-based radar detection devices which the enemy used for plotting and homing on to the British airborne radar no radio or any other counter-measures were devised before his night-fighter defence system collapsed in the summer of 1944, for the reasons discussed in Appendix 20 and Appendix 21. No 100 Group RAF did develop during the first few months of 1944 a new 'Mandrel' jamming screen for blanketing the enemy's ground-based early-warning *Freya* network. To ensure that it achieved maximum effect when *Overlord* was launched, this was not brought into use until June. From July it was used regularly and to great effect in conjunction with other forms of jamming and with the various tactical counter-measures that had been developed since September 1943; the latter included sorties by Mosquitoes to simulate major raids by dropping large amounts of 'Window', a form of deception which No 100 Group had introduced from the beginning of 1944.[18] These operations accelerated the decline in the efficiency of the German night-fighter defences, but the collapse of the defences in August was above all due to shortages of fuel and trained manpower and the retreat of the early-warning network in the face of the advance of the Allied armies.

---

15. *Bomber Command Counter-Measures*, p 66; Price, op cit, p 189.
16. Webster and Frankland, op cit, Vol II, p 208.
17. M Middlebrook, *The Nuremberg Raid* (1975), p 61.
18. Webster and Frankland, op cit, Vol III, pp 145 et seq; *Bomber Command Counter-Measures*, p 75 et seq; AIR 41/43, *The RAF in the Bombing Offensive against Germany*, Vol V, p 131.

APPENDIX 20

Lichtenstein SN2 Air Interception Set

Lichtenstein SN2 (FuGe 220) was an Air Interception (AI) set employing a frequency range from 80 to 85 M/cs which was immune from 'Window'. It began to replace earlier *Lichtensteins* in the equipment of the German twin-engined night-fighters, the only fighters big enough to mount its unusual aerials, sometime between August and October 1943.[1] In a crash programme, the Germans had produced 200 sets by February 1944 and 1,000 sets by May 1944.[2] SN2 enabled its fighter to make early contact with the bomber stream once it had been given a general idea of the enemy's whereabouts by other warning and location devices* and then enabled it to keep contact. This took place in total darkness, without the help of searchlights, flares and fires. With the help of *Benito* (and later *Egon*)† the German controller could direct other fighters to the shadowing fighter. Furthermore, as RAF Y soon revealed, SN2 night-fighters sometimes emitted a DF note while maintaining contact with the bomber stream, thus making it possible for other night-fighters to home on to the SN2 aircraft and find the bombers.[3] In these ways SN2 was essential to the process by which *Wilde Sau* was replaced by *Zahme Sau*, and it made a great contribution to Gemany's biggest victories against Bomber Command. That ADI (Sc) could derive some comfort in March 1944 from evidence suggesting that not many night-fighters were fitted with SN2 shows that *Zahme Sau* was not yet understood by the RAF, since the system worked effectively with comparatively few SN2 aircraft.[4]

The possibility that a new *Lichtenstein* was being introduced was raised in February 1944, after No 80 Wing RAF had noticed a decline in *Lichtenstein* transmissions.[5] By the beginning of March No 80 Wing had failed to find any unfamiliar signals, but the increase in bomber losses had made it 'painfully obvious' that the enemy was using a new AI set, and occasional references by agents and

---

* See Appendix 21 (i).
† See Appendix 23 for the use of *Benito* and *Egon* by German bombers.

1. AIR 41/10, *The Rise and Fall of the German Air Force*, p 279; Price, *Instruments of Darkness* (1967), p 179; Irving, *The Rise and Fall of the Luftwaffe* (1973), p 229.
2. Price, op cit, p 213.
3. Air Sunset 135 of 4 January 1944.
4. AIR 20/1656, ASI Report No 101 of 6 March 1944.
5. AIR 41/46, No 80 Wing RAF Historical Report, pp 92–93.

POW and in Enigma decrypts to new equipment under code names *Neptun* and SN2, and to such type-numbers as FuGe 216* and FuGe 220 had suggested to ADI (Sc) that SN2 was one of three types of *Lichtenstein* AI now in service, that 'fortunately it only exists on a small scale at present', and that one of the urgent problems was to establish its wavelength, which might be 80 M/cs and thus immune from 'Window'[6]. Unfortunately, this frequency was in that part of the radar frequency spectrum that was already cluttered with the transmissions of the latest *Freya* and other early-warning sets, and the search for it had still not succeeded by the middle of April.[7] Equally unfortunately, an agent had by then supplied a rough sketch of a new aerial array, seen in the nose of a night-fighter, which suggested that the array belonged to a wide-angle search AI on a frequency of about 150 M/cs.[8] On 25 April ADI (Sc), noting that SN2 was 'rapidly increasing in service', urged the importance of finding the frequency and developing counter-measures; he suggested that the frequency might be vulnerable to the new 'long' 'Window' that was then being introduced,† but accepted that the frequency might be about 165 M/cs.[9]

No further progress was made until June, when the Air Ministry's Technical Intelligence Section noticed in the film of a combat between a US fighter and a Ju 88 night-fighter that the Ju 88 was fitted with an aerial array similar to the rough sketch supplied by an agent in April; this had suggested a frequency of about 150 M/cs. The photographs were very good and they established beyond doubt that this was the SN2 and that its frequency was less than 100 M/cs. On 13 July an intact SN2 was taken from a Ju 88 which landed at Woodbridge and it emerged that the frequency was 85 M/cs.[10]

It was at once recognised that SN2 could indeed be jammed by 'long' 'Window'. Bomber Command brought this counter-measure into force within ten days, but by then SN2 had operated to great effect without interference for nearly nine months.

---

* *Neptun* (FuGe 216) was a rear-facing radar (see Appendix 23).

† 'Long' 'Window' was a form of 'Window' developed for use against the German naval *Seetakt* and the *Freya* ground radar sets on the Channel coast before the invasion of Normandy (see Volume III Part 2). These sets used a much longer wavelength than the *Würzburg*.

6.   ibid, pp 92–93; AIR 20/1656, ASI Report No 101 of 6 March 1944; Jones, *Most Secret War* (1978), p 393.
7.   Price, op cit, pp 213–214.
8.   *Air Ministry Intelligence*, pp 384–386.
9.   AIR 20/1657, ASI Report No 103 of 25 April 1944.
10. AIR 20/1658, ASI Report No 107 of 29 June 1944; *Air Ministry Intelligence*, p 386; Price, op cit, p 214.

APPENDIX 21

(i) Intelligence on the Radiation Detection Devices of the German Night-Fighter Organisation

FLAMMEN

In the first half of 1943, in the course of raising the *Freya* frequency to avoid jamming by 'Mandrel', the Germans accidentally reached the point at which *Freya* challenged the transmissions of the IFF sets in the British bombers. They regularly monitored these over distances of up to 350 km under the codeword *Flammen* from October 1943 with ground sets normally attached to their GCI stations, which used them to direct the night-fighters equipped with *Benito*.[1]

The fact that the enemy was reporting unidentifiable plots called *Flammen* was disclosed by decrypts of the Enigma key of the GAF Experimental Signals Regiment. GC and CS having resumed the decryption of this key (Brown) in the autumn of 1943, when other decrypts had shown in April that radar equipment was being despatched to Peenemünde, it was discovered that, while the signals of the 14th Company of the Regiment were reporting plots of the flying bomb trials in the Baltic, those of the 15th Company had in October begun to report *Flammen* plots from stations in Holland and Germany; GC and CS concluded that they were plots of British bombers. In December 1943 they were investigated by ADI (Sc) who, already aware that 'Oboe' was being plotted under the code-name *Bumerang* (see below), deduced that *Flammen* were plots of the bombers' IFF sets.[2] In January this deduction was confirmed by a proving flight by No 192 Squadron RAF, and this evidence persuaded Bomber Command to forbid the use of IFF over enemy territory; but the Enigma decrypts showed that IFF plotting continued until Bomber Command sealed the bombers' IFF sets in March.[3]

---

1. AIR 20/1656, ASI Report No 101 of 6 March 1944; Price, *Instruments of Darkness* (1967), p 171.
2. AIR 20/1668, ASI Report No VI of 8 January 1944.
3. AIR 20/1657, ASI Report No 103 of 25 April 1944; *Air Ministry Intelligence*, p 323; *Bomber Command Counter-Measures*, p 72; Jones, *Most Secret War* (1978), pp 389–390.

KORFU, NAXOS AND NAXBURG

All three were devices for detecting, homing on or plotting the centimetric radar emissions of Allied heavy bombers. *Korfu* was a ground receiver and direction finder developed against the centimetric radar, H2S, which the Germans had recovered from a British bomber in January 1943, very soon after it had come into service. *Korfu* was in operation by September 1943, from which date it plotted radiations from Bomber Command's H2S sets which for many months remained switched on from take-off to the end of a raid.[4]

Originally designed as an airborne search receiver against H2S, *Naxos* was from September 1943 developed into an airborne detector which could home on to H2S transmissions and also into a search receiver for use by U-boats against centimetric ASV.* It was used operationally by the German night-fighters for the first time on 28 November 1943; it could pick up a bomber stream at a distance of 60 miles. Thereafter it became capable of locating individual bombers and, in conjunction with SN2, was chiefly responsible for Bomber Command's heaviest losses.[5]

The *Naxburg* ground receiver combined the *Naxos* search receiver with the directional aerial dishes of the *Würzburg*. It determined the source of H2S transmissions with great precision; the first *Naxburg* registered H2S transmissions from an individual bomber at a distance of between 100 and 160 miles on 22 September 1943. In October, when the Germans began to set up a *Naxburg* network, the receiver was picking up H2S aircraft at distances of 250 and 300 miles.[6]

No evidence was obtained about the existence of *Naxburg* until December 1944, when it was mentioned in Enigma decrypts for the first time.[7]

When reporting on *Flammen* early in January 1944 ADI (Sc) gave the general warning that the Germans 'will probably try other radiations should we now thwart them on IFF and we shall therefore need to be even more circumspect than before in our use of all radio equipment which involves continual transmissions from our aircraft', and he mentioned, among that equipment, 'Oboe' and 'Monica'.[8]† But he did not refer to H2S. A few days before this the naval

---

* See above, p 225. † See below, pp 563–564.

4. Price, op cit, pp 135, 175; Webster and Frankland, *The Strategic Air Offensive against Germany*, Vol IV (1961), p 22; Irving, *The Rise and Fall of the Luftwaffe* (1973), p 237.
5. Price, op cit, pp 135, 143, 175, 179, 185, 195; Price, *Luftwaffe Handbook* (1977), pp 27, 29.
6. *Bomber Command Counter-Measures*, pp 55–57.
7. AIR 20/1654, ASI Report No 83 of 26 March 1945.   8. AIR 20/1668.

Enigma had confirmed something of which there had been 'strong indications' – also in the same traffic – in November. On 3 January the Admiralty had informed the operational authorities that the enemy now possessed information on the frequency and essential operating details of ASV Mk III (ie 10 cm) and had issued a search receiver – *Naxos* – to cover this waveband.* In the GAF Enigma traffic there was no reference to enemy knowledge of H2S or of centimetric radar until March 1944. It was assumed by the British that the GAF was in possession of this knowledge from equipment recovered from a Halifax of Bomber Command which had crashed near Rotterdam in March 1943 and from other bombers since then. The British scientists who had designed H2S did not believe, however, that the Germans could exploit their knowledge to help their night-fighters by furnishing them with plots and bearings.[9]†

Arrangements existed for informing ADI (Sc) of naval technical intelligence, but it is not known how soon the information reached him on this occasion.[11] It is true that as early as January 1943, in an attempt to avert the use of H2S over enemy territory, he had warned the RAF authorities that possession of the equipment would allow the Germans to devise receivers able to listen to centimetric transmissions, to use the technique for their own purposes and to devise jammers for it. But as 1943 wore on with none of these things happening the views of the British radar specialists must have seemed to be vindicated. There is no evidence that they changed their views when the naval Enigma revealed that the Germans had designed a search receiver to cover the 10 cm band, presumably because it was easier to listen to the transmissions than to use them for location and homing.[12] Whether or not ADI (Sc) was aware of this naval development, there is no reference to German knowledge or exploitation of centimetric radar in his routine reports on enemy radar developments until that of 6 March 1944. Here he mentioned that 'H2S [had] greatly surprised the Germans' and, for the first time in these reports referred to the existence of a German naval

---

* The German Navy started to issue this device to U-boats at the end of October 1943 (see Appendix 10).

† It is noteworthy that when the German naval radar specialists first learned in September 1943 of GAF possession of H2S they rejected the idea that the Allies would be able to use the centimetric technique to locate U-boats,[10] see above pp 515–516.

9. ADM 223/186, Ultra signal 1317/25 November 1943; ADM 223/188, Ultra signal 0317/3 January 1944; Naval Headlines Nos 865 of 16 November 1943, 918 of 8 January 1944.
10. ADM 234/68, BR 305 (3), p 4.
11. *Handling of Naval Special Intelligence*, pp 88, 101.
12. AIR 20/3062, ADI (Sc) minute to the VCAS of 23 January 1943; Jones, op cit, p 320.

search receiver, *Naxos*. In March he regarded modifications to the early-warning radars – *Würzburg*, *Freya*, *Mammut* and *Wassermann* – rather than the development of radiation detection as being 'the main German reaction to our counter-measures'.[13]

ADI (Sc)'s next report, dated 25 April 1944, again concentrated on the latest German counter-measures to 'Window' and to jamming; these were now known to include anti-jamming modifications to *Freya* and *Würzburg*, a new early-warning radar (*Würzmann*), and SN2, which was stated to be Germany's 'main hope' for evading 'Window'. The report noted, on the evidence of the Enigma, that *Flammen* had helped to destroy 210 bombers during January and February, and that plotting of the bombers' IFF had since been stopped; but in its list of the main problems remaining to be solved it did not mention other radiation detection devices.[14] Indeed, the report said that 'all the present counters to "Window" are now understood'. It has been claimed that POW had by then referred to *Naxos* as equipment in use by the German night-fighters,[15] but it is clear that they said nothing that carried conviction with the British technical experts. It was not until May that firm evidence that the Germans had centimetric radar, and were using H2S for detection and homing, was obtained from Enigma references to *Naxos* and *Korfu* which disclosed that they were an airborne and ground receiver respectively, for tracking H2S.[16] Not until after the war was it discovered that *Korfu* had been in service since September 1943.[17]

ADI (Sc)'s report of 29 June announced that 'a long foreseen phase of the war has now arrived when a serious effort [by the Germans] is being made to utilise the fact that a radiating aircraft thereby compromises its position'. The evidence, first received fragmentarily in May, had been confirmed in detail by documents captured in Normandy; these showed that before adapting it for use by U-boats the Germans had developed *Naxos* for the detection by their night-fighters of H2S from British bombers.[18] As late as August 1944 the British radar experts, still doubting whether the Germans could be exploiting H2S, attached one of their number to ADI (Sc)'s staff to examine the Enigma evidence.[19]

In the report of 29 June 1944 ADI (Sc) also circulated for the first time intelligence about *Bumerang* and *Flensburg*.

---

13. AIR 20/1656.   14. AIR 20/1657.
15. Price, *Instruments of Darkness*, p 213.
16. AIR 20/5804, ADI (Sc) minute, 4 May 1944.
17. Price, *Instruments of Darkness*, p 175.
18. AIR 20/1658, ASI Report No 107 of 29 June 1944.
19. Jones, op cit, p 392.

BUMERANG

This was a procedure based on the interception by ground receivers of the frequency used by 'Oboe', Bomber Command's navigation and bomb-aiming aid. 'Oboe' was first used in December 1942, but the Germans did not discover it until November 1943, when they tried to jam it. Bomber Command responded by introducing a centimetric frequency for 'Oboe' in January 1944, but transmissions also continued on the old frequency for some time. It has been said that this helped to prevent the Germans from discovering the new frequency until July 1944.[20]

An Enigma decrypt of 28 January 1944 disclosed that early warning obtained from 'Oboe' plots by *Bumerang* ground stations had helped to frustrate a bombing raid over Holland; at this time the old 'Oboe' frequency may still have been in use alongside the new one. As no further intelligence was received before May, it was presumably assumed that the centimetric 'Oboe' was safe. But an Enigma decrypt of 25 May 1944 congratulated the experimental Air Signals Regiment which operated the *Bumerang* on obtaining early warning of a raid at a range of 100 kilometres, and on having distinguished the main raid from a diversionary one. This leaves no doubt that the Germans were plotting the centimetric 'Oboe' before July 1944.

The discovery that 'receivers are being used on the ground for tracking Oboe Mark II' was reported in ADI (Sc)'s report of 29 June 1944.[21]

FLENSBURG

Flensburg was an airborne device for homing on to the rear-facing radar ('Monica') which gave the British bombers warning of night-fighters approaching from behind them. The Germans had developed it by the end of 1943, having recovered a 'Monica' set from a crashed bomber within a week of its introduction by Bomber Command in the spring. It could detect 'Monica' signals from a range of 130 miles and home with great accuracy on to individual bombers.[22]

Some time after the beginning of 1944 POW referred to *Flensburg*, together with *Naxos*, as devices fitted in night-fighters but gave no useful intelligence about them.[23] The Enigma first referred to *Flensburg* at the end of February, disclosing that it had been installed in

---

20.   Webster and Frankland, op cit, Vol II, p 95 (n); Price, *Instruments of Darkness*, pp 189–190, 218–219.
21.   AIR 20/1658.
22.   Price, *Instruments of Darkness*, pp 139, 165, 215; Price, *Luftwaffe Handbook*, p 27.
23.   Price, *Instruments of Darkness*, p 213.

two types of long-range maritime aircraft. In the light of this information it was assumed that it might be a type of ASV active search radar, whereas it was a passive detection device; and so much so that ADI (Sc), who had in January canvassed but dismissed the possibility that the *Flammen* plots were plots of 'Monica', did not associate *Flensburg* with 'Monica'.[24] As late as 29 June 1944 he believed that it was another new AI set with a considerably longer range than SN2, possibly 19 miles, which could also be used as an ASV.[25] Nor was it till July that captured documents, without revealing that *Flensburg* was the equipment used, established that the Germans were detecting 'Monica' radiations.[26]

On 13 July an intact *Flensburg* was recovered from the Ju 88 that had landed at Woodbridge. Its characteristics and capabilities were quickly established and 'Monica' withdrawn from all aircraft in Bomber Command.[27]

24.   AIR 20/1668.   25.   AIR 20/1658.
26.   AIR 20/1652, ASI Report No 73 of 13 July 1944.
27.   Price, *Instruments of Darkness*, p 215.

APPENDIX 21

(ii) The Nuremberg Raid, 30 March 1944

We summarise here existing accounts of the Nuremberg raid. We do so because, although it was exceptionally ill-fated, the raid illustrated particularly well the state of intelligence about the enemy's night-fighter defences in the first half of 1944.

The decision to make a raid with all available heavy bombers (in fact 795 took part) was prompted by the AOC-in-C's realisation that time was running out for the hope that the bombing would bring about a German collapse; it would soon be too late in the spring to go deep into Germany, and increasing demands were about to be made on Bomber Command for pre-invasion bombing.[1] As for the choice of target, the initial meteorological reports, which always exerted a major influence on such decisions, dictated that it should be in south Germany, where they forecast the possibility of cloud cover; and in south Germany the AOC-in-C preferred Nuremberg to the six priority targets listed in the current Air Staff directive, and particularly to Schweinfurt or Regensburg for which the weather forecast was equally favourable, primarily because Nuremberg had not yet been seriously damaged, because its Nazi associations made it a 'political target of first importance' and because it was believed that 'morale was always particularly shaky in Nuremberg'.[2] Such was the importance the AOC-in-C attached to these considerations, as also to the decision to make a raid in the first place, that although the weather forecast became less favourable in the afternoon of 30 March, and so much so that his staff expected him to cancel, he did not do so.[3] In the event the bombers had to make most of the outward flight not only without cloud cover and in moonlight but also in freak atmospheric conditions, unforeseen by the latest weather reports, which caused them to make long white condensation trails.[4]

It has been argued that the raid was handicapped not only by the weather but also because it was routed carelessly, perhaps with bravado; the route incorporated a long straight track which went

---

1. Middlebrook, *The Nuremberg Raid* (1973), pp 84–85.
2. ibid, pp 85, 87.   3. ibid, pp 100, 102, 282
4. Webster and Frankland, *The Strategic Air Offensive against Germany*, Vol II (1961), pp 208–209; Middlebrook, op cit, p 168; Price, *Instruments of Darkness* (1967), pp 197–198.

close to two night-fighter assembly beacons.[5] But Bomber Command knew the exact location of all the enemy beacons and still found it extremely difficult 'to plan a route that avoided all the beacons as well as the Flak-defended areas'; and since the route was planned with a view to prolonging the enemy's uncertainty as to the destination of the raid, there is no reason to question the conclusion that 'for a target as distant as Nuremberg it was as good a route as any, provided that the risk of fighter interception . . . in moonlight was appreciated'.[6] In the event the Germans did not identify Nuremberg as the target until long after they had made contact with the bomber stream – a fact which disposes of the rumour that information had been leaked to them – and if the raid was a disaster for Bomber Command it was because the risk of fighter interception was gravely under-estimated.

It seems reasonable to suppose that it was under-estimated partly out of the belief that the size and serviceability of the enemy's night-fighter force, and also, perhaps, its morale, were suffering from the heavy losses inflicted on the German fighters by the USAAF's daylight offensive since the beginning of March.* But the main reason is to be found in the fact that Bomber Command, while it was of course aware that the enemy had replaced target interception by route interception, had no conception of the efficiency of the *Zahme Sau* system of early interception because, except that they had acted to prevent the exploitations of IFF, the British intelligence authorities remained unaware of the various detection devices on which the system was based.† This is indicated by its assumption that most of the 73 bombers it had lost during the last raid on Berlin on 24 March were Flak casualties, whereas most of them had been shot down by *Zahme Sau* night-fighters.[7] With the assistance of this system, the night-fighters had been improving their performance against Bomber Command since at least December 1943. In the Nuremberg raid, when they were also favoured by the weather, the system tipped the scales further to their advantage.

On the night of 30 March, from their interception of the bombers' H2S transmissions, the defences detected that a large force was assembling over East Anglia and moving south-east, and were also able to distinguish between that force and a smaller force, which was routed across the North Sea to simulate a threat to Hamburg

---

* It has been noted above (see p 317) that the Enigma was confirming that these losses were high and was also showing that the Germans were using night-fighters against the daylight raids.

† See Appendix 21(i) for full details.

5. Webster and Frankland, op cit, Vol II, pp 208–209
6. Middlebrook, op cit, p 91; see also pp 64, 90, 104, 106.
7. ibid, pp 130, 282–293.

or Berlin, in sufficient time to have over 200 twin-engined night-fighters flying to the beacons in the Aachen and Frankfurt areas from all over the Reich before the bombers crossed the German frontier south of Aachen. Nor were they misled by Mosquitoes which made three other diversionary raids by using 'Window' to simulate major attacks on Aachen, Cologne and Kassel; they identified them as Mosquitoes because they knew from experience that Mosquitoes did not use H2S.[8] The fact that the Germans were able to identify the simulated raids may appear to give substance to the criticism that Bomber Command was at fault in concentrating its real effort against a single target.[9] By attacking more than one target it had on earlier occasions confused the defences. But it had done so at the expense of reducing the weight of its attacks; and dispersal was becoming less and less effective against increasingly accurate and flexible defences.

The jamming devices used by the bombers against the night-fighter running commentary were ineffective. So were the 'Serrate' aircraft accompanying the bombers, which were designed to home on to the obsolete *Lichtenstein* AI; the frequency of the SN2 AI remained unidentified and nothing was known about the detection and homing devices used by the waiting night-fighters and the German route-tracking organisation.[10] Three night-fighter divisions had made contact with the bomber stream before it reached the beacon in the Frankfurt area; they were there joined by a fourth and also by a bomber squadron which dropped above the bomber stream parachute flares that 'could be seen by fighters all over Germany . . .'[11] Most of the casualties – 94 failed to return and a further 71 were damaged – were shot down between this point and the target.[12] By the time they reached the target the bombers were so scattered by the fighters, and also by the wind, that their attack lacked accuracy and concentration; few bombs fell in Nuremberg.

It is not known how many of the casualties had fallen victim to *Schräge Musik*, the name given to the upward-firing cannon with which the German night-fighters were being increasingly equipped. Bomber Command had acquired no operational evidence of the use of this weapon; few bombers attacked by it managed to return, and those that did return knew little about what had hit them, the attacks having been made from a blind spot beneath them.[13] Nor

---

8.   ibid, pp 131–132, 134; Price, op cit, p 196.
9.   Webster and Frankland, op cit, Vol II, pp 208–209.
10. Middlebrook, op cit, pp 140, 163; Irving, *The Rise and Fall of the Luftwaffe* (1973), p 273.
11. Price, op cit, p 197.
12. Webster and Frankland, op cit, Vol II, pp 192–193.
13. Middlebrook, op cit, pp 70–74, 140, 177.

had the intelligence sources yet referred to the existence of the weapon. It might be supposed that information about it would have filtered through from the many civilians who worked on the night-fighter airfields in the occupied countries. But the first reference in intelligence papers to an upward-firing gun did not occur till 29 June; a report by ADI (Sc) then mentioned unconfirmed reports on the subject.[14] The first good evidence followed in July 1944, when a POW reported that Me 110 aircraft were equipped with it.[15] In the reports which AI 2(g) regularly made on night-fighter armament no reference was made to an upward-firing weapon until September 1944.

---

14.   AIR 20/1658, ADI (Sc) Report No 107 of 29 June 1944.
15.   Air Historical Branch, ADI (K) Report 348/44 of 12 July 1944.

APPENDIX 22

Minute to the Prime Minister from the Chief of the Air Staff, 3 January 1944*

PRIME MINISTER

1. When the Chiefs of Staff recommended to you in June 1943 that 'Window' should be used, we informed you that improvements in our RDF equipment and organisation, both ground and airborne, would partially by the end of 1943 and substantially by the middle of 1944, safeguard our own defences against the effects of 'Window'. At the Staff Conference on the 15th July, at which you finally approved the introduction of 'Window', it was stated that a reasonable degree of protection would be assured by the Spring of 1944. In your personal minute of the 2nd July you had already asked me for details of the rate at which the new equipments would become available. In my reply of the 4th July I informed you that it was hoped that 100 Mosquitoes would be fitted with SCR 720 by the end of November and that a new 10 cm type of GCI might be available for trials during the Autumn of 1943.

2. Unfortunately the programme for the fitting of SCR 720 and the development of 10 cm GCI have been set back by a series of unavoidable delays. The SCR 720 sets were late in arriving from America; they were found to be more difficult to instal in the aircraft than had been expected, and finally it was found that they caused serious interference with the VHF system. To overcome these technical troubles it has been necessary to screen all the SCR 720 wiring in the aircraft and to make other technical modifications. The result is that the first 100 Mosquitoes fitted with SCR 720 will not have been delivered before the end of February, and the first three Mosquito squadrons equipped with SCR 720 which I hoped would be ready by the end of 1943 are not likely to be operational before March.

3. Technical troubles were also experienced with the development of the 10 cm GCI. Instead of being ready for trials last Autumn as we hoped, the first equipment is not likely to be ready until the end of January. Five more should be ready by mid-March, and twelve further sets are due to follow. On the other hand, the 50 cm CHL

---

* Reproduced from CAB 120/293, PM Registered File PM 406/1/1.

and GCI equipments promised by the end of 1943 have all been provided.

4.   The failure to achieve the programme by the dates given to you in my minute of the 4th July is unfortunate but I do not think that it will necessarily cause us very great embarrassment. The effects of the delay will turn very much on the enemy intentions this winter which are still obscure.

5.   From recent Intelligence Reports you will be aware that the Germans have withdrawn from Italy their 6 long range bomber Gruppen (180 aircraft) and that some of these at least have been moved to the Western Front, though they are not yet operational. There are also 3 other Gruppen which have recently completed refit in Germany and may become operational. Finally, a further Gruppe, which is now engaged on anti-shipping work, might be brought in to augment the available bomber force. If all these reinforcements were available, the number of long range bombers which might be disposed for attack on this country would be 480 as compared with 150 in July, when authority was given for 'Window' to be used by Bomber Command. The scale of effort which might be achieved would be a maximum of 300–350 sorties on any one night compared with a maximum of 75–100 sorties which was possible in July.

6.   The above figures represent theoretical maxima but there is not yet any positive evidence that the Germans intend to use these reinforcements for attacks on this country in the near future. Although the personnel position in the German bomber force has improved during the last six months, the average level of training is still low and the use of the above force in intensive operations would certainly lead to fairly heavy wastage. With the conviction that everything must be ready for a possible attempt to liberate the Continent in the Spring, the GAF may well be most unwilling to carry out bomber operations which would result in heavy wastage and would interfere with badly needed training. On the other hand it cannot of course be excluded that the use of these reinforcements for bombing operations unconnected with OVERLORD might be ordered for political reasons. In particular, a special effort might be called for in conjunction with an initial CROSSBOW attack. Should this occur during the next two months, our lack of Mosquitoes fitted with SCR 720 might prevent us from inflicting the full casualties which we should hope to be able to inflict when the full programme has been achieved. I do not however think that the bombing which could be carried out by the augmented force would be likely to be very accurate or effective. Moreover, the enemy has not yet shown himself capable of making the best use of WINDOW.

7. To sum up, I consider that in spite of the various setbacks we shall achieve by the end of March the reasonable degree of protection which was forecast at the Staff Conference of the 15th July and that our failure to do so earlier is unlikely to have very serious results. I can assure you that every effort is being made to hasten the fitting of SCR 720 and the provision of 10 cm GCI and that other counter-measures, both technical and tactical, are being developed on the first priority. I will have a close watch kept on this question and report to you if anything should occur either to retard our preparations or to make the enemy threat appear more imminent or serious.

Signed C PORTAL
CAS

3rd January 1944

GAF Radar and Radio Navigational Aids from 1943–1944

DUEPPEL

Düppel, the German name for 'Window', was first used by the GAF over the United Kingdom on the night of 7–8 October 1943. No intelligence warning of its introduction was received, and it at first confused the radar defences; but by the end of 1943 it had had no great effect in reducing German casualties and POW interrogations had shown that the GAF aircrew placed little faith in it.[1]

Before *Düppel* was used, the Air Ministry had decided to develop a new Air Interception (AI) set (Mark X, a modification of the American SCR 720) that was expected to be a match for *Düppel*. It had hoped to equip the new Mosquito night-fighters with it by the end of the year, and also to install during January 1944 new GCI equipment that would be effective against *Düppel*. On 3 January 1944 the CAS notified the Prime Minister that the Mosquitoes were not likely to be fitted with the Mark X AI before March, and that only one of the new GCI sets would be ready by the end of January, but went on to assure him that these delays would not cause very great embarrassment. The augmented GAF bomber force was unlikely to deliver a very effective attack; moreover, the enemy has not yet shown himself capable of making the best use of 'Window'.*

During January and February 1944 the Germans used *Düppel* in every major raid on the United Kingdom. It has been calculated that during January, when only one of the new GCI sets was in service and only one Mosquito squadron was fitted with the Mark X AI, *Düppel* accounted for about 15 per cent of the British failures to intercept the bombers, and that in March, when more of the new equipment became available, this percentage dropped to between 7 and 9 per cent. In spite of *Düppel*, however, the British defences shot down 10 per cent of the enemy aircraft engaged in the bombing in the first half of 1944.[2]

---

* See Appendix 22.

1. AIR 41/49, *The Air Defence of Great Britain*, Vol V, p 206.
2. ibid, pp 217–218.

NEPTUN

Neptun (FuGe 216), a backward-looking warning radar which had been fitted to most German bombers by September 1943, had initially caused 'considerable embarrassment' to British fighters, and it took some time to develop counter-measures against its beamed transmissions even after the equipment had been recovered from crashed aircraft in October and November. No 80 Wing RAF introduced stop-gap jamming measures in February 1944, switching on when warning was received from Kingsdown that *Neptun* transmissions had been intercepted. Proper ground jammers were installed in May 1944, but by that time the German bomber pilots, who found *Neptun*'s echoes confusing and were perhaps discouraged by the stop-gap counter-measures, were using the apparatus only seldom over the United Kingdom.[3] The GAF introduced *Neptun* into their night-fighters after the middle of 1944, to protect them against British intruder Mosquitoes; by then the Mosquitoes were fitted with equipment which enabled them to home on to *Neptun*.[4]

KNICKEBEIN, BENITO AND EGON

Throughout 1943 No 80 Wing RAF's interceptions, POW reports, captured documents and PR evidence showed that the enemy was continuing to use *Knickebein**** and developing the *Benito* system for use in his bombers†. In addition to an increase in *Knickebein* transmissions, which might be aimed at confusing the British defences, *Knickebein* was used in conjunction with *Elektra* in an effort to avoid British jamming when guiding Pathfinder aircraft, and *Elektra* was being interchanged with *Sonne* in some circumstances.‡ Together with the expansion of the ground organisation for the *Benito* system and changes in its procedure, these developments necessitated a change in British jamming policy from the summer of 1943, area jamming replacing the jamming of specific targets. But because it was known from POW interrogations that the GAF pilots had little faith in *Knickebein* and *Benito*, the counter-measures authorities found it difficult to understand why the enemy was devoting so much effort to their expansion.[5]

In December 1943 it was noticed that I/KG 66, a Pathfinder unit which was known to have been experimenting with flare-dropping

---

* See Volume I, Appendix 11 (ii).
† For the use of *Benito* by night-fighters see Appendix 21 (i). ‡ See below, pp 571–572.

3. ibid, pp 210, 219; AIR 41/46, No 80 Wing RAF Historical Report, pp 59, 89; AIR 20/1656, ASI Report No 101 of 6 March 1944.
4. AIR 20/1658, ASI Report No 107 of 29 June 1944.
5. AIR 41/49, pp 43–44, AIR 41/46, 56, 60.

over the United Kingdom since the summer, was carrying out flare-dropping operations over London and the Home Counties which bore no relation to the enemy's bombing operations. It was not realised that I/KG 66 was practising for the forthcoming offensive, but it was suspected that its activities might be associated with the intention to introduce some new form of radio aid to navigation.[6]

When the offensive began in January 1944 the radio aids to navigation and bomb-aiming – one of them, *Egon*, an entirely new one – that were used by the German Pathfinders proved to be largely ineffective. It is not easy to judge how far this was due to operational factors such as the poor training and lack of experience of the German pilots and the bad weather, rather than to the British counter-measures, but there is some evidence that the counter-measures added to the enemy's difficulties. The counter-measures authorities were familiar with *Knickebein*, *Benito* and *Sonne* – and they had no difficulty in jamming them once they had studied the ways in which the enemy had modified their procedures in an effort to avoid jamming. The new *Knickebein* procedures were quickly detected, and POW interrogations testified to the fact that the German pilots continued to distrust it. POW also reported that *Benito*, which appears to have been used only sporadically, was also successfully jammed; there was, moreover, an Enigma reference to the fact that it was effectively jammed during the raid on Bristol on the night of 14–15 May, when the Pathfinders dropped their flares 40 miles from the target. *Sonne* was meaconed* without difficulty, as were the MF safety beacons; the use of the latter, on which the GAF depended heavily for navigation, had been made so complex by the middle of 1943, in an effort to avoid meaconing, that at the beginning of 1944 it had had to be made simpler in the interests of the German pilots.[7] It thus became more easily meaconed.

Egon, the new system, resembled the British 'Oboe' in one respect – the use of radar and transponder to measure the distance from the bombing control – and was capable of great accuracy. It was a system by which the bomber flew along the split beam of a *Freya* or *Mammut* radar set, which had been aligned on to the target, and was guided by R/T by the radar operator, who checked the bomber's position by means of the response of its IFF set, until it was told to drop its bombs or flares. It was first used on the night of 29–30 January in conjunction with *Benito*, but was not intercepted by

---

* For the technique of using masking beacons (meacons) to re-radiate a beacon signal see Volume I, pp 550–551.

6. AIR 41/49, pp 198, 201, 206.
7. ibid, p 223; AIR 41/46, pp 42, 49, 56, 58, 60.

Kingsdown until 19 February. In the light of the intercepts POW were persuaded to give further evidence about the system's method of operation, and *Egon's* R/T channel was then jammed by 'Cigarette', a device which had successfully jammed the R/T used by the German fighter-bombers during their attacks on London in the spring of 1943.* POW interrogations showed that the jamming was effective, as did the first Enigma references to *Egon*; these disclosed that it had been rendered useless by jamming during the raid on Bristol of 14–15 May and that jamming had made it only partly effective during a raid on Portsmouth on 15–16 May. By the end of May the Germans had abandoned the use of *Egon*.[9]

HYPERBEL AND TRUHE

In addition to the above aids, the GAF made use of British 'Gee' sets (German code-name *Hyperbel*) recovered from crashed British bombers, and of a German-manufactured copy of 'Gee' (called *Truhe*). A 'Gee' set was recovered from a German bomber shot down on 26 February 1944; this led to jamming precautions. The Enigma report on the raid on Bristol on 14–15 May attributed the failure of the raid to the fact that *Truhe* had been jammed, as well as *Egon* and *Benito*.[10]

ELEKTRA AND SONNE

Elektra – a fan system of beams on MF – was identified in September 1940. It was a long-distance navigational aid. *Sonne*, a development of *Elektra*, was first heard in February 1943. Both could be used by the RAF for its own location of targets. *Sonne* consisted of a fan of *Elektra* beams sweeping in azimuth which enabled an operator to determine his bearing from a *Sonne* transmitter to an accuracy of between one-third and one-sixth of a degree at intervals of two minutes; its additional advantage over *Elektra* lay in providing a true navigational aid anywhere within its range of cover. *Sonne*

---

* Particularly because it was feared that *Egon* might be used extensively against the *Overlord* landing beaches, efforts were also made to discover methods of jamming its other components. At ADI (Sc)'s suggestion, these included the development of a device ('Perfectos') which would enable British fighters to home on to the IFF sets of the German bombers. The Germans ceased to use *Egon* before 'Perfectos' was ready, but it was used from the summer of 1944 by RAF Mosquitoes against the German night-fighters.[8]

8. Jones, *Most Secret War* (1978), pp 397, 399.
9. AIR 20/1656, ASI Report No 101 of 6 March 1944; AIR 41/46, p 56; AIR 41/49, pp 219–220; Jones, op cit, pp 396–397.
10. CAB 120/293, PM Registered File 406/1/1, CAS Minute to the Prime Minister, 27 February 1944.

stations were installed during 1943 in the Brest area, in Holland, Norway and in north-west and south-west Spain. As in the case of *Elektra*, meaconing was employed on all *Sonne* transmissions which could be used against, and in the vicinity of, the British Isles. POW testified to the effectiveness of *Sonne* meaconing. *Elektra*, being more useful for homing, for marking a predetermined landfall and for approach runs to a target or turning-in point, was used at selected *Sonne* stations during the German offensive against Britain in the first months of 1944, *Sonne* changing to *Elektra* during or immediately before a raid. By adopting this system of interchange the enemy frequently gave warning of an attack, since on a number of occasions *Elektra* signals were intercepted from *Sonne* stations long before the aircraft were plotted by Allied ground radar stations.[11] But it became the German habit to switch on *Sonne* only when required for offensive and reconnaissance operations.

---

11. AIR 41/46, pp 23, 42, 49–50, 60 and Appendix L.

AI 2(g) Report on the Me 163*, 20 April 1944

Me 163

In view of the vitally important part which aircraft have played in this war and the vast amount of intensive development work which has been undertaken during the past 4½ years, the relative absence of unorthodox airframes and propulsion systems from the operational field is a matter for some surprise. Partly on this account, no doubt, the Me 163, although it has not yet been reported in action, has aroused great interest by virtue of its strikingly unconventional design. It may, indeed, be described as the mystery plane of the war, not because there is any particular dearth of consistent intelligence reports relating to its design, but because the picture which they portray implies a highly specialised aircraft, presumably involving peculiar operational tactics. The Me 163, which has been photographed at Peenemünde on several occasions, was briefly described in a recent AI2 (g) Report (No 2225), but since it has now made its appearance at Zwischenahn airfield (RAF Medmenham Report No L161), from which it might be employed operationally, it is considered timely to examine its possibilities more closely and to indulge in some speculations as to its tactical usage.

Propulsive System and Fuel Supply

All the available evidence indicates that the aircraft is powered by a liquid rocket. This method of propulsion offers several advantages but suffers from the inherent disadvantage of very high fuel consumption. So great, indeed, are the requirements in this respect that fuel stowage capacity is the determining consideration in the design and performance of a rocket aircraft. From a drawing of the Me 163, based on sketches and reconnaissance photographs, it has been estimated that a space about 100 cu ft might reasonably be devoted to fuel stowage.

It may be noted that one of the problems associated with rocket aircraft, where the fuel load must necessarily represent so large a proportion of the all-up weight, is to dispose that load in such a way that there is no appreciable change in the centre of gravity as it is

---

* Reproduced from AIR 40/2166.

consumed. The pronounced sweep-back on the wings of the Me 163, with its consequent effect upon the centre of lift, undoubtedly facilitates the disposal of a great weight of fuel in the after part of the fuselage. Having arrived at this stage in the design, it may have been decided to take advantage of the control possibilities afforded by the disposition of the wings to eliminate the conventional tail-plane and elevator.

A space of 100 cu ft would accommodate about 8,000 lb of a suitable rocket fuel. It has been stated by General Galland of the GAF, during the course of a lecture, that the full throttle endurance of the aircraft is about 8 minutes. Since this figure comes from a reliable source and is reasonable for this method of propulsion, it may be accepted as a basis for estimation.

Investigations undertaken in connection with the Hs 293 rocket propelled glider bomb have shown that the rocket propellant favoured by the enemy is almost certainly a concentrated hydrogen peroxide mixed with a small proportion of methyl alcohol, while a potassium permanganate solution fulfils the role of catalyst. On the reasonable assumption that a similar fuel is used for the Me 163 rocket, a specific thrust of the order of 180 lb/lb/sec might be expected. If 8,000 lb of fuel suffices for 8 minutes, then the maximum thrust developed by the unit on the above basis is approximately 3,000 lb. This is quite a modest figure for rocket propulsion, and would be readily provided by a small combustion chamber unit occupying very little space.

It may be recalled (see AI2 (g) Report No 2218) that General Galland spoke of "hot" and "cold" units. The term "cold" might well be applied to a rocket unit utilising a hydrogen peroxide base fuel with only a small addition of methyl alcohol, since such a unit may operate at a comparatively low temperature. This theory is supported by a statement that the "cold" unit produces a long vaporisation trail. The "hot" unit was not ready for operation at the time that General Galland spoke, but this description, coupled with more recent references by Ps/W to long flames from the jet orifice, suggests that attempts are being made to improve the overall efficiency by increasing the combustion temperature. This may imply the use of a more concentrated peroxide-methyl-alcohol mixture or some different fuel.

All-up weight

There have been no direct references in reports to the all-up weight of the aircraft, but deductions may be drawn from certain statements which permit of a reasonable approximation. One informant has stated that he has seen Me 163s launched by towing to a height of 10,000 ft, and that the aircraft glided in to land at a very low speed

(35 to 40 mph). Apparently during these flights the propulsive system was not in operation, and it is possible that the observer was witnessing aerodynamic tests of the airframe without armament and with a minimum of equipment. Even so, the very low wing loading which such a landing speed connotes, suggests that every effort has been made to lighten the structure. The weight of the operational aircraft without fuel, however, could hardly be less than, and would probably exceed, 3,000 lb, and making allowance for the catalyst in addition to the main fuel supply, an all-up weight of 11,500 lb will be assumed for purposes of estimation.

Performance

For the above weight and an approximate gross wing area of 220 sq ft, the wing loading at take-off would be about 52 lbs. This figure is not so high as to preclude unassisted take-off from a normal run-way. On the other hand there is definite photographic evidence to show that, at Peenemünde, experiments have been carried out on a special run-way in the form of a a shallow furrow, about 1,000 yards long, probably provided with rails. Such a run-way may imply some form of assisted take-off, possibly utilising a rocket propelled trolley, in order to conserve fuel. If special run-ways of this type prove to be essential to the launching of the aircraft, their appearance on reconnaissance photographs should provide a ready means of identifying those airfields from which the Me 163 is to operate. It is very significant to note that narrow extensions have been made to all the run-ways at Zwischenahn.

Under the assumed conditions the initial rate of climb with full fuel load would be about 5,000 ft per minute at sea-level, and allowing for compressibility would attain a value of the order of 10,000 ft per minute at 40,000 ft. A word of explanation of the marked increase in rate of climb with altitude may not be out of place. Unlike the conventional reciprocating engine and the turbo-jet, the rocket motor will develop its full rated thrust irrespective of speed or altitude. On the other hand, the thrust required to overcome drag falls off as the altitude increases. More important, however, is the rapid diminution in weight resulting from a fuel consumption of 1,000 lb per minute.

These high rates of climb suggests a steep angle, but contrary to what might be expected, a jet propelled aircraft does not show to advantage when climbing steeply at a comparatively low air speed. The explanations must be sought in the peculiar property of the jet prime mover that its equivalent horse power is dependent upon the speed of flight. For example, the equivalent thrust horse power of a 3,000 lb rocket motor at 250 mph. is 2,000, whereas at 500 mph it becomes 4,000. To obtain this thrust horse power with a recipro-cating engine and propeller combination, more than 5,000 bhp would be necessary, or double the power of any engine now in service.

The maximum speed of the aircraft is impossible to assess without a much more detailed knowledge of its aerodynamic characteristics than is at present available. Certainly it is in the critical range between 500 and 600 mph. The exact maximum, however, is mainly of academic interest. The aircraft undoubtedly has a substantial margin of speed in hand over anything that is likely to be opposed to it in the near future.

Tactical Employment

Having discussed briefly the probable performance of this rocket fighter, it is necessary to consider its purpose, and the manner in which it is likely to be employed. Obviously it would be a very unpleasant antagonist for any reconnaissance aircraft to encounter, and this is a possibility which should be borne in mind. At the same time, it is hardly likely that this would be its role, or, indeed, its primary function. It must be assumed, therefore, that its principal purpose is to attack bomber formations and/or the fighter escorts. That it possesses ample speed goes without saying, but how it will fare from the standpoint of manoeuvrability must, for the time being, remain a matter for speculation.

There remains the vexed question of endurance. At first sight it would appear that, after climbing to an operational height at the expense of, say, half the total fuel load, little could be achieved with the remainder. If the endurance at the operational altitude was only four minutes, very accurate timing and directional control would be necessary to permit of effective interception. On the other hand, in level flight only one-third to one-fourth of the maximum thrust would be necessary to maintain a high flying speed, and if the full thrust were maintained, much of the power would be uselessly expended upon the fringes of the "sonic wall". It is doubtful, however, whether the thrust of a rocket unit can be effectively regulated over any appreciable range, and the possibility of being able to cruise at part "throttle" for, say, 12 to 16 minutes, appears to be remote. Another way in which the endurance might be improved would be to employ the rocket at full thrust in short bursts interspersed with periods of gliding during which the potential and/or kinetic energy thus imparted to the aircraft would be gradually dissipated by the drag.

There is a growing weight of evidence, which cannot be ignored, to show that the latter expedient will be adopted, despite the apparent danger involved in this procedure. In other words, the aircraft will be used primarily as a glider, and the power will be switched on only as necessary to restore altitude or provide rapid acceleration. It has been stated that, by employing these tactics, the aircraft can remain airborne for as long as 2¾ hours. This figure may be rather optimistic, but there is no doubt that, as the weight is progressively reduced and the aircraft more nearly assumes the characteristics of a true glider, it will cruise for a considerable time with only a modest loss of altitude. Here it should be mentioned that, with the fuel expended, the wing loading is only about 14 lb per sq ft.

Ps/W have suggested that experience with gliders is desirable or even essential for prospective pilots of the Me 163, and the towed-take-off, motorless flights, referred to earlier in this report, may have been primarily intended for pilot training purposes. The possibility cannot be overlooked, however, that with the sacrifice of part of the fuel load so as to bring the wing loading within permissible bounds, the aircraft might be towed up to its operational height and only released when approaching its quarry. It is conceivable that a twin-engined fighter, also destined to take part in the attack, might serve as a tug.

Armament and Armour

If it is to be at all effective against fighters or heavily armed and armoured day bombers, the Me 163 must carry a reasonable armament comprising certainly two, and probably more guns of at least 20 mm calibre.

There have been references to armour and bullet-proof glass, but it seems unlikely that any extensive protection can have been provided in view of the necessity for keeping the landing weight to a minimum. Probably, therefore, the pilot must rely for his safety mainly upon the considerable advantage which his superior speed will confer. Even so, the rather corpulent fuselage should provide a good target for hostile gunners, and the fact that in the earlier stages of flight it is largely occupied by fuel would hardly add to the pilot's peace of mind. It must be admitted, however, that little is yet known of the probable effects of various types of projectiles upon tanks containing rocket fuel.

Drive for Auxiliaries

With a rocket propelled aircraft, there is no simple method of driving the various instruments and auxiliaries from the prime mover. This, no doubt, explains the presence of the small windmill at the nose of the Me 163 which probably drives a generator, the latter, in turn, providing the power for driving the auxiliaries including the fuel pump. When the aircraft is at rest the necessary current may be drawn from a small storage battery.

Conclusions

It seems probable that the Me 163 has now passed the experimental stage, and that it may make an operational appearance at no far distant date. Its performance will undoubtedly be startling, but its very unconventionality prohibits any reliable assessment of its fighting potentialities.

APPENDIX 25

Intelligence Report on the V-Weapons, 12 August 1943

1. There are two different Rocket secret weapons under construction:

  (a) Pilotless aircraft officially known as "PHI 7".
  (b) Rocket projectile officially known as "A4".

2. PHI 7 is being constructed by a specially selected body of persons sworn to secrecy. The Heereswaffenamt are not connected with the construction of this aircraft. Source is therefore unable to state how many are in existence or any details as to size, weight, etc. The PHI 7 is launched by catapult.

3. A4 is 16 metres long and 4.5 (sic) metres in diameter. The weight is not known but one-third of the weight is explosive charge and two-thirds propellant. The explosive charge is stated to have an effect equivalent to the British four-ton bomb. The A4 is launched from a projector ("Schlitten"). The structure of the projectile is stated to be almost exactly similar to the American rocket projectile on railway lines. The OKW have reports with drawings concerning trials proceeding with this projectile in North Africa. The A4 has vanes at the rear end like a bomb.

4. The range of the A4 is 200 km with maximum altitude approximately 35,000 m. The propulsion is too weak to enable the projectile to travel 200 km with lower trajectory. The projectile is therefore shot into the stratosphere and as no measurements exist for the stratosphere the coefficient of uncertainty of aim is exceptionally high. Both the PHI 7 and the A4 are equipped with radio steering, without which it would be impossible to determine where either would land.

5. The radio steering for both weapons is constructed partly at Siemens in Berlin. Most important and complicated parts were being built in the workshop at Friedrichshafen destroyed in the RAF raid and described in the BBC report as one in which radio locators were built. The OKW believe that the British must have discovered this important work in progress at Friedrichshafen. The destruction was a considerable handicap, but the shop has now been rebuilt and steering construction is at present in progress in other shops of the same works.

6. The construction of parts of both weapons is distributed throughout Germany so that the producers themselves do not know their purpose. Assembly and tests for both weapons are carried out at the experimental institute on the part of the coast described as the "nose" near Peenemünde.

7. The actual tests are carried out in the Baltic. So far approximately 100 A4 projectiles have been fired and a further 100 are at present in hand. The accuracy of aim is most unsatisfactory. Only 25 per cent landing within an extensive target area. Unless the radio control is improved projectiles can only be used for aimless destruction.

8. The Heereswaffenamt is in charge of the production of the launching projectors which are of simple construction of iron rails slanting upwards from which the rocket takes off under its own power. The lower rails are very strong to carry the weight. The lateral rails are not so strong. 100 projectors have at present been built, but any desired number can be produced by October owing to their simplicity.

9. Some concrete emplacements for A4 projectors are now ready near Le Havre and Cherbourg. More are under construction. These concrete emplacements are for protection but are not essential as the projectors can be placed in open fields if necessary.

10. It is probable that the weapons will be transported fully assembled from Peenemünde to the operation point, except for the fuses and delicate steering mechanism.

11. Hitler and members of his cabinet personally inspected both weapons at Peenemünde (date not given). About June 10th, Hitler told assembled military leaders that the Germans had only to hold out as by the end of 1943 London would be levelled to the ground and Britain forced to capitulate.

12. Despite continued opposition by experts, the decision reported on 9.8.43., has since been reversed by Hitler who insisted on reprisals for the Hamburg raids. October 20th is at present fixed at zero day for rocket attacks to begin. Hitler ordered the construction of 30,000 A4 projectiles by that day. This is, however, beyond the bounds of possibility, but the production of both weapons is to have first priority and 1,500 skilled workers have been transferred to this work from anti-aircraft and artillery production. Hitler has also ordered experiments to be made with A4 projectiles filled with gas.

13. At the same time Hitler ordered Milch to prepare 2,000 aircraft for a gas attack on England. The latter replied that aviation reserves were already exhausted and he could not assemble the necessary

force. In this connection source considers phosphorous bombs are unlikely to be used owing to the German shortage of phosphor which is already having an effect on the output of tracer ammunition.

APPENDIX 26

Air Scientific Intelligence Special Note on the Flakzielgerät 76*
14 September 1943

1. *Data.*

On 7/9/43, the following two telegrams were sent by section IA Op. 2 of Luftflotte 3:

Luftflotte 3 IA Op. 2 No 116 (figure smudged) O, signed Boehme, on 7/9 –

Reference (1) Luftlotte 3 Op. 2 No 11655 of 6/9 and (2) General der Flakwaffe No 2717 of 5/9 about Flak protection of ground organisation Flak target apparatus Flakzielgerät 76.

(1) Luftflotte 3 again requests the immediate bringing up of Flak forces to protect ground organisation Flak target apparatus 76. The urgency of this is emphasized by the following facts –

a. According to report of C in C West, Abwehr Station France reports the capture of an enemy agent who had the task of establishing at all costs the position of new German rocket weapon. The English, it is stated, have information that the weapon is to be employed in the near future and they intend to attack the positions before this occurs.

b. In fact, according to Ref. 2 above (General der Flakwaffe to GAF Ops Staff), 5 reception stations (Auffangstellen) have up to now been attacked, some repeatedly, with bombs and aircraft armament. This is confirmed by communication of Luftgau Belgium to Luftflotte 3.

(2) Luftflotte 3, in Ref. 1 above, has already pointed out that in its own area there are no further Flak forces available.

From IA, Op. 2 number 8404, dated 7/9:

For Flak protection of ground organisation of FZG 76, Luftflotte 3 is the sole competent authority vis à vis Luftgau Belgium – North France, and is solely responsible to C in C GAF Ops Staff.

In future therefore the chain of command will be respected and applications direct to offices outside Luftflotte 3 are to cease.

---

* Reproduced from AIR 20/1721.

2. *Deduction*

2.1. From the above telegrams it appears that there is an apparatus known as the Flakzielgerat 76 which has the following salient characteristics –

(a) A ground organisation for the apparatus is being, or has been, set up in the area of Luftgau Belgium – North France.

(b) This ground organisation is at present vulnerable, and requires Flak protection.

(c) The organisation is so important that the Luftflotte is taking direct responsibility for its protection: normally Flak protection arrangements are left to the Luftgau.

(d) The discrimination of ground organisations suggests that there may also be associated air activity.

(e) There are at least 5 reception stations (supply points, not radio stations), probably scattered. These have been attacked fortuitously by the RAF.

(f) An officer who knew the technical nature of the FZG 76 appeared to regard it as the object of British enquiries about the new German rocket weapon. It therefore probably has some form of rocket propulsion.

(g) It may be operated by the General der Flakwaffe.

3. *Nature of FZG 76*

3.1. The above facts all provide clues to the nature of FZG 76. A further clue may lie in its name, which can be interpreted in two ways: a target apparatus for Flak, or an aiming apparatus for Flak. The latter usage of 'Ziel' by the GAF occurs in the Bombenzielapparat, which is a bombsight, but is unlikely in the present case because the family of names for sighting apparatus for Flak (Flakmessgerät, Entfernungsmessgerät, Kommandogerät, and others) is already known. Moreover, it would be a peculiar Flak sighting apparatus which required a ground organisation in urgent need of Flak protection. Therefore, if the name Flakzielgerät is at all descriptive, it almost certainly refers to a target apparatus intended to be engaged by Flak. It is unlikely that in the present case the FZG 76 is to be so used, for this would make nonsense of the messages. It is therefore a code name for an important weapon, probably rocket driven, now being installed in Belgium or North France.

3.2. The two rocket weapons most likely to be used shortly from the area concerned are the large long range rocket and the pilotless aircraft. 'Flakzielgerät' is very much more likely to cover the latter than the former; a 'Queen Bee' used for Flak purposes may very easily have been developed into an offensive pilotless aircraft, and the name carried over. The true Flak is almost certain to have radio control, and so – apart from other evidence – this control should have been available, if the Germans wanted to apply it to the FZG 76.

3.3. The above messages therefore probably refer to the installation of the launching and storage facilities for pilotless rocket-driven aircraft in Belgium – North France. The purpose is not conclusively shown, and it could not be proved, for example, that they are not intended as anti-shipping weapons in case of invasion, but it is probable that these aircraft are to be used to attack England.

3.4. While there is no direct reference to site, or sites of installation, it is worth noting that three days before the same section of Luftflotte 3 was urgently discussing with C in C, GAF the Flak protection of Watten.

4. *Collateral Evidence*
4.1. The Oslo report of 4.11.39 accurately anticipated, among many other important developments, the recent appearance of the rocket-driven radio-controlled glider bomb used against ships. The secret development number, according to Oslo, of this bomb was FZ 21, the FZ standing for Ferngesteuerte Zielflugzeug (Remote controlled aiming or target aircraft); it was developed at Peenemünde. The same source also said that a remote control autopilot for pilotless aircraft was being developed at Diepensee for remote control under the designation of FZ 10 (Ferngesteuerte Flugzeug). The FZ series therefore, even if source's interpretations are not quite correct, does indicate remotely controlled air devices. Actually, such variations as indicated in the three different interpretations of FZ 10, 21 and 76 occur both in German and British usage. For example, FMG has been officially held to stand for both Flak and Funkmessgerät, while the interpretations of the letters RDF are several. It is probably coincidence that the numbers 10, 21 and 76 can all be expressed as (11n–1).

4.2. It may be worth remarking that the 1st (Flak) Abteilung of Artillery Regiment 760 was, on 30.8.43, envisaging changing its positions – which it had first occupied near St Omer a month before on the orders of OKH – because the British had presumably recognised its intention to construct some installation. The dates, place (Watten bombed on 27.8.43, is 10 kms from St Omer), and the Abteilung's sensitivity to British attention, suggest that it may be concerned in some way with the FZG 76 project.

4.3. There have been good reports from agents both of the development of the long-range rocket, and of the rocket-driven pilotless aircraft; sometimes both have been mentioned in the same report. The messages under discussion appear to confirm the fairly imminent use of the pilotless aircraft, but do not reflect on the question of the long-range rocket except that they add credibility to it in those reports, manifestly competent, which state the existence of both weapons.

5. *Conclusion*

5.1. The Germans are installing, under the cover name of FZG 76, a large and important ground organisation in Belgium – Northern France which is probably concerned with directing an attack on England by rocket-driven pilotless aircraft. It is more than possible that the construction at Watten is associated with this project. It appears that the aircraft are not to be launched from far back, but that supplies may be brought up to the forward areas.

A D I (Science)

14 September 1943

Intelligence on the Effects of Air Attack on the V-Weapon Sites in France from January to March 1944

ACAS(I)'s report of 22 January 1944 gave in some detail what was known of the construction dates for the sites, attacks by bombers on them and the strength of the Flak defences.[1]

Watten: Excavation had begun by 16 May 1943; buildings had been started by 17 July, but neither then nor at any later stage were they recognisable for any known purpose; the chief feature was great strength and solidity of construction. The site had been bombed by Eighth Air Force on 28 August and 7 September, causing great damage. No immediate attempt was made to clear the site but by 5 December it was clear that construction was under way. Rapid progress was being made by 24 December and this was confirmed on 14 January 1944. Strong Flak defences were now deployed, it had not been so defended before the August raid.

Wizernes: Activity was first noticed on 15 August with railway construction, the erection of stores and the dumping of stores. Tunnelling had started by 5 December and by 4 January a large area on a hill top had been covered by an elaborate camouflage. Flak had been heavily increased since the end of November and was now formidable.

Sottevast: First activity was seen on 20 October, and by 13 December a deep wide trench had been dug and various buildings were under construction. By 14 January a second long trench was seen, an L-shaped excavation and six tall cylindrical structures. There had been a considerable increase in light Flak defences since mid-December.

Martinvast: Was first reported on 28 July; two long trenches were seen under construction between then and 13 December. The site was similar to Sottevast both in regard to the trenches and the presence of six cylindrical structures. It was attacked on 11 November and 2 December with good results. Photographs of 14 January showed that the cylinders had been removed since 13 December. Defences had been reduced since the last attack.

---

1. CAB 121/212, SIC file B/Defence/2, Vol 2, COS (44) 59 (0) of 22 January.

Siracourt: Activity was first reported on 4 September. Two long parallel trenches were the main feature, other buildings and construction could be seen. Defences were remarkable light, thought due to immunity from attack so far.

Lottinghem: First photographs were taken on 24 September, and considerable construction had taken place by 3 November. The main feature was two long trenches as at Siracourt and Martinvast, and camouflaged structures similar to those at Siracourt were seen in the trenches. There were no defences or they were very light.

Mimoyecques: First indications were observed on 18 September when railway lines to two tunnels could be seen. A number of shafts appeared to be sunk from a hill top to meet the tunnels. The completed shafts were covered with a conical structure. Light railway lines were seen to enter these structures. The site was bombed on 5 and 8 November and activity was suspended until at least 25 November. Flak defences were considerably increased after the raids and ground reports, which had earlier suggested that rocket projectiles were to be fired from the shafts, indicated that work was continuing. That it had done so was seen from photographs on 24 December, when parallel trenches thought similar to the other sites were being dug.

Thus, at the end of January 1944, though nothing could be proved, these sites were suspected of being concerned with a rocket threat. This was partly due to agents' reports to this effect and partly because of an understandable inability to interpret in any other way the good photographic reconnaissance which was available.

The next ACAS (I) report on 28 January gave some details of continuing work at Watten. It noted that new trenches at Mimoyecques were being enlarged, and stated that it was clear that a circular emplacement about 280 feet in diameter was being constructed above the quarry at Wizernes immediately below the camouflaged area.[2] (Though it was not known at the time, this structure was a novel dome built on the hill top so that excavation and construction work could be carried out, unseen by reconnaissance and protected from air raids, to produce the A-4 bunker. This had been proposed by the head of the Todt organisation, who also had in mind a similar smaller platform to cover the new work on a limited facility at Watten). Much activity could be seen at the site.

Wizernes was the subject of a special note in ACAS (I)'s report of 5 February, as the Chiefs of Staff had asked for a recommendation about attacking it. It had been photographed on 21 January, when the construction of the circular emplacement on the hill top was

---

2.   ibid, COS (44) 94 (o) of 28 January.

shown to be still at an early stage, and a ground report, with information dating back to November, referred to cement being pumped through pipes to the works on the hill. A detailed description was given in the report, but no new opinion was offered as to what might be its purpose or function. ACAS (I) did not recommend that the emplacement should be bombed; it could wait until it was more damageable. But he remarked that very heavy bombs might have to be used. Harassing attacks against other features at the site were, however, recommended.[3]

The next site to receive special attention was Sottevast on 19 February. Work had progressed very rapidly during the previous month. The report offered no explanation of its use, however, but contented itself with a detailed description of the site based on an annotated PR photograph, taken on 6 February.[4]

Wizernes was again the subject of a report of 4 March. The progress of the work on the circular emplacement was described, but its purpose could not be explained.[5]

A fortnight later further progress was reported at Watten, where a tall rectangular building had reached a considerable height and was partially roofed. It was, however, Mimoyecques which received the greatest attention. Work had been resumed there by the time of a PR sortie on 24 December, and seemed to be similar to the work at the sites at Martinvast, Sottevast, and Lottinghem. But by mid-March it was realised that the resemblance was only temporary and that Mimoyecques had developed along different lines. As a result of the bombing attacks in November work on only one tunnel was in progress, and had not been resumed on the western tunnel. A recent report, presumably from an SIS agent, had drawn attention to this and had connected the tunnel and its shafts with the launching of a large rocket. It had gone on to say that the works in the neighbourhood of the shafts would include a concrete turret forming a chamber in which a tube 40–50 metres long would be installed. The tube was described as a rocket launching cannon. The shafts were described as 'air holes to allow for the expansion of the gases released by the explosion of the launching charge'. AI commented that the shafts were probably intended to contain launching tubes or mortars, since these require to be almost vertical, and concluded:

'The high level of activity at this site leaves no doubt that the installations are regarded by the enemy as being of great importance. The nature of the works supports the statement put forward in a recent intelligence report that they may be intended for the launching of a large rocket'.[6]

---

3.   ibid, COS (44) 130 (o) of 5 February.
4.   ibid, COS (44) 173 (o) of 19 February.
5.   ibid, COS (44) 219 (o) of 4 March.
6.   ibid, COS (44) 266 (o) of 18 March.

There were detailed reports on Wizernes and Watten at the end of March, together with descriptions and annotated photographs. The circular emplacement at Wizernes could be clearly seen and consisted of an apparently solid core surrounded by an annular trench and it was thought that all would be clad in concrete. Much activity was observed all around this unusual structure, but the interpreters could offer no explanation as to its function. At Watten the building with its heavy concrete roof appeared to be near completion, but again the purpose was inexplicable. The Wizernes photograph had been taken on 16 March, that of Watten on 13 March, and AI's report, dated 31 March, stated that since these had been taken both sites had been bombed. The report also contained a note about an interesting development at Sottevast, where a rectangular building was being constructed similar to that at Watten.[7]

---

7.   ibid, COS (44) 308(o) of 31 March.

Index

A-1 see under V-Weapons
A-2 see under V-Weapons
A-3 see under V-Weapons
A-4 see under V-Weapons: V2
A-5 see under V-Weapons
AA see under Guns
AAPIU, 83 fn, 465
Abbeville, 393, 408
Abe, Vice-Admiral, 245, 519-26
Abwehr
  SIS in touch with agent of, 19, 359;
  Intelligence from decrypts of, on
  Russian front, 20-1; Intelligence from
  decrypts of, on mining of Danube,
  42; Warning from official in (SIS
  agent), re-V-weapons, 46 fn;
  Intelligence from decrypts of, on
  Italian landings, 110; Reports heavy
  Naples bombing, to Berlin, 110;
  Decrypts of, on Yugoslav internal
  fighting, 141 & fn, 144 fn; Decrypts
  of, circulated in Cairo, 141 & fn;
  Decrypts of, available to SOE, 141 fn;
  Decrypts of, on Tito identification,
  147 fn; Decrypts of, on Cetnik
  collaboration, 150, 154 & fn, 155,
  159-60; Jevdjevic in contact with, 150
  fn; Decrypts of, warn on possible
  Cetnik revenge attack on German
  forces, 151; Decrypts of, show Italian
  forces' reaction to German take-over,
  156-7; Decrypts of, show Mihailovic/
  German collaboration, 159; Decrypts
  of, show interest of German Navy in
  midget submarines, 195; German
  Navy takes over KDK from, 195 &
  fn; Decrypts of, show Axis fears of
  Allied landing in Azores, 221 fn;
  Covoy intelligence by, for U-boats,
  223, 227; Agent of, reports on Arctic
  convoy preparations, 263; Agent of,
  landed in Iceland, 263 fn, 269; HQ
  of Kommandos of, at Arras, 426 fn,
  446; Decrypt of, re V 2s, from Arras,
  446; Seizure of documents by, in
  Balkans, 468; Decrypts of, disclose
  Obladen Kommando documents
  raids, 468 & fn; Capture of high-
  grade machine cypher of, by No 30
  Commando, 468; Decrypting of
  traffic of, in Balkans, 501-3;
  Handling of decrypts of, in Cairo,
  502; Collaboration of, with German

Army, in counter-guerrilla
  operations in Yugoslavia, 502;
  Ordered to investigate centimetric
  ASV, 515; Captures Allied agent
  investigating rocket sites, 589
ACAS (I), 296-7, 412, 419 fn, 436, 440-1,
  445-6, 450-1, 453, 455, 465, 593-5
Accolade, Operation, see under Rhodes
Achse, Operation (German), 12, 14,
  108-9, 115 & fn, 148, 151, 156
ACIU, 466
ACVs (Armoured Command
  Vehicles), 180
ADGB, see also under RAF – fighter
  Command, 283, 325, 553-4
ADI(K), 467, 471
ADI(Ph), 465-6
ADI(Sc), 309, 311-5, 365, 369, 374,
  389-90, 393-4 & fn, 398, 408, 410,
  417-8, 419 fn, 436, 444-5 fn, 446-7 &
  fns, 448-55, 554, 557-64, 576 fn,
  589-92
Admiral Scheer, German battleship, 252-3
Admiralty
  Evidence of new U-boat types
  received by, 47, 49-50 & fn, 195,
  240-5; Warns on use of underwater
  missiles on Anzio beachhead, 195;
  Decrypts give warning to, of renewed
  U-boat attack, 211; Enigma warnings
  to, help in location of escorts, 219;
  Enigma warnings to, on U-boat
  attack on Gibraltar convoy, 227;
  Reinforces Gibraltar convoy, 227;
  Orders of, for attack on refuelling
  points in Indian Ocean, 230; Warns
  of U-boat approach to
  Mediterranean, 233 & fn;
  Conclusions of, on U-boat
  construction, 242; Discussion by
  Naval Staff on new U-boat types,
  243; Preoccupation of, with
  protection of *Overlord* convoys, 243-5;
  Learns of delay in U-boat
  construction, 245; Importance
  attached to, to blockade-runners,
  249; Whereabouts of *Alsterufer*
  revealed to, by Sigint, 250; Speed of
  decrypting of blockade-runners
  Sigint for, 251; Announcement by, of
  movement of *Lützow*, 257-8;
  Confusion in, over movement of
  Lützow, 258; Unable to brief X-craft

597

Greece
  Possible Allied seizure of airfields in, 7; Move of German reinforcements to, 11, 80; Build-up of GAF in, 11–2, 122; Move of XXII Mountain Corps to, from Russia, 13; New GAF command in, 13; German forces in, 28–9, 31, 122, 144, 468; German forces moved from, to Hungary, 31; German fears of Allied landing in, 31; Axis assesses Allied threat to, 77–9, 120 fn; Allied landing in, suggested by *Husky*, deception, 78, 120 fn; Guerrillas in, 78, 120, 145; Reinforcement of German forces in, prior to *Husky*, 80, 120 fn; Strength of GAF in, prior to *Husky*, 80; Strength of GAF in, after *Accolade*, 122; Destroyers of, set out to attack Cos convoy, 123; Destroyers of, damaged in Aegean, 129; German forces move to, for attack on Samos and Leros, 131; GAF heavy bombers move from, 133; GAF Transport Gruppe sent to, 134; Hitler's belief in threat to, by notional British divisions, 134 fn; Sabotage of railways in, 145; Move of 1st SS Panzer Division from, to Russia, 153; Move of 1st Mountain Division from, to Yugoslavia, 158; Mihailovic/SS collaboration against volunteer bands in, 159; GAF fighters sent from, to counter Yugoslav supply drops, 170; GAF bombs Bari from, 184; GAF bombs Allied forces in Operation *Shingle* from, 187; SOE operations in, 463; Seizure of documents from British Army HQ in, 468; Little Sigint on, 501 fn, 502

Greenland, 225, 253 fn, 527–8
Greifswalder Oie, 375, 368 & fn, 369, 402, 441 fn
Grosseto, 499, 507–8, 513
Guadalcanal, US escort-carrier, 232
Guns, Allied, 413, 415 fn, 420 fn
Guns, Axis
  Ferdinand, promised to Allies by Russia, 19 fn; Losses of, in Russia, 39–41; Heavy, landed at Leros, 132; Numbers of, in Italy, revealed by Sigint, 180; Shortage of anti-tank, in Italy, 206; New AA, for U-boats, 211, 215–8, 220–1, 224, 252, 270; Whereabouts of AA defences against Operation *Tungsten*, 273; AA parties, on German coastal shipping, 279; Army 21 cm mortar, adapted for GAF, 296; AA defences of Germany, against bomber offensive, 308, 310, 312 fn, 548, 551–2; Armament of Me

262, 348; Reports on German long-range, 359, 361, 368, 376–9, 381–3, 392–3; War Office sets up units to spot long-range, 382; Flak defences of Watten, increased, 385; Testing of new types of, at Rechlin and Peenemünde, 391; Successes of No 30 Commando in capturing equipment and designs of AA, 469; German Flak defences, 551–2; AA sent to Italy, 551; Flak defences requested, for FZG 76, 589–90; Flak defences of rocket sites, 593–4
Gurnard (Fish link), 502–3
Gustav line, 26, 197 & fn, 202 & fn, 203

H2S (Navigational aid), 284, 291–2, 314 & fn, 315, 515, 560–1 & fn, 562, 566–7
H2X (Navigational aid), 314 & fn
Hagenuk or *Wanze* (Radar search receiver), 218, 220, 222–3, 516 & fn
Hamburg, 241, 244, 280, 292–3, 297, 299, 308, 310, 522–3, 551, 566–7, 586
Hanover, 294
Harris, Air Chief Marshal, 242 fn, 297–8, 301, 303, 305, 308, 550, 565
Harz Mountains, 384, 433
He (Heinkel), see under Aircraft, Axis Types
He 293 see under Hs 293
'Heidelager' see under Blizna
Heinemann, General, 423–4
Heinkel Factory, see also under Aircraft, Axis Types, 334
Hercegovina, 29, 140, 148, 150 & fn
Hermes see under Porpoise
HF (High Frequency), see also under VHF, 554 & fn, 556
Himmler, Heidrich, 116, 205, 374
Hitler, Adolf
  Decision by, to defend Italy, 14; Expects Allied landing in Balkans, 14–5, 78, 173; Opposes strategic bombing in Russia, 21; Speaks of move of forces to Balkans, 22–3; Speaks of withdrawal on eastern front, 22–3, 34; Gives priority to western front, 23; Informs Japanese Ambassador of moves on eastern front, 23; Vetoes evacuation of Crimea, 40–2; Warned of German oil shortages, 58; Personal liaison officer of, in Sicily, 76; Orders all forces in Sicily to attack, 89–90; Personally orders moves of forces in Sicily, 91; Views of, on Allied failure to stop Sicily evacuation, 99 fn; Fears of, of Italian collapse, 103; Fears of, of destruction of Rome, 116; Orders Tenth Army to Rome area, 116;

Yugoslavia—cont.

on Cetnik/German collaboration, 154–5; Abwehr sees as, in Russian sphere of interest, 155; Cetnik leader in Montenegro signs pact with Germans, 155 & fn; Tito acknowledged by Germans to be full military threat, 155 fn; Foreign Office and JIC agree on more supplies for Partisans, 155–6 & fn; London acknowledges that no Tito/ Mihailovic truce possible in, 156; Foreign Office to press government of, to replace Mihailovic as Cetnik leader, 156; Agreement at Tehran conference to switch aid to Tito, 156, 158, 160; Supplies sent to, by Allies, 156 & fn; Response of Partisans to Italian collapse in, 157; Sigint discloses renewed German advance in, 157–9, 166; Allied support to Partisans ties down large German forces in, 158–9; Allies formally break with Mihailovic, 158–61; German failure to conquer completely, 159, 168; Fresh evidence of Mihailovic's collaboration with Germans, 159–61; Report from liaison officers that some Cetnik leaders refused to obey Mihailovic's mobilisation order, 159; Liaison officers report on Cetnik/ Nedic collaboration, 159–61; PM convinced by Maclean, Deakin and others of Mihailovic's treachery, 160; PM tries to persuade government of, to sack Mihailovic, 160; PM tries to persuade King Peter to sack Mihailovic, 160, 162; Difficulties of proving case against Mihailovic, 160–1 & fn; Cairo sets Mihailovic a test of loyalty, 160; Refusal of Foreign Office to accept test of loyalty as evidence, 160–1; Fresh report by Deakin on Mihailovic's treachery, 161–2; Foreign Secretary concedes Mihailovic/Nedic collaboration, 162; COS judge Mihailovic on his military failures, 162; COS agree to withdrawal of missions to Cetniks, 162; Military situation in, December 1943 – February 1944, 162–5; 114th Jäger Division moves to Italy from, 163; Partisans lose, then recapture Jajce, 163; Allied air attacks on railways of, 163–4; Allied supply drops to, stepped up, 164 & fn, 170; Insecurity of Tito's cyphers, 164 fn, 166 & fn; Allied supply drops compromised by Tito's W/T traffic, 164 fn; GC & CS warning on pending attack on Tito's HQ sent to AFHQ, 165; GC & CS warning not sent to mission with Tito, 165; Mission in, not to receive high-grade Sigint, 165–6 & fn; Low-grade cyphers of mission in, 166 & fn; Allied air attack on GAF in, 166–7, 169; Tito's HQ evacuated to Bari, by air, 166; Tito's HQ returns to Vis, 166; Partisans resume active operations in, 166; German attack on islands of, 166–9; GAF postpones airborne attacks on Vis and Lagosta, 168; Axis supply system depends on holding islands of, 168; Shortage of German forces in, 168–70; Success of Allied air attacks on ports and coastal waters of, 168–70; Lack of GAF cover for Axis operations in, 168–70; AI calculates GAF strength in, 170; Transfer of GAF units from, to Bulgaria and Romania, 170; GAF sends fighters to, from Greece, to combat air lift, 170; Commando raids on islands of, 170–2; SOE operations in, come under military control, 463; Plethora of Sigint on, 501 fn; Police and Abwehr decrypts from, 502; Collaboration of Police and Abwehr with Army in, in counter-guerrilla operations, 502; Political situation in, revealed by Sigint, 502–3; Relations between Germans, Cetniks and Partisans, revealed by Sigint, 503; Partisan activities in, hold up German troop movements, 508

Z-Stoff (Sodium Permanganate), 341, 418, 428, 580
Zagreb, 12, 30, 138, 145, 150 fn, 157–9, 162, 165
Zahme Sau (German fighter interception system), 313–4, 555, 557, 566
Zaporozhe, 18, 22
Zara, 31, 156, 167–8
Zaunkönig see under Torpedoes
Zempin, 402, 408, 412–3, 427
Zhitomir, 18, 39
Zinnowitz see under Zempin
Zitronella, Operation (Axis), 234–5
Zwischenahn Airfield, 350, 579, 581

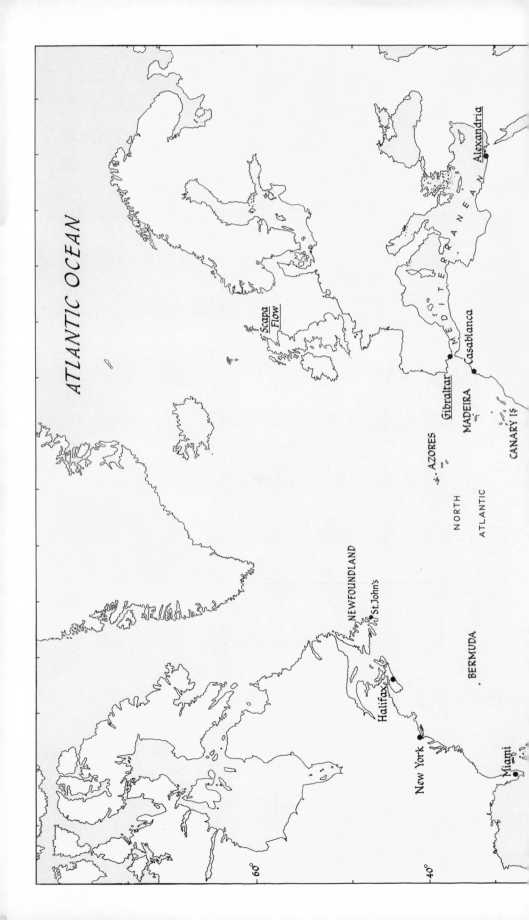